VOLUME 1

Dictionary

DAVID BOWMAN

Rhinegold Publishing Limited
London • 2002

First published 2002 in Great Britain by
Rhinegold Publishing Ltd
241 Shaftesbury Avenue
London WC2H 8TF
Tel: 020 7333 1721

© Rhinegold Publishing Ltd 2002

All rights reserved. No part of this publication may be reproduced, stored in a retrieval system, or transmitted in any form or by any means, electronic, mechanical photocopying, recording or otherwise, without the prior permission of Rhinegold Publishing Ltd.

Rhinegold Publishing Ltd has used its best efforts in preparing this dictionary. It does not assume, and hereby disclaims, any liability to any party for loss or damage caused by errors or omissions in the dictionary whether such errors or omissions result from negligence, accident or any other cause.

The Rhinegold Dictionary of Music in Sound comprises three volumes: Volume 1 the alphabetic entries and eight chapters of the 'Elements of music', Volume 2 the musical examples, and Volume 3 containing three CDs.

ISBN: 0-946890-87-0

Printed in Great Britain by Biddles Ltd, Guildford

Foreword

In 1968, at the Juilliard School of Music, the door to Room 308 opened directly to hell. Four years of hard work and study were about to be shattered. Conductors and composers who had gone through a rigorous curriculum called Literature and Materials of Music, known to most people as Harmony and Theory, would be put to the test, literally. This was the final exam. The one we had been warned about. Urban legends grew from this room.

Supposedly, on entering, one would be confronted with a set of open scores on a piano. Not only were we supposed to identify the piece and the composer, but we had to describe the style and audio features that the pages revealed. On a blackboard there were to be numerous words in many languages, all of them supposedly related to music. Our job was to translate them and explain how they applied to basic music theory. One year the words *al dente* were supposedly on the board. One poor student thought it meant to play the flute with your teeth. Each candidate was also given a piece of music, then sent into a room for 30 minutes, with the understanding that he or she would come back with a complete harmonic analysis of those pages.

I mention this because most musicians from past generations did not have access to a dictionary such as the one you are looking at. Of course, many people survived the interrogation and went on to do quite well for themselves. But many of us also came away from our musical education with a less than complete knowledge of the field we were about to enter.

Music in the western world should be a simple matter, just 12 notes and a seemingly endless number of sound combinations. However, it is very difficult to understand these matters without precise definitions of terms and, more importantly, examples of the places in which they occur. This dictionary goes a long way to filling a void, which has only been partially full for such a long time. It is now possible to understand the musical terms, see how they physically look in the music and then listen to their practical result. I am not sure that this knowledge would have aided me at the Juilliard School. I was not a particularly attentive student. But I do know that the understanding of the musical process would have been greatly enhanced by a volume such as this. All of a sudden, to give a very basic example, I can look up *basso continuo* and, if I have any questions, I will be referred to the

Foreword

text of a piece of music and subsequently to its audio component. There is nothing that brings music to life more than the hearing and performing of the material.

So, you have at your disposal an extremely valuable resource. It should be used wisely and often. If once in a while you feel overwhelmed, just remember that poor fellow who was trying to play the flute with his teeth.

Leonard Slatkin

Contents

Foreword
By Leonard Slatkin (page iii)

Preface
By David Bowman (page viii)

Introduction

How to use this dictionary
Page xi

Abbreviations and symbols peculiar to this dictionary
Page xii

Other abbreviations and symbols
Page xiii

Acknowledgements
Page xiv

Dictionary
Alphabetic entries (page 1)

Elements of music

1: Rhythm, metre and tempo (page 197)
- 1.1 Rhythm (page 197)
- 1.2 Accents (page 197)
- 1.3 Metre (page 198)
- 1.4 Simple and compound metres (page 198)
- 1.5 Complex metres (page 199)
- 1.6 Characteristic rhythms (page 199)
- 1.7 Metrical disruptions (page 200)
- 1.8 Triplets and duplets (page 202)
- 1.9 Polyrhythms (page 202)
- 1.10 Cross rhythms (page 202)
- 1.11 Polymetre (page 203)
- 1.12 Rhythmic modes (page 204)
- 1.13 Isorhythm (page 204)
- 1.14 Articulation (page 205)
- 1.15 Tempo (page 205)

2: Tonality, modality and atonality (page 208)
- 2.1 Pitch (page 209)
- 2.2 Intervals (page 209)
- 2.3 Scales and tonality (page 212)
- 2.4 Modality (page 214)
- 2.5 Modulation (page 219)
- 2.6 Bitonality and polytonality (page 220)

Contents

2.7 Tonality and atonality (page 220)
2.8 Modes of limited transposition (page 222)
2.9 Pentatonic music (page 222)

3: Melody, figuration and ornamentation (page 224)
3.1 Tune (page 224)
3.2 Theme (page 225)
3.3 Thematic transformation (page 226)
3.4 Leitmotif and unending melody (page 226)
3.5 Recitative, arioso and aria (page 227)
3.6 Recitation (page 228)
3.7 Klangfarbenmelodie (page 229)
3.8 Serial melody (page 229)
3.9 Figuration (page 230)
3.10 Ornaments and ornamentation (page 230)

4: Counterpoint (page 238)
4.1 Contrapuntal motion (page 238)
4.2 Two-part counterpoint (page 238)
4.3 Melodic decoration in two-part counterpoint (page 239)
4.4 Contrapuntal techniques (page 241)
4.5 Fugue (page 245)
4.6 Serial counterpoint (page 249)

5: Harmony (page 251)
5.1 Chord symbols (page 251)
5.2 Consonance and dissonance (page 254)
5.3 Triads (page 256)
5.4 Cadences (page 259)
5.5 Diatonic harmony (page 263)
5.6 Modulation and pivot chords (page 269)
5.7 Chromatic harmony (page 269)
5.8 Non-functional harmony (page 278)

6: Timbre and texture (page 281)
6.1 Timbre (page 281)
6.2 Harmonic series (page 281)
6.3 Tone colours (page 283)
6.4 Bowed and plucked string instruments (page 283)
6.5 Special string effects (page 286)
6.6 Timbres and special effects of woodwind instruments (page 289)
6.7 Timbres and special effects of brass instruments (page 293)
6.8 Percussion (page 296)
6.9 Keyboard instruments (page 300)
6.10 Electric and electronic instruments (page 303)
6.11 Texture (page 304)

7: The structure of music (page 309)
7.1 Motif (page 309)
7.2 Phrase (page 309)
7.3 Period (page 310)

7.4	Binary forms (page 310)	
7.5	Ternary forms (page 312)	
7.6	Rondo forms (page 313)	
7.7	Sonata forms (page 314)	
7.8	Variation forms (page 318)	
7.9	Vocal and instrumental forms of the middle ages and renaissance (page 321)	
7.10	Cyclic forms (page 323)	

8: Style, genre and historical context (page 325)

8.1	Style (page 325)	
8.2	Genre (page 330)	
8.3	Historical style-periods (page 331)	
8.4	Medieval monophony (c.500–c.1430) (page 331)	
8.5	Medieval polyphony (c.900–c.1430) (page 335)	
8.6	Renaissance music (c.1430–c.1600) (page 339)	
8.7	Baroque era (c.1600–c.1750) (page 346)	
8.8	Eighteenth-century pre-classical styles (page 357)	
8.9	Viennese classical styles (c.1770–c.1820) (page 359)	
8.10	Nineteenth-century romantic music (c.1820–c.1900) (page 364)	
8.11	Divergent trends in twentieth-century music (page 377)	

Preface

Any attempt to describe in words alone how music functions is likely to fail unless the reader already has a mental image of the sound of what is being described. This is because music itself has no words for the concrete realities upon which verbal languages depend. The nearest music can get to the naming of things is the primitive imitation of natural sounds, such as the bird calls in Beethoven's *Pastoral* Symphony. This is not to deny that there is a language of music, or, more accurately, a wealth of languages and dialects corresponding to the profusion of styles that have emerged throughout the ages and across the world. But these languages or styles are hermetic, so no amount of purple prose is going to reveal their own purely musical logic. However, all is not lost, for an understanding of musical styles can develop in the same way as a baby learns a language – by hearing it spoken (or played) often enough for patterns to begin to emerge from what was at first an apparently random series of sounds.

So why should it be necessary to understand the technical vocabulary of music? For professional musicians the answer is obvious. An expert craftsman needs to be able to say to an apprentice that mortise and tenon joints should be made at the corners of a wooden panel (because life is too short to describe how to make them every time such joints are needed). In the same way, a conductor needs to be able to ask for more emphasis on a series of appoggiaturas without the need to explain what these are every time one appears in the score. For the listener an understanding of musical terminology is essential if one wishes to probe beneath the surface of music to hear and delight in compositional details that may never register if one is not directed to them by an experienced guide. On a larger scale, one might well miss the structure of a great piece of music if a route map has not been provided. Just as cartography has its own essential symbols and technical vocabulary, so music has a technical vocabulary that enables the listener to appreciate the way in which the hills and valleys of music unfold as a composition progresses.

So this dictionary is based on the premise that words alone cannot explain the meaning of musical terminology. To this end every definition is illustrated by a music example (often several music examples) that takes two forms: a printed score (the route map) and a recording of the music represented in the score (the landscape itself). Thus, to take a simple example, the entry on 'quaver' refers the reader to music example B18 and to the entry on 'note'. For some it may be sufficient to look up the music example and listen to the corresponding track, since Handel's quavers can be seen and heard against an unvarying beat and in the context of longer and shorter note-values (identified in the score). Others may wish to follow the reference to 'note' and take up references to rhythm and pitch in the music examples and in the 'Elements of music'.

Preface

The dictionary is based on a second premise that, even when one has heard and understood the workings of a particular musical feature, it is necessary to hear it again in its original context (or perhaps in several different contexts). For instance, it is exceedingly unlikely that an isolated suspension will be encountered in a public recital. To this end complete pieces are included among the music examples and references are made to specific sections in the set of eight chapters that form part of this volume. These allow the reader to explore cognate terms. Thus the entry on 'theme' refers the reader to the first bar of a complete fugue in which the theme (or fugal subject) is heard several times in a contrapuntal context. The reader is also referred to the first 14 bars of a complete movement in sonata form in which the opening theme (or first subject) is heard again at the start of the recapitulation. Following the reference to 'EM 3.2' (the second section in Chapter 3 of the 'Elements of music') leads the reader on to a discussion of different types of thematicism, such as theme and variation forms and thematic transformation.

A third premise is that only through the works of real composers can the true significance of musical terminology be fully apprehended. Thus a discussion of types of scale starts from the music itself and shows how scales are theoretical concepts derived from the actual practices of composers. This can be seen in A82 and A83 where an undecorated version of a theme contains only the pitches of a harmonic minor scale, while its decorated version includes all of the pitches of the ascending and descending forms of a melodic minor scale. Similarly, different types of motion are illustrated by the same theme with its bass part in A85. All of these versions of the theme (with Jacquet de la Guerre's ornamentation) can then be heard on track A84 in a complete performance of the rondeau from which they are taken.

A final premise is that music is primarily the art of significant sound. It follows from this that terms relating to techniques that cannot be heard by most people have been excluded. An example is the serial phenomenon of combinatoriality. However, there are very few terms of this type. Where listeners are likely to find difficulty hearing a particularly complex device an effort has been made to find the simplest possible example of it. This is true of C40 in which a single unaccompanied melody of 12 pitches comprises a complete tone row that divides into four three-note motives, each containing intervals of a tone and semitone, with the whole tune rising through the notes of an ascending chromatic scale. The music is so simple that it is possible to tick off the notes of the row as they are heard even without the aid of the score. Similarly the verticalisation of the row in the four chords at the end of C40 is sufficiently simple for many to be able to hear that the outer parts consist of three-note segments of a chromatic scale that relate to one or other of the four cells identified by the letters A, B, C and D (though it takes a keen ear to detect that the same is true of the inner parts). The trouble with this approach is that such simple examples are unlikely to be typical of styles employing these techniques. To solve the problem the same devices are shown in more complex and more typical contexts in other examples. Thus another but much more complex twelve-tone melody is sung in bars 2–4 of C88, a row that, like the one in C40, is verticalised, this time to form the three chords heard in the first bar. There will be a tiny minority of people who will be able to detect these processes by ear alone. The rest of us will at least understand what Stravinsky is about, having first encountered the devices in their simplest forms in the extract from Hauer's song.

The nature of the dictionary and its length preclude a survey of the extensive terminology of non-western cultures (it would require a couple of dictionaries in sound to deal adequately with these types of music). Even within the canon of western art music a few rare terms, genres and instruments have had to be excluded. For example, I regret that neither 'caccia' nor 'catch' have made it, but hope that the underlying styles of both will be understood through other entries and music examples that are included.

David Bowman

Introduction

How to use this dictionary

Begin by looking up the relevant term in the dictionary's alphabetic entries in Volume 1. Most English terms are followed by a concise definition. It may be that this is all that is required. If not, a number of avenues may be followed.

(a) Take up the reference (or the first reference if there is more than one) to a music example. Thus under *Phrygian mode* reference is made to A37. In this example the mode is printed beneath the last two phrases of a phrygian-mode melody.

(b) Listen to the corresponding track. In the case of track A37 this will enable the listener to apprehend phrygian-mode music as sound rather than as just a theoretical conception expressed as a scale. The exact point at which the two phrases related to the scale begin can be pinpointed by the timing given at the start of this passage (0:45 = 45 seconds from the start of the track).

(c) Take up any other references. Under *Phrygian mode* reference is made to a transposed version of the last two phrases of the phrygian melody (A38). Reading the music and listening to the viola solo will enable the reader to understand how the phrygian mode (or any modal scale) can retain its identity when the melody is played at a higher or lower pitch level. Finally the reference to A39 leads to an extract in which harmonies derived from the phrygian mode accompany the original melody.

(d) Take up the reference or references to the 'Elements of music' (EM) given at the end of the entry. Under *Phrygian mode* the reference is EM 2.4.1. This subsection of Chapter 2 is concerned with authentic modes, so it is now possible to explore three similar modes, or, by reading the whole section (2.4 Modality), to become acquainted with all eight church modes and the modes that were added by Glareanus in the sixteenth century (all of them illustrated by printed and recorded music examples).

Where American terminology differs from British usage there are separate entries, with cross-references between them. Some entries are very short (particularly those on foreign terms that have English or well-known Italian synonyms). Nevertheless, it is possible to follow the avenues described above by taking up the cross-reference. Thus the German term *Abgestossen* is simply defined as 'Staccato'. For many, this, together with the reference to bar 1 of B41, will suffice. Others, wishing for a fuller definition, will look up *Staccato*. Under this head they will find not only a longer definition but also a longer music example in which staccato and legato phrases can be compared. They will also find a reference to a section in the 'Elements of music' on the larger subject of articulation.

Introduction

Abbreviations and symbols peculiar to this dictionary

Printed music examples and corresponding recordings bear the same identifiers. Thus A1 and A98 refer to the first and last tracks of compact disc A, and to music examples A1 and A98. Tracks B1–B79 and C1–C97 are contained on compact discs B and C respectively. The related music examples follow the same sequence (A1–98, then B1–79, then C1–97). In the alphabetic entries, references to both printed music and recordings are made by the use of these symbols (in some cases followed by bar and beat numbers). In the 'Elements of music', the same system is used except that, in the interests of prose style, titles and composers' names are sometimes given as well.

'EM' followed by a set of numbers at the end of an entry in Volume 1 refers the reader to the 'Elements of music'. The first number refers to one of the eight chapters, each of which begins with an introductory paragraph (so 'EM 7.0' means the first paragraph in the chapter on 'The structure of music'). A numeral after the first dot refers to a complete section within a chapter (so 'EM 1.2' means the section on accents in the chapter on 'Rhythm, metre and tempo'). Some sections are divided into several subsections. These are represented by numerals after a second dot. Thus 'EM 8.10.3' refers to the subsection on the romantic character piece within the section on the romantic era (8.10) in Chapter 8.

In Volume 2 (the music examples) timings from the beginning of a track are shown by two numerals separated by a colon within a box. These two numbers represent minutes and seconds elapsed from the beginning of the track (not from the first note of the corresponding printed music example). Timings are not given for very short examples or for examples where the text makes it easy to follow the music. These timings are rarely used in Volume 1, but the given bar numbers enable the listener to pinpoint the particular feature to which reference is made. Thus after the first definition of *Development* reference is made to bars 52–71 of B40. Above bar 52 the beginning of the development is identified by the symbol 1:00 (one minute from the start of the track) while above bar 72 the symbol 1:23 (one minute and 23 seconds) identifies both the end of the development and the beginning of the next section. Similarly for the other example cited (B36) the beginning and end of the development (bars 141–179) can be identified on disc by the symbols 2:09 and 2:41. Readers should note that references to the music examples in Volume 2 illustrate the sound of the instrument cited, whether or not the abbreviation in question appears in the musical example.

Other abbreviations and symbols

The following common abbreviations have been used in the Dictionary:

A. Augmentation
Arab. Arabic
Eng. English
f. Feminine
pl. Plural
Fr. French
Ger. German
Gk. Greek
Hung. Hungarian
I. Inversion
Ind. Indonesian
It. Italian
Jav. Javanese
Lat. Latin
m. Masculine
Mac. Macaronic
Mal. Malay
Pol. Polish
Port. Portuguese
sing. Singular
Span. Spanish

The following musical symbols have been used in the Dictionary:
For ♯ see *Sharp*
For ♭ see *Flat*
For ♮ see *Natural*
For × and ♯♯ see *Double sharp*
For ♭♭ and ♭♭ see *Double flat*

The Dictionary follows the convention of using Roman numerals thus:
I = tonic triad
II = supertonic triad
III = mediant triad
IV = subdominant triad
V = dominant triad
VI = submediant triad
VII = leading-note triad

Superscript and subscript numbers added to these Roman numerals indicate dissonant additions and inversions such as:

a) V^7 = root-position dominant-7th chord
b) V^9 = dominant-major-9th chord (with or without its root)
c) $V^{\flat 9}$ = dominant-minor-9th chord (with or without its root)
d) V^{13} = dominant-13th chord
e) V^6 = first-inversion dominant triad
f) V^6_4 = second-inversion dominant triad
g) V^6_5 = first-inversion dominant-7th chord
h) V^4_3 = second-inversion dominant-7th chord
i) V^4_2 = third-inversion dominant-7th chord

A flat sign before a Roman numeral indicates a triad on a flattened scale degree. Thus ♭II means a triad on the flattened supertonic (eg B58, bar 17), and ♭II⁶ means a first-inversion triad whose root is the flattened supertonic – a Neapolitan 6th (eg B65, bar 23).

Superscript numbers are also used to indicate the beat of a bar (bar 9^3 means the third beat of bar 9) and pitch (for details of which see the folded insert).

Acknowledgements

Hundreds of musicians have contributed directly or indirectly to this dictionary. Most of their names are recorded elsewhere, and I am deeply indebted to all of them. Here I should like to offer my more personal thanks to those who have given freely of their time and talents, and who are either not mentioned in an index or who are deserving of more explicit recognition.

Without the unwavering support and encouragement of my wife, Jill, I would never have had the courage to embark on the project. Without the tenacity of Sarah Williams, the general manager of Rhinegold Publishing, the dictionary would never have seen the light of day. Both of these good ladies, though heavily committed in their own professional lives, contributed in the most practical ways to ensure progress over many years. My special thanks go to all of the staff at Rhinegold, but especially to Keith Diggle and Lucien Jenkins.

Of the performers who contributed to the recordings I should particularly like to express my gratitude to Simon Wright, who not only performed splendidly on a range of keyboard instruments, but who also helped with the correction of the scores and offered invaluable advice. Among other performers I should like to thank my friends and colleagues who so magnificently organised and directed ensembles: Charles Cole (the Scarsdale Singers), Nicholas Cole (the Royal Academy of Music), and Magnus Johnston (the Johnston Quartet). My sincere thanks also go to Ian Little, the Director of Music of Ampleforth College, who not only performed brilliantly, but also facilitated recording venues in the college and the abbey church. Among other performers I should like to single out Nigel Cliffe who went to great lengths to ensure that we would be able to make a recording of Bodorová's Requiem with the Schidlof Quartet.

For half of my life I have been fortunate enough to call on the resources of the community of Ampleforth Abbey. Here I should like to record my thanks to the Abbot and Headmaster for permissions so freely given. My particular thanks go to Fr Adrian Convery, Fr Oswald McBride, Fr Alexander McCabe, Fr Lawrence McTaggart, Fr Anthony Marett-Crosby and Fr David Morland for their singing, translations and advice. My colleagues Paul Terry and Mike Weare read early drafts of the dictionary and saved me from many an error, as did Tony Barton and Tim Bayley of the University of York. I am also grateful to two other colleagues, Christopher Wilding for his translation of the somewhat obscure text of A30, and John Mackenzie for his thorough introduction to the art of guitar music.

With so much to do in what never seemed to be enough time, the success of the recording sessions was in no small measure attributable to the patience and professionalism of our recording engineers and producers, Alan Ferne, Michael McCarthy and John West. With his usual tenacity Peter Nickol worked wonders in tracking down the copyright owners of scores and recordings and in finding alternative recordings when licences were not forthcoming. In this connection my special thanks go to Roger Wright, the controller of BBC Radio 3, and Chris Hutchins, Felicity Williams and Mike Wood of Boosey and Hawkes. Finally I should like to offer my sincere thanks to Laura Davey who read every word and every note of the (almost) finished product. Her perceptive comments are reflected in text and music throughout the dictionary

I am deeply grateful to everyone who contributed to the dictionary, but whatever errors remain I acknowledge to be my sole responsibility.

Acknowledgements

The author and publishers would like to place on record their gratitude to the following people for their help with the production of the dictionary:

Hallam Bannister, Ann Barkway, William Carter, Michael Downes, Monica Leiher, Robin Newton, Chris Painter, Peter Skuce and Abigail Walmsley.

Copyright credits: score anthology
The publishers are grateful to the following who have granted permission for the use of copyright music:
Arco Diva for the extract from the *Terezín Requiem* by Bodorová.
Boosey and Hawkes Music Publishers Ltd for various examples taken from works by Bartók: *Mikrokosmos*, © copyright 1940 by Hawkes and Son (London) Ltd; String Quartet No. 6, © copyright 1941 by Hawkes and Son (London) Ltd; and the *Concerto for Orchestra*, © copyright 1946 by Hawkes and Son (London) Ltd; also for the extracts from: Symphony No. 7 by Shostakovich, © copyright 1941 by Boosey and Hawkes Music Publishers Ltd; *Serenade for Tenor, Horn and Strings* by Britten, © copyright 1944 by Hawkes and Son (London) Ltd; *Billy Budd* by Britten, © copyright 1951 by Hawkes and Son (London) Ltd; *Canticum sacrum* ('Surge, aquilo') by Stravinsky, © copyright 1956 by Hawkes and Son (London) Ltd; *Ave maris stella* by Maxwell Davies, © copyright 1976 by Boosey and Hawkes Music Publishers Ltd; *Quickening* by MacMillan with words by Michael Symmons Roberts, © copyright 1999 by Boosey and Hawkes Music Publishers Ltd.
Boosey and Hawkes Music Publishers Ltd also for *Abii ne viderem* by Kancheli, © copyright by Musikverlag Hans Sikorski, Hamburg. Sole publisher for the UK, British Commonwealth (excluding Canada), Eire and South Africa: Boosey and Hawkes Music Publishers Ltd.
Faber Music for the extract from *Fantasia on a Theme by Thomas Tallis* by Vaughan Williams, reproduced by permission of Faber Music Ltd, London.
International Music Publications for 'Danilo's Song' from *The Merry Widow*, music by Lehár, words by Viktor Leon and Leo Stein, translated by Paul Francis Webster, © 1994 Glocken Verlag Ltd/Chappell Music Ltd, Warner/Chappell Music Limited, London W6 8BS. Reproduced by permission of International Music Publications Ltd.
Alfred A. Kalmus Ltd for the extracts from: *Pierrot Lunaire* by Schoenberg, © 1914 by Universal Edition, copyright renewed 1941 by Arnold Schoenberg; *Five Pieces for Orchestra* by Webern, © 1923 by Universal Edition A. G., Wien, copyright renewed 1951 by Anton Webern's heirs; *Le marteau sans maître* by Boulez, © 1954 by Universal Edition (London) Ltd, final version ©1957 by Universal Edition (London) Ltd; Roumanian Folk Dance No. 3 for Violin and Piano by Bartók arranged by Székely, © 1926 by Universal Edition, copyright renewed 1953 by Boosey and Hawkes, Inc, New York. Reproduced by permission.
Robert Lienau Musik Verlag for the extract from *Hölderlin-Lieder*, Op. 21 No. 2 by Hauer, © 1922 by Robert Lienau Edition, Frankfurt/Main (Germany). All rights reserved.
Music Sales for the extracts from: *The Planets* by Holst, reproduced by permission of J. Curwen and Sons Ltd; *Hymn to the Holy Spirit* by Tavener, reproduced by permission of Chester Music Ltd; *Cry* by Swayne, reproduced by permission of Novello and Co Ltd.
Oxford University Press for the descant by Willcocks to *Unto Us a Child Is Born*,

Acknowledgements

© Oxford University Press 1961, licence no. 05277; and for the extract from *Façade* by Walton, licence no. 05126.

Peters Edition Limited, London, for the extract from *Till Eulenspiegel* by Strauss, © assigned 1932 to C. F. Peters, Leipzig.

Ricordi for the extracts from *Ionisation* by Varèse, © CASA Ricordi – BMG-Ricordi S.p.A.

Professor N. Sandon for the conductus *Pange melos lachrimosum* from the *Oxford Anthology of Music*.

Schott and Co Ltd (London) for the extracts from *Concierto de Aranjuez* by Rodrigo, © Joaquin Rodrigo, Madrid, and from *Concert Royal* No. 4 by Couperin.

SJ Music for the extract from *Élégie* by Bosanquet.

United Music Publishers for the extracts from *L'Ascension* by Messiaen, reproduced by permission of Editions Alphonse Leduc, Paris, copyright owner for the world, and from two works by Ravel, *Ma Mère l'oye* and *Le Tombeau de Couperin*, © 1912 and 1919 respectively, co-ownership Redfield and Nordice, exclusive representative Editions Durand, Paris.

Universal Edition (London) Ltd for the extracts from: *Háry János* by Kodály, © 1927 by Universal Edition, copyright assigned 1952 to Universal Edition (London) Ltd, London, copyright renewed 1955; *Clapping Music* by Reich, © 1980 by Universal Edition (London) Ltd; Roumanian Folk Dance No. 3 by Bartók, © copyright 1926 by Universal Edition, copyright renewed 1953 by Boosey and Hawkes, Inc, New York. Reproduced by permission.

Copyright credits: recordings

The publishers are grateful to the following who have granted permission for the use of copyright recordings:

℗ BBC 1999 for track C97. Released by arrangement with BBC Music.

BIS Records for track A89.

Brewhouse Records for track A60.

Chandos Records Ltd for tracks A15, A16 and C38.

Decca Music Group for tracks A12, A32, A35, A36, A39, A61, A75, B37, B59, B60, B63, B68, B73, C35 and C86 all licensed courtesy of Decca Music Group Ltd.

ECM Records for track C94, from the album *Abii ne viderem* ECM New Series 1510.

Hänssler Verlag GmbH for tracks B7 and B8.

Harmonia Mundi for tracks A13 and C34.

Hyperion Records Ltd for tracks A22, A58, B57, C69, C70, C71, C72 and C88.

Meridian Records for track B40.

Naxos for tracks A17, A18, A21, A23, A26, A27, A34, A44, A62, A63, A64, A65, A66, A68, A69, A88, A95, A96, A97, A98, B4, B5, B14(b), B15, B16, B17, B19, B21, B27, B28, B29, B30, B31, B32, B33, B34, B35, B36, B50, B58, B61, B65, B66, B74, B76, B77, C1, C2, C3, C4, C5, C6, C7, C8, C10, C11, C19, C20, C27, C28, C29, C32, C33, C36, C37, C41, C66, C67, C74, C75, C76, C77, C78, C79, C80, C81, C82, C83, C84 and C85.

Nimbus Records for track C92.

NMC Recordings Ltd and the BBC Singers for track C91.

Priory Records for track C30.

Sony Music for track C87.

Stradivarius Records for track B25.

Unicorn-Kanchana Records for track C90.

York Guitar Quartet for track C68.

Acknowledgements

Photographic acknowledgements
Paul Signac: *Sailing Boats in the Harbour of St Tropez*. © ADAGP, Paris, and DACS, London, 2000.
Georges-Pierre Seurat: *Bathers at Asnières*. National Gallery Picture Library, London.
Claude Monet: *Cathédrale de Rouen*. Réunion des Musées Nationaux – ADAGP, Paris.
Claude Monet: *Régates à Argenteuil*. Réunion des Musées Nationaux – ADAGP, Paris.
Francesco Guardi: *San Giorgio Maggiore, circa 1770*. The Wallace Collection, London.

For Jill,
without whom…

A

A. 1. The first of a series of letters denoting the relative or absolute pitches of notes. Unqualified, the letter A can refer to any of the nine pitches shown in A1. Each is an octave apart from its nearest neighbours. The A shown in the second space up on the treble stave is of particular importance since its pitch was fixed at 440 Hz (Hertz) by international agreement. This is the note (usually sounded by an oboist) by which most orchestras standardise their tuning before a concert starts. When the A string of a violin is in tune with this pitch it will vibrate along its whole length 440 times per second, whereas the longer A string of a cello, sounding an octave below the violin's A string, will vibrate half as fast (220 Hz). All nine A's shown in A1 are played on an organ, each succeeding A causing cycles of compression and decompression of the air that are twice as fast as those caused by the previous note. There are several systems of symbols that distinguish between the note A in different octaves. The combination of capital A or lower-case a with numbers above or below them (shown on the diagram of a keyboard on the folded insert) is a modified form of the widely accepted Helmholtz system used throughout this dictionary. **2.** An abbreviation of alto (A31, second stave down in second and third systems). See *Concert pitch*.

A 2, a 3, a 4, a 5. 1. Abbreviations of the Italian terms 'a due', 'a tre', 'a quattro', 'a cinque', meaning for two, three, four or five voices or instrumental parts. The most common title for a baroque trio sonata (A74) was 'Sonata a tre'. Mass settings are often catalogued according to the number of voice parts (A52 is the second Kyrie from Palestrina's *Missa Iste confessor a 4*). **2.** Performance directions having two opposite meanings that are only clarified by their context in a score: **a)** two solo instruments should play a single melodic line in unison (C82, bar 9), **b)** a section of instruments that normally plays in unison should divide into two or more groups to play the increased number of parts written for them (C28, bar 6).

ABA, ABACA. Symbolic representations of ternary form (C2) and simple rondo form (A84). Other combinations of capital letters are used to represent other musical structures.

Abbellimenti (It.). Ornaments. A66 is an ornamented version of A65.

Abgesang (Ger.). The last section of a piece in bar form (A13). *EM 7.9.1, 8.6.2*.

Abgestossen (Ger.). Staccato (B41, bar 1). *EM 1.14*.

Abnehmend (Ger.). Diminuendo (B79, bars 24–26).

Absolute music, abstract music. Music that can be understood only in its own terms, not by reference to extramusical ideas or images (B40). *EM 8.10.7*.

Absolute pitch. The ability to identify the pitch of a note without another pitch having been first identified. A person with absolute pitch would be able to tell that A95–A98 are played a semitone lower than notated without reading the footnotes. The term perfect pitch is synonymous with absolute pitch (though the latter more accurately describes the phenomenon). See *Relative pitch*.

Abzug (Ger.). The diminuendo often heard as an appoggiatura nears its resolution (B69(b)).

Academy, accademia (It.). Originally an Italian institution devoted to the promotion of arts, sciences, literature or music. Monteverdi's *Orfeo* (A62–A66) was first performed at a meeting of the Accademia degli Invaghiti at Mantua in 1607. The term is now most often encountered in the titles of teaching institutes such as the Royal Academy of Music, London, but the spirit of scholarly enquiry and creativity is still maintained in organisations such as the Accademia Monteverdiana founded at Columbia University, New York, in 1961.

A cappella, alla cappella (It.). Choral music sung without instrumental accompaniment (A44). Medieval and renaissance sacred music is usually performed in this manner today even though renaissance polyphony was originally often supported by an instrumental accompaniment. See *Chorus*.

Accelerando (accel.) (It.). Getting faster (C82, bars 1–8). See *Tempo markings*.

Accent

Accent. 1. A stress on certain beats or individual notes caused by: **a)** the prevailing metre (although accents are not marked in B9 a stress is implied by the changing intervals of the melody), **b)** dynamic changes (the triple metre of B38 is disrupted by Mozart's dynamic marks in bars 3–8), **c)** articulation (the second note of B10 is felt to be accented because the first note is played staccato whereas the second is sustained for its full value), **d)** the relative durations of notes (the second note of B6 is felt to be accented because it is twice the length of the first), **e)** changes of pitch (the first and third beats of bar 1 of A87 are felt to be accented because they both begin with the highest notes in this bar). **2.** From the late 16th to the 18th century, a French and German term for a springer (B25, bar 52) or appoggiatura (B1, bar 4, beat 2). See *Agogic accent. EM 1.2, 1.7.1, 3.10.2.*

Accented passing note. A dissonant note sounded on the beat and filling the gap between two harmony notes a third apart. In bar 9 of A30 the quaver D♯ in the soprano part forms a dissonant compound ninth with the bass and it fills the gap between the preceding E♯ and the ensuing C♯ (both of which are harmony notes in the chord of C major sounded on the last two beats of this bar). Chromatic accented passing notes may be heard on tracks B70 and B71 (they are identified in the corresponding printed examples). *EM 4.3.2.*

Acciaccatura (It.). A melodic decoration (♪) a step above or below the note it decorates. On keyboard instruments the notes are often played together, the acciaccatura being immediately released. On melody instruments the acciaccatura and the note it decorates are played in rapid succession (B73, bars 1–15). See *Ornaments. EM 3.10.2.*

Accidental. A symbol in front of a note that indicates a change of pitch or the cancellation of the effect of an earlier accidental. The flat sign (♭) in the first bar of C31 lowers the pitch of E by a semitone, while the first note of the triplet group in the next bar is unaffected by an accidental. The sharp sign (♯) on the next note raises the pitch of C by a semitone. The natural sign (♮) on the last note of the triplet cancels the effect of the sharp. The pitches of these four notes can be seen on the diagram of a keyboard on the folded insert (the C sounding at 65 Hz, the C♯ being the black note immediately above it, the E♭ being the black note immediately below E). A double sharp (𝄪 or ×) raises a note a whole tone (C25, bar 2), while a double flat (♭♭ or ♭) lowers a note a whole tone (C64, bar 3, beat 2).

Acclamation. 1. In the western Christian tradition, a corporate expression of praise (eg 'Alleluia') or assent (eg 'Amen'). An acclamation might be shouted or sung spontaneously in response to the words of a preacher (as it is in the joyful outpourings of African-American congregations), or it might be formalised as a plainsong or choral response (as it is in Roman Catholic and Anglican cathedrals and abbey churches). **2.** In plainsong, the chant sung immediately before the Gospel reading (A5), or any one of a number of responsorial chants such as 'Benedicamus Domino' (Let us bless the Lord) intoned by a priest or cantor, and 'Deo gratias' (Thanks be to God) sung by the whole choir or congregation (A8).

Accompagnato (It.). Accompanied. See *Recitativo accompagnato* and B16.

Accompanied recitative. See *Recitativo accompagnato* and B16.

Accompaniment. Music that supports one or more principal melodies. The continuo group in A68 accompanies the tenor soloist. The left-hand part of B74 is an accompaniment to the right-hand melody.

Accord (Fr.). Chord. 'Accord parfait' means 'triad' (A59, bars 1–2).

Accordatura (It.). The tuning of an instrument, usually to A at 440 Hz (A1), but sometimes to another standard (some of the instruments on the accompanying CDs are tuned to A at 415 Hz and so sound a semitone lower than printed, eg A88). The term is most often used of string instruments. Violin strings are tuned to g, d^1, a^1 and e^2. These open strings can be heard in bars 16–26 of B73.

Accordo (It.). Chord. C86 is composed of 20 different chords, some containing just three pitches (bar 10), others as many as 15 pitches (bar 6).

Achtel, Achtelnote (Ger.). Eighth-note or quaver (B18, variation 1).

Achtelpause (Ger.). Eighth note or quaver rest (the sign after the time signatures in the first bar of C7).

Aeolian mode

Acoustic bass guitar. For most musicians the term 'bass guitar' is a name for a guitar with a solid body and electronic components which is specifically designed to be used in conjunction with an electronic amplification system (C94). To distinguish this instrument from a large guitar reliant on a hollow body to amplify the sound 'bass guitar' is qualified by the adjective 'acoustic' (C68).

Acoustics. The science of sound. The four most important properties of a sound are its pitch (the middle c at the start of A57 has a frequency of 262 Hz, as shown in A2), its duration (it lasts roughly twice as long as the next note), its intensity (it is relatively quiet) and its timbre (it has the characteristic tone-colour of flue pipes). The last three of these properties are modified by the acoustics of the enclosed space in which the note is sounded (in this case a reverberant church) and the position and quality of the equipment used to record and play back the sound (the reverberant effects of the acoustics of the church were mitigated by close miking). See *Reverberation*.

Act. A principal section of an opera that is further subdivided into scenes and, in early operas, into recitatives (A62 and A63) and arias (A66). Operas can be divided by intervals into any number of acts: there are five in *Orfeo* but only two in *Die Zauberflöte* (B50). Since the early 19th century, many operas have fallen into three acts, each dramatically and musically unified. Britten's *Billy Budd* originally had four acts, but the extract shown in C86 comes from a revision in which the composer reduced the number of acts to three. In this more standard form the orchestral interlude comes at the dramatic crux of the last act.

Ad libitum (ad. lib.) (It.). A performance direction giving the player liberty to vary the tempo (C84) or in some other way to change the printed part (in bar 5 of C76 the flautist is allowed to repeat the printed semiquaver figure as often as desired).

Adagio (It.). Slow (B59). See *Tempo markings*.

Added-note harmony. See *Added-2nd chord*, *Added-6th chord*, C23 (bars 3–4) and C26. *EM 5.8.3*.

Added-2nd chord. A triad with a 2nd above the root (C26, bars 3–4). *EM 5.5.11.*

Added-6th chord. A triad with the note a major 6th above the root. In the first bar of B66 the damper pedal sustains all of the notes in the figuration above the tonic chord of F major. In addition to the notes of chord I (F, A and C) the note a major 6th above the root (D♮) is heard four times, thus producing an arpeggiated version of the added-6th chord shown on the extra stave. Added-6th chords in root position are also heard in bars 5, 9, 13 and 17. Major 6ths are added to second-inversion triads in bars 2, 6, 10 and 18. *EM 5.5.11.*

Additive rhythm. A term invented by Carl Sachs in 1953. Its meaning is imprecise because it has been used in reference to a range of rhythmic and metrical phenomena, notably in the works of Stravinsky, Bartók and Tippett. To overcome this problem Ian Kemp suggested in 1984 that two types of additive rhythms could be distinguished, namely fixed additive rhythm and free additive rhythm. The former category is sometimes called additive metre since it refers to two or more groups of short notes which, added together, form an asymmetric pattern of beats that is repeated in every bar of a substantial passage or an entire movement. This is illustrated in C66 in which short notes (quavers) are grouped 3+3+2 in every bar of the extract. Free additive rhythms consist of irregular groups of notes added together in patterns that are unpredictable and hence do not generate regularly organised metrical units. Even if, for convenience and ease of performance, the composer imposes regularly spaced barlines, these rhythms cut across them. Free additive rhythms are apparent in the last four bars of C64. Even though Bartók maintains barlines corresponding to his time signature, his phrase marks (and the performance on CD C) clearly define the additive rhythms shown above and below the two melodies in these bars (ie quavers grouped 6+5+4+3+3+3+5 in the right hand and quavers grouped 6+5+4+4+6 in the left hand). *EM 1.5.*

A due, a 2 (It.), **à deux, à 2** (Fr.). See *A 2* and A28 (Kyrie for two voices) and C82, bar 9 (unison).

Aeolian mode. A scale that can be reproduced by playing the white notes of the piano from any A♮ to the A♮ an octave above it (see the diagram of a keyboard on the folded insert). It was one of the modes added to the eight church modes by Glareanus in 1547 to help categorise melodies that did not

Aerophone

conform to any of these traditional scales. This scale (sometimes called the natural minor scale) is distinguished from other similar scales by the positions of the two semitones. They are formed between the second and third degrees (B–C) and the fifth and sixth degrees (E–F) making the scale identical in structure to the descending form of the melodic minor scale (A83). Provided the same order of tones and semitones is maintained the aeolian mode (like modern major and minor scales) and aeolian melodies can be transposed up or down by any interval. A12 shows the aeolian scale transposed to D. The B♭ is needed in order to maintain the same intervallic structure as the untransposed scale (semitones between the second and third degrees – E/F – and the fifth and sixth degrees – A/B♭). Aeolian modality is particularly strong in this ballade because: (a) every note comes from the aeolian scale, (b) three of its six phrases end on D (the final or first degree of the mode), (c) the other three phrases end on the characteristic flat seventh of the mode (the subtonic), and (d) the melody ends with a cadence formed by the subtonic and final. Aeolian modality pervades both right- and left-hand parts in bars 9–21 of C32 – a passage that contrasts strongly with the major tonality of bars 1–9^1 and 21–29. Just as a B♭ was needed to form an aeolian scale on D, so an F♯ (shown as a key signature) is needed to form an aeolian scale on E (with semitones between F♯ and G and between B and C). Aeolian modality is strongly asserted by the cadences in bars 16–17 and 20–21 in which both parts end on the final of the mode (E♮). Couperin's melody in bars 9–21 of C32 is in the authentic aeolian mode. This means that its range extends from the lower final (E on the bottom line of the stave) to the final an octave above (E in the top space of the stave). In its plagal form (called the hypoaeolian mode) the range extends from the note a 4th below the final to the note a 5th above it. B61 shows a hypoaelian scale on G and a melody (bars 3–11) in the hypoaeolian mode extending from dominant to dominant (d^1–d^2). In this case the final of the modal melody is established by the modal bass part which begins and ends on G. *EM 2.3.3, 2.4.1.*

Aerophone. A category of musical instruments that rely upon air to generate sound (eg the trombone and regal in A63). See *Brass instruments*, *Instruments* and *Woodwind instruments*.

Affection, Affekt (Ger.), **Affetto** (It.). A fixed emotion or passion such as indignation (A63). The baroque concept of the Doctrine of the Affections held that music moved the emotions through specific rhythms and melodic figures that evoked particular passions. Thus in B15 Bach arouses a feeling of awe at the vision of the 'Mighty Lord and strong King' by his deployment of martial arpeggios throughout the first part of this da capo aria. From an aural point of view this consistent use of a few sharply characterised motifs throughout entire movements is the most obvious legacy of the doctrine of the affections. The same unity of affection is evident in serious operatic arias of the 18th century (in B50 Mozart arouses the single emotion of rage throughout the whole aria).

After-beat. English for *Nachschlag* (B1, bar 3, last two semiquavers). See *Ornaments*.

Aggregate. See *Pitch aggregate* and the notes in a box in C64.

Agitato (It.). Agitated, excited. The direction 'Animato, molto agitato' in C69 means 'animated and very excited'. See *Tempo markings*.

Agnus Dei (Lat.). The fifth item of the Ordinary of the Mass (A19).

Agogic accent. An accent brought about by the articulation of the note itself and the notes around it. In B10 the first note is played staccato so the longer second note sounds accented. *EM 1.2, 1.7.1.*

Agréments (Fr.). Ornaments (A84 and B17).

Air (Eng. and Fr.). Song. The air was the most common type of solo vocal movement in French baroque operas and contemporary English operas and semi-operas (and so is a counterpart of the Italian aria). It was also a name given to independent art songs in both countries. A75 is an extract from an air upon a ground that, while being particularly Purcellian, also exhibits many of the features of earlier French airs. See *Aria* and *Arie*. *EM 8.7.1.*

Ais (Ger.). A♯ (B28, bar 5, last note).

Aisis (Ger.). A double sharp, A𝄪 (C79, second clarinet, bar 2, third note – which is a semitone lower than the B♯s on either side of it). See *Doppelkreuz*.

Akkord (Ger.). Chord. C86 is composed of

Altered chord

20 different chords, some containing just three pitches (bar 10), others as many as 15 pitches (bar 6).

Al fine (It.). An abbreviation of 'Da capo al fine' ([repeat] from the beginning up to the word 'fine' [end]) (B15, bar 120).

Al rovescio (It.). See *Rovescio* and B25.

Al segno (It.). An abbreviation of 'Dal segno al fine' (C2, bar 41).

Al tallone (It.). In string playing, a performance direction requiring the use of the heel of the bow (C70, bar 1). See *Au talon* and *Talon*.

Alberti bass, Alberti figuration. Originally a late 18th-century type of broken-chord accompaniment that lies well under the fingers of a keyboard player's left hand. This sort of figuration was soon transferred to accompanimental parts in orchestral textures. Alberti figuration is built on a constantly repeated four-note figure consisting of a low note, a high note, a middle note and the high note again (B37, second violins, bars 20–25). See *Ostinato*.

Alcuna, alcuno, alcun' (It.). Some. In the performance direction at the head of C4 'con alcuna licenza' means 'with some liberty' (ie with some rhythmic flexibility).

Aleatoric music, aleatory music. Chance music. There has always been an element of chance even in the most prescriptive scores (the composer cannot predetermine the precise timbres of the instruments for which he writes or the particular vocal qualities of a singer). But as the term is most commonly used it refers to 20th-century music in which composers such as Boulez and Stockhausen deliberately delegated important parameters of their works to the performer. Aleatoric music as such declined in importance in the closing decades of the 20th century, but aleatoric passages within otherwise prescriptive scores continue to be common. In bars 9–11 of C97 the precise music played by two complete orchestral sections is left to chance. The number of repetitions of the bell music (bar 36ff) is determined at the last minute by the conductor. In bars 39–41 each singer in the chorus is free to improvise a melodic line from the set of pitches prescribed by the composer, and treble voices are allowed similar licence in bars 50–67. *EM 8.11.10, 8.11.11*.

All'ottava (It.). A direction requiring the performer to play an octave above written pitch. It is most often indicated by *8va*............ or just *8*............ and is cancelled when the dotted line ends, sometimes reinforced by the word 'loco' (return to written pitch) (C9, bars 1–8).

All'unisono (It.). The simultaneous performance of the same melody by two or more instruments (B29, bars 1–10).

Alla breve (It.). The time signature shown immediately after the clef in A31. Nowadays it is usually interpreted as meaning two minim beats per bar. See *Cut time*.

Alla chitarra, quasi chitarra (It.). See *Chitarra* and C69. *EM 6.5.5*.

Alla tedesca (It.). In the German style. See *Tedesca* and B44.

Allargando (allarg.) (It.). Getting slower (bars 1 and 15–18 of C97). See *Tempo markings*.

Allegretto (It.). Moderately fast (B38). See *Tempo markings*.

Allegro (It.). Fast (C63). See *Tempo markings*.

Alleluia (Lat.). The third item of the Proper of the Mass. It is sung just before a reading from one of the New Testament Gospels and consists of the Alleluia proper and a verse from a psalm appropriate to the liturgical feast or season. It is characterised by lengthy melismas, the longest of these being the jubilus on the last syllable of the word 'Alleluia' (A5).

Allemande (Fr.). The first of the four most common dances in a baroque suite, the allemande is usually in slow $\frac{4}{4}$ time with anacrustic phrasing and complex contrapuntal textures (B17). *EM 7.4.4, 8.7.3*.

Almain, alman (Eng.). Allemande (B17).

Almglocken (Ger.). Cowbells (C28).

Alt (Ger.). **1.** Alto or contralto (A22). **2.** The phrase 'in alt' (from the Italian 'in alto') refers to the range of pitches from g^2 to $f\sharp^3$ shown on the folded insert.

Alteration. The change of pitch effected by an accidental. In B28 the diatonic pitch of C♮ in bar 1 is altered by a semitone in bar 2.

Altered chord. A chord in which one or more notes are chromatically inflected. For example, the Neapolitan 6th (B50, bars 80–

Alternatim

81) can be considered to be a chromatically altered supertonic triad in first inversion.

Alternatim (Lat.). The alternation of differing musical forces in the performance of a liturgical text. The principle is evident in the alternation of monophonic chant and polyphony in A10.

Alternativo (It.), **alternativement** (Fr.). An 18th-century performance direction indicating that the first of a pair of movements is to be repeated after the second has been played. In solo music it was common practice to add improvised ornaments to the first of the pair when it was repeated. In B25 compare the Menuetto (bars 1–20) with its embellished repeat (bars 45–64).

Altflöte (Ger.). Alto flute (C87).

Altissimo (It.). Very high. The phrase 'in altissimo' refers to the range of pitches from g^3 to $f\sharp^4$ shown on the folded insert.

Alto. 1. A low female voice (A22) or a countertenor (A12). See the folded insert for the approximate range of an alto. **2.** In French, viola (Track A38). **3.** The second highest part (whether for instruments or voices) in a four-part texture (crumhorn 2 in A35).

Alto clef. One of the moveable C clefs. It indicates that middle C is on the middle line of the stave. It is most often used nowadays for viola parts. Alto clefs may be found in old editions for alto voice and alto trombone parts, but this form of notation is now obsolete in these contexts. See *C clefs* and A38 (in which the same melody is shown in the bass clef and the alto C clef).

Alto flute, flute in G. A large flute pitched a 4th below the most familiar orchestral flute (see folded insert). Its entire range is explored in C87. *EM 6.6.1.*

Alto oboe, Althoboe (Ger.). Cor anglais (C88, bars 3–5). See *Reed instruments.*

Altus (Lat.). Alto (A52). See also *Alto* 3 and A35, crumhorn 2.

Am Frosch (Ger.). A performance direction requiring a string player to use the heel of the bow (C70).

Am Griffbrett (Ger.). A performance direction requiring a string player to bow near or over the fingerboard (C34, cello, bars 7–8).

Am Steg (Ger.). A performance direction requiring a string player to play with the hairs of the bow near to the bridge (C34, cello, bars 2–6). *EM 6.5.8.*

Ambitus (Lat.). The range of pitches covered by a modal melody. Together with the pitch of the final, the *ambitus* is the most important element that determines modality. Thus A40 belongs to Mode I (the authentic form of the dorian mode) chiefly because it ends on D (the final) and because its *ambitus* coincides with the lower and upper finals of the mode (ie D–D on the white notes of a piano). A8 also ends on D, but its *ambitus* extends from A to a, a perfect 4th lower than the range of the authentic dorian mode. This plagal form of the dorian mode is known as the hypodorian mode. See *Church modes. EM 2.4.2, 8.4.1.*

Amboss (Ger.). Anvil (C48).

Amen cadence. Plagal cadence (the last two chords of A91, and A39, bars 17–18).

Amoroso (It.). Amorous, amorously (C29).

Anacrusis. One or more off-beat or weakbeat notes preceding the first strong beat of a musical phrase. Compare B79 (anacrustic phrasing) with B25 (in which every phrase in bars 1–20 begins on the first beat of the bar).

Anacrustic, anacrusic. Adjective used to describe a phrase that begins with an upbeat and ends in the middle of a bar. All eight phrases of A22 are anacrustic.

Anche (Fr.), **ancia** (It.). Reed. Reed instruments can be heard on tracks A32 and A35.

Andamento (It). **1.** A fugal subject that, unlike a *soggetto*, is of a significant length (B9). **2.** A sequence (B7, bars 7–12). **3.** A fugal episode (B14, bars 5–6). See *Attacco.*

Andante (It.). Moderately slow (B27). See *Tempo markings.*

Andantino (It.). A confusing performance direction that in the 18th century probably meant a slightly slower tempo than andante, but which, sometime in the 19th century, came to mean the opposite (slightly faster than andante). It is in the latter sense that Tchaikovsky uses the term at the beginning of C6. See *Tempo markings.*

Anhalten, anhaltend (Ger.). To hold or to allow to continue to sound (it means the same as 'laissez vibrer' in C97, bar 9, cymbal and tam-tam).

Anhang (Ger.). In music, an appendix to a complete edition or thematic catalogue containing works not to be found in the main series of volumes. The abbreviations A or Anh. are usual in identifying such works (hence KA 229 in the title of B40).

Anhemitonic. Without semitones. The descending whole-tone scale at the start of C21 and the pentatonic scales used by Bartók in C60–C63 are all anhemitonic. *EM 2.9.2.*

Anima (It.). Soul, spirit, life. In B64(a) the direction 'Con anima' can be interpreted as 'spirited' (literally 'with spirit').

Animando (It.). Becoming more lively, getting faster (C84, bar 9). See *Tempo markings.*

Animato (It.). Animated, lively (C69). See *Tempo markings.*

Animé (Fr.). Animated, lively. 'Animé et très décidé' in C18a means 'lively and very resolute'. See *Tempo markings.*

Ansatz (Ger.). 1. Embouchure. In the performance of the trumpet part of B15 the embouchure needs to be tighter for the performance of passages in the clarino register than elsewhere in this solo. 2. Attack (compare the effect of the different types of bowing in C69 and C70).

Anschwellend (Ger.). Getting louder, as in crescendo (B73, bars 13–15).

Answer. In a fugal exposition, a statement of the subject pitched a 5th above or a 4th below the original statement (B9, upper part, bars 5–10). This is an example of a real answer, that is to say that every melodic interval of the subject (bars 0–5) is exactly replicated in the answer. In a tonal answer one of the intervals is modified to avoid unwanted modulation (at the beginning of B14 the initial fall of a 3rd in the subject is changed to a fall of a tone at the start of the answer). See *Fugue. EM 4.5.1ff.*

Antecedent and consequent. 1. In a melody, two phrases of equal length, the second sounding like an answer to the first. In B28 an eight-bar antecedent ends with an imperfect cadence, while the balancing eight-bar consequent repeats the first phrase until the last two bars, where a perfect cadence answers the imperfect cadence, thus completing the musical sense of the whole theme. 2. The subject and answer in a fugal texture. In B29 the upper part of bars 0–4 can be called an antecedent and the lower part of bars 9–13 a consequent. This nomenclature is rarely used nowadays. *EM 3.2.1, 7.3.*

Anthem. The English counterpart of the Latin motet sung in the post-reformation liturgies of the Anglican Church. There are two distinct types: **a)** the full anthem is scored for chorus alone, and in the 16th century was in a style similar to contemporary continental motets such as that recorded on track A44 (though with an English text), **b)** the verse anthem is scored for one or more solo voices with instrumental accompaniment alternating with passages scored for full choir and instruments. In the first 22 bars of A61 solo alto, tenor and bass (identified as verse alto, verse tenor and verse bass) are accompanied by a consort of viols. The full choir (also accompanied by viols) is heard in the last five bars of the extract. In the complete anthem these two contrasted groups constantly alternate.

Anticipation. A metrically weak ornament which is of the same pitch as the harmony note it precedes. In the cadence at the end of section A in A89 the quaver G♯ at the end of bar 7 (forming a dissonant 4th from the bass) anticipates the G in the next bar (which forms a harmonious octave with the bass). The same sort of anticipation precedes an octave in bars 11, 15 and 23 in the same extract. *EM 4.3.6, 4.3.9.*

Antiphon. A text (usually biblical) often sung before and after a psalm or canticle (A4).

Antiphona ad introitum (Lat.). The first item of the Proper of the Mass, consisting of an antiphon, a verse of a psalm and the antiphon again (A4).

Antiphoner, antiphonary, antiphonale (Lat.). A collection of chants for the Divine Office including psalms (A6) and hymns (A49) as well as antiphons (A4). A49 is taken from the *Antiphonale Monasticum*, Desclée, Tournai, 1934, page 655. See *Vespers.*

Antiphony. A method of performance in which two or more groups of singers and/or instrumentalists are heard alternately. In A58 three instrumental choirs play the same three-beat phrase (A) antiphonally, then the process is repeated with a new phrase (B). *EM 6.11.6.*

Antique cymbals. Small high-pitched cymbals that may be struck together or sus-

Anvil

pended and struck with a beater. They can be of indefinite or definite pitch: the latter type can be heard at the end of C19. See *Percussion instruments. EM 6.8.3.*

Anvil. A blacksmith's anvil or a metal bar struck with a steel mallet or a metal hammer to simulate the sound made by a blacksmith (C48 and C54). See *Percussion instruments. EM 6.8.4.*

Aperto and chiuso (It.). **1.** In horn music, a return to normal playing (*aperto*) after stopped notes (*chiuso*). Although not marked 'chiuso' and 'aperto' by Britten the effect of alternating stopped notes (indicated by a cross below the note) and unstopped notes can be heard in the last two bars of C85. **2.** In medieval music, open and closed phrase endings. In A18 *aperto* phrases end on the 6th degree of the mode and *chiuso* phrases end on the final (tonic). *EM 7.9.5.*

A piacere (It.). A direction indicating that the performer is at liberty to execute the music in any fitting manner. Its meaning is similar to that of 'ad libitum', the term used by Bartók in bar 5 of C76: in the passage marked 'quasi cadenza' the beat is suspended to allow the flautist considerable rhythmic latitude, and so to play 'at pleasure'.

Appassionato (It.). Impassioned (C85, bar 8).

Applied dominant. Secondary dominant (B16, bar 4, beat 3). See *Dominant chords. EM 5.7.1.*

Appoggiatura (It.). A dissonant note approached by a leap and usually resolved by stepwise motion. In bar 14 of B61 the F♯ forms a discord with the other two notes of the chord. It is approached by a leap of a 3rd and it resolves down a step to an E♮. The full impact of a romantic appoggiatura can be heard in bar 17 of B68. An extremely dissonant chromatic appoggiatura can be heard in bars 6–7 of B74 (A♮ resolving to A♭). Appoggiaturas are sometimes written as grace notes in small type (B27, bar 32 – the A♮ is dissonant with the dominant-7th chord played on the other instruments). See *Ornaments. EM 3.10.1, 3.10.2, 4.3.5.*

Appuy (Fr.). In the early 18th century, the appoggiatura or note that has the effect of an appoggiatura at the beginning of a trill. In B9, bar 4 the accented G heard at the start of the trill is an *appuy*, and so is the D heard at the start of the trill in bar 9. See *Ornaments.*

Appuyé, appuyée (Fr.). Accented, emphasised (C20, bar 4, last quaver).

Arabesque. A passage or complete work featuring florid melodic decoration. The arabesque in bar 8 of B64(a) is supported by the simplest possible accompaniment (B64(b)) that needs to be played with rubato to accommodate the plethora of notes above it. See *Ornaments. EM 3.10, 3.10.3, 8.10.4.*

Arch form. A symmetrical form in which a central section is flanked by identical sections. Ternary form (ABA) is the simplest type of arch form (A26). *EM 7.7.3.*

Archlute, archiluth (Fr.), **archiliuto** (It.), **archilaúd** (Span.). A six- or seven-course lute to which six or seven unstopped bass strings have been added. It was similar to, and was used for the same purposes as the theorbo (A75).

Arco (It.), **archet** (Fr.). Bow. As a performance direction in string music it indicates a change to bowing after the use of another technique such as pizzicato. At the start of C31 the contrabassoon solo is accompanied by plucked cellos and basses. They change to bowing at the word 'arco' in bar 9. *EM 6.5.4.*

Aria (It.). **1.** Song. The term is most often used of extended vocal solos in baroque and classical operas, oratorios and cantatas. Some composers used the term for song-like vocal duets and trios. In his cantatas Bach used the term 'Aria' for some 30 vocal duets and the term 'Aria Duetto' for about 20 other vocal duets, while the vocal trio in his Christmas Oratorio is entitled 'Aria Terzetto'.

In early opera the aria differed from recitative (A62), in that it was more obviously melodic and metrical. In the aria 'Possente spirto' Monteverdi provided both a simple vocal melody and a version with florid ornamentation. A65 shows a single phrase from this aria in its basic form, while A66 shows Monteverdi's ornamented version of it.

The da capo aria was the most common type of solo song in late baroque operas, oratorios and cantatas. The name comes from the instruction 'Da capo al fine' printed at the end of the second section of the aria (B15, bar 120). This means '[repeat] from the beginning to the word "fine" [end]'. Thus the aria shown in B15 is a ternary structure (ABA) in which the first section (A) begins and ends in the tonic key of D major (bars 1–80), and the second section (B) passes through several related keys (notably minor keys not heard in the first section). Finally the first section is repeated (sometimes with added improvised ornamentation, such as the appoggiatura shown above bar 20). A common feature of this type of aria was the inclusion of instrumental ritornellos – instrumental passages heard at the start that are repeated whole or in part, perhaps varied and in a different key. The opening ritornello of B15 (bars 1–14) is repeated at the start of the da capo (2:54 to 3:13) while a variant of it (bars 67–80) is heard at the end of both the first and last sections (1:36 to 1:56 and 4:30 to the end of the track).

The obbligato aria was also common in the late baroque era. The term refers to an obligatory instrumental solo heard in ritornellos, and in counterpoint with the voice elsewhere in the aria. The obbligato instrument in B15 is the trumpet. See *Air* (Eng. and Fr.) and *Arie* (Ger.).

2. An instrumental movement of a song-like character (B1). *EM 3.5, 8.2, 8.7.1.*

Aria di bravura (It.). An aria written to display a singer's virtuoso technique (B50).

Arie (Ger.). Song. This title is most often given to solo vocal movements in the 18th-century German *Singspiel*. It can be the counterpart of the Italian aria (apart from its vernacular text). B37 is in the rumbustious style of contemporary Italian opera buffa (comic opera), its chief features being diatonic triadic or scalic melody, homophonic textures and simple functional harmony (only three chords are heard in the whole extract). It can also parody the style of contemporary Italian opera seria. B50 exhibits the florid ornamentation of the Italian coloratura aria and, in its string tremolo, the *stile concitato* that was invented by Monteverdi. Simultaneously it acknowledges the influence of Haydn's *Sturm und Drang* symphonies (compare the minor mode agitation of this *arie* with the same mood in B21). See *Air* and *Aria*.

Arietta (It.), **ariette** (Fr.). Diminutives of aria (B15) and air (A75) thus designating shorter songs than these two examples.

Arioso (It.). **1.** A passage of more melodious music in the context of a recitative (B7, bars 7–18). **2.** A complete movement that is shorter than the contemporary baroque aria and partakes of the flexibility of recitative and the melodiousness of the aria (B5). *EM 3.5, 8.7.2.*

Armure (Fr.). Key signature (A82, the two flat signs after the treble clef).

Arpa (It.). Harp (C6).

Arpa doppia (It.). Double-strung harp with a fully chromatic range that was developed and became popular in the late 16th century (A66).

Arpège, arpègement, arpégé (Fr.). Arpeggio, arpeggiated. In classical French keyboard music a simple vertical wavy line usually means an upward arpeggiation, or *arpègement en montant*, as does a wavy line with a hook at the bottom (A84, last bar). A hook at the top indicates a downwards arpeggiation, or *arpègement en descendant*, as does a stroke through the stem of a chord (B17, letter c in bar 3). See *Ornaments. EM 3.10.2.*

Arpeggiando, arpeggiato (It.). In string music and some kinds of keyboard music these are performance directions indicating that the printed chords should be played as arpeggios (A96). See *Ornaments. EM 6.5.3.*

Arpeggiation. A sounding of the notes of a chord as an arpeggio, usually from the lowest note to the highest, as shown on the extra staves below the last bar of A84. See *Ornaments.*

Arpeggio (It.). A chord played as successive notes. The first chord of B66 is played as an arpeggio (indicated by the wavy vertical line), and the right-hand figuration is arpeggiated throughout the whole prelude. See *Ornaments. EM 3.10.2.*

Arrangement. A composition for one medium rewritten for another. C66 is an extract from a piano piece by Bartók and C68 is an arrangement of the same extract for four guitars.

Ars Antiqua (Lat.). The 'old art' of late 12th- and 13th-century French polyphony that began with the measured organum of the Parisian School of Notre Dame (A10). See also *Clausula, Conductus* and *Motet. FM 1.12, 8.5.1.*

Ars Nova

Ars Nova (Lat.). The 'new style' of the 14th century in which, released from the stranglehold of modal rhythm, melody became freer and more expressive (A22 and A23). Polyphonic music also became more eloquent, ranging in style from the modal simplicity of the anonymous *Messe de Tournai* (A19) to the complex isorhythmic textures of Machaut's *Messe de Nostre Dame* (A21). See also *Cantus firmus, Isorhythm, Motet* and *Plainsong. EM 7.9.4, 8.5.1.*

Ars veterum, Ars vetus (Lat.). Ars Antiqua (A10).

Arsis and thesis (Mac.). **1.** Upbeat, or weak beat (the first note of A24), and downbeat, or strong beat (the second note of A24). Imitative entries made on alternating strong and weak beats are said to be made 'per arsin et thesin' (A61, bar 1). **2.** 'Per arsin et thesin' can also mean the inversion of a contrapuntal theme. In bars 6–9 of C64 there is a canon *per arsin et thesin* (the lower part being an inversion of the upper part).

Articulation. The degree of separation between successive notes. At one extreme notes can be articulated with no perceptible break between them (as in the first oboe phrase in B68), at the other they can be articulated in a detached manner (as in the repeated violin notes at the start of C29). The first type of articulation (legato) can be indicated by a slur (the curved line above bars 2–3 in B68), the second (staccato) can be shown by dots above or below the notes (as shown in bars 1 and 3 of C29). The articulation of phrases is one of the most important aspects of musical interpretation. Thus in A57 the organist subtly draws attention to the phrases identified by the letters A and B by detaching the last note of each from the ensuing note (thereby clarifying Gabrieli's imitative counterpoint). *EM 1.14.*

Artificial harmonics. See *Natural and artificial harmonics* and C56.

Art music. Music that is composed and written down for the cultivated amateur or professional musician to play or to listen to, as opposed to folk music or popular music. Compare C33 (a sophisticated evocation of a courtly 18th-century French dance) with C56 (a setting of a Romanian folk dance). The distinctions between art music, folk music and popular music can be, and often are, deliberately blurred (C38). *EM 8.11.7–8.11.8.*

Art song. A composed and fully notated song as opposed to aurally transmitted folk songs. Compare B58 (an art song) with C57 (a folk song transcribed by Bartók).

As (Ger.). A♭ (B39, second note).

Ascending trill. A trill beginning on the lower note then ascending through the main note to the upper note. An ascending trill is identified by the letter f at the end of A84. See *Ornaments. EM 3.10.2.*

Ases (Ger.). A♭♭ (C64, bar 3, second note – which is a semitone higher than the G♭s on either side of it). See *Doppelbe.*

Assai (It.). Very. The direction 'Largo assai' at the beginning of B30 means 'very slow'. See *Tempo markings.*

Assez (Fr.). Fairly, quite, rather. The direction 'Assez vif et bien rythmé' at the head of C16 means 'quite fast and very rhythmic'. See *Tempo markings.*

A tempo (It.). Resume the original speed (after a change of tempo). In bars 15–18 of C97 there is a broadening of tempo ('poco allarg.'), with a return to the original tempo (of bars 5–14) marked by the direction 'a tempo' (bar 19). See *Tempo markings.*

Athematic music. Music which, lacking a theme, relies on elements such as timbre and texture for its effect (C35).

Atonal, atonality. Terms that refer to music that lacks tonality. In C34 Schoenberg ensures that tonal centres will not emerge by totally avoiding octaves (both melodic and harmonic), major or minor triads (both melodic and harmonic) and dominant-7th chords, and by never using a succession of more than four notes that could be construed as belonging to the scale of a particular key. See *Dodecaphony* and *Serial music. EM 2, 2.7, 2.8, 3.8, 5.8, 5.8.1, 8.11.3.*

A tre, a 3 (It.), **à trois, à 3** (Fr.). See *A 2* and A59 (madrigal for three voices), A74 (Sonata a tre) and C28, bar 6 (divided violins).

Attacca (It.). Begin the next section immediately. In B4 the term is enclosed in brackets to show that the performance direction is an editorial addition (between bars 1 and 2, and between bars 5 and 6).

Attacco (It.). A short motif used as the subject of a fugue or a passage of imitative counterpoint. See A80, bars 13–14, *Andamento* and *Soggetto.*

Attack, attaque (Fr.). The characteristics of the beginning of a note or chord. These can be precisely measured by scientific means, but the term is generally used when describing aurally perceived qualities such as the degree to which an ensemble of instruments begin unanimously. At one extreme the attack of the two parts playing semiquavers on track A87 is absolutely unanimous throughout the extract, and there is little difference in timbre or intensity between the attack and the rest of the note in the individual parts. At the other extreme the attack of individual performers and the orchestra as a whole is deliberately fuzzy in the first bar of C4. The precise mode of attack is one of the most important aspects of articulation and thus of musical expression. It is for these reasons that the leader of French orchestras is called the chef d'attaque.

Au chevalet (Fr.). In string music, a performance direction indicating that the instrument should be bowed near the bridge (the instruction 'sul ponticello', which means the same thing, is used to prescribe this technique in C72).

Au talon (Fr.). A performance direction requiring a string player to use the part of the bow near to the heel or frog (the part of the bow that the performer holds). This helps in the production of the somewhat coarse sound heard at the start of C70.

Auctoralis (Lat.). Authentic mode (A37, the melody of which is in the authentic phrygian mode). See *Church modes*.

Auf dem G (Ger.). A performance direction indicating that the melody should be played on the G string. From bar 22 of B68 the violins are instructed to play on the lowest (G) string, thus producing a different timbre from that produced by playing on the higher D and A strings. Other strings can be specified in the same way.

Aufgesang (Ger.). The first part of a piece in bar form comprising two identical *Stollen* (A13, bars 1–18). *EM 7.9.1.*

Auflösungszeichen (Ger.). The natural sign (♮). See *Natural* 2 and the symbol shown in front of the third note of B39 (which cancels the effect of the flat sign in front of the second note).

Auftakt (Ger.). Upbeat (A91, first note).

Augmentation. A lengthening of the time values of the notes of a theme. In bars 19–20 of B14 the time values of the subject (bar 1) have been doubled. *EM 3.3, 4.5.6.*

Augmented chord. See *Triad* and C21. *EM 5.3.3.*

Augmented 4th (interval). See *Intervals* and B9, bars 1 and 6. *EM 2.2.4.*

Augmented octave (interval). See *Octave* and B74, bar 6.

Augmented 2nd (interval). See *Intervals* and the violin part of C56. *EM 2.2.5, 2.3.3.*

Augmented 6th (interval). See *Intervals* and B9, bars 2 and 7. *EM 2.2.7.*

Augmented-6th chords. A chromatic chord consisting of a major triad on the flat sixth degree of a diatonic scale with an augmented 6th above the root of the triad. In the key of B major the flattened sixth degree of the scale is a G♮, a major triad on this note is G♮ (the root), B♮ (a major 3rd above the root) and D♮ (a perfect 5th above the root). An augmented 6th above the root is E♯. These are the notes that combine to make the prominent augmented-6th chord in bar 8 of B30. As with most augmented-6th chords, the root resolves down a semitone (G♮ to F♯) and the augmented-6th resolves up a semitone (E♯ to F♯) onto the outer notes of a cadential six–four.

There are three varieties of the augmented 6th: **a)** the four-note chord described above is a German 6th, **b)** the Italian 6th which is the same as a German 6th except that the 5th of the chord is omitted (B57, bars 38–40), **c)** the French 6th which is the same as an Italian 6th but with a tritone added above the root (the B♮ in bar 7 of B67). *EM 5.7.4.*

Augmented triad. See *Triad* and C21, bar 4. *EM 5.3.2, 5.5.5.*

Ausdruck, ausdrucksvoll (Ger.). Expression, with expression. See *Espressivo* and B79, bars 8–9ff.

Auszug (Ger.). An extract or arrangement. C73 is both an extract and an arrangement of orchestral parts for piano (a *Klavierauszug*).

Authentic and plagal modes. Authentic modes are those in which the outermost notes of the range of pitches used correspond more or less exactly with the lower and upper final (A40). Plagal modes are

Authentic cadence

those where the range of pitches fall about a 4th below the range of pitches in the corresponding authentic mode (A8). See *Aeolian mode*, *Church modes*, *Ionian mode* and *Plagal modes*. *EM 2.4.1, 8.4.1, 8.11.11.*

Authentic cadence. 1. Perfect cadence. **2.** A perfect cadence with chords V and I in root position. **3.** A perfect cadence with the tonic note in the uppermost part of chord I. All three definitions are illustrated in B46. See also *Full cadence*. *EM 5.4.1.*

Authentic instruments. With the acceleration of the early-music movement in the second half of the 20th century came the desire for ancient instruments or copies of them. Most of the instrumental music recorded for this dictionary is played on instruments used in the period when the music was written or, more often, on accurate replicas. In the first category is the fortepiano by Johann Schantz heard in track B25. It is undated, but was made in Vienna, probably in the 1790s, and now belongs to the Accademia Bartolomeo Cristofori in Florence. In the second category is the clavichord heard on B20. It is a fret-free, double-strung instrument made in 1995 by Alan Edgar of Hessle. The use of a modern grand piano on B14 allows a comparison with the more authentic performance of a toccata played on a Clavier (harpsichord) on B13.

Auto-brake-drums, automobile brake drums. Brake drums from motor vehicles used as percussion instruments (C97, bars 9–14).

Auxiliary note, auxiliary tone. A melodic decoration approached by step from a harmony note, it then returns to the same harmony note. The E major chord in bar 7 of B30 is decorated with a chromatic lower auxiliary (F$\times$) in the treble and a diatonic lower auxiliary (D♮) in the bass. *EM 4.3.4.*

Avant-garde (Fr.). Advance guard. Composers of modernist tendencies. Boulez was among the avant-garde of the 1950s and 1960s (C87). See *Modernism* and *Serial music*. *EM 8.11.9.*

Avec timbres (Fr.). With snares. On C44 drums with and without snares can be heard.

Ayre. Renaissance English for a song. Morley used the term for all types of secular vocal music of a light-hearted nature, including his canzonets (A59). The term is now most often used to mean English songs of the late 16th and early 17th centuries with accompaniments for lute, sometimes with other optional vocal parts printed in a way that allowed the performers to sing from a single copy while seated round a table. The first extant collection of such lute songs is Dowland's *First Booke of Songes or Ayres* of 1597.

B

B. 1. In English, any of the pitches with this letter name shown on the diagram of a keyboard on the folded insert. Example C1 begins on a B♮. See *A*. **2.** German for B♭ (B♮ being denoted by the letter H). The fourth note of B39 is a B♭. **3.** Abbreviation of bass (A30).

Bacchette di legno (It.). Hard or wooden sticks. In C36 wooden sticks are used on a kettle drum throughout the extract.

Backbeat. In jazz and pop, an instrumental articulation of weak beats. In the opening bars of C38 a cymbal emphasises the weak second and fourth beats of each bar.

Backfall. 17th-century English term for a downward-resolving appoggiatura (B1, bar 4, beat 2). See *Forefall* and *Ornaments*. *EM 3.10.2*.

Bagpipe. An ancient reed instrument in which a bag is inflated by means of a blowpipe or pair of bellows. The air is then expelled through a chanter (with fingerholes to allow the performance of melodies) and through one or more fixed-pitch drone pipes. On A17 a single drone is heard throughout the duet between the bagpipe chanter and a shawm. *EM 6.6.4*.

Baguette (Fr.). Drumstick (C53, bongos, bar 4). Specific types of drumstick that may be specified by the composer include:
 baguettes de bois – wooden drumsticks
 baguettes dures – hard drumsticks
 baguettes d'éponge – soft-headed drumsticks
 baguettes de timbales – timpani drumsticks
 baguettes timbales en feutre – felt-headed drumsticks
 baguettes de tambour – snare drumsticks.

Baguettes tambour, baguettes de tambour (Fr.). Side drum sticks. In C53 Varèse uses the term as a performance direction ('use side-drum sticks') in order to achieve a different timbre from the usual sound produced by small yarn mallets.

Baisser (Fr.). To lower. The term is most often used in reference to the lowering of the pitch of a string in order to play notes outside the normal range of an instrument. In order to perform the massive six-part chords in bars 13–15 of C83 the lowest string of the guitar (normally E) has to be lowered a tone to D.

Balance. A term in common use among musicians and recording engineers, though rarely found in dictionaries of music. It refers to the relative dynamic levels of the various strands that contribute to a musical texture. In the two-part texture of B74 the balance favours the melody at the expense of the subordinate accompaniment, but in the contrapuntal texture of B77 the two parts are equally balanced (because they are equally important).

Balanced phrasing. See *Periodic phrasing* and B41 (which falls into four balanced phrases).

Ballad opera. A satirical English operatic genre of the 18th century in which popular songs alternated with spoken dialogue. The first example was *The Beggar's Opera* (Gay and Pepusch, 1728). Coffey's *The Devil to Pay* (1731) was translated into German and gave rise to the *Singspiel* (B37). See also *Melodrama*.

Ballade (Fr.). **1.** One of the *formes fixes* of medieval France. A12 shows the AAB melodic structure that was repeated for each verse. Also typical is the varied repetition of a phrase (x) from the A section in the B section and the aeolian modality. As they have come down to us early medieval ballades appear to be monophonic, but it is possible that trouvères such as Richard the Lionheart would have improvised a simple instrumental accompaniment such as that played on a harp on A12. See *Troubadours*. *EM 7.9.2, 8.4.2, 8.6.3*. **2.** In the period c.1770–c.1850, a setting of a German narrative poem. Though most are strophic settings of poems running to many stanzas, some were more concise and through-composed. Schubert's famous *Erlkönig* is an exceptional example of the latter type. The stylistic development of this sort of ballade paralleled that of the contemporary German lied (B57 and B58). **3.** In the 19th century, an instrumental composition inspired by a narrative poem (eg Brahms's first Ballade, which the composer assures us is based on a Scottish ballad called 'Edward'). As such this type of ballade is closely related to contemporary characteristic pieces such as B61 and B74. *EM 7.9.2.*

Ballata (It.). The most important secular vocal genre of the Italian Ars Nova. Some ballatas display exactly the same ABBAA structure as the virelai (A22), all have a similar structure. *EM 7.9.2.*

Ballet. A dramatic entertainment in which costumed dancers are accompanied by instrumental music. A ballet may be a part of a larger work, such as an opera, or it can be an independent work in several acts in which a plot unfolds through mime and dance. C5 and C6 are extracts from full-length ballets and they show something of the range of styles that were encompassed by the classical ballet ('classical' in this context meaning late 19th-century). C5 is a wild Cossack dance while C6 is an extract from music written for a magical transformation scene.

Ballett (Eng.), **balletto** (It.). A simple, short, tuneful and predominantly homophonic madrigal of the late 16th and early 17th centuries. The triple-time dance-like rhythms and fa-la-la refrains of A59 are typical of the genre. *EM 8.6.3.*

Ballo (It.). **1.** Dance. **2.** A fast dance coupled with the slower *bassadanza*, or *basse danse* (A36). **3.** A professionally choreographed sequence of dances that in the 15th century included the *bassadanza* and and a courtly version of the saltarello (A18), and that in the 16th century included the galliard (A35). **4.** Any of the dances published in 16th-century collections, including the pavan (A32) and galliard. **5.** A dramatic work in which choreographed dances play a central role (eg Monteverdi's *Il ballo delle ingrate*).

Band, banda (It. and Span.), **bande** (Fr.). A group of instruments or instrumentalists of any size. In the 17th century the term was used for court orchestras such as Louis XIV's Grande Bande (Les Vingt-Quatre Violons du Roi) and Charles II's Private Band (which also comprised 24 string instruments). The sinfonia recorded on track A64 is played by a band consisting of a mixed group of string instruments and organ. Nowadays the term is used in a wide variety of senses and contexts including: **a)** a colloquial term for an orchestra, no matter how large (C28), **b)** a colloquial term for an orchestral section, such as the string band heard on track B19 and the wind band heard on track C27, **c)** an early-music ensemble of loud instruments, especially one associated with military affairs (A32). More specifically the term is associated with ensembles such as the brass band, jazz band (C38), military band, percussion band (C52–C54), symphonic band and wind band.

Bar. A metrical unit represented in print by all of the notes written between two barlines. The first complete bar of A91 is represented by the two notes sung to the word 'dulci' (one metrical unit of this piece in triple time). When numbering bars it is common practice to begin with the first complete bar (so the single note sung to the word 'in' in A91 is counted as bar 0). See *Metre*.

Bar form. Music with the structure AAB. Richard the Lionheart's ballade in A12 has this form (as shown by the letters above bars 1, 9 and 17). In Germany bar form was cultivated from the time of the minnesingers (A13) through to the chorale melodies that Bach harmonised (B6) and beyond to the famous Prize Song in Wagner's opera *Die Meistersinger*. In these songs the A sections are called *Stollen* (the two together making up the *Aufgesang*), and the B section is called the *Abgesang*. The *Stollen* and *Abgesang* are often united by the use of common melodic phrases (x and y in A13, and B at the ends of the *Stollen* and *Abgesang* in B6). *EM 7.9.1, 8.4.2, 8.6.2.*

Bar numbers. Numbers placed just above the start of a bar as an aid to conductors, performers and listeners. Numbering usually starts with the first complete bar, so an incomplete bar at the start is therefore regarded as bar 0 (the first bar of B78 is bar 0 because it contains only five of the 12 demisemiquavers that go to make up a complete bar in $\frac{3}{8}$ time). Bars are then numbered every five or ten bars, or, as in this dictionary, they are given at the start of each stave or system. In some lengthy orchestral or vocal movements bar numbers are replaced by rehearsal letters or numbers enclosed in boxes. In this dictionary letters in boxes are used to identify structural sections: these are unrelated to the bar numbers at the start of each stave or system of staves.

Basse

Bar rest. In order to avoid using too many rests a silence lasting for a complete bar is conventionally indicated by a semibreve rest no matter what time signature is used (C6, violins, bars 1–2).

Barcarole, barcarolle (Fr.). **1.** A Venetian gondolier's song. **2.** In the 19th century, a character piece whose melody imitated the songs of Venetian gondoliers and whose compound-time accompaniment suggested gently lapping waves (B61 and B74). *EM 8.1.*

Bare 5th. See *Open 5th* and A19, last bar.

Barlines. 1. Vertical lines that divide one metrical unit from another. The metrical unit in A25 is a group of four crotchet beats with a strong accent on the first one. Every four beats a barline separates one four-beat unit from the next. A double barline is used to indicate the end of an important section, movement or complete work. **2.** In plainsong, a vertical line that separates one phrase from the next (A4). See *Bar, measure.*

Bariolage (Fr.). The performance of the same note on two strings, one stopped and one open. In bars 2 and 3 of A98 notes played on the open A string are marked o (the other notes are played on stopped D or G strings). *Bariolage* continues throughout Variations 57–59 of this Chaconne and it is possible to detect the slight difference in timbre between open and stopped notes in this passage. *EM 6.5.10.*

Baritone. A high bass voice (C96), sometimes further qualified as bass-baritone (B5).

Baritone oboe. An alternative name for the *Bass oboe* (C36, bars 5–6).

Baroque. A style-period extending from about 1600 to 1750, though music characteristic of the renaissance era was written after 1600, and some early 18th-century compositions foreshadow early classical styles. See A62–B19. *EM 8.7.*

Baroque pitch. A tuning system used in modern 'authentic' performances of baroque music based on a^1 at 415 Hz instead of the usual modern standard of a^1 at 440 Hz (A1). Performances on instruments tuned at baroque pitch sound about a semitone below standard pitch (A88). See *Authentic instruments.*

Bas and haut (Fr.). **1.** Soft (*bas*) and loud (*haut*) instruments of the middle ages and renaissance. To the former belonged strings (A13) and recorders, to the latter belonged the bagpipe and shawm (A17). Soft instruments were considered suitable for indoor performances, loud instruments for outdoor performances. **2.** Low pitch and high pitch respectively.

Basic series, basic set. In serial music, the prime order (C40, bars 0–7).

Bass, basse (Fr.), **basso** (It.), **bassus** (Lat.). **1.** A low male voice (C40). See the folded insert for the approximate range of a solo bass. **2.** The lowest-sounding part of a passage of music. See *Real bass* and A27, bar 5, tenor F♯ (which sounds below the vocal bass A♮). **3.** The lowest-sounding member of a family of instruments (for example, the double bass in C7 is the lowest-sounding instrument of the modern string family).

Bass-baritone. A male voice with a range intermediate between a bass and a tenor (B5).

Bass clarinet. See *Clarinets* and C34, C38 and the folded insert. *EM 6.6.3.*

Bass clef. See *Clef* and the symbol at the start of A8.

Bass drum. A large single- or double-headed drum of indefinite pitch. It usually stands upright and is normally played with one or two large soft-headed sticks (C42 and C52). See *Percussion instruments. EM 6.8.2.*

Bass guitar. A large four-string electric guitar. Played loudly it can be heard above the largest of instrumental ensembles (C94, bar 12). See *Acoustic bass guitar.*

Bass oboe. The largest member of the oboe family, the bass or baritone oboe is pitched an octave below the ordinary orchestral oboe. Because its range is similar to that of a heckelphone the two instruments are used as alternatives in performance of such works as Holst's *Planets* suite (C36, bars 5–6). See *Woodwind instruments.*

Bass trombone. A low-pitched trombone given the number 3 (or III) in the standard orchestral instrumentation of three trombones and tuba (C75, bar 16). Its approximate range is shown on the folded insert. See *Brass instruments.*

Bassadanza (It.). *Basse danse* (A36). See *Dances.*

Basse (Fr.). Bass part, bass voice (C40).

Basse chiffrée

Basse chiffrée (Fr.). Figured bass (B4).

Basse continue (Fr.). Basso continuo (B4).

Basse danse (Fr.). A moderately slow (sometimes very slow) courtly dance of the 15th and 16th centuries that was common in France, Italy and the Low Countries. The name reflects the gliding movements of feet that barely left the ground. It is these steps that characterise the dance rather than metre since there are examples of the *basse dance* in both triple time and duple time. A36 is in moderate duple time (minim beat). See *Dances. EM 8.6.3.*

Basse à pistons (Fr.). Euphonium (C37). See *Brass instruments.*

Basse-taille (Fr.). Baritone voice (C96).

Basset-horn, bassett horn. A member of the clarinet family that was developed in southern Germany in about 1770. It is usually pitched in F, a 4th below the familiar clarinet in B♭. Mozart exploits almost its full range in B40. See *Clarone* and *Reed instruments. EM 6.6.4.*

Bassi (It.). **1.** In the 18th century, an abbreviation of cellos and double basses (B19, bars 5 and 11). **2.** An abbreviation of *contrabassi* (double basses).

Bassklarinette (Ger.). Bass clarinet (C38). See *Clarinets* and *Reed instruments.*

Basso (It.). Bass (C40).

Basso buffo (It.). A comic bass lead in an opera buffa. Osmin, though he sings in German, is a *basso buffo*, in terms of both the part he has to play in Mozart's *Singspiel*, and the buffo style of the music he sings (B37).

Basso continuo (It.). A bass part, often with figures below it. These indicate the chords that are to be realised on one or more harmony instruments (such as harpsichords, lutes or harps). In the absence of figures the performer was expected to improvise chords in accordance with contemporary performance practice. The bass part itself can be played on a melody instrument such as a bassoon or cello. A basso continuo part (with or without figures) was provided for almost all baroque ensemble music. B4 shows a figured basso continuo part. On an extra stave below bar 1 are the chords that are realised by the organist on track B4 (note that the music is performed a semitone lower than printed). See *Continuo* and *Figured bass. EM 8.7.1ff.*

Basso ostinato (It.). A short bass melody continuously repeated thoughout an entire movement. In A34 the basso ostinato is a romanesca, one of a number of bass melodies used for sets of variations in 16th- and 17th-century Italy and Spain. The English name for a basso ostinato is 'ground' or 'ground bass' (A75). See *Folia. EM 8.7.1.*

Basso ripieno (It.). In a concerto grosso, the bass part for tutti passages only (B19, bars 5–8, 11–12 and 15–16).

Bassoon, Basson (Fr.). A large double-reed instrument that provides the bass of the woodwind section in all but the largest of orchestras. A duet for two bassoons can be heard on track C77 and the instrument's range is shown on the folded insert. See *Reed instruments. EM 6.6.2.*

Bassposaune (Ger.). Bass trombone (C75, bar 16). See *Trombone.*

Basstuba (Ger.). Tuba (C28, bars 1–7). See *Brass instruments.*

Bassus (Lat.). In renaissance music, the lowest voice part in a polyphonic composition (A52). See *Bass.*

Baton. A stick used by conductors for beating time. Before the late 18th century large ensembles were directed from the harpsichord or chamber organ. Alternatively the principal violinist gave the lead, often using the bow as a baton. This practice continued well into the 19th century, but, beginning in the late 18th century, the use of a baton became ever more prevalent as orchestras and choruses increased in size. By the middle of the 19th century the use of a baton had become the norm for symphonic works such as B73 (Liszt's footnote on the first page of the score even tells the conductor how to beat time – one beat per bar). See *Conductor.*

Battaglia (It.). A programmatic composition depicting the sights and sounds of a battle field (A31 and A32).

Battement (Fr.). In the 17th and early 18th century a lower mordent (A84, bars 1 and 17, letter a) or trill (A84, bars 8 and 24, letter d). See *Ornaments.*

Batteria (It.). The percussion section of a symphony orchestra (C97, bar 9 – brake drums, cymbal, tam-tam, bass drum and timpani).

Batterie (Fr.). **1.** An orchestral percussion section (C97, bar 9 – brake drums, cymbal, tam-tam, bass drum and timpani). **2.** In jazz or music in jazz style, a drum kit (C38). **3.** A formulaic drum rhythm (C74). **4.** In guitar playing, the strumming style known as *rasgueado* (C83, bars 1–18). **5.** In the 18th century, broken-chord figuration (A96)

Battery. 1. The percussion section of an orchestra (C97, bar 9, bottom stave). **2.** A baroque term for the performance of written chords as broken chords (A96). See *Ornaments*.

Battuta (It.). **1.** Bar or measure. In A75 all of the notes set to the word 'sweetest' on its first appearance add up to one bar in $\frac{3}{4}$ time. **2.** Beat. In B73 Liszt directs the conductor to give one beat per bar. See *Bar*.

Bc, B.c. Abbreviation of basso continuo (B5).

Bck. Abbreviation of *Becken* (cymbals) (C47).

Bcl., B. Kl. Abbreviations of *Bassklarinette* (bass clarinet) (C38).

Be (Ger.). The flat sign (♭). See *Accidental*, *Key signature* and A86, bar 8.

Beam. A line joining the stems of two or more notes. B18 shows notes beamed together in twos (quavers or eighths), threes (triplets) and fours (semiquavers or sixteenths), and a group of eight notes beamed together (demisemiquavers or thirty-seconds). Notes joined with four beams are technically hemidemisemiquavers (sixty-fourths), but those shown at the end of B18 form a group of six: Handel's notation is, strictly speaking, incorrect, but his intention is clear (ie play the notes as fast as humanly possible). See *Flag*.

Bearbeitung (Ger.). Arrangement (C68 is an arrangement of C66).

Beat. 1. The regular underlying pulse of metrical music. The beat can coincide with the rhythm of the music. This is the case in bars 1 and 3 of A35 in which the underlying crotchet pulse is replicated in the three-crotchet rhythm of all the instruments. But the beat is still sensed in bars 2 and 4, in which the minim–crotchet rhythm of the crumhorns and the dotted rhythm of the tabor only correspond with the beat at the beginning and end of the bar. Sometimes the rhythms of the music never correspond with the duration of the beat. Apart from the last note A87 uses semiquaver rhythms but an absolutely regular crotchet beat is sensed throughout. (The beat is normally subject to greater or lesser variations in speed, but this last example is computer-generated to ensure absolute regularity throughout.) See *Tempo. EM 1.4, 1.15.* **2.** 17th-century English term for a lower mordent. The symbol used in France (A84, letter a in bar 1) and Germany (B1, bar 1) was used in England in the 18th century along with several other more ambiguous symbols. See *Ornaments*.

Bebung (Ger.). Vibrato on a clavichord achieved by striking a key then wiggling the finger. The effect can be heard on the note marked with four dots and a slur near the start of B20. See *Ornaments. EM 3.10.2, 6.9.2, 8.8.3.*

Bécarre (Fr.), **becuadro** (Span.). The natural sign (♮). See *Natural* 2 and the symbol shown in front of the third note of B39 (which cancels the effect of the flat sign in front of the second note). See also *Accidental* and *Key signature*.

Becken (Ger.). Cymbals (C47).

Begleitung (Ger.). Accompaniment (the piano part in B57).

Beisser (Ger.). 18th-century term for a lower mordent (B1, bar 1). See *Ornaments*.

Bel canto (It.). Beautiful singing. A term coined in the 19th century to describe the vocal style that was thought to have prevailed in the performance of songs (especially operatic arias) in the period from about 1650 to 1800. Many of the features of bel canto are apparent in the singing on track B50, particularly effortless agility in florid roulades (bars 69–73), apparent ease in taking high notes (bars 30–32), and an extensive range with even tone in all registers (the vocal part of B50 encompasses two octaves). In other styles of aria bel canto demanded faultless breath control in long legato phrases and, above all, beautiful tone throughout the whole vocal range.

Belebend, belebt (Ger.). Animato (C69, bar 4). See *Tempo markings*.

Bell. 1. A hollow metal percussion instrument that vibrates when struck. Composers have specified church bells (B60 and B62), but have usually had to make do with tubular bells (C97, bars 36ff), or, more recently, electronically synthesised bell sounds. **2.** The flared end of a brass instrument. See *Campane in aria* (C97, bars 23–26) and *Stopped notes* (C85, the last two bars).

Bemol (Span.), **bémol** (Fr.), **bemolle** (It.). The flat sign (♭). The second note of B39 is *La bémol* (A♭). See also *Accidentals* and *Key signature*.

Ben, bene (It.). Well, very. The direction 'ben ritmico' in bar 1 of C63 means 'very rhythmical'.

Benedicamus Domino (Lat.). A versicle sung at the end of a Roman Catholic service. It means 'Let us bless the Lord', to which the response is 'Deo gratias' (Thanks be to God). See A8.

Benedictus (Lat.). The second part of the Sanctus (one of the texts of the Ordinary of the Mass). A20 and A21 show two complete settings of the Benedictus ('Blessed is he who comes in the name of the Lord'). *EM 8.4.1.*

Bequadro (It.). The natural sign (♮). See *Natural* 2 and the symbol shown in front of the third note of B39 (which cancels the effect of the flat sign in front of the second note). See also *Accidental* and *Key signature*.

Berlin School. A group of composers working at the court of Frederick the Great in the second half of the 18th century. The most famous was C. P. E. Bach (B20).

Bes (Ger.). B♭♭. See *Doppelbe*.

Beschleunigend (Ger.). Accelerando (C82, bars 1–8). See *Tempo markings*.

Bewegt (Ger.). Agitato (C69, bar 4). See *Tempo markings*.

B. gtr. Abbreviation of bass guitar. In C94 it refers to the electric bass guitar.

Bichord. See *Polychord* and the brass chords in bars 62–67 of C82.

Bicinium (Lat.). A two-part composition for voices or instruments that was a common feature of musical education from the 15th to the 17th centuries. Bartók, among others, revived the bicinium with similar didactic intentions (C58).

Biedermeier. A derogatory term derived from Papa Biedermeier, a fictional poet invented by Ludwig Eichrodt in 1854. It refers to the cosy bourgeois styles of poetry, furniture and painting that were popular in Germanic cultures from about 1815 to 1848. During this period the piano was an indispensable adjunct of middle-class life, and Biedermeier sensibility was expressed through lieder such as B57 and characteristic pieces such as B61 (both intended for private delectation or the more public ambience of the *soirée*).

Bien (Fr.). There are many common meanings of this word, but in music it usually means 'very' ('bien rythmé' at the head of C17 means 'very rhythmic'). See *Tempo markings*.

Bimodality. The simultaneous or successive combination of melodies or harmonies (or both) displaying differing modalities. In bars 9–19 of C63 Bartók combines a minor-mode pentatonic melody on E with a major-mode pentatonic melody on D. *EM 8.11.7.*

Binary form. A musical structure in two sections (A and B), both of them marked with repeat signs (but note that only in B76 are these repeats observed in performance in this dictionary). It was the most common form for dance movements in baroque suites, and the same structure is found in the themes of many later sets of variations. Since most binary-form movements are based on a few short motifs that dominate the whole movement, it is tonality that largely determines structure.

In early binary-form movements section A was usually shorter than section B, and often ended with a perfect cadence in the tonic. The longer second section sometimes included modulations to related keys before returning to the tonic key and another perfect cadence. In A67 the first section (bars 1–10) begins and ends in D minor and includes an intermediate imperfect cadence in the relative major (bars 5–6). Section B modulates through A minor (with an imperfect cadence in bars 12–13) and C major (with an inverted perfect cadence in bars 15–16) before returning to the tonic key of D minor by way of a harmonic sequence (bars 17–21).

By the beginning of the 18th century the first section usually modulated to a related key and ended with a decisive perfect cadence in this new key. This is the case in A89 (which is recorded a semitone lower than printed). The tonal structure has by now become much clearer. The first section consists of two balanced four-bar phrases, the first ending with a perfect cadence in the tonic (bar 4), the second modulating to the relative major and ending with a perfect cadence in the new key (bars 7–8). Section B is exactly twice as long as the first section, comprising four four-bar phrases that end with perfect cadences in A minor and B minor, an imperfect cadence in the tonic (bars 19–20) as well as the final perfect cadence in the tonic.

Large-scale binary structures of the early 18th century sometimes ended with a partial reprise of material from the first section. This is evident in B17 in which, having regained the tonic key of A minor in bars 29–30, Rameau recapitulates bars 3–4 of the first section and ends (bars 32–38) with a reprise of the last six bars of section A transposed from the dominant (E minor) to the tonic. It was from this sort of structure (often called rounded binary form) that sonata forms emerged in the second half of the 18th century.

The minuet was the only binary-form dance to survive into the classical era. From a tonal point of view the first section of B25 might have come from a very early binary-form movement since there are no modulations and it ends with a simple imperfect cadence in the tonic key of A♭ major. The surprise comes in the second half which turns out to be a retrograde version of the Section A (ie exactly the same music played backwards). The same is true of the following binary-form trio. B76 is equally simple and even shorter (the simpler the theme the greater the potential for creative variation).

B41 conforms with the most common tonal scheme of short binary-form movements of the late 18th century: an eight-bar excursion from the tonic to the dominant in Section A and an early return to the tonic in Section B. See also *Corrente*, *Form* and *Rounded binary form*. *EM 7.4ff*.

Bind. Tie, a curved line joining two notes of the same pitch to make one longer note (A62, bass, bars 1–2).

Bindung (Ger.). Tie (A62, bass, bars 1–2) or slur (A90, bar 1).

Bisbigliando (It.). Whispering. In harp music, a fast to-and-fro movement of the fingers producing a whispering tremolo (C97, bars 50–67).

Biscroma (It.). Demisemiquaver (thirty-second-note). See B18, Variation 5, bar 7, beat 3.

Bitonality. The simultaneous use of two different tonalities. The right-hand part of C59 uses the first five degrees of the scale of F♯ major, the left-hand part uses the same degrees of the scale of D minor. *EM 2.6, 8.11.7.*

B. Kl. in B, Bkl. in B (Ger.). Abbreviation of *Bassklarinette in B* (ie bass clarinet in B♭). See *Clarinets* and C34.

Bkl. (Ger.). Abbreviation of *Bassklarinette* (C38).

Blanche (Fr.). Minim or half-note (the first note of A26).

Blasinstrument (Ger.). Wind instrument. See *Brass instruments*, *Woodwind instruments* and C86.

Bleat. A vocal ornament consisting of a rapid reiteration of a single note, usually at a cadence. In 17th-century Italy the *trillo caprino* was simply called a *trillo* (A62, bar 3). In the 19th century Wagner used the *Bockstriller* with humorous intent in *Die Meistersinger*. See *Ornaments*.

Blechinstrumente (Ger.). Brass instruments (C86).

Bloc de bois (Fr.), **blocco di legno** (It.). Wood block (C51 and C53). See *Percussion instruments*.

Bloc de métal (Fr.). Anvil (C48 and C54).

Blocco di legno cinese (It.), **Blocs chinois** (Fr), **Bloque de madera china** (Span.). Chinese wood blocks (C51 and C53).

Block chords, block harmony. A homorhythmic texture such as that in a simple hymn-tune harmonisation (A37, bars 1–3).

Blockflöte (Ger.). Recorder (A69). See *Woodwind instruments*.

Blue note. In jazz, a note sung or played deliberately out of tune and falling somewhere between two adjacent notes of a chromatic scale. The effect (but not the style) can be heard in C70, bars 6 and 8, in which one of the violinists plays a quarter of a tone flat (thus the F♯ in bar 6 actually sounds a note halfway between this F and the E a semitone below). On instruments incapable of such microtonal inflections blue notes are played a whole semitone flatter than the corresponding note in a diatonic scale (C20, bars 15, 22 and 23). *EM 8.11.8.*

Bn. Abbreviation of bassoon (C77).

Bockstriller (Ger.). Bleat or trillo (A62, bar 3).

Bogen, Bog. (Ger.). The bow of a string instrument and hence a performance direction requiring the resumption of bowing after pizzicato. It can therefore be used in the same sense as the Italian 'arco' (C75, bar 4).

Bogenform (Ger.). Arch form. A26 is in ternary form (ABA), the simplest type of arch form.

Bois (Fr.). **1.** 'Les bois' means 'woodwind instruments' (C77–C80). **2.** 'Avec le bois' means 'col legno' or 'with the wood [of the bow]' (C36).

Bombard (Ger.). Tenor or bass shawm (A32).

Bombo (Span.). Bass drum (C42 and C52).

B^{on} (B^{ons}). (Fr.). Abbreviations of basson(s) (C77).

Bongos. A pair of single-headed conical or cylindrical drums tuned about a 5th apart and struck with bare hands or sticks (C45 and C52). See *Percussion instruments. EM 6.8.2.*

Bouché (Fr.). Abbreviation of *sons bouchés* – stopped notes on a horn (the two notes with crosses above them in the last two bars of C85).

Bourdon (Fr.), **bordone** (It.), **Bordun** (Ger.). **1.** A drone or an instrument that produces a drone (A15). **2.** An organ flue stop (C55). *EM 4.4.6.*

Bourrée (Fr.). One of the 'optional' movements of the baroque dance suite, the bourrée is in moderate to fast duple time with anacrustic phrases starting on the last half-beat. Like other dance-suite movements it is in binary form (the two sections are marked A and B in A89). *EM 7.4.5, 8.7.3.*

Bowing. The manner in which the bow is used in string music. The two basic strokes are the up-bow and the down-bow (C70, bar 2). See *Au talon* (C70, bar 1), *Col legno* (C36), *Sul ponticello* (C72, bars 1 and 2) and *Sul tasto* or *am Griffbrett* (C34, bars 7–8).

Br. Abbreviation of *Bratsche*, the German word for viola. See A38 and A39.

Brace. A vertical bracket joining two or more staves at the left-hand side to show they belong to the same system (and therefore that the music on them is played simultaneously). Instrumental families are usually braced together in a score (C97, bar 9) and keyboard instruments have their own type of brace (B48).

Brake drum. An ordinary motor-car brake drum struck with a variety of sticks or brushes. The approximate pitch is determined by size. In bars 9–14 of C97 three brake drums of different pitch levels are combined with brass chords. See *Percussion instruments. EM 6.8.4.*

Brass band. An ensemble consisting wholly or mainly of brass instruments. A typical brass band contains cornets (C3), a variety of horns and euphoniums (C37), trombones (the last two bars of C75) and tubas (C28, bars 1–7).

Brass instruments. Metal wind instruments in which sound is generated by the vibrations of the performer's lips against a funnel or cup-shaped mouthpiece. Examples include euphonium (C37), cornet (C3), horn (C84), sackbut (A60), trombone (A62, tenor trombone, and A63, bass trombone), trumpet (B15, in D, and B36, in B♭) and tuba (C28). Of these, horns, trumpets, trombones and tuba form the brass section of a normally constituted large-scale symphony orchestra. Sustained chords for various groupings of these instruments can be heard on track C86. *EM 6.7.*

Bratsche (Ger.). Viola (A38 and A39). See *String instruments.*

Bravura (It.). A display of virtuoso technique such as that displayed by the Queen of the Night in B50.

Break. 1. In woodwind instruments, the join between the lowest register of fundamental notes and the first octave of overblown tones. On clarinets the break comes between the B♭ and B♮ a 7th above middle C (written pitches). Clarinettists devote much time to making the join between registers as smooth as possible. In C75 the clarinet crosses the break four times (bars 3–4, 5, 7 and 9) but it is so well covered by the performer that there is no perceptible change of timbre. **2.** A term used for the join between head voice and chest voice. See *Chest voice and head voice* and A63 and B50 (bars 74–79), *Ponticello* 2 and C30.

Breve (Eng. and It.), **brève** (Fr.), **brevis** (Lat.). Double whole-note (𝅜). A note that has the duration of two semibreves. It is not in common use nowadays, but is shown in three of its possible notations beneath bars 19–20 of A13 (where the tied semibreves played on the vielle last for four minim beats, the same length as a breve). *EM 1.12.*

Bridge. 1. The curved piece of wood set at 90 degrees to the longitudinal axis of a string instrument over which the strings are stretched. It carries the vibrations of the strings to the body of the instrument where they are amplified and disseminated. When bowed on or near to the bridge a string instrument produces a distinctive rasping sound. See *Sul ponticello* and the start of C72.

Bridge passage. Transition (B40, bars 18–25).

Brillant, brillante (Fr. and It.). Brilliant, sparkling, glittering. The adjective is used in the title of B64 and the mood is perfectly expressed in the virtuoso Arabesque in bar 8.

Brisé (Fr.). **1.** Arpeggiation (B20, opening, left hand). **2.** Detached bowing (A80, bars 13–38). See *Ornaments* and *Style brisé*.

Broderies (Fr.). **1.** Ornaments. French baroque ornaments are shown by conventional signs above and below the stave in B17 and five types of broderie are shown in written-out form below bars 1–4. **2.** Auxiliary notes (neighbor notes). See A98, bars 2 and 3 (the B♭ in both bars).

Broken chord. Notes of a chord heard successively rather than simultaneously (A98, bars 14–17). See *Ornaments*.

Broken consort. In 16th- and 17th-century England, an ensemble of solo instruments from different families. The consort song on track A60 is accompanied by a broken consort played on recorders, sackbut and *gedackt* bass curtal.

Btb. Abbreviation of bass trombone (C75, bar 16).

Buffa, buffo (It.). Comic. See *Basso buffo* and *Opera buffa*. B37 is an extract from a *Singspiel*, but the style is typical of the contemporary opera buffa.

Bühnenmusik (Ger.). **1.** Incidental music for a play (for example, Mendelssohn's music for *A Midsummer Night's Dream*). **2.** Music played on stage in an opera (B45).

Bulgarian dance. The most obvious feature of Bulgarian folk music is its wide variety of asymmetric metres in which two-, three- or four-beat groups are repeated in patterns such as 3+2 or 2+3 ($\frac{5}{8}$ time) or 2+2+3 ($\frac{7}{8}$ time). In his Dance in Bulgarian Rhythm No. 6 (C66 and C67) Bartók consistently exploits the asymmetric pattern 3+3+2. The title of these six dances should be noted. They are not transcriptions of folk music: their harmonic and melodic style is Bartók's own.

Burden, burthen. 1. A refrain in a 15th-century English carol (in A24 there are two burdens, both of them sung at the start and after each of the two verses). **2.** The lowest part in 14th- and 15th-century English polyphony (in A24 this is the second tenor part). **3.** Bourdon 1(A15). *EM 8.5.2.*

Burgundian cadence. Named after Burgundian composers of the 15th century (in whose style it is a characteristic feature), this cadence consists of a stepwise descent to the final in the lowest voice, the interposition of the sixth degree of the mode between the leading note and the final, and a sharpened fourth degree rising to the dominant. All of these features are evident in the cadence in bars 16–17 of A24. In addition an F♯ is interposed between the secondary leading note (G♯) and the dominant (A♮). See *Cadence. FM 2.4.3, 5.4.9.*

Burlesque. A musical trifle or a satire involving grotesque exaggeration. It is in the latter sense that Bartók uses the term 'Burletta' as a title in his sixth quartet (C70).

Burletta (It.). In 18th- and early 19th-century England, an Italian comic opera, or a satire of opera seria. In the USA the term was sometimes used as a synonym for burlesque (C70).

Burthen. See *Burden* and A24.

BWV. Catalogue numbers for Bach's complete works. Those given for A86–B16 come from the *Bach Werke Verzeichnis, Kleine Ausgabe* (*Catalogue of Bach's Works, Small Edition*), Breitkopf and Härtel, Wiesbaden, 1998.

C

C. 1. In English and German, any of the pitches shown in A2. Middle C is often taken as a point of reference because it comes approximately halfway up most keyboard instruments. On track A3 this note is played twice, once on a nasal-sounding organ reed pipe, then on a flute-like flue pipe. See the folded insert. **2.** A sign indicating $\frac{4}{4}$ time (A81). See also *C clefs*.

C. A., C. Angl. Abbreviations of cor anglais (C88, bars 3–5 and 9–10).

Cadence. A point of repose at the end of a musical phrase. The effect can be one of partial closure if the phrase ends on any note other than the tonic (the open endings in A13) or complete closure if the phrase ends on the tonic (the closed endings in the same example).

When chords are added to the ends of phrases four principal types of cadence may be perceived: **a)** Perfect cadence: A91, bars 7–8 (V–I in E major), 15–16 (V–I in A major) and 19–20 (V–I in F♯ minor), **b)** Plagal cadence: A91, bars 3–4 and 31–32 (both IV–I in A major), **c)** Imperfect cadence: A91, bars 23–24 (IV⁶–V in F♯ minor), **d)** Interrupted cadence: B69 (V⁷–VI in A minor).

Any of these cadences may be inverted: ie one or both of the chords might have the third or fifth in the bass (A91, bars 11–12 and 27–28).

See *Burgundian cadence* (A24), *Double-leading-note cadence* (A24), *Feminine and masculine cadences* (B30 and B46), *Landini cadence* (A24), *Medial cadence* (A91, bars 11–12), *Phrygian cadence* (A37, bars 3–4) and *Radical cadence* (A91, bars 7–8). EM 2.4.3, 2.5, 4.3.9, 5.4, 7.3.

Cadence (Fr.). In the 17th and 18th centuries, a trill (B17, letter f in bar 4) or turn (A84, the letter b in bars 1 and 17). See *Ornaments*. EM 3.10.2.

Cadent. In 17th-century England, an anticipation (A80, bar 12), shown by a line slanting down to the anticipated note. See *Ornaments*.

Cadential six-four. A triad in second inversion resolving to the dominant to form an imperfect cadence (B40, bars 66–68) or perfect cadence (B46). See *Six-four chord. EM 5.5.2.*

Cadenza. An improvised or written-out solo towards the end of a concerto movement (C76, bar 5).

Caisse claire (Fr.). Side drum (C43 and C53).

Caisse roulante (Fr.). Tenor drum (C43 and C53).

Caja clara (Span.). Side drum (C74).

Caja militar (Span.). A deep-sounding military side drum with snares (C45, *tambour militaire*).

Caja rodante, redoblante tenor (Span.). Tenor drum (C43 and C53).

Cakewalk. In the early 20th century, a type of African-American jazz in march-tempo $\frac{2}{4}$ time with the characteristic syncopated rhythm identified by the letter x in the first bar of C20. See *Ragtime. EM 8.11.8.*

Calando (It.). Declining or waning in volume or speed or both (B79, bars 25ff). See *Tempo markings*.

Call-and-response. Vocal music in which a soloist sings a phrase to which a group of vocalists responds. Although the term is properly used of African musics, African-American work-songs, jazz and pop, some use it of similar styles in western music (A5, in which a cantor sings the first phrase of the Alleluia and a group of monks respond with the complete Alleluia).

Calmo (It.). Calm, peaceful (C76).

Cambiata, nota combiata (It.). A three-, four- or five-note figure common in late medieval and renaissance polyphony, the cambiata is characterised by a dissonant off-beat note (the *nota cambiata*) that leaps a 3rd to a consonant note. A three-note cambiata is identified in A47, where the note marked x (the *nota cambiata*) forms a dissonant 4th with the soprano before leaping down a 3rd to form a consonant 5th with the soprano B♭. The same cambiata (now identified as a four-note figure) can be heard in a three-voice texture in A48, and in its original context in the four-voice polyphony at the end of Victoria's Kyrie from his *Missa O mag-*

Canon

num mysterium (A46, bars 37–38, bass). Near the beginning of A61 a common five-note cambiata is repeated in the soprano sequence of bars 1–3 (the G♯ is the *nota cambiata* in the first figure, the A♮ is the *nota cambiata* in the second figure). The doubling of the first cambiata in 3rds by the second viol is less common, but by no means rare. The *nota cambiata* is sometimes called a changing note ('cambiare' being the Italian infinitive 'to change'). *EM 4.3.7.*

Camera and chiesa (It.). A 'camera' is a room or a chamber; 'chiesa' is a church. Baroque sonatas and concertos often bear the appellation 'da camera' or 'da chiesa'. The first indicates that the composer intended the work to be performed domestically, the latter that it was intended to be performed in the context of a church service. Generally speaking the former type of composition contained dances or dance-like movements and the latter contained more serious movements. But there are many exceptions to this rule, and A74 is one of them. It is the last movement of a *sonata da chiesa*, yet it is, in all but name, a gigue (which was often the last movement of a *sonata da camera*).

Camerata (It.). In the 16th century, an informal group of intellectuals gathered to discuss some aspect of science, art, literature or music. Nowadays the term usually refers to the Camerata that met in Florence in the late 16th century at the home of Count Bardi. It was the deliberations of this select society on the nature of Greek drama that was chiefly responsible for the genesis of early opera (A62–A66).

Campana (It.). **1.** Bell (B60). **2.** The flaring end of a wind instrument, especially a brass instrument. The instruction 'campane in aria' directs the performer to play with the bell raised (C97, bars 23–26).

Campanaccio, campanelli da mucca (It.). Cowbells (C28).

Campane in aria (It.). Bells up. A performance direction requiring wind instrumentalists (most often brass players) to raise the bells of their instruments so they are pointing directly at the audience. This affects the tone quality to such a degree that it is possible even on a recording to distinguish between the timbre of brass played in the ordinary position (C27) and with bells up (C97, bars 23–26).

Campane, campane tubolare (It.). Tubular bells (C97, bars 36ff).

Campanelli (It.). Glockenspiel (C3, bars 6–7).

Cancrizans (Lat.). Music played backwards. In B25 bars 1–10 are played backwards in bars 11–20.

Canon. In its simplest form a canon is a contrapuntal device in which a melody called the *dux* (leader) is later repeated note for note by another part called the *comes* (follower) while the melody of the *dux* continues to unfold. Thus the two canonic parts combine, each phrase of the *dux* being shadowed by the *comes* a few beats later. This process of exact imitation continues for the duration of the canon. On track A91 a soprano sings the familiar carol *In dulci jubilo*. With only very slight modification Bach uses this melody as the theme of a two-part canon (A92). The *comes* enters with the same theme as the *dux* a bar later and an octave lower. This is known as a canon 2 in 1 at the octave below (ie a two-part canon on one theme in which the *comes* is pitched an octave below the *dux*). A93 is also a canon 2 in 1 at the octave below.

Any number of imitative voices can be employed in a canon. A14 shows a Latin hymn which, with English words, is used to build a canon 4 in 1 at the unison (A15). The canonic voices enter in bars 7, 9, 11, and 13, all singing exactly the same melody at the same pitch. This is an example of an infinite or perpetual canon in which each voice, having sung the complete melody, returns to the beginning and sings it again an infinite number of times (since this is hardly practical A15 simply fades out towards the end of the second canonic cycle). A more familiar name for this type of canon is a round (and a more familiar round is *Three blind mice*).

Another and more complex four-part canon can be heard on track A94. In it Bach combines the two canons heard on tracks A92 and A93. This is a canon 4 in 2 (four canonic parts using the two contrasing themes that begin together in bar 1 of track A94) sometimes called a double canon. The carol can be heard played on flue pipes in the uppermost part and on reed pipes in the

Canon by inversion

tenor register. The dancing triplets of the second canonic theme appear in the alto register and are imitated an octave below by a part that also provides the bass part of the entire composition.

Canonic writing can form part of larger musical designs. B22 shows a short canon at the 7th below (ie the violin melody is transposed down a 7th to provide the imitative cello part). Strict canonic writing ends when the solid lines turn into dotted lines. The next example (B23) shows a canon at the 4th above on a different theme. These two canons combine to form a canon 4 in 2 in bars 28–33 of B21 (repeated in a different permutation in bars 37–41). In these passages the first canonic theme is labelled b2, the second is labelled d, and it will be seen that b2 is derived from the second four-bar phrase of the unison theme with which this symphonic finale begins. The canons are thus integral parts of the first subject of what is in fact an abbreviated sonata-form structure (of which only the first subject is shown in B21).

In a canon by inversion (canon *per arsin et thesin*, canon *per moto contrario*) every interval of the original theme is turned upside down by the *comes*. Immediately after the rest in bar 6 of C64 a canonic theme enters in the right-hand piano part (*dux*) and this is followed half a bar later by a melodic inversion of the same theme (*comes*): where the *dux* begins with a falling semitone, 4th and semitone the *comes* begins with a rising semitone, 4th and semitone: this process continues until the canon ends at the start of bar 9. Like the canons in B21 this canon is completely integrated into a larger design: motif x is first heard in the bare octaves at the start of the extract, it is then extended to form the theme of a canon at the 6th below, then follows the canon by inversion, and finally the first three notes of motif x are heard in contrapuntal cross-rhythms. See *Counterpoint*, *Double canon* and *Imitation*. *EM 4.4.4–4.4.6, 4.5, 7.8.5.*

Canon by inversion. A canon in which the *comes* is an inversion of the *dux*. See *Canon*, paragraph 5, and C64, bars 6–8. See also C82, bars 34–41. *EM 4.4.4.*

Canon cancrizans (Lat.). A canon in which the *comes* is a retrograde or retrograde inversion of the *dux*. In bars 2–4 of C88 the *dux* is the tenor solo. This is shown in simplified form below bars 2–4. C88(ii) shows the same theme played backwards (retrograde), and C88(iii) shows the retrograde with every interval turned upside down. It is this retrograde inversion that forms the *comes* played on cor anglais, flute and harp in bars 3–5 of C88, thus forming a canon cancrizans with the tenor.

Canon per arsin et thesin (Mac.), **canon per moto contrario** (It.). Canon by inversion (C64, bars 6–8). See also C82, bars 34–41.

Canone al contrario riverso (It.). A canon in which the *comes* is a retrograde inversion of the *dux* (C88, bars 2–5, in which the tenor part is the *dux* and the cor anglais, flute and harp parts form the *comes*).

Canonic. Adjective from 'canon' describing passages of music shorter than a complete canon (B26 is a canonic passage from B27). *EM 7.9.3.*

Cantabile (cant.), cantando (It.). In a singing style. The direction 'Poco adagio cantabile' at the beginning of B32 means 'somewhat slow and in a singing style'.

Cantata. A baroque secular or sacred vocal composition in several sections or movements. In Germany the church cantata was particularly associated with Lutheran liturgies. Most of these cantatas contained more or less elaborate settings of chorale melodies (B6 and B8), recitatives and ariosos (B7) and arias (B15). See also *Oratorio*. *EM 8.7.2.*

Canticum (Lat.). Song, canticle. C88 is an extract from Stravinsky's setting of a text from the Canticum canticorum (the biblical Song of Songs) which is itself a movement from his *Canticum sacrum* (*Holy Song*).

Canticle. A biblical song such as the Magnificat (C30).

Cantilena (Lat.). **1.** Medieval sacred or secular song (A14 and A22). **2.** In the 19th and 20th centuries, a lyrical vocal or instrumental melody (B57 and C6 respectively).

Cantino (It.). The highest string of a string instrument, especially the E string of a violin (C9, first violin, bars 13–18).

Cantio (Lat.). Song, especially medieval monophonic song (A22).

Canto (It. and Span.). **1.** A song or melody (A23). **2.** In renaissance polyphony, the highest vocal part (A52). See *Bel canto*.

Canto de órgano (Span.). Polyphonic music (A44–A46) as opposed to plainsong (A40)

Canto fermo (It.). Cantus firmus (A26 and A27).

Canto figurato (It.). **1.** A song characterised by florid runs and leaps that require great vocal agility (B50). **2.** Polyphonic music (A19) as opposed to plainsong (A20). **3.** Ornate polyphony (A27) as opposed to simple polyphony (A19).

Canto fiorito (It.). See *Canto figurato* 1 and B50.

Canto gregoriano, canto piano (It.). Plainsong (A4 and A5)

Cantor. A solo singer in a church service (A4).

Cantus (Lat.). **1.** A plainsong melody or collection of plainsong melodies (A4–A6). **2.** In renaissance polyphony, the highest vocal part (A52).

Cantus figuralis, cantus figuratus, cantus indentatus, cantus mensuratus (Lat.). Mensural music (A10, bars 1–29) as opposed to unmeasured plainsong (A10, bar 30).

Cantus firmus (Lat.). A pre-existent melody used as the basis for otherwise freely composed polyphonic music. In early music the part containing the cantus firmus is called the tenor (Lat. 'tenere' – to hold) because it 'holds on to' the plainsong melody. In A10 the cantus firmus is the melismatic portion of A8 rendered in long notes in the tenor part. In A21 the plainsong Benedictus of A20 is subjected to isorhythm and becomes a part of a four-voice polyphonic complex. In A27 Dufay uses a secular song for his cantus firmus (A26).

In the baroque era the cantus firmus still played a prominent role in sacred music, notably in Lutheran Germany. In A94 Bach uses a well-known carol (A91) as the cantus firmus in an organ chorale (the melody being treated in strict canon as shown in A92). In B8 Bach breaks up the chorale melody shown in B6 into short phrases (the first of which is heard in bars 13–17) which he embeds in a contrapuntal orchestral texture that in itself derives from Luther's melody (see bars 1–3). *EM 1.13, 7.9.4.*

Cantus firmus Mass. A setting of the Ordinary of the Mass in which a pre-existent sacred or secular melody is heard in long notes in one part (usually the tenor) while the other parts weave independent contrapuntal parts around it. The secular monophonic song *L'homme armé* (A26) was used in this way by several renaissance composers. In the extract from Dufay's *Missa L'homme armé* (A27) the first nine bars of the original melody can be heard in the tenor part of bars 5–20.

Cantus planus (Lat.). Plainsong (A4). *EM 8.4.1.*

Cantus prius factus (Lat.). Cantus firmus (A26 and A27). *EM 1.13, 8.5.1, 8.6.1.*

Canzona, canzone. A 16th- and 17th-century instrumental genre that derived from the French chanson. A comparison of Janequin's chanson *La Bataille de Marignan* (A31) with Gabrieli's *Canzona noni toni* (A58) reveals common elements – lively dance-like rhythms, simple chordal and antiphonal textures (throughout the chanson and at the start of the canzona) and tonal harmonies (C major in the chanson, D minor at the start of the canzona). After the first 12 bars Gabrieli indulges in some offhand imitation on the short motifs labelled C and D. Alternating chordal and imitative sections like these were also a feature of the chanson (though this is not apparent in the short extract in A31). Gabrieli's canzona begins with a rhythm (repeated in the following antiphonal exchange) that was such a cliché of both the chanson and the canzona that it is often referred to as the 'canzona rhythm' (see bar 1 of A58). See *Polychoral music. EM 8.6.3.*

Canzonet (Eng.), **canzonetta** (It.). A short, tuneful, dance-like madrigal of the late 16th and early 17th centuries (A59).

C. à p., C. à pist. Abbreviations of *cornet à pistons* (cornet), the brass instruments heard in bars 3–6 of C3.

Cappella (It.). Chapel. See *A cappella* and A44.

Capellmeister (Ger.). Old-fashioned spelling of Kapellmeister. Bach wrote the instrumental works from which A87–A90, A95–98 and C94 are taken while he was Capellmeister at Cöthen.

Capriccio (It.), **caprice** (Fr.). A term, first used in the 16th century, for any work in which the composer follows the whim of the moment and so often disregards the stylistic conventions of the day. Tchaikovsky's *Capriccio italien* is a fantasia on Italian folk

Carol

songs. In the extract shown in C3 a pair of cornets in 3rds ('molto dolce espressivo') warble an Italian ditty over a Verdian oom-pah-pah accompaniment. *EM 8.10.6.*

Carol. 1. A medieval song of English origin celebrating Christmas and other church festivals, the seasons of the year, or a notable historical event. The 'Agincourt song' (A24) exhibits many of the characteristic features of the late medieval polyphonic carol. Alternating one-, two- and three-part textures lend variety to the repetitive chorus-and-verse structure. In this case there are two choruses (burdens I and II), both setting the same words but with different music for each of them. The reverse is true of the strophic setting of the verses (all sung to the same music). Both burdens are sung at the start and after every verse (only two of which are sung on A24). Thus the overall form is AB C1 AB C2 AB etc (in which A and B are the first and second burdens, and C1 and C2 are the first and second verses). **2.** As generally understood nowadays, a simple strophic song celebrating the birth of Christ. Most carol melodies date from post-reformation times. The melody of A25 dates from before 1582, but the harmony and descant are modern. The melody of A91 dates from the 14th century, but the harmony at the cadences is by Bach. *EM 8.5.2.*

Carrée (Fr.). Breve (A13, below bars 19–20).

Cascabeles (Span.). Sleigh bells (C49 and C52). See *Percussion instruments*.

Cassa (It.). Drum (C42–C45, C49, C50, C52, C53). The term 'cassa' with no further qualification can mean 'gran cassa' (bass drum). See *Percussion instruments*.

Cassa di legno (It.) Wood block (C51). See *Percussion instruments*.

Cassa rullante (It.). Tenor drum (C43). See *Percussion instruments*.

Cassation. A multi-movement instrumental work of the classical period, similar to a serenade or divertimento (B40) but probably designed for outdoor performance or as the final item in a concert. See *Finalmusik*. *EM 8.9.3.*

Castanets, castagnettes (Fr.). A pair of wooden shells clapped together (C50 and C52). See *Percussion instruments*. *EM 6.8.5.*

Catch. A vocal entertainment for gentlemen popular in English taverns and coffee houses from 1580 onwards (the Noblemen and Gentlemen's Catch Club celebrated its bicentenary in 1961). All who were capable took part in rounds that were stylistically not unlike the Reading Rota (A15). There were, however, two significant differences between the rota and the catch. Firstly, instead of the modal alternation of the tonic and supertonic chords generated by the polyphony of *Sumer is icumen in*, most catches were based on primary triads. Secondly, the 'catch' itself was usually an indelicate verbal pun that was not evident to the eye, but was all too evident once all parts had entered.

Cauda (Lat.). Tail, the melismatic ending of many conductus (A11). *EM 8.5.1.*

Cavata (It.). An epigrammatic arioso at the end of a recitative. In B7 the words of the recitative ('Do not let Satan have any part in your life; do not let your sins convert the heaven within you into a wilderness; repent of your sins with sorrow') are drawn together in the cavata ('that the spirit of God may be united with you'). Bach drives the point home by text repetitions and melodic sequences.

Cb., C.b., C.B. Abbreviations of *contrabasso* (double bass). See B21, bar 26 or B73, bar 1.

C clefs. Clefs that fix the pitch of middle C on a stave. In modern plainsong notation the C clef takes the form shown on the four-line stave at the start of A4. Like other C clefs it can be placed on any line, so allowing chants in any of the church modes to be shown without more than one ledger line above or below the stave. In A4 the C clef theoretically fixes the pitch of notes on the top line as middle C (compare the plainsong notation with the modern staff notation, noting that the little 8 below the treble clef indicates that the chant sounds an octave lower than it would with an ordinary treble clef). In practice singers often transpose the chant to any convenient pitch, but on track A4 the music is sung at the printed pitch.

In later music C clefs took the form shown on the extra staves beneath A30. The soprano C clef fixes the bottom line as middle C and is consequently sometimes referred to as C1. Similarly the mezzo-soprano, alto and tenor C clefs fix the second, third and fourth lines up as middle C and so are also referred to as

C2, C3 and C4 respectively. Only the alto and tenor C clefs are in common use nowadays. The former is used for viola parts (compare A38(a) with A38(b)), the latter for tenor trombone parts, and for cello and bassoon parts when appropriate (rather confusingly, alto trombone parts are now usually printed with a tenor clef). Apart from the examples discussed above, music originally notated with C clefs has been transcribed using treble, bass or tenor F clefs throughout this dictionary.

Cebell, cibell. An English vocal or instrumental piece of the late 17th century and early 18th century with duple-metre rhythms, similar to the contemporary gavotte (B18).

Celesta (Eng., Ger., It. and Span.), **celeste** (Eng.), **célesta** (Fr.). A keyboard instrument that looks like a small upright piano, but instead of strings it has a set of steel plates with resonators beneath them. Its approximate range is shown on the folded insert. It can be heard playing the chords shown in bars 7–13 of C28, and, more clearly, playing a tremolo in bars 15–18. *EM 6.8.7.*

Céleste, voix céleste (Fr.). An organ stop with two ranks of pipes, one tuned slightly sharper than the other to produce an undulating sound that is meant to suggest celestial voices. It makes an obvious contribution to the registration used in the performance of C55. This French term should not be confused with the English 'celeste', the name most commonly used by orchestral musicians for celesta.

Cell. Motif. The term is most frequently used of small groups of notes in 20th-century music. In C40 the twelve-tone row of the first 8 bars divides into four closely related three-note cells (A, B, C and D) which are later used to form piano chords. See *Serial music. EM 3.8.*

Cello. This abbreviation of violoncello is the most commonly used name for the second largest of the modern bowed string family. Its approximate range is shown on the folded insert. An unaccompanied cello solo can be heard on track A90. A plucked (pizzicato) cello can be heard on track C13. An unaccompanied glissando is heard in bar 3 of C69 (rising to the uppermost register of the instrument). All of the commonly used natural harmonics are played on the lowest string of the instrument (C) on track C95. A full section of cellos plays an extended melody above the rest of the orchestra in bars 27–36 of B59. See *String instruments. EM 6.4.1.*

Cembalo (It.). Abbreviation of clavicembalo, a harpsichord (B17).

Cencerro (Span.). Cowbell (C28).

Cento (Lat.). A composition, such as a quodlibet (B2 and B3), that consists of a patchwork of quotations of pre-existent musical materials. The term also applies to plainsong melodies (A4) and Mass texts that evolved through the combination of melodies and literary texts from a number of different sources.

Cephalicus (Lat.). A two-note neume. See *Pes* 1 and A4

Ces (Ger.). C♭ (B75, bar 4, beat 1).

Ceses (Ger.). C♭♭. See *Doppelbe.*

Cetera, cetra (It.). See *Cittern* and A13.

Ceterone (It.). A large plucked string instrument of the late 16th and 17th centuries, it was often employed in continuo groups in early baroque music (A66).

Cf, c.f. Abbreviations for cantus firmus (A27)

Chacona (Span.), **Chacony** (Eng.). Chaconne (A95).

Chaconne and passacaglia. Though differing in their origins, by the beginning of the 18th century there was little difference between these two forms. Both were continuous variations based on an ostinato which could be a repeating bass pattern (like the four-bar ground shown in A75) or a harmonic progression (like the four-bar progression shown at the start of A95) or both. In fact, from the earliest days, both types of ostinato were often subjected to variation in the manner shown in A34 (where the romanesca bass acquires passing notes in the second variation). Bach's Chaconne in D minor (A95) is no exception. As early as the first variation (indicated, like the other variations, by a bold number in a box) Bach subtly varies his harmonic ostinato (compare bars 3 and 7). Harmonic changes in the second and third variations occur where Roman numerals are shown beneath the staves. Even greater changes are made in Variation 23 (A96), but all of the variations begin with the tonic chord (I) and they all end with a perfect cadence (V–I). In some variations the bass is retained unaltered (Variation 6, A95), yet this

Chalumeau

is supposed by some historians to be the chief characteristic of the passacaglia. *EM 7.8.4, 8.7.3, 8.7.7.*

Chalumeau (Fr.). **1.** A 17th-century single-reed woodwind instrument of the clarinet family. **2.** The lowest register of a modern clarinet (two clarinets in this register can be heard above the pizzicato bass in bars 25–30 of B59). See *Clarinets. EM 6.6.3.*

Chamber music. Music for domestic performance and delectation, with only one instrument per part. In its broadest sense the term embraces music for a single soloist (A95 and B25) and music for voices or instruments (or both) from any century. This classification includes the early 16th-century frottola (A30) on the one hand and the 20th-century quartet (C69–C72) on the other. Another, perhaps more widely accepted definition excludes music for one performer, music written before the 17th century and vocal music. This categorisation includes the following genres represented in the music examples of this dictionary: duets (C57), trio sonatas (A73), string quartets (B30–B35, B38, C17 and C69–C72) and piano quintets (C9). *EM 8.9.1, 8.10.8.*

Chamber orchestra. An orchestra with a complete string section, though of smaller numbers than in the standard symphony orchestra, but only a limited number of wind instruments. In his earlier symphonies Haydn frequently scored for a chamber orchestra of strings, two oboes, two horns and one or two bassoons (B21).

Chamber organ. See *Positive organ* and A62, A68, B4(a) and B7.

Chamber sonata. *Sonata da camera.* See *Trio sonata* and A74.

Chance music. Aleatoric music (C97, bars 9–11).

Changing note. See *Cambiata* and A47 (in which the changing note is identified by the letter x). *EM 4.3.7.*

Chanson (Fr.). In its literal sense the term encompasses any song with French words, from a medieval trouvère song to a 20th-century café song. But as used by most historians it usually means a secular French polyphonic song of the late Middle Ages and Renaissance. A31 displays some of the most characteristic features of the early 16th-century chanson: dance-like rhythms, homorhythmic textures enlivened by simple antiphonal exchanges, syllabic word underlay, and a diatonic melodic and harmonic style. Janequin was particularly famous for chansons that imitated natural sounds (in this extract the noises of a battlefield). The term 'programme chanson' is sometimes used to categorise this subgenre. *EM 8.4.2, 8.6.3.*

Chant. 1. Plainsong (A4) or Anglican chant. **2.** To sing. **3.** In French, a vocal melody as distinct from its accompaniment (the tenor part in C73). *EM 8.11.11.*

Chanter. The pipe on a bagpipe that has finger-holes to allow the performance of a melody such as that recorded on track A17. *EM 6.6.4.*

Chanterelle (Fr.). The highest string of any bowed instrument, especially the E string of a violin. The first violin part in bars 13–18 of C9 is played on the E string.

Chapel, capilla (Span.), **cappella** (It. and Lat.), **chapelle** (Fr.). **1.** A place of Christian worship. From a musical point of view the most important chapels were those attached to a university college or to an aristocratic or royal residence, such as St. George's Chapel in windsor Castle. **2.** The clergy and musicians of such a chapel. In the most important establishments, such as the English Chapel Royal, singers and instrumentalists accompanied the monarch as they progressed from one royal residence to another providing secular as well as sacred music. Gibbons spent half his life as organist of the Chapel Royal, and it is almost certain that his verse anthem 'See, see, the Word is incarnate' (A61) was written for this establishment.

Character piece, characteristic piece, Charakterstücke (Ger.). In the 19th century, a single-movement instrumental work intended to express a particular mood or evoke an image of a particular scene. Most character pieces were for solo piano and were given vague titles such as 'Prelude' (B66), 'Nocturne' (B67) and 'Intermezzo' (B78 and B79). Others had more explicit titles (B61 and B74). Both types continued to be written in the 20th century: Debussy gave the generic title *Préludes* to his two sets of character pieces, but each of them also has a programmatic title (C21 – 'Sails', and C22–C26 – 'The sunken cathedral').

Chorale

Not all character pieces were for solo piano. *The Carnival of the Animals* by Saint-Saëns is a set of programmatic character pieces for instrumental ensemble (C7 and C8).

Dances that had a particular national flavour were sometimes called characteristic dances by their composers. This is the case with the 'Russian dance' shown in C5 (it comes from a set of 'Danses caractéristiques' in Tchaikovsky's ballet, *The Nutcracker*). Some writers therefore broaden the term to include stylised national dances written by composers such as Chopin (B64 and B65).

Many character pieces were in ternary form (in C2 a fast middle section is flanked by the same 16 bars in waltz tempo). See *Programme music. EM 8.10.3, 8.10.6*.

Chest of viols. In 16th- and 17th-century England, a matching set of viols (usually pairs of trebles, tenors and basses) kept in a specially constructed chest. There is no way of knowing whether the viols heard on A61 come from the same chest, but it is unlikely, since it comprises a treble viol, a tenor viol, two bass viols and a violone (double-bass viol).

Chest voice and head voice. Chest voice, in which the chest is used as a resonator, is the lowest register of a singer's range. Chest voice production is essential in the performance of parts that require depth of tone and power in a low register. In A63 Charon's powerful chest voice easily matches the tone of the trombone that shadows his melodic line. Head voice, in which the cavities of the skull act as resonators, is used for the highest register of a singer's range. The tone is exceptionally clear and flute-like (B50, bars 30–31 and 74–80). There is a natural break between head voice and chest voice. Singers spend much time developing techniques to make the join between the two registers (the ponticello or 'little bridge') as smooth as possible. In treble voices the break comes about an octave above middle C, but in C30 the break is so well covered by the performers that it is inaudible in the melodic line that descends from the head-voice register of the opening bars to the chest-voice register of the closing bars of the extract. See *Break* and *Ponticello 2*.

Cheute (Fr.) Alternative spelling of *chute* – an appoggiatura (B1, bar 4, beat 2) or anticipation (A80, bar 12). See *Ornaments. EM 3.10.2*.

Chevalet (Fr.). The bridge of a string instrument. 'Au chevalet' means the same as 'sul ponticello' (C72, bar 1).

Chevrotement (Fr.). See *Bleat* and the trillo in A62.

Chiave (It.). Clef. A variety of clefs is shown in A30.

Chiesa (It.). Church. See *Camera and chiesa* and A74.

Chifonie (Fr.). Hurdy-gurdy (A18).

Chimes. Tubular bells (C97, bars 36ff). *EM 6.8.3*.

Chinese blocks. A set of hollow hardwood blocks. They are clamped to a stand, often in a set of five that approximate to a pentatonic scale, and are usually beaten with rubber-headed mallets (C51 and C53). See *Percussion instruments*.

Chitarra (It.). Guitar (C83). 'Alla chitarra' and 'quasi chitarra' are performance directions requiring a guitar-like strumming technique on a violin, viola or cello (C69).

Chitarrone (It.). A large 17th-century lute with six courses of double strings and eight unstopped bass strings. It was chiefly used in the accompaniment of solo songs (A65). *EM 6.4.2*.

Chiuso (It.). See *Aperto and chiuso*, the last two bars of the horn part in C85 and the cadences in C18.

Choeur (Fr.). A chorus of voices (C30) or instruments (there are three instrumental choirs in A58).

Choir. 1. That part of a church where the liturgy is sung. **2.** A group of singers, especially those who sing in the choir of a church (C30). **3.** A group of instruments of the same type (four crumhorns in A35). **4.** Contrasted groups of singers and/or instruments in antiphonal textures (A58).

Chor (Ger.). Chorus (B4).

Choral (Ger.). **1.** Plainsong (A4). **2.** Chorale (B6).

Choralbearbeitung (Ger.). A composition based on a sacred melody such as plainsong (A10) or a chorale melody (A91–A94 and B6 with B8).

Chorale. A Lutheran hymn tune with Ger-

Chorale prelude

man words. Some were metrical adaptations of pre-reformation plainsong melodies (eg *Allein Gott in der Höh' sei Ehr* is an adaptation made in 1524 of the Easter plainsong *Gloria in excelsis*). Others were adaptations of folk songs (for example *Innsbruck, ich muss dich lassen* comes from a book of secular songs published in 1539, the tune later being adapted and harmonised by Bach). A third category comprises those melodies that were specially composed for Lutheran congregations. The text of *Ein' feste Burg ist unser Gott* is a paraphrase of Psalm 46 made by Luther himself. The melody, like many chorales, is in bar form, consisting of a repeated section (*Stollen* 1 and 2) and a longer concluding section (the *Abgesang*). In B6 the first *Stollen* is shown in the form it takes in Klug's *Geistlich Lieder* of 1533. The second *Stollen* shows how Bach changed the irregular rhythms of the original *Stollen* so as to form a perfectly regular four-bar phrase. As in many bar-form melodies a phrase from the *Stollen* is repeated in the *Abgesang* (in this case phrase B). In B6 this phrase is shown as Bach harmonised it in Cantata No. 80 (bars 16–18). *EM 8.6.2, 8.7.2.*

Chorale prelude, Choralvorspiel (Ger.). An organ composition based on the melody of a chorale. In Bach's chorale prelude *In dulci jubilo* (A94) the melody sung on A91 is heard in the uppermost part and in canon at the octave below. *EM 8.7.2.*

Chord. Two or more notes sounded simultaneously. A succession of two-note chords is shown in A7(a). For more complex chords see *Augmented-6th chords, Dominant chords, Neapolitan 6th, Quartal harmony, Quintal harmony, Secondary-dominant chords, Seventh chords, Thirteenth chord* and *Triads. EM 2.2.2, 5.*

Chord cluster. See *Cluster chord* and C91, bar 2.

Chord progression. In tonal music, a series of chords related to each other by the prevailing key of the music. The chord progression in B48 explicitly defines the key of G major by means of tonic and dominant chords. The chord progression in B49 functions in the same way, but this time using a wider variety of chords and a modulation to D major.

Chord stream. Parallel chords (C24). *EM 5.8.3.*

Chord symbols. Numbers and/or letters beneath a bass part to show **a)** what chords should be improvised by a continuo instrument (see *Figured bass* and B16) or **b)** how chords relate to the prevailing key of a passage of music. See *Roman numerals* and B25. *EM 5.1.*

Chordal textures. See *Homorhythmic textures* and C86. *EM 6.11.4.*

Chordophone. A category of musical instruments that generate sound by the vibrations of stretched strings (eg the lute, cello and clavichord on A89, A90 and B20 respectively). See *Instruments*.

Chorus. 1. A body of singers whether performing in unison or in parts and usually with more than one voice to a part. A mixed chorus consists of females and males (C97, bars 27–36), and a chorus that sings without instrumental support is described as 'a cappella' (A27). The total range of an average chorus extends from E to c^3 (see the folded insert). **2.** On an organ, a complete set of unison, octave and 5th-sounding ranks, all of them with the same tone-colour (A86, manual parts). **3.** In a song, a refrain that is repeated after each verse. The two burdens in A24 together form a chorus that is repeated after each of the two verses shown in bars 17–36.

Christmas music. The second most important feast of the liturgical calendar has been celebrated with special music from earliest times. There is an extensive repertoire of plainsong, the antiphon *Hodie Christus natus est* being particularly famous because of Britten's use of it in his *Ceremony of Carols*. Strictly speaking the medieval carol was a strophic song in English or Latin (or both) with one or two refrains sung after each verse, and by no means were all about the Nativity (A24). But the term is now used for ancient and modern melodies with non-liturgical texts about Christ's birth (A25 and A91). Polyphonic settings of Latin texts about the Incarnation abound (A44), and there is a large repertoire of English polyphony with sacred texts set as consort songs (A60) and anthems. In Germany cantatas and oratorios told the story of the birth of Christ in semi-dramatic form, the most notable being Schütz's *History of the Joyful and Merciful Birth of Jesus Christ, Son of God and Mary* (A68 and A69) and Bach's

Christmas Oratorio (B15 and B16). There is also a large repertoire of organ chorales based on carol melodies, one of the most famous being Bach's joyful chorale prelude *In dulci jubilo* (A94, based on A91).

Chromatic chord. Any chord containing notes other than those in the scale of the prevailing key. See *Augmented-6th chords* and B30, bar 8; *Neapolitan 6th* and B50, bars 80–81; *Secondary-dominant chords* and A81, bar 8.

Chromatic bullock. A strange English name for the ophicleide (B63) which nevertheless more accurately describes the capabilities and timbre of the instrument than the usual Greek-derived name.

Chromatic harmony. Harmony that includes pitches other than those contained in the diatonic scale of the prevailing key. In these terms chromatic harmony does not include chromaticism arising from inflexions of a mode in the polyphony of composers such as Machaut (A21, bars 11, 14, 18, 24–25, 27 and 29). Nor does it include chromatic inflexions in tonal music connected with modulations (A73, where the A♯s and G♯s in bars 7–8 are diatonic to the new key of B minor). But with the overthrow of modality and the establishment of major/minor tonality in the 17th century chromatic harmony followed apace (A81). By the early 18th century chromatic harmony had become an accepted resource: see how Bach evades a diatonic perfect cadence in bars 7–8 of A86 then highlights the chromatic Neapolitan 6th of the tonic key of F major (bars 14–16) before eventually returning to a diatonic cadence at the end of the toccata. There is no straight evolutionary development of chromatic harmony (classical composers more often than not reacted against baroque excess), but by the middle of the 19th century chromatic harmony threatened the very foundations of tonality (B68–B72) leading to what Schoenberg saw as its demise (C34). Despite this, late 20th-century composers have often returned to chromatic harmony in tonal contexts as an expressive resource (C97, bars 27–39). *EM 5.7.*

Chromatic music. See *Diatonic and chromatic music* and B38 (which is chromatic in bars 3–10 and diatonic in bars 11–19). *EM 5.7, 8.10.1.*

Chromatic passing note. An unessential note not belonging to the scale of the prevailing key which is approached and quitted by step in a rising or falling melodic line. The prevailing key in bar 10 of B40 is F major. The chromatic passing note G♯ does not belong to the scale of this key (and is therefore chromatic), it does not belong to chord V (and is therefore unessential), and it is approached and quitted by a semitone in a rising melodic line. In bar 105 of the same example two chromatic passing notes (A♭ and B♮) can be heard in an ascending scale linking the essential notes F, A♮ and C. A strikingly romantic chromatic passing note can be heard in bar 21 of B59. *EM 2.3.2.*

Chromatic scale. A scale of 12 pitch classes in which the interval between any note and an adjacent note is a semitone. B39 shows that composers can make use of all 12 chromatic notes without abandoning tonality (B38), but the systematic exploitation of the scale in serial music (C40 and C88) inevitably leads to atonality. *EM 2.7.*

Church modes. See the box on page 32. See also *Ecclesiastical mode. EM 2.4, 8.4.*

Church music. Music specifically written for performance in church, as distinct from sacred music (which includes settings of sacred texts in works designed for the concert hall).

In the middle ages church music was dominated by plainsong, whether as unaccompanied melody (A4) or as the basis for polyphonic composition (A21). The following types of plainsong can be found in the music examples: acclamation (A8), Alleluia (A5), hymn (A49), introit (A4), melismatic (A5), neumatic (A4), Ordinary of the Mass (A20, A42), psalm (A6), sequence (B62), syllabic (A6), versicle and response (A8).

In the later middle ages and renaissance, plainsong had an essential part to play in sacred polyphonic compositions such as the clausula (A10), isorhythmic Mass (A21), and paraphrase Mass (A52).

Alongside these types of church music were compositions that were not directly based on plainsong, but where the flowing style of the chant is evident in the independent contrapuntal lines (even in those compositions based on a secular melody): cantus firmus Mass (A27, which is based on the secular song shown in A26), conductus (A11), cyclic Mass (A28 and A29), motet (A44), parody Mass (A45 and A46).

After the reformation new sacred genres

Church sonata

emerged in Protestant countries, most of them involving instruments as well as, or instead of, voices: cantata (B6–B8), chorale prelude (A94), *historia* (A68 and A69), Lutheran chorale (B6), metrical psalm (A37), oratorio (B15–B16), organ Mass (A81), passion (B4 and B5), service (C30), verse anthem (A61).

Church sonata. *Sonata da chiesa*. See *Trio sonata* and A74.

Chute (Fr.). In 17th- and 18th-century France, an anticipation (A80, bar 12) or an appoggiatura (B17, bar 3, beat 1, G♯). See *Ornaments*.

Ciaconna (It.). Chaconne (A95).

Cibell. Cebell (B18).

Cimbalom. A Hungarian percussion instrument shaped like a trapezoidal table. It has exposed horizontal strings like those in a grand piano. Using a pair of double-ended hammers the performer can play single notes, chords and the tremolo so characteristic of the instrument. The full range of a modern cimbalom can be heard on track C41. See *Percussion instruments. EM 8.11.6.*

Cinelli (It.). Cymbals (C47). The term 'piatti' is now more commonly used.

Cinfonía (Span.). Hurdy-gurdy (A18).

C. ing. Abbreviation of *corno inglese* (cor anglais). See C88, bars 3–5 and 9–10.

Circle of 5ths. 1. A theoretical series of pitches,

Church modes

Eight collections of pitches, each of which can be arranged in the form of a scale as follows:

Church mode	Approximate range on the white notes of the piano	Final (tonic)
I (dorian)	D–D	D
II (hypodorian)	A–A	D
III (phrygian)	E–E	E
IV (hypophrygian)	B–B	E
V (lydian)	F–F	F
VI (hypolydian)	C–C	F
VII (mixolydian)	G–G	G
VIII (hypomixolydian)	D–D	G

Modes I, III, V and VII (in which the outermost notes of the approximate ranges and the lower and upper final coincide) are known as authentic modes. Modes II, IV, VI and VIII (in which the approximate ranges are a 4th below the final) are known as plagal modes. Music in these modes can be heard on the following tracks:

Mode	Track	
I	A40	(dorian mode on D)
II	A8	(hypodorian mode on D)
III	A37	(phrygian mode on E)
IV	A5	(hypophrygian mode on E)
V	A19	(lydian mode on F)
VI	A18	(hypolydian mode on F)
VII	A28 (tenor)	(mixolydian mode on G)
VIII	A4	(hypomixolydian mode on G)

All of these modes can be transposed. The essential feature that must be retained is the intervallic relationship between consecutive degrees of the scale. Thus the semitones between the second and third degrees and the sixth and seventh degrees of Mode I (dorian) that are evident in A40 are also seen in the dorian mode transposed down a tone in A22 and transposed up a third in A26. Similarly Vaughan Williams transposes the phrygian modality of A37 to G in his *Fantasia* (A39). Also see A11, A17, A20–A21, A24, A49, B61, B62, C33 and C57.

each a perfect 5th apart, which returns to the original pitch displaced by seven octaves, eg C_1–G_1–D–A–e–b–f♯^{1}–c♯^{2}–g♯^{2}–d♯^{3}–a♯^{3}–e♯^{4}–b♯^{4} (=c^5 in equal temperament). These pitches are shown (in a different notation) arranged as a circle at the foot of B78. **2.** In diatonic music, a series of notes that are all a perfect 5th apart except for one pair of notes which are a diminished 5th apart. This diminished interval allows the series to return to the starting note in seven instead of 12 steps. In C93 a diatonic circle of 5ths starting on a^2 and descending in 5ths is shown on the extra stave beneath bars 7–14 (a^2–d^2–g^1–c^1–f–B–E–A_1, in which a diminished 5th is formed between f and B). In practice Bach displaces every other note by an octave, thus producing alternate rising 4ths and falling 5ths. **3.** A harmonic sequence based on chords whose roots are a 5th apart. The term 'circle of 5ths' is loosely used for harmonic sequences that cover only a part of the complete circle (the bass of B78 covers a six-note segment from B♭ to C). Composers sometimes use a segment of a circle of 5ths in order to modulate through a variety of keys to a new tonal goal. This is the case in bars 6–13 of B17 where Rameau, starting in C major, modulates through a series of keys, each a perfect 5th above the last, to reach his tonal goal of E minor. This sort of harmonic sequence is known as a modulating circle of 5ths. *EM 5.5.10.*

Circles above notes. Depending on the context these can indicate harmonics (C35, bars 10–11) or open strings (A98, bars 2–3).

Cis (Ger.). C♯ (A24, alto, bar 7, beat 3).

Cisis (Ger.). C double sharp (C79, second clarinet, bar 1, third note – which is a semitone lower than the D♯s on either side of it). See *Doppelkreuz.*

Citole (Fr.). A medieval plucked string instrument (A13). *EM 6.4.2.*

Cittern, cistre (Fr.), **Cister** (Ger.), **cetula** (It.). A developed form of the medieval citole (A13), this renaissance string instrument was plucked with a plectrum. It was almost as popular as the contemporary lute, and was used as both an accompanimental and a solo instrument (often featuring in English broken consorts).

Cl. Abbreviation of clarinet, *clarinete* (Span.), *clarinette* (Fr.) and *clarinetto* (It.). See C79.

Cl. B. Abbreviation of *clarinetto basso* (bass clarinet). See C34 and C38.

Cl. bas. in Si♭. Abbreviation of *clarinetto basso in Si♭* (bass clarinet in B♭). See C38.

Cl. in Si♭., Cl. in La. Abbreviations of *clarinetto in Si♭/La* (clarinet in B♭ or A). In the original score C79 is notated for clarinets in A. The composer's choice between clarinets in A or B♭ is governed more by ease of performance than by any timbral differences between them.

Cl. picc in Re, Cl. picc. in Mi♭. Abbreviations of *clarinetto piccolo in Re/Mi♭* (little clarinet in D or E♭). Both are transposing instruments that sound a tone or a minor 3rd above written pitch (C10).

Clairon (Fr.). An organ reed stop. On a classical French organ it contributed to loud registration (such as the *grand jeu*) at four-foot pitch (ie sounding an octave above the pitches shown in A81).

Clappers. 1. Any of a variety of concussion ideophones consisting of two pieces of material clapped together. See *Castanets* (C50), *Claves* (C51) and *Whip* (C46). **2.** Persons clapping (C89). **3.** The metal tongues in instruments such as cowbells (C28).

Clarinets, clarinette (Fr.), **clarinetto** (It.), **clarinete** (Span.). A family of single-reed woodwind instruments. The clarinet in B♭ is the most commonly used member of the family and its approximate range is shown on the folded insert. The larger clarinet in A has a range a semitone lower than the B♭ instrument. Solos for clarinets in B♭ and A can be heard in a variety of registers in B68 (bars 6–7), C4 (bars 6–7), C41 (bars 16–17), C75 (bars 2–10) and C79 (a duet for two clarinets).

The bass clarinet is pitched an octave lower than the B♭ clarinet (see the folded insert). Almost the whole of its range is covered in C34, and in bars 3–5 the effect of flutter-tonguing can be heard.

Clarinets in D and E♭ are pitched a major 3rd and a perfect 4th above the B♭ clarinet. In C10 a clarinet in D reaches the extremity of its upper register before plunging three octaves to its lowest register. The clarinet in D is now a rarity, its parts usually being played on the little E♭ clarinet (it is impossible to tell which of these instruments is used on track C10 since their timbres are so similar). See *Reed instruments. EM 6.6.3.*

Clarino register

Clarino register. The highest register of the baroque trumpet in which complete scales could be played (B15, bars 79–80).

Clarone (It.). **1.** Basset-horn (B40). **2.** Bass clarinet (C38). See *Reed instruments*.

Clashed cymbals. A pair of large cymbals, each with a leather strap, that are played by crashing them together with an oblique movement (C47).

Classical or classic guitar. A term used to describe the acoustic guitar with six metal strings (C83), distinguishing it from other acoustic and electric guitars (C94).

Classical music. 1. In common parlance, any western music other than jazz, folk or pop (though the adjective 'classical' is sometimes applied to jazz and pop numbers that have stood the test of time). **2.** Music in the Viennese styles of the late 18th and early 19th centuries (B21–B55). **3.** In France, music of the late 17th and early 18th centuries (A81, A84, B17 and C32).

Clausula (Lat.). A section of organum based on a melismatic passage from a plainsong melody. The two-part polyphony of A10 forms a clausula in which the tenor corresponds with the plainsong melisma on the word 'Domino' shown in A8. *EM 8.5.1.*

Clavecin (Fr.), **clavecín** (Span.). Harpsichord (B17).

Claveciniste (Fr.). **1.** A harpsichordist. **2.** 'Les clavecinistes français' were composers of the French classical period who wrote extensively for the harpsichord (A84, B17 and C32).

Claves (Span.). A pair of hardwood sticks, one held in a cupped hand, the other used as a beater (C51 and C53). See *Clappers* and *Percussion instruments. EM 6.8.5.*

Clavicembalo (It.). Harpsichord (B17).

Clavichord. A keyboard instrument of great antiquity. It is very soft-toned but, within its restricted dynamic range, is capable of the most subtle dynamic variations, including crescendos and diminuendos. Because the performer was in almost direct contact with the string it was capable of vibrato – a technique available on no other keyboard instrument. This made it the most suitable keyboard instrument for the performance of intimate and highly expressive works such as the fantasias of C. P. E. Bach (B20). See *Bebung. EM 3.10.2, 6.9.2.*

Clavier (Ger.). Old spelling of *Klavier*. Keyboard, or keyboard instrument. Unless qualified 'Clavier' now refers to the harpsichord (B10), clavichord (B20) or piano (B56). It should be noted, however, that Bach's *Clavier-Übung* (*Keyboard Practice*), from which examples B10–B12 are taken, includes organ music.

Clavis (Lat.). Clef. See A30 for a variety of clefs.

Clef. A symbol at the beginning of a stave fixing the pitches of notes written on it. In A1–A3 bass clefs are used for the pitches of notes at or below middle C, and treble clefs for the pitches of notes at or above middle C. Nowadays music for tenor voices is commonly written using a treble clef with some indication that the pitches should sound an octave lower than written (in A10 this is shown by the figure 8 attached to the bottom of the clef). With only three exceptions these are the only clefs used in this dictionary (see *C clefs* and the extra staves in A4, A30 and A38). See also *Alto clef*.

Climax. A point of maximum tension, excitement or elation relative to passages of music before and after it. A climactic effect can be achieved by thickening the texture, and increasing the range and level of dissonance. All three elements are evident in A58, which begins with antiphonal exchanges between three four-part instrumental choirs (bars 1–8). The texture thickens and the range increases with the imitative counterpoint of bars 8–14, and the climax is reached at bar 17, where all 12 instruments are playing and the first cornett sounds a dissonant A♮. Tension is dispersed when dominant harmony resolves to the tonic in the last bar. A climax can also be reached by rising melodic lines, increasing speed and volume, modulation to unrelated keys, and the use of chromatic harmony. All of these elements are evident in B58. The build-up to the climax begins with a modulation from A minor to the distant key of C♯ minor (bars 1–5), and continues as the baritone rises from b♯ to the climactic e^1 in bars 6–10. At the climax a chromatic German 6th resolves back to the tonic (bars 9–11). In romantic music common ways of building to a climax include the use of melodic or harmonic sequences (or both), repetition, fragmentation and unexpected resolution of discords. The climax in bars 16–17 of B68 is preceded by a three-bar phrase (first system) twice

Combination pedal

repeated in a rising sequence (second and third systems). Then the last phrase is repeated an octave higher (bars 12–13), a fragment of it is also repeated an octave higher (bars 14–15), then the expected resolution of dominant harmony (bar 16) to the tonic is avoided by the climactic use of chord VI with a searing appoggiatura (bar 17). In C97 a series of climaxes (bars 9, 23 and 35) are achieved by similar means, but the last three climaxes are brought about by the alternation of very soft and very loud passages of music (bars 39–48).

Clivis (Lat.). A two-note neume (A4). See also *Pes*.

Cloches (Fr.). Bells (B63).

Cloches de vache (Fr.). Cowbells (C28).

Clos (Fr.). See *Ouvert and clos* (A13).

Close. Cadence (B48, bars 3–4).

Close harmony, close position, close spacing. Chords in which the constituent notes are close together. In the first two beats of bars 30–34 in A59 the chords are in close position (as opposed to the wider spacing of the chords on the third beats of these bars).

Closing section, closing theme. In sonata form, the last section or last theme of the exposition in which a secondary key is strongly asserted. In B40 this is identified as a codetta (bars 48–51). Although it appears to be no more than a series of perfect cadences in the dominant key of C major, it turns out to be thematic when the development begins to unfold (compare z in bars 50–51 with the use of this figure in bars 52–68). *EM 4.5.7*.

Cluster chord. A chord comprising a set of adjacent pitches (C91, bar 2). *EM 8.11.9, 8.11.11*.

Coda. The final section of a composition. In the last 16 bars of B36 finality is manifested by a tonic pedal, repeated perfect cadences, and, in the last three bars, repeated tonic chords.

Codetta. 1. In a fugal exposition, a linking passage between entries of the subject and answer, or vice versa (B10 and B14). **2.** In sonata forms, a passage at the end of the exposition that confirms the tonality of the second subject by devices such as repeated perfect cadences in the key of the second subject (B40, bars 48–51). *EM 4.5.1, 7.7.1*.

Col legno (It.). A performance direction indicating that a bowed string instrument should be played with the reverse, wooden side of the bow. In C36 *col legno* strings contribute to the dry sound of the ostinato that runs through the whole extract. *EM 6.5.11*.

Col, coll', colla (It.). With, with the. In C36, bar 1 'col legno' means 'with the wood' (ie the strings are directed to reverse their bows and play the strings by tapping them with the wood of the bow). In C76 Bartók instructs the strings to play 'colla parte'. This means they must sustain their chord until the flautist has finished the cadenza. Likewise the instruction 'colla voce' means that accompanimental instruments should follow the voice part, moving at the moment dictated by the soloist.

Color (Lat.). A repeated pitch pattern in an isorhythmic tenor. Not all isorhythmic tenors contain such repetitions. The repetition of both pitch and rhythm in the first 16 bars of A21 stems from the repetition in the plainsong melody (A20) that Machaut uses as a cantus firmus.

Coloration. Elaborate ornamentation of the type commonly written at cadences in 16th-century lute or keyboard music (A57), and similar embellishment (whether written-out or improvised) in 17th- and 18th-century vocal music (A66). See *Coloratura* and B50.

Coloratura (It.). Extravagant melodic ornamentation, especially in vocal music such as that shown in B50, bars 24–31. A coloratura soprano has a high range (up to f^3 in bar 31) and the technique to negotiate such virtuosic vocal melodies. See *Voice*. *EM 8.9.6*.

Colour. A word sometimes used to mean timbre. Thus one could say that the organ registration used in the performance of C55 is coloured by the presence of the *voix céleste* (Messiaen often used the word in reference to registration, instrumentation and modality, as in his *Couleurs de la cité céleste* of 1963). *EM 3.7, 8.11.3*.

Combination pedal, combination piston. Knobs operated by an organist's feet or fingers allowing more than one division of the organ to be played on a single manual. In C55 the right-hand melody is played on a rank of pipes in the positive department combined with (or coupled to) four ranks of pipes in the swell department (*récit*). See *Coupler*.

Combo

Combo. In jazz, a combination of instruments such as clarinet, saxophone, trumpet, drum kit and pizzicato double bass (in C38 a cello is used instead of a bass, while the flute is an instrument that features rarely in a combo).

Come sopra (It.). As above. This performance direction saves printing the same details of articulation twice (in bar 4 of C70 the words refer the performer back to the similar passage in bar 2).

Come (It.). As, like. 'Come prima' (as at the start) at bar 38 of C2 indicates a return to the tempo and style of bars 1–16. 'Come sopra' (as above) at bar 4 of C70 saves printing the details of articulation twice (compare bars 2 and 4).

Comes (Lat.). See *Dux and comes* and B26.

Comic opera. A generic term for musical dramas in which comic elements are more pervasive than serious elements. The term is vague and can encompass many types of opera including *Singspiel* (B37) and operetta (C73). See *Opera buffa*.

Commedia dell'arte (It.). A comic theatrical entertainment popular in Italy and France (where it was referred to as 'comédie Italienne') from about 1545 to 1800. It included improvised songs accompanied by the masked players themselves. Some of the stock characters survived in 19th- and 20th-century art music. In Schumann's *Carnaval* (1835), for instance, Arlequin is the madcap servant Arlecchino, Pantalon (Pantalone) is a Venetian magnifico, and Colombine (Columbina) is a lover. Another stock character was Pedrolino (Little Peter), a mad clown who makes his appearance in *Carnaval* as Pierrot. It is this character who is the eponymous anti-hero of Albert Giraud's 21 poems which, in a German translation, Schoenberg set as his Op. 21, *Pierrot lunaire* (1912). The composer said of this seminal 20th-century masterpiece that he intended it to have a light, ironic, satirical mood. This is true of some of the songs, but 'Nacht' (C34) reveals the sinister depths of Pierrot's moonstruck madness.

Common chord. In England, any major or minor triad. All of the chords heard in C86 are common chords. In the USA only major triads are classed as common chords. *EM 5.3.1, 5.3.2.*

Common time. $\frac{4}{4}$ time (A25) sometimes indicated by the letter C (A17). See *Time signature*.

Communion, communio (Lat.). The last of the six items of the Proper of the Mass. It is sung while the consecrated elements are consumed. At this point a polyphonic motet is often sung. *O magnum mysterium* (A44) is sometimes used in this way during Christmastide, even though the text is part of a responsory associated with the Divine Office.

Compass. Range. The compass of A5 is an octave from c to c^1.

Complement. 1. The difference between any interval less than an octave and the octave itself. In C95 bar 11 begins with a leap of an octave. This is followed by a leap of a 5th. The difference between a 5th and an octave is a 4th (as shown in beats 3–4 of the same bar). When an interval is inverted by transposing one of the two notes up or down an octave the resultant interval is the complement. Thus, when intervallically inverted a perfect 5th becomes a perfect 4th (as in bar 11), a major 6th becomes a minor 3rd, a major 2nd becomes a minor 7th, and so on. **2.** In serial music, the six notes that are left after abstracting a hexachord from a 12-tone row. In bars 5–6 of C88 the tenor sings the first hexachord of the retrograde form of the prime order that was sung in bars 2–4. The complement of this hexachord comprises the remaining six notes of the retrograde order (ie the last six notes of C88(ii)).

Composite organum. See *Organum* and A7(b). *EM 5.8.2, 8.5.1.*

Composition. The term derives from the Latin 'componere': to put together. This central aspect of composition is evident in medieval music that strives, not for originality, but for an enlargement of what already exists (A9, A10 and A21 are based on plainsong melodies that would have been familiar to everyone who heard the music in the middle ages). The same was true in the renaissance (a secular melody invades A27 and plainsong is again at the core of A40–A52).

With the advent of humanism composers found, perhaps for the first time in western music, means of expression that were not derived from pre-existent materials (though they thought they were following the ancients in establishing the 'new music' of the early baroque – A62–A66). The reformation ironically continued the old traditions in encouraging an art that was often based on pre-reformation song (A91–A94), but by the end of the 18th century a new and vibrant secular instrumental tradition was soon established that owed little to the past (B21–B36).

The role of the composer radically changed in the 19th and 20th centuries. Instead of being a servant of Church or State the composer became a potentially revolutionary figure whose subjective insights challenged later composers (B68, C27–C29 and C34). In the 20th century composers fought a battle over the pre-eminence of post-romanticism (C84–C86) and recherché modernism (C87, C88 and C90). In the late 20th century many composers returned to their roots (and tonality) in an attempt to bridge the chasm between modernism and romanticism. Posterity will judge the degree to which composers such as Swayne, Tavener, Kancheli, Bodorová and MacMillan (C91–C97) have succeeded in the task of returning to the original role of the composer without sacrificing originality.

Compound intervals. Intervals greater than an octave. The leaping 9ths and 10ths in A90 can be described as compound 2nds and compound 3rds respectively (the same principle can apply to greater intervals such as 11ths, 12ths and so on).

Compound stop. On an organ, a stop containing more than one rank of pipes, usually sounding octaves and compound fifths above eight-foot pitch. The French cornet also contains a rank sounding a compound third above eight-foot pitch. It is this compound stop that adds brilliance to the reedy timbre of the other stops in A81.

Compound time, compound meter. See *Simple and compound time* and A14, A18, A86, A90, B19, B61, B68, B74, C3, C4 and C72. *EM 1.4, 1.8.*

Con (It.). With. 'Allegro con spirito' at the head of C83 means 'fast with spirit' (fast and lively).

Con sordino (con sord.) (It.). With mute. The plural, 'con sordini', is used when more than one performer is required to add a mute (C19).

Concert. A public performance of music for a soloist or an ensemble of instruments or voices (or both) before an audience gathered with the specific intention of hearing it.

Before the 18th century secular music-making was largely the preserve of the aristocracy, but, with the rise of the middle classes in the 18th century, academies in Italy and musical guilds in Germany began to present concerts for their members. From these sprang the public concerts given by societies that still exist today (eg the Gewandhaus concerts in Leipzig that were inaugurated in the middle of the 18th century). By the end of the 18th century, subscription concerts had become the norm in most European capitals, but they were held in theatres and halls not specifically designed for music (eg the Hanover Rooms in London). After the completion of the concert hall in the Paris Conservatoire (1811) concert series in specially built halls spread throughout Europe and America.

The increasing popularity of concerts in the late 18th century and 19th century was accompanied by an expansion of the symphony orchestra from the modest requirements of Haydn (B21 is scored for a wind section of five and a small string ensemble) to the gargantuan forces gathered under Mahler's baton (C27 and C28 are taken from a symphony that calls for a wind section of 40, two harps, strings and five percussionists). Throughout the 20th century prophets of doom have suggested that concerts of this magnitude would, from sheer economic necessity, suffer the same fate as the dinosaurs. Yet the construction of new concert halls in Birmingham and Manchester and the performance of works such as MacMillan's *Quickening* (C97) on the eve of the millennium suggest otherwise.

Concert grand. A grand piano about nine feet long used in large halls, particularly for the performance of romantic piano concertos. B64 was recorded on a concert grand. Its sonorous tone should be compared with the thinner sound of the upright piano used in the recording of C73.

Concert pitch. Sounding pitch, usually in relation to a^1 at 440 Hz (A1). The term is used to distinguish between the written or printed pitch of music for transposing instruments and the pitch at which they actually sound. Music for transposing instruments is notated at concert pitch in Volume 2 of this dictionary.

Concertante. An adjective describing the solo role of voices and/or instruments in a

Concertato style

larger ensemble. In A69 there are two concertante groups, three recorders and three solo voices. Both are supported by a continuo group. The term was used in a similar sense in the late 18th century when the title 'Sinfonia concertante' indicated a work for two or more soloists and orchestra (eg Mozart's Sinfonia concertante K297B for oboe, clarinet, horn and bassoon soloists accompanied by a chamber orchestra). There are concertante roles for bassoons, oboes, clarinets, flutes and trumpets (among other instruments) in Bartók's Concerto for Orchestra (C77, C78, C79, C80 and C81 respectively).

Concertato style. A baroque style in which contrasting groups of instruments and/or singers are accompanied by continuo instruments. A trio of recorders and a trio of singers alternate and combine in A69, both being supported by continuo instruments (organ and cello).

Concertino. 1. A group of solo performers in a concerto grosso. In B19 the group comprises two violinists and a cellist. 2. A small-scale concerto. See *Ripieno. EM 8.7.5.*

Concertmaster. The leader of an orchestra, one of whose duties is to play solo violin parts (C97, bars 53–65).

Concerto. 1. In the early 17th century, a work for concerted voices and instruments. Although A69 is taken from a *historia*, the interplay of voices and instruments supported by a continuo group is no different from sacred works that Schütz himself called 'concerti'. The term was used in this sense as late as the time of Bach (who gave the title 'Concerto' to many of the works that are now known as cantatas). 2. In the late 17th and early 18th centuries, a concerted work in several movements for one or more solo instrumentalists, string ensemble and continuo group. Early examples of such concerti were characterised by the contrasting textures of passages written for a solo group (the concertino) and a larger group composed of the concertino reinforced by an ensemble of strings (the ripieno) that could comprise anything from one instrument per part to what, even in modern terms, constituted a large string orchestra. In these concerti grossi the concertino most often consisted of two violins, cello and a continuo group – the same forces that were employed in the contemporary trio sonata (A74). Indeed Corelli's concerti grossi could be regarded as trio sonatas with textural contrast brought about by a ripieno group that, apart from an added viola part, simply doubled the concertino at certain points. Handel followed Corelli's lead in his 12 Grand Concertos Op. 6. B19 shows how the concertino play throughout doubled by the ripieno group in bars 5–8, 11–12 and 14–16 (in which passages the texture is also thickened by the addition of viola and double bass parts). **3.** In the classical era, an instrumental work, most often for a single soloist and most often in three movements (fast–slow–fast). Like other genres of the period the first movement was often in a type of sonata form that contained two expositions, the first purely orchestral, the second for soloist and orchestra. Similar modifications were made to sonata-rondo form in finales such as that shown in B36. **4.** In the 20th century the concerto survived divergent stylistic developments, often making self-conscious references to the past (C77–C81). *EM 8.9.2.*

Concerto for orchestra. A concerto in which individual members, pairs or groups from the orchestra are given prominent solos. Among scores of solos in Bartók's *Concerto for Orchestra* the cadenza for flute solo (C76) and the passages for pairs of woodwinds (C77–C81) are particularly noteworthy.

Concerto grosso. A 'grand concerto' (Handel's title for his Op. 6 concerti). See *Concerto* 2 and B19. See also *Concertino* and *Ripieno. EM 8.7.5.*

Concierto (Span.). 1. Concerto (C83). 2. Concert.

Concitato (It.). See *Stile concitato* and the start of B50.

Concord. See *Consonance and dissonance.* Every chord in the fa-la-la refrains of A59 and every chord in C86 is a concord. *EM 5.2.*

Conduct of parts. The manner in which individual parts or voices move from note to note, especially in contrapuntal textures. At the end of the first burden of A24 the conduct of all three parts is in keeping with the stylistic norms of the period, the two sharpened notes rising a semitone as the bass moves down to the final of the mode in contrary motion. See *Voice leading.*

Consonance and dissonance

Conductor. A person who by conventional and expressive gestures coordinates the performance of a group of musicians. The task of a modern conductor includes the indication of tempo and metre, giving cues for vocal or instrumental entries, ensuring proper balance between parts and the correct articulation of them, and, ultimately, bearing the responsibility for the final interpretation of the music. In the 16th century a conductor would simply indicate the tactus. In the 17th and 18th centuries the role of a conductor was often combined with that of harpsichordist or principal violinist who indicated tempo changes by a nod of the head or by using the bow as a baton. Weber is often credited with being the first conductor in the modern sense of the term, and in 1820, the year of the first performance of *Der Freischütz* (B59), the term was used for the first time in a concert programme. Berlioz (B62) was among a new breed of composer-conductors, and by the second half of the 19th century a conductor was essential for the performance of romantic operas (B68) and the complex orchestral works of composers such as Liszt (B73) and Richard Strauss (C10). See *Dirigent*.

Conductus (Lat.). **1.** Non-liturgical (but often sacred) rhyming Latin poems of 12th- and early 13th-century Spain and France (A11). **2.** Monophonic or polyphonic musical settings of such poems. Unlike contemporary organum, the polyphonic variety was based on a freely composed tenor and written in the syllabic, note-against-note style called discant. The exception is the melismatic *cauda* with which many conductus end (A11). Conductus (pl.) were sometimes sung as alternatives to the plainsong salutation 'Benedicamus Domino' (A8). See *Discant. EM 8.5.1.*

Confinalis (Lat.). The pitch a 5th above (or a 4th below) the final of a mode. A4 is in Mode VIII (the hypomixolydian mode) and the ambitus (range) stretches from the lower *confinalis* (D♯) to the *confinalis* an octave above it.

Congregation. An assembly of people at an act of worship. Congregational music tends to be melodically simple and metrically four-square (A25).

Conjunct motion. See *Motion* and the melody of A36.

Consecutive 5ths and octaves. Two vocal or instrumental parts moving in the same direction while maintaining the vertical interval of a 5th (A7a) or an octave (A26, bars 1–11) between the parts. Although parallel motion and consecutive motion are technically synonymous, the latter term is often used disapprovingly when referring to 'forbidden' parallel motion in classical tonal music.

Consequent. See *Antecedent and consequent* and B28. *EM 7.3.*

Conservatory (Eng.), **conservatoire** (Fr.), **conservatorio** (It.). An institution devoted to the practical and theoretical education of aspiring musicians. The performers on tracks C42–C54 are all students at the Royal Academy of Music, a conservatory in London, UK.

Console. The keyboard (or keyboards or manuals), pedals and stop knobs that control the various departments of an organ. A86, A94 and C55 were recorded on an organ with four manuals, pedals and nine departments (including the usual great, swell, choir, positive and solo departments).

Consonance and dissonance. The relative stability (consonance) or instability (dissonance) of two or more notes sounded simultaneously. Because perceptions of consonance and dissonance have changed through the centuries it is impossible to categorise intervals and chords as concords and discords in a way that hold good for all styles of music. Nevertheless certain intervals that have for several centuries been accepted as consonant still give an impression of stability. They include the 3rds and 6ths heard in Variation 33 of Bach's Chaconne in D minor (A97, bars 0–4), which, compared with the other variations, sounds entirely concordant. Equally consonant are chords built up from perfect octaves and perfect 5ths. A19 begins and ends with such a chord, and, because all the other chords are built from these intervals together with 3rds and 6ths, the whole Kyrie sounds concordant. Dissonant intervals include 2nds, 7ths and the tritone. After the consonant 3rds and 6ths of the first phrase of C58 these dissonant intervals are particularly striking. Even more unstable is the first three-part discord heard in bar 3 of A81. At the end of this track the instability of the penultimate chord (containing a tritone) resolves to the stability of the final chord (containing a perfect octave and a major 3rd). *EM 4.3.6, 5.2.*

Consonant 4th. Throughout the renaissance and for much of the 17th century the interval of a 4th from the bass was regarded as a dissonance that needed to be treated as a suspension when it occured on the beat. One of the very few exceptions was the sounding of a 4th from the bass on a weak beat just before a cadence. An example is identified by the asterisk in A47. Listening to this consonant 4th one is struck by its similarity to a suspension: it is as though the B♭ on the second beat of the bar were a preparation for a suspension on the third beat of the bar (which is resolved to the A♮ on the last beat of the bar). This becomes more obvious when Victoria's tenor part is added (A48). Now there are stronger dissonances before and after the consonant 4th (the suspended 7ths shown by the vertical brackets). Compared with these dissonances the 4th from the bass sounds relatively consonant. An even more striking example can be heard at the end of A58. *EM 5.2.*

Consort. In 16th- and 17th-century England, an ensemble of solo instruments. A whole consort consisted of instruments all of the same family (eg the consort of viols heard on track A61). A broken consort contained instruments from more than one family (eg the recorders, sackbut and curtal heard on A60).

Consort anthem. A verse anthem with solo and choral parts accompanied by an instrumental ensemble (A61). *EM 8.6.2.*

Consort song. An English song for solo voice or voices with an ensemble of solo instruments, the consort song flourished from about 1550 to 1650. The imitative contrapuntal texture of A60 is typical of a genre that could be performed by one solo voice with equally important instrumental polyphony (as here), or by any combination of voices and instruments. *EM 8.6.2.*

Continuo. Abbreviation of basso continuo. A continuo part can be realised by a single harmony instrument (on track A79 the violin is accompanied by a solo harpsichord), but more often there are at least two instruments, one to play the printed bass line, the other to realise the figuring beneath it (on track B4 the Evangelist is accompanied by a cello and chamber organ). The term is also used in reference to the group of instruments or instrumentalists that realise a basso continuo. A variety of continuo groups can be heard on A62–A66, namely: trombone, harpsichord and chamber organ (A62), trombone and regal (A63), chitarrone and harps (A65), and organ and plucked strings (A66). See *Figured bass. EM 6.4.4, 6.9.2, 8.7.1.*

Contrabass, contrebasse (Fr.), **contrabasso** (It.). Double bass (C7), often abbreviated as 'cb' in orchestral scores (B59, bar 26). See *String instruments.*

Contrabass viol. Sometimes called a violone in the 16th and 17th centuries, the contrabass viol (or double-bass viol) is the largest instrument of the viol family and a precursor of the modern double bass (A36). See *Viol.*

Contrabassoon, contrebasson (Fr.). The largest double-reed woodwind instrument in common use. Its approximate range is shown on the folded insert. The solo played on track C31 descends to its lowest register and it provides a strong bass to the wind chorale on track C27. See *Double-reed instruments. EM 6.6.2.*

Contradanza (It.), **contredanse** (Fr.). Country dance. A fast dance in duple time that was popular throughout Europe in the late 18th century (B43).

Contrafactum (Lat.). A vocal work in which new words have been substituted for the original text. The Latin hymn *Perspice Christicola* (A14) is a contrafactum of the melody of the English round *Sumer is icumen in* (A15).

Contrafagotto (It.). Contrabassoon (C31). See the folded insert for the approximate range of the instrument.

Contralto. The lowest female voice (A22). See the folded insert for the contralto's approximate range.

Contrappunto (It.), **contrapunctus** (Lat.). Counterpoint (C93).

Contrapuntal. Adjective describing musical textures made up of two or more melodic lines sounded together (A28, in which the two melodic lines are of equal importance). *EM 4.1.*

Contrapuntal inversion. The inversion of two contrapuntally combined melodies so that the melody that has been above another melody in one passage of music becomes the lower melody in a second passage. The two melodies d and b^2 are contrapuntally inverted in B24 (they can be heard in their true context in bars 29–41 of B21). In fugal textures the subject and countersubject are commonly inverted (compare bars 0–4 with bars 9–13 in B29). See also *Invertible counterpoint. EM 4.4.5.*

Contrary motion. See *Motion* 2 and A85, bar 4. *EM 4.1.*

Contratenor (Lat.). In the 14th and 15th centuries, a vocal part that occupied the same range as the tenor. In A27 the tenor sings a cantus firmus derived from A26, and has a range of a 6th from e to $c\sharp^1$. The part sung by basses in the same example is free and has a range from c♯ to $c\sharp^1$ (almost the same as the tenor and often crossing parts with it), thus qualifying it as a contratenor part. In fact this music is on the cusp of the progression from equal-voice polyphony to the more stratified textures of composers such as Victoria (A44–A46) and Palestrina (A52).

Contrebasse (Fr.). Double bass (C7).

Contrebasson (Fr.). Contrabassoon (C31).

Contredanse (Fr.). *Contradanza* (B43).

Cor (Fr.). Horn (C84).

Cor à pistons (Fr.). Valve horn (C85, bars 8–25).

Cor anglais. A tenor oboe pitched a 5th below the ordinary oboe (see the folded insert). A duet for tenor voice and cor anglais can be heard in bars 3–4 of C88 and its lowest register can be heard at the end of the same extract. Also called the English horn. See *Reed instruments. EM 6.6.2.*

Cor chromatique en Fa (Fr.). Valve horn in F (C85, bars 8–25).

Coranto. Corrente (A67).

Corda (It.), **corde** (Fr.). String. Composers sometimes specify which string should be used by Roman numerals. Thus in bars 5–10 of C70 the Roman numeral IV indicates that the violin's lowest string (G) should be used instead of the D string (on which this passage would normally be played).

Cordes, les (Fr.). Strings (B19).

Cori spezzati (It.). Plural of *coro spezzato* (A58).

Cornamusa (It.), **cornemuse** (Fr.). Bagpipe (A17).

Cornet (Eng.). A brass instrument similar to a trumpet, but with a wider bore and different tonal qualities. This difference in timbre can be heard on track C3 in which a pair of cornets play a melody in 3rds shortly followed by a fanfare figure on a pair of trumpets. See *Brass instruments. EM 6.7.4.*

Cornet (Fr.). A French name for an organ stop made up of several ranks of pipes most commonly sounding at written pitch, and at the octave, 12th (an octave and a 5th), 15th (two octaves) and 17th (two octaves and a major 3rd) above written pitch. The cornet contributes the highest-sounding pitches and adds brilliance to the *grand jeu* heard on A81.

Cornet à pistons (Fr.). Cornet (C3). *EM 6.7.4.*

Cornett (Eng.), **cornetto** (It.). A wooden wind instrument with finger-holes like a recorder and a cup-shaped mouthpiece like a trumpet. It flourished from the end of the 15th century to the end of the 17th century. Cornetts and sackbuts were often paired together in ceremonial ensemble music of the period (A58, bars 1–2). The cornett should not be confused with the modern cornet (C3). *EM 6.7.5.*

Cornetta (It.). Cornet (C3). Not to be confused with 'cornetto'.

Corno (It.). Horn (C84).

Corno di bassetto (It.). Basset-horn (B40).

Corno inglese (It.). English horn (C88, bars 3–5).

Coro (It. and Span.). Chorus, choir (C30).

Coro spezzato (It.). Broken choir. Music written for spatially separated vocal and/or instrumental forces (A58).

Corona (It.). The sign for a pause on a sustained note or chord (B15, bars 64 and 80; B68, bars 11 and 13). The Italian synonym 'fermata' is often used, but the Italians themselves prefer 'corona'.

Corrente (It.), **courante** (Fr.). Originating in the 16th century, but more characteristic of the baroque era, the corrente or courante was a dance in triple time that was usually in binary form. Although composers often used the titles interchangeably two types emerged in the 17th and 18th centuries. The Italian corrente (A67) was usually in moderate or fast triple time ($\frac{3}{4}$ or $\frac{3}{8}$), basically homophonic, and with simple triadic or scalic melodies. The contemporary French courante was usually slower than the corrente (some authorities describing it as having the same pulse as the sarabande) and was characterised be hemiolaic cadences and, in many cases, contrapuntal or *style brisé* textures. Together with the allemande (B17), sarabande (A88) and gigue (A90) the courante was one of the most common movements in the baroque suite. See *Courante. EM 8.7.3.*

Corthol. Curtal (A60).

Coulé (Fr.). **1.** A descending appoggiatura (B1, bar 4, beat 2). **2.** A slide (A84, letter e in bar 12). See *Ornaments*. **3.** As a performance direction in French baroque music, legato (C32, bar 9). *EM 3.10.2.*

Coulé de tierce, coulé sur une tierce (Fr.). In French baroque music, a slide through the interval of a 3rd (A84, letter e in bar 12). See *Ornaments*.

Counter-exposition. In a fugue, a complete set of redundant entries heard after all voices have stated the subject or answer in the opening fugal exposition. In B14(a) all three voices state the subject or answer in the exposition of bars 1–5[1]. In the counter-exposition of bars 7–11[1] the subject and answer are restated in all three voices in the tonic key (with very slight changes to the pitches of the answers and with two rhythmic changes in the subject).

Counter-melody. An independent melody sounding against another melody that might already have been heard. In B21 melody c (bars 12–18) is a counter-melody to b[1] (a shorter version of which has already been heard in bars 4–8).

Counterpoint. 1. The combination of two or more independent melodic lines (B13). **2.** A single melodic line in a contrapuntal texture. In the first two bars of B13 subject 1 is a counterpoint of subject 2 (and vice versa). See *Counter-melody. EM 4, 6.11.5.*

Counter-subject. A contrapuntal part sounded against the subject or answer of a fugue (B9, lower part, bars 5–10). *EM 4.5.1, 4.5.9.*

Countertenor. A male alto falsettist (A12).

Country dance. A name given to a variety of English folk dances of the 16th century. Some were taken up at the court of Elizabeth I and, in the 17th century, by the French court, where the fast duple-time variety became known as the 'contredanse' (B43).

Coupler. On an organ or harpsichord, a device allowing more than one department to be played on a single manual. See *Combination pedal* and C55.

Couplet (Fr.). An episode in a French rondeau. The couplets in A84 are identified by the letters B and C. *EM 7.6.2.*

Courante (Fr.). Like the Italian *corrente* (A67), the French *courante* was originally a fast 'running' dance in triple time (hence the title). In the early 17th century the styles of the two dances began to diverge, the typical *courante* being slower and more contrapuntal than the *corrente*, and often characterised by hemiolaic rhythms in $\frac{3}{2}$ time. Composers themselves, however, often took a cavalier attitude to these stylistic norms. The *Courante* from Bach's French Suite No. 4 (BWV 815), for instance, is in $\frac{3}{4}$ time and its style is indistinguishable from that of the *Corrente* in his Partita No. 1 (BWV 825) – they are both in the Italian style. In fact the title *courante* (which Bach uses in all six French Suites) is applicable only to those in the first and third suites, the other four being in $\frac{3}{4}$ time and Italianate in style. Both types were usually in binary form and commonly appeared as the second of the four regular dances of the baroque suite. See *Corrente*.

Course. One, two or three strings tuned to the same pitch or to the octave on plucked string instruments such as the theorbo (A75) and lute (A89). Multiple stringing enriches the timbre and increases the volume of sound produced by these delicate instruments.

Cowbells. Hollow metal percussion instruments that can be mounted on a stand and struck with a variety of sticks. Mahler uses them to evoke the image of distant cattle in an Alpine landscape (C28). In this context cowbells with clappers are gently shaken to produce a more naturalistic effect. See *Percussion instruments. EM 6.8.3.*

Cps. Abbreviation of cycles per second measured in Hertz. See A1, A2 and the folded insert.

Crab canon. A canon in which the *comes* is a retrograde or retrograde inversion of the *dux*. See *Canon cancrizans* and C88, bars 2–5.

Creed, credo (Lat.). The third sung item of the Ordinary of the Mass, the creed is a confession of faith. The style of the most commonly used plainsong settings is syllabic (like A6). The style of polyphonic settings also tends to be simpler than settings of the other parts of the Ordinary (because of the considerable length of the text).

Crescendo (cresc.). Gradually getting louder (C27, bar 1). Increasing volume is also indicated by a sign that most musicians call a 'hairpin' (C27, bar 4). See *Dynamics*.

Croche (Fr.). Quaver or eighth-note (B18, Variation 1).

Croches égales, notes égales (Fr.). In baroque French and French-style music, a direction requiring the performer to play quavers (*croches*) as written rather than treating them according to the conventions of *notes inégales* (uneven notes). In the first eight bars of C32 the notes beamed together in threes are played *inégales*, but in bars 9–21 all of the quavers are played as *croches égales* in conformity with Couperin's direction 'notes égales' (bar 9). *EM 1.6.4.*

Croma (It.). Quaver, eighth-note (B18, Variation 1).

Cromorne (Fr.). **1.** Crumhorn (A35). **2.** A reed stop on an organ. It contributes to the *grand jeu* heard on track A81.

Crook. A length of tubing inserted into a brass instrument to alter the total length of tubing and so alter its basic pitch. In B59 two horns are crooked in F and two are crooked in C, thus permitting the four-part chords heard in bars 18–24. *EM 6.7.1.*

Cross-phrasing. Phrases (indicated by slurs) that cross the barline causing mild conflict with the prevailing metre. In bars 0–7 of B79 Brahms's slurs emphasise the triple metre, but in bars 8–15 the slurs cross the barlines, so emphasising the cross-rhythm engendered by the harmonic rhythm in this passage. A similar effect can be heard in bars 30–37.

Cross-relation. See *False relation* and the last two bars of A81.

Cross-rhythm. A rhythm that conflicts with the regularly stressed beats of the prevailing metre. A simple example can be heard on track C2 where, in bars 21–24 and 29–31, repeated three-quaver groups conflict with the prevailing triple metre. More subtle examples of cross-rhythm can be found in bars 8–15 and 30–37 of B79. The term also applies to the simultaneous combination of conflicting rhythms within a single beat, eg the three-against-two effect heard in the second half of each bar in C15. *EM 1.10.*

Crossing of parts. In counterpoint, a situation in which a part that is normally higher than another moves beneath the lower voice or vice versa. In A27 crossing of parts occurs between the tenor and bass in bars 5, 16, 20 and 23. When two parts are printed on the same stave it is possible to see as well as hear the crossing of parts by the direction of the stems. Thus in bar 6 of A30 the soprano crosses the alto part on beats 2 and 3 as it pursues its descending quaver figure while the alto remains on a G♮.

Crotales (Fr.). Small, tuned brass or bronze discs like the antique cymbals at the end of C19. They can be struck together or, when mounted, struck with a variety of beaters. *EM 6.8.3.*

Crotchet. Quarter-note (♩). See *Note* and the first stave of B18.

Crumhorn. A woodwind instrument of the 16th and 17th centuries. It has a double reed covered by a wind cap and the bottom of the instrument is curved upwards like a hockey-stick. An ensemble of four sizes of crumhorn plays a galliard on track A35. *EM 6.6.4.*

Crushed note. Acciaccatura. In bars 29–30 of B27 asterisks identify the three acciaccaturas. See *Ornaments* and the first 15 bars of B73.

Crustic. Phrases that begin and end on a downbeat. All four four-bar phrases in A36 are crustic.

Cuivré (Fr.). A harsh tone-colour used for special effect on brass instruments (C97, bars 9–15).

Cuivres (Fr.). Brass (C97, bars 23–26).

Curtal, curtall. The precursor of the bassoon, this double-reed 16th- and 17th-century derivative of the shawm family was made in several sizes of which the bass curtal was the most important. It can be heard in the

Cut time

broken consort playing on A60. See also *Dulcian. EM 6.6.4.*

Cut time. Another name for *alla breve* or $\frac{2}{2}$ time indicated by the sign shown after the clef in A31.

Cycle. 1. In acoustics, one complete vibration of a string or column of air etc. Hence the measurement of the frequency of vibrations as the number of cycles per second (cps) or Hertz (Hz). The number of cycles per second is one of the most important factors determining the pitch of a note (A1–A3). **2.** See *Song cycle* and B57. **3.** See *Cyclic Mass* and A28 and A29. **4.** See *Cyclic form* and C18.

Cyclic form. Any musical structure in which two or more movements are linked by the use of the same or similar thematic material. C18 shows how Debussy unifies three contrasting movements of his string quartet by introducing into each of them transformations of the theme heard in the opening bars of the first movement. *EM 7.10.*

Cyclic Mass. A Mass in which all movements make use of the same musical materials. A28 and A29 come from the first and last movements of a Mass by the late 15th-century composer Obrecht. It is easy to hear that the head motif (a) of Kyrie I appears in rhythmic diminution at the start of Agnus Dei II, but other motifs (b, c and d) reappear in subtly varied forms, thus ensuring a sense of unity between these two movements (and between the other movements of the Mass which are not shown in this example). *EM 7.10.1, 8.6.1.*

Cymb. Abbreviation of cymbals. See C47 and C54.

Cymbales antiques (Fr.). Antique cymbals (C19).

Cymbale chinoise (Fr.). A Chinese cymbal that has a timbre akin to that of a tam-tam but in the higher cymbal register (C47).

Cymb. sus. Abbreviation of *cymbale suspendu* (suspended cymbal). See C97, bars 7–9.

Cymbalon, czimbalom (Hung.). Cimbalom (C41).

Cymbals. A pair of dish-shaped metal plates that are either clashed or, more rarely, rubbed together. On C47 both techniques can be heard. Alternatively a single cymbal may be suspended and played with beaters or wire brushes. Single strokes and a roll on a suspended cymbal can be heard on C47. Clashed and suspended cymbals can be heard in combination with other percussion instruments at the start of C52. The penetrating sound of a roll on a suspended cymbal can be heard in bars 7–9 of C97. See *Percussion instruments. EM 6.8.3.*

D

D. In English and German, any of the pitches with this letter name shown on the diagram of a keyboard on the folded insert. A14 begins on a D♯. See *A*.

Da capo (It.). Repeat from the beginning. As usually printed in modern scores the Menuetto recorded on track B25 consists of bars 1–44 with the performance direction 'Menuetto da Capo' beneath bars 43–44. This means that the Menuetto should be repeated after the Trio. It was, however, standard practice to add improvised ornaments to such repeats, so in B25 the words 'Menuetto da capo' have been printed at the beginning of the ornamented version (bars 45–64, which form a transcription of what is actually played on track B25).

Da capo al fine (It.). Repeat from the beginning until the word *fine* (end) (B15, bar 120).

Da capo aria. An aria in ternary form (ABA), is so named because only the first two sections are written out, the repeat of the first section being indicated by the instruction 'Da capo al fine' (repeat from the beginning, ending at the word *fine*). In common with many baroque arias bars 1–80 of B15 form a closed first section that begins and ends in the tonic key of D major. The second section (bars 81–120) obviously needs to be completed by a repeat of the first section, since, after passing through a number of related keys, it ends in the dominant key of A major. It was (and still is) common practice for the soloist to embellish the repeat of the first section. The complexity of the texture of this aria prohibits more than the few ornaments that are noted on extra staves above the vocal part (marked D.C.). *EM 3.10.1, 7.5.1, 8.2, 8.7.2.*

Dal segno (It.). Sometimes abbreviated to D.S., this phrase indicates that the performer should repeat the music from the sign. At the end of C2 the phrase 'Dal segno al fine' means that the pianist should repeat the music from the sign at bar 5, ending the piece at the word 'fine' (end) (bar 16).

Damper pedal. The right-hand pedal on a piano. It lifts the dampers from the strings, so allowing them to continue vibrating after the keys have been released. The shimmering haze of sound at the start of B74 is attributable to the use of the damper pedal (notice particularly how the sound of the A flat in bar 4 carries through to the next bar despite the fact that the key has been released in conformity with the rest printed in bar 5).

Dämpfer. (Ger.). Mute. See C19 (horns), C72 (strings), C81 (trumpets). In the original score of C35 Webern marks the trumpet, trombone and string parts with the abbreviation 'mit Dpf'. (with mutes).

Dances. See: *Allemande* (B17), *Ballet* (C6) *Basse danse* (A36), *Bourrée* (A89), *Bulgarian dance* (C66), *Corrente* (A67), *Country dance* (B43), *Deutsche* (B44), *Ductia* (A16), *Estampie* (A18), *Forlana* (C32), *Furiant* (C9), *Galliard* (A35), *Gavotte* (B18), *Gigue* (A90), *Mazurka* (B65), *Minuet and trio* (B25), *Pavan* (A32), *Polonaise* (B64), *Romanian dance* (C56), *Saltarello* (A18), *Sarabande* (A88), *Siciliana* (B19), *Trepak* (C5), *Waltz* (C2).

See also *Ballo, Jig, Kujawiak, Ländler, Mazur, Oberek, Padovana, Partita, Passamezzo, Rant, Tarantella, Tedesca, Tourdion, Traquenard, Varsovienne* and *Volta. EM 8.7.3, 8.10.4.*

D. bn., D. bsn. Abbreviations of double bassoon (C31).

DC, D.C. Abbreviations of da capo (B25, bar 45).

Dead interval. An interval formed between the last note of one phrase and the first note of the next. In bars 29–30 of A59 there is a dead interval of a perfect 4th between the E♮ and the ensuing A♮ in the alto part (and between the C♮ and F♮ in the tenor part). Dead intervals are not subject to the normal conventions of voice leading. Thus the overlapping of the alto and tenor parts (reckoned to be a solecism in most circumstances) is considered to be acceptable in this context (on track A59 a short silence has been introduced between bars 29 and 30 to allow the overlapping to be more clearly heard).

Decay. In acoustics, the manner in which a sound declines in volume as vibrations die away in the instrument or voice and in the ambient vibrating system. In the resonant acoustic in which A86 was recorded the

Deceptive cadence

organist is obliged to play in a very detached manner because the decay from the end of each note to zero intensity is so prolonged (the last chord can be heard for five seconds after the organist has released it). But in A87 decay from maximum to zero intensity is almost immediate (the minim at the end stops dead with no perceptible after-resonance).

Deceptive cadence. Interrupted cadence (B69). See *False cadence*. *EM 5.4.4.*

Decibel (dB). A unit of measurement used in comparing the difference in intensity (volume) between two sounds. One decibel is about the minimum difference of intensity that most people can detect by ear alone. The difference between the threshold of hearing and the threshold of pain is approximately 120 decibels. It is impossible to illustrate these extremes on a compact disc because of the many limitations imposed by machinery, from the microphones used to record the sound through to the loudspeakers that play it back. A vague impression of a difference of about 100 decibels may be gained by comparing bars 48–50 of C97 with bar 68.

Décidé (Fr.). Resolute. 'Animé et très décidé' in C18(a) means 'animated and very resolute'.

Declamation. The relationship between text and music, particularly with regard to the coincidence of textual stress and melodic accent. Monteverdi went to great pains to ensure that the rhythms of spoken Italian should be reflected in his musical notation, especially in recitatives. This is apparent in the score of A63 which, sung exactly as printed, does not falsify the rhythms and stresses of the text. But, as is normal in authentic performance practice, the singer takes certain liberties with Monteverdi's rhythms in the interests of even better declamation. Most of these changes are extremely subtle, but the shortening of bar 8 is immediately obvious (it should be noted that in the original score of 1607 regular barring is infrequent in recitatives). Partly because Schütz's declamation is less scrupulous than Monteverdi's, the singer on track A68 takes much greater liberties, singing with such speech-like rapidity that it is not until bar 5 that a regular beat can be discerned.

Decoration. 1. A melodic ornament such as a mordent or turn, whether represented by a conventional symbol (A84, bar 1) or written out (A84, bar 17). **2.** The process of embellishing the repetition of a melody. In B18 Variations 1, 3 and 5 are decorated versions of the theme. *EM 4.3.*

Decrescendo (decresc.). Diminuendo (B65, bar 33). See *Dynamics*.

Degree. Any note of a diatonic scale in relation to the tonic, or, in the case of a mode, the final (B18). See *Scale degrees*.

Dehors (Fr.). See *En dehors* and C17.

Demisemiquaver. Thirty-second-note ($\:$). See *Note* and B18, Variation 5, bar 7, beat 3.

Department. In an organ, several ranks of pipes on the same wind chest and controlled by a single manual. In A94 the flue pipes belong to the positive department and are played on a manual keyboard while the reed pipes belong to the pedal department and are played on the pedalboard.

Des (Ger.). D♭. In B74 the last flat (♭) in the key signature on the lower stave makes every note on the middle line a D♭.

Descant. 1. A counter-melody sung by trebles or sopranos above a hymn tune (A25). **2.** A name for one of the highest of a family of instruments (eg the descant recorders heard at the start of A69). **3.** Discant (A11).

Descending trill. A trill beginning on the upper note then descending through the main note to the lower note before the trill proper (B1, bar 3, beat 2). See *Ornaments*. *EM 3.10.2.*

Deses (Ger.). D♭♭. See *Doppelbe*.

Dessus (Fr.). Treble (C30) or uppermost part or voice.

Détimbrée (Fr.). Side drum without snares or with the snares relaxed so they do not rattle (C44).

Deutsche, Deutscher Tanz (Ger.). A late 18th-century south German and Austrian dance in fast triple time that was superseded by the waltz in the first half of the 19th century (B44). See also *Ländler*. *EM 8.10.4.*

Development. 1. The central section of a movement in sonata form (B40, bars 52–71) or sonata-rondo form (B36, bars 141–179). *EM 7.7.1, 7.7.3.* **2.** A process involving modifications to the melodic contour of a theme, expansion or fragmentation of it, combination with other themes, transposition, reharmonisation and reorchestration of it and so on. In the development section of a movement in sonata or sonata-rondo form the theme or themes that are subjected to such developmental processes will normally have been heard previously in the exposition. Thus in the development section of B40 a fragment of the codetta (z in bars 50–51) is transposed and its melodic contour changed by altering the octave leap to a diminished 7th. Processes such as this continue in a variety of keys until, in the last four bars of the development, a variant of the last two notes of z is detached and reharmonised four times to form a link (retransition) with the recapitulation.

In many sonata-form movements developmental processes are not confined to the development section proper. B21 is an extract from the exposition of a movement in abbreviated sonata form. It begins with a theme (bars 1–8) which falls into two clearly differentiated phrases, a and b. Phrase a is immediately repeated, but phrase b is subjected to developmental processes in bars 12–18. Firstly it is extended to six bars by a sequential repetition of its first two bars. Secondly it is combined with a new counter-melody (c). Similar sequences and a new cadence expand phrase a from four bars to ten bars in the first tutti (bars 18–28). Phrase b is even more radically developed in bars 28–42. Its melodic contour is changed (b^2) and it is combined with a new counter-melody (d). Both b^2 and d are treated canonically (see B22 and B23) and are contrapuntally inverted (see B24). The brackets and letters above the staves in bars 28–42 show the full extent of Haydn's contrapuntal development of his first subject theme within the exposition of his sonata-form structure.

Devil in music. Tritone (B60). See *Diabolus in musica* and C96, bars 1–27.

Diabolus in musica. Latin for 'the Devil in music', this being the dissonant tritone. To avoid emphasising the tritone between the first and fourth degrees of Mode V (F–B or B–F in the modal scale shown in A19), the fourth degree was often flattened (as in the melisma on the last syllable of 'Hosanna' in A20). In harmony, too, a tritone between the bass and an upper part was avoided by flattening the fourth degree of Mode V (bar 6 of A19). See *Intervals*. *EM 8.10.1*.

Dialogue. 1. Vocal exchanges between parts in the frottola and madrigal (Morley's *Phillis, I faine wold die now* is a fine example). **2.** A texture in which musical phrases are passed from one instrument to another. In B38 the phrase heard in the first violin in bars 4–5 passes to the cello in bars 6–7.

Diapason. In American and British organs, the principal open flue stop of the great organ. The stop can be used on its own, but more commonly it is used as a foundation upon which a chorus of higher-sounding ranks is built (A86).

Diaphonia (Gk.), **diaphony.** Medieval two-voice polyphony (A9).

Diatonic and chromatic music. Diatonic notes are those whose pitches correspond with one of the degrees of the scale of the prevailing key. Diatonic notes in C major are C, D, E, F, G, A and B. Diatonic notes in A minor are A, B, C, D, E, F (♯ or ♮) and G (♯ or ♮). All of the notes in C93 are diatonic to the keys of A minor (at the start) and C major (at the end).

Chromatic notes are those that are foreign to the scale of the prevailing key. In B38 the prevailing key is G major, so all notes other than G, A, B, C, D, E and F♯ are chromatic. B39 shows that all chromatic notes (black notes) and diatonic notes (white notes) are present in the first eight bars of the minuet. This chromatic music contrasts strongly with the entirely diatonic melody in the last eight bars of B38, in which all seven degrees of the scale of G major are heard, with no chromatic notes at all. *EM 2.3.2*.

Dièse (Fr.), **diesis** (It.). The sharp sign (♯). The third note of C40 is *La dièse* (A♯).

Dies irae (Lat.). A medieval sequence that forms part of the Mass for the Dead (Requiem). Part of the plainsong setting can be heard on track B62. The well-known melody has been used with programmatic intent in many 19th- and 20th-century instrumental compositions. Berlioz used it in his *Symphonie fantastique* to conjure up supernatural visions (B63). A modern setting of the same text can be heard on track C96. *EM 8.4.1, 8.10.6*.

Diferencias (Span.). Literally 'differences', but in 16th-century Spain it was also a term for variations. A34 is taken from a set of *diferencias* based on *Guárdame las vacas*, a secular song used as a theme by many

Dim

16th-century Spanish composers. The song was accompanied by a romanesca, one of several repeating bass melodies that were used as a basis for variations in the 16th century (it functions in the same way as the ground bass in A75). The opening of the song is shown above the first four bars of Variation 1 and the dotted lines show how the anonymous composer incorporates the bare bones of the melody in his figuration. In the first variation the romanesca is heard on the vihuela almost unaltered, but in the second variation (the lowest stave of both systems) the composer varies the romanesca bass by changing some of the rhythms and adding passing notes (from 0:24 one can hear that the melody is further disguised by more elaborate figuration, but this is not shown in the partial score of A34). *EM 8.6.3.*

Dim., dimin. Abbreviations of diminuendo (B79, bar 24).

Diminished chord. See *Triad* and B20 (first chord).

Diminished 5th (interval). See *Intervals*. There are three prominent intervals of a diminished 5th in the bass of bars 37–39 of B65. *EM 2.2.4.*

Diminished 4th (interval). In a minor scale, the interval between the sharpened leading note and the mediant above it. A diminished 4th can be formed on any note, but in tonal music this is the most easily identifiable type (A95, bar 30). See *Intervals*. EM 2.2.6.

Diminished 7th (interval). In music in a minor key, the interval between the sharpened leading note and the sixth degree of the scale above it. In the key of A minor, G♯ and the F♮ above it (heard three times in the first six bars of C93 and once very clearly on a solo viola in bars 1–2 of C94). Diminished 7ths can be formed on any degree of any scale, but this is the one that occurs most commonly in diatonic music. See *Intervals*. *EM 2.2.8.*

Diminished-7th chord. A four-note chord made up of superimposed minor 3rds (or their enharmonic equivalents), the interval between the lowest and highest notes being a diminished 7th. In bars 8 and 9 of A81 a diminished-7th chord on F♯ is immediately followed by a diminished-7th chord on F♮ (the relationship of these chords to the key of C minor is shown on the extra staves beneath these bars). Similar diminished-7th chords are heard more dramatically towards the end of the Queen of the Night's aria from Act 2 of Mozart's opera *Die Zauberflöte* (B50, bars 93–94).

Depending on the context, the same diminished-7th chord can belong to any one of four different keys (eight if both major and minor modes are included). B20 begins in the key of E minor and the second arpeggiated chord is a diminished 7th that functions as a dominant chord in this key. The fifth chord comprises the same pitches, but here it functions as a dominant chord in G minor (it resolves to the tonic chord of this unrelated key). The ability of the diminished-7th chord to change its tonal function so easily made it perhaps the most typical chord of the romantic era. See *Dominant chords* (e) and *Half-diminished-7th chord. EM 5.5.7.*

Diminished 3rd (interval). An interval notated as a 3rd, but with only a tone between the two notes. In tonal music the interval most commonly occurs when one of the notes is chromatic. Bar 30 of A95 is in the key of D minor. In this key the C♯ in the third group of semiquavers is diatonic, but Bach has chromatically altered the second degree of the scale to form a diminished 3rd between the E♭ and the C♯.

Diminished triad. In major keys (and in minor keys when the seventh degree of the scale is sharpened) a diminished triad can be formed on the leading note. Because of the tritone between the root and 5th this leading-note triad (chord VII) is rarely used in root position, but an example can be heard in bar 7 of A73. In this context its use is justified by contrary motion between the outer parts. A similar use of chord VII (this time in D minor) is evident in bar 3 of A95. See *Triad* and the first arpeggiated chord in B20. *EM 5.3.3, 5.5.5.*

Diminuendo (dim.). Getting softer (B79, bars 24–26). 'Decrescendo' (decresc.) and the sign that musicians call a 'hairpin' mean the same (B79, bar 38). 'Diminuendo a niente' means 'becoming gradually softer until inaudible' (C97, bar 68). See *Dynamics*.

Diminution. A compositional technique in which the durations of the notes of a motif or phrase are proportionally reduced in a restatement of it. In bar 1 of C34 the three-note motif of equal minims marked x (piano bass part) is repeated three times in the next bar, each time in equal quavers. *EM 3.4, 3.10.1.*

Diminutions. The ornamentation of a melody by dividing some or all of the notes into shorter note values. In B18 the crotchets of the theme are divided into quavers (Variation 1), triplet quavers (Variation 3) and semiquavers (Variation 5). The term refers to a wide variety of music ranging from 16th-century *diferencias* (A34) to 18th-century coloratura passage work (B50, bars 69–73). See *Ornaments*. *EM 3.10.3.*

Direct. A conventional symbol which indicates the pitch but not the duration of a note. In this dictionary directs are sometimes used to show the pitch but not the note-value of the last note of an extract (B9, bar 10, upper stave).

Direct fifths and octaves. See *Consecutive fifths and octaves*, A7a and A26, bars 1–11.

Dirge. The term derives from the first word of an antiphon in the Office for the Dead. Hence the term is used for the office itself. In more common usage it refers to any composition written as a memorial for the deceased. A95 is an extract from an elegy written as a memorial for the distinguished cellist and teacher, Joan Dickson (whose command of harmonics was legendary).

Dirigent (Ger.). Conductor. Liszt addresses conductors directly in a footnote on the first page of the full score of his *Mephisto Waltz* (B73): 'Das Stück ist fast durchgängig im Vierviertel-Takt zu dirigieren' (This piece is to be conducted almost throughout in $\frac{4}{4}$ time). It is left to the conductor to explain to the orchestra that the music will be conducted with one beat per bar in the down-left-right-up gestures normally used for $\frac{4}{4}$ time. See *Conductor*.

Dis (Ger.). D♯ (A89, bar 1).

Discant, discantus (Lat.). **1.** A voice part added to a plainsong cantus firmus, eg the *duplum* in A10. **2.** A medieval style of vocal polyphony in which melodic lines are set predominantly note against note. The style is characteristic of early organa (A7) and early 13th-century conductus (A11). *EM 8.5.1.*

Discord. See *Consonance and dissonance*. Compared with the chords in C24, every chord in C25 is a discord.

Disis (Ger.). D double sharp. See *Doppelkreuz*.

Disjunct motion. See *Motion* and B7.

Displacement, octave displacement. In 12-tone music, the notion that any of the constituent pitches of a tone row can be moved up or down one or more octaves without altering its function in the row. In C88 the retrograde inversion of the prime order is shown in its simplest form at the foot of the page (labelled RI). In the cor anglais part of bars 3–4 notes 1, 3, 4 and 5 of RI are displaced by an octave so that, instead of the smooth stepwise movement shown in RI the cor anglais part is characterised by jagged leaps of a 7th and 9th.

Disposition. The manner in which the stops of a harpsichord or organ are assigned to particular keyboards (and pedalboard if there is one). In A94 the manual part is played on flue stops while a reed stop is assigned to the pedals.

Dissonance. See *Consonance and dissonance*. Compared with C32, C33 is dissonant. *EM 4.3.6, 5.2.*

Ditty. A short, simple song such as A25, hence the refrain or burden of a song (A24). In the 17th century even a relatively complex song such as A75 could be described without offence as a ditty, but the term has now acquired a pejorative sense.

Div. Abbreviation of *divisi* (C28, bar 6).

Divertimento (It.). A title for keyboard or ensemble compositions written in the second half of the 18th century. Haydn used the title for his early string quartets, but after about 1775 the more familiar classification of late 18th-century ensemble music into 'serious' genres (such as the quartet and sonata) and 'diverting' genres (such as the divertimento and serenade) became apparent, particularly in Austria. Divertimenti written in the last quarter of the century usually contain between three and eight movements and are light and entertaining in style. B40 is the first movement of a divertimento for three basset-horns in five movements (Allegro–Minuet–Adagio–Minuet–Rondo). See *Finalmusik*. *EM 8.9.3.*

Divertissement (Fr). **1.** Divertimento (B40). **2.** A sequence of dances, vocal solos or ensembles within an act of an opera or ballet. The term originated in late 17th-century France and is still in use in the context of the ballet. C5 is a characteristic dance from a

Divine Office

divertissement within Act 2 of Tchaikovsky's ballet *The Nutcracker.*

Divine Office. A series of non-Eucharistic services sung each day in the Roman Catholic Church. See *Office* 1, *Vespers*, A6, A8 and A49. *EM 8.4.1.*

Divisi (div.) (It.). Divided. A term applied chiefly to orchestral string sections that the composer wishes to divide into groups to play chords (instead of the usual single notes). A single string section is sometimes divided in order to produce a different texture. This is the case in bars 6–14 of C28 where the first violins are divided into three then four parts while the second violins and violas are silent. In the last two bars of C85 a solo horn is accompanied by a cello section divided into four groups ('divisi a 4').

Divisions. An instrumental and vocal technique popular in England in the 17th and 18th centuries in which long note-values were broken up into shorter notes whilst retaining the overall shape of the bass or melody so treated. In B18 Handel retains the same crotchet bass throughout a set of variations, but the crotchet melody is divided into ever more complex figurations, first in quavers, then triplets of quavers, then semiquavers and, right at the end demisemiquavers and hemidemisemiquavers. The dotted lines show how the simple melodic outline of the theme is retained in all of the divisions. See *Ornaments. EM 3.10.1, 3.10.3, 7.8.6, 8.7.7.*

Divisés (Fr.). Divisi (C28, violins, bars 6–14).

Do (It. and Span.). C♮. See *C,* the diagram of a keyboard on the folded insert and A1. Not to be confused with the tonic sol-fa syllable *doh* (the first degree of any major scale).

Doble bemol (Span.). The double-flat sign (♭♭). The second note in bar 3 of C64 is *Sol doble bemol* (A♭♭) which is a semitone above the G♭s on either side of it.

Doble sostenido (Span.). The double-sharp sign (×). The uppermost note in the first two bars of B65 is *Fa doble sostenido* (F×) which is a semitone above the F♯ in bar 3.

Dodecaphony. Music without tonality (see *Atonality* and C34) or music based on a tone row (see *Serial music* and C40). *EM 3.8, 8.11.4.*

Doh. The first degree of any major scale in the British system of tonic sol-fa. The first note of A25 is *doh* in the key of D major.

Dolce (It.). Sweet, gentle (B79, bars 26ff). For a guitarist this performance direction is usually interpreted as meaning *sul tasto* (C68, bar 21).

Dolcissimo (dolciss.) (It.). Very sweetly (B70).

Dominant. The fifth degree of a scale. The dominant of F major (C♮) is heard throughout the first seven bars of A86.

Dominant chords. In tonal music, any chord built on, or derived from, the fifth degree of the scale of the prevailing key. Dominant chords commonly create an expectation of resolution to a tonic chord. Thus the dominant triad of C major on the first beat of bar 25 in B40 creates expectation that it will be followed by the tonic chord of C major – an expectation that is fulfilled in the next bar.

There is a wide variety of dominant chords, nearly all of them containing the leading note, the degree of the scale with the strongest tendency to resolve to the tonic:

a) A dominant triad consists of the fifth degree of the scale (the dominant) plus notes a 3rd and a 5th above it. In the key of A minor these are E, G♯ and B, and they are the notes of the first organ chord heard in B6. As expected, the leading note (G♯) resolves up to the tonic (A) as the chord changes from the dominant to the tonic triad (A, C, E), thus forming a perfect cadence. *EM 5.1.3.*

b) The dominant 7th (V^7) consists of the dominant triad plus the note a minor 7th above the root. In the third bar of B48 the violin repeats the 7th of the complete dominant-7th chord of G major played by the pianist. The dominant-7th chord of E major in first inversion (ie with the 3rd of the chord in the bass) resolves to the tonic chord in bars 2–3 of B30. The dominant-7th chord of B major in second inversion (ie with the 5th of the chord in the bass) resolves to chord I in bar 6 of the same example. The dominant-7th chord of E major in third inversion (ie with the 7th of the chord in the bass) resolves to chord I^6 in the third and fourth beats of bars 1 and 3 in the same example.

c) The triad on the leading note (VII) functions like a dominant-7th chord shorn of

Dominant chords

its root. It is rarely used in root position because of the prominent tritone between the root and fifth. But in first inversion it is used in exactly the same way as a dominant triad or dominant 7th. The first phrase of A33 ends with the progression VII^6–I forming as obvious a perfect cadence as the progression V–I does at the end of the second phrase.

d) The dominant major 9th (V^9) consists of a dominant-7th chord plus the note a major 9th above the root. At the start of A86 a variety of dominant chords can be heard over the dominant pedal of F major. The chord of the dominant major 9th can be seen in bar 4. The two chords on the extra stave below this bar show that one note is omitted in Bach's chord (the 5th of the chord, G♮), but the four notes it does contain (the root with the 3rd, 7th and major 9th above it) are sufficient to identify the chord as a dominant major 9th in root position. This chord is rarely heard. More commonly the root and possibly one other note are omitted. In the key of E major a complete dominant major 9th consists of the root (the dominant note, B♮) with a 3rd above it (D♯), a 5th above it (F♯), a 7th above it (A♮) and a major 9th above it (C♯). This is the chord shown on the extra stave below bar 4 of B30, and it will be seen that Haydn omits the root and 5th from this chord. This makes no difference to its dominant function: it resolves to chord I in the next bar just as did the dominant-7th chords discussed under (b) above. The incomplete dominant major 9th is sometimes known as chord VII^7 (in major keys), but the change of nomenclature makes no difference to its dominant function.

e) The dominant minor 9th ($V^{♭9}$) consists of a dominant-7th chord plus the note a minor 9th above the root. In G minor the chord consists of the dominant-7th chord (D, F♯, A and C) plus the minor 9th above the root (E♭). This is the chord shown on the extra stave below bar 9 of B5. The minor 9th is heard in the second viola d'amore part and, as expected, it resolves down a semitone to a consonant D♮. The complete dominant-minor-9th chord is infrequently heard. More commonly the root is omitted leaving a diminished-7th chord like those in bars 4–5 of B31. The chords on the extra stave beneath these bars show the origin of these chords in the prevailing key of E major and their eventual resolution to the tonic. The dominant minor 9th is sometimes known as chord VII$^{♭7}$ (in minor keys or when the ninth is a chromatic note), but the change of nomenclature makes no difference to its dominant function.

f) The dominant 11th (V^{11}) is rare (B79, bar 39). It more often proves to be a dominant chord sounding against a tonic pedal (A70, bar 6).

g) The dominant 13th (V^{13}) most commonly consists of a dominant-7th chord plus a major or minor 13th above the root (rarely does such a chord contain a 9th). The second chord heard on C30 is a dominant 13th in the key of C major, the origin of which is shown on the extra stave beneath bar 2. It will be seen that, as is the case in a majority of chords of this type, Stanford only uses four of the seven notes that make up a complete dominant 13th (the root, 3rd, 7th and 13th). There is a dominant minor 13th in the same piece four bars later. The same components of the complete chord are used as in bar 2, but it is heard in its third inversion (with the 7th of the chord in the bass).

h) Chord III^6 contains the leading note and so can (and often does) behave as a dominant chord. In C minor chord III consists of E♭ (the root), G♮ (the 3rd) and B♮ (the 5th). In first inversion the 3rd is sounded in the bass (as shown on the extra stave at the foot of A81). This is the penultimate chord of the extract, and it will be seen that it can be viewed as another version of the dominant 13th (containing just the root, 3rd and 13th).

i) In jazz and other 20th-century styles a substitution chord sometimes functions as a surrogate dominant once the tonality has been firmly settled. The penultimate chord of C38 is a complex dominant chord that can be broken down into two components. On the bass stave an ordinary dominant 7th of F major resolves to the tonic (this chord can be heard on its own on track C39(a)). On the treble stave are three chromatic notes (D♭, B♮ and G♯) together with a major 9th (D♮). When this four-note chord is abstracted (as it is on track C39(b)) the resultant substitution chord sounds like a dominant because the key of F major has been so clearly established and the substitution chord immediately resolves to the tonic. See *Secondary-dominant chords*. EM 5.5.5, 5.5.6.

Dominant-11th chord

Dominant-11th chord. See *Dominant chords* and B79, bar 39. *EM 5.5.5.8.*

Dominant key. The key whose tonic note is a perfect 5th above the prevailing key. Thus the prevailing key of bars 1–18 in B40 is F major. A perfect 5th above the tonic note of F major is C♮, and C major is the key of bars 26–51: in relation to the F major tonality of bars 1–18 this is the dominant key. Also see B49.

Dominant-9th chord. See *Dominant chords* and A86, bar 4 (dominant major 9th) and B31, bar 5 (dominant minor 9th). *EM 5.5.7.*

Dominant pedal. See *Pedal, Pedal point* (b) and bars 1–7 of A86.

Dominant preparation. The use of dominant chords to arouse expectation for a resolution to the tonic. This expectation can be fulfilled or denied. Mozart's use of dominant chords in the key of D minor in bars 82–87 of B50 does indeed lead to the tonic in bar 88, but the expectation of the tonic of F major after the dominant preparation in the first seven bars of A86 is defeated by the dramatic interrupted cadence in bars 7–8.

Dominant-7th chord. See *Dominant chords* and B48, bar 3. *EM 5.5.3.*

Dominant-13th chord. See *Dominant chords* and the penultimate chord of B75. *EM 5.5.9.*

Doppelbe, Doppel-b, Doppel-be, Doppel B, Doppel-Be (Ger.). The double-flat sign (♭♭). The second note in bar 3 of C64 is *Ases* (A♭♭) which is a semitone above the G♭s on either side of it. The other German names for notes lowered a tone by a double-flat sign are *Bes* or *Heses* (B♭♭), *Ceses* (C♭♭), *Deses* (D♭♭), *Eses* (E♭♭), *Feses* (F♭♭), and *Geses* (G♭♭). See *Accidental*.

Doppelgriff (Ger.). See *Double stopping* and A97.

Doppelkreuz (Ger.). The double-sharp sign (× or ♯♯). In the second clarinet part of C79 the third note in bar 1 is *Cisis* (C×), the third note in bar 2 is *Aisis* (A×), and the last note in bar 3 is *Fisis* (F×). In each case these notes are a semitone below the notes on either side of them. In the right-hand part of B65, the lower of the two semiquavers in bar 33 is *Gisis* (G×) which is a semitone below the A♮s on either side of it. The other German names for notes raised a tone by a double-sharp sign are *Disis* (D×), *Eisis* (E×), and *Hisis* (B×). See *Accidental*.

Doppelschlag (Ger.). Turn (A84, bars 1(b) and 17(b)). See *Ornaments*.

Doppeltaktnote (Ger.). Breve or double whole-note (A13, below bars 19–20).

Doppelt-cadence (Mac.). A term used by J. S. Bach, C. P. E. Bach and others for a trill beginning with a turn (A84, letter f in bar 44 and B1, bar 3, beat 2). See *Ornaments*. *EM 3.10.2.*

Doppeltriller (Ger.). A trill with a turn at the end. All of the trills in B11 are of this type (though Bach called the ornament a 'trillo und mordant'). The turned endings are shown by two demisemiquavers in every case. See *Ornaments*.

Doppelzunge (Ger.). Double-tonguing (C97, bars 27–32). See *Tonguing*.

Doppio (It.). Double, as in 'doppio movimento' (twice as fast). In A80 the passage from bar 13 to the end is twice as fast as the first 12 bars (implied by the tempo marks and change of time signature). 'Doppio movimento' is sometimes used as a performance direction without a change of time signature.

Doppio bemolle (It.). The double-flat sign (♭♭). See *Accidental* and C64, bar 3, beat 2.

Doppio diesis (It.). The double-sharp sign (×). See *Accidental* and B65, bar 1.

Dorian mode. This, the first of the church modes, is a scale that can be reproduced by playing the white notes of the piano from any D♮ to the D♮ an octave above it (see the diagram of a keyboard on the folded insert and the ascending dorian scale shown in bars 2–4 of A67). It is distinguished from other similar scales by semitones between the second and third degrees and between the sixth and seventh degrees. The scale can be transposed up or down by any interval. Music in the transposed dorian mode can be heard on tracks A17, A22, A26 and B62. All of these melodies are in the authentic dorian mode – their ranges roughly extend from the final to the note an octave above it. In its plagal form (Mode II or the hypodorian mode) the final is the same, but the range (*ambitus*) extends from the note a 4th below the final to the note a 5th above it (A8). Like melodies in the authentic mode

Double fugue

the hypodorian mode can be transposed up or down by any interval (A11). See *Church modes*. *EM 2.4.1*.

Dots. 1. Dots above or below notes indicate a detached, staccato performance (compare bars 1 and 2 of B41). **2.** In modern notation dots after notes increase their lengths by half. There are three crotchet beats per bar in A59. In bar 8 the dots increase the length of the minims from two to three beats. Two dots after a note increase its length by three quarters (compare A76 and A77).

Dotted rhythms. A two-note figure consisting of a dotted note plus a note a third its length can be a characteristic feature of a melody or, if often repeated, a musical style. In A76 two types of dotted rhythm (x and y) are shown in a melody by Purcell. In the performance of baroque music containing rhythms such as x it is common practice to add another dot (double dotting) to lengthen the first note of the pair and shorten the second (x^1 in A77). This practice is known as over-dotting. Some performers replace the extra dot with a rest. These *silences d'articulations* (marked x^2) can be heard on track A78. When the short and long notes of a dotted rhythm are interchanged (so the short note is sounded on the beat) a characteristic Lombardic rhythm or Scotch snap is heard (z in A79). These dotted rhythms can be heard in the context of a complete French overture on track A80. *EM 1.6.1*.

Double 1. An early 18th-century French term for a type of variation consisting of the elaborate ornamentation of a melody. In B18 each variation is a double of the theme, and the dotted lines show how the original pitches are retained in the increasingly elaborate figuration. *EM 3.10.2, 7.8.6, 8.7.7*. **2.** To perform the same note or notes an octave apart on more than one instrument and/or voice. In B29 the flute (fl.) is doubled at the unison by oboe (ob.) and violin I (vln 1) in bars 0–10. In the same passage the bassoon (fag) is doubled at the octave below by double basses (cb).

Doublé (Fr.). In French baroque harpsichord music, a turn (B17, letter e in bar 4). See *Ornaments*.

Double bar, double barline. See *Barlines*. B17 is a complete piece so it ends with a double barline. B19 is an extract so there is no double barline at the end.

Double bass. The largest and deepest-sounding member of the modern bowed string family. The approximate range of a four-string bass is shown by the solid line on the folded insert. A five-string bass with the lowest string tuned to C_1 or B_2 extends the bass range by a 3rd or a 4th (as the pecked line shows). A double-bass solo can be heard in C7 and double-bass harmonics can be heard at the start of C88. See *String instruments*. *EM 6.4.1*.

Double-bass viol. Sometimes called a violone in the 16th and 17th centuries, the double-bass viol (or contrabass viol) is the largest instrument of the viol family and a precursor of the modern double bass (A36). See *Viol*.

Double bassoon. Contrabassoon (C31). See *Double-reed instruments*. *EM 6.6.2*.

Double bémol (Fr.). The double-flat sign (♭♭). See *Accidental* and C64, bar 3, beat 2.

Double cadence. (Fr.). A short trill ending with a turn. In bar 8 of A84 this is indicated by a wavy line with a hook at the end. The same ornament is written out in bar 24 with the turned ending identified by the letter x. In bar 4 of B17 the hook is replaced with two demisemiquavers and the whole ornament is identified by the letter f. See *Ornaments*. *EM 3.10.2*.

Double canon. The combination of two canons in a single four-part contrapuntal texture. In A94 Bach combines a canon at the octave on the carol *In dulci jubilo* (A91 and A92) with a freely-composed canon at the octave (A93). This type of canon is also known as a canon 4 in 2 (a canon for four voices on two canonic subjects).

Double counterpoint. Two-part invertible counterpoint (B24). *EM 4.4.5*.

Double croche (Fr.). Semiquaver, sixteenth-note (B18, Variation 5, bars 1–6).

Double dotting. See *Dotted rhythms* and A77. *EM 1.6.2*.

Double dièse (Fr.). The double-sharp sign (×). See *Accidental* and B65, bar 1.

Double flat. A sign (♭♭) that lowers a note a whole tone from its uninflected pitch. See *Accidental* and C64, bar 3, beat 2 (the pitch of this note is equivalent to G♮).

Double fugue. A fugue with two subjects. In B10 the first of the two subjects is heard in a

Double harpsichord

normal fugal exposition with the subject answered at the 5th above (bars 2–4) and the final entry in the bass at the end of bar 6. The same is true of the contrasting second subject (B11), though the order of entries is changed. Finally the two subjects are contrapuntally combined (B12).

Another type of double fugue introduces both subjects simultaneously so they act as each other's counter-subject (B13). The answers (at the 5th above and the 4th below) are also stated simultaneously while the first two voices continue with counter-subjects in a dense four-part contrapuntal texture. For the rest of the fugue the two subjects are always heard together, once in contrapuntal inversion. *EM 4.5.8, 8.7.6.*

Double harpsichord. A harpsichord with two manuals. It is possible to tell that A84 has been recorded on a double harpsichord because of the sudden dynamic changes in bars 5, 9, 17, 21, 25, 33 and 41. These are achieved by jumping from the lower manual (set with a loud registration) to the upper manual (set with a soft registration) and vice versa.

Double horn. The most common type of horn in use nowadays, the double horn is so called because it has a fourth valve that enables it to function as a horn in F or a horn in B♭. The other three valves allow a chromatic range of notes to be played with F or B♭ as the fundamental pitch (C85, bars 8–25). There are double horns based on other combinations of fundamental notes, but they are rare. See *Valve horn.*

Double-leading-note cadence. A characteristic cadence of the 14th and 15th centuries in which the usual semitonal rise to the final (tonic) is accompanied by a similar semitonal rise in another part, most often the dominant. This is the case in bars 7–8 of A24: the alto rises a semitone to the final of Mode II (C♯–D) while simultaneously the tenor rises a semitone to the dominant of the mode (G♯–A). *EM 2.4.3, 5.4.7.*

Double pedal. See *Pedal* and bars 5–8 of B65.

Double-reed instruments. See *Reed instruments* and A32 (shawm and rauschpfeife), A35 (crumhorn), A60 (curtal), B8 (oboe d'amore and oboe da caccia), C31 (contrabassoon), C77 (bassoon), C78 (oboe), C88 (cor anglais). *EM 6.6.2.*

Double sharp. A sign (either 𝄪 or ×) that raises a note a whole tone from its uninflected pitch. See *Accidental* and B65, bar 1 (the F× is equivalent in pitch to a G♮).

Double stopping. The performance of a two-note chord on a bowed string instrument. See *Stopping* and A97.

Double tonguing. See *Tonguing* and C97, bars 27–32 (brass).

Double whole-note. Breve (𝅂) (A13, below bars 19–20).

Doubles cordes (Fr.). Double stopping (A97, bars 0–3).

Doubling. The simultaneous performance of the same melody at the identical pitch or in octaves. In the fourth bar of B15 violins double the trumpet at pitch. In the first nine bars of B29 flutes and oboes are doubled by violins while bassoons, violas and cellos are doubled at the lower octave by double basses. *EM 5.3.1.*

Douce, doux (Fr.). **1.** Sweet, and therefore synonymous with the German *zart* (C35). **2.** Soft, and therefore synonymous with the Italian *piano* (B19).

Dovetailing. A term sometimes used to describe the contrapuntal technique of overlapping entries that disguise a cadence (A52, bar 4, where the bass cadences on D as the alto enters while the soprano is in mid-phrase).

Downbeat. The first beat of a bar. Both sections and all phrases of the Menuetto in B25 are downbeat phrases (they all begin on the first beat of a bar). The term derives from the downward motion of a conductor's baton at the start of each bar.

Down-bow. Unless instructed to the contrary string players decide for themselves when to use up-bows (a stroke from the tip of the bow to the heel – the end of the bow the performer holds) and when to use down-bows (a stroke in the opposite direction). In a good performance it is usually difficult for listeners to detect which of these strokes the player is employing at any given moment. However, if the composer instructs the performer to play consecutive down-bows at a loud dynamic level the tone will be strident. This is the case in bar 2 of C70, where Bartók indicates down-bows by the symbols above each slur. The effect is particularly violent because the players are also bowing near the heel of the bow (as instructed by the performance direction 'au talon'). See *Bowing*.

Doxology. A liturgical offering of praise to God the Father, Son and Holy Spirit. The Greater Doxology is the 'Gloria in excelsis Deo'. The Lesser Doxology is the text that is sung at the ends of psalms (A6) in the Divine Office of the Roman Catholic Church, and at Matins and Evensong in the Anglican Church. The text of the Lesser Doxology reads 'Gloria Patri et Filio et Spiritui Sancto; sicut erat in principio, et nunc, et semper, et in saecula saeculorum. Amen.' ('Glory be to the Father, and to the Son: and to the Holy Ghost; as it was in the beginning, is now and ever shall be: world without end. Amen.' – English translation from the Book of Common Prayer.)

Drag. A side drum figure consisting of two rapidly executed grace notes before an accented note (C43, bar 1).

Dramma giocoso (It.). An 18th-century comic opera with some serious elements. The plots of such operas involve a tragi-comic interaction between aristocrats, servants and rustics (B45 is taken from a scene in Mozart's dramma giocoso *Don Giovanni* in which three onstage bands play a courtly minuet and two plebeian dances simultaneously).

Dramma per musica (It.). The libretto of a serious baroque opera (A62–A66).

Drehleier (Ger.). Hurdy-gurdy (A18).

Dreiklang (Ger.). Triad (A59, bars 1–2).

Dreiviertelnote (Ger.). A dotted minim (A59, bar 8).

Drone, drone bass. One or more notes held or repeated throughout an extended passage of music (A13, A15, A17 and A18). Drones were used for picturesque effect in later romantic and post-romantic music: in bars 1–10 of B57 Schubert suggests bucolic bliss by repeated tonic and dominant notes. At the start of the *Mephisto Waltz* (B73) Liszt suggests the devil's fiddle by a four-note drone consisting of superimposed perfect 5ths. In Debussy's 'La Cathédrale engloutie' ('The sunken cathedral') a drone supports the 'organum' of the upper parts (C24). At the start of 'Mars' in Holst's *The Planets* (C36) the repeated G♯s form a drone against dissonant wind instruments.

Drum. A percussion instrument consisting of a circular frame, cylinder or hollow vessel with a round top over which a membrane is stretched and struck with hands, mallets or sticks. See: *Bass drum* (C42), *Bongos* (C45), *Side drum* (A32, C43 and C74), *Tabor* (A35), *Tambour militaire* (C45), *Tambourine* (C42), *Tenor drum* (C43), *Timpani:* rolls (B36, bars 255–263), strokes (C27), glissando (C82, bars 68–69). An exception to the rule is the friction drum, in which the membrane is made to vibrate by friction with a string or stick positioned on the surface of the membrane, or passing through a hole in it. See *Lion's roar* (C46) and *Rommelpot* (A36). EM 6.8.1, 6.8.2.

Drum kit, drum set. In jazz and pop, a set of drums and cymbals played by one performer. On track C38 two characteristic drum kit timbres are heard – a suspended cymbal struck with wooden sticks on the backbeat (bars 1–3) and a side drum played on the rim then in the usual way on the membrane (bars 4–7). Other instruments such as wood blocks and cowbells are often added to the standard kit, but the triangle (heard in the last two bars of C38) is rare in jazz combos.

Drum roll. On instruments such as the kettle drum (last three bars of B36) and side drum (C44), a rapid repetition of a single note produced by alternate strokes with two sticks.

Dry recitative. See *Recitative* and A68.

DS, D.S. Abbreviations of dal segno (C2, bar 41).

Duct flute. See *Fipple flute* and A69.

Ductia (medieval Lat.). A medieval dance-form with pairs of phrases, the second a repeat of the first except for the cadence (the first phrase has an open ending on a note other than the final, the second a closed ending on the final). It differs from the *estampie* only in its regular phrasing. A16 shows the first four phrases of an anonymous English *ductia* that continues to fall into similar four-bar phrases after the extract has ended. The second rebec part of phrases A1 and A2 are identical, but the varied first rebec part forms an open cadence (ending on the *confinalis* or dominant) in the first phrase and a closed cadence (ending on the final or tonic) in the second phrase. These two phrases constitute the first *punctus* and the second (bars 9–16) is organised in a similar manner. EM 7.9.5, 8.5.2.

Dudelsack

Dudelsack (Ger.). Bagpipe (A17).

Dudy (Pol.). One of a number of types of Polish bagpipes. In his mazurkas Chopin often imitates both the drones and the fast ornaments played on the chanter (B65, bars 5–8).

Due corde (It.). Two strings. Because bass strings are more resonant than treble strings, the highest pitches on a piano are each assigned three strings, pitches in mid-range have two, while each bass note has just one string. On a grand piano the left-hand or *una corda* pedal (the 'soft pedal') shifts the whole keyboard and its mechanism to the right so the hammers strike only two of the treble strings (or one in early pianos). Beethoven, among others, distinguishes between 'tre corde' (three strings) when the soft pedal is not depressed at all (B51–B55), 'due corde' (two strings) when the soft pedal is half-depressed, and 'una corda' (one string) when the soft pedal is fully depressed (B74).

Duet. Chamber music for two solo performers (C58) or two concertante instruments in an orchestral work (C77–C80). The term also applies to music for two solo voices (with or without accompaniment) and is sometimes used for a passage of two-part counterpoint in polyphony for more than two voices, whether or not the voices are doubled (A28 and A29 are duets from a Mass for four voices).

Dulcian, dulzian (Ger.). An alternative name for the curtal (A60). *EM 6.6.4.*

Duo. 1. Two solo performers. C56 is played by a duo consisting of a violinist and pianist. **2.** Duet (C58).

Duole (Ger.), **duolet** (Fr.). See *Duplet* and C14.

Duple time, duple meter. Music in which the underlying pulse is organised in regular patterns of alternating strong and weak beats. The beat is a crotchet in C63 and a dotted crotchet in C17, but both are in duple time. *EM 1.3.*

Duplet. Two equal-length notes played in the time of three notes of the same type. In C14 four sets of duplets are heard in the context of a melody that contains six three-quaver groups in compound time. In C15 duplets in the cello part are played against three-note groups in the violin part.

Duplum (Lat.). A second voice added to the plainsong cantus firmus in medieval organum (A10). *EM 8.5.1.*

Dur (Ger.). Major. B10 is in G major.

Duration. The time that a note or rest lasts.

Dynamics

The relative loudness and softness of music. Alternating loud and soft orchestral chords can be heard on C86. Composers indicate relative dynamic levels with the following performance directions:

pianissimo (*pp*)	very soft	B59, bar 1
piano (*p*)	soft	B59, bar 3
mezzopiano (*mp*)	moderately soft	C94, bar 3
mezzoforte (*mf*)	moderately loud	B59, bar 17
forte (*f*)	loud	B59, bar 30
fortissimo (*ff*)	very loud	B59, bar 33
crescendo (cresc.) (also indicated by a hairpin opening to the right)	gradually becoming louder	B73, bars 13–15 B59, bar 1
rinforzando (rinf., *rf*, *rfz*)	quickly becoming louder	B79, bars 2–3
decrescendo (decresc.) or diminuendo (dim.) (also indicated by a hairpin closing to the right)	gradually becoming softer	B79, bars 24–26 B59, bar 33–36
fortepiano (*fp*)	loud then immediately soft	C5, bars 1 and 3
sforzando (*sf* or *sfz*)	strongly accented	C5, bar 2

Exceptionally composers indicate extreme dynamics by using more than two *p*s or *f*s (C94).

In absolute terms duration can be measured in seconds (in C95 the timings show that the low cello C lasts for 18 seconds), but durations in music are usually measured by the relative time values of printed notes and rests. Thus in the first bar of C95 the crotchets are each approximately a third of the duration of the dotted minim, but their absolute durations are determined by the performer's response to the tempo mark (Lento).

Durchführung (Ger). **1.** The exposition of a fugue (B10). **2.** The development section of a work in sonata form (B40, bars 52–71).

Durchkomponiert (Ger.). Through-composed. The term is most often used to distinguish songs that have different music for each verse (B57 and B58) from strophic songs, in which each verse is set to the same music (A24, bars 17–36).

Dux and comes (Lat.). Terms for the leader and follower in canonic music (violin 1 and 2 respectively in B26). *EM 4.4.1, 4.4.4, 4.4.6.*

Dyad. Two pitches sounded successively or together (C34, *sf* in the last bar). The term is most often encountered in discussions about atonal or serial music.

Dynamic accent. An emphasis on a note or chord brought about by singing or playing it more loudly than surrounding notes or chords. In bar 1 of B51 the two-note staccato chord on the treble stave is unaccented, but when it reappears in bar 3 it is marked *sf*, so the pianist plays it more loudly, thus causing an emphatic syncopation. The same is true of the four single notes marked *sf*. See *Agogic accent* and *Tonic accent. EM 1.2, 1.7.1.*

Dynamics. See the box on page 56.

E

E. Any of the pitches with this letter shown on the diagram of a keyboard on the folded insert and played on track A3. See *A*.

Early music. A term coined in the 1960s that now has as many meanings as 'classical music'. But just as the latter term is used in record stores to segregate sheep from goats, so 'early music' is generally thought of as music that needs some historical awareness on the part of the listener and extensive knowledge of historical performance practice on the part of the performer. Whereas a quarter of a century ago early music would have encompassed A4–B25, now the boundary has been pushed well into the 19th century (notice John Eliot Gardiner's use of the once obsolescent ophicleides in B63). See *Authentic instruments*.

Ecclesiastical mode. Rare name for one of the eight church modes (A4, A5, A11, A18, A19, A28, A37 and A40).

Échappée (Fr.). An unaccented dissonant melodic decoration that leaves an essential note by step and returns to the next essential note by a leap in the opposite direction. The *échappée* at the start of A97 forms a dissonant 4th with the bass and is quitted by a leap of a 3rd to the consonant E♭ in the next bar. See *Ornaments*. EM 4.3.8.

Échelle (Fr.). Scale (B18)

Echo. The immediate repetition of one or two chords or a short phrase on different voices or instruments and often at a lower dynamic level. In C3 a glockenspiel and a pair of flutes echo the last notes of the cornet melody (bars 6–7). In bars 52–57 of B50 a loud one-bar orchestral figure is repeated twice, each time echoed by upper strings at a much lower dynamic level.

Éclatant (Fr.). Brilliant (see the title and bar 8 of B64).

Eguale (It.). See *Equale* and C58.

E.H. Abbreviation of English horn (C88, bars 3–5).

Eight-foot stop. A rank of organ pipes of which the longest measures approximately eight feet. Music performed on an eight-foot stop sounds at printed pitch. C55 is played on five eight-foot stops – *flûte harmonique*, *flûte*, *bourdon*, *voix céleste* and *gambe*. Eight-foot pitch is a term that is sometimes used to classify a range of pitches (for any instrument or voice) based on C (see A2 and A3). See also *Fifteenth* and *Four-foot stop*.

Eighth-note. Quaver (♪). See *Note* and B18, Variation 1.

Einklang (Ger.). Unison (B59, bars 3–4 and 7–8).

Einleitung (Ger.). Introduction or prelude (B68).

Einstimmig (Ger.). Monophonic (A4).

Eis (Ger.). E♯ (B67, bar 2, beat 1).

Eisis (Ger.). E double sharp. See *Doppelkreuz*.

Élargissant (Fr.). See *Allargando* and bars 1 and 15–18 of C97.

Electric and electronic instruments. 1. Instruments that resemble acoustic instruments in appearance and performance techniques, but in which the initial acoustic sound is modified and amplified electronically. See *Electric guitar* and C94. **2.** Instruments in which sound is generated, modified and amplified electronically. A87 was recored on a synthesiser in which sound-elements such as attack, decay, intensity and timbre had been automatically adjusted to simulate the sound of a harpsichord (compare this track with the sound of a real harpsichord on Track A84).

Electric guitar. An electronically amplified guitar. The extremely resonant bass notes in the last bar of C94 owe much to the amplification of the bass guitar.

Electro-acoustic music. Music of the late 20th century and today that depends on the electronic modification of natural sounds (often including the sounds of recorded or live performers), the synthetic production of the pitches and timbres of acoustic instruments, or the electronic origination of new sounds (or all three). Experimental electro-acoustic music is often characterised by the creative manipulation of new timbres and textures and the exploitation of spatial effects in large halls.

C91 is a partial score of a work for electronically modified solo voices (bars 1–11) and an electronically amplified chamber choir (bars 12–15). It is impossible to do justice to the composer's full intentions on a recording because, in a concert performance, each of the 28 singers has a microphone linked to a mixing desk where the balance is adjusted and artificial reverberation and phasing is added. The sound-complex is then relayed to seven 200-watt loudspeakers laid on their backs so that the sound bounces off the ceiling and completely envelops the audience. But the remote, almost inhuman sound-quality of the soloists is clear from the recording.

Electrophone. A category of musical instruments in which sound is generated by a loudspeaker set in motion by electrical impulses (eg the synthesiser on A87). See *Instruments*.

Elegy. 1. A mournful song (C85). **2.** A mournful instrumental work, often written in memory of a dead person (the *Elégie* from which C95 has been taken is written in memory of a famous cello teacher, hence the exploration of the highest harmonics on the lowest string).

Eleventh chord. See *Dominant chords* and B79, bar 39.

Elision. In common speech, the omission of a vowel sound in words such as 'don't' (where the vowel sound of the word 'not' is omitted). This process has become so common in English that what was originally a three-syllable word such as 'darkenéd' could, by the early 17th century, be set as a two-syllable word without any indication of the elision (as in bar 12 of A61). In other contexts an elision can be indicated by an inverted comma (eg A37, bar 1, where the second syllable of 'fumeth' is elided) or by a curved line (eg A62, bar 1, in which the last syllable of lasciate is elided). See *Oda* for a discussion of the metrical implications of elision.

Embellishment. An ornament or melodic decoration. A85 is a simplified version of the opening bars of a rondeau embellished with just a few quaver passing notes. In bars 1–8 of A84 the same passage can be heard with the composer's embellishments, all of them written out in full in the repeat of the refrain (bars 17–25). See *Ornaments. EM 3.10.1.*

Embouchure. In performance on wind instruments, the disposition of the lips, facial muscles and jaw. A player's embouchure is one of the most important variables not only in playing a range of notes, but also in achieving timbral beauty. The performance of baroque brass music (such as the obbligato part in B15) requires virtuosic control of embouchure.

Empfindsamer Stil, Empfindsamkeit (Ger.). Terms derived from the German noun 'Empfindung' (feeling, emotion, expression). They refer to a north German style of the mid-18th century that gave expression to the most intimate and often melancholy feelings, especially in the unbarred and highly chromatic keyboard fantasias of C. P. E. Bach (B20). This extract is characterised by chromatic instability (beginning in E minor, it passes rapidly through the unrelated keys of G minor and F minor to end in E♭ major), the use of diminished-7th chords, and constantly altering dynamics. These are all typical features of the *empfindsamer Stil* and of the music of the romantic era (to which the *empfindsamer Stil* might be regarded as a prelude). *EM 8.8.3.*

En dehors (Fr.). Prominent. In the lower string parts of C17 there are three ostinatos. Above these the first violin plays a melody that is meant to stand out a little from the accompanying string parts ('un peu en dehors').

En descendant and en montant (Fr.). In French or French-style baroque ornamentation suffixes to *arpègement*, *chute* and *port de voix* to indicate descent (B17, bar 3, beat 1, and B1, bar 4, beat 2) or ascent (A84, bar 45, and B1, bar 8, beat 2). See *Ornaments*.

Enclume (Fr.). Anvil (C48 and C54).

Eng. Hr., Englh. (Ger.). Abbreviations of English horn or Englischhorn (cor anglais, C88, bars 3–5).

Engführung (Ger.). See *Stretto* and B14, bars 14–18.

English flute. Recorder (A69). See *Woodwind instruments*.

English horn, Englischhorn, Englisches Horn (Ger.). Cor anglais (C88, bars 3–5). *EM 6.6.2.*

Enharmonic notation. The same pitch notated in two different ways. For instance, G♭ and F♯ both refer to the lowest of any group of three black notes of a keyboard

Ensalada

(see the folded insert). Similarly B♮ and C♮ both refer to the white note immediately above the highest of any group of three black notes. In bar 33 of B65 G♯ is renotated enharmonically as A♭ and the same sort of enharmonic notation is used in the next two bars (F♯♯/G♮ and E♯/F♮). *EM 2.1.*

Ensalada (Span.). Literally 'salad', but in music the name of a humorous 16th-century mixture of verses and tunes from diverse sources. Similar to the quodlibet (B2 and B3). *EM 4.4.7.*

Ensemble. 1. A group of singers or players (or both) of any size, though the term is most often used of groups smaller than a chorus or orchestra. A31 is sung by a four-part vocal ensemble, A32 is played by an ensemble of five instrumentalists. **2.** The degree of unanimity between performers in an ensemble.

Entr'acte (Fr.). Music, usually instrumental, between the acts of a play or opera. Although situated between scenes, C86 serves the same purpose since it covers the change of scene from the captain's cabin to the gun deck.

Entfernt (Ger.). **1.** Distant (C28, cowbells and tubular bells). **2.** Remote (key). In bars 1–8 of B58 Schubert moves from A minor to the remote key of C♯ minor.

Entry. 1. The point at which an instrumental or vocal part begins, or begins again, after resting. In C28 there are entries for a solo horn at the start of bars 9 and 13. **2.** In a fugue, a statement of the subject or answer. In B10 there are fugal entries at the opening (subject), at the end of bar 2 (answer) and at the end of bar 6 (subject).

Epilogue. Coda. Strauss calls the coda of *Till Eulenspiegel* (C11) an 'Epilog'.

Épinette (Fr.). Spinet (A67) or virginal.

Episode. 1. In general terms, a passage of music between two statements of the same musical material, eg the central section of a movement in ternary form (C2, bars 17–37). **2.** The contrasting sections between the statements of the refrain in a movement in rondo form (B and C in B36). In a classical French rondeau (A84) episodes are called couplets. **3.** In a fugue, passages between statements of the subject after the completion of the exposition. The three episodes in a fugue by Bach are identified in B14. *EM 4.5.4, 7.6.2.*

Equal temperament. A method of tuning instruments in which the octave is divided into 12 equal semitones. As a result only octaves are perfectly in tune, all other intervals having to be slightly modified (tempered) to accommodate equal intervals of a semitone. All of the keyboard music specially recorded for this dictionary is played on instruments tuned to the equally tempered scale, but one of each pair of strings on the clavichord recorded on B20 has been slightly detuned, to give 'bite' to the timbre. See *Temperament* and *Tuning. EM 2.1.*

Equal voices. Two or more voices with the same compass. The ranges of the two voice parts in the *pes* of A15 are exactly the same.

Equale, aequale (Lat.), **eguale** (It.). A composition for two or more voices or instruments of the same type (C58). The term is most often used as a title for solemn music for trombones (eg Beethoven's *Equale* of 1812).

Erhöhungszeichen (Ger.). The sharp sign (♯). See *Accidentals*, *Key signatures* and B21 (in which there is a key signature of one sharp and an accidental D♯ in the first complete bar).

Erniedrigungszeichen (Ger.). The flat sign (♭). See *Accidentals*, *Key signatures* and B4(c) (in which there is a key signature of one flat and an accidental E♭ in the first bar).

Es (Ger.). E♭ (B64(a), first chord, left hand).

Escape note, escape tone. *Échappée* (A97). *EM 4.3.8.*

Esercizio (It.). A technical exercise or study. Although entitled 'Prelude', B66 is like a short study in that it consistently explores widely spaced broken chords that are to be played with the greatest delicacy.

Eses (Ger.). E♭♭. See *Doppelbe*.

Espressivo (espress.) (It.), **expressif** (Fr.). Expressive, with feeling (B79, bars 8ff).

Essential note. A note, sometimes called a harmony note, belonging to the chord against which it is heard. A chord consisting of the notes D, F♯ and A sounds throughout the first phrase of B37 (bars 1–6) so all of the notes of the printed melody are essential notes with the exception of the G♯s (which are unessential notes or non-harmonic tones). *EM 4.3, 4.3.3*.

Estampie (Fr.). *Istampita* (A18). *EM 7.9.5.*

Estinguendo, estinto (It.). Dying away to nothing and barely audible respectively (C97, last bar)

Étouffer (Fr.). To damp (eg piano or harp), to mute (eg strings) or, on horns, to stop the sounds (C19, horns and violins).

Étude (Fr.). Study. Although one of Chopin's 24 Preludes Op. 28, the continuous semiquaver arpeggios in the right-hand part of B66 are in the style of an *étude*. See *Esercizio*.

Etwas (Ger.). A little, rather, somewhat (C34).

Euphonium. A type of tenor tuba (C37). See *Brass instruments*. *EM 6.7.4.*

Evangelist. In a Passion, the narrator. In Bach's *Johannes-Passion* the Evangelist is St John and the Gospel narrative is set throughout as recitative (B4).

Exchange of parts, exchange of voices. See *Voice exchange* and the first four bars of A15.

Exercise. See *Esercizio* and B66.

Evensong. In the Anglican Church, the service of Evening Prayer. The items that are usually sung include responses, psalms, the Magnificat (C30) and Nunc dimittis, and an anthem (A61).

Exposition. 1. The first section of a fugue in which all of the contrapuntal parts state the subject or answer. B10 is a complete fugal exposition. The exposition of the fugue shown in B14(a) ends in the first beat of bar 5. *EM 4.5.4.* **2.** The first section of a movement in sonata form in which a theme or themes are stated in the tonic key followed by a decisive move to a contrasting key (B40, bars 1–51). *EM 7.7.1, 7.7.3.*

Expression. A term referring to those elements of music or musical performance that have to do with the emotions. Though the term is vague, there can be no doubt that the expression of emotions has been central to the work of most western composers. In some periods there was an attempt to formulate precise criteria for the types of melody that could be associated with specific emotions (see *Affection*). In more general terms expression is often associated with the affective aspects of interpretation (compare the articulation, the use of rubato and the dynamic nuances in B61 and B74).

Expression marks. All of those words and symbols other than those relating to pitch and duration that guide performers in their interpretation of a score. See *Articulation*, *Dynamics* and *Tempo markings*. C97 contains more expression marks than any other example in Volume 2.

Expressionism. An early 20th-century artistic, literary and musical movement that sought to give expression to the innermost passions and obsessions of the psyche. Schoenberg vividly described his own expressionism in his diary for the year 1912. Writing about one of the movements of *Pierrot lunaire* he declared that the sound it made was a 'bestially direct expression of sensual and spiritual impulses – almost as if everything [had been] directly transmitted' (the transmission came, of course, from the depths of his subconscious mind). The text of C34 provides the concrete images beneath which Schoenberg's music burrows to seek direct transmissions from the darkest recesses of his mind:

'Out of the dense fumes of the lost depth arises a mind-destroying scent.
Huge black wings obscure the sunlight, and from heaven to earth the wings of unseen monsters beat down,
battening on the hearts of men …'.

Apart from the disorienting lack of tonality, Schoenberg achieves his aims by his use of *Sprechstimme*, low-pitched instruments (which descend to their very lowest registers at the end), obsessively repeated motifs, angular and chromatic melodic lines, and extreme dynamics. See also *Atonality*. *EM 8.11.3.*

Extemporisation. Improvisation (C97, bars 9–11).

Extrèmement (Fr.). Extremely. 'Extrèmement lent' at the head of C55 means 'extremely slow'. See *Tempo markings*.

F

F. In English and German, any of the pitches with this letter name shown on the diagram of a keyboard on the folded insert. A20 begins on an F♮. See *A*.

F (*f*). Abbreviation of *forte* (B59, bar 2).

Fa (Fr., It. and Span.). F♮. See *F*, the diagram of a keyboard on the folded insert and A3. Not to be confused with the tonic sol-fa syllable *fah* (the fourth degree of any major scale).

Fa-la-la-la, fa-la-la-la. Nonsense syllables in some types of madrigal, notably the Italian balletto or the English ballett (A59).

Faburden. An English improvisational technique of the 15th and early 16th centuries in which a pre-existent melody was used as the basis for polyphony. Parallel melodies improvised a 3rd below and a 4th above the original tune produced a series of first inversion chords (with a bare 5th and octave at cadence points). The technique is similar to *fauxbourdon*, but is quite unlike *falsobordone*. Though not based on a pre-existent melody, bars 5–8 of A24 are in the style of faburden. See *Falsobordone* and *Fauxbourdon*. EM 5.3.3, 8.5.2.

Fag., Fg. Abbreviations of *Fagott* (Ger.) and *fagotto* (It.). See *Bassoon* and C77.

Fagotto (It.), **Fagott** (Ger.). Bassoon (C77). See *Double-reed instruments*.

Fah. The fourth degree of any major scale in the British system of tonic sol-fa. The fourth note of A25 is *fah* in D major.

False cadence, false close. Interrupted cadence (A86, bars 7–8). EM 5.4.4.

False entry. In a fugue, an incomplete statement of the subject or answer (B14, bar 26). EM 4.5.7, 4.5.9.

False relation, cross relation. The simultaneous or adjacent occurrence in different parts of a note in its natural form and its chromatically inflected form. The E♭ in bar 13 of A81 forms a false relation with the E♮ in the next bar. The C♮ at the top of the first chord of C86 forms a false relation with the C♯ under the treble stave in the second chord. Simultaneous false relations can be heard in B36, bar 232 (A♮/A♭), and B40, bar 57 (E♭/E♮). There are three false relations (marked 'fr') in bars 1–4 of C77.

Falsetto (It.). A vocal technique by which a normally constituted male extends his range upwards to cover the range of notes available to a female or boy alto (A12).

Falsobordone (It.), **fabordón** (Span.). A style of vocal music dating from the late 15th century and cultivated particularly in Italy and the Iberian peninsula. Three voice parts were added note-for-note to an existing plainsong melody such as a psalm tone (A6) so that a homophonic texture of mainly root-position chords was formed. *Falsobordone* differs from faburden and *fauxbourdon* in that all four parts were written out and root position chords (rather than first inversions) predominate.

Familiar style, stile familiare (It.). Chordal writing, particularly four-part syllabic vocal styles (A37).

Fancy. The 16th- and 17th-century English counterpart of the continental fantasia. It was usually contrapuntal in style, its structure being based on a succession of points of imitation like some types of ricercar (A57).

Fanfare. A loud and strongly characterised call to attention played on brass instruments, sometimes with drums. The term is used of short passages of this nature that announce the beginning or end of an important section of a symphonic movement (the last three bars of B36).

Fantasia (It.), **fantaisie** (Fr.), **Fantasie** (Ger.), **fantasy** (Eng.). A title for a composition of no particular genre or set form in which the composer's fantasy can be given free rein. In the 16th and 17th centuries fantasias (and English fancies) were usually contrapuntal compositions like the ricercar (A57). Another type of fantasia was improvisatory in style (B20), which, having no bar lines or obvious pulse is bound to sound as though it were improvised. A third type made imaginative use of one or more pre-existent melodies. A39 is an extract from a fantasia of this type. The psalm tune shown in A37 can be heard in the tenor register played on violas, with the other strings playing accompanimental chords above it and a pizzicato bass below it. *EM 8.8.3*.

Fauxbourdon. A 15th-century French term for two-part vocal music consisting mainly of parallel 6ths, but with some melodic decoration in the upper part and an octave at each cadence. To these written parts a third part would be improvised moving mostly a 4th below the uppermost part, so producing chains of first inversion triads that moved to a bare 5th chord at cadence points. Bars 5–8 of A24 illustrate the technique. In the original only the outer parts of these four bars were written down. Of the seven intervals between the outer parts in this passage, four are 6ths and the last is the expected octave at the cadence. The second tenor part has been added in accordance with contemporary performance practice. In all but one of the chords it is pitched a 4th below the alto. This 'improvised' faburden produces four first inversion triads (labelled $^6_3$) and the expected bare 5th chord at the cadence.

Favola in musica (It.). A fable set to music, a subtitle in some 17th-century operas (A62–A66).

Favorita (It.). A 16th- and 17th-century dance-type in compound duple time and based on the same harmonic structure as the romanesca (A34).

F clef. Another name for the bass clef. See *Clef* and the symbol at the start of A38(a).

Female voices. See: *Coloratura* (B50), *Contralto* (A22), *Mezzo-soprano* (C91), *Soprano* (A91).

Feminine and masculine cadences. In a feminine cadence the second of the two chords forming the cadence falls on a weak beat (B40, bar 10), in a masculine cadence it falls on a strong beat (B46). A variety of feminine cadences in which a dominant-7th chord is heard over the tonic note is a stylistic fingerprint of late 18th-century music (the last bar of B30 and B31). *EM 5.4.5*.

Fermata (It. and Span.), **Fermate** (Ger.). Pause (B15, bars 64 and 80).

Ferne (Ger.). Distance. In C28 Mahler's original marking for the cowbells (bars 4–14) is 'Herdengl. In der Ferne' (cow bells in the distance).

Fes (Ger.). F♭ (B74, upper stave, bar 8, second note).

Feses (Ger.). F♭♭. See *Doppelbe*.

Ff (*ff*). Abbreviation of *fortissimo* (B59, bar 33).

Fff (*fff*), *ffff*. Very, very loud and very, very loud indeed (C97, bars 42ff).

Ficta (Lat.). See *Musica ficta* and A19 and A20.

Fiddle. 1. A colloquial name for a violin. **2.** A medieval name for any of a range of bowed string instruments such as the vielle (A13). *EM 6.4.3*.

Field drum. A large snare drum called a *tambour militaire* in French (C45 and C52). See *Percussion instruments*.

Fife. A small transverse flute with a narrow range and a high shrill sound similar to a piccolo (an instrument that can be clearly heard over the orchestral tutti with which B37 begins).

Fifteenth. On an organ, a rank of pipes sounding two octaves above printed pitch. The highest notes of A3 are played on a rank of pipes based on two-foot pitch, so that all of the notes sound two octaves above pipes based on eight-foot pitch (ie ranks that reproduce the pitch notated in printed organ music).

Fifth. 1. See *Degree* and the fifth note of B18. **2.** See *Intervals* and C80.

Figural, figurate, figured. 1. Adjectives describing the florid counterpoint of late 15th-century composers such as Obrecht (A28 and A29). **2.** In the 15th and 16th centuries, polyphony (A52) as opposed to plainsong (A49). **3.** A passage of music characterised by figuration (eg the semiquaver figuration in A87).

Figuration. A type of non-thematic melody composed of any number of repeated figures. The scalic figuration in the first episode of B14 forms contrapuntal parts against motifs derived from the theme of the fugue (the subject heard at the start), but the figuration is not itself thematic. Broken-chord figuration suggests the sound of a babbling brook throughout B57, and arpeggio figuration dominates the whole of the prelude by Chopin recorded on B66. *EM 3.9*.

Figure. A short melodic idea with its own characteristic identity. The six notes in bar 4

Figured bass

of B10 that are identified by the letter x might be described as a semiquaver figure, and the three notes below (y) could be described as a quaver figure. Repeated in a rising sequence, figure x generates continuous semiquaver figuration in the remainder of this codetta. *EM 3.9.*

Figured bass. A basso continuo with figures and accidentals that indicate the type of chords that should be played on a harmony instrument such as a harpsichord, organ or plucked string instrument. The extra stave below A68 shows the original figured bass. On the two staves above it is shown the organist's realisation of the figured bass part heard on A68. For bass notes without figuring a five-three chord is played. The flat sign indicates a minor triad. The figure 6 indicates a six-three chord. The bracketed figures do not appear in the original part, but the improvisation of a 4–3 suspension would have been an option within the stylistic parameters of the period. *EM 5.1.1.*

Figuring. See *Figured bass* and the figures shown beneath the continuo part in B4. *EM 5.1.1ff.*

Final, finalis (Lat.). The pitch on which a melody in a particular mode ends. It functions in modal terms in much the same way as the tonic in tonal music. Every phrase of A49 ends on the final of Mode VIII. See *Church modes. EM 8.4, 8.4.1.*

Final entries. In a fugue, the last entries of the subject (B14, bar 23, beat 3, to bar 26, beat 3).

Finale. The last movement of a multi-movement work. Many classical finales were lively in style and written in sonata-rondo form (B36).

Finalis (Lat.). Final. In Mode IV the *finalis* is E♮ (A5). See *Church modes.*

Finalmusik (Ger.). In the classical period, a composition of the cassation, divertimento (B40) or serenade type performed at the end of a concert or ceremony, especially out of doors (both Mozart and his father, Leopold, wrote *Finalmusik* to be performed at the end of the summer term at Salzburg University).

Fine (It.), **fin** (Fr.). End. The word is used at the end of a section of music that should be repeated (B15, bar 80). See also *Da capo al fine.*

Finger-picking. In guitar technique, the performance of individual notes by a plucking action of the fingers (C83, bars 19–26).

Fingerboard. On string instruments, a strip of wood under the strings that allows the player to stop the strings by pressing them against it, so producing notes that are higher than the open string. In B42 the cellist can play the first and third note on open G and D strings, but the second and fourth notes have to be played by stopping these strings against the fingerboard.

Fioriture (It.). Improvised or written-out flourishes. The melody shown in A65 is decorated with elaborate fioriture in A66 and the cadences of A57 are similarly embellished. See *Ornaments. EM 3.10.1.*

Fipple flute. Any flute in which sound is generated by air blown through a mouthpiece and directed at a sharp edge (as it is in a whistle). See *Flageolet* and *Recorder* (A69). Organ flue pipes work on the same principle (A3 and A93).

First-inversion chord. A triad with the 3rd sounding in the bass. It is also called a six-three chord because the intervals formed between the bass note and the upper parts are a 6th and a 3rd. Four six-three chords can be seen in bars 5–7 of A24. See *Sixth chord. EM 5.3.3, 5.5.1.*

First-movement form. Sonata form (B40). The term is unhelpful because first movements are not always in sonata form.

First subject. 1. The first part of the exposition of a sonata-form movement in which one or more themes are presented in the tonic key (B40, bars 1–18). Sometimes called a first subject group. *EM 7.7.1.* **2.** In a double fugue, the first of the two themes treated in fugal imitation (B10 and B12).

First-time bar, second-time bar. Bars marked with a horizontal bracket and the numbers 1 and 2 respectively. They are used to indicate repeated passages which differ only in the last bar or two. The penultimate bar of B37 is marked with a bracket, the number 1 and repeat marks (the dots in front of the double bar). This indicates that bars 26–32 should be repeated and the first-time bar omitted so the extract ends with the second-time bar (marked 2.). See also *Prima volta* and C5, bars 7, 15, 39–40 and 47–48.

Fis (Ger.). F♯ (A82, third note).

Fisis (Ger.). F double sharp (B65, bars 1–2, uppermost note, which is a semitone higher than the F♯ in bar 3). See *Doppelkreuz*.

Five-eight time. A metre in which five quaver beats form the repeating patterns strong–weak–strong–weak–weak or strong–weak–weak–strong–weak. Maxwell Davies groups the quavers of bar 2 of C90 in the latter pattern, but the overall rhythmic flow is so irregular that it is difficult to perceive. The metre is indicated by the time signature $\frac{5}{8}$.

Five-four time. A metre in which five crotchet beats form the repeating patterns stong–weak–strong–weak–weak or strong–weak–weak–strong–weak. C36 is of the latter type, the strong–weak–weak grouping of the ostinato being defined by the initial triplet, the strong–weak group by a pair of quavers. When the wind begin their ascent in bars 9–14 they reinforce this pattern by moving on the first and fourth beats of the bar. Five-four time in which there is an accent on the first beat only, or in which a subsidiary accent moves from the third to the fourth beat and back, is very rare. The metre is indicated by the time signature $\frac{5}{4}$.

Five-three chord. Any root-position triad, so called because the notes above the bass form intervals of a 3rd and a 5th with it. All of the chords in A35 are five-three chords with the exception of the two marked with the figure 6.

Fl. Abbreviation of *flauto* (It.) or flute. The sound of two flutes can be heard in C80.

Fl. Alto. Abbreviation of *flauto alto* (alto flute in G). The sound of an alto flute can be heard in C87.

Flag. In musical notation, a hook-shaped symbol attached to the end of a stem. The vocal part of B5 begins with notes with one flag. These are quavers (eighths). The last note of bar 2 has two flags. This is a semiquaver (sixteenth). To form shorter individual notes more flags are added – three for a demisemiquaver (thirty-second), four for a hemidemisemiquaver (sixty-fourth) and so on. See *Beam* and B18.

Flageolet. 1. A high pitched variant of the recorders heard on A69. It had four fingerholes and two thumb-holes and was popular in the late 16th century and the 17th century (particularly in England). **2.** A very high-pitched organ flue stop, the highest pipes of which can be heard at the end of the scale played on A3.

Flageolett-Töne (Flag.) (Ger.). Harmonics (C34, bar 1).

Flam. A two-note side-drum figure (♪♪) (C43, bar 2).

Flat. A sign (♭) that lowers a note a semitone from its uninflected pitch. See *Accidental, Key signatures* and B39, bar 1, beat 2.

Flatten. To lower the pitch of a note. A flat sign (♭) means that the note should be played a semitone lower than the unqualified note (C70, bar 5). In bar 6 of C70 the first violin is directed to play the two notes a quarter of a tone flat while the second violin plays the same notes in tune. The result is the acidic folky sound heard in this bar and in bars 8 and 9.

Flatterzunge (Ger.). Flutter-tonguing. See C34, bars 3–5 (clarinet), and C35 (flute, bar 1). *EM 6.6.1*.

Flauta dulce (Span.). Recorder (A69).

Flautando, flautato (It.). A performance direction in string music requiring the player to bow over the fingerboard (C34, bars 7–8 in which context 'am Griffbrett' means the same as 'flautando'). *EM 6.5.9*.

Flauto (It.). Flute (C76, bars 1–5), except in baroque scores where it means recorder (the horizontal flute being designated by the terms 'flauto traverso' or just 'traverso'). See *Woodwind instruments*.

Flauto a becco, flauto diretto, flauto dolce (It.). Recorder (A69).

Flauto piccolo (It.). Piccolo (C76, bars 9–11).

Flautone, flauto contralto (It.). Alto flute (C87).

Flexa (Lat.). A two-note neume (A4).

Fliessend (Ger.). Flowing. The term is entirely appropriate to the flowing semiquaver accompaniment that symbolises the brooklet in B57, but Schubert's intentions are so clear that he had no need of the term.

Florid. An adjective applied to: **1.** Elaborately ornamented melody (A66). **2.** Elaborate figuration (A98). **3.** Counterpoint of the late 15th century (A28 and A29).

Flöte, grosse Flöte (Ger.). Flute (C76, bars 1–5).

Flttz. Abbreviation of *Flatterzunge* (flutter-tonguing). See C34, bars 3–5 (bass clarinet).

Flue pipes

Flue pipes, flue-work. Organ pipes that work on the same principle as a recorder. On track A92 the sound of flue pipes (upper part) can be compared with the sound of reed pipes (lower part). *EM 6.9.1.*

Flügel (Ger.). Literally 'wing', the term refers to the grand piano because of its shape (B64).

Flute, flûte (Fr.). As commonly used in English, a woodwind instrument held horizontally and played by blowing across a hole towards a sharp edge on the opposite side to the lips. This is one of a number of transverse flutes (the others most commonly heard being the piccolo and alto flute). A cadenza for solo flute can be heard on track C76 and a flute duet can be heard on track C80. See *Transverse flute* and *Woodwind instruments*. *EM 6.6.1.*

Flûte à bec, flûte douce (Fr.). Recorder (A69).

Flûte en sol, flûte alto en sol (Fr.). Flute in G. See *Alto flute* and C87.

Flûte harmonique (Fr.). An organ stop of open flue pipes pierced with a hole so that the first harmonic is particularly pronounced. The hollow sound of these pipes is coloured by four ranks of pipes in the swell organ in the right-hand part of C55.

Flute in G. Alto flute (C87).

Flutter-tonguing. Rolling the letter r while blowing a wind instrument. It produces a trill-like sound that is a characteristic of 20th-century music. See C34, bars 3–5 (bass clarinet) and C35, bar 1 (flute). *EM 6.6.1.*

Folia, follia (It.). Like the romanesca (A34) this was a basso ostinato dating from the early 16th century and used by composers from then until the 20th century as a vehicle for sets of variations. Unlike the romanesca the most famous example also has a simple melody so that the treble and/or the bass could be varied. See *Glosa*.

Folk music. Before World War Two, a term distinguishing music of the oral traditions of the rural lower social classes as opposed to the composed art music of the urban middle and upper classes. The styles of folk music were at least as varied as those of art music, ranging from the simple diatonicism of B3 to the plangent Gypsy modality of the violin melody of C56 (the piano accompaniment is by Bartók). Throughout the ages art music has been influenced by folk music. Among the music examples in Volume 2 this is most apparent in B43 (a country dance), B65 (which contains an evocation of rustic drones), C5 (a Russian dance), C9 (a Bohemian dance), C41 (a Hungarian folk song) and C66 (a dance in Bulgarian rhythm). After World War Two rural folk music (at least in the sense defined above) largely died out in England, and it is now difficult to distinguish between urban folk music and pop in its many and varied manifestations. See also *Nationalism*. *EM 8.10.4, 8.11.6, 8.11.7.*

Follower. See *Dux and comes* and B26.

Forefall. 17th-century English term for an upward-resolving appoggiatura or *port de voix* (B17, letter b in bar 1). See *Backfall* and *Ornaments*. *EM 3.10.2.*

Forlana (It.), **forlane** (Fr.). In the 17th and early 18th centuries, an elegant but lively French courtly dance in compound time with dotted rhythms (C32 and C33). *EM 8.11.5.*

Form. The structure of a musical composition. The overall structure is often symbolised by capital letters (AAB in A12 shows that the first phrase is repeated, and that the song ends with a new phrase). Repetitions of motifs are often symbolised by small letters (x and x^1 in A12 show that a motif from phrase A reappears in phrase B in a slightly modified form).

See *Bar form* (A13), *Binary form* (A67), *Chaconne and passacaglia* (A95–A98), *Cyclic form* (C18), *Formes fixes* (A12, A22 and A23), *Fugue* (B9–B14), *Ritornello form* (B15), *Rondo forms* (A84 and B36), *Sonata form* (B40), *Ternary form* (C2), *Variations* (B18 and B32–B35). *EM 7.*

Formes fixes (Fr.). French musico-poetic forms of the middle ages including the ballade (A12), rondeau (A23) and virelai (A22).

Fort (Fr.), **forte** (It.) (*f*). Loud (B59, bar 2). See *Dynamics*.

Fortepiano. 1. A term now used to distinguish the late 18th-century wooden-framed piano from the modern pianoforte. The difference in timbre is evident when B25 (played on a Viennese fortepiano dating from the last decade of the 18th century) is compared with B64 (played on a Steinway concert grand piano built nearly two centuries later). *EM 6.9.3.* **2.** *fp*. Loud then

Freistimmigkeit

immediately soft (B50, bars 32–33). See *Dynamics*.

Fortissimo (*ff*). Very loud (C86). See *Dynamics*.

Fortspinnung (Ger.). The process of spinning out a short motif by continuous manipulations of it. In A98 the motif of a repeated A♯ alternating with notes above and below it (bar 2) is spun out throughout variations 57, 58 and 59. *EM 3.9*.

Forza (It.). Force. The octaves at the start of C10 are played 'con forza' (with force) while all instruments play 'con tutta forza' (with all possible force) in the repeat of bars 42–44 in C97.

Fouet (Fr.). Whip (C46).

Foundation stop. On an organ, a rank of flue pipes of 16-, eight- or four-foot pitch to which stops of other pitches can be added to build a chorus such as that heard on track A86. In Britain the eight-foot bourdon and four-foot principal are commonly used as foundation manual stops.

Four-foot stop. A rank of organ pipes of which the longest measures approximately four feet. Music performed on a four-foot stop sounds an octave above printed pitch. In its original form Bach's Chorale Prelude BWV 608 has a pedal part printed an octave lower than shown in A94. By playing this part on a four-foot reed stop the organist achieves Bach's intention that this melody should sound above the left-hand manual part. Four-foot pitch is a term that is sometimes used to classify a range of pitches (for any instrument or voice) based on c (see A2 and A3).

Four-four time. A type of metre in which the underlying crotchet pulse is arranged in the repeating pattern strong–weak–strong–weak. It is indicated by the time signature $\frac{4}{4}$ or C immediately after the first clef (A87 and B2 respectively).

Four-part textures. Any musical texture in which four pitches are heard simultaneously throughout a whole movement (B41) or a substantial passage (B35). With some notable exceptions it became the most common type of texture from the 15th century on, whether contrapuntal (A27) or homophonic (A37). For a wide variety of four-part textures see also A30–A33, A35, A44–A46, A52, A94, B2, B21 (bars 26–42), B31, B32, B72, C17 and C92 (bars 6–10).

Four-three suspension. A prepared dissonance in which a note a 4th above the bass resolves down a step to a consonant note a 3rd above the bass. In A54 the two alto notes labelled 'sus' form dissonant 4ths with the tenor (the real bass in this example) and both resolve down a step to form a 3rd with the tenor. Four-three suspensions are common in baroque cadences (A68, bar 5). See *Suspension*.

Fourth. 1. See *Degree* and the fourth note of B18. **2.** See *Intervals* and C65.

Fourth chord. A chord built from superimposed fourths (C65) as opposed to the superimposed thirds of the tertian harmony that was the norm in most Western music before the 20th century (A59).

Fp (*fp*). Abbreviation of *fortepiano* (B50, bars 32–33).

Fragmentation. A developmental procedure in which a theme is broken down into its constituent motifs. B40 contains a four-bar codetta (bars 48–51) which Mozart fragments in the ensuing development section (bars 52–71). First, motif z is detached and treated imitatively in bars 52–68, then an even smaller fragment (motif y) is detached and reharmonised (bars 68–71) to form a link to the ensuing recapitulation. In bars 26–30 of B27 the four-note figure n is abstracted from motif a^3 to form the sequential fragments in bar 27. Then the first two notes of n are abstracted to form fragment p. *EM 3.2.2, 3.4*.

Frame drum. A generic name for a variety of portable drums that have a shallow frame (usually circular) over which one or two membranes are stretched. They are held with one hand and struck with the other (or with a stick). Some, like the tambourine (C42), have jingles mounted in the frame. See *Percussion instruments*.

Free rhythm. Rhythm in which the constituent notes are unrelated to an underlying pulse or beat. Plainsong as it is almost universally performed nowadays is free of a regular beat (A4 and A5).

Freistimmigkeit (Ger.). Freedom in the number of voices making up a quasi-contrapuntal texture. This term is most often used to describe music (usually for

French horn

keyboard or a plucked string instrument) that gives an impression of strict counterpoint, but in which the number of parts varies from chord to chord (B1).

French horn. See *Horn* and C84. *EM 6.7.1.*

French overture. A baroque instrumental genre that originated in France as an introduction to the ballet, but spread throughout Europe as a prelude to operas, oratorios, cantatas and suites. It falls into two sections, the first characterised by stately dotted rhythms, the second by a fast tempo and imitative textures (A80). Some French overtures return to a slower tempo and dotted rhythms in the closing bars. *EM 8.7.1.*

French-6th chord. A type of augmented-6th chord containing the root and notes a major 3rd, an augmented 4th and an augmented 6th above it (B67, bar 7). *EM 5.7.4, 5.7.5.*

Frequency. The rate of repetition of a vibration measured in Hertz (cycles per second). See A1–A3, C95 and the folded insert.

Frets. Raised strips running at right angles across the fingerboard of some string instruments. On western instruments they are normally spaced a semitone apart, thus allowing the performer to strike the correct pitch without having to position the finger in precisely the correct location. Moveable gut frets are used on the vihuela (A34), viols (A61) and lute (A89); fixed metal, ivory or wooden frets are used on the modern guitar (C83).

Fricassée (Fr.). A 16th-century vocal quodlibet (similar to B2) with silly or obscene words. *EM 4.4.7.*

Friction drum. A drum that usually consists of a hollow vessel or cylinder with a membrane stretched over the opening. It is played by rubbing the hand over the membrane, or by pulling, turning or rubbing a stick or a string that is attached to it or passes through it. The *Rommelpot* (A36) and the lion's roar (C46) are both friction drums.

Frog, Frosch (Ger.). The part of the bow of a string instrument that the performer holds and that contains the mechanism for adjusting the tension of the hairs. 'Am Frosch', 'au talon' and 'al tallone' are all directions requiring the performer to use the section of the bow nearest the frog (C70, bar 1).

Front line. Wind instruments of a jazz combo. The front line most often comprises a clarinet or saxophone, a trumpet or cornet and a trombone. In C38 these are replaced by a bass clarinet, saxophone and flute. See *Jazz band*.

Frottola (It.). A secular song, common in late 15th- and early 16th-century Italy, for three or four solo voices, sometimes adapted for solo voice and lute. A30 shows the simple homophonic texture and vocal ornamentation of the uppermost part that was typical of the genre. It was a precursor of the more sophisticated Italian madrigal. *EM 8.6.3.*

Frullato (It.). Flutter-tonguing (C34, bass clarinet, bars 3–5).

Frusta (It.). Whip (C46 and C52).

Fuga (Lat. and It.). **1.** In medieval music, a canon. Voices I–IV of A15 form a special type of canon known as a rota or round. **2.** In renaissance music, imitation (A52). **3.** From about 1600, a fugue (B14).

Fugal. Adjective from 'fugue'. It often refers to textures that have some of the characteristics of a fugue but are not in themselves complete fugues (C82, bars 14–46).

Fugal exposition. See *Exposition* 1 and B11 (which is a complete fugal exposition). *EM 4.5.1.*

Fugato. A fugal passage within a larger structural design. The first subject of an extended movement in sonata form is shown in B28. From this Haydn fashions the subject of a fugato (B29) that is an integral part of the development section of a symphonic finale. *EM 4.5.9.*

Fughetta. A short fugue, sometimes consisting of just a fugal exposition. Although taken from a proper fugue, B10 could be an independent *fughetta* of unusual brevity. *EM 4.5.8, 8.7.6.*

Fugue. A vocal or instrumental composition that explores the potential of a theme (called the subject) in a variety of imitative contrapuntal textures. There is no set form for a fugue except that they nearly all begin with an exposition in which each of the contrapuntal parts enters with a statement of the subject. B14 illustrates many common features of the fugue. Its most unusual feature is that it begins as a three-part fugue, but at bar 19 a fourth part enters with a consequent enrichment of the fugal texture. B14(a) shows the fugue in skeletal form to reveal its underlying structure. On track B14(a) the fugue is performed as printed. On track B14(b) it is performed as Bach wrote it.

The subject of the four-bar fugal exposition of this fugue contains two motifs (x and y) that suffuse the ensuing textures, even when the subject is absent. This is evident in the first episode in which an inversion of the semiquaver figuration (z^1) is accompanied by a variant of x. In the counter-exposition the tonal answer is modified by the introduction of a B♮, and the subject is rhythmically varied (bars 7–8). The brief second episode is based on motive y from the subject. The same procedures are evident in the third episode. In the stretti of bars 14–18 the subject is contrapuntally combined with its own rhythmic augmentation, and the second half of this augmentation is contrapuntally combined with a free inversion of the answer. Three-part texture ends with statements of the subject in *stretto maestrale* (bars 16–17). Four-part texture begins with statements of the augmented subject and inverted answer in a fourth contrapuntal part not heard before (bass, bars 19–21). After the perfect cadence in the tonic (bar 23), the coda begins with another *stretto maestrale* in the upper two parts, and the fugue ends with an elaborately decorated perfect cadence. See also *Double fugue* and B10–B13. *EM 4.5, 8.7.6.*

Full cadence, full close. Perfect cadence (B48). *EM 5.4.1.*

Full orchestra. An orchestra comprising complete wind, percussion and string departments (B50) as opposed to a chamber orchestra (B21), string orchestra (B19) or instrumental ensemble (C87).

Full organ. A vague term meaning a very loud registration consisting of a full flue chorus and as many reed stops as are required to achieve an appropriate effect for a specific composition. The term does not imply that all of the organ stops should be drawn since multiple stops at the same pitch would deprive the organ tone of the brightness heard on track A86. See *Grand jeux, Organo pleno* and A81 (in which the sound of reed stops is much more prominent than on track 86). *EM 6.9.1.*

Full score. A comprehensive representation of what is played or sung (C52) as opposed to a short score on two staves (A33) in which certain details may be omitted (eg the precise underlay of the text in the last nine bars of A33). There are very few full scores in this dictionary, most orchestral scores being represented by reductions (A97 is a reduction of a full score printed on as many as 32 staves per system).

Functional harmony. Harmony that establishes clear tonality. This is brought about chiefly by the use of primary triads and dominant discords (see B25, in which nearly all of the chords are of this type). In functional analysis all other chords are deemed to behave like one of the three primary triads. For instance chords II, III and VI are regarded as relative minor chords of chords IV, V and I respectively and so are thought to function as variant subdominant, dominant and tonic chords.

Fundamental. The lowest pitch of a harmonic series. In C95 the fundamental is the open C string (bars 7–11) and all of the other notes in this extract are harmonics (from the second to the tenth) played on the same string. *EM 6.2, 6.3.*

Fundamental bass. A theoretical bass consisting of the roots of a succession of chords. In bars 77–79 of B50 the fundamental bass of Mozart's circle of 5ths is shown on an extra stave. It will be seen that, in the original progression, first-inversion chords alternate with root-position triads, but the fundamental bass consists of the roots of all of Mozart's chords. The fundamental bass of bars 1–2 of B41 is a G♮, the inverted chords (labelled $^6_3$ or $^6_4$) being regarded as derivatives of the tonic triad (I). The theory of the fundamental bass was first postulated by Rameau in his treatise on harmony of 1722, and the concept now forms the core of modern harmonic analysis.

Furiant (Czech). An energetic Bohemian folk dance in very fast triple time with frequent hemiolas. It was one of a number of folk dances that were incorporated into the instrumental works of Dvořák (C9). *EM 8.10.4.*

Furlana (It.). See *Forlana*, C32 and C33.

G

G. In English and German, any of the pitches with this letter name shown on the diagram of a keyboard on the folded insert. A36 begins and ends on G♮. See *A*.

Gagliarda (It.), **gaillard** (Fr.). Galliard (A35).

Gai, gaiement (Fr.). Gay, lively, allegro (C32, bar 1). See *Tempo markings*.

Galant (Fr.). Literally 'gallant'. The term is used to describe the light, sophisticated, melodious and largely homophonic style that ousted the serious, contrapuntal styles of the baroque era in the mid-eighteenth century. See *Style galant* and B25.

Galanterie (Fr.). Any short, elegant and modish dance in the French taste of the early 18th century. The style of *galanteries* foreshadowed the galant style of the early classical period. The term is sometimes reserved for the 'optional' movements of the late baroque suite (A89, B18 and B19). See *Suite. EM 8.7.3, 8.8.2*.

Galliard, gallarda (Span.). A 16th-century dance in moderate triple time characterised by the dotted rhythms shown in the tabor part of A35. It was sometimes paired with the pavan (A32). *EM 8.6.3*.

Galoubet (Fr.). A pipe with three finger-holes used in southern France in combination with a string drum and elsewhere in combination with a tabor (the two instruments being played by one performer). See *Pipe and tabor* (A35) and *Rommelpot* (A36).

Gamba, Gambe (Ger.). **1.** Abbreviation of viola da gamba, the Italian name for any type of viol (A61 and A64). **2.** An organ stop meant to imitate the sound of a viola da gamba (C55).

Gamelan (Ind. and Mal. from Jav.). A large instrumental ensemble of Southeast Asia. In its most familiar form it includes an array of gongs (C48) and metallophones tuned to a five-note *slendro* scale or a seven-note *pelog* scale. The exact tunings of these two scales differ from one gamelan to another. It is probable that Bartók had the sound of a particular gamelan in mind when he wrote *From the Island of Bali* (C64) with its pentatonic scale (bars 2–3) that is possibly based on a particular *slendro* tuning. *EM 8.11.7*.

Gamme (Fr.). Scale (eg the notes labelled 1–8 in B18).

Gamut. 1. In medieval theory, the entire range of pitches from G to e^2 (as shown on the diagram of a keyboard on the folded insert). **2.** The lowest note of this range. **3.** The compass of any instrument, voice or melody (one octave in the case of A4).

Ganze, ganze note, Ganze Taktnote (Ger.). Semibreve, whole-note (A41, first note).

Ganzton, Ganztonleiter (Ger.). Whole-tone and whole-tone scale respectively (C21)

Gapped scale. A scale of six notes or less that includes an interval greater than a tone. Any pentatonic scale is by definition a gapped scale (C60–C63). *EM 2.9.1*.

Gavotte. In the 17th and 18th centuries, a stylised dance in moderate $\frac{2}{2}$ time, usually with four-bar anacrustic phrases beginning with two crotchets. All of these characteristics are evident in B18. A gavotte, together with other 'optional' dances, often appeared between the sarabande and gigue in baroque suites. See *Suite. EM 8.7.3*.

G clef. Another name for the treble clef. See *Clef* and the symbol at the start of A22. See also *Tenor clef* and the symbol at the start of A23.

G^{de} Fl. Abbreviation of *grande flûte* (the ordinary transverse flute). See C80.

Gebrauchsmusik (Ger.). Functional music; music that was of immediate usefulness for films, radio, amateurs and especially for use in schools. The term was invented in the 1920s and is particularly associated with Hindemith and Weill, but its ideals soon spread. In 1930 a distinguished German violin teacher asked Bartók to write a set of pieces for elementary- and intermediate-level youngsters. The result was 44 violin duets which were published in *Das Geigen-Schulwerk*. These were of immediate usefulness since they could be played by teacher and pupil, or by two pupils, or even by a whole class of violinists without the need for a piano (the repertoire of such duets being almost non-existent at the time). See C58.

Gebunden (Ger.). See *Legato* and B67.

Gedackt, Gedeckt, Gedäckt (Ger.). Covered. This German term can be used to indicate covered or veiled vocal or instrumental tone. It can also mean a stopped organ pipe (or rank of pipes), the stopper being an adjustable wooden block fitting into the upper end of the pipe: this effectively doubles the length of the column of air so that it sounds an octave lower than an unstopped pipe of the same length. In the case of the *gedackt* bass curtal (A60) the cover serves as a mute.

Gedämpft (Ger.). Muted (C19, horns and violins).

Gegenbewegung (Ger.). Contrary motion (A85).

Gegenthema (Ger.). A fugal counter-subject (B14).

Geige (Ger.). Violin (A95).

Geistlich (Ger.). Sacred. In the 17th century a 'geistliches Konzert' (sacred concerto) was a German sacred work in several sections, often making use of concertato style in some if not all movements (A69).

Gemshorn. 1. A medieval instrument of the recorder family, the gemshorn was named after the chamois (Ger. 'Gemse'), from the horns of which animal this type of flute was originally made (A36). **2.** An organ stop of similar timbre. *EM 6.6.4.*

Gemächlich (Ger.). Comfortably slow (C11). See *Tempo markings*.

Generalbass (Ger.). Basso continuo (B5).

Generalpause (Ger.). A rest for the whole orchestra. This is usually indicated in the printed music by the abbreviation GP., but Wagner achieves the same effect by placing a pause mark above each of the rests in bars 11 and 13 of B68.

Genre. A species or type of composition. B61, B67, B71 and C2 belong to a romantic genre known as the character piece. *EM 8.2.*

German dance. See *Deutsche* and B44.

German flute. Transverse flute (C76, bars 1–5).

German-6th chord. A type of augmented-6th chord containing the root and notes a major 3rd, perfect 5th and augmented 6th above it (B30, bar 8). *EM 5.7.4.*

Ges (Ger.). G♭ (B74, bar 8, upper stave, first beat).

Gesamtkunstwerk (Ger.). The unified artwork that encompassed music, poetry and drama in Wagner's vision of the ultimate art form. In terms of pure sound the most impressive manifestation of the ideal was Wagner's unending melody (B68, bars 17–24, and many bars beyond this point in the opera itself).

Gesang (Ger.). Song (C73).

Geschwind (Ger.). Fast, rapid. The term is more or less synonymous with Liszt's direction 'Allegro vivace, quasi Presto' at the head of B73. See *Tempo markings*.

Geses (Ger.). G♭♭. See *Doppelbe*.

Gesprochen (Ger.). Spoken (C34, bar 1).

Gestopft (Ger.). Stopped horn notes (C85, the notes with crosses above them in the last two bars). See *Horn*.

Geteilt (get.) (Ger.). Divided. The first violins are divided into three parts to perform the chords shown in bars 6–14 of C28.

Ghironda (It.). Hurdy-gurdy (A18)

Gigue (Fr.), **Giga** (It.). The last movement of many baroque dance suites, the gigue is in fast compound time and, in its Italian version, is characterised by regular four-bar phrasing (shown by brackets under the first 20 bars of A90). Like other dance-suite movements, gigues are usually in binary form. The texture of gigues in the French style is often contrapuntal with imitative entries in the first section (letter A in A74) that are inverted in the second section (letter B in the same example). See *Suite*. *EM 8.7.3.*

Giocoso (It.). Playful, humorous. Mozart's opera *Don Giovanni* is subtitled 'Dramma giocoso' and the composer's playful combination of dances in different metres (B45) reflects the meaning of his subtitle.

Gis (Ger.). G♯ (B17, bar 1, third semiquaver).

Gisis (Ger.). G double sharp (B65, bar 33, the lower of the two semiquavers, which is a semitone lower than the A♯s on either side of it). See *Doppelkreuz*.

Gitarre (Ger.). Guitar (C83).

Giusto (It.). Just, proper, correct. 'Allegro giusto' at the head of C20 means 'at the correct [fast] tempo [for a cakewalk]'. See *Tempo markings*.

Glck. Abbreviation of glockenspiel (C35, bar 2)

Glissando

Glissando (gliss.). A slide from one pitch to another. A true glissando is one of the most characteristic effects on a harp. It is achieved by sweeping the fingers over strings that have been set to a predetermined scale: in C27 it is the scale of G major from D to d^2. A two-note glissando on a marimba can be heard at the end of C90.

On some instruments a microtonal slide (portamento) is possible. This happens near the start of C69 where an unaccompanied cello slides up an octave. Pizzicato glissandi are performed by plucking a stopped string once then sliding the finger up or down while the string is still vibrating (C71, bars 7 and 9–13). Trombone glissandi are performed by gradually moving the slide in or out (C75, bars 16 and 17). A glissando can be played on chromatic timpani by playing a roll while altering the tension of the membrane by means of a foot pedal (C82, bars 68–69).

Many authorities try to maintain a distinction between glissando (as a slide in which discrete pitches can be heard) and portamento (as a microtonal slide), but such distinctions are rare except in technical discussions about vocal and string techniques. See *Ornaments*. *EM 3.10.2, 6.5.7.*

Glissé (Fr.). In harp music, a glissando (C27, bars 4–5).

Globular flute. Sometimes called a vessel flute, globular flutes have any shape other than the familiar tube of the flute and recorder families. Globular flutes are common in Africa. The ocarina (A18) is a familiar western example dating from the mid-19th century.

Glock. Abbreviation of glockenspiel (C35, bar 2).

Glocken (Ger.). Bells (B63).

Glockenspiel. A high-pitched tuned percussion instrument with a set of metal plates arranged like a keyboard. These are struck with wooden, rubber, plastic or metal hammers. Its range is shown on the folded insert, and it can be heard unaccompanied in the second bar of C35 and with flutes in C3. Some orchestral glockenspiels are fitted with a keyboard, and marching bands use a portable version. See *Percussion instruments*. *EM 6.8.7.*

Gloria (Lat.). The second sung item of the Ordinary of the Mass, the Gloria is a hymn of praise to God the Father, Son and Holy Spirit. Like the introit shown in A4, plainsong settings are neumatic in style. Polyphonic settings often divide the text up into its three component parts and these become individual movements in the symphonic masses of the classical and romantic eras.

Glosa (Span.). In 16th-century Spanish music, variations or embellishments, particularly of formulaic harmonic schemes such as the folia, passamezzo and ruggiero. A34 shows how both the melody and bass of a romanesca are embellished with arpeggios and passing notes in a piece from Valderrabáno's anthology of 1547. See *Ornaments*.

Glsp. Abbreviation of glockenspiel (C35, bar 2).

Goat horn. Gemshorn (A36).

Goat's trill. See *Bleat* and the *trillo* in A62.

Gondellied (Ger.), **gondoliera** (It.). Gondola song, a type of barcarole (B61 and B74).

Gong. A large circular metal plate suspended in a frame and beaten with sticks or padded mallets (C48 and C54). The centre is sometimes raised to form a boss. This type of gong is of definite pitch (C97, bar 5). In English-speaking countries 'gong' is a generic term that encompasses all types of gong and tam-tam. In continental Europe 'tam-tam' is the generic term. See *Percussion instruments*. *EM 6.8.3.*

Gorgheggio (It.). Warbling. A modern term for 17th-century Italian 'gorgia' (A66) and for more recent improvised warblings in the style parodied by Mozart in B50.

Gorgia (It.). Improvised ornamentation, especially that of the early baroque era. A65 shows a phrase from an aria as originally composed, A66 shows the same phrase elaborately embellished with *gorgie*. See *Ornaments*. *EM 3.10.1.*

GP, G.P. Abbreviation of *Generalpause* (B68, bars 11 and 13 where the rests and pause marks have the same effect).

Grace notes, graces. Any of numerous melodic ornaments printed in small type adjacent to a principal note of the tune. They normally rob the following note of a part of its value. Grace notes are typical of music performed on the chanter of a bagpipe and are sometimes too complex to be represented in normal notation (A17). In some cases grace notes can flower in such profusion that, although they are printed in small type, they totally supplant a single melody note (compare bars 3 and 7 of B64). In most cases the composer does not expect the performer to play the graces in time – rubato is of the essence. A stream of grace notes is sometimes called an arabesque (bar 8 of B64). See *Embellishment* and *Ornaments*. *EM 3.10, 3.10.2, 3.10.3.*

Gradual, Graduale (Lat.). The second item of the Proper of the Mass. It is sung immediately after a reading from one of the New Testament Epistles. Plainsong settings tend to be as melodically florid as those of the Alleluia (A5).

Gran cassa (It.). Bass drum (C42 and C52).

Gran tamburo (It.). Bass drum (C50 and C52).

Grand couplet (Fr.). The refrain in a French baroque rondeau. *Grands couplets* are identified as refrains in A84 and C32. *EM 7.6.2.*

Grand jeu, grands jeux (Fr.). A loud and brilliant-sounding organ registration based on reed and mutation stops. It is one of the most characteristic timbres of the classical French organ, and is most often used for very slow contrapuntal music (A81). See also *Full organ*.

Grand orgue (Fr.). The most important and largest division of a French organ, the *grand orgue* is the equivalent of the English great organ (A86).

Grand piano. See *Pianoforte* and B64–B67.

Graphic notation. Visual symbols that, while they might approximate to some form of conventional notation, are intended to suggest and inspire rather than prescribe what is to be performed. These symbols can be accompanied by verbal instructions. See C97, bars 9–11 (wind and strings) and 39–41 (chorus). *EM 3.10.3.*

Grave (Fr. and It.). Slow and solemn (A81). See *Tempo markings*.

Gravicembalo (It.). Harpsichord (A84).

Grazioso (It.). Graceful (C1).

Gr. C. Abbreviation of *gran cassa* (bass drum). See C42 and C52.

Great organ. 1. A large organ (A86) as opposed to a chamber organ (A57). **2.** The principal department on an organ with two or more manuals. Since a wide range of timbres is available from a single department, and since departments can be coupled together, the unaided ear cannot usually distinguish between the different departments of a large organ.

Gregorian chant. Plainsong supposedly collected by Pope Gregory I (c.540–604), but the term is used freely of chants that date from much later periods, eg the 13th-century sequence *Dies irae* (B62). *EM 8.4.1.*

Grelots (Fr.). Sleigh bells (C49 and C52, bars 18–20).

Gr. Fl. (Ger.). Abbreviation of *grosse Flöte* – the ordinary transverse flute (C76, bars 1–5).

Griffbrett (Ger.). The fingerboard of a string instrument. See *Am Griffbrett* and C34 (cello, bars 7–8)

Groppo (It.) See *Gruppetto* and A66, bar 5.

Grosse caisse (Fr.). Bass drum (C42 and C52).

Grosse Flöte (Ger.). The ordinary transverse flute, as distinct from the piccolo (C76, bars 1–5).

Grosses Orchester (Ger.). Full orchestra (C86).

Grosse Trommel (Ger.). Bass drum (C42 and C52).

Ground, ground bass. English name for a basso ostinato (A75, in which a theorbo plays a four-bar ground three times beneath an unfolding vocal melody). *EM 7.8.1, 8.7.1.*

Group. Two or more themes in the first or second subjects of a sonata-form movement. Thus bars 26–47 of B40 can be described as the second subject group.

Gr. Tr. Abbreviation of *grosse Trommel* (bass drum). See C42 and C52.

Gruppetto, gruppo, groppo (It.). A trill ending in a turn (A66, bar 5) or the turn itself. See *Ornaments*.

Gsp. Abbreviation of glockenspiel (C35).

Guárdame las vacas (Span.). A melody and bass widely used in 16th-century Spanish variations (A34).

Guitar, guitare (Fr.), **guitarra** (Span.). A fretted string instrument that is plucked or strummed. Unqualified the term refers to the six-string acoustic bass guitar that has a range from E to about e^2 (C68, C83 and C87). See also *Quasi chitarra*, *Requinto* and *Tenor guitar*. *EM 6.4.5.*

Güiro

Güiro (Span.). A hollow gourd with a serrated surface that is scraped with a small stick (C51 and C53). See *Percussion instruments. EM 6.8.5.*

Gypsy scale. A scale containing two augmented 2nds (shown by brackets in C56) that was characteristic of much 19th-century Hungarian Gypsy music.

H

H (Ger.). **1.** B♮. See *B,* the diagram of a keyboard on the folded insert, and A3. **2.** Abbreviation of Anthony van Hoboken. See *Hob* and the titles of B21–B36.

Hairpins. Symbols representing a crescendo or diminuendo (B59, bars 29 and 30 respectively).

Halbe, Halbe Note, Halbe Taktnote (Ger.). Minim or half-note (A26, the first note).

Halbe Pause (Ger.). A minim or half-note rest (C30, bar 1).

Halbton (Ger.). Half step, semitone (all intervals marked x in C85).

Half cadence, half close. Imperfect cadence (A67, bars 5–6). *EM 5.4.1.*

Half-diminished-7th chord. A chord built on any degree of a scale and consisting of the root and a minor 3rd, a diminished 5th and a minor 7th above it. In C1 the chord heard from the third beat of bar 17 to the first beat of bar 19 is a half-diminished 7th chord in which the root is C♯, the minor 3rd is E♮, the diminished 5th is G♮ and the minor 7th is B♮ (VII^7 of V in G major). The term is related to the diminished-7th chord (which contains a diminished 5th and a diminished 7th, however notated), and, like the latter term, 'half-diminished 7th' does not explain the function of the chord within a key. The *Tristan* chord (C68, bar 2) has been analysed as a half-diminished 7th, and Debussy uses Wagner's exact pitches (enharmonically notated) in bars 10–11 of his 'Golliwogg's Cakewalk' (C20) – a piece in which he later parodistically quotes the opening cello motive of B68. See also bars 37–42 of B65. *EM 5.5.7.*

Half-note. Minim (♩). See *Note* and the first note of each voice part in bars 1–4 of A52.

Half-step. Semitone (x in bar 1 of C85). See *Note*.

Hand bells. Bells of definite pitch that come in a range of sizes. Since only one bell can be held in each hand they are most frequently played by an ensemble of ringers (C97, bars 36ff, 42ff and 48ff).

Hand stopping. In the normal playing position for a French horn the performer places the right hand part of the way into the bell of the instrument. When the hand is thrust further into the bell a dramatic alteration of tone-colour is heard. At low dynamic levels the tone is muted and distant-sounding (like the sound of the horns in C19). When played loudly the timbre is biting. In the last two bars of C85 hand-stopped notes are marked with a cross (the conventional symbol for this effect). Stopping can alter pitch as well as timbre.

Harfe (Ger.). Harp (A66, C6, C27 and C35, bars 10–11).

Harmonic flute. See *Flûte harmonique* and C55.

Harmonic interval. See *Intervals* and C58. *EM 2.2.*

Harmonic inversion. See *Inversion of chords* and B41, bar 1 (in which the tonic chord in root position and first and second inversions are heard on successive beats).

Harmonic minor scale. One of three minor scales, the harmonic minor is characterised by the interval of an augmented 2nd between its flattened sixth degree and its sharpened seventh degree. All of the notes of a harmonic minor scale are heard in the melody of A82. *EM 2.3.3.*

Harmonic progression. Any series of chords whether or not they are related to one another by the prevailing key of the music. See *Chord progression* and B48 (a progression of tonic and dominant chords in G major), B49 (the same progression leading to a more complex progression in D major) and B72 (an atonal progression). *EM 7.8.4.*

Harmonic rhythm. A rhythm generated by chord changes. In the first eight bars of B79 the harmonic rhythm confirms, indeed helps, to generate the triple metre indicated by the time signature (because there is a change of chord at every barline). In bars 8–15 however the chords change irregularly so that the triple metre is temporarily disrupted (only the underlying harmonic progression is shown in this passage, and Brahms's barlines on the bass stave have been shifted to correspond with what is actually heard). In bar 21 (originally notated

Harmonic sequence

in $\frac{3}{4}$ time) the harmonic rhythm (two dotted crotchets) effectively introduces a bar of compound time. Similar metrical disruptions occur in bars 30–37, but in this passage no changes have been made to Brahms's original notation: instead extra time signatures beneath the bass staves show how the harmonic rhythm crosses the composer's barlines. *EM 1.3.*

Harmonic sequence. See *Sequence* and B68, bars 2–3 and 5–6. See also *Harmony*.

Harmonic series. See *Harmonics* and C95 (a harmonic series on C is shown on the extra stave below bars 11–14). *EM 5.2, 6.2.*

Harmonics. The individual pure sounds that in varying intensities contribute to the timbre of a complex musical sound of defined pitch. They can be isolated on string instruments by lightly touching the string at particular points along its length (called nodal points). For instance, if a vibrating string is lightly touched half-way along its length it will sound a note an octave above the fundamental (the pitch produced by an unfingered open string). This is how all of the cello notes in C95 are produced (with the exception of those without a small circle). All of these harmonics are played on the open C string (the deepest-sounding string on a cello) by touching it lightly at the nodal points shown at the bottom of the page (where the frequencies of these harmonics are also shown).

These are the first ten pitches of a harmonic series on C (all of which are played in ascending order in the last four bars of C95). If the fundamental is changed a new harmonic series will be formed, but the intervals between adjacent notes will remain the same. If, for example, the cellist had played natural harmonics on the G string, the harmonic series would be G (the fundamental), g (the second harmonic, an octave above the fundamental), d^1 (the third harmonic, a 5th above g), g^1 (the fourth harmonic, a 4th above d^1) and so on.

Harmonics on other instruments can be heard on tracks C35, bars 10 and 11 (harp), C56 (violin), C84 (horn) and C88, bar 1 (double basses). See *Natural and artificial harmonics. EM 6.2, 6.3, 6.7.1.*

Harmonie (Fr. and Ger.). **1.** Harmony. **2.** Wind band or wind instruments of a symphony orchestra (C27).

Harmoniemusik (Ger.). Late 18th- and early 19th-century name for a wind band, the primary function of which was to provide musical entertainment at social events (B40).

Harmony. The simultaneous combination of musical sounds to produce a succession of chords. In homophonic textures the succession of chords that gives rise to a harmonic progression can be quite obvious (in A35 it is clear that the first three chords are all of the same type and that two new chords appear in bar 2 before a return to the first type of chord in the next bar). In more complex textures harmony may be implied by the interaction of two or more parts (in A87 the chords shown on the bass stave form a harmonic progression that is implied by the interaction of the monophonic right-hand and left-hand parts heard on track A87). In tonal harmony, chord progressions can establish a key (in B48 just two types of chord establish the key of G major). In atonal harmony, chords are often a by-product of the exploitation of other musical elements (the four chords at the end of C40 are by-products of the combination of four three-note cells derived from the tone row heard in the first seven bars). *EM 5.*

Harmony note. See *Essential note* and bars 1–6 of B37 (in which all of the notes of the printed melody are harmony notes of chord I of D major – D, F♯, A – with the exception of the G♯s). *EM 4.3.3.*

Harp, harpe (Fr.). The medieval harp probably dates from the 10th century. It had many fewer strings than the modern harp but was constructed on the same principles (A12). The double harp of the 16th and 17th centuries had two rows of strings covering a range of four octaves. Monteverdi exploits most of its range in A66.

The range of the modern harp is almost as great as that of the modern piano (see the folded insert). Two of the most characteristic harp effects can be heard in C6 and C27. In the former, harp arpeggios are heard linking the four-bar phrases of the violin melody. In the latter a three-octave G-major scale is played as a glissando. Unaccompanied harp harmonics can be heard just before the end of C35. A less resonant sound can be produced by plucking the strings near the soundboard ('prés de la table'). Confusingly this effect is indicated in German by the direction 'Resonanztisch!', or (as in bar 7 of

C28), just 'Resonanz'. *Bisbigliando* is a much less common technique. A rapid to-and-fro movement of the fingers across the strings produces a rustling tremolo (C97, bars 50–67). *EM 6.4.4.*

Harpégé (Fr.). In French baroque music, a term indicating that a chord should be arpeggiated (A84, last chord) or an entire passage should be played in an arpeggiated manner ('arpeggio' in A96 is the Italian equivalent.

Harpsichord. A keyboard instrument of the 15th to the 18th centuries. It was superseded by the piano in the 19th century, but was revived in the 20th century for authentic performances of early music, and 20th-century composers such as Stravinsky, de Falla, Poulenc and Górecki have written for it. One or more sets of strings are plucked by plectra operated by one, two or even three manuals. Harpsichords come in a range of sizes and shapes. The virginal and spinet often had a range of no more than three and a half octaves (A67 can be played on a short-octave spinet) while 18th-century French harpsichords had a range of five octaves or more (C17 explores four octaves extended by the use of 16-foot and 4-foot registers). A84 is a recording of a performance on a two-manual harpsichord that allows changes of dynamics (the first phrase is played *forte* on the lower manual, the second *piano* on the upper manual). In the baroque era the harpsichord was one of the most common instruments to be found in continuo groups (A73). *EM 6.9.2.*

Hauptmotiv (Ger.). Wagner's preferred term for what he described as the 'so-called leitmotif'. See B68(i) and (ii), which identify the three *Hauptmotive* heard on track B68.

Hauptsatz (Ger.). In sonata form, the first subject (B40, bars 1–18).

Hauptstimme (Ger.). **1.** In an opera, a principal part or role, eg the Queen of the Night in Mozart's *Die Zauberflöte* (B50). **2.** Schoenberg's term for the principal instrumental or vocal part in atonal and serial music. In the closing bars of C34 the vocal part becomes the *Hauptstimme* supported by subterranean instrumental parts. Schoenberg later devised a bracket formed from the letter H to identify the principal part in complex serial textures (and a bracket formed from the letter N to identify the *Nebenstimme* or next most important part).

Hauptwerk (Ger.). Great organ (A86).

Hausmusik (Ger.). House music, music intended for domestic performance and delectation (B57 and B61). See *Gebrauchsmusik*.

Haut, haute (Fr.). **1.** High pitched. **2.** See *Bas and haut* (A13 and A17).

Hautb., Hb. (Fr.). Abbreviation of *hautbois*, oboe (C1, bars 1–4)

Hautbois (Fr.) Oboe (C78).

Hautboy (Eng.). Old spelling of oboe (C4, bars 2–5).

Head motif. A melodic fragment appearing at the start of each section of a multi-movement composition that helps unify the whole work. Compare the opening bars of A28 and A29. *EM 8.6.1.*

Head voice. See *Chest voice and head voice* and B50, bars 74–79.

Heckelphone. A double-reed woodwind instrument invented in 1904, the bass heckelphone (the only one of a family of three instruments still in common use) has a range similar to the bass oboe. Although Holst specifies a bass oboe in his *Planets* suite its part is often played on a heckelphone (C36, bars 5–6).

Heel. The end of the bow that the performer holds (the frog). The performance direction 'au talon' at the start of C70 requires bow strokes using the hair near the heel of the bow.

Hemidemisemiquaver. Sixty-fourth-note (𝅘𝅥𝅲). See *Note* and the last six notes of bar 7 of Variation 5 in B18.

Hemiola. A temporary change of metre from strong–weak–weak/strong–weak–weak to strong–weak/strong–weak/strong–weak while maintaining the same unit of time. In A59 Morley maintains triple time (in this case crotchets arranged in the pattern strong–weak–weak) for the first 24 bars, but at bar 25 the metre changes to duple time for three bars. The strong–weak/strong–weak/strong–weak pattern of these three bars is a hemiola. See also A71 for an example of a hemiola in $\frac{6}{8}$ time (the upper system shows the music as Corelli wrote it, the lower shows the metrical effect of the hemiola). *EM 1.7.2.*

Hemitonic. Music characterised by semi-

Heptachord

tones. See B39, in which there is a semitone between each successive note of the chromatic scale. See also B38 in which the hemitonic motifs a and b of B39 can be heard in their original context

Heptachord. Any collection of seven different pitch classes, but especially diatonic scales (A82, A83 and B18) and modes (A4, A5, A8, A18, A19, A28, A37 and A40).

Herabstimmen (Ger.). To tune the pitch down. In order to achieve the low D in bars 13–15 of C83 the lowest string of the guitar (usually E) is tuned down a tone. The opposite is herausstimmen.

Hertz (Hz). The unit of frequency. One Hertz = one cycle per second (eg one complete vibration of a stretched string). See A1–A3.

Herdengeläute, Herdenglocken (Ger.). Cowbells (C28).

Hervorgehoben, hervortretend (Ger.). Brought out, emphasised, The terms are equivalent to the French 'en dehors' (in C17 the direction above the first violin part means 'somewhat prominent').

Hes (Ger.). A less common name for B♭ (which the Germans call B). The fourth note of B39 is Hes (B♭) and the next note is H (B♮).

Heses (Ger.). B♭♭. See *Doppelbe*.

Heterophony. The simultaneous performance of a melody and a variant of the same melody. In bars 20–25 of B37 Osmin sings a simple triadic melody which is doubled two octaves above by violins except for bars 23–24 where the strings play a variant of Osmin's repeated A♮s. Also see C82, bars 1–8. *EM 6.11.3*.

Hexachord. Any collection of six different pitch classes. Many folk tunes are based on a hexachord (B3, alto, bars 2–3 and soprano, bars 3–4). The whole-tone scale (C21) is hexatonic. Messiaen's seventh mode of limited transposition (C55) is a scale that divides into two overlapped hexachords. Bars 1–9 of C82 are based on the hexachord shown on the extra stave. In serial music the term is used to distinguish between the first and last sets of six pitches contained in a 12-tone row (C88, R 1–6 and RI$_6$ 1–6 in bars 5–7). *EM 4.6*.

Hfe. Abbreviation of *Harfe* (harp). See C27.

His (Ger.). B♯ (B30, bar 9, beat 2).

Hisis (Ger.). B double sharp. See *Doppelkreuz*.

Historia (Lat.). A setting of a biblical story which, in the baroque era, was akin to an oratorio, containing narrative recitatives and concerted movements for solo voices or chorus accompanied by an instrumental ensemble. Schütz's *historia* known to English speakers as *The Christmas Story* (A68 and A69) is actually entitled *Historia von der Geburt Jesu Christi* (*Story of the Birth of Jesus Christ*). *EM 8.7.2*.

Hn. Abbrevation of horn or *Horn* (Ger.). See B59 (bars 10–24), C84 and C85 (bars 8–25).

Hob. 1. Abbreviation of Anthony van Hoboken (1887–1933) who published two thematic catalogues of Haydn's compositions in which works are identified by Roman numerals (standing for particular genres) and Arabic numbers (standing for particular works within each genre). Hob. numbers used in B21–B36 are taken from *The New Grove Dictionary of Music and Musicians* (London, Macmillan, 1980), Volume 8, pages 360–401. **2.** Abbreviation of the German *Hoboe* (oboe) or *Hoboen* (pl.).

Hoboe (Ger.), **Hoboen** (pl.). See *Oboe* and C1.

Hocket, hoquet (Fr.), **hoquetus** (Lat.). A medieval vocal technique in which melodic lines are interrupted by frequent short rests. Hocketing voices usually appear in pairs, one resting while the other sings (A21). *EM 8.5.1*.

Holzblasinstrument (Ger.). Woodwind instrument (C77–C80).

Holzblock (Ger.). Wood block (C51).

Holzklapper (Ger.). Whip (C46).

Holzschlägel, Holzschlegel (Ger.). Wooden drum stick. In C36 a kettle drum is beaten with wooden sticks throughout the extract.

Home key. The key in which a movement begins and ends. The home key of B40 is F major. See *Tonic key*.

Homophony. A texture in which one part (most often the uppermost part) has all the melodic interest, the other parts providing a subservient accompaniment. Chordal homophony consists of a series of chords that support a treble melody (A37). Such absolute homophony is sometimes described as homorhythmic (ie all four parts have the same rhythm). More often homophonic music includes some independent movement in the lower parts. The dominance of the first violin melody in B41 is never in doubt, but at the end of each two-bar phrase in the A section attention is briefly diverted to movement in the lower parts. In the B section the viola, instead of simply playing one of the notes of the chord in each beat, provides broken chords that enliven the still subordinate accompaniment. Textbooks sometimes describe this sort of texture as melody-dominated homophony. *EM 6.11.4.*

Homorhythmic texture. A type of homophony in which all parts move at the same time, thus forming a series of chords. C86 is homorhythmic throughout. Other adjectives describing textures of this type include isometric (A7), note-against-note (A19), familiar (A37) and chordal (B58, piano part). *EM 6.11.4.*

Hook. The hook-shaped symbol attached to the stem of a note. See *Flag* and the first three notes sung in B5.

Horn. The subject of this entry is the French horn, a brass instrument that acquired its name in the late 17th century when it was first imported from France to England. In both English and German, however, the single word 'horn' is commonly used in scores and in conversation among musicians (in French 'cor' and in Italian 'corno' suffice to identify the same instrument).

The original *corno da caccia* (hunting horn) of the late 17th century was an instrument that could only play the natural harmonics of the key it was built in. Thus, without the specialised technique of hand stopping, a natural horn in F could play only the pitches shown on the extra stave below C84. The invention of crooks – different lengths of tubing that could be plumbed into the horn – allowed the fundamental pitch of an instrument to be altered so it could be played in a range of keys. By specifying two horns crooked in different keys classical composers were able to write parts that covered a range of pitches in the two principal keys of a symphonic movement. Thus in bars 19–59 of B21 horns crooked in E and G play in the tonic key of E minor and the related key of G major. The same principle is at work in Weber's much larger orchestra (B59), but now there are four horns, two crooked in C and two crooked in F. The horn parts are printed in bars 10–24 where it will be seen that these instruments allow Weber to write four-part harmony in C major and F major. Nevertheless a full chromatic range was not easily achieved until valve horns (invented in 1815) became widely available. In developed versions of these instruments a complete chromatic range of more than three octaves can be played (see the folded insert). In bars 8–25 of C85 Britten explores a large part of this compass (from $B\flat_1$ in bar 17 to f^2 in bar 21) in an extremely chromatic melody that displays the extremes of the horn's dynamic range.

In the last two bars of the same extract Britten exploits *sons bouchés* (stopped notes), by a type of muting that produces one of the most characteristic effects of the instrument. By playing loudly and inserting the hand further into the bell of the horn than usual the pitch is lowered by a semitone and the timbre changes to the harsh muted sound heard on the notes printed with crosses (the conventional sign for hand stopping). The slanting line between the last two notes indicates a microtonal slide achieved by gradually withdrawing the hand to its normal position in the bell. As in other brass instruments a muted effect can also be achieved by inserting a hollow, conical stopper into the bell. When played softly with such a mute the horn's timbre changes to the veiled sound heard in C19. At the other extreme horns played very loudly without mutes can produce an extremely powerful brassy effect known as *cuivré*. In bars 23–26 of C97 the effect is magnified by the raised bells of all brass instruments ('campane in aria'). *EM 6.7.1.*

Horn 5ths. A common figure for a pair of natural horns consisting of a stepwise ascent of a 3rd in the upper part and a lower part which forms intervals of a 6th, a 5th and a 3rd with the upper part. The figure is sometimes prolonged by a similar descent. Horn 5ths are most often found at or just before a cadence (B36, bars 38 and 40).

Hörner (Ger.). Horns (B59, bars 10–24).

Hosanna (Lat. from Gk. and Hebrew). 'Hosanna in the highest', an acclamation sung after the Sanctus and after the Benedictus in the Mass (A20 and A21).

Hr

Hr. Abbreviation of horn (C84).

Htb., H^{tb}**.** Abbreviation of hautboy (oboe). See C78.

Humanism. Perhaps the most important aspect of the renaissance, humanism sought to replace the theocentric doctrines of the middle ages with a revitalised, man-centred philosophy based on early Greek and Roman culture. In music its most obvious achievement was the invention of opera which was intended to be the rediscovery of classical Greek drama (A62–A66).

Hungarian mode, Hungarian scale. See *Gypsy scale* and C56.

Hurdy-gurdy (Lat.). A string instrument in which the sound is produced by a hand-cranked rosined wheel in contact with the strings. The upper strings are stopped by a key mechanism so melodies can be played, while the lower strings can produce a permanent drone tuned to a perfect 5th (A18) or octave (A15 – bourdon was an alternative English name for the hurdy-gurdy). *EM 6.4.3.*

HWV. Abbreviation of *Händel Werke Verzeichnis* (*Catalogue of Handel's Works*) which refers to the *Thematisch-systematisches Verzeichnis* prepared by Bernd Baselt. This forms the first three volumes of the *Händel-Handbuch, herausgegeben vom Kuratorium der Georg-Friedrich-Händel-Stiftung*, Leipzig, Eisen and Eisen, 1978–85. See the titles of B18 and B19.

Hymn. A song in praise of God or his saints in strophic form. In the early middle ages these were in Latin and sung to plainsong melodies (A49). Some were contrafacta of secular songs (A14). The melodies of some Lutheran *Kirkenlieder* (Chorales) were adaptations of pre-reformation plainsong or contemporary secular song, while others were specially composed (the first two phrases of B6 show the words and music of *Ein' feste Burg* as Luther composed them). The metrical psalms of the infant Anglican Church (A37) were forerunners of familiar 19th- and 20th-century four-part hymns. *EM 8.4.1.*

Hypoaeolian mode. See *Aeolian mode* and B61. *EM 2.4.2.*

Hypodorian mode. See *Dorian mode* and A11. *EM 2.4.2.*

Hypoionian mode. See *Ionian mode* and A13. *EM 2.4.2.*

Hypolydian mode. See *Lydian mode* and C57. *EM 2.4.2.*

Hypomixolydian mode. See *Mixolydian mode* and A49. *EM 2.4.2.*

Hypophrygian mode. See *Phrygian mode* and A5. *EM 2.4.2.*

Hz. Abbreviation of Hertz (A1–A3).

I

Idée fixe (Fr.). Berlioz's term for a theme that represents the beloved and which recurs obsessively in every one of the five movements of his *Symphonie fantastique*. See B63(i) and (ii), *Cyclic form* and *Thematic transformation* (C18). *EM 7.10.2*.

Idiomatic. An adjective describing music that exploits the capabilities of particular instruments and that is unsuited to other types of instrument. The marimba solo shown in C90, though extremely difficult, is idiomatic to that instrument and would be impossible or very nearly impossible to play on most other instruments. Early instrumental music was often not idiomatic. It would be quite possible to play A35 using numerous other ensembles or on any contemporary keyboard instrument.

Idiophone. A category of musical instruments in which the body of the instrument is made to vibrate, most often by striking or scraping it (eg the güiro, claves and wood blocks on C51). See *Instruments*. *EM 6.8*.

Illustrative music. See *Programme music* and A31, A32, B61, B63, B73, B74, C7, C8, C10, C11, C19, C21–C26, C31, C36 and C37.

Imbroglio (It.). A scene in an 18th or 19th-century comic opera in which confusion on stage is mirrored by musical complexity. There can be few instrumental passages in the operatic repertoire that can match the rhythmic complexity of B45, in which two plebeian dances (the country dance and German dance) are combined with an aristocratic dance (the minuet). This musical complexity mirrors the on-stage confusion as Don Giovanni attempts another seduction while his servant tries to get rid of all the other on-stage characters (including the fiancé of the woman Giovanni is about to seduce). In addition to the instrumental music shown in B45 there are seven singing parts, all with melodies reflecting their social status and their intentions or reactions in the unfolding drama.

Imitation. A contrapuntal device in which a melodic idea presented in one part is copied at pitch or transposed in another part while the melodic line of the first part continues. Only the opening notes of the original melody need be repeated. In A54 the first four notes of the alto part are imitated in the tenor part. A55 shows the same melodic idea in three-part imitation, and the same imitative idea pervades the four-part texture of A52. See *Counterpoint* and *Fugue*. *EM 4.4.1, 4.5, 6.11.6*.

Imperfect cadence. The end of a phrase harmonised with two chords, the second of which is a dominant chord (B6, bar 16). *EM 5.4.1*.

Imperfect consonances. Major and minor 3rds (C78) and major and minor 6ths (C77) as opposed to the perfect consonances (perfect 4ths, 5ths and octaves).

Impressionism. A term that has been applied to musical styles that are thought to mirror the impressionist paintings of artists such as Monet and Pissarro. Just as these painters sought to blur the outlines of concrete objects and scenes by concentrating on the play of light and colour, so Debussy blurred classical tonality and metre by concentrating on the intrinsic colour of chords (rather than their functions within a clearly established key) and by allowing his music to flow freely, often without a clearly defined beat. Both of these techniques are evident in C19. The quaver beat is so slow and the first, fifth and ninth chords so long that the semiquavers seem to float freely between them without any suggestion of a regular beat. A sense of tonality is maintained by the tonic pedal and the E-major chord at the beginning of the extract, but the semiquaver triads are unrelated to this tonal centre. The scoring for muted horns and violins aids the vague impression engendered by the rhythm and harmony. Until the last two pizzicato chords E-major tonality is blurred by the chromatic A♯ on the violins. See *Parallel chords* and C21–C26. *EM 8.10.6, 8.11.2*.

Improvisation. The creation or realisation of a composition while performing it. In bars 9–11 of C97 the composer requires wind and string instrumentalists to improvise their own parts within his prescribed parameters. On track A68 the organist improvises a chordal accompaniment from a figured bass. In the first of these examples the composer's

In alt

notation has been left unaltered. In the second a transcription of the organist's realisation appears in the score. See *Jazz*.

In alt (from the It. 'in alto'), **in altissimo** (It.). Terms often used in relation to high and very high notes in vocal music. In bar 31 of B50 Mozart writes an F 'in alt' (one of the very highest notes in the soprano repertoire). Pitches *in altissimo* (above f^3) are extremely rare in vocal music, but not unknown in instrumental music (see C97, violin, bar 63 and the folded insert).

Incalzando (It.). Pressing on, getting faster. The effect can be heard in the last few seconds of track C5. See *Tempo markings*.

Incipit (Lat.). The opening few bars of a composition used for the identification of a piece in a thematic catologue. The fugal subject of B9 is an incipit shown in the *Bach Werke Verzeichnis* (*Kleine Ausgabe*, Wiesbaden, Breikopf and Härtel, 1998, page 320).

Incudine (It.). Anvil (C48).

Indeterminacy, indeterminate music. A term coined by John Cage to describe aleatoric music (C97, bars 9–11, wind and strings).

Inégales (Fr.). See *Notes inégales* and B17.

Infinite canon. Round (the four uppermost voices of A15).

Inflection, inflexion. 1. In plainsong, a deviation from a reciting note (the D♮ on the second syllable of 'operibus' which returns to the reciting note on the third syllable in A6). 2. In later music, a deviation from a set of pitches already established, eg chromatically altered notes (the C♯s, D♯s and A♮ in B28) and blue notes (C20).

Inharmonicity. The tone-colour of sounds in which the partials do not match the pitches of the harmonic series (an example of which is shown on the extra stave in C95). Inharmonicity is evident to the unaided ear in gongs (C48 and C54) and bells (B60, in which the midnight bell sounds an A♭ that is distorted by other clearly audible discordant pitches).

Inner part. A melodic strand between the treble part and the bass part. In B40 the bass melody of bars 95–100 is repeated in bars 103–108 and becomes an inner part in bars 105–108.

Inner pedal, internal pedal, middle pedal. A sustained or repeated note in an inner part (B75, the repeated A♭s in the left-hand piano part).

Inno (It.). Hymn (A49).

Instrumentation. So far as the listener is concerned the term means the choice and combination of instruments. In early music instrumentation was not specified by the composer: A35 is played on crumhorns, but could be played equally effectively on a consort of viols. In later music instrumentation is often of vital importance: the effectiveness of C86 is largely determined by Britten's choices of contrasting choirs of orchestral instruments. See also *Orchestration*.

Instruments. Any device, other than the human voice, used for producing musical sounds. There are two chief methods of classifying instruments. The first, in general use amongst musicians, divides instruments into four groups: **a)** strings, both plucked (eg the lute, A89) and bowed (eg the cello, A90), **b)** winds, both woodwind (eg flutes, C80) and brass (eg trumpets, C81), **c)** percussion, both tuned (eg the xylophone, C8) and untuned (C42–C54), **d)** keyboards, both mechanical (eg the piano, B75–B79) and electronic (A87).

The second, more scientific categorisation divides instruments into five main groups according to the physical characteristics of sound production: **a)** chordophones, in which sound is generated by plucking, rubbing, or striking stretched strings (eg A89, A90 and B20 respectively), **b)** aerophones, in which sound is generated by a vibrating column of air set in motion by the performer's breath or by compressed air from a pair of bellows (eg the recorders and organ heard on track A68), **c)** idiophones, in which vibrations are set up in the body of the instrument, most often by striking or scraping (eg the güiro, claves and wood blocks on C51), **d)** membranophones, in which a stretched membrane is made to vibrate by striking or rubbing it (eg the bongos on track C45 and the string drum on track C46), **e)** electrophones, in which a loudspeaker is made to vibrate by electrical impulses (eg A87).

Intensity. A measurement of the physical energy of a sound. From a subjective point of view the term is almost synonymous with volume or dynamic level. An extreme range of intensities can be heard on track C97.

Introduction

Interchange of voices, interchange of parts. See *Voice exchange* and the *pes* in bars 1–8 of A15.

Interlude. Music played between sections of a larger composition, especially the acts or scenes of an opera (C86 is played as Captain Vere leaves a naval court martial to inform the eponymous hero of Britten's *Billy Budd* that he has been sentenced to death).

Intermedio (It.), **intermedium** (Lat.). In the 16th century, a musical work, such as a madrigal (A33), performed between the acts of a play. The genre was an important progenitor of early operas such as Monteverdi's *Orfeo* (A62–A66). Schütz used the term in the 17th century for musical tableaux in which three or four voices represented shepherds (A69), the three kings and the high priests in the story of Christ's nativity. *EM 8.7.2.*

Intermezzo (It.). **1.** A short comic operatic work between acts of a 17th-century serious opera that later became an independent genre as the opera buffa (B37, though an extract from a Singspiel, gives some idea of the style of this type of opera). **2.** In the 19th century, a type of character piece, most often for solo piano, often lyrical in style and in no set form (B78 and B79). *EM 8.10.3.*

Internal pedal. Inner pedal (the repeated A♭ in B75).

Interpretation. In a musical performance, all those matters that go beyond the written or printed music.

In early music, interpretation might include an element of improvisation. A65 shows an unornamented phrase from an early 17th-century aria. A66 shows the same phrase with Monteverdi's own written-out ornamentation. On the basis of this (and hundreds of other extant examples of early baroque embellishment) a proper interpretation of similar unornamented music of this period requires historically informed embellishment of a similar nature. Even when conventional symbols are used to represent ornamentation (B1 and B17) the precise interpretation of them is often as much a matter of good taste as of knowledge of contemporary ornament tables (which are, in any case, sometimes contradictory). The realisation of a figured bass (A68) is not simply a matter of the correct intervals above the bass indicated by the figures. Instead of the spare chords shown in the transcription of this recording, it would be quite possible to play sustained eight-part chords embellished with all manner of ornaments between them (though most would find the results ludicrous).

With the advent of romanticism and more prescriptive scores expressiveness began to play a central role in interpretation. B61 and B74 are both character pieces to do with Venice, both are barcaroles with sustained melodies over rocking broken-chord accompaniments, they share the same tempo marks and time signatures, and both are in minor keys. Yet the interpretations of the two pianists differ widely, the Mendelssohn being played with almost classical restraint, the Liszt with considerable rubato. One interpretation is not better than the other since they are both well within the bounds of accepted performance practice and good taste. They simply reflect each pianist's subjective view of the musical significance of each piece.

Interrupted cadence, false cadence. At the end of a phrase, a dominant chord followed by almost any chord other than the tonic chord. The second of these two chords interrupts the expected resolution of the dominant chord to the tonic. B69 shows the most common type of interrupted cadence – V^7–VI (which can be heard in its original context in bars 16–17 of B68). More unusual is the cadence in bars 21–22 of B79 (V–IV). Interrupted cadences can lead to a change of key (A86, bars 7–8). *EM 5.4.4.*

Intervallic inversion. See *Inversion* and C95, bar 11 (the perfect 4th is an intervallic inversion of the perfect 5th).

Intervals. See the box on page 84. *EM 2.2, 5.3.1.*

Intonation. 1. The first few notes of a plainsong melody sung by a cantor to set the pitch for the choir (A4). See *Intonatione* (A57). **2.** The degree to which a singer or performer is in tune. The poor intonation of the first violinist in bars 6 and 8–10 of C70 is deliberate.

Intonatione (It.). An organ prelude designed to set the pitch and mode for a vocal composition sung immediately after it. See *Ricercar* and A57.

Introduction. A preparatory section before the main body of a composition. The instrumental ritornello at the start of a baroque

Intervals

An interval is the distance between two pitches. Intervals can be calculated by counting the number of letter names between the lower and higher pitch including both first and last letters. Thus the interval between c^1 and d^1 (see the folded insert and A3) is a 2nd, the interval between c^1 and e^1 is a 3rd, and so on. All intervals have greater and lesser forms. Thus a major 3rd is a semitone wider than a minor 3rd, an augmented 4th is a semitone wider than a perfect 4th, and so on. Although in absolute terms some differently named intervals are made up of two notes that have the same pitches (eg F–G♯ is an augmented 2nd while F–A♭ is a minor 3rd), yet in their tonal contexts their aural effects are quite different. Intervals can be heard harmonically (as two notes sounded simultaneously) or melodically (as two notes sounded one after the other). The following chart attempts to place both types of interval in their tonal contexts.

Melodic interval	**Example number and bar number(s)**
Minor 2nd (semitone)	C85, any of the two-note figures marked x
Major 2nd (tone)	A91, any of the three-note figures marked x
Augmented 2nd	C56, any two notes marked with a bracket
Minor 3rd	B9, bars 1 and 6
Major 3rd	A91, bars 1–2 and 5–6
Perfect 4th	C65, bar 1–2
Augmented 4th (tritone)	B9, bars 1 and 6
Diminished 5th (tritone)	C11, bar 2
Perfect 5th	C95, bar 11
Minor 6th	B68, the first two cello notes
Major 6th	B68, bars 4–5 and 8–9
Augmented 6th	B9, bars 2 and 7
Diminished 7th	A96, bar 2
Minor 7th	B5, vocal part, bars 2 and 3
Major 7th	A90, bars 28–29
Perfect octave	C95, bar 11

Harmonic interval	**Example number and bar number(s)**
Minor 2nd (semitone)	C58, bar 8, beat 3
Major 2nd (tone)	C81, trumpets throughout
Augmented 2nd	B30, bar 5
Minor 3rd	C78, oboes, bars 1–3
Major 3rd	C58, bar 1
Perfect 4th	C65, bars 1, 3 and 5
Augmented 4th (tritone)	C96, cello bar 1
Diminished 5th (tritone)	C96, cello bar 5
Perfect 5th	C80, flutes throughout
Minor 6th	C77, bassoons, bars 0–2
Major 6th	C58, bar 3, beat 1
Augmented 6th	B57, bars 38–40
Diminished 7th	B20, between the D♯ and C in the second chord
Minor 7th	C79, clarinets throughout
Major 7th	C85, cellos, bar 7
Perfect octave	A29, last bar

See also *Augmented octave*, *Compound intervals*, *Diminished 3rd* and *Diminished 4th*.

Ionian mode

aria may be considered an introduction to what is primarily a vocal composition (B15, bars 1–14).

Introit, introitus (Lat.).The first item of the Proper of the Mass (A4). In its most usual form it consists of an antiphon ('Ad te levavi … non confundentur') followed by a verse from a psalm ('Vias tuas Domine … et semitas tuas edoce me'). Finally the antiphon is repeated.

Invention. An original product of a composer's imagination; the term implies no set form or genre. Bach's original title for the two-part invention shown in C93 was 'Praeambulum' (prelude) which he later changed to 'Inventio'.

Inversion. 1. Melodic inversion. A melody is said to be inverted when every interval between adjacent notes is retained but moves in the opposite direction to the original. The first bar of A72 is inverted in the first bar of A73. **2.** See *Contrapuntal inversion* and B24. **3.** Intervallic inversion occurs when one note of an interval remains fixed while the other moves an octave above or below its original position. In the harmonic series played by the cello at the end of C95 the interval of a perfect 5th in bar 11 is followed by its inversion, a perfect 4th. **4.** See *Inversion of chords* and A24, bars 5–7 (where $^6_3$ identifies first inversion triads). **5.** See *Inverted cadence* and A91 bars 27–28. *EM 4.4.5, 4.5.6.*

Inversion of chords. A chord is said to be inverted when a note other than the root is heard in the bass. See: *First-inversion chord* and A24, bars 5–7 (the chords labelled $^6_3$), *Second-inversion chord* and B46 (the first chord), *Third-inversion chord* and B30 (the second chord). *EM 5.3.3.*

Inverted cadence. A cadence in which one or both chords are inverted. In bars 11–12 of A91 the first chord of the cadence is inverted, and in bars 27–28 the second chord of the cadence is inverted. *EM 5.4.1.*

Inverted canon. See *Canon* and C82, bars 34–41.

Inverted mordent. An ornament consisting of the written note, the note above it, then the written note again. It can be written out (B65, bars 5, 7, 13 etc.) or indicated by a symbol (bars 6, 8, 14 etc in the same example). There is still considerable confusion about what constitutes an inverted mordent (the meaning changed over time) so the term upper mordent is preferred in this dictionary. See *Ornaments, Upper mordent* and B25, bar 56.

Inverted pedal. See *Pedal* and bars 5–7 of A70. An inverted pedal can be heard throughout C67.

Invertible counterpoint. Counterpoint so composed that what was the upper part in one statement can become the lower part in the next (and vice versa). B24 shows the process in two-part counterpoint, and the same music can be heard in the context of four-part invertible counterpoint in bars 28–42 of B21. Fugal subjects and counter-subjects are often written in invertible counterpoint (compare bars 0–4 and 9–13 of B29). *EM 4.4.5.*

Ionian mode. A scale that can be reproduced by playing the white notes of the piano from any C♮ to the C♮ an octave above it (see the diagram of a keyboard on the folded insert). It was one of the modes added to the eight church modes by Glareanus in 1547 to help explain melodies that did not conform to any of these traditional modes. Between them the two rebec parts of A16 encompass all of the notes of the ionian mode. But a comparison of this ionian music with the major tonality of the music in bars 1–25 of B59 reveals that Glareanus's ionian mode and the scale of C major are in fact identical. Both have semitones between the third and fourth, and between the seventh and eighth degrees, and both begin and end on C♮. Ionian alias major-mode melodies are common in early music, especially early secular music. A31 and A32 are both in (ionian) C major and A14 and A15 are both in D major (the ionian mode transposed up a tone).

Between them the two rebec melodies of A16 cover the range of the authentic ionian mode, their combined ranges extending from the final/tonic (middle C) to the note a tone above the upper final. In its plagal form (the so-called hypoionian mode) the final is the same, but the range extends from the note a 4th below the final to the note a 5th above it (G–G). Like all modes and major or minor scales, the ionian mode can be transposed to any of the 12 chromatic pitches. In A13 the melody cadences three times on D♮. This is the final of the ionian mode transposed up a tone. But the range is from the A a 4th below the final (tonic) to the A a 5th above it.

Irregular resolution

Glareanus would have classified this melody as a member of the hypoionian mode. To us it sounds like a tune in D major with a range extending from the dominant to the upper dominant. *EM 2.4.1.*

Irregular resolution. A discord is said to resolve irregularly when the part containing the discord leaps to a consonant note instead of resolving by step to an adjacent concord. In bar 11 of B5 the B♭ in the vocal part forms a dissonant 7th with the bass C♮. It resolves regularly by moving down a tone to A♭ (which forms a consonant 6th with the bass). At the beginning of the next bar the C♮ in the vocal part forms another dissonant 7th, this time with the bass D♮. It resolves irregularly by leaping a 5th to F♮ (which forms a consonant 3rd with the bass).

A chord is said to resolve irregularly when the conventions of voice leading are similarly disregarded. Thus according to 18th-century conventions it would be normal for the G♮, A♯ and E♮ in bar 4 of B31 to resolve as shown by the arrows on the extra stave below. Instead they lead to the D♯, A♮ and C♮ respectively in the next bar. *EM 5.7.1.*

Isometric. Homorhythmic (A37).

Isorhythm. A 20th-century term for a compositional device of the Ars Nova (14th century) in which a rhythmic pattern is repeated throughout a voice part. A20 shows how Machaut superimposed a repeating rhythmic pattern (*talea*) on a plainsong melody. The resulting isorhythmic cantus firmus can be heard in the tenor of A21. *EM 1.13, 7.9.4, 8.5.1.*

Istampita (It.). A medieval instrumental form in which several phrases (*puncta*) are repeated, the first with an open ending (like a first-time bar ending on any note but the tonic), the second with a closed ending (like a second-time bar ending on the tonic). The melodic formulae of these two types of cadence remain the same throughout. In A18 the open endings (marked 'aperto') all finish on D and the closed endings (marked 'chiuso') all end on F (the tonic or final of the hypolydian mode). In the same example the start of each pair of phrases is identified by a letter (A–D) and a number (1 being a phrase with an open ending and 2 a phrase with a closed ending). Thus the form of the whole istampita is AA'BB'CC'DD'. *EM 7.9.5.*

Italian-6th chord. A variety of augmented-6th chord containing the root and notes a major 3rd and an augmented 6th above it (B57, bars 38–40). *EM 5.7.4.*

J

Janissary music. 1. Turkish military instruments introduced into 18th-century orchestras, particularly opera orchestras. The orchestra for Mozart's 'Turkish' opera *Die Entführung aus dem Serail* (*The Abduction from the Harem*) includes a piccolo, triangle, cymbals and bass drum (the last of these played with a stick on one side, and a switch of twigs on the other. **2.** A style of music intended to imitate Turkish music (B37).

Jazz. In its early 20th-century form, a fusion of African and western styles of music characterised by vocal and instrumental improvisation, an insistent march-like beat, complex syncopation, blue notes, and simple formulaic harmonic progressions (often limited to chords I, IV and V). It is beyond the scope of this dictionary to cover what became the single most important and influential idiom of 20th-century music, though the influence of jazz on 20th-century art music is evident in many of the music examples, particularly C20 and C38.

The cakewalk originated in 19th-century African-American parodies of plantation owners' swaggering gait. In the early 20th century it became a popular dance characterised by the rhythm marked x at the start of C20 and the marching stride bass. Other features of this example are common to all types of early 20th-century jazz, such as the weak-beat syncopation at the end of bar 5 (and in the right-hand part thereafter) and blue notes formed by flattening the third, sixth and seventh degrees of the scale (as shown in the context of a descending scale of E♭ major).

By the third decade of the 20th century jazz had become a worldwide phenomenon, the sophistication of which may be judged by Walton's parody of one of its styles (C38). Rhythmic subtleties are set against the marching oom-pah rhythm of the cello (with cymbal backbeats). Although conventionally notated in $\frac{4}{4}$ time, the dotted rhythms of the melody are often performed like the swung rhythms shown above the first bar. The exact inequality of these rhythms is determined by the bass clarinettist, in the same way that *notes inégales* are determined by the harpsichordist on B17 (though there is no historical link between the two styles).

The clarinet, saxophone and drum kit (or drum set) are all instruments that regularly feature in jazz combos. Finally the complex chord on the second beat of the last bar is composed of a dominant-7th chord (on the bass stave) and a substitution chord (on the treble stave).

Both of these parodies of jazz style, however, lack the vital ingredient of real jazz – improvisation. *EM 8.11.8*.

Jazz band, jazz combo. In the first half of the 20th century, a jazz ensemble typically comprising melody instruments (the 'front line') such as the cornet, trumpet, clarinet, saxophone and trombone together with a rhythm section comprising a drum kit and harmony instruments such as the piano, guitar and banjo. The bass line was usually supplied by pizzicato double bass. Not all of these instruments would find a place in a typical jazz band, and other instruments might find a place according to the availability of instrumentalists. C38 is a pastiche of 1920s jazz, and the constitution of the band is atypical. Although saxophone and drum kit are represented, the front line includes a bass clarinet and a flute, while pizzicato cello doubles as a replacement for a piano, guitar or banjo (playing harmonies by triple and quadruple stopping). This type of jazz band was called a jazz combo to distinguish it from the big bands (in which instrumental melodies were doubled by several instruments) that developed in the mid-20th century.

Jazz quavers. The unequal performance of quavers in a range of jazz idioms. In C38 Walton notated the rhythms in the second to fourth beats of bars 1–3 as dotted rhythms in $\frac{4}{4}$ time, but jazz musicians often play such rhythms as approximate triplet groups. This is in keeping with the performance conventions of jazz, and it is, in fact, impossible to convey in conventional notation the exact degree of inequality in the performances of jazz musicians. *EM 1.6.5*.

Jeu de timbres (Fr.). Glockenspiel (C35, bar 2).

Jig. 1. An energetic dance of the British Isles dating back to at least the 16th century. Variants of it are still popular in contemporary

Jingles

folk music. **2.** An English name for a gigue (A90), which some think derived from the dance described above.

Jingles. 1. Sleigh bells (C49). **2.** The small thin metal discs set in the frame of a tambourine (C42).

Jubilus (Lat.). The lengthy melisma on the last syllable of a plainsong Alleluia (A5).

K

K, KV. Abbreviation of *Köchel-Verzeichnis*, a thematic catalogue of Mozart's works by Ludwig von Köchel. The K numbers given for B37–B50 are taken from *The New Grove Dictionary of Music and Musicians* (London, Macmillan, 1980), Volume 12, pages 725–747 (using Köchel's original numbering rather than K6). KA refers to items in the *Anhang* (appendix) of editions of the catalogue published before 1964.

Kadenz (Ger.). **1.** Cadence (A91 contains eight different cadences). **2.** Cadenza (C76, bar 5).

Kanon (Ger.). Canon (A92–A94).

Kantor (Ger.). A director of music in a Lutheran church. As *Kantor* of St Thomas's Church in Leipzig, Bach's duties included training choirs, conducting and writing cantatas (B7 and B8) and Passions (B4 and B5).

Kapellmeister (Ger.). Literally a 'chapel master', but by Bach's time a princely *Kapelle* was a musical establishment that could perform secular as well as sacred music. Indeed secular music would occupy more of a *Kapellmeister*'s time at a Calvinist court (where the role of church music in the liturgy was circumscribed). From 1717 to 1723 Bach was *Kapellmeister* at such a court (Cöthen), and it was during these years that he wrote some of his finest instrumental music (A87, A88, A90, A95–A98 and C93).

Kastagnetten (Ger.). Castanets (C50 and C52).

Kb. Abbreviation of *Kontrabass* (double bass). See C7.

Kesselpauke, Kesseltrommel (Ger.). Kettle drum (C27, timpani).

Kettle drums. Timpani (B36, bars 255–263, C27 and C82, bars 62–69). *EM 6.8.1.*

Key. 1. In tonal music, the relationships between pitches that establish the pre-eminence of one pitch above all others. The tonality of a particular passage of music is described in terms of this pre-eminent note (the tonic). B18 is described as being in the key of G major because the pre-eminence of G♮ has been established as early as the seventh note (which seeks resolution to the tonic, and achieves it two notes later). Similar relationships in A82 also establish G as the tonic, but here there is a B♭ and E♭ (instead of the B♮ and E♮ in B18). To distinguish the tonality of this music from the tonality of B18 the rondeau is described as being in the key of G minor. **2.** A lever on a keyboard that, when depressed, activates a mechanical or electronic device that causes a sound to be made. *EM 2.5, 2.6, 2.7.*

Key chord, tonic chord. A triad on the first degree of a scale. The first chord of B30 is the key chord of E major.

Key note. The tonic or first degree of a major or minor scale. The first note of A25 is the key note of D major.

Key signature. A group of flats or sharps placed immediately after the clef at the beginning of a stave (B64(a), bar 1) or immediately after a double bar (B64(a), bar 5). These flat and sharp signs indicate which notes are to be played flat or sharp whenever they appear on the same stave (unless they are contradicted by accidentals). In most cases key signatures give some indication of the tonality or key of the music written on the same stave. This is the case in B64(a) where the first key signature indicates the key of A♭ major and the second indicates the key of G major.

Keyboard. A set of keys on instruments such as the piano and organ. See the folded insert.

Keyboard instruments and keyboard music. See: *Clavichord* (B20), *Fortepiano* (B25), *Harpsichord* (B17), *Pianoforte* (B64–B67), *Regal* (A63), *Spinet* (A67), *Synthesiser* (A87). *EM 6.9.*

Keyed trumpet. In the late 18th century attempts were made to overcome the limitations of the natural trumpet (B15) by boring sound holes in the tube (similar to those in woodwind instruments). These were opened and closed by keys. The experiments were successful, and 1796 Haydn wrote a trumpet concerto for Anton Weidinger and the keyed trumpet in E♭ which he had developed. The solo part of this concerto contains passages that show off the ability of the keyed trum-

K. Fag

pet to play chromatically (B36, bars 92–97). Despite this the keyed trumpet was superseded by the valve trumpet (C81) in the early 19th century.

K. Fag., K-Fag. Abbreviations of *Kontrafagott* (contrabassoon). See C31.

Kirchenkantate (Ger.). Church cantata (B6–B8).

Kirchenmusik (Ger.). Church music (A68–A69, A91–A94, B4–B8, B15–B16).

Kirchenschluss (Ger.). Plagal cadence (A91, bars 3–4 and 31–32).

Kirchenton (Ger.). Church mode (A4 and A5).

Klagelied (Ger.). Elegy (C95).

Klangfarbenmelodie (Ger.). Tone-colour melody, a term invented by Schoenberg to describe a melody consisting of a succession of changing instrumental timbres. Five different timbres are heard in the seven-note melody at the start of C35. The term is also used of changing timbres on a single pitch (bar 12). See *Instrumentation* and *Orchestration*. *EM 3.7, 6.11.8, 8.11.3.*

Klarinette (Ger.). Clarinet (C79).

Klavier (Ger.). Keyboard, or keyboard instrument. When used without further qualification, *Klavier* now refers to the piano (B78).

Kleine Flöte (Ger.). Piccolo (C76, bars 9–11).

Kleine Trommel (Ger.). Snare drum (A74).

Kl. Fl. Abbreviation of *kleine Flöte*, German for piccolo (C76, bars 9–11).

Kl. in A, Kl. in B. Abbreviation of *Klarinette in A/B*, German for clarinet in A or B♭ (C79).

Klingen lassen (Ger.). Let it continue to sound. See *Laisser vibrer* and C97, bar 9.

Kl. Tr. Abbreviation of *kleine Trommel*, German for snare drum (C74).

Köchel numbers. See *K* and B37–B50.

Kontra C-Saite (Ger.). The fifth string that extends the range of a double bass down to the C three octaves below middle C (though many bass players prefer to tune it to B_2). With this extra string the sustained D heard in the first ten bars of C28 can be played.

Kontrabass (Ger.). Double bass (C7).

Kontrafagott (Ger.). Contrabassoon (C31).

Kontrapunkt (Ger.). **1.** Counterpoint (B13). **2.** Countersubject (B9).

Konzert (Ger.). **1.** Concerto (B36). **2.** Concert.

Konzertmeister (Ger.). The leader of an orchestra. Among many other duties the leader is expected to play solo parts (C97, bars 53–65).

Kornett (Ger.). Cornet (C3).

Kortholt (Ger.). Double-reed instruments of the 16th and 17th centuries including the early bassoon known as the dulcian or, in England, the curtal (A60).

Kreuz (Ger.). The sharp sign (♯). See *Accidental*, *Key signature* and B28, bars 0–3.

Krummhorn (Ger.). Crumhorn (A35).

Kujawiak (Pol.). A Polish folk dance and song in moderate triple time with prominent accents on the second and third beats of the bar. It is the slowest and most melancholy of the three main types of mazurka. B65 is a mazurka in the style of a Kujawiak.

Kunstlied (Ger.). Art song (B57) as opposed to folk song (B3).

KV., Kv. See *K* and B38–B50.

Kyrie (Gk.). Abbreviation of 'Kyrie eleison' (Lord have mercy on us), the first item of the Ordinary of the Mass. The full text reads 'Kyrie eleison, Christe eleison, Kyrie eleison'. The two Kyries are usually set to different music, hence Kyrie I and Kyrie II (A27, A28, A42, A43, A45, A46 and A52). *EM 8.4.1.*

L

La (Fr., It. and Span.). A♮. See *A*, the diagram of a keyboard on the folded insert and A3. Not to be confused with the tonic sol-fa syllable *lah* (the sixth degree of any major scale).

Lady Mass. A Mass setting devoted to the Blessed Virgin Mary. See *Votive Mass* and A21.

Lah. The sixth degree of any major scale in the British system of tonic sol-fa. In A25 the third note of bar 3 is *lah* in the key of D major.

Laissez vibrer (Fr.). A performance direction (often abbreviated to l.v.) requiring the performer to allow an instrument to continue to vibrate until the sound dies out naturally (C97, bar 9, cymbal and tam-tam).

Lament. An expression of grief or mourning. See *Elegy* (C95) and *Tombeau* (C33).

Landini cadence. Named after the 14th-century composer Francesco Landini, this was, in fact, a common cadence in 15th-century polyphony. Its essential feature was the interposition of the sixth degree of the mode between the leading note and its resolution to the final (A24, bars 24–25). *EM 5.4.8.*

Ländler (Ger.). An Austrian, south-German and German-Swiss folk dance dating from the 17th century. It was originally in slow triple time, but in the 18th century it became faster and was eventually superseded by the much faster 19th-century waltz (C2). *EM 8.10.4.*

Langsam (Ger.). Slow. 'Langsam und schmachtend' at the beginning of B68 means 'slow and languishing'. This direction is taken to mean very slow (quaver beat) in this context. See *Tempo markings*.

Largamente (It.). Broadly (C97, bar 27). See *Tempo markings*.

Largo, Larghetto (It.). Slow. There is some dispute about quite how slow a Largo should be, but there can be no doubt about Haydn's intentions in B30, 'Largo assai' clearly meaning 'very slow'. Larghetto is a slightly faster tempo than Largo. See *Tempo markings*.

Laute (Ger.), **Lauto** (It.). Lute (A89).

Lavolta (from the It. 'volta' – 'turn'). A late 16th-century dance described by contemporary authorities as resembling the galliard (A35).

Leadback. Retransition (B40, bars 68–71).

Leader. 1. An English name for *dux* (the part that first states a canonic melody). The 'follower' is the *comes* (A92). **2.** In an orchestra, the principal first violinist who is directly responsible to the conductor for technical matters ultimately affecting the whole orchestra. Among these duties the leader is expected to play solo passages when required (C97, bars 53–65).

Leading motif, leading motive. Leitmotif. The motif marked x in B68 is a leading motif.

Leading note, leading tone. The seventh degree of a major or minor scale. The leading note of G major is shown in context in B18 (note 7).

Leading-note-7th chord (chord VII^7). In its complete form, a leading-note triad with the addition of the note a 7th above the root. A complete secondary 7th on the flat leading note of B♭ minor is shown in B78(iii) where it is identified by the symbol ♭VII^7. It can be heard in the middle of a sequence of secondary-7th chords in bar 3 of Brahms's Intermezzo where it is presented as an arpeggio lacking the 5th of the chord (E♭) above the root (A♭) in the left-hand part. Built on the sharp leading note this particular 7th chord often has a strong dominant function. In E major the leading-note 7th consists of D♯ (the root), F♯ (the 3rd), A (the 5th) and C♯ (the 7th). In B30 a complete version of VII^7 is shown beneath the barline separating bars 4–5. The black note-head represents the 3rd of the chord which Haydn omits in his version of the chord (bar 4). A comparison of this chord with the complete dominant 9th (V^9) shows how similar they are. As expected of a chord with such strong dominant tendencies, VII^7 resolves to the tonic just as V$^9_5$ did in bars 2–3. A chromatic version of the leading-note 7th can be heard resolving to the tonic in bars 5–6 of B31.

Leading-note triad. A triad formed on the

leading note. In major keys (and minor keys when the seventh degree is sharpened) this is a diminished triad. In A73 the leading-note triad (VII) of B minor can be heard at the end of bar 7. *EM 5.1.3.*

Leap. A melodic interval greater than a tone. See A90, which begins with leaps of a rising fourth and a falling octave followed by a conjunct scale. *EM 4.3.7.*

Lebhaft (Ger.). Lively, animated. The term is synonymous with the Italian 'vivace' (B55). See *Tempo markings.*

Ledger lines. See *Leger lines* and B54.

Legato (It.). A smooth articulation of music without any breaks between successive notes. The melody of B67 is played legato. *EM 1.14.*

Leger lines, ledger lines. Extra short lines drawn above or below a stave to accommodate notes that are too high or too low to be represented on the stave itself (A3 and B54).

Leggero, leggiero, leggeramente (It.). Light, lightly (B73, bar 28).

Legni, i (It.). Woodwind. See *Woodwind instruments* and C77–C80.

Legno (It.). Wood. See *Col legno* and C36.

Leiter (Ger.). Scale (B18).

Leitmotif (Fr.), **Leitmotiv** (Ger.). A distinctive melodic fragment or musical idea that represents an emotion, idea, object or person in German romantic opera. A leading motive can be a simple varied repetition (compare the harmony and orchestration of bars 25–30 of B59 with bars 4–11 of B60), but in Wagner's music leading motives are more complex.

The first 24 bars of the Prelude to *Tristan und Isolde* contain the three leitmotifs shown in B68(ii). These have been identified with Tristan's grief (leitmotif 1), the lovers' desire for each other (leitmotif 2) and the fateful glance (leitmotif 3), but, whether or not Wagner had these ideas in mind, the way the potential of these motifs is exploited is of more importance. Motifs 1 and 2 are contrapuntally combined in the first seven bars, but as the opera unfolds it becomes increasingly obvious that, apart from the first note of motif 1, the two are closely related (x in bars 2–3 being an inversion of y in bars 1–3). In bars 8–11 Wagner adds one more chromatic step to both motifs, partly to increase the emotional intensity, partly to reach the dominant of the dominant of A minor (the tonic key of B68). Leitmotif 3 contains two smaller motives (a and b) which, in various forms, generate the extended melody of bars 19–23. *EM 3.4, 5.7.5, 8.10.1.*

Lent (Fr.), **Lento** (It.). Slow (C55 and C95). See *Tempo markings.*

Lesson. In England from the late 16th century to the 18th century, an instrumental composition of any type (rarely did the term imply any connection with musical education). By the beginning of the 18th century the term was most often used for keyboard dance movements (B18).

Letter names, letter notation. A type of musical notation that uses letters of the alphabet to identify the pitches of notes. In English the letters A to G signify the pitches shown on the keyboard on the folded insert (played as a scale on track A3). Unless qualified these letters refer to pitch classes (all A♯s, all B♭s, and so on). In this dictionary lower-case letters, upper-case letters, subscript numbers and superscript numbers identify the precise registers of letter-name pitches (as shown on the folded insert). In German the letter B means B♭ and the letter H means B♮.

Liaison (Fr.). **1.** Legato (C32, bars 9–21). **2.** A slur (C22, bar 1). **3.** A tie (A22, bar 8).

Liber usualis (Lat.). A book of liturgical texts and chants combining the most important items from other books devoted specifically to the Mass and Divine Office. A20 comes from the *Liber usualis.*

Libretto (It.). As commonly understood today, the text of an opera (A62–A63), oratorio (B15–B16) or cantata (B7–B8).

Licenza (It.). **1.** In the 17th and 18th centuries, passagework or cadenzas added by a soloist to the original composition (compare A65 with A66), or an epilogue added to a stage work for a particular occasion. **2.** In the phrase 'con alcuna licenza' (C4) the term means 'licence' or 'liberty' (ie with some rhythmic flexibility).

Lié (Fr.). **1.** Legato (C32, bar 9ff). **2.** Slurred (C33, left hand, bars 20–23). **3.** Tied (C33, bar 30).

Lied (Ger.), **Lieder** (pl.). Song. In this sense

the term can refer to any German song from the medieval *Minnelied* to the latest pop number. However, the term is most often reserved for German romantic songs with piano accompaniment. B57 and B58 illustrate the range of style and structure that the lied could encompass. Both are through-composed, but in 'Wohin?' a characteristic and continuous piano figuration suggests the babbling brook, whereas the chordal piano part of 'Der Doppelgänger' relies on extreme harmonic dissonance and chromaticism for its effect. Similarly the vocal part of 'Wohin?' is a periodically phrased cantabile melody, whereas the vocal part of 'Der Doppelgänger' is a sort of recitative that rises to a declamatory climax in bars 9–11. *EM 8.10.2.*

Lied ohne Worte (Ger.). Song without words, a term used by Mendelssohn for a character piece. Of the many piano pieces he wrote under this title B61 is one of the few that have programmatic subtitles.

Liederkreis, Liederzyklus (Ger.). Song cycle. B57 is a song from Schubert's cycle *Die schöne Müllerin*.

Ligature. 1. From the 12th to the 16th century, a single symbol representing two or more notes. Ligatures of this type have been rendered in modern notation in Volume 2. **2.** A slur over two or more notes to show they are to be sung to the same syllable (B50, bars 13 and 15). **3.** Some use the term to mean a tie (B50, bars 8–9).

Line. A melody as a single entity, or as part of a contrapuntal texture. Thus one may speak of the smooth melodic line sung by a soprano on A51, or of the line of the same melody considered as part of the four-voice imitative texture of bars 9–14 of A52.

Lion's roar, tambour (tambourin) à corde (Fr.). A drum with a string attached to the centre of the membrane. It is played by dragging a piece of well-rosined leather along the string (C46 and C52). *EM 6.8.2.*

Liquescent neume. A neume of two or more notes in which some are sung lightly in order to ensure a smooth delivery of the text. The notes that are to be treated in this way are notated in small print. In the first neume of A4 (a *cephalicus*), the second note is liquescent and is sung lightly in order to avoid too much emphasis on the adjacent consonants d and t ('Ad te').

Litany. A responsorial prayer in which a cantor sings a series of invocations or petitions, each of them answered by a phrase such as 'Ora pro nobis' (pray for us) or 'Kyrie eleison' (Lord have mercy) sung by the full choir or congregation (A42).

Liturgy. An officially approved Christian rite, the texts of such a rite, and (in some cases) the type of music to which these texts are sung (A4–A6, A8, A20, A40, A42, A49, A56, B4–B8, B15, B16, B62, C30). Not all sacred music is liturgical: A60 is chamber music, and C88 is concert music.

Liuto (It.). Lute (A89).

Livret (Fr.). Libretto (eg the texts of A62–A65).

Loco (It.). A performance direction countermanding an octave sign. At bar 21 in C9 the word 'loco' countermands the direction 'col 8' (played with the octave above) and reinforces the return to normal pitch shown by the end of the dotted line.

Lointain (Fr.). Distant. The second version of the *idée fixe* from Berlioz's *Symphonie fantastique* shown beneath B63 can be played by an off-stage clarinettist or by an on-stage performer playing so softly that the melody appears to come from the distance.

Lombard rhythm, Lombardic rhythm. See *Dotted rhythms* and z in A79. *EM 1.6.3.*

Long, longa (Lat.). A note, now obsolete, that is four or six times as long as a semibreve (depending on the mood). Below bars 7–10 in A13 the length of a long in minor mood is related to the tied semibreves on the stave. *EM 1.12.*

Lontano (It.). Distant. The recording on C97 was made at a performance in the Royal Albert Hall in London. The treble voices (bars 50–67) were positioned in the uppermost gallery a very long way indeed from the main body of performers and from most of the audience.

Loudness. The apparent strength or power of sound, loudness is roughly synonymous with intensity. The ear is not equally sensitive to sounds throughout the entire audible range of frequency. the highest and lowest pitches seem to have lower intensity levels. With age the ear becomes more insensitive to these extremes no matter how intense they are. Young people will find no difficulty in hearing all of the pitches shown in A1–A3

Loud pedal

while those of a certain age will be unable to hear several of the highest pitches and might hear a distorted version of the lowest pitches. See *Decibel* and *Intensity* and listen to A97 for extremely loud and extremely soft music.

Loud pedal. A colloquial term for the right-hand pedal of a piano. See *Sustaining pedal* and B66.

Lower auxiliary. See *Auxiliary note* and B30, bar 7 (F× and D♯). *EM 4.3.4.*

Lower mordent. A term used by some writers to describe a mordent consisting of the written note, the note a step below it, and the written note again (marked a in bars 1 and 17 of A84). See *Ornaments. EM 3.10.1, 3.10.2.*

Luftpause (Ger.). In vocal and wind music, a pause for breathing. In A22 the pause for breath (represented by a crotchet rest) can clearly be heard in bar 4 and (even though a rest is not marked) in bar 8.

Lugubre (It.). Mournful. The title of B74 refers to a gondola carrying the body of the deceased in a funeral cortège.

Lunga, lungo (It.). Long, as in 'lunga' above the chords and rests in the last two bars of C97 (indicating they are to be held longer than their printed time values).

Lusingando (It.). Caressing, coaxing. Even though C11 is marked 'Gemächlich' (taken from the start of the tone poem and meaning 'comfortable'), the term 'lusingando' exactly fits the mood of this passage.

Lustig (Ger.). Merry. The full title of the work from which C10 is taken is 'Till Eulenspiegels lustige Streiche' ('Till Eulenspiegel's Merry Pranks').

Lute, luth (Fr.). A fretted plucked string instrument of great antiquity. One of the most ubiquitous instruments of the late renaissance and baroque eras, it was used as an accompanimental instrument in lute songs, as one of the instruments in a continuo group, as an obbligato instrument (B5) and as a solo instrument (A89). *EM 6.4.2.*

Lutheran church music. A central tenet of Luther's reforms was an insistence on the use of vernacular (German) texts in all but a few items of new liturgies. He was also adamant that the congregation should play as full a part as possible in singing what had previously been the domain of trained choirs. To this end he adapted plainsong and secular songs to newly composed sacred German texts and himself composed new texts and melodies for congregational hymns that have come to be known as chorales. Bars 1–6 of B6 show the text and melody of a chorale that was almost certainly composed by Luther, while the rest of the example shows the melody as adapted by Bach. After Luther's death the prominent place assigned by him to such melodies continued to be apparent in the Lutheran cantata in which concerto-style orchestral music supported chorale melodies with which congregations would be familiar (B8). In Lutheran cantatas and Passions other elements that had developed in 17th-century Italy included dramatic recitatives and choruses (B4), arias (B15) and ariosos (B5).

Lydian cadence. An alternative name for the double-leading-note cadence (A24, bars 7–8). It gets its name from the lydian (sharpened) fourth degree of the mode (G♯). See *Lydian mode. EM 2.4.3.*

Lydian mode. A scale that can be reproduced by playing the white notes of the piano from any F♮ to the F♮ an octave above it (see the diagram of a keyboard on the folded insert and the scale shown beneath the last five bars of A19). This, the fifth church mode, is distinguished from other similar scales by semitones between the fourth and fifth and between the seventh and eighth degrees of the scale. Like most melodies in the untransposed lydian mode, the alto melody of the Agnus Dei in A19 ends on F♮ (appropriately called the final or *finalis*). The mode is altered in bar 6 by the appearance of a B♭. This is used to avoid a tritone between the outer parts at this point: otherwise every note of A19 conforms to the lydian mode. In fact such modal purity is uncommon in lydian mode melodies. Even in plainsong, melodies that are nominally in Mode V are frequently modified by the introduction of B♭s, thus effectively changing them to melodies in F major (as in the plainsong Benedictus shown in A20).

This plainsong melody is theoretically in the authentic lydian mode (even though B♭s are used) – its range extends from the final (F♮) to the note an octave above it. In its plagal form (Mode VI or the hypolydian mode) the final is the same, but the range (ambitus) extends from the note a 4th below the final to the note a 5th above it. In its untransposed form this means that all of the white notes from C–C are used, but the melody ends on F. Like major and minor scales the hypolydian mode can be transposed up or down by any interval. Such transposed scales will still be in Mode VI provided the same intervals are maintained between each pair of pitches. C57 shows a melody in the hypolydian mode transposed to A. The distinctive sound of the so-called 'lydian 4th' (D♯) is its most characteristic feature. Such pure lydian modality is very rare (notice that Bartók's added counter-melody in C58 studiously avoids D♯) but A18 is in the hypolydian mode throughout. *EM 2.4.1.*

Lyric. 1. Tuneful. C2 is one of Grieg's numerous *Lyric Pieces*. **2.** A light-toned voice, usually a soprano or tenor (B57).

M

Madrigal. 1. One of the most important secular musico-poetic forms of the Italian Ars Nova (14th century), it consisted of two (sometimes three) three-line stanzas sung to the same music followed by a couplet set to new music in a contrasting metre. This AAB (or, more rarely, AAAB) structure is similar to that of the French ballade (A12), but its two-part texture and melodic floridity contrast strongly with the style of its French counterpart. There is no connection between the medieval madrigal and the 16th-century madrigal. **2.** An Italian part song descended from the early 16th-century frottola (A30), it came to maturity in the 16th and early 17th centuries. A33 shows that even the earliest examples displayed a sophisticated blend of textures ranging from the homophonic style of the frottola (bars 1–10) to imitative counterpoint deriving from the contemporary motet (bars 23–29) as well as affective word-painting (eg the sustained chords on the flattened seventh degree of the scale to underline the word 'piangendo' in bars 6–7).

The English madrigal began life in 1588 when English words were added to Italian madrigals, but a native school soon developed. Morley acknowledges his debt when he calls the madrigal shown in A59 a canzonet (It. 'canzonetta'). It is in the light homophonic style that was typical of the genre, and the recurring fa-la-la refrains entitle it to be further classified as a type of madrigal known as a ballett (Italian 'balletto'). *EM 8.6.3.*

Madrigalism. Word-painting in 16th-century madrigals. In bars 6–7 of A33 a reference to 'weeping' brings with it the first chromatically inflected chord (a triad on the flattened seventh). In the closing bars the 'thousand deaths' are reflected in the first and only imitative passage (so the words are repeated over and over again like the thousand deaths).

Maestrale (It.). See *Stretto* and B14, bars 16–18.

Maestro (It.). In America and Italy a courtesy title for a conductor. In Britain a colloquial title for any musician of superior (or supposedly superior) ability. In Italy Sir Andrew Davis (the conductor of C97) would be addressed without irony as 'maestro Davis'. In Britain the same appellation would be used in a companionable manner among members of his orchestra. In the baroque era a *maestro di cappella* was the Italian equivalent of the German *Kapellmeister* (who often directed performances from the harpsichord as a *maestro al cembalo*).

Maestro di cappella (It.). Director of music of an important church or a princely chapel or court. Palestrina was *maestro di cappella* at St Peter's in Rome. His *Missa Iste confessor* (A52) was probably written for the choir of St Peter's (the Cappella Giulia).

Magadize (Gk.). To play or sing in octaves (C92, bars 1–5, tenor and first bass).

Maggiore (It.). Major. The term sometimes indicates a section in the major in a composition that is otherwise in the parallel minor key (A97).

Magnificat (Lat.). The song of the Blessed Virgin Mary (Luke 1, verses 46–55), this canticle is sung in the Roman Catholic service of Vespers and in the Anglican service of Evensong (C30).

Majeur (Fr.). Major. The term sometimes indicates a section in the major in a piece which is otherwise in the parallel minor key (A97).

Major. See *Chord* (the first four chords of C86), *Interval* (C58, bars 1 and 3), *Key* (the whole of A14 is in D major), *Scale* (the notes numbered 1–8 at the start of B18), *Triad* (A59, bar 1).

Major and minor triads. From the beginning of the 14th century the two most important types of chord in western music, major and minor triads are built from superimposed 3rds. In root position a major triad consists of a major 3rd plus a minor 3rd (A59, bars 1–2) while a minor triad consists of a minor 3rd plus a major 3rd (A35, bar 1). The expressive potential of these triads has been exploited from the renaissance to the present day, nowhere more overtly than in romantic compositions (compare the six-part trumpet chords in bars 5–6 of C27). *EM 5.3.2.*

Major mode and minor mode. See *Minor mode and major mode* and A96 (minor mode) and A97 (major mode).

Major pentatonic. Anhemitonic pentatonic music in which a major tonality is implied (C60).

Major 2nd. The interval between the first and second degrees of a diatonic major scale, and other intervals encompassing the same range. A major 2nd encompasses the same interval as two semitones. See *Intervals* and C81 (in which trumpets play in major 2nds throughout). *EM 2.2.3.*

Major 3rd. The interval between the first and third degrees of a diatonic major scale, and other intervals encompassing the same range. A major 3rd encompasses the same interval as four semitones. See *Intervals* and C58, bar 1. *EM 2.2.3.*

Major 6th. The interval between the first and sixth degrees of a diatonic major scale, and other intervals encompassing the same range. A major 6th encompasses the same interval as nine semitones. See *Intervals* and B68, bars 4–5 and 8. *EM 2.2.3.*

Major 7th. The interval between the first and seventh degrees of a diatonic major scale, and other intervals encompassing the same range. A major 7th encompasses the same interval as 11 semitones. See *Intervals* and A90, bars 28–29. *EM 2.2.3.*

Male alto. A name sometimes given to a countertenor (A12).

Male voices. 1. In a narrow sense, a term used for adult male voices excluding falsettists. This category includes tenors, baritones and basses (A8–A11). **2.** In a broader sense, a term used for male voices of all ages, including boy trebles, countertenors, tenors, baritones and basses. Stanford's Magnificat in C major was written for male-voice church choirs. An extract from it is sung by a male-voice cathedral choir on track C30.

Malinconico (It.). Melancholy, an expression mark not far removed from the Italian 'mesto' (mournful) that Bartók uses at the end of his sixth quartet (C72).

Mandolin, Mandoline (Fr. and Ger.), **mandolino** (It.), **mandolina** (Span.). A small plucked string instrument dating from the 16th century or earlier. There are usually four pairs of strings tuned like a violin (g, d^1, a^1, e^2) that are played with a plectrum. Its most characteristic sound is a tremolo (C29, bars 8, 10 and 12), but melodies that do not need much sustaining power are effective too (bars 5–7, 9 and 11 in the same example). The mandolin commonly used in the orchestra has a range of three octaves from the g a 4th below middle C. *EM 6.4.6.*

Manicorde (Fr.), **manicordio** (Span.), **manicordo** (It.). Clavichord (B20).

Manieren (Ger.). In the 18th century, ornaments (B1).

Manual. The keyboard of an organ or harpsichord. A84 was recorded on a harpsichord with two manuals, one loud (bars 1–5), the other soft (bars 5–9). *EM 6.9.1.*

Manualis (Lat.), **manualiter** (Ger.). A performance direction indicating that a composition is to be played on one or two manuals of an organ without the use of the pedals (A57).

Maracas. A pair of hollow gourds (or similarly shaped synthetic vessels) filled with dried seeds, beads or metal balls. The player grasps the attached handles and shakes the gourds to produce a rattling noise (C46 and C52). *EM 6.8.5.*

Marcato (marc.) (It.). Accented, marked, stressed, emphasised. In bars 78 and 86 of B73 accents are already marked: Liszt intends that the whole tune should be emphasised so that it becomes more prominent than the accompanying parts.

March. A composition in duple or quadruple time intended to accompany the formalised rituals of the military parade ground or battlefield. The essential element of a military march is a repeated drum rhythm such as that shown in the first two bars of C74. Marches have been used with programmatic intent in symphonic music since the early 19th century. C74 is meant to represent the distant sound of German troops approaching the beleaguered city of Leningrad in World War Two.

Marcia (It.). March (C74).

Marimba. A percussion instrument that looks like a large xylophone and is pitched an octave below it (see the folded insert). Its keys are much thinner than those of a xylophone, and, played with soft sticks, its tone

Markiert

is more mellow (compare C8 with C90). *EM 6.8.7.*

Markiert (Ger.), **marqué** (Fr.). See *Marcato* and bars 78 and 86 of B73.

Markig (Ger.). Vigorous. The term is almost synonymous with the Italian 'molto vivace' (C5). See *Tempo markings*.

Marsch (Ger.). March (C74).

Martellato (It.). A 'hammered' style of performance on a piano (C67, the semibreves in bars 11–14 where the effect is indicated by arrow heads beneath each note).

Masculine cadence. See *Feminine and masculine cadences* and B46. *EM 5.4.5.*

Mass. The most important service of the Roman Catholic Church in which the Last Supper is commemorated and the consecrated elements of bread and wine are consumed. Those parts of the Mass that are normally sung divide into two types: **a)** The Ordinary consists of those texts that never change – Kyrie (A27, A28, A45, A46 and A52), Gloria, Credo, Sanctus (the second part of this – the Benedictus – is shown in A21), Agnus Dei (A19 and A29). **b)** The Proper consists of those texts that change according to the time of year or the saint commemorated on a particular day – Introit (A4), Gradual, Alleluia (A5) or Tract, Offertory (A81 is played while the offertory text is said privately), Communion. *EM 8.4.1.*

Mass for the Dead. See *Requiem* and B62.

Mässig (Ger.). Moderate (B57). See *Tempo markings*.

Mastersinger. See *Meistersinger* and B6 (an example of a melody in bar form).

Mazur, mazurek (Pol.). A passionate Polish folk dance and song from the plains around Warsaw. It is in triple time with strong accents on weak beats and was one of the stylistic sources for Chopin's mazurkas (though B65 is too slow and melancholy to be classed as a *mazurek* itself).

Mazurka. A Polish national dance in triple time (B65). It is characterised by dotted rhythms (such as that labelled x in bar 6) and second- and third-beat accents (the former heard in bars 21, 23, 25 and 27, the latter in bars 7 and 15). The original dance was often accompanied by a bagpipe and its drones are suggested in B65 by the arpeggiated chords (containing the tonic, C♯, and dominant, G♯) in bars 5–8 and 13–16. See *Kujawiak. EM 8.10.4.*

Me. The third degree of any major scale in the British system of tonic sol-fa. The third note of A25 is *me* in the key of D major.

Measure, mesure (Fr.), **misura** (It.). Bar. In metrical music, a unit of time containing a fixed number of beats or pulses. In staff notation a measure is contained between two vertical barlines. In A35 the metrical unit is a measure of three quarter-note pulses in the pattern strong–weak–weak. Each measure contains note-values (or, in the last measure, a note-value and a rest) that equate with three quarter-notes.

Measured and unmeasured music. Early neumatic notation (A4) precisely represented the relative pitches of a melody but gave little indication of its rhythm. This unmeasured music is now usually performed monophonically and without an obvious beat, the freely flowing rhythms being largely governed by the Latin text (except for lengthy melismas). It was not until the turn of the 12th century that a notational system was developed which allowed rhythms to be accurately represented. The difference between unmeasured and measured music may be judged by listening to A9 and A10 (though we have no way of knowing whether the singing on A9 accurately reflects contemporary practice).

Measured organum. See *Organum* and A10.

Medial cadence. 1. Any cadence in which the penultimate chord is inverted (A91, bars 11–12). **2.** In plainsong, a cadence on a note other than the final (A4, end of first stave). *EM 5.4.1, 5.4.2.*

Mediant. The third degree of a diatonic scale. It is shown in the context of a G major scale in B18 (third note).

Mediant-7th chord (chord III[7]). In its complete form, a mediant triad with the addition of the note a 7th above the root. A complete mediant 7th in B♭ minor is shown in B78(iii) where it is identified by the symbol III[7]. It can be heard in the middle of a sequence of secondary-7th chords in bar 4 of Brahms's intermezzo where it is presented as descending and ascending arpeggios above the root (D♭) in the left-hand part.

Mediant triad (chord III). A three-note chord consisting of the mediant (the root) and notes a 3rd and 5th above it. In the key of G minor the mediant is B♭, so the mediant triad consists of B♭ (the root), D♮ (the 3rd), and F♮ (the 5th). Because in minor keys the major triad on the mediant contains the flat leading note it is often found in modal-sounding progressions. This is particularly true in B61 where it is preceded by a triad on the flat leading note (♭VII). Nevertheless the key of G minor is emphasised by the cadential progression that follows (VI–I$^6_4$–V^7–I). When in minor keys the 5th of the mediant triad is sharpened a startling augmented triad is formed. This is the chord shown on the first of the extra staves below A81. Couperin uses it in first inversion in the wonderfully astringent harmony of bars 13–14. See *Triad*. *EM 5.1.3*.

Medieval music. Music from the 6th to the early 15th centuries. The beginnings of medieval music are obscure because staff notation was unknown until the 11th century and even then it is too vague to be rendered into modern notation with any degree of rhythmic precision. What is known of early medieval music derives from treatises such as *Musica enchiriadis* (from which A7 is taken). As with all historical periods in music there is no clear boundary between medieval and renaissance music, but most would agree that Machaut (A21–A23) was one of the last and greatest medieval composers and that Dufay's works (A27) are among the first flowerings of renaissance polyphony. See *Ars Antiqua* (A10–A11, A15 and A16) and *Ars Nova* (A19–A23).

Meistersinger (Ger.). Master singer. A member of one of the guilds of musicians that flourished in Germany from the 14th to the 17th century. The chorale melody of B6 is a typical example of the bar-form songs of the mastersingers (though it is reputed to have been composed by Martin Luther).

Melisma (Gk.). A group of notes sung to one syllable (A9).

Melismatic organum. See *Organum* and A9. *EM 8.5.1*.

Melismatic style. A type of plainsong characterised by lengthy melismas (A9). *EM 8.4.1*.

Melodic interval. See *Intervals* and C95, bars 11–13. *EM 2.2*.

Melodic inversion. See *Inversion* and C82, bars 14–33.

Melodic minor scale. A minor scale in which the sixth and seventh degrees are raised a semitone ascending and returned to key-signature pitch descending. All of the notes of both forms of a melodic minor scale on G are included in A83 and the scale itself is shown on an extra stave. *EM 2.3.3*.

Melodic sequence. See *Sequence* and B7, bars 7–12.

Mélodie (Fr.). **1.** Melody (A22). **2.** A solo art song of the 19th or 20th centuries, it was the French counterpart of the German romantic lied (B57). Perhaps the most famous example of the genre is Fauré's *Après un rêve*. *EM 8.6.3*.

Melodrama. A dramatic presentation in which spoken words are accompanied or punctuated by instrumental music. Complete works of this type were written from the 18th century on, but the technique is best known in certain scenes from operas such as Weber's *Der Freischütz* (B60). Not to be confused with 'melodramma'. *EM 8.10.1*.

Melodramma (It.). A text written to be set to music. Alessandro Striggio's libretto for Monteverdi's *Orfeo* (A62–A66) is an early example. The term has been used for many different types of libretto and opera including several of Verdi's operas. It should not be confused with 'melodrama'.

Melody. A rhythmically organised succession of single pitches coherently related to each other. Rhythmic organisation is most often related to metre (A41) but need not be (A40). The succession of single pitches may be heard alone (A41), or as one strand in a contrapuntal texture (A44, soprano, bars 1–9), or as a melody that dominates a subservient accompaniment (B49). Coherent relationships between individual pitches might contribute to and derive from overarching tonality (E♭ and B♭ major in C20) or the use of some other organising principle (restriction to six pitch classes in C21). See *Interval* and *Key*. *EM 3, 4.4.1*.

Membranophone. A category of musical instruments that generate sound by the vibration of a stretched membrane (eg the drums on track C45). See *Instruments*. *EM 6.8*.

Meno (It.). Less. The direction 'un poco

Mensural music

meno mosso' above bar 69 of C82 means 'a little less fast'. See *Tempo markings*.

Mensural music. Medieval music written down in such a way that it is possible to determine its rhythms (A10 and A11 show some very early mensural music transcribed into modern notation). See *Measured and unmeasured music*.

Menuet (Fr.), **Menuett** (Ger.). Minuet (B25)

Menuetto. A late 18th-century neologism for a non-Italian minuet (B25).

Messe (Fr. and Ger.). Mass (see the titles of A19 and A21).

Mesto (It.). Sorrowful (C72).

Mesure (Fr.). Bar or metre (A35 is in triple metre with three crotchet beats per bar).

Metallophone. A category of musical instruments consisting of rows of tuned metal bars that are struck with mallets. They are of great antiquity and are found throughout the far east. Several western percussion instruments are modelled on them, notably the celesta (C28, bars 15–18), the glockenspiel (C35, bar 2) and the vibraphone (C87).

Metamorphosis. See *Thematic transformation* and C18.

Metre, meter. The organisation of regular pulses (heard or implied) into repeating patterns of strong and weak beats. These patterns are called bars, and when the music is written down one bar is separated from the next by a vertical line known as a barline. In B36 each bar contains two beats (strong–weak) which establish duple metre (or duple time). In A26 each bar contains three beats (strong–weak–weak) which establish triple metre (or triple time). In A25 each bar contains four beats (strong–weak–strongish–weak) which establish quadruple metre (or quadruple time).

When the beat divides into shorter notes based on the ratio 2:1 (as in B36) the music is said to be in simple time (in this case, simple duple time). When the beat divides into shorter notes based on the ratio 3:1 the music is said to be in compound time. In A14 the beat is represented by the dotted crotchets shown beneath the first four bars of the melody. In bar 2 it can be seen that this beat can divide into a group of three quavers (unlike the groups of four or two quavers in B36). Nevertheless this music is also in duple time since it divides into metrical units with the pattern strong–weak. So the metre of the hymn can be fully described as compound duple time.

Not all music is metrical (no regular pulse can be felt in A4) and metrical patterns can be more complex than those described above. In *Stollen* 1 of B6 duple and triple time, and simple and compound time alternate. Yet it is possible to feel a regular crotchet beat (like that in *Stollen* 2) against which these complex rhythms are projected (so there is no complete metrical disruption when Luther's melody flows straight into Bach's metrically simple version of it). In addition to a strong accent on the first beat of the bar, quintuple metres often have a secondary accent on the third or fourth beat of the bar, thus making for what is aurally perceived as an alternation of duple + triple time, or triple + duple time. This is the case in C36 where every bar divides into 3+2 units (emphasised by the triplet rhythm on beat 1 and the two quavers on beat 4, and further emphasised by the rhythm of the melody which moves on the same beats). A similar sort of asymmetrical metre (3+3+2) can be heard on tracks C66 and C67. *EM 1.3*.

Metrical psalm. See the box on page 101. *EM 8.6.2*.

Metrical rhythm. Rhythm that is governed by an underlying metrical unit. In B15 the metrical unit is a minim (half-note) that divides into two crotchet (quarter-note) pulses repeated throughout the aria in the pattern strong–weak. The note-values in every bar add up to a minim, and the rhythms are governed by the strong–weak metre that underpins the whole aria.

Metronome. A mechanical or electronic device that maintains a steady beat heard as clicks or seen as flashes (or both). Most metronomes are calibrated to allow tempos ranging from about 40 to 208 beats per minute to be set. Metronomes are not intended to be used throughout a piece to maintain a rigid beat since one of the most important expressive elements in music is rhythmic flexibility whilst maintaining the same overall tempo. The mechanical sound of A87 is in large measure attributable to an absolutely rigid tempo of 96 beats per minute (ensured by the electronic controls of the synthesiser that generated the performance). Compare this with the musical interpretation of the opening of a fugue heard on B9.

Metallico (It.). Metallic. In the context of bars 9–16 of C68 this performance direction is observed by plucking the strings as near to the bridge as possible.

Mezza voce (It.). Half voice, restrained (B30, bar 1).

Mezzoforte (*mf*) (It.). Moderately loud (B59, bar 17). See *Dynamics*.

Mezzopiano (*mp*) (It.). Moderately soft (C94, bar 3). See *Dynamics*.

Mezzo-soprano. A female voice intermediate in range between a soprano and a contralto (C91).

Mezzo-soprano clef. One of the moveable C clefs. It shows that notes on the second line up of the stave are middle Cs. The mezzo-soprano clef is now obsolete, but can be found in 19th-century vocal scores. See A30.

Mf (*mf*). Abbreviation of *mezzoforte* (B59, bar 17).

Mi (Fr., It. and Span.). E♮. See *E*, the diagram of a keyboard on the folded insert and A3. Not to be confused with the tonic sol-fa syllable *me* (the third degree of any major scale).

Microphone technology. The use of microphones to enhance, distort, manipulate or amplify the sound of instruments or voices (C91).

Microtone. An interval smaller than a semitone. In bars 6, 8 and 9 of C70 the second violin plays the written notes while the other violinist plays these notes a quarter of a tone flat. Thus there is a microtonal interval between the two instruments.

Middle C. The C♮ nearest the centre of most keyboards. It usually has a frequency of 261.63 Hz and can be written on a leger line immediately below a treble stave or on a leger line immediately above the bass stave (see the folded insert, A2 and A3).

Middle entry. A statement of the subject in the central section of a fugue (B14, bass, bars 11–12). *EM 4.5.5*.

Military drum, Militärtrommel (Ger.). A large snare drum or field drum with snares (C45 and C52).

Military band. The use of trumpets and drums to give signals on the battlefield dates back to ancient times. By the 16th century these were supplemented by a range of wind instruments including shawms (A32), cornetts and sackbuts (A58). By the late 18th century the foundations of the modern military band had been established. Typically it would consist of trumpets (B15), horns (C84), oboes

---

Metrical psalm

A version of a psalm in which a metrically free English translation of the Bible or Book of Common Prayer is rendered in metrical rhyming verse. For instance:

Why do the heathen so furiously rage together:	Why fum'th in fight the Gentiles' spite, in fury raging stout?	8 6 A
And why do the people imagine a vain thing?	Why tak'th in hand the people fond, vain things to bring about?	8 6 A
The kings of the earth stand up, and the rulers take counsel together:	The Kings arise, the Lords devise, in counsels met thereto,	8 6 B
Against the Lord, and against his Anointed.	Against the Lord with false accord, against his Christ they go.	8 6 B
Book of Common Prayer, Psalm 2, verses 1 and 2	*Archbishop Parker: The Whole Psalter Translated into English Metre (A37)*	

The right-hand columns show the absolute metricality of Parker's verse and his use of rhyming couplets (AA, BB). Tallis's homophonic setting loosens this rigidity by constant metrical shifts (A37). But it was Parker's relentless metricality that enabled Vaughan Williams, as musical editor, to choose Tallis's lovely psalm tune for the *English Hymnal* of 1906 (though new words by Addison with the same metre replaced Parker's doggerel). So, although Tallis's melody began life as a metrical psalm tune, it was most widely disseminated as a hymn (like many other metrical psalm tunes).

Mineur

(C78), bassoons (C77) and percussion (perhaps including Janissary instruments).

In addition to these instruments a modern military band contains most if not all of the following: flute and piccolo (C76), clarinets (C10 and C79), saxophones (C38), cornets (C3), trombones (C75), euphoniums (C37), tubas (C28, bars 1–7).

Mineur (Fr.). Minor. The term sometimes refers to a passage in the minor in a piece that is otherwise in the parallel major key (C32, bars 9–21).

Minim, minima (It. and Lat.). Half-note ($\rfloor$). See *Note* and the first note of each voice part in bars 1–4 of A52.

Minimalism. A late 20th-century reaction against the complexity of modernist compositions such as *Le marteau sans maître* by Boulez (C87) and Stravinsky's *Canticum sacrum* (C88). In *Clapping Music* (C89) Steve Reich strips music to the bare minimum – no melody, no harmony, no instruments, no voices – just a single rhythmic pattern clapped by two performers. *EM 8.11.10, 8.11.11.*

Minnelied (Ger.). One of the three main types of *Minnesang* written in Germany from the late 12th century to the early 14th century. Some had the same strophic AAB form as the trouvère ballade (A12). This bar form is evident in the true *Minnelied* shown in A13, in which the first two sections (AA) are called *Stollen* and the last section (B) is called the *Abgesang*. As with the French ballade, phrases from the *Stollen* often crop up in the *Abgesang* (compare x and y in the first *Stollen* with the same phrases in the *Abgesang*).

A13 is in a major key (by no means were all medieval songs modal), and this makes it easy to hear the typical open and closed endings. These are like the first-time and second-time bars in a phrase that is to be repeated (the second four-bar phrase of each *Stollen* being a repeat of the first apart from the cadence). The effect is of an imperfect cadence (bars 5–6) being answered by a perfect cadence (bars 9–10).

Der Unverzagte was a late 13th-century German Minnesinger who specialised in character portraits (sometimes character assassinations) of royal figures such as Emperor Rudolf I. The instrumental performance on A13 features a plucked citole (*Stollen* 1 and *Abgesang*) and a bowed vielle (*Stollen* 2), the whole accompanied by the drones of a second vielle. *EM 7.9.1, 8.4.2.*

Minnesang (Ger.). German courtly monophonic song of the 12th to 14th centuries. One of the three main forms of *Minnesang*, the *Minnelied* (A13), may be taken as an example of the extant melodies that owe much to contemporary trouvère songs.

Minnesinger (Ger.). German poet-musicians of the 12th to 14th centuries. They cultivated a variety of genres, among which the *Minnelied* (A13) is particularly famous.

Minor. See *Chord* (C86, bar 5), *Intervals* (the first two notes of B68), *Key* (the whole of A95 is in D minor), *Scale* (A82 and A83), *Tonality* and *Triad* (A35, bar 1).

Minor mode and major mode. Terms used to distinguish between the minor and major tonalities of passages of music sharing the same tonic. A96 is in the minor mode, A97 is in the major mode, the tonic of both being D.

Minor pentatonic. Anhemitonic pentatonic music in which minor tonality is implied (C61).

Minor 2nd. The interval between the second and third degrees of a diatonic minor scale and other intervals encompassing the same range. A minor 2nd encompasses the same interval as one semitone. See *Intervals* and x in bars 11–12 of C85 (all pairs of notes identified by the letter x are semitones, but some of them are not notated as minor 2nds). *EM 2.2.3.*

Minor 3rd. The interval between the first and third degrees of a diatonic minor scale and other intervals encompassing the same range. A minor 3rd encompasses the same interval as three semitones. See *Intervals* and C78, bars 1–3 (in which the oboes play in parallel minor 3rds throughout). *EM 2.2.3.*

Minor 6th. The interval between the first and sixth degrees of a harmonic minor scale and other intervals encompassing the same range. A minor 6th encompasses the same interval as eight semitones. See *Intervals* and B68, bars 0–1. *EM 2.2.3.*

Minor 7th. The interval between the first and seventh degrees of the dorian mode (A40) and other intervals encompassing the same range. A minor 7th encompasses the same interval as ten semitones. See *Intervals* and C79 (in which the clarinets play in parallel minor 7ths throughout). *EM 2.2.3*.

Minore (It.). Minor. See *Mineur* and bars 9–21 of C32.

Minstrel. Professional itinerant musician of the middle ages often employed as accompanists by aristocratic southern French troubadours, northern French trouvères (A12) and German minnesingers (A13).

Minuet and trio. The minuet was a courtly French dance of the baroque era in moderate triple time, and one of the many binary-form 'optional' dances of the late baroque suite. In this context minuets often appeared in pairs with the first repeated after the second to form an overall ternary structure: Minuet 1–Minuct 2 Minuet 1. The second minuet was sometimes called a trio, a name deriving from the 17th-century practice of reducing the scoring of ensemble minuets to three instruments (thereafter the term lost this meaning).

In the classical era the minuet and trio combination survived as a movement in orchestral and chamber works. A complete minuet and trio is shown in B25. Its structure is typical of both the baroque and classical minuet and trio save for the fact that the repeats of the two sections in both the minuet (AB) and trio (CD) are not observed in the recording on B25 (but the da capo is performed, giving an overall structure AB–CD–A'B'). When the minuet is repeated (A'B') it is embellished with the sort of elegant ornamentation that is typical of the gallant style of 18th-century minuets. Later in the 18th century such ornamentation tended to be written out, and the textures of minuets, particularly those that formed the third movement of string quartets, became more varied (B38). *EM 7.5.2, 8.8.2, 8.9.1.*

Minuetto (It.). Minuet. The Italians would have called Haydn's 'Menuetto' (B25) a 'minuetto'.

Mirror canon. A canon in which the *comes* is a retrograde inversion of the *dux*. In the mirror canon in bars 2–5 of C88 the *dux* is the tenor part which is imitated by the retrograde inversion played by cor anglais, flute and harp. The term is also used of canons in which the *comes* is a retrograde or inversion of the *dux*. See *Mirror composition* and C64, bars 6–9.

Mirror composition. 1. A composition in which original material can be performed backwards (in B25 the first ten bars are played backwards in bars 11–20). **2.** A composition in which a melody is inverted (in the canon heard in bars 6–9 of C64 the *comes* is an inversion of the *dux*).

Missa (Lat.). Mass (A52 is a Kyrie from a Mass).

Missa pro defunctis (Lat.). Latin name for Mass for the Dead. It is better known as a Requiem Mass, a title taken from the Introit 'Requiem aeternam dona eis Domine' (Grant them eternal rest O Lord). As well as familiar items of the Ordinary (Kyrie, Sanctus and Benedictus, and Agnus Dei) and Proper (Introit, Gradual, Offertory and Communion) the Missa pro defunctis includes the sequence 'Dies irae' (B62 and C96).

Misterioso (It.). Mysterious (C97, bar 50).

Misura (It.). **1.** Beat. **2.** Bar (measure). **3.** Metre (time, meter).

'Senza misura' means 'in free time' (as in bar 5 of C76). 'Alla misura' means 'in strict time' (as in bars 6–13 of the same example).

Mixed voices. A group containing both female and male singers. A33 is sung by a female soprano and male alto, tenor and bass.

Mixolydian mode. A scale that can be reproduced by playing the white notes of the piano from any G♮ to the G♮ an octave above it (see the diagram of a keyboard on the folded insert and the scale shown beneath A28). This, the seventh church mode, is distinguished from other similar scales by semitones between the third and fourth and between the sixth and seventh degrees of the scale. Like most melodies in the untransposed mixolydian mode, the tenor melody of A28 ends on G♮ (appropriately called the final or *finalis*). The mode is altered by the singer's B♭ in bar 5. Such *musica ficta* is used here to avoid outlining the interval of a tritone between B♮ and the F♮ two notes earlier. The modal purity of the alto melody is similarly altered by F♯ in the same bar (used to form a more definitive cadence). B♭s are common in plainsong, but the inclusion of an F♯ in Obrecht's Kyrie is indicative of the gradual move from modality to modern major/minor tonality that is evident in sacred styles from the 15th century through to the 17th century.

The tenor part of A28 is in the authentic mixolydian mode – its range extends from

Mixture stop

the final (G♮) to the F♯ a 7th above it. In its plagal form (Mode VIII or the hypomixolydian mode) the final is the same, but the range (ambitus) extends from the note a 4th below the final to the note a 5th above it. The plainsong melody shown in A4 conforms precisely to this definition of Mode VIII. A49, like many modal melodies, has a range that only approximates to modal theory. *EM 2.4.1.*

Mixture stop. An organ stop containing a mixture of ranks. In A86 the mixture stop contributes to the brilliance of the full organ (*organo pleno*).

MM, M.M. Abbreviations of Maelzel's metronome. The letters are conventionally followed by a note and a number, although it is more common nowadays to take the letters for granted and give only note and number. These indicate how fast the beat is in terms of beats per minute, and they give a much more accurate impression of the composer's intention than Italian tempo marks. Bartók uses both at the head of C70. See *Tempo markings*.

Modal music. Music characterised by the use of modes. Ancient music can be entirely modal (A5). But the use of a B♭ (the only accidental found in Gregorian chant) can so alter modality that the music sounds as though it is founded upon one of the modern diatonic scales. This is the case in A20 where a plainsong melody nominally in Mode V (F to F on the white notes of a piano) is actually in F major because the characteristic lydian fourth degree of the mode (B♮) is negated by the accidentals.

The practice of sharpening the leading note in renaissance music further eroded the modal system (compare A50 and A51 – the first is in the mixolydian mode, but the F♯ introduced at the cadence of the Kyrie suggests the key of G major). Many medieval compositions, although theoretically in the so-called ionian mode, are, to all intents and purposes, in a major key (A14). Conversely music of the last 150 years is sometimes completely modal (A57), or contains modal passages (C33). See *Modes* 1. *EM 8.11.5, 8.11.6.*

Modal rhythm. See *Rhythmic modes* and A10.

Modality. Those characteristics of a composition that can be explained by reference to modal theory. In A4 phrases 1, 5, 7, 9, 11 and 13 end on G and the pitches used span a range (*ambitus*) from D to D. It is thus a textbook example of music in Mode VIII (the hypomixolydian mode). Modal theories attempted to categorise music that had already been written, but from earliest times modal music often included pitches that could not be explained by these theories. Thus, although the Benedictus shown in A20 is ascribed to Mode V (F to F on the white notes of the piano) in officially approved collections of plainsong, the characteristic B♮ of this mode is flattened by the only accidental that regularly appears in Gregorian plainsong. The result of this use of accidentals is a melody which to modern ears sounds as though it is F major. Machaut's isorhythmic version of the same melody includes both a B♮ and a B♭, and this modal ambivalence is evident in other voices of his polyphonic setting (A21). See *Aeolian mode, Church modes* and *Ionian mode*. *EM 2, 2.4, 2.4.4.*

Mode of vibration. The manner in which a stretched string or a column of air vibrates. In bar 11 of C95 a stretched string is made to vibrate throughout its whole length (first note), then in halves (second note), then in thirds (third note), then in quarters (fourth note). As the table of nodes shows, this process continues until the string is vibrating in ten discrete parts of its length in the last note the cellist plays. This is a somewhat simplified explanation of modes of vibration because it describes only the patterns of vibration pertaining to the perceived pitch of each note (the fundamental). In fact higher modes of vibration are also present even when the cellist reaches the tenth harmonic (bars 13–14). See *Harmonics. EM 6.2.*

Moderato (It.). At a moderate tempo (B66). See *Tempo markings*.

Modéré (Fr.). Moderato (C21). See *Tempo markings*.

Modernism. 1. A term commonly used in America in the second quarter of the 20th century encompassing the then modern styles of composers such as Schoenberg (C34), Webern (C35), Varèse (C42–C54) and Bartók (C69–C72). **2.** As most commonly used in the second half of the 20th century, a term that encompassed the styles of composers such as Boulez (C87), whose chief inspiration came from the serial music of Webern. Stravinsky, whose many-faceted musical styles reflected most of the enduring strands of 20th-century music, adopted a typically idiosyncratic version of serialism towards the end of his life (C88). *EM 8.11.9, 8.11.11.*

Modes. 1. For dorian and hypodorian modes, see *Dorian mode*, A40 (Mode I) and A8 (Mode II);
for phrygian and hypophrygian modes, see *Phrygian mode*, A37 (Mode III) and A5 (Mode IV);
for lydian and hypolydian modes, see *Lydian mode*, A19 (Mode V) and A18 (Mode VI);
for mixolydian and hypomixolydian modes, see *Mixolydian mode*, A28 (Mode VII) and A4 (Mode VIII);
for aeolian and hypoaeolian modes, see *Aeolian mode*, A42 (Mode IX) and B61 (Mode X);
for ionian and hypoionian modes, see *Ionian mode*, A16 (Mode XI) and A13 (Mode XII).

Modes I–VIII are the ancient church modes. Modes IX–XII were added to modal theory by Glareanus in the 16th century. The purely theoretical locrian mode (B–B on the white notes of a keyboard) was avoided because of the tritone between the final and the dominant. It is not illustrated in this dictionary. *EM 2.4.* **2.** See *Rhythmic modes* and A10. *EM 1.12.* **3.** See *Mode of vibration* and C95.

Modes of limited transposition. A term invented by Messiaen to describe scales that can be transposed only a few times before the same set of notes is repeated. They are all 'artificial' scales that are unrelated to the church modes or to major and minor scales. None of them generates a tonal centre. Instead they produce consistent and distinctive harmonic colours that can be distinguished from one another by the unaided ear. Messiaen's Modes 1 and 2 have been used by many 20th-century composers. The first of them is the same as a whole-tone scale. An example of it is shown at the start of C21. It consists of the notes G♯–A♯–C–D–E–F♯–G♯ (reading up). If this is transposed up a semitone a new whole-tone scale will be produced (A–B–C♯–D♯–F–G–A). But if it is transposed up a further semitone the same set of pitches as those in the original scale will emerge (A♯–C–D–E–F♯–G♯–A♯). Further transpositions of this sort produce either the original set of pitches, or a set of pitches identical to the pitches contained in the first transposition. Thus a whole-tone scale can be transposed only once. Messiaen's second mode is an octatonic scale. One version of this scale of alternating tones and semitones is shown in C64. It can be transposed up a semitone and a tone, but a third transposition (up a minor 3rd) produces the same set of pitches as those in the original scale. The scale shown in C55 consists of two structurally identical hexachords (three semitones, a tone and a semitone reading up). This is Messiaen's seventh mode of limited transposition, and the pitches he selected from this mode to form the first five chords of the organ piece are identified on an extra stave beneath the organ part. Mode 7 can be transposed six times before the set of pitches in the original scale is repeated. *EM 2.8, 8.11.2.*

Modo (It.). Mode (A8).

Modulating sequence. See *Sequence* and B17.

Modulation. The process by which the key of one passage of music is supplanted by another key. In phrase 1 of B49 the key of G major is established by the violin melody and the tonic and dominant chords that accompany it. The introduction of C♯ at the start of the second phrase destabilises the tonality of G major, and the modulation to D major is finalised by the cadence D–C♯–D in the last two bars of the melody and by the tonic and dominant chords in the new key. See also *Harmony* and *Tonality*. *EM 2.5, 4.5.1, 5.6, 7.4.5.*

Modus (Lat.). Mode. See *Church modes*, *Modes*, and *Rhythmic modes* (A10)

Moll (Ger.). Minor. A87 is in C-moll.

Molta, molto (It.) Very. 'Con molta espressione' at the head of B78 means 'with much expression' and 'Molto rall.' at the end of C84 means 'getting very much slower'. See *Tempo markings*.

Monacordio (Span.). Clavichord (B20).

Monocordo (It.). In string playing, a performance direction requiring that a certain passage of music be played on one string. The Roman numeral IV in C70 indicates that bars 5, 7 and 9 should be played on the lowest (G) string of the violin.

Monody

Monody. 1. A synonym of monophony (A4 and A22). **2.** Any of the many types of solo song with continuo accompaniment that flourished in Italy during the first half of the 17th century, especially recitatives (A62 and A63) and arias (A65). *EM 6.11.2, 8.7.1.*

Monophony. Music consisting of a single unaccompanied melody whether sacred (A4–A6, A8, A20) or secular (A22 and A23). *EM 6.11.1, 8.4.*

Monothematic. An adjective describing compositions based upon one theme. A fugue is usually monothematic since it is dominated by its subject or motifs derived from the subject. Apart from non-thematic figuration (z and the music in the last two bars) B14 is based on the subject and the two motifs that are its constituent parts (x and y). Monothematicism can prevail in other types of composition. The sonata-form Andante that opens Haydn's string quartet Op. 42 is almost entirely based on motifs a, b, c and d shown in bars 1–8 of B27 (which also shows how they are manipulated in the exposition of the movement). *EM 3.2.2, 8.9.1.*

Monotone. A single sustained note or a succession of notes of the same pitch (C69, bars 1–2).

Montre (Fr.). A principal stop on a French baroque organ. The pipes are displayed on the front of the organ case, hence 'montre' (meaning 'show'). It acts as an 8-foot foundation stop in the *grand jeu* heard on track A81.

Mood. In medieval mensural notation, the relationship between the durations of the long (*longa*) and breve (*brevis*). In minor mood (*modus minor*) the long is worth two breves or four semibreves (see A13, bars 7–10 and 19–20).

Morceau (Fr.). Piece (A84).

Mordent. A melodic ornament of two types: **a)** The lower mordent consists of the written note, the note a step below it and the written note again. The conventional symbol for a lower mordent is shown in bar 1 of A84 (letter a) and its written-out form appears in bar 17 (also marked with the letter a). In German this is simply called a *Mordent*. **b)** The upper mordent consists of the written note, the note a step above it and the written note again (B25, bars 56, 58 and 62). In baroque music upper mordents usually begin with the upper note sounded on the beat. The conventional symbol for an upper mordent is shown in bar 5 of A84 (letter c), and its written-out form appears in bar 21 (also marked with the letter c). In German this baroque upper mordent is called a *Pralltriller*. See *Ornaments*.

Morendo (It.). Dying away (C28, the last two bars).

Mosso (It.). Movement (speed). The direction 'un poco meno mosso' above bar 69 of C82 means 'a little less movement' (slower). See *Tempo markings*.

Motet. 1. In the middle ages a vocal genre that grew out of organum by adding new words (Fr. 'mots') to the *duplum* of a clausula (A10). To begin with these textual additions were in Latin, later in French, and the *duplum*, changing its name to 'motetus', gave its name to a new genre that became independent of the liturgical organum from which it sprang. Later still a third voice (the *triplum*) might be added with another new text, thus giving rise to the polytextual motet (sometimes with sacred words, sometimes with secular words, most often with a mixture of the two). This medieval version of the motet achieved its highest point of sophistication in works of 14th- and 15th-century composers such as Machaut and Dufay (whose polyphonic style may be judged by A21 and A27). **2.** An independent and freely composed Latin sacred composition of the 16th to 20th centuries. The texts could be taken from the Proper of the Mass, but they could also be taken directly from the Bible. Recent evidence suggests that 16th-century motets (of which there are thousands of examples) would have been performed as an ornament of the liturgy, not as an essential part of it. Later polyphonic Latin motets were sung as substitutes for plainsong settings of texts such as the Introit or Alleluia. Along with settings of the Ordinary of the mass, the motet was the most important sacred polyphonic genre of the renaissance (A44). *EM 8.5.1, 8.6.1.*

Motetus (Lat.). **1.** Latin for motet (A44). **2.** In medieval sacred music, the first texted part above the tenor (A19).

Motif (Eng. and Fr.), **Motiv** (Ger.), **motive** (Eng.). A short melodic or rhythmic idea that is sufficiently distinctive to allow it to be modified, manipulated and possibly combined with other motifs while retaining its own identity. In B41 there are three motifs from which nearly all of the melodic material derives. Motif x (bar 1) reappears transposed but otherwise unchanged in bars 3, 5, 9 and 11. The cadential motif z (bars 7–8) is repeated in the final cadence. Mozart's handling of motif y (bar 2) is more complex. Its rhythmic identity is evident in bars 6, 7, 10, 12 and 14 (the last two being transpositions of y^2 in bar 6), and bar 15 (a transposition of y^3 in bar 7). Bar 13 begins with another transposed version of y^2, but its last note (the first G♮) becomes the first note of the repeated quavers that characterised motif x (bar 1). Thus a new motif has been forged from the characteristic elements of motifs x and y. This leaves just one motif unaccounted for – y^1 in bar 4. The four short motifs in B47 show a possible derivation of it. B47(b) and (c) do not appear in the minuet, but they show stages in the evolution of motif y^1 from y^2. The final stage (B47(d)) is achieved by decorating B47(c) with a passing note (C♮) and an extra essential note (the semiquaver B♮). For yet more complex motivic manipulation see B27 and bars 17–23 of B68. *EM 3.1, 3.4, 4.5.1, 7.1, 7.7.1, 7.7.2, 7.10.1.*

Motion. 1. The characteristic movement of a single melodic line. In conjunct motion the melody moves wholly or predominantly by step from one pitch to an adjacent pitch (A36). In disjunct motion the melody leaps from one pitch to another (B7). Most melodies include both conjunct and disjunct motion (at the start of A4 the setting of the words 'Ad te' is disjunct while the setting of 'levavi' is conjunct). **2.** The simultaneous movement of two melodies in relation to each other. A85 illustrates four types of contrapuntal motion: **i)** in contrary motion the parts move in opposite directions (bar 4), **ii)** in oblique motion one part remains stationary while the other moves towards or away from it (bar 8), **iii)** in parallel motion the parts move in the same direction and maintain the same interval between them (bars 6–7), **iv)** in similar motion the parts move in the same direction without maintaining the same intervals between them (bar 2).

Moto (It.). Movement (speed). 'Con moto' at the beginning of C4 means 'with movement'. See *Tempo markings.*

Moto perpetuo (It.). *Perpetuum mobile* (B66 (right-hand part)).

Motto, motto theme. 1. A motif that is repeated at the start of each section of a 15th- or 16th-century Mass (a in A28 and A29). See *Head motif.* **2.** In 17th- and 18th-century motto arias, a short vocal idea sung before the first instrumental ritornello. **3.** In later music, a motif that unifies a multi-movement composition (C18).

Mouvement (Fr.), **movimento** (It.). **1.** See *Movement* 1. B40 is a complete movement from a divertimento. **2.** Tempo. 'Mouvement de valse modéré' at the head of C31 means 'in moderate waltz tempo'. See *Tempo markings.* **3.** Motion (A85).

Movement. 1. A discreet section of a large composition. Movements are usually sharply contrasted in style, tempo and metre. For example, the allemande (B17), courante (A67), sarabande (A88) and gigue (A90) are strongly characterised dance movements of the baroque suite. **2.** See *Motion* 1.

Movimento (It.). **1.** See *Movement* 1 and B17. **2.** Tempo, as in 'Doppio movimento', double the speed of the beat (in A80 the passage from bar 13 is played twice as fast as the first 12 bars).

Mp (*mp*). Abbreviation of *mezzopiano* (C94, bar 3).

Multiple stopping. The performance of two-, three- or four-note chords on a bowed string instrument. See *Stopping* and A95.

Musette (Fr.). **1.** In 17th- and 18th-century France, a small bagpipe that achieved great popularity among the aristocracy and at Versailles. Rameau, among others, composed for it. **2.** In the French classical period, a term for a mock-pastoral dance featuring drone-like pedals or similar effects. Although imitating some of the stylistic features of country dances, pieces such as Couperin's *Muséte de Choisi* display the utmost sophistication (Couperin was born in the small country town of Choisy-en-Brie, and one of his favourite pupils, the Princesse de Conti, owned a small chateau there). The sophisticated simplicity of musette style is evident in bars 9–21 of C32 and bars 16–24 of C33.

Music, musica (Lat.). Organised sound designed to uplift (A5 and C97), stir (A17 and B73), entertain (A18 and C73), express (B37 and B50), instruct (C58–C67) or provoke (B63 and C89).

Music drama. A term for operas in which

music, poetry, drama and staging are of equal importance. In Wagner's mature operas the aims of music drama are met in purely musical terms by doing away with separate arias, duets and ensembles and replacing them with a continuous symphonic evolution notable for its manipulation of leitmotifs to form what he called 'unending melody'. The beginning of such a melody can be heard in bars 17–24 of B68.

Music-hall songs. Tuneful ditties that were sung, often with rowdy audience participation, in places of entertainment where programmes also included comic turns, soulful monologues and numbers from contemporary operettas such as *The Merry Widow* (C73). Music-hall songs were popular on both sides of the Atlantic from about 1850 to 1940. Walton's 'Popular song' (C38) is a parody of this type of song. *EM 8.11.8.*

Music theatre. A 20th-century term for compositions that involve some sort of dramatic presentation, but which are not necessarily fully staged and acted. The vocal part of Schoenberg's *Pierrot lunaire* (C34) was written for a costumed and made-up actress whose gestures and facial expressions underlined the expressionism of the text and music. See also C38. *EM 8.11.8.*

Musica ficta (Lat.). The medieval and renaissance practice of introducing notes foreign to the prevailing mode in order (a) to avoid melodic or harmonic tritones, or (b) to form conclusive cadences. The only chromatic alteration to the mode to be encountered in plainsong was B♭. In later polyphonic music other chromatic alterations begin to appear as early as the 14th century (A21). Fictitious accidentals may be introduced into ancient music by editors trying to follow the principles of early performance practice, eg the flat sign printed above the B♮ in bar 5 of A28 (introduced to avoid a tritonal sound between this note and the F♯ two notes before it). *Ficta* of category (b) can be heard at the final cadences of A28 and A29. In both cases the seventh degree of the prevailing mixolydian mode (F♮) is raised a semitone to form more conclusive cadences. *EM 2.4.3, 5.4.7.*

Musica mensurata, musica mensurabilis (Lat.). Mensural music. Compare A9 (unmeasured) with A10 (measured organum).

Muta (It.). Change. The term is used as an instruction to a performer to change the fundamental pitch of an instrument or to change to a different instrument (C52, bar 9).

Mutes. Devices that are attached to instruments to change the timbre and reduce the overall dynamic level. On string instruments a clamp is placed on the bridge to reduce its vibration. The effect of violin mutes can be appreciated by comparing the unmuted chords in bars 4–6 of C72 with the muted chords in the last three bars of the same example. Brass players have a wide variety of mutes to choose from, each changing the timbre in a different way. Having selected a mute the performer wedges it into the bell of the instrument. A pair of muted horns can be heard at the start of C19, muted trumpets play throughout C81, and a muted trumpet and trombone can be heard in bars 6–7 of C35. On a horn a muted effect can be achieved by hand stopping (see *Stopped notes* and C85, bars 24–25). On a piano a muted effect is caused by the use of the left-hand (una corda) pedal (B74). *EM 6.5.13.*

N

Nacchera (It.). Kettledrum (B36, last 7 bars). Not to be confused with *Nacchere* (castanets).

Nacchere (It.). Castanets (C50). Not to be confused with *Nacchera* (kettledrum).

Nachschlag (Ger.). **1.** As most commonly used nowadays, the final two notes of a turn at the end of a trill (the two demisemiquavers at the end of bar 3 in B1). **2.** In baroque music, a single-note unaccented ornament played or sung just before a strong beat. The most common types are the springer (B25, bar 52) and the anticipation (A95, bar 15, beat 3, semiquaver D♯). See *Ornaments. EM 3.10.1.*

Nachtmusik (Ger.). In the late 18th century, instrumental works in the style of a serenade (such as Mozart's *Eine kleine Nachtmusik*). The fourth movement of Mahler's seventh symphony (C29) is entitled 'Nachtmusik'. It is in the style of a serenade and includes parts for guitar and mandolin that evoke images of a lover seranading his mistress in the traditional manner. Britten's Seranade consists of an evocative horn solo (C84) that frames six settings of poems about dusk and night, some of them with nightmarish imagery (C85).

Nachtstück (Ger.). Nocturne (B67).

Naked 5th. Open 5th (A19, last bar).

Nasard, nazard (Fr.). An organ stop sounding an octave and a 5th, or two octaves and a 5th above printed pitch. These stops add brilliance to the full organ registration in A86.

Nationalism. A movement within 19th- and early 20th-century romanticism marked by the incorporation of some of the stylistic characteristics of folk music into almost all types of art music, as well as direct quotations from folk sources.

Tchaikovsky's 'Russian Dance' from his ballet *The Nutcracker* (C5) evokes a Cossack dance by its very fast tempo and its duple metre. A characteristic feature of folk dances throughout Europe is the repetition of a short melodic or rhythmic cell. In this trepak the cell marked x pervades the whole dance.

The *furiant* is an energetic Bohemian folk dance in triple time. C9 contains an obsessively repeated rhythmic cell (x) similar to that in Tchaikovsky's dance. Specifically characteristic of the *furiant* are the two hemiolas at the end.

Modality is a feature of genuine folk music (C57), and it colours much newly composed nationalist music. In C9 it is apparent in the root-position minor triads (III and VI in bars 26–30) and the avoidance of dominant chords in the last seven bars. In C41 modality is apparent in the oboe melody at the start and the flute and clarinet melody at the end (more specifically Hungarian is Kodály's use of a cimbalom in this extract).

Kodály toured eastern Europe with his compatriot Bartók and between them they collected thousands of folk melodies. C56 is an extract from Bartók's arrangement of a Romanian folk dance which again exhibits a constantly repeated melodic cell as well as the all-pervading augmented 2nd of the so-called Gypsy scale. Bartók's lifelong researches into folk music bore fruit in his own freely composed music. This is particularly evident in the asymmetrical metres of his *Dances in Bulgarian Rhythm* (C66), but the rhythmic energy of dances like these spills over into most of his compositions (C70) and asymmetrical rhythms are equally common (B75, bars 1–2).

Elements of Spanish folk music are evident in the extract from Rodrigo's *Concierto de Aranjuez* (C83), notably the strumming (*rasgueado*), the parallel triads over a pedal, the three-bar phrasing and the frequent hemiolaic rhythms. England's heritage of modal melodies was exploited by Vaughan Williams, notably in his *Fantasia on a Theme by Thomas Tallis* (A37–A39).

Not surprisingly, nationalist sentiments and nationalist music barely survived World War Two. *EM 2.4.4, 8.10.4, 8.11.6.*

Natural (nat.). 1. An uninflected note corresponding with any of the white notes on a keyboard (see the folded insert and A3). All of the notes in A16 are naturals. **2.** A sign (♮) cancelling the effect of one of the symbols in a key signature, or cancelling the effect of a previous accidental. In B39 the A♮ on the

Natural and artificial harmonics

third beat of the first bar cancels the effect of the A♭ on the second beat, and the F♮ in the cello part cancels the effect of the key signature. See *Accidental* and *Key Signature*. **3.** See *Naturale* and C94, bars 11–12 (the term 'ordinario' is synonymous with 'naturale').

Natural and artificial harmonics. Natural harmonics are produced on an unstopped vibrating string by touching it lightly at a node. All of the notes with a circle above them in C95 are natural harmonics. Artificial harmonics are produced by stopping the string with one finger and lightly touching a node with another finger. All the notes played by the violinist on C56 are artificial harmonics apart from the D♯s in bars 8, 12 and 16.

Natural horn. A horn without valves and therefore only capable of playing notes of the harmonic series (or stopped notes). Although C84 is played on a valve horn Britten instructs the performer to play without valves, deliberately using 'out-of-tune' harmonics as a special effect. *EM 6.7.1.*

Natural minor scale. A to A on the white notes of the piano. Also called the aeolian mode (A42 and A43). *EM 2.3.3, 2.4.1.*

Natural notes, natural tones. The pitches of the harmonic series, particularly those that can be produced on brass instruments without the use of valves (C84).

Natural trumpet. A trumpet without valves and therefore only capable of playing the notes of the harmonic series (B15). *EM 6.7.2.*

Naturale (It.), **naturel** (Fr.), **natürlich** (Ger.). A return to normal performance after a special effect. The synonym 'ordinario' (often abbreviated to 'ord.') is more common. See *Normale* and the last bar of C94.

Neapolitan 6th. A major chord on the flat second degree of a diatonic scale (usually a minor scale) in first inversion. In bars 80–81 of B50 a Neapolitan 6th is heard in the key of D minor. The flat second degree of the scale of D minor is E♭, and a major chord built on this note is shown beneath these bars together with its first inversion (♭II^6). The Neapolitan 6th usually resolves to the dominant (B65, bars 23–24, 25–26 and 27–28). *EM 5.7.3.*

Nebendreiklang (Ger.). See *Secondary triad* and B25, bar 7, beat 3 (chord VI is the only secondary triad in the Menuetto).

Nebennote (Ger.). Unessential note or non-harmonic tone (B25, bar 46, semiquaver A♭)

Nebensatz, Nebenthema (Ger.). Secondary theme. The second subject of B40 (bars 26–48) is a secondary theme in relation to the first subject (bars 1–18).

Nebenstimme (Ger.). In complex atonal or serial textures, Schoenberg's term for the next most important part after the *Hauptstimme*. As heard on track C34, the vocal part in bar 13 of 'Nacht' is the *Hauptstimme*, the bass clarinet is the *Nebenstimme*, and the other parts fulfil less important accompanimental roles. From 1909 Schoenberg often identified *Nebenstimmen* by a bracket formed from the letter N.

Nebentonart (Ger.). Any key other than the tonic key of a movement (B41, bars 5–8 which are in the dominant key of D major).

Neighboring tone, neighbor note. Auxiliary note (A87, bar 1, all four D♮s). *EM 4.3.4.*

Neoclassicism. An early 20th-century movement that sought to replace the grandiloquence of late romantic styles with a tonal language deriving from pre-romantic styles. In this context the new classicism did not necessarily refer to Viennese classical styles: in fact, more often than not, it sought inspiration from the works of baroque composers. This is the case with Ravel's *Le Tombeau de Couperin,* a suite of pieces that pays homage to one of the greatest of French baroque composers. The structural and stylistic elements that link C32 and C33 include the following: **a)** both are forlanas, **b)** both are rondeaux (though the refrain of Ravel's rondeau is not shown in C33), **c)** both fall into four- and eight-bar phrases, **d)** both are decorated with *pincées* and *tremblements* (Couperin's represented by symbols, Ravel's written out), **e)** both contain modal passages (notably the aeolian mode in the couplet of Couperin's forlana and in the first phrase of the extract from Ravel's forlana).

Additionally, there are pedal points in bars 8–11 and 16–24 of Ravel's forlana. There is no direct connection here with Couperin's forlana, but pedal points such as these occur in many other of his compositions. In both Ravel and Couperin these are meant to evoke the sound of the pastoral musette.

One of the new elements of Ravel's neoclassicism is his free use of unprepared and unresolved discords such as the 7th chords on the first beats of bars 1–3 and the 9th chord on the first beat of bar 6. Another is his exploration of keyboard textures that include many three- and four-note chords. They sound as crystalline as Couperin's two-part textures because they are all pitched above e. *EM 2.4.4, 8.11.5.*

Neoromanticism. A term sometimes used to categorise the styles of composers who, in the second quarter of the 20th century, continued to embrace late romantic tonality and tunefulness, partly in reaction against the perceived inhumanity of serialism. Samuel Barber's opulently romantic *Adagio* (originally a movement in his string quartet of 1936) and Benjamin Britten's *Serenade* of 1943 (C85) exemplify the elegiac strain that runs through much of the music of later American and English neoromantic composers. *EM 8.11.1.*

Nera (It.). Crotchet, quarter-note (B18, theme).

Net (Fr.) Neat, clear, tidy. The performance direction above bar 10 of C20 means 'very clear and dry'.

Neuma, pneuma (Lat.). **1.** In plainsong notation, a neume (the symbols on the four-line stave in A4). **2.** In plainsong, a melisma, especially the lengthy melismas of an Alleluia (A5). *EM 8.4.1.*

Neumatic style. A style of plainsong in which there is, generally speaking, one neume per syllable. In A4 the modern notation of the first phrase is underlaid with the original neumatic notation, and it will be seen that each syllable except the last is set to a single neume (identified as the single-note *punctum*, the two-note *cephalicus*, *clivis* and *pes* or *podatus* and the three-note *torculus*). See *Melismatic style* and *Syllabic style*. *EM 8.4.1.*

Neume. A symbol for a note (*punctum*) or group of notes (*cephalicus*, *clivis*, *pes* etc) appearing on a four-line stave in the unmeasured system of notation that predated modern staff notation. Some of the commoner neumes are shown at the start of A4.

New music. A term that frequently appears in the history of music to identify a perceived change of style. Thus the Ars Nova of the 14th century (A21–A23) repudiated the rhythmic formalism of the Ars Antiqua (A11), the 'nuove musiche' of the early 17th century (A62–A66) rejected the old polyphony of the 16th century (A52), and the New German School of Wagner and his associates (B68, B70, B73, B74) spurned the continuing development of classical genres by composers such as Brahms (B76 and C1). The battle continued to be fought in the 20th century when the forces of modernism (C87) were ranged against post-modern eclecticism (C94).

New German School. A group of progressive 19th-century composers led by Liszt who supported Wagner's quest for the 'art-work of the future' (B68). In fact Liszt anticipated Wagner in many respects (compare B70 and B71) and in his old age went much further than Wagner in his exploration of new harmonic resources (B74). They regarded the absolute music of composers such as Brahms (B75–C1) as reactionary.

Niente (It.). Nothing, to nothing. The term is most often used as a performance direction after a diminuendo to indicate that the music should fade away into silence (C97, bar 68).

Nine-eight suspension. See *Suspension* and A33, bar 16, beat 4, to bar 17, beat 2. The soprano C♮ is suspended over the barline to form a dissonant 9th with the bass. The resolution occurs when the soprano moves down to the minim B♮ to form a consonant octave with the bass (the quaver B♮ being an anticipation of the resolution).

Nine-eight time. A compound triple metre in which three dotted-crotchet beats form the repeating pattern strong–weak–weak in moderate or fast tempi. Alternatively nine quaver beats can form the repeating pattern strong–weak–weak, strong–weak–weak, strong–weak–weak in slower tempi. It is indicated by the time signature $\frac{9}{8}$ immediately after the first clef. In C72 the beat is a quaver (see the metronome mark), and in bar 2 violin 1, violin 2 and cello enter in that order on the strong first, fourth and seventh quavers of the bar. In bars 6–8 plucked violin notes emphasise the strong beats and support the legato viola melody.

Ninth. 1. An interval spanning nine letter-name pitches (including the first and last). In bar 10 of C35 the first two harp notes form the interval of a major 9th. **2.** A chord containing the interval of a 9th above the

Nocturne

root (A81, bar 3). See also *Dominant chords* and *Secondary-dominant chords*.

Nocturne. A romantic character piece evoking images of the night, often through the use of left-hand broken-chord figures supporting a smoothly flowing cantabile melody (B67). *EM 8.10.3.*

Node. A point on a vibrating string in which one or more of its modes of vibration can be halted by lightly touching the string, so producing a harmonic. Nodes lie at those points shown beneath C95. Nodes are also found in the vibrating columns of air in wind instruments. *EM 6.2.*

Noire (Fr.). A crotchet or quarter-note (see the theme at the start of B18).

Non troppo (It.). Not too much (B78). See *Tempo markings*.

Non-dominant 7th chords. See *Secondary-7th chords* and B78, bars 2^3–5^1.

Non-functional harmony. See *Functional harmony* and B25. Compare the functional harmony of this example with the non-functional harmony of C55. *EM 5.8.*

Non-harmonic note, non-harmonic tone. Unessential note. A note (tone) that is not part of the chord sounded against it. In A30 three types of non-harmonic note are identified. In bar 6 the two notes labelled 'pn' are passing notes (passing tones) that are not parts of the G-major chord heard in the first half of the bar. Similarly the note labelled 'en' (*échappée* or escape note) and the accented passing note labelled 'apn' are not parts of the C-major chord heard in the second half of the bar.

Normale (It.). A return to normal performance after a special effect. The synonym 'ordinario' (often abbreviated to 'ord.') is more common. In bar 3 of C94 the composer instructs the pianist to pluck the strings of the piano. A return to the normal practice of playing on the keyboard is indicated by the direction 'ord.' at the end of the extract.

Nota cambiata (It.). Literally a 'changed note' (sometimes called a changing note). An unaccented unessential decoration that leaves an accented essential note by step then leaps a third to the next accented essential note. The *nota cambiata* in the second bar of A47 is identified by the letter x. See *Cambiata*. *EM 4.3.7.*

Notation. Any system for representing musical sounds on paper. See *Aleatoric music* (C97); *Bar, Barline, Time signature* (B6); *Crotchet, Demisemiquaver, Hemidemisemiquaver, Minim, Quaver, Semibreve, Semiquaver* and B18; *Clef,* (A30), *Pitch* (A1–A3), *Stave*; *Dotted rhythms* (A76–A80); *Neume* (A4); *Rests* (C34). *EM 1.12, 8.5.1.*

Note. A symbol that in most types of notation shows the relative length (duration) and pitch of musical sounds. Length is indicated by the nature of the symbol itself, pitch by the position of the note-head on a stave.

The durations of short notes may be judged by listening to track B18 in which a constant crotchet pulse is maintained in the bass. Against this pulse the following note-lengths are heard (and shown in B18): **a)** crotchets (quarter-notes) in the theme, **b)** quavers (eighth-notes) in Variation 1, **c)** triplets of quavers (each triplet group played in the time of one crotchet) in Variation 3, **d)** semiquavers (sixteenth-notes) in bars 1–6 of Variation 5, **e)** demisemiquavers (thirty-second-notes) in bar 7, beat 3, of Variation 5, **f)** hemidemisemiquavers (sixty-fourth-notes) just before the final note of Variation 5.

The durations of longer notes may be judged by listening to A52 (which has a slightly slower crotchet pulse than B18). Minims (half-notes) occur at the start of each vocal part in bars 1–4, and it can be heard (and seen in the first bar of A52) that they last twice as long as crotchets. Semibreves (whole-notes) are the longest notes commonly used in modern notation. A comparison of the bass and soprano parts in bar 3 reveals that the semibreve is four times as long as a crotchet (a fact that can be verified by counting carefully while listening to the bass part).

The pitches of notes on bass and treble staves covering almost the entire range that is commonly notated will be found in A3. All of these pitches are recorded on an organ on the corresponding track. See *A* for a more scientific explanation of pitch.

Note cluster. See *Cluster chord* and C91, bar 2.

Note row. See *Serial music, Tone row* and C40, bars 1–7.

Note sensible (Fr.). Leading note (B18, note 7).

Note-against-note style. Music in which parts move in the same rhythm (A7) or similar rhythms (A11).

Notes égales (Fr.). A performance direction in French baroque music indicating that the performer must play the notes as written: *notes inégales* are not an option (C32, bar 9).

Note-head. The circular or oval-shaped symbol placed on a stave to show the pitch of a note (A5).

Notes inégales (Fr.). The performance of equal notes (such as a run of quavers) as unequal notes (as a run of dotted quaver–semiquaver rhythms, for example). The conventions governing such inequality developed to their fullest extent in late 17th- and 18th-century France, but they applied with equal force to music in the French style written in other European countries. The principle can be seen in bars 37–44 of A84. When the equal quavers of bars 37–40 of the refrain are repeated in bars 41–44 they are converted into dotted rhythms (some of them Lombardic). The performance on A84 was made especially to illustrate the principle: in an authentic performance such inequality would apply to most, if not all, conjunct quavers. This is the case with the allemande performed on B17, where the sort of inequality shown on the extra stave below bar 1 is maintained consistently throughout the piece for conjunct runs of semiquavers (the semiquaver arpeggios in bars 32–33 and triplets throughout are played as written). See *Notes égales. EM 1.6.4, 3.10.2, 8.7.3.*

Notturno (It.). **1.** Nocturne (B67). **2.** In the 18th century, a multi-movement concerted composition for solo instrumentalists of the serenade/divertimento type (B40). Its function is captured by the title of the most famous example of the genre, Mozart's *Eine kleine Nachtmusik* (*A Little Night Music*). *EM 8.9.3.*

Nuance (Fr.). Any expressive changes of rhythm, tempo, dynamics or timbre. All but the last of these types of nuance are very evident on track B67.

Number opera. An opera consisting of many separate and structurally distinct numbers (arias and ensembles) that can be performed independently. In a *Singspiel* individual numbers (B37 and B50) are linked by spoken dialogue.

Nuove musiche, Le (It.). The title of a collection of monodic vocal pieces by Caccini that was published in 1602 and lent its name to the 'new music' of the *seconda prattica*, particularly operatic recitative (A62 and A63) and aria (A65 and A66).

Nut. 1. The part of the bow of a string instrument that the performer holds and that contains the mechanism for adjusting the tension of the hairs. 'Am Frosch', 'au talon' and 'al tallone' are all directions requiring the performer to use the section of the bow nearest the nut (C70, bar 1). **2.** A ridge at the narrow end of the fingerboard of a string instrument. Unless stopped the strings vibrate between the nut and the bridge.

O

O. Circles over notes can indicate the use of open strings (A98) or harmonics (C35, bars 10–11).

Ob. Abbreviation of oboe (Eng., Ger. and Span.). See C78.

Obbligato aria. A song, usually from a cantata, opera or oratorio, with an obligatory instrumental solo that is often as important as the vocal part (B15, in which the obbligato trumpet part is almost as extensive as the vocal part). *EM 8.7.2.*

Obbligato parts. Essential instrumental solos in baroque compositions. There are three obbligato parts in B5, two for viole d'amore and the other for lute.

Oberek, obertas (Pol.). A lively Polish folk dance and song in triple time with prominent weak-beat accents. It is one of the stylistic sources for Chopin's mazurkas (though B65 is too slow and melancholy to be classed as an *oberek*).

Oblique motion. See *Motion* and A85, bar 8. *EM 4.1.*

Oboe. A treble double-reed woodwind instrument that has been a standard member of the symphony orchestra since the 18th century. Its approximate range is shown on the folded insert and oboe solos can be heard in the first four bars of C1, in C4, bars 2–5, and throughout C78. *EM 6.6.2.*

Oboe d'amore. An alto oboe dating from the early 18th century and pitched a 3rd below the normal orchestral oboe. In B8 it is often doubled by violins, but its reedy timbre can be distinctly heard, especially in bars 9–13. *EM 6.6.4.*

Oboe da caccia. A tenor oboe of the 18th century pitched a 5th below the modern oboe. In B8 it is doubled by string instruments, except in bars 3–4 where its throaty tone is distinctly audible. It is sometimes called a *taille* (French for tenor). *EM 6.6.4.*

Ocarina. An egg-shaped flute with a mouthpiece similar to that of a recorder, invented (and mass-produced) in the 19th century. Because its sound is similar to that of primitive pipes it is sometimes used in ancient music (A18).

Ochetus, oketus (Lat.). Hocket (A21).

Octatonic scale, octatonic collection. A scale of alternating tones and semitones, or a collection of pitches that can be arranged to form such a scale. In C64 the canon at the 6th below is made from the eight pitch classes shown in the octatonic scale beneath it. The right-hand part uses four of these pitches, and the left-hand part uses the other four. This and other factors make it relatively easy to hear that the music is octatonic. When a passage of music based on an octatonic scale is buried in a more complex texture it is difficult to detect with the unaided ear (C88, bars 5–7). See also *Modes of limited transposition*. *EM 2.7.3, 2.8.*

Octave. The interval between notes whose frequencies differ in the ratio 2:1, eg c and c^1 (see A1). An octave encompasses the same interval as 12 semitones. Technically this interval is called a perfect octave, but used without qualification 'octave' is taken to mean 'perfect octave'. A perfect octave can be heard melodically between the first and second notes of B59, and the same interval can be heard harmonically in bar 2 of the same extract. Augmented octaves are rare and very dissonant: they can be heard in bars 6, 9, 13 and 17 of B74. *EM 2.1.*

Octave displacement. See *Octave equivalence* 2 and C88, bars 2–4, cor anglais. *EM 4.6.*

Octave equivalence. 1. The subjective perception that notes an octave apart are in some sense the same. Thus men and women singing the same song an octave apart are thought to be singing the same pitches (A26). **2.** In serial composition and analysis, the notion that any note in a tone row may be transposed any number of octaves without losing its functional identity in the row. Thus the retrograde inversion of Stravinsky's prime order in C88 (shown on the lower of the two extra staves below bars 3–4) retains its identity when presented with the first, third, fourth and fifth pitches displaced by an octave to produce the extremely angular melody played on the cor anglais.

Octave species. The distribution of tones and semitones in a diatonic scale. It is this distribution that determines the type or species of scale (not absolute pitches, since any diatonic scale can start on any of the 12 notes used in most western music). In an ascending major scale the distribution of tones and semitones will always be TTSTTTS (where T = tone and S = semitone) whether the scale starts on D (A25) or G (B18). Similarly the distribution in the dorian mode will always be TSTTTST whether the scale starts on D (A40) or F (A17).

Octet. 1. Any group of eight solo performers. A69 is performed by three solo vocalists and two solo recorder players accompanied by a continuo group consisting of a cellist, a bassoonist and an organist. **2.** A type of chamber music for eight solo performers, eg Mendelssohn's Octet Op. 20 for four violins, two violas and two cellos.

Oda (It.). One of the verse forms of the frottola. It consisted of four-line stanzas with a rhyme scheme such as ABBC (valle, pace, iace, cristalli in A30). The first three lines of each stanza have seven syllables, the last from four to eleven syllables. This is true of A30 in which vowel sounds are elided in bars 1, 3, 7 and 9. In a typical fashion the first and second seven-syllable lines are set homorhythmically, but the third seven-syllable line is extended by a melisma to form a three-bar phrase, while the final eleven-syllable line is set to a four-bar phrase including a short melisma.

Offbeat. The term refers, strictly speaking, to notes which do not coincide with any of the beats of the bar, like the upper notes of the ragtime bass in bars 6–13 of C20. However, it has come additionally to refer to notes articulated on weak beats of the bar (C38, cymbal in bars 1–3). See *Backbeat* and *Metre*.

Offertoire (Fr.), **Offertorium** (Lat.). Offertory (A81) *FM 8.7.2.*

Offertory. The fourth item of the Proper of the Mass. It is sung while the offerings of bread and wine are brought to the altar. Like the Alleluia (A5) plainsong offertories are melismatic in style. A81 is an extract from the offertory of an organ mass *FM 8.7.2.*

Office. 1. Non-Eucharistic services of the Roman Catholic Church originally sung at about three-hour intervals: Matins at about 3am, Lauds at daybreak, Prime at 6am, Terce at 9am, Sext at noon, None at 3pm, Vespers at nightfall and Compline before retiring. In contemporary monastic houses some of these services are combined, but the basic pattern of psalms (A6), antiphons (A4), canticles, hymns (A49) and responses (A8) is retained. **2.** The services of Morning Prayer (Matins) and Evening Prayer (Evensong) of the reformed Church of England. They are conflations of the Roman Catholic services of the Divine Office. For instance, Evensong usually includes responses, an office hymn, psalms, and the canticles Magnificat (C30) and Nunc dimittis (the last two items coming from the Roman Catholic services of Vespers and Compline respectively).

Oketus (Lat.). Hocket (A21).

Oktave (Ger.). Octave (B59, bars 1–2).

Ondeggiando (It.), **ondulé** (Fr.). In string playing, a bow stroke alternating between two adjacent strings. It is this type of bowing that is used in *bariolage*, where the undulation is usually between a stopped and an open string (A98, bars 2–13).

Oom-pah accompaniment. A type of accompaniment in which accented low notes alternate with unaccented high notes or chords (C73, orchestral reduction). This simple accompanimental pattern is common in marches, particularly when played by marching bands (Bartók parodies the style in bars 4–10 of C75).

Op. Abbreviation of opus (B30).

Open and closed endings. See *Ouvert and clos* and A16. *EM 7.9.5.*

Open 5th. A chord with a root and 5th but no 3rd. Medieval and renaissance polyphonic compositions often end on such a chord (A19, last bar).

Open note. 1. Natural harmonics on a brass instrument (C84). **2.** See *Open string* and C95, bars 7 11[1].

Open position, open harmony. A spacing of a chord in which there is a large gap between parts, especially between the lowest two parts. Compare the first chord of B25 (which is in open position) with the first chord of bar 3 (which is in close position).

Open score and short score. In an open score each instrumental or vocal part has its own stave (as shown on the extra staves beneath A30). In a short score these parts are compressed onto as few as two staves

Open string

(the first four bars of A30 represent exactly the same music as that written on the four-stave system at the end of the example).

Open string. A string that is bowed or plucked but not stopped with the fingers of the left hand. Open strings produce a resonant sound, but vibrato is impossible (C95, bars 7–11). In bars 16–26 of B73 all of the violins play on all four open strings (g, d^1, a^1 and e^2). See also *Sympathetic strings*.

Opera. A dramatic fusion of words, music, spectacle and sometimes dancing. The term covers a multitude of types such as: *favola in musica* – a fable set to music, Monteverdi's title for *Orfeo* (A62–A66); opera buffa – baroque comic opera (the musical style is represented in B37); *dramma giocoso* – opera buffa with serious elements (B41–B45); opera seria – baroque serious opera (the musical style is represented in B50); *Singspiel* – German opera with spoken dialogue (B37, B50 and B60). See *Aria* (A65 and A66), *Arie* (B37 and B50), *French overture* (A80), *Interlude* (C86), *Melodrama* (B60), *Music drama* (B68), *Overture* (B59 and B68), *Recitative* (A62 and A63), *Sinfonia* (A64). *EM 8.7.1, 8.11.1.*

Opera buffa. 18th-century comic opera with an Italian libretto that is sung throughout. Although taken from a *Singspiel*, B37 illustrates many aspects of buffo style. The tempo is very fast, so the words have to be rapidly enunciated by the buffo bass. Melodic lines, both orchestral and vocal, are triadic or scalic, so making them easy to remember. The harmony is simple, often remaining static on the tonic or dominant (bars 20–27), and limited (only chords I, IV^6_4 and V are used in B37). Finally the melody dominates the homophonic accompaniment throughout.

Opéra comique (Fr.). In the late 18th and early 19th centuries, a French music drama with spoken dialogue. As such it was the French equivalent of the German *Singspiel* (B50 and B60).

Opera seria. One of the two main types of 18th-century Italian opera (the other being opera buffa). Librettos were based on heroic or tragic themes and were mostly set to music as recitatives and arias (B15 is not from an opera, but its da capo form is typical of most early 18th-century operatic arias). The style of opera seria may be judged by the Queen of the Night's vengeful aria shown in B50. It expresses just one *Affekt* (rage), through a vocal part that is characterised by angular leaps, chromaticism and virtuosic coloratura displays. The harmony is also chromatic (note particularly the colourful Neapolitan 6th in bars 80–81 and the diminished-7th chords in bars 93–94). The instrumentation is lavish (double woodwind and brass were largely reserved for the opera house in the 18th century) and the orchestral textures are vivid (note the string tremolo at the opening and the dramatic detached tutti chords at the end). Finally, the wildly changing dynamics add to the dramatic impact of this aria. *EM 8.9.5.*

Operetta. 1. In the 17th and 18th centuries, a generic name for short or unpretentious operas such as opera buffa and *Singspiel* (B37 and B50). **2.** In the late 19th and early 20th centuries, a popular light opera with spoken dialogue and tuneful songs (C73).

Ophicleide. A 19th-century bass keyed bugle that was superseded by the tuba in both bands and orchestras but has been revived for authentic performances of romantic scores (B63). See *Chromatic bullock. EM 6.7.5.*

Opus (Lat.). Work. The term is used by composers and others to identify particular pieces. For short pieces an opus number is often followed by another number. Thus Chopin wrote over 50 mazurkas, but each one can be identified by its opus number and its position within that opus (B65 is the fourth mazurka of his Opus 30). Composers (and those who attempted to catalogue their works) being human, there is no guarantee that opus numbers are either comprehensive or chronological (hence the proliferation of thematic catalogues of composers' works in the 19th and 20th centuries).

Oratorio. A sacred libretto set to music and intended for concert rather than theatrical performance. Like opera, the oratorio could include recitative (A68), concerted movements (A69) and arias (B15). See also *Cantata* and *Historia. EM 8.7.2.*

Orchestra. As most commonly understood, a body of string instruments (with more than one player to each part) to which may be added any number of wind and percussion instruments. The composition of orchestras varies according to their function and the date of composition of the score. Thus in the early 18th century a concerto grosso was most often scored for soloists and a string orchestra (B19). In the later 18th century the orchestra for an opera was often larger than that for a symphony (B50 is scored for strings and two each of flutes, oboes, bassoons, horns, trumpets and drums, whereas B21 only requires strings, two oboes and two horns). By the turn of the century the four sections of the modern symphony orchestra had been established (woodwind, brass, percussion and strings). In the tutti sections of B36 the woodwind section comprises two flutes, two oboes and two bassoons, the brass section includes two horns and two trumpets (in addition to the solo trumpet), and the percussion section consists of two timpani.

In the 19th century every section of the orchestra grew in size, and new instruments were introduced: B59 includes prominent parts for four horns, B68 includes parts for English horn and bass clarinet, the loudest chords on track B73 include three trombones and a tuba, C3 calls for a pair of cornets and a glockenspiel, and a harp and antique cymbals are heard on track C19.

In his nine symphonies Mahler calls for some of the largest orchestral forces ever assembled. The brass section heard on track C27 includes eight horns and six trumpets, C28 has parts for cowbells, celesta and tubular bells, and C29 includes a prominent part for a mandolin. Despite predictions to the contrary, the symphony orchestra survived the 20th century, as C97 shows. The loudest passages of MacMillan's *Quickening* (1999) are played by strings, organ, 24 wind instruments, and a percussion section including timpani, handbells, clashed and crash cymbals, tam-tam, tuned gong, tubular bells, brake drums and piano.

Orchestral exposition. The first section of many classical concerto movements in which some or all of the themes are played by the orchestra alone in the tonic key (B36, bars 1–43). An orchestral exposition is usually followed by a solo exposition in which some or all of the themes heard in the orchestral exposition are taken up by the soloist in the tonic and in a contrasting key (B36, bars 44–140). See also *Sonata form*.

Orchestration. The art of creating orchestral textures by designating melodies or notes of chords to particular instruments.

Before 1600 it was rare to specify instruments in this way. Monteverdi (A62–A66) was among the first to do so. By the end of the baroque era, instruments were usually specified, but the ensembles that performed instrumental music were not necessarily orchestras in the modern sense.

By the second half of the 18th century the core of the modern orchestra was beginning to emerge, and special orchestral effects became more common (eg Mozart's dramatic use of wind and timpani at the start of B50).

In the early 19th century composers continued this trend, particularly in illustrative music (note the use of bells, string tremolo, pizzicato double bass and soft kettle-drum strokes in B60).

At the beginning of the 20th century Ravel was among the most subtle and witty orchestrators (C31), and on the eve of the 21st MacMillan showed masterful ability in creating new orchestral textures from the most diverse resources (C97). See also *Instrumentation*.

Ordinario (It.), **ordinaire** (Fr.) **(ord.)**. A direction requiring an instrumentalist to play in the normal way after a passage in which an unusual performance technique has been used. In the last bar of C94 the pianist is required to play the chord in the ordinary way (on the keyboard) instead of plucking the strings (bars 3–4). The terms 'naturale' and 'normale' are synonymous with *ordinario*.

Ordinary of the Mass, ordo missae, ordinarium missae (Lat.). Those texts which are said or sung at almost every celebration of the Mass: Kyrie (A27 and A52), Gloria, Credo, Sanctus and Benedictus (A20 and A21) and Agnus Dei (A19 and A29). *EM 8.4.1.*

Ordo (Lat.). In the medieval rhythmic modes of the School of Notre Dame in Paris, an order or series of repeating rhythmic units making a phrase that is usually defined by a rest after the last note of the series. There are six rhythmic modes, and the units that go to make up an *ordo* are shown at the foot of A10. In a complete *ordo* these rhythmic units can be repeated any number of times before ending with the single note-value with which the *ordo* began (or the two note-values with which the *ordo* began in the case of Mode 4). Complete Mode 3 *ordines* are identified by brackets in bars 9–13 and 22–26 (in which the rhythmic unit is heard four times) and 18–21 (in which it is heard three times). All three *ordines* end with the dotted crotchet with which the *ordo* began, followed by a dotted crotchet rest before the next phrase begins. See *Rhythmic modes*.

Ordre (Fr.). In French baroque music, a large collection of instrumental pieces all in the same key. Most *ordres* contain binary-form dances found in contemporary suites (such as the allemande shown in B17), programmatic pieces with fanciful titles (such as 'La virginité, sous le domino couleur d'invisible' in Couperin's 13th *ordre*), and rondeaux (such as that shown in A84). It is improbable that all of the pieces in an *ordre* were intended to be performed together in the manner of a suite (there are 16 pieces in Couperin's 13th *ordre*): such collections were more likely to have been treated as anthologies from which selections were made to suit individual circumstances.

Organ. A wind instrument of great antiquity consisting of bellows that supply compressed air to sets of pipes controlled by a keyboard. The full compass of a modern organ can be heard on track A3 and solo organ music can be heard on tracks A57, A81, A86, A94 and C55. Small positive organs used in continuo groups can be heard on tracks A68, B4 and B7. *EM 6.9.1.*

Organ Mass. A setting of the Ordinary and Proper of the Mass in which plainsong and organ solos alternate. Sometimes a complete text may be replaced by an organ fantasia. This is the case in the Offertoire from Couperin's *Messe pour les paroisses* (A81 comes from the central section of the offertory which is in the style of a monothematic ricercar). *EM 8.7.2.*

Organ chorale. Chorale prelude (A94). *EM 8.7.2.*

Organ point. Pedal point (A86, bars 1–7).

Organa. Plural of organum (A7, A9 and A10). *EM 7.9.4.*

Organistrum (Lat.). Hurdy-gurdy (A18).

Organo (It.), **Orgel** (Ger.), **orgue** (Fr.). Organ. See A57 (Italian renaissance registration), A81 (French baroque registration) and A86 (German baroque registration).

Organo pleno (Lat.). In northern European baroque music, the full flue chorus, with or without reed stops. In A86 pedal reed stops are drawn. *EM 6.9.1.*

Organum. Medieval polyphony in which one or more parts are added to a plainsong melody.

Parallel organum consists of the plainsong melody (*vox principalis*) with another voice (*vox organalis*) singing the same melody a perfect 4th or 5th above or below it (A7(a)). Alternatively two or even three voices can be added to the *vox principalis* as shown in the composite organum of A7(b).

In melismatic organum (A9) the plainsong melody (A8) is sung in long notes that are embellished by the ornate melismas of the *vox organalis*.

The most extensive collection of organa is that of the Parisian School of Notre Dame (c.1150–1250). These differ from earlier examples in that their dance-like triple-time rhythms (derived from poetic metres) were accurately notated. In A10 the melismas in the plainsong setting of 'Domino' (A8) are rendered in long notes in the tenor while the added voice (*duplum*) sings a limited number of short rhythmic patterns derived from the rhythmic modes.

Some 20th-century composers imitated organum for pictorial effect. At the start of 'La Cathédrale engloutie' (C22) Debussy uses the parallel 5ths and 4ths of composite organum, but later adds parallel 9ths (C23) and 3rds (C24). *EM 8.11.11.*

Orgel (Dutch and Ger.), **orgue** (Fr.). Organ (A92–A94)

Ornaments. Decorative notes that flesh out a melodic skeleton. The melodic skeleton of the opening bars of a rondeau by Jacquet de la Guerre is shown in A82, while A83 shows the ornamented version of the same melody heard in bars 37–41 of A84. Ornaments may be improvised: bars 45–64 of B25 show a transcription of the embellished version of Haydn's Menuetto (bars 1–20) that the pianist improvised in accordance with late 18th-century performance practice. Ornaments may be represented by conventional symbols such as those shown above the first eight bars of A84 or they may be written out in full (compare bars 1–8 of A84 with bars 17–24). *EM 3.10, 8.7.3.*

The following are some of the most important types of ornament and ornamentation.

Accent (Fr.) **a)** appoggiatura (B1, bar 4, beat 2), **b)** springer (B25, bar 52).

Ornaments

Acciaccatura, short appoggiatura (C1, bar 1).
Anticipation, cadential ornament (A80, bar 12).
Appoggiatura, unprepared dissonance (B69(b)).
Appuy (Fr.), appoggiatura at the beginning of a trill (B9, bar 4).
Arabesque, extended ornamentation (B64(a), bar 8).
Arpègement (Fr.) **a)** *en montant* (A84, bar 45), **b)** *en descendant* (B17, letter c in bar 3).
Arpeggio **a)** arpeggiation (B66, bar 1), **b)** arpeggiando (A96).
Ascending trill, trill beginning on the lower note (A84, letter f in bar 44).
Backfall, type of appoggiatura (B1, bar 4, beat 2).
Battement (Fr.), lower mordent (A84, letter a in bars 1 and 17).
Battery, broken chords (A96).
Beat, type of lower mordent (A84, letter a, bars 1 and 17).
Bebung (Ger.), tremolo on clavichord (B20, second minim).
Beisser (Ger.), type of lower mordent (B1, bar 1);
Brisé (Fr.), arpeggiation (A84, bar 45).
Broken chord, successive articulation of chord-notes (A98, bars 14–17).
Cadence (Fr.) **a)** trill (B17, letter f in bar 4), **b)** turn (A84, letter b in bars 1 and 17).
Cadent, anticipation (A80, bar 12).
Chute (Fr.) **a)** appoggiatura (B17, bar 3, letter c, G♯–A), **b)** anticipation (A80, bar 12).
Coulé (Fr.) **a)** descending appoggiatura (B1, bar 4, beat 2), **b)** *coulé sur une tierce* or slide (A84, bar 12).
Descending trill, trill beginning on the upper note and descending to the lower note before the trill proper (B1, bar 3, beat 2).
Diminutions and divisions, types of ornamental variations (B18).
Doppelschlag (Ger.), turn (B1, bar 6, beat 3).
Doppelt-cadence (Mac.), ascending or descending trill (A84, letter f in bar 44 and B1, bar 3, beat 2).
Doppeltriller (Ger.), trill ending with a turn (all of the ornaments in B11).
Double cadence (Fr.), short trill ending with a turn (B17, letter f, bar 4).
Doublé (Fr.), turn (B17, letter e, bar 4).
Échappée (Fr.), escape note (B25, bar 52, semiquaver E♭).

Fioriture, ornaments (A66).
Forefall, type of appoggiatura (B17, letter b, bar 1).
Glissando, type of slide (C27, harp).
Glosa (Span.), ornamentation (A34).
Gorgie (It.), embellishments (A66).
Grace notes, ornaments printed in small type (B65, bars 7 and 9).
Gruppo and *gruppetto* (It.), trill ending in turn (A66, bar 5).
Lower mordent, ornament containing a lower auxiliary (A84, letter a in bars 1 and 17).
Mordent **a)** lower mordent (A84, letter a in bars 1 and 17), **b)** upper mordent (A84, letter c in bars 5 and 21).
Nachschlag (Ger.) **a)** turn at the end of a trill (B1, bar 3, beat 3), **b)** springer (B25, bar 52), **c)** anticipation (A95, bar 15, beat 3, semiquaver D♮).
Passaggio (It.), florid ornamentation (A66).
Pincé (Fr.), lower mordent (B17, letter a in bar 1).
Portamento, vocal slide (C96, baritone, bars 29–35).
Port de voix (Fr.), appoggiatura (B17, letter b in bar 1).
Pralltriller (Ger.) **a)** short trill (A84, letter c in bars 5 and 21), **b)** upper mordent (B25, bar 58).
Relish, trill ending with a turn (A84, letter d in bars 8 and 24).
Ribattuta (It.), trill in uneven notes (A62).
Schleifer (Ger.), slide (B25, bar 60).
Schneller (Ger.), upper mordent (B25, bar 56).
Shake, trill (A80, bars 12 and 37).
Slide, conjunct ascent to main note (A84, letter e in bar 12).
Springer, *échappée* (B25, bar 52).
Tirade (Fr.), rapid scale (B20, penultimate system).
Tremblement (Fr.), trill **a)** *tremblement détaché* (A84, letter d in bars 8 and 24), **b)** *tremblement coulée* (A84, letter f in bar 44), **c)** *double cadence* (B17, letter f in bar 4).
Tremolo **a)** *trillo* (A66), **b)** strumming on one note (C29, mandolin), **c)** alternation of notes more than a step apart (C69, bars 4–9, violins).
Trill **a)** *tremblement* (A84, letters d in bar 8 and f in bar 44; B17, letter f in bar 4), **b)** without *Nachschlag* (B9, bars 4 and 9), **c)** with *Nachschlag* (all of the ornaments in B11).

Osanna

Trillo (It.) **a)** vocal tremolo (A62), **b)** trill (B36, bars 248–252).

Turn, main note with upper and lower auxiliaries (A84, letter b in bars 1 and 17).

Upper mordent **a)** baroque (A84, letter c in bars 5 and 21), **b)** classical (B25, bar 56).

Vibrato **a)** string (C18(c)), **b)** vocal (C96, bars 29–34).

Vorschlag (Ger.) **a)** appoggiatura (B69(ii)), **b)** grace note (B1, the small notes in bar 2).

Osanna. Alternative spelling of Hosanna (A20)

Ostinato. A rhythmic, melodic or harmonic pattern repeated many times in succession. The rhythm shown in the first bar of C36 is repeated 15 times in this extract (and many more times in the complete movement). The melodic pattern played by a viola in the first two bars of C12 is heard six times on tracks C16 and C17. The one-bar ostinato figure heard four times on track C13 is repeated nine times on track C17 (where it combines with two other ostinato figures played on the second violin and viola). A longer ostinato forms a ground bass in A75. *EM 7.8.1.*

Ottava (It.). The interval of an octave (C95, bar 11). 'All'ottava', 'ottava alta', 'ottava sopra' (or the abbreviations 8va or 8 above the stave) all indicate that the music is to be performed or sounds an octave higher than written (C76, bars 9–11). 'Ottava bassa', 'ottava sotto' (or the abbreviations 8vb or 8 below the stave) indicate that the music is to be performed or sounds an octave lower than written (C7).

Ottavino (It.). Piccolo (C76, bars 9–11).

Ouvert and clos (Fr.). Open and closed endings to phrases that are repeated in medieval songs. In A13 each *Stollen* consists of two four-bar phrases, the second identical to the first except for the open and closed endings (which here sound just like modern perfect and imperfect cadences). The same is true of the two pairs of phrases in A16.

Ouverture (Fr.). **1.** Overture (B59). **2.** French overture (A80). **3.** A suite named after its first movement when it is entitled ouverture. Bach's four orchestral suites are thus entitled.

Over-dotting. See *Dotted rhythms* and compare A76 with A77. *EM 1.6.2.*

Overblowing. In wind instruments, the process by which pitches higher than the fundamental tones (ie harmonics) are produced. In C76 the flute is overblown in bars 1–3 but fundamental tones are used in bar 4.

Overlapping. 1. In contrapuntal textures, a passage where a new entry starts before another part has completed its phrase. In A61 Gibbons allocates a different musical phrase to each new phrase of the text. In bar 11 the tenor is still singing the three-note setting of the words 'the earth quakes' as the alto and then the bass enter with a new five-note setting of the words 'the sun is darkened'. It is by this technique of overlapping that the six points of imitation are unified in an uninterrupted flow of counterpoint lasting 22 bars. **2.** In counterpoint, voice leading such that a lower voice moves to a higher note than the note just vacated by a higher voice (or vice versa). In bars 29–30 of A59 the lowest voice (tenor) moves up a perfect 4th from C♯ to F♯, thus overlapping with the alto part (the tenor F♯ in bar 30 being higher than the alto E♮ in bar 29). On track A59 a brief silence has been introduced between these two bars to allow the effect to be heard more clearly.

Overtone. Any component of a single musical sound other than the fundamental. In C95 all of the notes of the harmonic series other than the bottom C are overtones. The more complex vibrations of a bell include non-harmonic overtones (B60).

Overture. 1. An instrumental prelude to vocal works such as operas and oratorios. Romantic overtures often make reference to music that will later be heard in the opera itself (compare bars 25–30 of B59 with bars 4–11 of B60). **2.** An independent orchestral piece in one movement, often based on an elaborate programme. A68 shows the start of an operatic overture that Wagner modified to make it suitable for performance in the concert hall. **3.** French overture (A80).

P

P (*p*). Abbreviation of *piano*, ie soft (B59, bar 3).

Padovana, padoana (It.). A dance from Padua. In the 16th century it could refer to dances in the style of the pavan (A32) or passamezzo.

Paired imitation. 1. Imitation in which two voices enter simultaneously and are imitated by two more voices entering simultaneously (A31). **2.** Imitation in which two voices engage in close imitation followed after some time by two more voices that also engage in close imitation. In A44 the soprano and alto enter as a pair at the start then, after several bars, the tenor and bass enter as a pair using the same imitative motive as the soprano and alto. See also *Counterpoint*.

Palindrome. In literature, a sentence or word that reads the same forwards and backwards, eg the name Anna. In music the same effect is achieved when a given passage is immediately followed by the same passage played backwards (B25, bars 1–10 and 11–20 respectively). *EM 7.4.1.*

Pandiatonicism. A term invented by Nicolas Slonimsky to describe 20th-century styles that use all of the pitches of a diatonic scale to form dissonant harmony or counterpoint which is nevertheless clearly tonal because of the absence of chromatic pitches. Slonimsky specifically refers to the opening pages of Prokofiev's Piano Concerto No. 3 and the use of added-6th and -9th chords. But, as in many other respects, Debussy anticipated pandiatonicism in some of his most characteristic music. In the first two bars of C23 he uses all but one of the seven degrees of a C-major scale. Yet, although every chord is dissonant (particularly featuring added-9th chords), the tonality of C major is clear because of the C♯s in the bass and the lack of chromaticism. In the next two bars of the same example added 2nds and added 6ths do nothing to obscure the D-major tonality of the passage.

Pans. Steel drums, steel pans (C97, bars 54–66).

Pantonality. As used by Schoenberg, music that is 'inclusive of all tonalities' (C34). The term is rarely used, the music to which Schoenberg was referring now being almost exclusively described as atonal (a term he detested). Some authorities claim the term was invented by Rudolph Réti in 1958. See also *Polytonality. EM 8.11.3.*

Parallel chords. A succession of chords all having the same intervals and spacing. In C22 a succession of bare-5th chords moves upwards in parallel motion. In C25 a succession of chords having the same intervallic structure as a dominant 7th moves downwards in parallel motion. These chords do not function as dominants because they all fail to resolve to a tonic chord. In fact the repeated use of parallel chords of this type undermines classical tonality. In its stead there is a succession of chords that are valued for their intrinsic tonal colours (rather than their ability, in other contexts, to establish a key). Harmony of this sort was an important element of musical impressionism.

Parallel 5ths and octaves. See *Consecutive 5ths and octaves, Parallel motion*, A7a (parallel 5ths) and A26, bars 1–11 (parallel octaves).

Parallel key, parallel major, parallel minor. Major and minor keys sharing the same tonic. D major (A97) is the parallel major key of D minor (A98).

Parallel motion. Two or more vocal or instrumental parts moving in the same direction and maintaining the same vertical interval. A variety of types of parallel motion is featured among the recordings, notably: **a)** parallel 2nds (C81, trumpets), **b)** parallel 3rds (C78), **c)** parallel 4ths (C65, bars 8–12), **d)** parallel 5ths (A7(a) and C80), **e)** parallel 6ths (C77), **f)** parallel 7ths (C79), **g)** parallel octaves (A26, bars 1–11), **h)** parallel 9ths (C23). See also *Motion* and A85, bars 6–7.

Parallel organum. See *Organum* and A7. In C22 Debussy imitates the effect of parallel organum to suggest the legendary medieval cathedral of Ys rising from the waves. *EM 8.5.1.*

Paralleltonart (Ger.). Relative key. In B27 the first subject is in D minor (bars 1–8) while the second subject (bars 13–33) is in the relative key of F major.

Paraphrase

Paraphrase. 1. A metrical version of scripture, especially of a psalm, set to music in homophonic, hymn-like style. The text of A37 comes from Archbishop Parker's *The Whole Psalter Translated into English Metre* (1567). It is a paraphrase of the first two verses of Psalm 2: 'Why do the heathen rage, And the people imagine a vain thing? The kings of the earth set themselves up, And the rulers take counsel together, Against the Lord, and against his anointed' (Authorised Version). The chordal style of the first phrase is maintained throughout the whole setting. In its original form the melody appears in the tenor part. **2.** See *Paraphrase Mass* and A49–A52. **3.** In the 19th century, a fantasia on popular or operatic melodies. They are most often written for piano and are of great virtuosity. Liszt wrote more than 70 operatic paraphrases, some of which he called fantasias or reminiscences.

Paraphrase Mass. A polyphonic Mass of the renaissance era that utilises a pre-existent secular or sacred melody in one or more voices. A50 and A52 show how Palestrina modifies the second phrase of the plainsong hymn *Iste confessor* (A49) to form one of the contrapuntal lines in his Mass of the same name. Versions of this melody can be heard in all voices of the imitative counterpoint of A52. *EM 7.10.1, 8.6.1.*

Parlando (It.). A performance direction indicating a speech-like delivery of melody and text. Hauer directs that the performance of his songs (C40) should 'follow the poet's speech'. See also *Sprechgesang*.

Parody. 1. A work that makes satirical use of material from another composition. Beneath the score of 'Fossils' (C8) the opening bars of the first theme of Saint-Saëns's own *Danse macabre* is shown. Although confined within a minor 3rd the composer skilfully manipulates the opening motive (x) to produce a continuous melody with a sting in its tail (the final A♭ of the quotation). The composer's parody ('Allegro ridicolo') distorts this theme by diverting the tonality from the sinister key of G minor to the cheery key of B♭ major, and by subjecting motive x to the sort of sequential development that is a commonplace of classical styles. Then, at the very last moment, he modulates back to the original key of G minor (a process that would not have received the approval of composition professors at the Paris Conservatoire). **2.** A vocal composition in which the original music is retained but a new text substituted in place of the old one. In the middle ages this was known as a contrafactum (compare A14 and A15). **3.** A radical reworking of pre-existent music to create a new work. A comparison of C93 and C94 reveals the way in which Kancheli uses motifs from Bach's invention to create cluster chords and how, by opposing dissonant harmony in two unrelated keys (A minor and C minor), he has completely altered Bach's serene progression through a circle of 5ths to the related key of C major. See *Parody Mass* and A44, A45 and A46. *EM 8.11.5, 8.11.6.*

Parody Mass. A Mass of the renaissance era that utilises complete sections of a pre-existent polyphonic composition (such as a chanson or motet). On track A44 the first 39 bars of Victoria's motet *O magnum mysterium* can be heard, while on tracks A45 and A46 the same composer's parody of two sections of it can be heard. A44 (ordinary note-heads), and A45 and A46 (diamond note-heads) show how Victoria has adapted these two sections of his motet to form the first and second Kyries of his *Missa O magnum mysterium*. *EM 7.10.1, 8.6.1.*

Part. 1. In music for more than one performer, the printed music for an individual musician, or the sounding melody or harmony that is heard when the printed part is played or sung. In B3 there are three parts/melodies (one each for soprano, alto and tenor voice). **2.** In polyphonic music for a soloist, a single melodic strand. B2 begins in two parts which may be identified as tenor and bass parts even though they are not sung. In bar 2 two more parts are added which may be similarly identified as soprano and alto parts. The texture of the whole of this extract may be described as four-part counterpoint, the individual melodic strands being identified by analogy with vocal music as soprano (the uppermost part), alto (the second part down), tenor (the third part down) and bass (the lowest part).

Part crossing. The rising of a voice that normally sings a lower part above a voice that normally sings a higher part, or vice versa. In bar 6 of A30 the soprano part (shown with stems pointing up) crosses the

Passing note

alto part (shown with stems pointing down) on the third beat.

Part song. 1. In a narrow sense, a 19th- or 20th-century secular composition in several parts for unaccompanied voices. **2.** In a broad sense, any unaccompanied secular vocal composition in several parts, including the frottola (A30), chanson (A31), madrigal (A33), ballett (A59) and quodlibet (B3). *EM 8.6.3.*

Part writing. The art of composing and combining melodies within the limitations of a particular style. In A52 Palestrina's smoothly flowing parts are governed by self-imposed stylistic limitations. For instance, the tritone, major 6th, the 7th and intervals greater than an octave are avoided altogether, and when there is a leap it is followed either by conjunct movement or a leap in the opposite direction. The harmony that these melodic lines engender is also strictly governed, so that, for example, any part forming an on-beat discord (such as the D♮ that clashes with the E♮ at the start of bar 4) is followed by a descent to a concord (in this case the C♯ on the second beat of the bar).

Palestrina's immaculate part writing has been admired since the 16th century, but it is not only in complex contrapuntal textures that composers strive for lucid part writing. In B30 Haydn's harmony, particularly the discords, are the main focus of attention in this homophonic style, but he makes sure that each part has a melodic as well as harmonic role to play (though the viola's melodic interest is not obvious until the last two bars). See *Voice leading*.

Partial. One of the component modes of vibration in a compound tone. The term is usually reserved for overtones that are generated by instruments such as a bell (B60), the tone of which includes non-harmonic partials. *EM 5.2.*

Particella (It.), **Particell** (Ger.). A detailed sketch of a composition on fewer staves than a full score. It is not intended for performance (like the piano reduction used in C73); rather it is a stage in the compositional process (like an artist's sketch for an oil painting). C6 gives some idea of how a particella might look and how it relates to the eventual orchestral sound (which, in the original score, is represented on 13 rather than three staves).

Partita (It.), **Partie, Parthia** (Ger.). **1.** In the 16th and 17th centuries, a single piece or a variation (most often on a well-known melody such as that shown above A34). **2.** In the late baroque era, an alternative title for a suite (A88 is an extract from one of the movements in Bach's Partita in D minor for unaccompanied violin). *EM 8.7.3.*

Partition (Fr.), **Partitur** (Ger.), **partitura** (It.). Score (B32–B35).

Passacaglia (It.), **passecaille** (Fr.). See *Chaconne and passacaglia* and A95–A98. Schoenberg's subtitle for 'Nacht' (C34) is 'Passacaglia', but the ostinato on which it is based (x in bar 1) is so short and subjected to so much manipulation that some might think the subtitle inappropriate. *EM 7.8.4.*

Passage. Any part of a composition, of any length and not necessarily of structural significance. The term is used to avoid words such as part or section which can have other meanings. One might, for instance, refer to 'the passage of dotted rhythms in bars 41–42' of A84, but refer to 'the section beginning at beat 2 of bar 41' because the latter is the complete *petite reprise*.

Passage work. Scales, arpeggios and other types of figuration perhaps linking important thematic material (B50, bars 47–50) or displaying the performer's virtuosity (compare A65 and A66).

Passaggio (It.). **1.** Florid ornamentation (A66). See *Ornaments.* **2.** A transition or modulation (B40, bars 18–25). **3.** The point at which a singer's head voice and chest voice meet or overlap. See *Break* and C30.

Passamezzo. A 16th-century duple-metre Italian dance similar in style to the contemporary pavan (A32), but structurally similar to the contemporary romanesca (A34). Like the romanesca it had stock harmonic progressions upon which it was common for the composer to write variations. There were two such progressions, one in the minor (for the *passamezzo antico*) and one in the major (for the *passamezzo moderno*).

Passing modulation. See *Transitory modulation* and bars 11–15 of B57 in which there is a fleeting modulation to A minor.

Passing note, passing tone. An unessential note filling the gap between two consonant notes a 3rd apart. The passing note identified by a cross in A47 links the E♭ (which is

Passion

consonant with both bass notes) to the C♮ (which is consonant with the A♭ below it). Like most passing notes the D♭ is dissonant. This is more evident in A48 where the same passing note forms the dissonant interval of a minor 9th with the tenor C♮. Taken in context, however (A46, bar 37), offbeat passing notes such as this are not registered as dissonant; they sound like what they are – passing melodic decorations. *EM 4.3.1.*

Passion. A musical setting of the story (*historia*) of the Last Supper, the arrest and trial of Jesus and his crucifixion as recorded in one of the Gospels. In the baroque era a singer representing the Evangelist narrated the biblical text in recitative (B4(a)), while the words of the crowds (*turbae*) were set as short, fast choruses (B4(b)). The Gospel story was punctuated by meditative arias and ariosos (B5), while harmonised chorales introduced melodies with which Lutheran congregations would already have been familiar. *EM 8.7.2.*

Pastiche (Fr.). An imitation of the style of another composer or school of composers. C29 is a pastiche of classical music (such as B40) which verges on sardonic parody. *EM 8.11.1, EM 8.11.8.*

Pastorale. A composition that, by its style, suggests idyllic (or idealised) scenes of rural life. The pastoral tradition in music dates back to the middle ages, but its most famous manifestations are 18th-century instrumental works in the style of the siciliana (eg the 'Pastoral Symphony' in Handel's *Messiah*). See B19.

Pauken (Ger.). Timpani (C27).

Pausa (It.), **pause** (Fr.), **Pause** (Ger.). Rest. Quaver (𝄾) and crotchet (𝄽) rests are shown in B68. Note that the pause marks (⌢) in this extract are *fermate* in Italian and should not be confused with the *pausa*.

Pause. In music of the 19th and 20th centuries a pause mark (⌢) means what it says and is usually observed by performers (B70). In baroque music pause marks were often a conventional symbol at the end of a section which might or might not be respected by performers (Bach's pause mark in bar 80 of B15 is rightly disregarded at the end of the first performance of bars 1–80, but is respected when this section is repeated). On the other hand, pauses are sometimes introduced (in conformity with baroque practice) where the composer did not write a pause mark (as in bar 64 of the same aria).

Pavan, pavane (Fr.), **Paduana** (Ger.), **pavana** (It.). A stately dance of the 16th century in slow to moderate duple time. Although the extract from the famous pavan *La Bataille* (A32) has fast rhythms (evoking the sounds of battle), the underlying duple-time minim pulse is in a moderate tempo. A pavan was often followed by a saltarello (A18) or galliard (A35). *EM 8.6.3.*

Pavillon(s) en l'air (Fr.). A performance direction found in wind parts indicating that the bells of the instruments should be raised. In bar 23 of C97 this is indicated by the synonymous Italian phrase 'campane in aria'.

Ped. Abbreviation of pedal. In the first two bars of B66 Chopin's original pedal marks are shown. The bracket after Ped indicates that the sustaining pedal should be engaged for a whole bar then changed at the bar line. In B78 Brahms's performance direction 'col ped.' literally means 'with pedal'. This implies that the sustaining pedal should be used in such a way that a legato effect is produced without one chord running into the next throughout the extract.

Pedal, pedal point. A sustained or repeated note against which changing harmonies are heard. Pedals are categorised according to their harmonic function and their position in the musical texture: **a)** tonic pedal: a pedal on the first degree of the scale of the prevailing key. The E♭ that is repeated many times in the first two and a half bars of B5 is the tonic note of E♭ major, **b)** dominant pedal: a pedal on the fifth degree of the scale of the prevailing key. The C♮ that is repeated several times in the first seven bars of A86 is the dominant note of F major, **c)** double pedal: a two-note pedal, usually consisting of tonic and dominant notes. The C♯ and G♯ at the bottom of the arpeggiated chords in bars 5–8 and 13–16 of B65 are the tonic and dominant notes of the prevailing key of C♯ minor, **d)** inverted pedal: a pedal sounding above changing harmonies beneath it. The tied A♮s in bars 5–7 of A70 form an inverted tonic pedal in the prevailing key of A major. An inverted pedal can be heard throughout C67, **e)** inner pedal, internal pedal: a pedal in an inner part. The repeated A♭s throughout B75 are enclosed by right-hand chords and the left-hand bass part.

Pedal (Eng. and Ger.). A foot-operated lever on an organ (see *Pedals* 1 and C55), a piano (see *Pedals* 2 and B74), or timpani (see *Pedal drums* and C82, bars 68–69). On a harp a set of pedals allows the performer to set the pitches of the strings to allow a variety of scales and arpeggios to be played. In C27 the harpist sets the pedals so the scale of G major can be played, while in C81 the pedals are set for a whole-tone scale. Pedal-operated drums and cymbals are found in pop and jazz bands (C38). Foot-operated levers that can change the registrations of the manuals, pedals or the whole instrument are found on some organs and harpsichords. See also *Pedalboard* and *Pedaliter*.

Pedal drums, pedal timpani. Timpani fitted with pedals that can change the tension of the membrane to allow instantaneous changes of pitch. Also called chromatic timpani. The most characteristic effect of a pedal drum is a glissando which is achieved by playing a roll while gradually altering the position of the pedal (C82, bars 68–69). *EM 6.8.1.*

Pédale (Fr.), **pedale** (It.). Pedal. In C55 Messiaen's use of the term simply confirms that the music on the lowest stave of each system is to be played on the pedalboard of the organ. Brahms's macaronic performance direction at the start of B75 ('sempre les deux pédales') means that the *una corda* pedal should be engaged throughout, but the sustaining pedal should be changed to produce a legato effect without one chord running into the next (see also B74). In C56 Bartók uses the Italian plural of *pedale* to indicate that both pedals should be engaged throughout the extract

Pedalboard, pedal organ. On most modern organs the pedalboard is a keyboard ranging from C–f[1] designed to be played by the performer's feet. Although the pedal department of an organ contains ranks of pipes at 16-foot, 32-foot or even 64-foot pitch (sounding one, two and three octaves below printed pitch), higher-pitched ranks can add brilliance to a bass part (A86, bars 17–20) and can also provide melodic lines at or above the pitch of the manual parts (A94).

Pedalpauke (Ger.). Pedal drum (C82, bars 68–69).

Pedals. 1. On an organ, a set of keys operated by the feet. Both pitch and timbre can be changed by the organist's choice of pedal stops. On track A86 a range of pedal stops produces very deep sounds (some lower than the printed notes). On track A94 pedal reed pipes of high pitch are used for a melody that sounds above the real bass (played by the performer's left hand). Many organs have a set of levers mounted above the pedal board that allow the performers to change the registration of the manuals, pedals or the whole organ instantaneously. **2.** On a piano two (sometimes three) foot-operated levers. The *una corda* pedal (left-hand pedal) reduces volume and changes the timbre of the instrument. The damper or sustaining pedal (right-hand pedal) allows strings that have been struck to continue sounding after the keys have been released. The effects of both of these pedals can be heard on track B74. A third pedal (not available on all grand pianos) allows a single chord to be sustained leaving the pianist free to play other notes that would normally be out of reach with great clarity (C67, bars 15–17). **3.** On a harp a set of foot-operated levers that allow the performer to set the pitches of the strings to allow a variety of scales and arpeggios to be played. In C27 the harpist is directed to set the pedals so a scale of G major can be played, while in C81 the harpist is directed to set the pedals so that a whole-tone scale can be played. **4.** On some large harpsichords, one or more foot-operated levers that allow the performer to couple or uncouple the manuals, so allowing a wide range of dynamic levels without having to move the hands from the keyboards. **5.** Kettle drums are usually tuned by a set of screws round the circumference of the head, but some modern timpani are fitted with a pedal that allows instantaneous changes of pitch. On such an instrument a glissando can be achieved by simultaneously playing a roll and changing the tension of the membrane by means of the foot-pedal (C82, bars 68–69). **6.** Pedal-operated drums and cymbals are found in pop and jazz bands (C38).

Pellet bell. A small spherical metal ball containing a piece of metal that rattles when the bell is shaken. Sleigh bells consist of several of these bells mounted on a stick (C49 and C52).

Pentachord. A collection of five pitches such as the first five degrees of a scale (G–D

Pentatonic scale

in B18) or the five-note chords derived from Messiaen's seventh mode of limited transposition at the start of C55. *EM 2.9.2.*

Pentatonic scale. A scale of five pitch classes. The most familiar is the scale that can be produced by playing the black notes on a piano. In transposed form music based on this scale can be heard on track C63. It consists of the notes G, A, B, D and E (with G repeated an octave above the first G to complete the scale). This anhemitonic scale is tonally ambiguous. If it ends on G the music will sound major (C60), if it ends on E the music will sound minor (C61). Another collection of pitches that can be arranged as an anhemitonic pentatonic scale can be heard on track C62 and in the left-hand part of the complete piece (C63, bars 9–19). Pentatonic scales containing semitones are common in non-western cultures. In bars 2–3 of C64 five pitches of a pentatonic scale include semitones between the first and last pairs of notes. *EM 2.9, 8.11.7.*

Per arsin et thesin. See *Arsis and thesis* and B14, bars 23–26. See also C64, bars 6–8. *EM 4.5.7.*

Percussion instruments. Instruments that are struck (eg drums), clashed (eg cymbals), scraped (eg the güiro) or shaken (eg maracas).

For tuned percussion see *Antique cymbals* (C19), *Celesta* (C35), *Cimbalom* (C41), *Glockenspiel* (C3), *Hand bells* (C97, bars 36–38), *Marimba* (C90), *Piano*, plucked strings (C94, bar 3), *Steel drums* (C97, bars 54–66), *Timpani* (C27), *Tubular bells* (C97, bars 36–38), *Vibraphone* (C87), *Xylophone* (C8).

For percussion of indefinite pitch see *Anvil* (C48), *Bass drum* (C49), *Bells* (B60), *Bongos* (C45), *Brake drums* (C97, bars 9–14), *Castanets* (C50), *Claves* (C51), *Cowbells* (C28), *Cymbals* (C47 and C97, bars 21–22), *Gong* (C48), *Güiro* (C51), *Maracas* (C46), *Rommelpot* (A36), *Side drum* (A32), *Siren* (C44), *Sleigh bells* (C49), *String drum* (C46), *Tabor* (A35), *Tambourine* (C42), *Tam-tam* (C48), *Tarole* (C43), *Tenor drum* (C43), *Triangle* (C47), *Whip* (C46), *Wood blocks* (C51). *EM 6.8.*

Percussione (It.). See *Percussion instruments* and C42–C54.

Perdendosi (It.). Dying away. Although MacMillan does not use the term, this is the effect in the closing bars of C97.

Perfect cadence. A dominant chord (V) followed by a tonic chord (I) at the end of a phrase (B6, bars 11–12, 14–15 and the last bar). *EM 5.4.1.*

Perfect 5th. The interval between the first and fifth degrees of a diatonic scale and other intervals encompassing the same range. A perfect 5th encompasses the same interval as seven semitones. A40 begins with a rising perfect 5th ('A-ve'), and the second phrase of this hymn ('Dei Ma-') begins with a falling perfect 5th. The interval can be heard harmonically on C80 in which two flutes play parallel 5ths throughout. See *Intervals. EM 2.2.2, 5.2.*

Perfect 4th. The interval between the first and fourth degrees of a diatonic scale and other intervals encompassing the same range. A perfect 4th encompasses the same interval as five semitones. See *Intervals* and C65 in which both melodic and harmonic perfect 4ths are identified by brackets. *EM 2.2.2, 5.2.*

Perfect interval. An interval (the distance between two pitches) in which the ratio of their frequencies can be expressed in small numbers. A1 shows that the ratio of two pitches a perfect octave apart is 2:1. For instance a^1 is produced by a body vibrating 440 times per second, twice as fast as the a an octave lower (440:220 = 2:1). The other perfect intervals are the 5th (3:2) and 4th (4:3). All of them can be heard in bar 11 of C95 and their frequencies are shown below the extra stave (perfect octave 128:64 Hz = 2:1, perfect 5th 192:128 Hz = 3:2, perfect 4th 256:192 Hz = 4:3). These were the intervals that were regarded by the ancient Greeks and medieval theorists as absolute concords (A7). In the modern equally tempered scale to which keyboard instruments are now tuned these ratios cannot be precisely maintained (except for the perfect octave, which always has a ratio of 2:1). See *Perfect 5th*, *Perfect 4th* and *Perfect octave. EM 2.2.2, 5.2.*

Perfect octave. See *Intervals*. All consecutive notes in A1 and A2 are an octave apart. *EM 2.2.2, 5.2.*

Perfect pitch. See *Absolute pitch*. A listener with perfect pitch would be able to hear without reference to any other source of sound that A95–A98 were not being performed at standard modern pitch.

Performing practice. Those aspects of performance that are not immediately obvious in written or printed notation. This is vividly exemplified in the performance of an aria by Monteverdi in which the original printed notation (A65) gives no idea of what was expected of a virtuoso vocalist in the early 17th century (A66). Similarly the printed notation of B17 gives little idea of what was expected of a harpsichordist of the French classical school.

Period. 1. In tonal music, a complete statement brought to a conclusion by a definitive cadence. The antecedent and consequent form a period in B28 and B49. **2.** The time taken to complete one cycle of a vibration (see *Hertz* and A1–A3). *EM 7.3, 7.4.2.*

Periodic phrasing. Phrasing that consists of a regular series of two-, four- or eight-bar units that are repeated or answer each other like antecedents and consequents. B41 falls into four periodic phrases, each of them four bars long.

Perpetual canon. Round (the four upper voices of A15).

Perpetuum mobile (Lat.). A piece featuring continuous rapid motion, often using the same time-value throughout. The right-hand part of B66 is in semiquavers throughout.

Pes (Lat.). **1.** A two-note rising figure sung to one syllable (or the same vowel sound in a melisma). The *pes* (or *podatus*) was one of a variety neumes (notes or groups of notes) in the medieval system of pitch notation that predated mensural notation (A4). **2.** The lowest part (tenor) in some medieval English polyphony. *Pes* is Latin for foot, and it is in this sense that the anonymous scribe of *Sumer is icumen in* refers to the two-voice ostinato sung below the four canonic voices throughout A15. (This *pes* is also literally at the foot of the famous manuscript in the British Library.) *EM 4.4.6.*

Pesante (It.). Heavily emphasised. Although not so marked, the effect can be heard in bar 2 of C70.

Petite flûte (Fr.). Piccolo (C76, bars 9–11).

Petite pédale (Fr.). The left-hand (soft) pedal on a piano. In B70 its use is indicated by the direction 'una corda'.

Petite reprise (Fr.). The restatement of the final phrase at the end of a French baroque piece. The last four bars of the *grand couplet* are repeated at the end of A84. *EM 7.6.2.*

Pezzo (It.). Piece (A67).

Pf., Pft. Abbreviations of pianoforte (B65).

P. Fl., P^{te} Fl. Abbreviations of *petite flûte* (piccolo). See C76, bars 9–11.

Phantasie (Ger.). Fantasia (B20).

Phrase. The musical equivalent of a verbal phrase, a group of notes forming an incomplete entity. B28 consists of two phrases. The partial musical sense of the first (an eight-bar antecedent) is completed by the second (an eight-bar consequent). Together they form a complete musical period. The extent of a phrase is sometimes made explicit by the use of a phrase mark (an extended curved line). This is the case in the first 8 bars of C2 where two phrase marks indicate the extent of the two four-bar phrases heard in this passage. *EM 3.1, 7.2, 7.3.*

Phrase exchange. A more accurate term for voice exchange favoured by some musicologists (A15, in which the two two-bar phrases x and y are exchanged by the two voices of the *pes*).

Phrasing. The manner in which a melody is articulated as a group of phrases, and the manner in which a performer realises those phrases in sound.

In early music phrasing is not indicated in the score, but it is nonetheless usually quite obvious. A84 begins with a pair of four-bar phrases, the second being a varied repeat of the first. The harpsichordist responds to this phrasing by allowing a very short pause between phrases, and by playing the second phrase on a different manual (so it sounds like an echo of the first).

In later periods composers might indicate the extent of each phrase by an extended curved line (called a phrase mark) drawn over each phrase. Like A84, C2 begins with a pair of four-bar phrases, this time indicated by a pair of phrase marks. The pianist realises these phrases by waiting a moment before beginning the second phrase. In bars 8–22 of B79 Brahms's phrase marks coincide with the implicit cross-rhythms generated by chord changes. Every last detail of this phrasing is realised in the pianist's performance of this passage (and of a similar cross-phrased passage in bars 30–38).

Phrygian cadence. A cadence formed by a first inversion chord on the second degree of the phrygian mode followed by a root position major triad on the final (A37, bars

Phrygian mode

2–3). The same name is given to an imperfect cadence consisting of chords IV^6 and V in later tonal music (A91, bars 23–24). *EM 5.4.2, 5.4.6.*

Phrygian mode. A scale that can be reproduced by playing the white notes of the piano from any E♮ to the E♮ an octave above it (see the diagram of a keyboard on the folded insert, and the descending and ascending scale shown beneath the last four bars of A37). This, the third church mode, is distinguished from other similar scales by semitones between the first and second and between the fifth and sixth degrees of the scale. Like most melodies in the untransposed phrygian mode, Tallis's psalm tune (A37) ends on E♮ (appropriately called the final or *finalis*). The scale can be transposed up or down by any interval. In his *Fantasia on Tallis's theme* (A39) Vaughan Williams transposes the mode up a minor 3rd (the complete melody is stated in the viola part). A38 shows how the last two phrases of the melody contain all of the pitches of this transposed version of Tallis's phrygian melody. A37 is in the authentic phrygian mode – apart from the note labelled 'subtonium' its range extends from the final to the note an octave above it. In its plagal form (Mode IV or the hypophrygian mode) the final is the same, but the range (*ambitus*) theoretically extends from the note a 4th below the final to the note a 5th above it. But in practice the range is often slightly different. In A5 it extends from the C♮ a third below the final to the C♮ an octave above. *EM 2.4.1.*

Pianissimo (*pp*) (It.). Very soft (B59, bar 1). See *Dynamics*.

Piano (*p*) (It.). **1.** Soft. See B59, bar 3. See *Dynamics*. **2.** Abbreviation of pianoforte (C22–C26).

Piano reduction, piano score. A two-stave score of an orchestral composition that is intended to be played on a piano (C73).

Piano trio, piano quartet, piano quintet. Unless qualified these terms refer to ensembles of piano and two, three or four solo strings. C9 is an extract from a work for piano and string quartet.

Pianoforte. A keyboard instrument in which a set of strings is struck by a set of felt-covered hammers. There are two basic designs: the grand piano (C22–C26) is usually more sonorous than the upright piano (C73). Some composers have extended piano techniques and piano timbres by requiring the pianist to perform directly on the strings (C94, bars 3–4 where the sound of plucked piano strings can be distinctly heard). The range of a modern piano is shown on the folded insert. *EM 6.8.7, 6.9.3.*

Piatti (It.). Cymbals (C47).

Picardy 3rd. *Tierce de Picardie* (see the last chord of A81).

Piccolo. A small flute with a range pitched an octave above that of the flute (see the folded insert). Its shrill tones can be heard above the loudest orchestral tutti (B37). *EM 6.6.1.*

Piccolo trumpet. A small trumpet in B♭ (with an extension to change its basic pitch to A♮) that sounds an octave above the standard trumpet in B♭. It was developed to facilitate the performance of works such as Bach's Brandenburg Concerto No. 2. It is often used for less extreme parts (such as B15), but in the hands of a good performer it is difficult for the listener to detect any difference in sound between a trumpet in D and a piccolo trumpet, unless the latter is playing in its extreme upper register.

Pick. 1. A plectrum such as that used to play the mandolin on track C29. **2.** As a verb, to pluck a guitar or similar instrument (C83, bars 19–26) as opposed to strumming it (bars 1–18 in the same example).

Pickup. Anacrusis or upbeat (the first note played on the citole in A13).

Piece, pièce (Fr.). An independent composition or part of a composition. A84 is a piece from Jacquet de la Guerre's *Pièces de clavecin* published in 1707.

Pieno (It.). Full, as in 'organo pieno' (full organ, A86) and 'a voce pieno' (full voice, C96, bar 35).

Piffaro, piffero (It.). Shawm (A32).

Pikkoloflöte, kleine Flöte (Ger.). Piccolo (C76, bars 9–11).

Pikkolotrompete (Ger.). See *Piccolo trumpet* and B15.

Pincé, pincement (Fr.). **1.** Lower mordent (B17, letter a in bar 1). See *Ornaments*. *EM 3.10.2.* **2.** Pizzicato (C71). *EM 6.5.4.*

Pipe and tabor. This combination of instruments played by a single entertainer was popular throughout the middle ages and renaissance. The pipe was held in one hand while the other beat the tabor (A35) with a stick. The pipe had as few as three finger-holes (see *Galoubet*), but achieved a useful range by overblowing (the ocarina in A18 is a modern substitute for a pipe).

Pitch. The depth or height of a note (the pitch of first note sounded on A1 is very low, the last very high). Pitch can be measured in absolute terms by counting the number of vibrations per second of the source of a sound. Thus the note a^1 in A1 is caused by a column of air vibrating 440 times per second (440 Hz). This is the absolute pitch of a^1 that has been accepted as a standard measurement throughout most of the world for most western music. Other pitches can be determined in relation to this fixed pitch. For instance, the notes an octave above and below a^1 have frequencies of 880 Hz and 220 Hz respectively.

Pitch can also be relative. Most authentic performances of baroque music are based on a^1 at around 415 Hz, so printed music performed on authentic instruments will often sound lower in pitch than performances on modern instruments (A88). *EM 2.1, 6.2.*

Pitch aggregate. In certain types of 20th-century music, an unordered collection of pitches. In C88 the notes enclosed in a box in bars 5–7 form an unordered pitch aggregate that can be reordered to form an octatonic scale (as shown on the extra stave below these bars).

Pitch class. A set of notes all having the same letter name. All of the notes sounded on track A1 belong to the same pitch class (A), and the same is true of track A2 (in which the organist plays all of the C♯s that are in common use).

Pitch names. See *Letter names*, A1–A3, the folded insert and *Tonic sol-fa*.

Più (It.). More. After the *accelerando* near the start of C75 the direction 'più mosso' means 'more movement' (faster than *Allegretto*). See *Tempo markings*.

Pivot chord. A chord belonging to two keys and used as a means of modulation from one to the other. The G-major chord in bar 4 of B49 is the tonic chord of G major and the subdominant chord of D major. Acting in these two roles it facilitates a smooth modulation between the two keys. *EM 5.6.*

Pizzicato (pizz.) (It.). Plucked. The different sounds of a plucked violin and a bowed (arco) viola can be heard on C12. Pizzicato chords are played on a cello in C13. Strummed chords (played in the same way as a guitar) are played on a viola in C69. A snap pizzicato (in which the string is plucked vigorously so that it rebounds off the fingerboard) can be heard on C71 (the first beats of bars 1 and 5). A pizzicato glissando is performed by plucking with the right hand then sliding a left-hand finger up or down the string to a new note (C71, bars 7 and 9–13). *EM 6.5.4.*

Pk. Abbreviation of *Pauken* (timpani). See C27.

Plagal cadence, Amen cadence. A subdominant chord (IV) followed by a tonic chord (I) at the end of a phrase (A91, bars 3–4 and 31–32). *EM 5.4.3.*

Plagal modes. Modes with a theoretical *ambitus* (range) from the note a 4th below the final (tonic) to the note a 5th above it. The prefix 'hypo' indicates the plagal form of a mode:

For the hypoaeolian mode (Mode X) see *Aeolian mode* and B61, bars 3–11.

For the hypodorian mode (Mode II) see *Dorian mode* and A8.

For the hypoionian mode (Mode XII) see *Ionian mode* and A13.

For the hypolydian mode (Mode VI) see *Lydian mode* and A18.

For the hypomixolydian mode (Mode VIII) see *Mixolydian mode* and A4.

For the hypophrygian mode (Mode IV) see *Phrygian mode* and A5.

Plainsong, plainchant. Monophonic liturgical chant of the Roman Catholic Church. Most chants date back to the early middle ages and are classified according to their texts and their function in the Mass or monastic office as in the following examples: psalm – monastic office (A6), Benedictus – from the Sanctus of the Mass (A20), hymn – from the monastic office of Vespers (A49), sequence – from the Requiem Mass or Mass for the Dead (B62). See also *Introit* (A4), *Alleluia* (A5), *Acclamation* and *Versicle* (A8). *EM 6.11.1, 8.4, 8.4.1, 8.5.1, 8.11.11.*

Plainte (Fr.). See *Lament*, C33 and C95.

Plaisanterie (Fr.). An early 18th-century harpsichord piece of an unpretentious nature (compare the *plaisanterie* shown in

Planctus

A84 with the extended and serious allemande shown in B17).

Planctus (Lat.). Lament (A11).

Plectrum. A piece of plastic, horn, quill or similar material used for plucking the strings of instruments such as the mandolin (C29) or harpsichord (B17).

Plenum (Lat.). Full organ (A86) or harpsichord (B17).

Pneuma (Lat.). See *Neuma*, A4 (the neumes on the four-line stave) and A5 (the jubilus).

Poco (It.). Little, a little. 'Poco allargando' at the start of C97 means 'growing a little broader'. 'Diminuendo poco a poco' in bars 34–35 of B65 means 'getting quieter little by little'. See *Tempo markings*.

Podatus (Lat.). See *Pes* 1 and A4.

Point, point of imitation. 1. In England, a theme or subject treated imitatively (A60, sackbut, bars 1–2). **2.** A set of imitative entries which, in many renaissance compositions, overlap with the next point of imitation to produce a seamless polyphonic flow. There are three points of imitation in A57. The first is based on a subject (A) that is probably derived from the phrase of plainsong shown in A56. The second (B) is based on a new subject which at bar 9 overlaps with the third point of imitation (again based on the plainsong extract). These points of imitation are easy to hear because the imitative voices are in canon, because the first point of imitation does not overlap with the second, and because the overlap of the second and third points is just one beat long. A more complex instance of the technique can be found in A61 in which six points of imitation overlap to produce a seamless flow of three- and four-part counterpoint in bars 1–22. *EM 4.4.2, 4.4.3*.

Point d'orgue (Fr.). **1.** Pedal point (A86, bars 1–7). **2.** Pause mark ($\frown$ in B70). **3.** A cadenza, which often begins with a pause (A76, bar 5).

Pointer (Fr.). To point, ie to dot. The term is used of the French baroque practice of replacing even conjunct notes with *notes inégales* (compare bars 38–39 with bars 42–43 in A84).

Pointillism. A 20th-century style perfected by Webern in his Five Pieces for Orchestra (C35). Instead of sustained melodies, conventional counterpoint, or block chords, the texture of the music is made up of individual points of sound and melodic fragments. *EM 6.11.8, 8.11.3.*

Polacca (It.). Polonaise (B64).

Polarised texture. A texture common in baroque music where one or two high-pitched melody instruments are accompanied by a continuo group. Polarisation is evident in A70, particularly in the last chord where there is a space of three octaves between the cello and the second violin (and only a 3rd between the two violin parts).

Polonaise. A stately Polish dance in triple time with phrases beginning on the first beat of the bar. In Chopin's stylised piano versions the dance was characterised by the left-hand rhythm shown in bars 1, 3, 4 and 5 of B64(a). *EM 8.10.4.*

Polychoral music. Music for two or more choirs of voices or instruments (or both). Most often these resources are exploited by spatial separation, by antiphonal exchanges and by combination at the approach to important cadences. All of these features are evident in Gabrieli's canzona for three four-part instrumental choirs (A58). *EM 6.11.6.*

Polychord. A complex chord made up of two or more simpler chords, usually belonging to different keys. In bars 62–67 of C82 the whole orchestra plays E♭-major triads and C-major triads simultaneously.

Polymetre. 1. The simultaneous combination of music in two or more different metres. In B42 four bars of a minuet in $\frac{3}{4}$ time can be heard, in B43 five bars of a country dance in $\frac{2}{4}$ time are played, and in B44 8 bars of a German dance in $\frac{3}{8}$ time can be heard. These three metres are combined in B45. **2.** The juxtaposition of two or more rhythmic patterns in different metres. In the first *Stollen* of B6 rhythmic patterns in four different metres are juxtaposed. *EM 1.11.*

Polyphonic instruments. Instruments capable of playing more than one note at a time. These range from ancient instruments such as the vihuela (A34) through to relative newcomers such as the marimba (C90). With the popularisation of electronic keyboards and synthesisers (track A87) in the late 20th century the term polyphony regained its original meaning. Thus a 'fully polyphonic keyboard' means a keyboard capable of realising any chord no matter how many notes it contains (not a keyboard designed to play counterpoint).

Polyphony. 1. As most commonly understood, polyphony is an approximate synonym of counterpoint – the weaving together of two or more melodic lines. In this sense polyphony can be largely note-against-note (A11), imitative (A52), or the parts can be completely independent (A28 and A29). **2.** In early sacred music polyphony means any vocal music that is not monophonic. Thus there is an opposition between plainsong (A6) and polyphony (A7). These quite distinct usages of the same word can cause serious confusion. Far from being heard as polyphony most people nowadays will hear the parallel organum on A7 as a succession of chords – the most absolute form of homophony! *EM 6.11.5, 8.5.*

Polyrhythm. The simultaneous combination of two or more distinctly different types of rhythm. In C12 the complex rhythm played on a viola is combined with a simple quaver rhythm played on a violin. A third rhythm played on a cello (C13) is combined with the simple quaver rhythm in C15 (with conflicting duplets and triplets). In C16 the viola ostinato is combined with a violin melody that contains both duplets and triplets. Finally all four rhythms are combined in C17. *EM 1.9.*

Polythematic. Adjective describing a movement containing more than one theme. This is most often the case in classical sonata form movements (see B40 in which the first and second subjects are contrasted).

Polytonality. The simultaneous combination of melodies or chords from two or more different keys. In C59 the music represented on the upper stave is in the key of F♯ major while that on the lower stave is in the key of D minor. See also *Pantonality. EM 2.6.*

Pommer (Ger.). Old German name for alto, tenor or bass shawm (A32). *EM 6.6.4.*

Pomposo (It.). Pompous (in C7 the term is used ironically).

Ponticello (pont.) (It.) Literally 'little bridge', the term is used in two senses: **1.** The bridge of a string instrument. See *Sul ponticello* and C72, bars 0 and 1. **2.** The join between registers in a singer's voice. See *Chest voice and head voice* and A63, B50 and C30.

Port de voix (Fr.). In 17th- and 18th-century French music (or music in French style), an appoggiatura that usually resolves upwards a step (B17, bar 1, letter b). The *port de voix* is often combined with other ornaments. In the same example, for instance, it is combined with an *arpègement* (letter c). When sung, the ornament was usually embellished with a portamento or vocal slide. It was from this practice that the ornament gained its name, since 'port de voix' literally means a 'carrying of the voice'. See *Ornaments. EM 3.10.2.*

Portamento (It.). Carrying the voice from one note to the next by sliding between them (C96, baritone, bars 29–35, and C97, trebles, bars 52–67). The effect is available on string instruments and some wind instruments, but the term glissando is more often used in this context (C75, bars 16–17). See *Ornaments. EM 3.10.2, 6.5.7.*

Pos. 1. Abbreviation for *Posaune* (trombone, B73, bars 57–58). Also see **Position** 2 and 3. **2.** *Pos. nat.* is an abbreviation of the French performance direction *position naturale*. It indicates a return to a normal bowing position after effects such as *sul ponticello* (C72, bars 0–2, where Bartók uses the Italian equivalent of *pos. nat. – ordinario*).

Posaune (Ger.). Trombone (B73, bars 57–58).

Position. 1. In harmony, the proximity of the constituent notes of a chord. In close position (A59, bar 1) the parts are as close together as possible. In open position (bar 9 in the same example) they are spread over a wider range. **2.** The location of the left hand relative to the fingerboard of a string instrument. In first position on a violin the performer can play up to a perfect 5th above the pitch of the open E string, so in first position the available range on this string is e^2–b^2 (both parts of C58 can therefore be played in first position). By moving the hand up the fingerboard so that the index finger can stop successively higher pitches, so successively higher pitches can be played with the fourth finger. In the late 18th century good violinists would be expected to have mastered the seventh position, thus taking the range up to a^3. Later the range of the violin was pushed ever upwards. The first note in bar 63 of C97 (d^4) might have been played in the tenth position, but at this

Positive organ

altitude one enters a mysterious realm of virtuosity where ordinary mortals fear to tread. Similar positions are used on the viola, but positions on cello and double bass are completely different (because the fingerboards are so much longer). **3.** There are seven positions of the slide on a trombone, each a semitone apart. This allows a performer to play glissandi of up to a tritone (C75, bars 16 and 17).

Positive organ, positif (Fr.), **Positiv** (Ger.). **1.** A small organ commonly used as a continuo instrument in early operas (A62), oratorios (A68) and cantatas (B7). In England this type of instrument is commonly known as a chamber organ. **2.** A separate division of a large organ that is often situated behind the player's back in baroque instruments (when it is known as the *Rückpositiv*). It can include a full chorus of flue pipes that can complement or even compete with the great organ (A93). *EM 6.9.1.*

Possibile (It.). Possible. In the performance directions above bar 9 of C97 'prestissimo possibile' means 'as fast as possible'.

Post-modernism. A vague term referring to any of the many late 20th-century styles developed as a reaction against the complex music of modernist composers such as Boulez (C87). At one extreme post-modernism could be expressed through the new simplicity of minimalism and neominimalism (C89 and C92), while at the other extreme the whole arsenal of 20th-century techniques could be ransacked to devastating effect in eclectic compositions that refuse to be pigeon-holed (C91, C94, C96 and C97). *EM 8.11.11.*

Postlude. 1. A section forming the conclusion of a composition. C11 is an extract from the concluding section of a tone poem. It restates the theme of the opening section, remains in the tonic key throughout and is separated from the main body of the work by a general pause. Strauss calls it an epilogue, but in this context the term is synonymous with postlude. **2.** Organ music played at the end of a church service. This may be improvised, or it may be a composition that suits the overall spirit of the service: A86 could be played at the end of a joyful celebration of Christ's resurrection, while C55 would suit a meditative service on the feast of the Ascension.

Post-romanticism. Music of 20th-century composers such as Mahler (C27–C29) who continued to write music that expressed the ideals of 19th-century romanticism.

Poynct, poynte. Old spelling of point (A60).

Pp (*pp*). Abbreviation of *pianissimo* (B59, bar 1).

Praeambulum, praeludium (Lat.). Prelude (A87).

Pralltriller (Ger.). **1.** In baroque music, a trill of four notes beginning on the upper note on the beat (A84, letter c in bars 5 and 21). The first note of this type of *Pralltriller* is often tied back to the previous note. **2.** In modern German usage, an upper mordent (B25, bar 56). See *Ornaments*.

Pre-classical music. 1. A term covering a range of styles of the mid-18th century, including the *empfindsamer Stil* (B20) and the *style galant* (B25). **2.** All music composed before the second half of the 18th century.

Préambule, prélude (Fr.). Prelude (A87 and B66).

Prelude. 1. An improvised or notated instrumental work played before a more substantial composition, or performed as a preamble to an item in a church service. In northern Europe from the 15th century onwards 'prelude' was a title given to pieces that were similar in style and function to ultramontane instrumental genres such as the fantasia and ricercar (A57). Other preludes were more improvisatory in style. This was particularly true of the 17th-century French *prélude non mesuré*, a harpsichord piece that was notated in such a way that the performer was at liberty to choose how to interpret most of the rhythmic values (in much the same way as C. P. E. Bach wrote out his unbarred fantasias a century later – see B20). In the 17th and 18th centuries north German composers such as J. S. Bach developed a type of organ prelude that was based on a Lutheran chorale melody (A91–A94), as well as freely composed preludial movements that were coupled with organ fugues (A86). The latter type was also cultivated in contemporary secular keyboard music. For instance, the improvisatory Prelude in C minor shown in A87 is, like the majority of Bach's preludes, linked with a fugue in the same key (it could be played before the fugue shown in B14, though the two pieces come from different volumes of Bach's *Well-tempered Clavier*). Sets of preludes and fugues continued to be written in the next two centuries, notably by Mendelssohn and Shostakovich. **2.** In the 19th and 20th centuries, an independent instrumental piece in any form or style. Most of these one-movement compositions are in fact character pieces, the majority of them written for piano solo (B66 and C21), though the title was sometimes used for orchestral tone poems (C19). **3.** An orchestral movement closely connected with an ensuing act of an opera. After the mid-19th century many composers followed Wagner's lead in preferring such integrated preludial music to the more independent overture of earlier periods (B68). *EM 8.7.6.*

Preparation. The sounding of a note as a concord immediately before the same note is sounded as a dissonance. In A54 the alto E♮ on the second beat of bar 6 forms a consonant 3rd with the C♮ below it. This is the preparation for the dissonant suspension heard on the next beat. *EM 4.3.6, 5.2.*

Près de la table (Fr.). In harp music, an instruction that the strings should be plucked near the soundboard (ie near the bottom of the strings). This produces the less resonant sound that can be heard at the bottom of the chords in bars 7–13 of C28 (Mahler uses the German 'Resonanz' to indicate this effect).

Près du chevalet (Fr.). See *Sul ponticello* and C72.

Prestissimo (It.). Extremely fast (C90, bar 14). See *Tempo markings.*

Presto (It.). Very fast (B21). See *Tempo markings.*

Prick song. In England from the late 15th century to the early 17th century, polyphony as opposed to plainsong (the former requiring to be 'pricked out' in mensural notation). See A37 (but note that Tallis's notation has been modernised).

Prima donna (It.). The principal female soloist in an opera company, or the singer performing the principal female role. Although other ladies of the cast of Mozart's *Die Zauberflöte* might question the Queen of the Night's entitlement to the term, she certainly portrays the overbearing arrogance that has come to be associated with the prima donna (B50).

Prima prattica, seconda prattica (It.). First practice and second practice respectively. The terms were used in the early 17th century to distinguish between the styles of 16th-century composers such as Victoria (A44–A46) and Palestrina (A52) and the new early baroque styles of composers such as Monteverdi (A62–A66). Composers who adopted the new styles of the *seconda prattica* thought, with some justification, that perfection of part writing was more important than musical expression of the texts in music of the *prima prattica*. In his *a cappella* Masses Monteverdi continued to observe the stylistic norms of the first practice, but in his secular vocal music he put into practice the guiding principle of the second practice, namely that the words should be 'the mistress of the harmony, not the servant'. To this end angular melodic lines (such as those in A63) could be justified because they reflected the mood of the text (in this case indignation). By the same token irregular treatment of dissonance could be justified. This is evident in bar 4 of A66 where the unprepared C♯s of the *trillo* clash with a G-minor chord and the B♭ at 'cieco' clashes with an F-major chord then resolves irregularly upwards. Again it is the text ('through blinding darkness') that justifies these harmonic irregularities.

Prima volta, seconda volta (It.). Commonly called first-time and second-time bars (C5, bars 7–8 and 15–16), the numbers 1 and 2 and the horizontal brackets show two endings to a passage of music, the first used for the repeat, the second for a continuation. In the full score of the *Nutcracker* the repeats are written out. In C5 the original bar numbers are retained (because this is what is actually heard). Hence bar 7 for the first-time bar and 15 for the second-time bar (similarly with bars 39 and 47).

Primary triads. Triads on the tonic (I), subdominant (IV) and dominant (V). They are so called because they are of primary importance in establishing tonality. In classical music the dominant triad often had a 7th above the bass added to it. This is the case in bars 1–8 of B41 in which all other chords are root-position or inverted primary triads that establish the keys of G major and its dominant, D major. See B49 for a simplified version of this passage. See also *Harmony, Key* and *Tonality. EM 5.5.1.*

Prime

Prime, prime order. In serial music, the basic order of the 12 chromatic notes (C40, bars 0–7). *EM 4.6, 5.8.1.*

Principal. 1. On American and British organs, a foundation stop of open flue pipes of four-foot pitch on the manuals and eight-foot pitch on the pedals (A86). **2.** The leader of an orchestral section. The principal first violinist is called the leader in England and the concertmaster in America. Among other duties a principal is expected to play important solos such as the flute cadenza in C76.

Principale, Prinzipal, Prinzipale (Ger.). The lower register of a natural trumpet (B15, bars 15–22). *EM 6.7.2.*

Programme chanson, program chanson. A polyphonic chanson of the 16th century that depicts natural sounds such as the noise of battle (A31).

Programme music, program music. Music intended to evoke extramusical images, whether or not they are explicitly stated by the composer in a programme note. Even without the programme that Berlioz provided for his *Symphonie fantastique*, his intentions are perfectly clear in the passage of the 'Witches' Sabbath' where he quotes the plainsong melody of the 'Dies irae' to the accompaniment of tolling bells (B63). In 'La Cathédrale engloutie' Debussy's performance directions explicitly refer to the legendary cathedral of Ys hidden in the mist (C22) which gradually becomes clearer as the mists disperse (C23) and finally appears resplendent in the full light of day (C24). *EM 8.10.6, 8.11.1.*

Programme symphony, program symphony. A symphony in which every movement is linked to a central non-musical theme. See *Programme music* and B62–B63. *EM 8.10.6.*

Progression. A series of two or more chords. The most familiar progression is probably the two chords that form a perfect cadence (B46). A longer progression is used as a theme in the set of variations that forms a chaconne (A95, bars 0–4).

Prologue. Normally a spoken or sung introduction to a dramatic work. Britten uses the term in C84 in the same metaphorical sense that Mendelssohn used the term 'Song without Words' for B61 (Britten's Prologue is repeated as an Epilogue at the end of the *Serenade*).

Proper. Those parts of the Mass that change according to the time of the liturgical year or the particular saint whose life and death is commemorated in the Mass. The Proper includes the Introit (sung at the start of Mass), the Gradual (sung after the reading from one of the New Testament Epistles), the Alleluia (sung before the reading from one of the New Testament Gospels), the Offertory (sung while the offerings of bread and wine are brought to the altar), and the Communion (sung while the congregation consumes the consecrated elements). A4 is an introit sung at celebrations of the Mass in the first week of Advent. Like most items of the Proper the text is taken from the psalms. A5 is an Alleluia sung at celebrations of the Mass during the fifth week of Eastertide.

Proposta (It.). The subject of a fugue (B9, bars 0–5) as opposed to the answer or *riposta* (bars 5–10 in the same example).

Proprium Missae (Lat.). The Proper of the Mass including the Kyrie (A52), Benedictus (A20) and Agnus Dei (A19).

Proprium Sanctorum, Proprium de Tempore (Lat.). Those parts of the Mass that are designated for saints' days (Proprium Sanctorum) and those that are appropriate for a day or a season in the church's calendar (Proprium de Tempore). A4 and A5 are both from the Proprium de Tempore, the first for the first week of Advent (the season before Christmas), the second for the fifth week after Easter Sunday.

Prosula (Lat.). In the middle ages, a text added to a lengthy plainsong melisma such as those found in Alleluias (A5). The words were underlaid syllabically, perhaps suggesting that they were an *aide mémoire* as well as an additional source of spiritual meditation.

Psalm, psalmus (Lat.), **psaume** (Fr.). Any one of the sacred poems contained in the biblical Book of Psalms. They are sung in Roman Catholic monastic offices such as Vespers and Compline and in the Anglican offices of Matins and Evensong. A verse of Psalm 104 sung to a psalm tone can be heard on track A6. Verses of psalms appropriate for particular days in the church's year are used in the Proper of the Mass. The introit shown in A4 is typical of the more florid style of chant to which these texts are set. See *Metrical psalm*. *EM 8.4.1.*

Psalm tone. A simple melodic formula that

is repeated, with appropriate modifications, for each verse of a psalm (A6).

Psalm tune. A melody added to a metrical psalm (A37).

Puncta (Lat.). Plural of *punctus* (A16). *EM* 7.9.5.

Punctum (Lat.). A neume representing a single note (A4). See also *Pes*.

Punctus (Lat.). A pair of phrases in an *istampita* (A18) or *ductia* (A16). The first phrase of each pair has an open ending, the second a closed ending. *EM 8.5.2.*

Punktierte (Ger.). Dotted. See *Dots, Dotted rhythm* and A76–A79.

Punteado (Span.). A guitar technique in which individual strings are plucked (C83, bars 19–26) as opposed to the strumming technique called *rasgueado* (bars 1–18). *EM 6.4.5.*

Q

Quadrat (Ger.) The natural sign (♮). See *Accidental, Key signature* and B39, third note.

Quadruple counterpoint. Invertible counterpoint involving four contrapuntal voices (B21, bars 28–42). *EM 4.4.5.*

Quadruple fugue. A fugue containing four subjects which are contrapuntally combined in the same manner as a double fugue (A10–A12). See the last movement of Haydn's String Quartet in C, Op. 20 No. 2.

Quadruple metre, quadruple time. Music governed by a repeating metrical unit consisting of strong–weak–strongish–weak beats, whether in simple time (B30, in which the beat is a crotchet) or compound time (B19, in which the beat is a dotted crotchet). *EM 1.3.*

Quadruple stopping. The performance of four-note broken chords on a bowed string instrument. See *Stopping* and the first chords of bars 1 and 2 of A88.

Quadruple-croche (Fr.). Hemidemisemiquaver or sixty-fourth-note (B18, Variation 5, bar 7, beat 4). See *Note.*

Quadruplet. Four equal notes performed in the time of three equal notes in metres in which the beat is divisible by three. In $\frac{9}{8}$ time there are three dotted-crotchet beats that normally divide into three equal quavers (or the equivalent). In bar 4 of C90 the upper stave of the marimba part consists of three groups of three quavers, each group occupying one dotted-crotchet beat. Against this the lower stave shows a quadruplet of dotted semiquavers on the first beat of the bar. See also *Duplet* and *Triplet. EM 1.8.*

Quartal harmony. Harmony in which chords are constructed from superimposed 4ths (C65). *EM 5.8.2.*

Quarte (Ger.). The interval of a 4th (C65).

Quarter-note. Crotchet (♩). See *Note* and the first stave of B18.

Quarter-tone. Half a semitone. In bars 6, 8 and 9 of C70 arrows in the first violin part show that the affected notes should be played a quarter-tone flat. The effect is particularly acidic because the second violinist plays the same notes in tune.

Quartet. 1. A group of four solo instrumentalists or vocalists. The group singing A33 is a vocal quartet and C87 is performed by a quartet of instrumentalists. **2.** A type of chamber music for four players. The most important genre of this kind is the string quartet (B27, B30–B35, B38, C17, C69–C72).

Quartole (Ger.), **quartolet** (Fr.). See *Quadruplet* and C90, bar 4.

Quasi (It.). Almost, like. The direction 'quasi corno' at the start of C95 means 'like a horn'.

Quasi chitarra (It.). See *Chitarra* and C69 (viola). *EM 6.5.5.*

Quatuor, quatuor à cordes (Fr.). Quartet, string quartet (C17).

Quattro (It.). Four. Thus A33 could be described as a *madrigale a quattro voci* (a madrigal for four voices).

Quaver. Eighth-note (♪). See *Note* and B18, Variation 1.

Querflöte (Ger.). Transverse flute (C76, bars 1–5).

Querflügel (Ger.). Spinet (A67).

Quintal harmony. Harmony based on chords consisting of superimposed 5ths (as opposed to the tertian harmony that dominates most western music). This superimposition of 5ths can be heard building up from a low E♭ in bars 1–12 of B73 (and, in a more complex form, bars 17–19). *EM 5.8.2.*

Quinte (Fr. and Ger.). The interval of a 5th (A40 begins with this interval).

Quintet. 1. A group of five solo performers (C96). **2.** A type of chamber music for five performers. Since the late 18th century the piano quintet has been one of the most important genres of this kind. Unless qualified this term means a work for piano and string quartet (C9).

Quintole (Ger.), **quintolet** (Fr.). Quintuplet (B64(a), bar 2).

Quintsaite (Ger.). The highest (E) string of a violin. Bars 13–18 of C9 are played on the E string.

Quintuor (Fr.). Quintet (C9).

Quintuple metre, quintuple time. Music based on a metrical unit of five beats (C36).

Quintuplet. A group of five equal notes occupying the time normally taken by four notes of the same type (B64(a), bar 2, where a quintuplet of semiquavers is played in the time of four normal semiquavers). See also *Duplet*, *Quadruplet* and *Triplet*. *EM 1.8*.

Quire. An almost obsolete term for 'choir' that is still used of some British cathedral choirs (C30).

Quodlibet (Lat.). A musical structure in which several different pre-existent melodies are contrapuntally combined. In Variation 30 of his *Goldberg Variations* (B2) Bach combines two rustic songs (1 and 2 in B3) with the bass melody and harmonies that pervade the Aria (B1) and all of the other variations. *EM 4.4.7, 8.7.7.*

R

R. Abbreviation of the catalogue of Liszt's works edited by Busoni, Raabe and others, Leipzig, 1907–36. See B70, B73 and B74. (Confusingly, the same letter is sometimes used for Rinaldi's catalogue of Vivaldi's works, but most use Rv. as an abbreviation of Rinaldi/Vivaldi.)

Rabāb, rabōb, rbāb, rebāb, ribāb (Arab.). Any of a number of bowed or plucked string instruments found throughout the Islamic world. A tenth-century description of a bowed rabāb makes it clear that it was this type of instrument that was the progenitor of the western European rebec (A16).

Radical bass. See *Fundamental bass* and B41 (in which the radical bass of bars 1–2 is G♮).

Radical cadence. A cadence in which the last two chords are in root position (A91, bars 7–8, 15–16, 19–20 and 31–32). *EM 5.4.1.*

Radleier (Ger.). Hurdy-gurdy (A18).

Ragtime. An African-American style of the late 19th and early 20th centuries. It was most often for solo piano and was characterised by march-style diatonic 'oom-pah' accompaniments, syncopated melodies (sometimes featuring blue notes), and simple four-bar phrasing. The cakewalk (C20) was one of the dances that were performed to ragtime accompaniments. *EM 1.7.1, 8.11.8.*

Ralentir (Fr.). To slow down (although not marked as such, this is the effect throughout C19). See *Tempo markings*.

Rallentando (rall.) (It.). Slowing down (B75, bars 5–6). See also *Ritardando, Ritenuto* and *Tempo markings*.

Range. The span of notes from lowest to highest that a particular voice or instrument can produce or the compass of a printed instrumental or vocal part. On track A3 almost the entire range explored by composers writing for acoustic instruments can be heard. The approximate ranges of other common instruments are shown on the folded insert. It is not possible to be more precise about these ranges because some instruments are modified to allow notes below the normal range (eg an extra string added to the normal four strings of a double bass allows the performer to reach C_1 or B_2). Similarly the upper limit of the range of many instruments is determined by the proficiency of the performer (C97, solo violin, bars 53–65). See also *Scordatura*. *EM 2.4.2, 6.11.7, 8.4.1.*

Rank. A set of organ pipes of the same timbre. A57 is played on two ranks of flue pipes of the same timbre one at eight-foot pitch, the other at four-foot pitch.

Rant. A fast Scottish dance in the style of a jig. The first printed examples date from the late 17th century and it is still danced north of the border. It has anacrustic phrases in compound time or simple duple time. All of these features are apparent in the baroque gigue (A90).

Rappresentativo (It.). See *Stile rappresentativo*, A62 and A63.

Rasch (Ger.). Lively, quick (C34, bar 1).

Rasgueado, rasgardo, rasqueado (Span.). Strumming technique on a guitar (C83, bars 1–18) as opposed to finger plucking (bars 19–26). *EM 6.4.5.*

Rattle, Ratsche (Ger.). **1.** A percussion instrument consisting of a vessel filled with beads, seeds or similar small objects that are made to rattle by shaking (A36). The rattle of this type most commonly used in an orchestra is a pair of maracas (C46). **2.** Ratchet or cog rattle. A wooden stick with a cogwheel and a frame containing a flexible tongue fixed to the outer edge of the frame. The instrument is played by whirling the frame round in circles so the tongue passes over the cogs and snaps back into the grooves producing a rapid, loud clicking noise. This is the type of cog rattle often used at football matches. It can be heard in bars 137–147 of Srauss's *Till Eulenspiegel* where it is identified by the abbreviation *gr. Rtsch.* (*grosse Ratsche* = large rattle).

Rauschpfeife. A double-reed wind instrument of the 16th and early 17th centuries. It is similar to the contemporary shawm, but in some examples the reeds are enclosed in a reedcap. Its loud incisive tone makes it suitable for outdoor performances (A32). *EM 6.6.4.*

Recitative

Ravvivando (It.). Quickening. The term is an instruction to return to a faster tempo. In the context of MacMillan's *Quickening* the term is synonymous with 'a tempo' at bar 19 of C97. See *Tempo markings*.

Ray. The second degree of any major scale in the British system of tonic sol-fa. The second note of A25 is *ray* in the key of D major.

Rbāb, rebāb (Arab.). See *Rabāb, Rebec* and A16.

Re (It. and Span.), **Ré** (Fr.). D♮. See A3 and the folded insert. Not to be confused with the tonic sol-fa syllable *ray* (the second degree of any major scale).

Real and tonal answers. In a fugue a real answer replicates all of the intervals between the successive notes of the subject (B9). In a tonal answer one of the intervals of the subject is altered to avoid unwanted modulation. The fugal subject of B10 begins with a rising 2nd. This is changed to a rising 3rd at the start of the answer. *EM 4.5.2.*

Real bass. The lowest-sounding part, whether or not it is actually sung by basses or played by bass instruments. In bar 5 of A27 the real bass is the F♯ sung by the tenors (it is a minor 3rd lower than the A♮ sung by the basses).

Realisation, realization. The conversion of conventional symbols that are less than exact into real sounds. On track A68 the organist converts the figured bass part of A68 into the chords shown above it. On A84 the harpsichordist realises the ornaments shown above bars 1–8 in the manner shown in bars 17–24. *EM 5.1.1.*

Rebec, rebacq, rebecke, rebecquet, rebekke, rebet (Fr.), **rebeca** (It. and Lat.), **rebecum** (Lat.), **rebequin** (Span.). A bowed string instrument of the middle ages and renaissance, usually with just three strings tuned in 5ths. A duet for two rebecs can be heard on A16. *EM 6.4.3.*

Recapitulation. The repetition of music heard previously, particularly the repetition of all or part of the exposition in the tonic key at or towards the end of a movement in sonata or sonata-rondo form (B40, bars 72–123, and B36, bars 180–294, respectively). *EM 7.7.1, 7.7.3.*

Recercar (It.). One of many alternative spellings of ricercar (A57).

Récit (Fr.). **1.** In 17th- and 18th-century French music a composition for solo voice in recitative or aria style. The term was later applied to instrumental solos. **2.** A division of the French baroque organ containing a *cornet* (A81). **3.** An enclosed division of the 19th-century French organ with a full chorus and *céleste* (the latter clearly heard in the soft registration of C55). It is the equivalent of the American and British swell organ. *EM 6.9.1.*

Recital. A public performance given by one or a few soloists, often with piano accompaniment. The term was invented by Liszt in 1840 for bravura performances of his own and other composers' piano music (of which B74 is quite untypical)

Recitando, recitato (It.). In the style of a recitative (C90, bar 1).

Recitation. In music, a text, particularly a poem, declaimed with the speaking voice (C38). The spoken dialogue in a melodrama (B60) is not regarded as recitation, but Schoenberg's *Sprechgesang* is (C34). *EM 3.6.*

Recitative. A type of solo vocal music in which the text is of paramount importance. The singer declaims the words, usually in accordance with natural speech-rhythms, often representing the emotional significance of individual words or phrases by particular melodic intervals and characteristic melismas. For instance, in B4(c) the noun 'Mörder' (murderer) is set to a melodic tritone (associated from earliest times with the devil) and the phrase 'und geisselte ihn' (and scoured him) is set to a lashing melisma.

Recitative was introduced in early opera (A62 and A63) to meet the ideals of the *stile moderno*: music was to be the handmaid of the text (rather than a vehicle for complex polyphony as it was in the *stile antico*).

In *recitativo secco* (dry recitative) the singer is accompanied by a continuo group that provides unobtrusive support and follows the flexible rhythms of the vocalist (rather than the nominal time signature). Although modern scores reproduce the sustained bass notes that composers wrote, most modern performers follow baroque performance practice by playing short, detached chords, sometimes with a more sustained style when the sense of the music demands it (A68).

Recitativo accompagnato

In *recitativo accompagnato* (or *stromentato*) the singer is accompanied by an ensemble of instruments in addition to the continuo group. B16 begins as a dry recitative for the Evangelist (narrator), but the direct speech of the angel is accompanied by a halo of sustained string chords (in Bach's *St Matthew Passion* the words of Jesus are similarly set as accompanied recitatives). *EM 3.5, 8.7.1.*

Recitativo accompagnato (It.). Accompanied recitative. See *Recitative* and B16. *EM 8.7.2.*

Recitativo arioso (It.). A type of recitative that is more melodious and metrical than ordinary dry recitative. The term (if used at all) is generally abbreviated to arioso in many of Bach's recitatives (B7, bars 7–16).

Recitativo secco (It.). Dry recitative. See *Recitative* and A68. *EM 3.5, 8.7.2.*

Recitativo stromentato (It.). Instrumental recitative. The same as *recitativo accompagnato*. See *Recitative* and B16. *EM 8.7.2.*

Reciting note, reciting tone. A single pitch in a psalm tone that is repeated as often as the words demand (A6).

Reco-reco, reso-reso (Port.). A notched bamboo instrument that is scraped like a güiro (C51) and specified in the works of some Latin-American composers such as Villa-Lobos.

Recorder. See the box below. *EM 6.6.4.*

Recording and reproduction of music.
From 1857, when the phonautograph etched patterns of sound for the first time, recording techniques have become ever more sophisticated until, with the popularisation of the compact disc in the 1980s, it could fairly be claimed that it was possible to reproduce an almost exact aural image of the original performance. But despite this seeming fidelity there are still many factors that make it impossible to recreate the experience of listening to live music. Not least is the almost inhumanly perfect level of performances heard on recordings that actually consist of a patchwork of short takes. (It is reported that a certain singer's top notes remained so stubbornly out of tune in the recording studio that another singer's top notes had to be patched in before the compact disc could be sold to a large and appreciative market). Outside the controlled conditions of the recording studio it is impossible to reproduce the acoustic effect of large reverberant building. In such an environment a listener is better able to distinguish the strands that go to make a complex musical texture which, recorded faithfully, can sound out of focus. To compensate an engineer may choose to use directional microphones (A94), but this creates a performance that is different from the live aural experience. Most recordings of music with a wide dynamic range have to be compressed – very soft passages boosted and very loud passages suppressed – and decisions about compression are in the

---

Recorder

An end-blown flute in which sound is generated by air passing over a sharp edge in a duct. Originating in the middle ages, the recorder acquired its name in 14th-century England and became the pre-eminent soft-toned wind instrument of the renaissance and baroque eras. There was a whole family of seven different sizes of recorder, each with a fully chromatic range of just over two octaves. They were used as solo instruments, as a whole consort, in broken consorts (A60), and as concertante instruments (A69).

There is considerable confusion about the names given to the recorder, not just because each language has its own names, but because musicians often use names foreign to their native tongue. For this reason the names in the table below are categorised by country rather than language. It should be particularly noted that when Bach (and many of his German contemporaries) specified 'flauto' he meant the recorder, not the transverse flute (which he identified with the term 'flauto traverso' or simply 'traverso').

England	America	France	Germany	Italy	Spain
recorder or English flute	recorder	flûte à bec or flûte douce or *douce* or flûte	Blockflöte or *Flauto* or Schnabelflöte	flauto dolce or flauto a becco or flauto diretto	flauta dulce or *dulce* or flauta de pico

hands of engineers and producers, not conductors or performers. Thus it is that the devastating effect of the original performance of C97 is impossible to reproduce with absolute fidelity. Despite these and many other technical difficulties there can be little doubt that recordings have been one of the most important means of musical communication in the 20th century.

Recte et retro (Lat.). Forwards and backwards (B25 bars 11–20 is a retrograde of B25 bars 1–10).

Reduction. The representation of vocal or orchestral music in a two-stave score. Reductions are most common in vocal scores in which the voice parts are shown complete and the reduction is used for vocal rehearsals (C73). Elsewhere in this dictionary orchestral reductions are for illustrative purposes only (C86).

Redundant entry. In a fugue, a statement of the subject or answer in the tonic key after all contrapuntal parts have given the subject or answer in the exposition. In B14(a) all three contrapuntal voices state the subject (bars 1–2^1, alto, and bars 4–5^1, bass) or answer (bars 2–3^1, treble) in the fugal exposition of bars 1–5^1. In bars 7–8^1 the answer is heard again in the tonic key of C minor. This redundant entry is followed by two more (a rhythmically varied subject in bars 8–9^1, and the answer again in bars 10–11^1). When a complete set of redundant entries like these is heard they form a counter-exposition (bars 7–11^1). *EM 4.5.9.*

Reed instruments. Instruments in which sound is generated by the vibration of a single piece of cane compressed between the player's lip and the mouthpiece, eg the clarinet (C79), or two pieces of cane compressed between the lips, eg the bassoon (C77). These are known as single- and double-reed instruments respectively. In organ reed pipes (A92) a thin tongue of brass enclosed in a chamber is made to vibrate when air is pumped into the chamber. Examples of reed instruments include bagpipes (A17), bass clarinet (C38), basset-horn (B40), clarinet in D (C10), contrabassoon (C31), cor anglais (C88), crumhorn (A35), curtal (A60), oboe (C78), oboe d'amore and oboe da caccia (B8), *rauschpfeife* (A32), saxophone (C38) and shawm (A32).

Reed organ. An organ in which sound is generated by blown reeds sometimes amplified by short pipes. The regal (A63) is a porable reed organ.

Reformation. A religious movement of the 16th century inaugurated by Martin Luther, a priest who sought to reform the corrupt practices of the Roman Catholic Church. Instead the reformation led to a break with Rome and the foundation of a number of Protestant churches in northern Europe, the doctrines of which differed to greater or lesser degrees from the doctrines of the Roman Catholic Church that continued to dominate southern Europe. Luther himself helped establish new protestant musical styles and genres (B6) that grew out of vernacular liturgies. For music of Anglican rites see A37, A61 and C30. For music of Lutheran rites see B4–B8, B15 and B16.

Refrain. A repeated passage of music. The refrains in a French baroque rondeau are identified by the letter A in A84. *EM 7.6.2.*

Regal. A small portable reed organ of the 16th and 17th centuries, it was sometimes used as a harmony instrument in a continuo group (A63). *EM 6.9.1.*

Register. 1. A set of pipes or strings controlled by a stop knob or lever on an organ or harpsichord. Part of the art of playing the organ or a large harpsichord is choosing the right registers for the style of music played. The registration on track A94 is chosen for maximum clarity – essential if the listener is to hear all four contrapuntal lines of this complex texture. **2.** A specific part of the range of a voice or instrument. This could be a vague description such as high or low, or more precise, as in the registers of a baroque trumpet shown in B15.

Registration. The selection and combination of organ stops to produce differing dynamic levels and timbres (compare the registrations on the same organ of A81 and A94).

Regular counter-subject. A melody sounding against the subject and answer in the exposition of a fugue which remains the same (apart from transposition and possibly a change to one of the intervals) every time the subject or answer appears. Subject 2 and answer 2 in B13 could be regarded as regular counter subjects.

Related keys. Keys that have five or six common pitches in their scales. Thus:

Relative major and relative minor keys.

C major and G major share C, D, E, G, A and B;
C major and F major share C, D, E, F, G and A;
C major and A harmonic minor share C, D, E, F, A and B;
C major and D harmonic minor share D, E, F, G and A;
C major and E harmonic minor share C, E, G, A and B.

So the related keys of any music in the major are the relative minor (VI), the dominant (V) and its relative minor (III), and the subdominant (IV) and its relative minor (II). All of the related keys of D major are visited in B15: G major (IV) in bars 51–54, A major (V) in bars 55–58, E minor (II) in bars 83–84, B minor (VI) in bars 89–92, and F♯ minor (III) in bars 96–104.

In relation to a minor key, the relative major (III), the dominant (V) and its relative major (♭VII) and the subdominant (IV) and its relative major (♭VI). B17 is in A minor, and all but one of its related keys are heard in the first section: C major (III) in bars 6–7, G major (♭VII) in bars 7–8, D minor (IV) in bar 9, and E minor (V) in bars 12–18.

Some writers include the tonic major (or tonic minor) in the list of related keys, others say the term has no meaning because all keys are related in some way (which is as true and as helpful as saying we are all relatives since we all spring from the loins of Adam and Eve).

Relative major and relative minor keys. Two keys that share the same key signature but whose tonic notes are a minor 3rd apart. In B27 bars 1–8 are in D minor and bars 13–39 are in the relative major key of F.

Relative pitch. 1. Any pitch in relation to a given pitch. Relative pitches remain the same whatever the standard of pitch used for a particular performance. For example, A95 is performed at 'baroque pitch', in what sounds like C♯ minor instead of D minor to ears accustomed to the modern pitch standard of A=440 Hz. The interval between the outer notes of the first printed chord of A96 is a perfect 5th. In the recorded version this interval is still a perfect 5th, even though the absolute pitches of both notes have been changed. **2.** The ability to identify any pitch in relation to a given pitch. See *Absolute pitch*.

Relish. In 17th- and 18th-century England, a term for a trill ending with a turn (A84, letter d in bars 8 and 24). See *Ornaments*.

Renaissance music. Music of the period c.1430–c.1600 (A27–A61). *EM 8.6.*

Repeat signs. A passage of music that is to be repeated is usually shown by double bars at either end with two or four dots arranged vertically after and before them (C12, bars 3–4). See *First-time bar* and C5. See also *Da capo al fine* and B15.

Replica (It.). A repeat. Most commonly the term is used in the negative. For instance 'da capo senza replica' means to return to the beginning and repeat the first section of a composition without the marked repeats. In B25 the repeats of sections A, B, C and D have been edited out of the recording, but the final repetition of sections A and B are presented as they were played originally – *senza replica* (but with lavish ornamentation).

Réponse (Fr.). A fugal answer (B9, bars 5–10).

Reports. A 17th-century English term defined by Henry Purcell meaning imitative or contrapuntal textures (A80, bars 13–38).

Reprise. Repeat. In French baroque music the term can refer to the refrain of a rondeau (A84, bars 1–9, 17–25 and 33–41) or a short passage repeated at the end of a movement (a *petite reprise*, A84, bars 41–45). The term is sometimes used as a synonym for recapitulation (B40, bars 72–123).

Requiem. The first word of the introit at the start of the Missa pro Defunctis: 'Requiem aeternam dona eis Domine' (Grant them eternal rest O Lord). It is now commonly used as a short title for settings of the Ordinary and Proper of the Mass for the Dead. Among the texts that are usually sung is a sequence that has no place in any other Mass: 'Dies irae, dies illa, solvet saeclum in favilla' (Day of wrath and terror when the earth will burn to ashes). The plainsong melody associated with this text (B62) used to be so well known that, for the romantics, it became an aural symbol of humanity's terror of death. This is how Berlioz uses it (with the added frisson of tolling bells) in the 'Dream of a Witches' Sabbath', the last movement of his *Symphonie fantastique* (B63). See also C96. *EM 8.4.1.*

Requinto, requinte (Span.). A five-string guitar with a higher range than the normal six-string guitar. It has a solo in bars 9–16 of C68.

Reso-reso. See *Reco-reco, Güiro* and C51.

Resolution. The release of tension that is perceived when music moves from a discord to a concord. In A54 the suspended E in bar 6 resolves to a D, and in the next bar the suspended D resolves to a C♯, both resolutions forming consonant 3rds with the tenor. *EM 2.2.3, 4.3.6, 5.2.*

Resonanz, Resonanztisch! (Ger.). See *Près de la table* and C28, bars 7–13.

Resonator. That part of an instrument which amplifies the initial vibrations set in motion by the performer. In an organ (B9) the resonators are the columns of air in the pipes which amplify the vibrations of reeds or edge tones in flue pipes. On a piano the resonator is the sound board which amplifies the vibrations of strings set in motion by the action of hammers.

Response. A short text sung by choir or congregation in response to a versicle sung by the priest or cantor. In A8 the versicle is 'Benedicamus Domino' (Let us bless the Lord) to which the choir responds 'Deo gratias' (Thanks be to God).

Rest. A symbol indicating a silence. This can be total silence when no one is singing or playing, or silence in an individual instrumental or vocal part. Both kinds are evident in B68.

There is a total silence lasting seven long quaver beats between phrases 1 and 2. This is indicated by two quaver rests on both staves in bar 3 and by the three rests (crotchet, quaver, crotchet) on both staves in bar 4. A pause mark over a rest (bars 11 and 12) indicates that silence can be extended to any length the conductor wishes.

The silence between phrases 1 and 2 is broken by the cellos at the end of bar 4. While they play in bar 5 the rest of the orchestra remains silent. This is indicated by the semibreve rests (a semibreve rest can be used to indicate a whole bar of silence no matter how many beats there are in a bar). The symbol for semibreve and minim rests is the same, but on a five-line stave semibreve rests usually hang from the second line down while minim rests sit on the middle line (compare the first rest on the bass stave of B20 with the rest immediately after the first arpeggiated chord).

Short rests are indicated by adding extra flags to the quaver rest. Thus the semiquaver rests in bar 7 of B27 have two flags, and the demisemiquaver rests after the pause marks in B20 have three flags.

Restatement. In discussions of musical form, a repetition of a significant passage of music after a contrasting passage, for instance the recapitulation in a movement in sonata form (B40, bars 72–123).

Retardation. Obsolete term for an upward-resolving suspension. In bar 9 of B5 the tied F♯ in the first viola d'amore part is concordant with the bass D♮: this is the preparation. When the bass moves to G♮ a dissonant 7th is formed: this is the suspension or retardation. Finally the F♯ resolves up to G♮ forming a concordant octave with the bass: this is the resolution of the retardation. *EM 4.3.6.*

Retenu (Fr.). Held back, slowing down (C19). See *Tempo markings*.

Retransition. The function of a transition in a sonata-form movement is to link the first subject to the second and bring about a modulation to the new key of the second subject (B40, bars 18–25). The function of a retransition is to link the development to the recapitulation and bring about a modulation back to the tonic key of the recapitulation (bars 68–71).

Retrograde. Played backwards. Bars 11–20 of B25 are the same as bars 1–10 played backwards (in the trio the same is true of bars 13–24 in relation to bars 1–12). The device is common in serial music (C88), but the atonal style makes it much harder to detect by ear alone. *EM 4.6, 5.8.1.*

Retrograde inversion. Played backwards (retrograde) and melodically inverted, ie every rising interval becomes a falling interval of the same type and vice versa. In C88 a series of 12 notes is shown (i). The same set of pitches is then shown in reverse order (ii). Finally the retrograde is inverted (iii). In Stravinsky's music the tenor sings the original series of 12 notes in bars 2–4 (with repetitions of the seventh, eighth and eleventh notes) and the retrograde inversion can be found in the cor anglais, flute and harp parts in bars 3–5. *EM 4.6.*

Reverberation

Reverberation (reverb.). 1. The continuous reflection of sound waves between the walls, floor and ceiling of an enclosed space. Reverberation time (the time it takes for a sound of specific intensity to decay to an imperceptible level) is an important factor governing the quality of the sound of music heard in a live performance (and, to a lesser extent, the quality of recorded sound). The organ music on track A86 was recorded in a highly reverberant church while the music on track A68 was recorded in the less reverberant acoustic of the chapel of Hertford College, Oxford. **2.** The simulation of reverberation by the electronic modification of the sound of instruments or voices (C91), or of electronically generated sounds.

Reversed dotting. The term refers to two-note dotted rhythms in which the shorter note falls on the beat and is followed by an offbeat dotted note. In bar 42 of A84 the most common type of dotted rhythm (long–short) is heard in the first two beats. The dotting is reversed in the last two beats (and in the whole of the next bar) to produce the short–long dotted rhythm known as a Scotch snap or Lombardic rhythm. *EM 1.6.3.*

Rezitation (Ger.). Recitation, the term used by Schoenberg for the vocal part of *Pierrot lunaire* (C34). See also *Sprechgesang*.

Rhythm. A group of two or more sounds which form a pattern in time chiefly determined by the relative durations of the notes that go to make up the rhythm. See *Cross-rhythm* (B79, bars 8–15, 21 and 30–37), *Dotted rhythms* (A76–A80), *Duplet* (C14–C17), *Hemiola* (A59, bars 25–27), *Lombard rhythm* (A79, z in bar 2), *Polymetre* (B45), *Polyrhythm* (C12–C17), *Syncopation* (B51–B54, *sf* and the notes with crosses) and *Triplet* (B54). *EM 1.1.*

Rhythm section. In a jazz band, the section that provides harmonic and rhythmic support for melody instruments. It comprises any or all of drum kit, piano and pizzicato double bass (or electric bass guitar). In C38 a pizzicato cello stands in for the piano and double bass by providing a regular on-beat bass line in bars 1–4 and three- or four-note chords that clarify the F-major tonality. The kit drummer provides a cymbal backbeat in the first three bars and punctuates the vocal solo with on- and offbeat side drum and cymbal strokes.

Rhythmic augmentation. See *Augmentation* and compare bar 1 of B14 with bars 19–20.

Rhythmic diminution. See *Diminution* and the left-hand piano part in bars 1–2 of C34.

Rhythmic modes. A modern term for various patterns of long and short notes found in the polyphony of the late 12th-century and early 13th-century School of Notre Dame in Paris. Medieval scholars discerned six modes made up of the patterns shown below A10. These patterns, rather like metrical feet in poetry, could be repeated as often as desired to make a complete phrase known as an *ordo* (pl. *ordines*). In Mode 1 the pattern consists of just two time-values, long–short. In the table at the foot of A10 this is represented as a crotchet–quaver pattern. In Mode 2 the rhythmic pattern is reversed (short–long). With the exception of Mode 4 an *ordo* was described as perfect if it ended with a note of the same length as the first note of the phrase (a crotchet in Mode 1, a quaver in Mode 2). One *ordo* was marked off from the next by rests. In Mode 4 a perfect *ordo* ended with the two initial time-values.

In the clausula itself there are three Mode 3 *ordines* identified by brackets. In the first and last the rhythmic pattern is heard four times, in the second it is heard three times. All end with the dotted crotchet with which they began (so they are all perfect), and they are all separated from ensuing phrases by a dotted-crotchet rest.

In the actual practice of composers of the Notre Dame school rhythmic patterns from different modes were often combined in a single phrase (as bars 1–8, 14–17 and 27–29 show). But the importance of the rhythmic modes cannot be overstated: they enabled composers to notate rhythms precisely and so provided the necessary prerequisite for the development of polyphonic music. *EM 1.12, 8.5.1.*

Rhythmic ostinato. See *Ostinato* and C66 and C67.

Ribāb (Arab.). See *Rabāb, Rebec* and A16.

Ribattuta (It.). In the 17th and 18th centuries a type of trill in dotted rhythms beginning on the main note on the beat. In early 17th-century music it was usually followed by a *trillo* (tremolo) at a cadence (A62). See *Ornaments*.

Ribibe, ribible, rubebe, rubible, rybbe (Eng.). See *Rebec* and A16.

Ricercar, ricercare (It.). A name deriving from an Italian verb meaning 'to seek'. What is sought after in the most familiar type of this instrumental genre of the 16th and 17th centuries is the contrapuntal potential of one or more melodic subjects. In A57 the principal theme (A) is immediately imitated in a passage of two-part counterpoint. After a shorter point of imitation on a new phrase (B), the first theme returns in denser three-part imitative counterpoint (bars 10–17). The way in which these points of imitation overlap in a seamless contrapuntal flow leads some musicologists to suppose that the ricercar was an instrumental offshoot of the contemporary motet (A44).

Some 17th-century ricercars were monothematic (built on a single subject). A81 is an extract from the central section of a movement from a late 17th-century organ Mass. This extended passage of music is, in all but name, a monothematic ricercar that explores the contrapuntal potential of the four-note subject heard at the start. The connection between this type of composition and the late baroque fugue (B14) is evident.

The keyboard ricercar sometimes functioned as a prelude to a vocal composition in a church service. Since the subject of Gabrieli's ricercar (A in A57) bears a striking resemblance to the first phrase of the plainsong hymn *Aeterna Christi munera* (A56) it is quite possible that this piece was written as an *intonatione* before the hymn itself, or before a polyphonic paraphrase of it. *EM 8.6.3.*

Ridicolo (It.). Ridiculous, absurd. The term is rare and, as used by Saint-Saëns in C8, it underlines his humorous parody of the famous *Danse macabre* (the principal melody of which is shown on an extra stave below the extract from 'Fossils').

Ridotto, riduzione (It.). A reduction or arrangement, most often of an orchestral score for piano (C73).

Rigaudon (Fr.), **rigadoon** (Eng.). A moderately fast baroque dance in duple time. It shares many characteristics with the bourrée (A89) and is usually in binary form with symmetrical anacrustic phrasing.

Rim shot. On a side drum, a loud report produced either by striking the rim and the head simultaneously with one stick or, less effectively, by placing one stick so that it touches the rim and the head, and then striking it with the other (C43 and C53). *EM 6.8.2.*

Rinforzando (rinf., *rfz*, *rf* **)** (It.). Quickly becoming louder (B79, bars 2–3). The term is also used as a synonym of *sforzando* (*sf* in the last bar of C34).

Ripieno (It.). **1.** In a concerto grosso, the ensemble that periodically doubles or complements the solo group and fills out the texture with added parts for instruments such as the viola and double bass (as in bars 5–8, 11–12 and 14–16 of B19). **2.** Tutti, a passage that is to be played with doubled parts in any baroque instrumental genre. *EM 8.7.5.*

Riposta (It.). In a fugue, an answer (B9, bars 5–10). The subject is called the *proposta*.

Risoluto (It.). Determined (C57).

Ritardando (ritard., rit.) (It.). Gradually slowing down. It is difficult to tell definitively whether a composer means *ritardando* or *ritenuto* when the abbreviation 'rit.' is used (B79, bar 37), but the context often reveals the composer's intention (there are no abrupt changes of tempo in B79 so it may be assumed that Brahms meant *ritardando*). See *Rallentando* and *Tempo markings*.

Rite. Any religious or solemn ritual such as those associated with marriage or burial from time immemorial. In this dictionary the term is used of Anglican, Lutheran and Roman Catholic rituals and the music to which the officially approved texts of these rituals are sung. See A37, A61 and C30 (Anglican), A68, A69, B4–B8, B15 and B16 (Lutheran) and A4–A11, A19–A21, A27–A29, A40–52, B62 (Roman Catholic).

Ritenuto (rit.) (It.). Immediately slowing down (B67, bar 7). See *Rallentando*, *Ritardando* and *Tempo markings*.

Ritmico (It.). Rhythmical. The direction 'ben ritmico' in bar 1 of C63 means 'very rhythmical'.

Ritornello (It.), **ritournelle** (Fr.). **1.** In baroque vocal music, a recurring instrumental section heard at the opening and at other points in the movement. A ritornello may be repeated in whole or in part, restated in its original form or varied, and recapitulated in

Ritornello form

the tonic or in other related keys. The ritornello for trumpet and strings in the first 14 bars of B15 provides material for the ritornelli that punctuate the vocal solo. In bars 67–80 motifs from phrase x (bars 1–4) are freely inverted and extended, and phrases y^1 and y^2 (bars 8–14) are modified towards the end to form a perfect cadence in the tonic in bars 79–80. The next ritornello (bars 96–104) is in the related key of F♯ minor. It begins with phrase y^2, continues with a syncopated figure like those in bars 1–2 and 5–6, and ends with a cadence figure (z) almost identical to that played by the violins in bars 13–14. When the first section is repeated the first and second ritornelli are also repeated. **2.** In some late baroque concerto movements, recurring passages for the full instrumental forces similar to the ritornelli discussed above. These are separated not by vocal music but by episodes for one or more solo instruments and continuo. *EM 7.6.3, 8.7.2.*

Ritornello form. The structure of many late baroque instrumental and vocal movements (especially the fast movements of some concerti grossi) in which repeated instrumental passages punctuate vocal or instrumental solos. In the aria 'Grosser Herr' from the *Christmas Oratorio* (B15) Bach combines the ternary structure of the da capo aria with ritornello form. Viewed as a ritornello structure its form may be summarised as:
  Ritornello in the tonic key of D major, cadencing on chord V (bars 1–14);
  Vocal solo in the tonic with passing modulations to G major and A major (bars 15–66);
  Ritornello (bars 67–80) (modified) in the tonic, cadencing on chord I (bars 79–80);
  Vocal solo modulating through related keys and ending with a perfect cadence in F♯ minor (bars 81–96);
  Ritornello (partial) in F♯ minor (bars 97–104);
  Vocal solo modulating through B minor to the dominant key of A major (bars 105–120);
  Repeat of bars 1–80 (first ritornello, fist vocal solo and second ritornello).
This differs from a ritornello movement in a concerto grosso in that, if there is a complete restatement of the opening ritornello in the concerto movement, it will be heard at the end, rather than at an intermediate point (as in Bach's aria). *EM 7.6.3.*

Rococo. A term borrowed from the visual arts which, transferred to music, most appropriately refers to small-scale French (or French-style) lute and harpsichord compositions of the end of the 17th century and the early 18th century (A84, A89, B17 and C32). Some authorities apply the term more widely to encompass longer forms and pre-classical and galant works such as B25. *EM 8.8.1.*

Röhrenglocken (Ger.). Tubular bells (C97, bars 36ff).

Roll. A rapid reiteration of a single pitch on a percussion instrument. See *Side drum* (C44) and *Timpani* (B36, bars 255–262).

Roman numerals. Numerals beneath a bass part that indicate how particular chords relate to the prevailing key of a passage of music. Thus in B25 the Roman numeral I under the first chord identifies it as the tonic chord (built on the first degree of the scale) of A♭ major. V^7 indicates a dominant 7th (built on the fifth degree of the scale) in the same key. Roman numerals are sometimes used to designate keys. *EM 5.1.3.*

Romanian (Rumanian) dance. Romania did not free itself from Turkish rule until 1878, and this partly explains why its folk music displays elements of both west-European diatonic modality and east-European chromatic modality. The latter is evident in the violin part of C56 (one of the thousands of folk melodies that Bartók transcribed during his frequent tours of Eastern Europe, Turkey and North Africa). Its most obvious characteristic is the often-repeated interval of an augmented 2nd (F–G♯). Bartók's original title for the piano pieces that Székely later arranged for violin and piano was *Romanian Folk Dances from Hungary*. Characteristics of folk music that developed in one country were often disseminated to neighbouring states. The national styles of Romania and Hungary in particular often became amalgamated in styles that Gypsy musicians carried with them throughout Europe.

Romanesca. One of a number of harmonic basses that were used by 16th- and 17th-century composers as ostinati, the romanesca appears to have originated as the bass part of a popular Spanish song (the first phrase of which is shown in A34). Both the song melody and the basso ostinato were widely used for sets of *diferencias* (variations). A34 shows how successive notes of

Guárdame las vacas are incorporated into the upper part of the first variation and how the romanesca bass is decorated with passing notes in the second variation. Similar bass melodies of the same period used in the same way include the folia, passamezzo and ruggiero. *EM 8.6.3.*

Romantic music. Music in which emotional expressiveness and pictorialism are generally more evident than perfection of form. Music of the 19th and early 20th centuries. Both of these generalisations can be misleading, for, on the one hand, there are romantic works which are extremely expressive yet also perfectly formed (B66), and, on the other, there are works outside the 19th and early 20th centuries that are as emotionally expressive as any written within the period (B20). Nevertheless the generalisations hold good in a majority of cases. See B57–C11 and C27–C29. *EM 8.10.*

Rommelpot. (Ger.). Rumble pot. A Flemish friction drum that is played by an up-and-down motion of a stick attached to or passing through the membrane (A36).

Ronde (Fr.). Semibreve, whole-note (A29, last note). See *Note*.

Rondeau (Fr.). **1.** One of the medieval *formes fixes*, the rondeau was both a musical and a literary form. In its most common manifestation two musical phrases are repeated in the setting of an eight-line poem containing repeated lines known as refrains. The poetic form (see the French text printed at the foot of A23) typically has the structure abcadeab, in which a and b are refrains. This represents the structure in terms of complete lines. The rhyme scheme – which is the same as the musical structure – is ABAAABAB. Together the music and poetry make a composite form that can be represented as ABaAabAB, in which capital letters identify poetic refrains and lower-case letters signify musical but not poetic repetitions. It is this composite form that is represented by the boxed letter at the start of each stave of A23. **2.** A French baroque form that can be represented as ABACADA etc, in which A is the refrain (or *grand couplet*) and B, C, D etc are episodes called *couplets*. The refrain is always in the tonic (ending with a perfect cadence), the *couplets* usually in or modulating through related keys. In A84 the form is as follows:

A: refrain (G minor, ending with a perfect cadence)
B: first *couplet* (G minor – B♭ major – G minor, ending with an imperfect cadence)
A: refrain (G minor, ending with a perfect cadence)
C: second *couplet* (G minor – F major – D minor, ending with a perfect cadence and *tierce de Picardie*)
A^1: refrain decorated with additional quavers (G minor, ending with a perfect cadence)
A^2: *petite reprise* (a repeat of the second four-bar phrase of the refrain).
EM 7.6.1, 8.4.2.

Rondellus (Lat.). A medieval English composition employing the technique of voice exchange in a manner similar to the *pes* of the Reading Rota (A15).

Rondo forms. 1. See *Rondeau* 2 and A84. Simple rondo structures of the type ABAC... A continued to be written in the late 18th and early 19th centuries, sometimes as independent pieces, sometimes as a movement (usually the last) in a symphony, sonata, concerto or chamber music genre. **2.** Sonata-rondo structures combine the form of the simple rondo with the structural principles of sonata form. The elements that are common to all manifestations of sonata-rondo form are:
a) a rondo theme (or first subject) in the tonic,
b) an episode (or second subject) in a different key,
c) a reprise of the rondo theme in the tonic,
d) a second episode (or development) moving through a number of keys,
e) a recapitulation of the whole or parts of the rondo theme or first episode (or both).

The finale of Haydn's trumpet concerto (B36) incorporates these elements in a movement that illustrates some of the other features that may be found in classical sonata-rondo structures.

The movement begins with an orchestral exposition containing:
A: the rondo theme (or first subject) in E♭ major (bars 1–25)
B: the first episode (or second subject) in E♭ major (bars 26–43).

The solo exposition is the first section of the sonata rondo structure proper. It contains:
A: a repeat of the rondo theme (or first subject) in E♭ major (bars 44–66)

Rondo theme

followed by a transition modulating from E♭ major to B♭ major (bars 67–78)

B: the first episode (or second subject) in B♭ major (bars 79–123) which begins with material derived from B in the orchestral exposition but continues with new thematic ideas

A: a shorter version of the rondo theme in E♭ major (bars 124–140).

C: a lengthy central episode (or development section) (bars 141–179) that modulates through a number of related keys and is based on thematic materials derived from the rondo theme.

The recapitulation remains in the tonic throughout and contains:

A: another short version of the rondo theme or first subject (bars 180–190) followed by a varied repeat of the transition (bars 191–198)

B: a varied reprise of the first episode/second subject (bars 199–236)

A^1: a much expanded version of the rondo theme (bars 237–278) that sounds like a second development (though the tonic key is never seriously threatened by the chromatic harmony)

A^2: A coda based on the rondo theme (bars 279–294).

Thus without the orchestral exposition, Haydn's sonata-rondo structure can be represented as $ABACABA^1A^2$, a form typical of many classical rondo finales. *EM 7.6, 7.7.3, 8.9.1.*

Rondo theme. See *Rondo forms* and B36, bars 1–25, 44–66, 124–140, 180–190 and 237–294.

Root. In tonal music, the fundamental pitch of any chord built from superimposed thirds. The root of a C-major chord is C♮ (C30, bar 1). On the extra stave beneath bar 2 a seven-note chord is constructed on the dominant. When the root is sounded in the bass in this way the chord is said to be in root position (as is Stanford's chord above it). Beneath bar 6 in the same example another chord of the same type is shown on the dominant of D minor, but now Stanford places the 7th of the chord (G♮) in the bass, thus inverting the chord. Despite this the root of the chord is still the A♮ (heard in the inner parts) that is the fundamental pitch from which Stanford's chord can be seen to derive. *EM 5.3.1.*

Root-position chords. Chords that have the root sounding in the lowest part. All of the chords in the first four bars of A35 are in root position. *EM 5.3.1, 5.3.3, 5.5.1.*

Rosalia (It.). A derogatory term for a sequence in which melody and harmony are transposed up a tone or semitone while maintaining exactly the same melodic intervals and harmonic progression in the new key. In A86 the broken-chord figuration and dominant–tonic harmony of bars 10–11 are repeated a tone higher in bars 12–13, the only alteration being the substitution of a D♭ for a D♮ (precise rosalias are uncommon in the works of reputable composers).

Rota (Lat.). Round. A15 is the only extant rota that is given this name in the original manuscript. *EM 7.9.3.*

Roulade. An ornamental passage, especially in 18th-century vocal music (B50, bars 69–73). *EM 3.10.3.*

Round. An infinite canon. In A15 each canonic voice (labelled I, II, III and IV), having reached the end of the melody, returns to the beginning, repeating this process ad infinitum, or at least for as long as the singers' patience lasts. *EM 4.4.6, 7.9.3, 8.5.2.*

Rounded binary form. A two-part structure (AB) in which section B ends with a recapitulation of material from section A (transposed to the tonic if necessary). See *Binary form* and B17. *EM 7.4.4.*

Rovescio, Al (It.). **1.** Retrograde. In the form in which Haydn originally notated the Menuetto shown in B25, bars 11–20 and 33–44 were not written out because his title, Menuetto al Rovescio was sufficient indication that bars 1–10 and 21–32 should each be followed by the same passage played backwards. **2.** Inversion. In C64 the canon by inversion in bars 6–8 can also be called a *canone al rovescio*.

Row. An abbreviation of note row or tone row (C40, bars 1–7).

Rubato, tempo rubato (It.). A rhythmically flexible interpretation of a score. A comparison of the performances of the two barcaroles performed on B61 and B74 reveals two different approaches to similar music. In the first the pianist maintains a fairly constant tempo, in the second the tempo varies from bar to bar. See *Tempo markings.*

Rückpositiv (Ger.). A department of an organ situated behind the performer. See *Positive organ* and A93.

Ruff. A common snare-drum figure consisting of three rapid grace notes just before an on-beat stroke (𝄾). In C78 the ruff in bar 8 can be easily identified because it occurs just after the only rest in the oboe duet.

Ruggiero (It.). One of a number of stock basses used as an ostinato in 16th- and 17th-century arias, dances and variations. See *Romanesca* and A34.

Ruhig (Ger.). Peaceful. See the performance direction at the head of C35 and *Tempo markings*.

Rührtrommel (Ger.). Tenor drum (C43).

Rumanian dance. See *Romanian dance* and C66.

Rythmé (Fr.). Rhythmic. The tempo mark at the head of C17 means 'quite fast and very rhythmic'.

Rythmes saccadés (Fr.). In string music, rhythms performed with jerky, sharply articulated bow strokes, especially rhythms associated with the first section of a French overture (A76–A80).

S

S. Abbreviation of soprano (A30).

Saccadé (Fr.). In string music, jerky, sharply articulated bow strokes. See *Rythmes saccadés* and A76–A80.

Sackbut. An early trombone originating in the late 15th century and soon developed to a point where it resembled the modern instrument in both appearance and versatility. The bell, however, was less flared, giving it a softer, mellower tone than the modern trombone (A60). Sackbuts were often combined with cornetts in 16th- and 17th-century ensemble music (two cornetts and two sackbuts can be clearly heard at the start of A58).

Sackpfeife (Ger.). Bagpipes (A17).

Sagbut, saggbutt. Sackbut (A60). *EM 6.7.5.*

Saiteninstrumente (Ger.). String instruments of any family including harp (A12), citole and vielle (A13), rebec (A16), hurdy-gurdy (A18), vihuela (A34), viola (A38), viol (A61), theorbo (A75), lute (A88), cello (A90), violin (A95), viola d'amore (B5), double bass (C7), mandolin (C29), cimbalom (C41) and guitar (C68).

Salmo (It. and Span.). Psalm (A6).

Saltarello (It.). A fast Italian dance in compound time (sometimes notated in triple time with a dotted-minim beat). It was popular from the 14th to the 16th centuries. A18 is a saltarello in the form of an *istampita* with typical *aperto* and *chiuso* cadences at the ends of the repeated phrases (A1–A2, B1–B2, C1–C2, D1–D2). As a folk dance the saltarello remained popular until the end of the 19th century. Mendelssohn reintroduced it into the world of art music in his *Italian Symphony*.

Sampling. The electronic process of recording live sounds and storing them so they can be reproduced on a synthesiser (A87).

Sanctus (Lat.). The fourth item of the Ordinary of the Mass. Its Latin text (Holy, holy, holy Lord God of hosts, heaven and earth are full of your glory) comes from the Old Testament and is among the most ancient texts of the Mass. The second part of the Sanctus is called the Benedictus (Blessed is he who comes in the name of the Lord), settings of which can be heard on tracks A20 and A21. *EM 8.4.1.*

Saqueboute (Fr.). Sackbut (A60).

Sarabande. The third of the four most common dances found in the baroque suite. The characteristic features of a French or German sarabande are exemplified on track A88: slow triple time with accents on the second beat of the bar (caused by longer note-values and changes of harmony). Bars 1, 2 and 6 display the characteristic dotted rhythm of the sarabande. Like other movements of the baroque dance suite, Bach's sarabande is in binary form (but only the first section is shown in this example). *EM 8.7.3.*

Sassofono (It.). Saxophone (C38, bar 9).

SATB. Abbreviation of soprano, alto, tenor and bass (A30).

Satz (Ger.). **1.** Movement of a concerto, symphony etc (B36). **2.** Subject or theme (B28). *Hauptsatz* and *Seitensatz* (or *Nebensatz*) refer to the first and second themes of a movement (B40, bars 1–14 and 26–48 respectively). **3.** Style, structure or texture. *Strenger Satz* (strict style) could describe the fugue recorded on track B14, and *freier Satz* (free style) could apply to the fugato recorded on track B29.

Sauterelle (Fr.). Saltarello (A18).

Saxophone, Saxophon (Ger.), **saxofón** (Span.). A family of wind instruments invented in about 1840. Although it has a metal body (often brass) it is usually classed as a woodwind instrument because it has a single reed (like a clarinet) and keys opening and closing holes in the body of the instrument (like most other woodwind instruments). An alto saxophone can be heard in bar 9 of C38. *EM 6.6.3.*

Scala (It.). Scale (B18, the notes marked 1–8 in the theme).

Scale. A collection of pitches that can be derived from a piece of music and arranged in an ascending or descending order. In the examples in Volume 2 discussed below, dotted lines between the printed music and a scale show

Scherzando

how the latter may be derived from the former.

Scale types are defined by the intervals between successive notes, not by the pitch upon which they begin and end. For instance the phrygian mode (Mode III) can be realised by playing the white notes on a keyboard from E to e (see A3 and the scale shown in A37). The order of tones (T) and semitones (S) reading up this scale is S–T–T–T–S–T–T (in all of the scales printed with musical examples a pointed bracket indicates a semitone and a curved bracket a tone). The same intervals will be found in the scale shown in A38(a) making this the phrygian mode transposed to G (the key signature having the effect of flattening the appropriate degrees of the scale to conform with Mode III).

Diatonic scales are those that contain five tones and two semitones between adjacent notes, namely:

Major scale (or ionian mode)	A16
Hypoionian mode	A13
Melodic minor scale ascending	A83
Melodic minor scale descending (or natural minor scale)	A83
Aeolian mode (or natural minor scale)	A12
Hypoaeolian mode	B61
Dorian mode (Mode I)	A40
Hypodorian mode (Mode II)	A24
Phrygian mode (Mode III)	A37
Hypophrygian mode (Mode IV)	A5
Lydian mode (Mode V)	A19
Hypolydian mode (Mode VI)	C57
Mixolydian mode (Mode VII)	A28
Hypomixolydian mode (Mode VIII)	A4

The harmonic minor scale contains three semitones, three tones and an augmented 2nd (A82). It is closely related to the Gypsy scale (or Hungarian scale) which has two augmented 2nds (C56).

There is no standard form for a blues scale, but all of them are characterised by the flattening of certain degrees, most often the third, sixth and seventh (C20).

Pentatonic scales, having only five pitches, are tonally ambiguous, but a tonal centre can be established by repeating one note more than the others and by ending a piece on the repeated note (C63). Those pentatonic scales that contain semitones are often atonal (C64).

Of itself a chromatic scale is also atonal (C40), but it is possible to use all 12 notes of a chromatic scale within a short passage of tonal music without negating the prevailing key (B38 and B39).

Like the chromatic scale, whole-tone scales have the same intervals between all adjacent degrees. The whole-tone scale used in C21 is the same as Messiaen's first mode of limited transposition: his seventh mode is shown beneath C55.

In the music of some 20th-century composers there are passages based on eight pitch classes that can be arranged to form an octatonic scale of alternating tones and semitones (C64 and C88). *EM 2.3, 2.3.2, 2.7.*

Scale degrees. The individual pitches of a major or minor scale. These seven pitch classes are either numbered (using Roman numerals) or named with terms that give some indication of their functional relationships in tonal music. For instance, in the G-major scale at the start of B18 the scale degrees are:

8 (I)	G♮	upper tonic
7 (VII)	F♯	leading note or leading tone
6 (VI)	E♮	submediant
5 (V)	D♮	dominant
4 (IV)	C♮	subdominant
3 (III)	B♮	mediant
2 (II)	A♮	supertonic
1 (I)	G♮	tonic

Scalic. Adjective from scale, sometimes used to describe a melodic line that traces all or some of the notes of an ascending or descending scale (B37, bars 26–27).

Scena (It.). **1.** A scene in an opera. B60 is an extract from music for a scene representing the Wolf's Glen in Weber's *Der Freischütz*. **2.** The opera stage and the scene represented on it. **3.** In Italian opera, a subdivision of an act containing a recitative and aria etc.

Schalmei (Ger.). Shawm (A32).

Schalltrichter auf, Schalltrichter in der Höhe (Ger.). See *Campane in aria* and C97, bars 23–26.

Schellen (Ger.). Sleigh bells (C49).

Schellentrommel (Ger.). Tambourine (C42). 'Tamburin' is the term more frequently used in Germany.

Scherzando (It.), **Scherzhaft** (Ger.). Playful, joking. Bartók's use of the term in C77–C81 is particularly apposite since the title of the movement means 'Game of the Couples'

Scherzo

(the music is a series of parodies of classical figuration in 3rds and 6ths).

Scherzo (It.). **1.** In the 16th and early 17th centuries, a short, light, dance-like madrigal similar to the contemporary *balletto*. **2.** A fast movement that superseded the minuet as the third movement of classical symphonies, chamber works and sonatas. Like the minuet it was usually coupled with a trio, and like the minuet it was usually in triple time, but it was often so fast that the beat was in reality a dotted minim (B55). **3.** In the 19th century, an independent work (often for piano solo) with something of the character of the classical scherzo. *EM 8.9.5.*

Schlaginstrumente (Ger.). See *Percussion instruments* and C42–C54.

Schleifer (Ger.). Slide (A84, letter e in bar 12, and B25, bar 60). See *Ornaments. EM 3.10.1.*

Schleppen (Ger.). To drag. Mahler's performance direction at the head of C27 ('Nicht schleppen') means 'do not drag'.

Schluss (Ger.). **1.** Cadence (B6, bars 11–12 and 14–15). **2.** Conclusion of a movement or work. A *Schlusschoral* is the simple harmonisation of a chorale melody with which most of Bach's cantatas end and a *Schlussatz* is the last movement (finale) of a multi-movement instrumental composition (B36).

Schlüssel (Ger.). Clef. Six different clefs are identified in A30: treble and bass at the start of the first and second staves, and four C clefs on the last four staves.

Schmachtend (Ger.). Languishing. The direction 'Langsam und schmachtend' at the head of B68 means 'slow and languishing'. See *Tempo markings.*

Schnabelflöte (Ger.). Recorder (A69).

Schnell (Ger.). Fast. A German synonym for allegro (B36). See *Tempo markings.*

Schneller (Ger.). A late 18th-century term for an upper mordent (B25, bar 56). See *Ornaments. EM 3.10.1.*

Schola, schola cantorum (Lat.). A choir that sings Gregorian chant (A4).

Schusterfleck (Ger.). Rosalia (A86, bars 10–11 and 12–13).

Schwer (Ger.). Heavy, ponderous (C27). See *Tempo markings.*

Scordatura (It.). The tuning of one or more strings of instruments such as the violin to non-standard pitches for special effects, or to permit the performance of notes outside the instrument's normal range. The most famous example is the solo violin in Saint-Saëns's *Danse macabre* (the opening phrase is shown at the foot of C8) which has its E string detuned to E♭ to permit the performance of devilish tritones (A–E♭) on open strings. The massive six-part guitar chords in bars 13–15 of C83 can only be performed with the lowest string tuned to D (a tone below the normal pitch of this string). *EM 6.5.14.*

Score. Music notated so that all instrumental or vocal parts are vertically aligned. An open score shows each part on a separate stave (C87), a short score compresses a few or many parts (C86) onto a very few staves.

Scoring. The choice of instruments or voices (or both) and the manner in which they are combined. The instruments for which C35 is scored are flute, clarinet, trumpet, trombone, celesta, glockenspiel, harp and strings, and the scoring could be described as pointillist.

Scotch snap. See *Dotted rhythms* and z in A79. *EM 1.6.3.*

Scraper. Any striated percussion instrument that is scraped with a stick or metal rod. See *Güiro*, C51 and C53.

Sdrucciolando (It.). Harp glissando (C27).

Sec (Fr.), **secco** (It.). Dry, staccato. The performance direction above bar 10 of C20 means 'very clear and dry'.

Secco recitative. See *Recitative* and A68.

Sechzehntel, Sechzehntelnote (Ger.). Semiquaver, sixteenth-note (B18, Variation 5, bars 1–6). See *Note.*

Sechzehntelpause (Ger.). Semiquaver/sixteenth-note rest (B78, the symbol immediately after the left-hand time signature).

Second. 1. See *Intervals* and C81. **2.** See *Degree* and the second note of B18. **3.** See *Added-2nd chord* and C26, bars 3–4.

Second-inversion chord. A chord with the fifth degree of the scale sounding in the bass. The first chord of B41 is a G-major triad in root position (with the root, G♮, sounding in the bass). The other components of this triad are B♮ (a 3rd above the root) and D♮ (a 5th above the root). The G-major chord on the last beat of bar 1 is a second-inversion triad because the 5th (D♯) is sounding in the bass. *EM 5.3.3, 5.5.2.*

Second subject. In a sonata-form exposition, the theme or group of themes heard in a key other than the principal key of the first subject. In B40 the key of the first subject (bars 1–18) is F major, and the key of the second subject (bars 26–48) is C major. In the recapitulation the second subject will normally be transposed to the tonic key of the whole movement (B40, bars 95–119). The thematic material of the second subject may be derived from the first subject without altering the tonal structure of the movement (B27, bars 13–39). Because the second subject might contain more than one theme some writers prefer the term second subject group. *EM 7.7.1.*

Second-time bar. See *First-time bar* and the last bar of B37.

Second Viennese School. A group of composers working in Vienna in the early 20th century, especially Schoenberg (C34) and his pupils Berg and Webern (C35). See *Atonality*, *Expressionism* and *Serialism*.

Seconda prattica (It.). See *Prima prattica*, A44–A46 and A52 (*prima prattica*) and A62–A66 (*seconda prattica*).

Seconda volta (It.). See *Prima volta* and C5, bars 15 and 47.

Secondary-dominant chords. A chromatic dominant chord built on the 5th of any diatonic triad other than the tonic triad itself. The first five bars of B16 are firmly in the key of D major and there is only one chromatic chord – the secondary dominant on beat 3 of bar 4. The origin of this chord is shown on the extra stave at the end of Bach's recitative. The 5th of chord V of D major is E (as shown in the first chord). A dominant 7th built on this note (ie with E as its root) contains the notes shown in the second chord. If this chord is inverted so the 3rd rather than the root is in the bass then a version of Bach's first-inversion dominant-7th chord will be formed (the third chord on the extra stave). Like all dominant-7th chords there is a strong tendency for the 7th to resolve down a semitone (D resolving to C♯ in this case) and for the 3rd to resolve up a semitone (G♯ to A in this case). So the chord to which this secondary dominant resolves is chord V. It is as though the secondary dominant had momentarily turned chord V of D major into the tonic chord of A major. This process of tonicisation ends with the ensuing perfect cadence in D major (bar 5) so that, in retrospect, the secondary dominant (V^6_5 of V) is perceived as nothing more than chromatic colouring of the underlying I–V–I progression in bars 4 and 5.

Secondary dominants can resolve onto other secondary dominants. This is the case in bars 99–100 of B40. Despite the chromaticism in this recapitulation of the second subject the key of the whole passage (bars 95–120) is F major. Chord II in this key consists of the notes G (the root), B♭ (the 3rd) and D (the 5th). The secondary dominant of this chord is built on its 5th and consists of the notes D (the root), F♯ (the 3rd), A (the 5th) and C (the 7th). This is the chord heard on the first beat of bar 99 (minus its 5th since there are insufficient bassett-horns to form a four-note chord). As in B16 the 3rd of the chord resolves up a semitone and the 7th resolves down a semitone. However, the chord onto which this secondary dominant resolves is not chord II (it has a B♮, not a B♭ as its 3rd) but another secondary dominant, V of V. The tonicisation of the dominant is of even shorter duration than was the case in B16 because Mozart immediately cancels the chromatic B♮ with the diatonic 7th (B♭) of the real dominant (chord V^7, which itself resolves to the tonic chord of F major in beat 3 of bar 100).

Any of the various types of dominant chord can function as secondary dominants. In bar 8 of A81, for instance, the chromatic diminished-7th chord is the dominant of the dominant. It resolves irregularly not to a simple G-major chord (V in the prevailing key of C minor) but to another diminished-7th chord (the dominant minor 9th of C minor). The same progression with even more irregular part movement can be heard in bars 4–5 of B31. See also *Dominant chords. EM 5.7.1.*

Secondary-7th chords. Diatonic chords of the 7th other than dominant 7ths. With the exception of V^7 all of the chords shown at (iii) beneath B78 are secondary-7th chords in the key of B♭ minor. Brahms uses all of them in bars 2–5 (see (i) below the intermezzo). The term non-dominant 7th is sometimes used for these chords. See also *Seventh chords. EM 5.5.10.*

Secondary triad

Secondary triad. In tonal music, any triad other than chords I, IV and V (the primary triads). In B1 chords VI and II^6 are secondary triads, the rest are primary triads.

Segno (It.). The sign shown at the start of bar 5 in C2. It marks the point where a repeat should begin (as indicated by the phrase 'Dal segno al fine' at the end of the printed music). The same sign is sometimes used to mark the end of a repeated section, but the word 'fine' is more common (bar 16).

Segue (It.). **1.** A direction requiring the performer to continue in a similar manner. The use of this term in bar 3 of C83 indicates that the guitarist should continue the rapid strummed arpeggiation (*rasgueado*) marked in the first two bars (until *punteado* has to be used from bar 19). **2.** *Attacca* (B4).

Sehr (Ger.). Very. 'Sehr langsam' at the opening of B58 means 'very slow'. See *Tempo markings*.

Seitensatz, Seitenthema (Ger.). In sonata form, the second subject (B40, bars 26–48).

Semibiscroma (It.). Hemidemisemiquaver, sixty-fourth-note (B18, Variation 5, the last six notes of bar 7). See *Note*.

Semibreve (Eng. and It.). Whole-note (𝅝). See *Note* and A17, bars 10–12 (shawm part).

Semicroma (It.). Semiquaver, sixteenth-note (B18, Variation 5, bars 1–6). See *Note*.

Semidemisemiquaver. Synonym for hemidemisemiquaver (B18, bar 7). See *Note*.

Semiquaver. Sixteenth-note (𝅘𝅥𝅯). See *Note* and B18, Variation 5, bars 0–6.

Semitone. The interval between any two adjacent notes (including the black notes) of a piano. The horn part in C85 consists almost entirely of pairs of notes, the first note of each pair falling a semitone to the second note (x). There are just three other intervals, all of them rising semitones (x'). *EM 2.2.1.*

Semplice (It.). Simple, without added ornaments or rhythmic alterations. Couperin does not use this term (or its French equivalent) in bars 9–21 of C32, but the music itself and the harpsichordist's performance of it is simple, rhythmically unaltered and contains only the three cadential trills marked by the composer (compare this passage with the flanking sections).

Sempre (It.). Always, throughout. The direction 'sempre ad libitum' at the head of C84 means 'play with rhythmic freedom throughout'.

Sensible (Fr.). Leading note (B18, note 7 at the beginning of bar 3). See *Scale degrees*.

Sentence. A complete musical idea. In this sense the term can be synonymous with period (B49), though some authorities maintain that a sentence is intermediate between a phrase (B48) and period.

Senza (It.). Without. The direction 'senza sord.' in bar 23 of C97 is an abbreviation of 'senza sordini' (without mutes).

Septet, septuor (Fr.). **1.** A group of seven solo performers (C38). **2.** A type of chamber music for seven solo performers, eg Beethoven's Septet Op. 20 for clarinet, bassoon, horn, violin, viola, cello and double bass.

Septuplet. Seven equal notes played in the time of four notes of the same type (C94, bar 7).

Sequence. 1. The immediate repetition of a motif or phrase of a melody in the same part but at a different pitch. The phrase labelled a at the start of B21 is a melodic sequence consisting of a seven-note motif that is immediately repeated one step up by the same instruments. **2.** The immediate repetition of a harmonic progression at a different pitch. The two chords heard in the first phrase of B68 (bars 2–3) are repeated a minor 3rd higher in the second phrase (bars 6–7). **3.** A type of hymn added to the official corpus of liturgical plainsong. It originated in the early medieval practice of adding words to the jubilus of an Alleluia (A5). During the course of the middle ages it became independent of its host and a number of sequences were newly composed. The *Dies irae* (B62) is a fine example of the genre. It is one of only a handful of sequences to survive the reforms of the Council of Trent in the 16th century. It retains its place to this day in the liturgy of the Mass for the Dead. *EM 8.4.1.*

Sequentia (Lat.). The textless, extended melody of chants such as the Alleluia (eg the jubilus shown in A5) to which words were later added to create a sequence (see *Sequence* 3).

Serenade. 1. An 18th-century instrumental composition in several movements intended

Seventh chords

for performance in the evening. Like the divertimento (B40) the serenade tended to be lighter in style than the contemporary symphony. **2.** Any composition to do with night, sunset, twilight and sleep (C84 and C85). *EM 8.9.3.*

Serenata (It.). See *Serenade* 1 and B40.

Serial harmony. See *Serial music*, C40 (bars 9–12) and C88, bar 1. *EM 5.8.1.*

Serial music. Music based on a predetermined succession of musical elements such as durations and dynamics of notes, and, most commonly, pitches of notes.

There is a series consisting of all 12 chromatic notes in the first seven bars of C40, and in the closing bars the series (or tone row) is manipulated to produce four chords (by superimposing cells A, B, C and D on top of each other).

A similar process can be heard at the start of C88. If the first 12 notes sung by the tenor are regarded as Stravinsky's original tone row (the prime order, basic series or basic set), then the first three chords can be heard as verticalisations of four-note segments of its retrograde order (the prime order played backwards – as shown below the first bar and in (ii) following C88). This is one of the standard manipulations of the row found in serial music, and it can be heard as a melody (marked R) in the last phrase of the tenor part (with decorative oscillations between notes 5–6 and 11–12). Another type of manipulation is melodic inversion. The inversion of the retrograde order is shown at (iii) following C88 and it can be heard in the instrumental parts of bars 3–5. The four basic orderings of the row (prime, inversion, retrograde and retrograde inversion) can start on any of the 12 chromatic notes: (iv) following C88 shows the first six notes of the retrograde inversion transposed up six semitones. This hexachord can be heard in the tenor part of bars 6–7 (again with oscillations between adjacent notes). *EM 3.8, 4.6, 8.11.4, 8.11.9.*

Series. An ordered succession of musical events used as a basis for composition, for instance, a tone row (C40, bars 1–7). See *Serial music. EM 4.6.*

Serrant (Fr.). Getting faster, as in the final seconds of track C5. See *Tempo markings.*

Service. Although the term has many meanings, it is chiefly associated with acts of communal worship in general and musical settings of items regularly sung in the Anglican services of Matins, Evensong and Holy Communion in particular. The Magnificat (C30) is one of the canticles that are said or sung in the service of Evening Prayer (Evensong).

Set. In serial music, a tone row (C40).

Setting. Music added to a text so that the words are sung instead of spoken. A48 and A52 are settings of the same text by Victoria and Palestrina respectively.

Seven-six suspension. See *Suspension* and A24, bars 20, 24 and 32.

Seventh. 1. See *Degree* and the seventh note of B18. **2.** See *Intervals* and C95. **3.** See *Seventh chords* and B78.

Seventh chords. A chord consisting of a triad surmounted by a 7th above the root. Seventh chords can be formed on any degree of a tonal scale. B78(iii) shows seventh chords formed on every degree of a natural minor scale on B♭. These chords can be heard as arpeggiated root-position chords in bars 2^3–5 of track B78. Since the 7th is a discord it is usual for it to resolve by step to a consonant note. On the extra stave below Brahms's music the 7ths are identified by a bracket linking the root and 7th. It will be seen that all but the last of these dissonances resolve down a step to a note that forms a consonant interval with the bass. For instance, the A♭ at the end of bar 2 (which forms an interval of a 7th with the bass B♭) resolves down to a G♭ at the start of the next bar (where it forms a consonant 3rd with the bass E♭). Similarly the dissonant D♭ in chord IV^7 resolves down to a consonant C♮ in bar 3. Like the dominant 7th, chords of the 7th built on other degrees of the scale take their names from the scale degrees upon which they are formed. Thus the chord on beat 3 of bar 2 is known as a tonic 7th, and the chord on the first beat of bar 3 is known as a subdominant 7th.

Like triads, 7th chords can be inverted. The dominant 7th of E major is shown with black note heads on the extra stave below bar 1 of B30. The next chord on this stave has the 3rd of the chord as its lowest note, thus forming a first-inversion dominant-7th chord of E major (V^6_5, heard in bar 2 of the extract). Similarly the first chord of bar 6 has the 5th of the chord as its lowest note, thus forming a second-inversion domi-

Sextet

nant-7th chord of B major (V_3^4). Finally, the second chord in bar 1 has the 7th of the chord as its lowest note, thus forming a third-inversion dominant-7th chord of E major (V_2^4).

A diminished-7th chord consists of a diminished triad surmounted by a diminished 7th above the root. It is most often formed on the leading note and so, like VII^7, it has a strong dominant function (compare the resolutions of these two chords to the tonic in bars 4–5 of B30 and bars 5–6 of B31).

See *Diminished-7th chord, Dominant chords* (b and c), *Half-diminished-7th chord, Secondary-dominant chords* and *Secondary-7th chords*.

Sextet, sextuor (Fr.). **1.** A group of six solo performers. Maxwell Davies's *Ave maris stella* is composed for a sextet comprising flute, clarinet, marimba, piano, viola and cello soloists (C90). **2.** A type of chamber music composed for six soloists, eg Schoenberg's *Verklärte Nacht* for six solo string players (later arranged by the composer for a full string orchestra).

Sextuplet, sextolet. A group of six notes performed in the time of four notes of the same kind (B51, in which the left-hand sextuplets can be heard against groups of four semiquavers in the right-hand part).

Sforzando, sforzato (*sf*, *sfz*) (It.). Strongly accented (B51, B53 and B54).

Sfp (*sfp*) (It.). Abbreviation of *sforzando-piano*, ie a strong accent immediately followed by a soft performance of the same note or notes (B50, wind, bar 2).

Sfz (*sfz*) (It.). Abbreviation of *sforzando* (B51).

Shagbutt. A 17th-century English name for a sackbut or trombone (A60).

Shake. Trill (A80, bars 12 and 37). See *Ornaments*. *EM 3.10.1*.

Sharp. A sign (♯) that raises a note a semitone from its uninflected pitch. See *Accidental, Key signature* and A23, bar 4.

Shawm. A double-reed woodwind instrument made in several sizes, the shawm was the principal loud instrument of professional wind players from the 14th to the late 16th century (and is still played in China, India, Morocco and Barcelona). A shawm can be heard playing a duet with a bagpipe on track A17 and an ensemble of shawms plays a pavan on track A32. *EM 6.6.4*.

Short score. A score on a few staves representing what was originally written on many staves. C86 is a reduction onto two staves of what Britten wrote on 20 staves. See *Open score and short score*.

Si (Fr., It. and Span.). B♮. See *B*, the diagram of a keyboard on the folded insert and A3.

Siciliana, siciliano (It.), **sicilienne** (Fr.). A pastoral dance in moderate $^6_8$ or $^{12}_8$ time characterised by the rhythm marked x in B19. The style is evident in many late 17th- and 18th-century arias and instrumental movements entitled 'pastorale'. *EM 8.7.3*.

Side drum, Snare drum. A small two-headed drum of indefinite pitch usually played with two wooden sticks. Its most characteristic sound is caused by gut, silk, nylon or metal snares stretched across the lower head of the drum. These rattle against the membrane when the upper head is struck causing a sound like that made by the *tambour militaire* on C45. When the snares are released the sound is more subdued (C44, which begins with two rolls on a side drum without snares). Further examples of side-drum rhythms can be heard in context on C52.

Characteristic side-drum strokes are shown in C43. The flam and drag consist of an accented note preceded respectively by one or two very fast unaccented strokes. The four-note ruff may be heard in C78, bar 8. This ornament should not be confused with the characteristic march rhythms played on tracks A32 and C74. Explosive rim shots are produced by striking the rim and membrane simultaneously, or by placing one stick so that it touches both rim and skin then striking it with the other stick. These effects can be heard in context on track C53. *EM 6.8.2*.

Signature. A symbol found just after the clef at the beginning of a stave. There are two types. A key signature consists of one or more flats (C8) or sharps (C9) that indicate which notes are to be lowered or raised a semitone throughout the stave. The two numbers forming a time signature indicate the number and type of beats in each bar (two minim beats in C8 and three crotchet beats in C9). Alternatively the letter C can be used instead of $^4_4$ (B76) and C with a vertical stroke through it instead of $^2_2$ (B21).

Silence (Fr.). Rest, eg the silence between

Simple and compound time

the second and third chords of B30 (indicated by symbols that look like the figure 7).

Silence d'articulation (Fr.). A short rest inserted by the performer between two notes to clarify a rhythm (compare B77 with B78). *EM 1.6.2.*

Silofono (It.). Xylophone (C8).

Sim. (It.). Abbreviation of *simile* (B73, bars 5–6).

Simfony, sinfony, symphony. Hurdy-gurdy (A18). *EM 6.4.3.*

Similar motion. See *Motion* and A85, bar 2. *EM 4.1.*

Simile (sim.) (It.). Continue in the same way. In B73 'cb simile' means that the double basses continue playing a pizzicato E♮ at the start of every odd-numbered bar.

Simple interval. An interval of an octave or less (eg the intervals between any two adjacent notes in the first ten bars of A90) as opposed to a compound interval (eg the 10th in bar 11 of the same example).

Simple and compound time, simple and compound meter. Simple time is a type of metre in which the main beat is an undotted note that is divisible into two, four, eight, 16 or 32 shorter note values, or mixtures of note values that equate with these groups. In B18 the main beat is a minim or half-note (as indicated by the time signature). In the theme this underlying beat divides into two crotchets (quarter-notes). In Variation 1 it divides into four quavers (eighths). In bars 0–6 of Variation 5 it divides into eight semiquavers (sixteenths). If other subdivisions of the beat are required numerals above or below each group of notes show how many notes should be fitted into a beat. In Variation 3 two groups of triplet quavers fit into one minim beat, and in B57 sextuplets fit into one crotchet beat. The following are the most common simple metres:

- $\frac{2}{2}$ = two minim beats per bar (A13 is in simple duple time)
- ¢ = $\frac{2}{2}$ = two minim beats per bar (A31 is in simple duple or *alla breve* time)
- $\frac{3}{2}$ = three minim beats per bar (A28 is in simple triple time)
- $\frac{2}{4}$ = two crotchet beats per bar (B15 is in simple duple time)
- $\frac{3}{4}$ = three crotchet beats per bar (A12 is in simple triple time)
- $\frac{4}{4}$ = four crotchet beats per bar (B9 is in simple quadruple time)
- c = $\frac{4}{4}$ = four crotchet beats per bar (A17 in simple quadruple or common time)
- $\frac{3}{8}$ (in a slowish tempo) = three quaver beats per bar (B78 is in simple triple time)
- $\frac{4}{8}$ = four quaver beats per bar (C11 is in simple quadruple time)

Compound time is a type of metre in which the main beat is a dotted note that is divisible into three, six, 12, 24 or 48 shorter note values, or mixtures of note values that equate with these groups. In A70 the main beat is a dotted crotchet (violin 1, bar 2 etc) which divides into groups of three quavers (violin 1, bar 1 etc). In C6 the beat is again a dotted crotchet, but this divides into groups of six semiquavers in the woodwind parts. Both of these extracts are in $\frac{6}{8}$ time. (In a slow tempo the same time signature can indicate a quaver beat (B68) with relatively strong accents on the first and fourth quavers of the bar.) If other subdivisions of the beat are required numerals above or below each group of notes show how many notes should be fitted into a beat (in bars 4–5 of C4 duplet quavers in the oboe and horn parts fit into the same beats as the normal three-quaver groups played in the bass part). The following are the most common compound metres:

- $\frac{3}{8}$ = one dotted-crotchet beat per bar in fast (A86) or moderate tempi (C93)
- $\frac{6}{8}$ = two dotted-crotchet beats per bar in moderate to fast tempi (A14)
- $\frac{9}{8}$ = three dotted-crotchet beats per bar in moderate to fast tempi, or nine quaver beats per bar with relatively strong accents on the first, fourth and seventh quaver beats in slow tempi (C72)
- $\frac{12}{8}$ = four dotted-crotchet beats per bar in moderate to fast tempi (B19)

These are the usual interpretations of the time signatures given above. But tempo plays a considerable role in determining how conductors beat the music and how the metre is perceived by a listener. Thus although B5 is notated in common time ($\frac{4}{4}$) Bach's slow tempo mark (Adagio) means that most conductors beat eight quavers to the bar. Contrariwise C2 is played so fast that, without the score, it might well be perceived as being in compound duple time ($\frac{6}{8}$), with every one of Grieg's bars being equal to a dotted-crotchet beat. *EM 1.4, 1.8.*

Simultaneity

Simultaneity. 1. Any collection of notes sounded at the same time. **2.** In serial music, a chord consisting of adjacent notes of a row. The first chord of C88 is a simultaneity in this sense because it consists of the first four pitches of the retrograde order of Stravinsky's row (ie A, B, C and B♭ in the tenor part of bar 5).

Sinfonia (It.). **1.** Symphony (B21 and B28). **2.** In Italian baroque operas an overture, interlude or postlude. The sinfonia from Act 3 of Monteverdi's *Orfeo* (A64) is, like most instrumental interludes in 17th-century opera, in one movement. It is played three times (twice in Act 3 and once in Act 5) and so acts as a unifying device in much the same way as a ritornello does on a smaller timescale. **3.** An alternative title for instrumental compositions such as the canzona, trio sonata or preludial movement in a baroque suite (Bach calls the first movement of his second keyboard partita a sinfonia). *EM 8.7.1.*

Sinfonie, symphonie (Ger.). Symphony (C1 and C27–C29).

Sinfonische Dichtung (Ger.). Symphonic poem (C10 and C11). Strauss preferred the synonym *Tondichtung* (tone poem).

Singing. The articulation of musical sounds through the open mouth. For centuries it dominated the art of music, a fact demonstrated both by the preponderance of compositions for voices, and by the influence that vocal music had on instrumental styles (compare A31 and A32, also A56 and A57). With the development of idiomatic instrumental styles in the baroque era singing lost its pre-eminence and vocal styles began to be influenced by new instrumental idioms (compare the vocal part of B15 with the trumpet and violin parts). The development of virtuoso singing techniques began at the beginning of the baroque era (A66) and continued throughout the 18th and 19th centuries (B50). By the 20th century extended vocal techniques (C34) pushed singing to the verge of incantatory speech (C91 and C97).

Single-reed instruments. See *Reed instruments*. Examples include basset-horn (B40), bass clarinet (C38) and clarinet (C79). *EM 6.6.3.*

Singspiel (Ger.). A vernacular German opera with spoken dialogue of the late 18th and 19th centuries. It could contain buffo-style arias (B37), arias in the style of opera seria (B50) and melodrama (B60). *EM 8.9.6, 8.10.1.*

Siren, sirène (Fr.), **Sirene** (Ger.), **sirena** (It. and Span.). A hand-cranked or electric machine identical to the device used in the Second World War to warn of impending air raids. The rising and falling wailing of a pair of sirens can be heard on tracks C44 and C52. *EM 6.8.6.*

Sitole. Citole (A13).

Six-eight time. A compound duple metre in which two dotted-crotchet beats form the repeating pattern strong–weak in moderate or fast tempi (A14). Alternatively six quaver beats can form the repeating pattern strong–weak–weak–strong–weak–weak in slower tempi (B74). It is indicated by the time signature $^6_8$ immediately after the first clef.

Six-four chord. A triad in second inversion. In the first bar of B41 the tonic chord of G major is heard in root position, first inversion (with the 3rd of the chord in the bass) and second inversion (with the 5th of the chord in the bass). The chord is described as a six-four because the intervals from the bass are a 6th (D up to B) and a 4th (D up to G). The same chord can be heard more clearly on track B46, first at the start (a), then sandwiched between two other chords (b). Finally the same chord can be heard in context in the two principal cadences of the minuet (B41, bar 7 and bar 15). This, the most common manifestation of the chord in classical music, is known as a cadential six-four. *EM 5.3.3., 5.5.2.*

Six-four time. A compound duple metre in which two dotted-minim beats form the repeating pattern strong–weak in moderate or fast tempi. Alternatively six crotchet beats can form the repeating pattern strong–weak–weak–strong–weak–weak in slower tempi. It is indicated by the time signature $^6_4$ immediately after the first clef. Debussy uses two time signatures at the beginning of 'La Cathédrale engloutie' (C22) because the music shifts between $^3_2$ and $^6_4$ time (or combines both metres). But in bars 3–4 of C23 the music is unambiguously in $^6_4$, with accents on the first and fourth beats.

Six-three chord. A first inversion triad. See *Sixth chord* and A24, bars 5–7.

Sixteen-foot stop. A rank of organ pipes of

which the longest measures approximately 16 feet. Music peformed on a 16-foot stop sounds an octave lower than printed. The registration of the pedal part in A86 (stems down on the bass stave) includes two 16-foot stops sounding an octave *below* printed pitch, but an octave *above* the lowest-sounding pitches (which are played on a 32-foot stop).

Sixteenth-note. Semiquaver (♪) (B18, Variation 5, bars 1–6).

Sixth. 1. See *Degree* and the sixth note of B18. **2.** See *Interval* and C95. **3.** See *Six-three chord* and A24, bars 5–7.

Sixth chord, six-three chord A triad in first inversion (ie with the 3rd of the chord in the lowest-sounding part). In the first bar of B41 a G-major triad can be heard in root position, then in first inversion (ie with the 3rd of the triad in the bass). The chord is so named because of the intervals formed between the bass note and the upper parts: in this case B up to G (a 6th) and B up to D (a 3rd). The difference between a six–three chord and the same triad in root position can be heard more clearly in the first two bars of B50 where the strings alone play a first-inversion triad of D minor followed by the whole orchestra playing the same triad in root position. See *Added-sixth chord* and B66, bar 1; *Augmented-6th chord* and B30, bar 8; *French-sixth chord* and B67, bar 7; *German 6th chord* and B30, bar 8; *Italian-6th chord* and B57, bars 39–40; *Neapolitan 6th* and B50, bars 80–81.

Sixty-fourth-note. Hemidemisemiquaver. (♬). See *Note* and the last six notes in bar 7 of Variation 5 in B18.

Slancio (It.). Rush, dash, impetus. 'Con slancio' (with dash, with rhythmic impetus) exactly describes the whole of B73.

Slapstick. A type of whip (C46 and C52).

Sleigh bells. A set of jingles on a stick, a leather strap or a wire frame shaken by the player (C49 and C52, bars 18–20). *EM 6.8.3.*

Slentando (It.). Slowing down (B65, bars 40–43). See *Tempo markings.*

Slide. 1. A melodic ornament consisting of two grace notes ascending rapidly by step to the main note. The first of the grace notes is played on the beat, so both grace notes rob the value of the main note. In bar 12 of A84 the most common conventional sign for a slide is shown on the main stave with the ornament as played written out on the stave. See also *Schleifer* and B25, bar 60. See *Ornaments. EM 3.10.1, 3.10.2.* **2.** A length of tubing that slides in and out of the body of a trombone, thus effectively shortening (in) or lengthening (out) the total length of tubing. The seven standard positions of the slide allow a full chromatic range as well as glissandi (C75, last 2 bars).

Slur. A curved line above or below a group of notes. It indicates: **a)** that the notes are to be played legato (in B79 the cross-bar slurring in bars 8–15 can be distinctly heard, and it emphasises the cross-rhythms engendered by the harmony), **b)** that the notes are to be played in one bow-stroke (C12, viola, bars 1–2), **c)** that a wind player should play all but the first note without tonguing (C31, contrabassoon in bars 1–4 and clarinets and bassoons in bars 5–8), **d)** that all of the notes under a long slur are to be regarded as parts of a single melodic phrase (B67, bars 1–3, 3–5, 5–7 and 7–9), **e)** that slurred notes should be sung to a single syllable (B5, bar 2). *EM 1.14.*

Smorzando (It.). Dying or fading away (B66, bars 20–22).

Snap pizzicato. A type of pizzicato in which the string is plucked vigorously so that it rebounds off the fingerboard (C71, bars 1 and 5). Also known as a Bartók pizzicato. *EM 6.5.6.*

Snare drum. Side drum. Despite its name the snare drum can be played without activating the snares (C44 and C45).

Snares. A set of gut, silk, nylon or metal wires stretched across the lower head of a side drum or snare drum. They rattle against the membrane when the upper head is beaten with a stick (C44). The snares can be released so changing the timbre of the drum (C52, bars 1–3).

Soave (It.). Sweet, gentle. See *Dolce* and B64(a), bar 9.

Sofort (Ger.). *Attacca* (B4).

Soft pedal. See *Una corda* and B74.

Soggetto (It.). In the 18th century, a short fugal subject (B14) similar to the imitative subjects of the older ricercar (A57, bars 1–2). See *Andamento* and *Attacco.*

Soh

Soh. The fifth degree of any major scale in the British system of tonic sol-fa. In A25 the first note of bar 3 is *soh* in the key of D major.

Sol (Fr., It. and Span.). G♯. See *G,* the diagram of a keyboard on the folded insert and A3.

Sol-fa. See *Tonic sol-fa* and A25.

Soli (It.). Soloists. Compare the passages marked 'soli' with those for the full orchestra (marked 'tutti') in B19.

Solo (It.). Music for a single voice (A22) or instrument (A88) or a single performer with accompaniment (B57).

Solo exposition. In a concerto movement beginning with an orchestral exposition, the second principal section, in which the main themes are played by the soloist and orchestra (B36, bars 44–140).

Son (Fr.). Sound. Thus *son étouffé* (muted, as in the horn and violin parts of C19).

Sonagli, sonagliera (It.). Sleigh bells (C49 and C52, bars 18–20).

Sonata. An instrumental composition, usually in several movements or sections, and written for a single instrument or a small ensemble. The term has changed its meaning over the centuries.

In the first half of the 17th century it could mean a canzona, but after about 1650 the term was used for a multi-movement composition for one or two soloists with continuo accompaniment. The latter type (the *sonata a tre*) is now known as a trio sonata, a genre that often contained binary-form dance movements (A74).

In the classical period sonatas were usually in three or four extended movements and were written for solo piano or a soloist with piano accompaniment (multi-movement works for larger ensembles were called trios, quartets, divertimentos etc). The first movement was often a sonata-allegro (B52 comes from the first subject of the opening movement of a piano sonata by Beethoven, and B53 comes from the second subject of the same movement). The second movement was usually slower and more lyrical (B56). If there were four movements the third was most often a minuet and trio (though early classical sonatas in three movements sometimes ended with a minuet). In later classical sonatas the minuet and trio (B25) was superseded by a scherzo and trio (B55). The last movement was fast and often in rondo form.

Although sonatas continued to be written in the 19th and 20th centuries, they are so varied in style and structure that generalisations about them would be misleading. For instance Brahms's gigantic Piano Sonata Op. 5 (B75) is in five movements, while Liszt's equally massive Piano Sonata in B minor is in one continuous and highly integrated movement. *EM 8.9.5.*

Sonata a tre, sonata a 3 (It.). Trio sonata (A74). *EM 8.7.4.*

Sonata-allegro. A fast movement (usually the first in multi-movement works) in sonata form (B40).

Sonata da camera and sonata da chiesa (It.). Chamber sonata and church sonata respectively. See *Trio sonata* and A74. *EM 8.7.2, 8.7.4.*

Sonata form. A name for many different musical structures composed from the mid-18th century onwards. They have in common a tripartite structure.

In the first section, called the exposition, a passage in the tonic is followed by a substantial passage in an opposing key. The two are often linked by a transition (or bridge) in which the music modulates from the key of the first passage to the key of the second. This tonal conflict is most apparent in sonata-form movements in minor keys. In these the minor mode of the first passage (called the first subject) conflicts with the major mode of the second subject. B27 is a complete exposition from a sonata-form movement. In the first subject (bars 1–8) the key of D minor is firmly established by tonic and dominant chords and a perfect cadence (V–I in bars 7–8). In the transition (bars 9–12) a modulation from D minor to its relative major (F major) is effected by the use of dominant harmony in the new key (V^7) and a perfect cadence (V^7–I in bars 12–13). This cadence overlaps the start of the second subject (bars 13–32) which never leaves the new key of F major. It is evident that the first and second subjects are linked by common motives derived from the theme of the first subject (notably motives a and c). Such monothematicism does not inhibit the tonal conflict between the two subjects since the common motives are heard in an entirely new light when they are transposed from a minor key to a major key. It is also evident that the second sub-

Song without words

ject divides into two subsections, the first (IIa) based on motive c, the second (IIb) based on motive a. Because the second subject (and, more rarely, the first subject) may contain more than one thematic idea some writers prefer to use the term second subject group. Most expositions end with a little tail (the codetta, bars 33–39) that emphasises the key of the second subject group by its repeated perfect cadences.

In the second section of the tripartite structure (the development) tonal conflict is usually more apparent than in the flanking sections, and, more often than not, the melodic ideas that are manipulated here derive from themes already heard in the exposition. Both of these generalisations hold good for the development in the finale of Haydn's *Oxford* Symphony. B28 shows the G-major theme at the start of the movement, while B29 shows how Haydn derives a fugal subject from it. The simple homophonic texture and almost static harmony of the first subject are replaced by tumultuous contrapuntal textures that pass rapidly through a series of minor keys (B minor, E minor and A minor) never heard in the exposition.

In the final section of the tripartite structure (the recapitulation) most if not all of the themes of the exposition are repeated, but the tonal conflicts of the first two sections are reconciled by the transposition of the second subject into the tonic key of the whole movement. The balancing function of the recapitulation is best understood in the context of a complete sonata-form movement. B40 begins with a first subject (bars 1–18) in F major. The transition (bars 18–25) modulates from the tonic chord of F major to the dominant chord of C major to prepare the ground for the second subject group (bars 26–48) that remains in the dominant key of C major throughout (confirmed by the repeated perfect cadence of the codetta, bars 48–51). The development (bars 52–71) is based on a figure from the codetta (z) and is tonally unstable (references are made to several keys, but none of them is confirmed by a perfect cadence). In the recapitulation the first subject is repeated without any changes at all, but the transition is modified so that, instead of ending on chord V of C major, it ends on chord V of the tonic key of F major (bar 94). This leads to the second subject which is reconciled with the first by being transposed from C major to F major. The repositioning of the melodies so that the treble part of bars 26–31 becomes the bass part of bars 95–100 and the bass of bars 34–39 becomes an inner part in bars 103–108 is wonderfully deft, but makes no difference to the tonal scheme. Mozart extends the chromatic figure of bars 41–42 and 44–45 in bars 113–118 so that the perfect cadence at the end of the second subject (bars 119–120) sounds even more conclusive. Finally a four-bar coda sets the seal on the tonal reconciliation by its repeated perfect cadences in the tonic. *EM 7.7, 8.9.1.*

Sonata-rondo form. See *Rondo forms* and B36. *EM 7.7.2, 8.9.2.*

Sonatina. Literally a 'little sonata', the sonatina retains the formal structures of the sonata but is shorter and, very often, easier to play. It was cultivated in the late 18th and early 19th centuries and was most often written for young pianists. The sonata-form movement shown in B40 was arranged with other movements from Mozart's Divertimenti KA229 as the last of a set of six *Sonatines pour le forte-piano*. This sonatina has four movements – a sonata-allegro, a minuet and trio, a binary-form adagio and the movement shown in B40 (but in the key of C major). Its compact sonata form and simple style are characteristic of many contemporary sonatina movements.

Song. A self-contained accompanied or unaccompanied vocal composition, most often for one singer. See *Ballade* (A12), *Carol* (A24), *Consort song* (A60), *Lied* (B57, B58 and C40), *Operetta* (C73), *Rondeau* (A23) and *Virelai* (A22). *EM 8.7.1, 8.10.2.*

Song cycle. A set of songs linked by a poetic theme and intended to be performed together. B57 is an extract from the second of a cycle of 20 lieder with texts by Wilhelm Müller telling of a youth's wanderlust, his first love, and his eventual despair. C85 is an extract from a song from an orchestrally accompanied cycle based on the theme of evening and nightfall.

Song form. Ternary form (ABA), such as that in a da capo aria (B15). The term is a misnomer since most songs are not in ternary form, and ternary form is much more common in short piano pieces such as C2.

Song without words, Lied ohne Worte (Ger.). A title invented by Mendelssohn for a type of lyrical character piece with a song-like melody and simple accompaniment. The titles given in many editions are not Mendelssohn's own with the exception of the three 'Venetian gondola songs' (of which B61 is one). Tchaikovsky used the title in two of his piano pieces, though he preferred to render it in French ('Chant sans paroles' is the title of Op. 40, No. 6).

Sonority. Although the adjective 'sonorous' usually means having a rich, deep or loud sound (C97, bars 23–26), the noun 'sonority' is now often used in a musical context in something nearer its original sense (of or pertaining to sound). Thus in modern writing about music the term can mean: **1.** The particular tone-colour of an instrument (compare the sonorities of a flute, a muted trumpet and a celesta in the last bar of C35). **2.** The tone-colour of combined instruments and/or voices (compare the sonority of the combined timbres of harp and muted trumpet playing the first note of C35 with the sonority of the combined timbres of celesta, muted viola and harp playing the second note of the same piece). **3.** The sound of a particular chord (compare the sonorities of the first three chords of C88). The last meaning of sonority has come to replace the term 'chord' because of the association of this word with the tertian harmony of earlier periods. See *Simultaneity*.

Sons bouchés (Fr.). Stopped notes on a horn (the notes with crosses in the last two bars of C85).

Sopra (It.). Above, on, over, upon. The direction 'sopra una corda' in bar 91 of B50 means 'upon one string' (the violin D string).

Soprano. 1. The highest female voice (B50). The range of a solo soprano is shown on the folded insert. **2.** A treble voice (C30). **3.** An adjective describing a high-pitched instrument. The recorders in A69 are soprano or treble recorders sounding an octave above written pitch. **4.** The highest-sounding part of a composition, whether written for voices or instruments. Thus the tonal answer heard in bars 2–3 of B14 can be described as a soprano entry even though all the parts of this fugue are played on the piano.

Soprano clef. One of the moveable C clefs. In A30 this is the clef on the top stave of the four-stave system beneath the modern transcription. It shows that the bottom line represents middle C (from this it is easy to determine that the first note of the soprano part of this frottola is c^2, an octave above middle C). The clef is now obsolete but can be found in 19th-century vocal scores.

Sordino (It.), **sourdine** (Fr.). Mute. 'Con sordini' and 'avec sourdines' mean 'with mutes' (C19, horns and violins). 'Senza sordini' and 'sans sourdines' mean 'without mutes' (C97, bar 23).

Sordone (It.), **sourdine** (Fr.), **Sordun** (Ger.). A double-reed woodwind instrument of the late 16th and early 17th centuries. Because its cylindrical tube doubles back on itself (like a bassoon) it had a low range for its relatively small size. Praetorius described five sizes and said that they sounded like crumhorns. A35 probably gives a fair impression of the sort of sound Praetorius's sordone made.

Sostenido (Span.). The sharp sign (♯) (A23, bar 4). See *Accidental* and *Key signature*.

Sostenuto (It.). Sustained (B61, bar 1) or slowing down (C1, bars 19–22). See *Tempo markings*.

Sostenuto pedal. The central pedal on pianos with three pedals. It allows the pianist to sustain a chord against which unsustained notes can be played. In bars 15–17 of C67 the pianist uses the sostenuto pedal to sustain the tonic triad while playing unsustained quavers above it.

Sotto voce (It.). Literally 'under the voice', the term is used metaphorically in instrumental music to indicate that a hushed or whispered performance is required (B65, bar 5).

Sound. 1. A disturbance of any elastic medium, especially the air. **2.** The perception of such a disturbance conveyed via the eardrum to the brain. As well as musical pitches, sound includes such non-musical phenomena as the clatter of the action of the clavichord heard on B20.

Soundboard. A thin sheet of wood that acts as a resonator on clavichords (B20), harpsichords (B17) and pianos (B61).

Soundbox. The hollow body of a string instrument which amplifies the vibrations of the strings (A88).

Sounding pitch. As used in this dictionary,

Staff notation

perceived sound as opposed to written or printed notation. Thus the clarinet part in C10 is printed at the pitches that are actually heard when *Till Eulenspiegel* is performed – despite the fact that Strauss wrote the part a tone lower for a clarinet in D and the fact that it is usually performed on a clarinet in E♭ (the performer being required to transpose Strauss's notation to achieve what is shown in C10).

Soupir (Fr.). Crotchet rest (the symbol at the end of each stave in A23).

Sourdine (Fr.). Mute. See *Sordino* and C19.

Soutenu (Fr.) See *Sostenuto* and the tempo mark in B61.

Spacing. The way in which notes of a chord are disposed in relation to each other. On the first beat of bar 5 in C29 the three notes of an A♭ major chord (A♭, C and E♭) can be heard in close spacing, then in bar 8 the same pitch classes can be heard in open spacing. *EM 6.11.7.*

Species counterpoint. A method of teaching Palestrinian counterpoint (A52) devised by Fux in 1725. The simplest exercise in species counterpoint consists of a cantus firmus to which the pupil adds a single part, note-against-note, while observing the 'rules' that Fux derived from Palestrina's style. This is the first species. In the second species two notes are added to each note of the cantus firmus, while the other three species gradually introduce more complex rhythms and more complex dissonance treatment. Many classical and romantic composers were taught species counterpoint and, adapted to contemporary styles, its influence is evident in contrapuntal passages such as those shown in B21–B24.

Speech-song. See *Sprechgesang* and C34.

Spinet, Spinett (Ger.), **spinetta** (It.). A plucked-string keyboard instrument similar to but smaller than a harpsichord. Spinets were domestic instruments, usually with only one manual, that were suitable for the performance of intimate miniatures such as the corrente recorded on A67.

Spinto (It.). A lyric soprano or tenor capable of dramatic power when required. In B57 the lyric qualities of Ian Bostridge's voice are paramount.

Spirito, spiritoso (It.). Spirit and spirited respectively. 'Allegro con spirito' at the head of C83 means 'fast with spirit' (fast and lively). See *Tempo markings*.

Spread chord. A colloquial term for an arpeggiated chord (A84, last bar).

Sprechgesang (Ger.). A type of vocal production halfway between speech and song. On track C34 the vocalist sings the pitches Schoenberg wrote, but with a breathy tone that changes in response to the text. Schoenberg wrote that the singer should 'give the pitch exactly, but then immediately leave it in a fall or rise [to the next note]'. There is, however, no standard way of delivering *Sprechgesang*: performances range from the virtual speech of melodrama (B60) to performances which treat pieces such as C34 almost as songs. *EM 8.11.3.*

Sprechmelodie (Ger.). Speech-melody, a term used by Schoenberg (C34). See *Sprechgesang*.

Sprechstimme (Ger.). Literally 'speaking voice', but the term was used by Schoenberg as a synonym for *Sprechgesang* (C34). *EM 3.6, 8.11.3.*

Sprezzatura (It.). Abbreviation of *sprezzatura di canto* (disdain of melody). A term coined at the beginning of the 17th century to describe the deliberate emphasis on correct declamation of the text at the expense of melody in the *stile rappresentativo* (A62 and A63).

Springer. A melodic decoration which can be an auxiliary note or an *échappée* articulated just before the next melody note (B25, bar 52). See *Nachschlag* and *Ornaments*. *EM 3.10.1.*

Staccato (stacc.) (It.). A detached method of articulating notes indicated by the term itself, its abbreviation (stacc.) or dots above or below the printed notes. The crotchets in bars 1–8 of B21 are staccato, the quavers are legato (indicated by the slur beneath the notes). *EM 1.14.*

Staff notation. Music represented on a number of horizontal lines called a staff or stave. These range from the single-line staff used for untuned percussion (eg the cowbells and bass drum parts in C28), through the four-line staves (staffs) used in modern transcriptions of plainsong (A4), to the five-line staff notation of A98. For keyboard music two staves are braced together to form a system (A57). In organ music, three

Stampita

staves represent the manual parts (braced together as in A93) and pedals (as in A94). In more complex scores any number of staves may be linked by the vertical line at the left-hand side of a system (in B5 the vocal part, the two viole d'amore parts, the lute part and the continuo part form a four-stave system in the first two bars). In this dictionary complex orchestral scores have been reduced to two staves, but other scores have been left in the form of staff notation used by the composer. Thus C86 is a reduction of the 21 staves of the original full score to just two staves, but C87 represents the original staff notation of the composer. See *Clef* and *Leger lines*.

Stampita (It.), **stantipes** (Lat.). *Istampita* (A18).

Stave, staff. Horizontal lines on and between which notes and rests are printed (A3). See *Staff notation*.

Steel drums, steel pans. Percussion instruments made out of the top section of oil-drums (the larger the section, the deeper the overall pitch). The top surface of the oil-drum is divided into a number of different shapes that, when struck, produce sounds of precise pitch. Rolls on steel drums can be heard in bars 54–66 of C97.

Steg (Ger.). The bridge of a string instrument. See *Am steg* and C34, cello, bars 2–6.

Stem. Sometimes called a tail, a stem is the vertical line attached to a note-head for all note-values shorter than a semibreve. Stems can be added to black note-heads to signify crotchets (A25, bars 1–3), or they can be added to white note-heads to signify minims (bar 4 in the same example). See *Note*.

Step. 1. A degree of a scale. The steps of a G-major scale are numbered at the start of B18. **2.** The intervals between these steps. In the same example steps of a tone are shown with a curved bracket, and steps of a semitone with a pointed bracket.

Stepwise motion, stepwise movement. Conjunct motion, ie melodic movement between adjacent pitches (A14, bars 1–2).

Stgs. A common abbreviation of strings (C94).

Stil (Ger.), **stile** (It.). Style. See *Empfindsamer Stil* (B20) and *Stile concertato* (A69).

Stile antico (It.). A term coined in the early 17th century for contemporary music written in the style of Palestrina (A52) as opposed to the *stile moderno* of the early 17th century. Most of Monteverdi's music is written in the 'modern style' (A62–A66), but, like many other composers of the 17th and even 18th centuries, he adopted a style similar to that of Palestrina in some of his liturgical compositions (most of his *Messa a 4 voci da cappella* published in 1641 is in the 'old style'). *EM 8.7.*

Stile concertato (It.). Concertato style (A69). *EM 8.7.2.*

Stile concitato (It.). Agitated style. The term was used by Monteverdi to decribe dramatic repeated semiquavers on a single pitch or chord in his *Combattimento di Tancredi e Clorinda* (1624). Mozart uses the same effect with the same intent at the start of the Queen of the Night's angry aria in Act 2 of *Die Zauberflöte* (B50).

Stile familiare (It.). Familiar style (A37). *EM 6.11.4.*

Stile moderno (It.). The 'modern style' of the early 17th century (A62–A66). See *Stile antico*. *EM 8.7.*

Stile monodico (It.). The style of solo song with continuo accompaniment practised by composers in the early 17th century. Monodic compositions of the period included both recitatives (A62 and A63) and songs that might now be classed as arias or ariosos (A65 and A66).

Stile rappresentativo (It.). The declamatory recitative style of early 17th-century opera (A62 and A63). It is characterised by rhythmic freedom, expressive and often angular vocal melody, and a subservient continuo accompaniment, the bass line of which often forms casual dissonances with the melody. *EM 8.7.1.*

Stile recitativo (It.). The style of early 17th-century recitative (A62 and A63).

Stimme (Ger.). A vocal or instrumental part (A60, soprano and curtal respectively), or an organ stop (A57, which is played on two flue stops).

Stimmtausch (Ger.). Voice exchange (A15, in which two two-bar phrases are exchanged between the two singers of the *pes*).

Stimmungsbild (Ger.). In romantic music, a

String instruments

mood picture, such as the mournful evocation of a funeral gondola in B74.

Stollen (Ger., sing. and pl.). The repeated first section of a piece in bar form (B6, bars 1–6 and 6–10). *EM 7.9.1, 8.6.2.*

Stop. 1. A knob on an organ which controls the flow of air to a rank of pipes, or a similar device on a harpsichord that controls a register of strings. **2.** A rank of pipes. On A92 ranks of flue pipes are used for the upper melody and a rank of reed pipes is used for the lower melody. *EM 6.9.1.*

Stopftöne (Ger.). On a horn, stopped notes (C85, bars 24–25).

Stopped notes, stopped tones. 1. Notes on a horn that are produced by pushing the right hand up the bell, thus altering both pitch and timbre. The G♯s played in the last two bars of C85 (marked with a circle) are open notes, the G♯s (marked with a cross) are stopped notes (the line joining the last two notes indicates a microtonal glissando produced by gradually withdrawing the hand from the bell). **2.** On a string instrument, notes produced by pressing a string firmly against the fingerboard, so shortening the length of the string that is free to vibrate and thus raising the pitch. There is a subtle difference between the sound of open (unstopped) strings and that of stopped strings: the first four notes of A98, bar 2, are played on stopped, open, stopped and open strings (in that order). *EM 6.7.1*

Stopping. On a string instrument, pressing a string firmly against the fingerboard to raise its pitch (see *Stopped notes*). It is possible to play two notes simultaneously by bowing two strings at once: this technique is called double stopping, even if one or both of the strings are unstopped (A97, bars 0–3). All the notes of a three-part chord can also be played simultaneously (the penultimate chord of B50) or implied by rapidly drawing the bow over three strings (bar 3 of A88). In both cases this is called triple stopping. In its literal sense quadruple stopping is impossible on modern string instruments, but four-part chords can be performed as rapid arpeggios (the first chords of bars 1 and 2 in A88).

Storm and stress. See *Sturm und Drang* and B21. *EM 8.8.4.*

Storto (It.). Crumhorn (A35).

Streichinstrumente (Ger.). Bowed string instruments (A38, A88, A90 and C7).

Streichorchester (Ger.). String orchestra (B19).

Streichquartet (Ger.). String quartet (B30–B35).

Strepitoso (It.). Noisy, exuberant. The term accurately describes B37.

Stretto (It.). **1.** In a fugue, imitation of the subject at a shorter interval of time than in the exposition. In the exposition of B14 the subject is imitated by the answer a bar afterwards. In bars 16–18 the subject is imitated after four quavers (this is a *stretto maestrale* involving all three contrapuntal parts). In the coda of the same fugue (bars 23ff) the gap is narrowed to just two quavers. **2.** As a performance direction it signifies a quickening of the tempo (B65, bars 29–32). See *Tempo markings*. *EM 4.5.6, 4.5.7.*

Stretto maestrale. See *Stretto* 1 and B14(a), bars 16–18.

Stride bass. A type of solo jazz piano accompaniment consisting of wide left-hand leaps between two chords. It originated in ragtime dance styles such as the cakewalk and was perfected in the second decade of the 20th century. The bass shown in bars 6–13 of C20 is similar to Scott Joplin's rag-style, stride-bass accompaniments.

String band. 1. A colloquial term for the string section of a symphony orchestra (B50, in which the music for the string band is printed on the two lowest staves throughout the score). **2.** See *String orchestra* and B19.

String bass. Double bass (C7).

String drum. A type of friction drum in which a string of rosined horsehair or a gut string is pulled through the membrane. Alternatively the string can be attached to the centre of the membrane: this is the lion's roar or *tambour à corde* heard on C46 and C52.

String instruments. Instruments in which sound is generated by vibrating strings set in motion by bowing, plucking or striking.

Examples of bowed string instruments include bourdon (A15), cello (A90), contrabass viol (double bass viol) (A36), double bass (C7), fiddle (A18), rebec (A16), vielle (A13), viol (treble, tenor, bass and contra-

String orchestra

bass) (A61), viola (A38), viola da braccio (A64), viola da gamba (A64), viola d'amore (B5), violin (A95–A98), violone (A64).

Example of plucked string instruments include ceterone (A66), chitarrone (A65), citole (A13), guitar (C68 – *requinto*, tenor and bass), harp (A66), lute (A89), piano (plucked strings, C94, bars 3–4), theorbo (A75), vihuela (A34).

The strings of a cimbalom (C41) are struck with hammers. *EM 6.4.*

String orchestra. Usually an orchestra comprising first and second violins, violas, cellos and double basses (B19).

String quartet. 1. A chamber ensemble consisting of two violins, a viola and a cello (B35). **2.** The most important type of chamber music from the late 18th century onwards. In classical string quartets there were usually four movements, the first most often in sonata form (B27), the second a slow movement (B30 and B31) sometimes in variation form (B32–B35), the third a minuet and trio (B38), the last a fast movement, often in sonata-rondo form. The four-movement pattern was retained in most 19th-century string quartets, but, in common with other instrumental genres, composers often linked the movements by the use of transformations of the same theme (C18). Perhaps the most important string quartets by a 20th-century composer are the set of six by Bartók (C69–C72). *EM 8.9.1.*

Stringendo (It.). Tightening the tempo, getting faster (C72, bars 2–3). See *Tempo markings*.

Strings. 1. The string section of an orchestra (B21, bars 1–18). **2.** An independent string orchestra (B19). **3.** A term used to identify the resources reqired for the performance of a work for a non-standard conbination of instruments (C85, which is an extract from a work with the full title of *Serenade for Tenor, Horn and Strings*).

Strisciando (It.). Glissando (C27, harp).

Stromentato (It.). With instrumental accompaniment. In *recitativo stromentato* other instruments are added to the normal continuo group (B16).

Strong beat. In metrical music, the first beat of the bar in any metre (A12 and A14). In some metres there may be subsidiary strong beats. For instance, in $\frac{4}{4}$ time the third beat as well as the first beat is strong in relation to beats 2 and 4 (A87).

Strophic song. A song in which every verse has the same melody. See *Carol* and A24, bars 17–36. *EM 8.10.2.*

Structure. An analytical term that is almost synonymous with form. Thus one may refer to the binary *structure* of the Menuetto shown in B25 (bars 1–20) and the ternary *form* of the whole movement (the italicised words could be interchanged without altering the sense of the observation). The term is most often used when referring to a particular element that helps define the form of a composition. Thus one may show how tonal structure helps define sonata form in B40 (in this case the two terms are not interchangeable).

Stück (Ger.). **1.** As most commonly used nowadays, a piece. B79 is an extract from an intermezzo that is one of a set of six *Klavierstücke* (piano pieces) that were published together as Op. 118 in 1893. **2.** In late 17th- and early 18th-century Germany, an alternative name for a church cantata (B7 and B8).

Study. A piece designed to develop an important aspect of a performer's technique. Although entitled 'Prelude', B66 is in the style of a study designed to develop the ability to play fast but quiet right-hand arpeggios (the semiquaver figuration shown at the opening continues throughout B66).

Sturm und Drang (Ger.). Storm and stress, a style cultivated by Haydn and others in the 1760s and 1770s. B21 displays the characteristic features of the style. The symphony is in a minor key, the movement is fast and agitated, the melodies are often angular (note the leaping 6ths and 7ths in phrase b^1), dynamic levels change frequently and are strongly contrasted, the harmony is often dissonant (note the 7ths formed between the slow-moving upper part and the fast-moving lower part on the first beats of bars 20, 22, 24 and 26), and the textures are highly contrasting (note the bare octaves at the start and the complex contrapuntal web of bars 28–42). *EM 8.8.4.*

Style. All those elements of a composition or a performance that distinguish it from other compositions or performances. The term can be used to distinguish between individual works by the same composer. B21 and B25 are both instrumental compositions by Haydn, but the former could be described as an example of *Sturm und Drang* style, the latter as an example of galant style. At the other extreme, style can be associated with historical periods so that both of these examples could be regarded as manifestations of late 18th-century classical style. In performance, similar stylistic comparisons can be made. B61 and B74 both exemplify the 19th-century character piece, but the pianist playing B61 takes fewer liberties with tempo than the pianist playing B74, so the interpretation of Liszt's piece could be described as being more romantic in style than the interpretation of Mendelssohn's piece. *EM 8.1.*

Style brisé (Fr.). The 'broken' baroque lute and keyboard style in which melodies are discontinuous and the number of parts varies from chord to chord (the chords themselves being broken up or arpeggiated). In B1 every chord shown in the harmonic reduction is articulated as a broken chord in the Aria, with each note sustained so that the texture varies between two and four parts. In bars 6–7 the bass and then an inner part become melodic, briefly suggesting a more contrapuntal texture before returning to their original harmonic role. *EM 8.7.3.*

Style galant (Fr.). Gallant or courtly style. An 18th-century term describing the light, elegant style of the mid-18th century which supplanted the serious contrapuntal styles of late baroque music and prefigured the mature classical style of the late 18th century. It is characterised by simple triadic or conjunct melodies supported by subservient homophonic accompaniments of thin-textured block chords or broken-chord figuration. Melodic ornamentation was decorative rather being an integral part of a melodic line (as it had been in French baroque music). Harmonies were largely diatonic, with tonic and dominant chords in all inversions delineating clear tonal structures such as sonata form (in first movements) and binary form (in minuets and trios). All of these features are evident in B25. Figure x is triadic (outlining chord V), and figures y and z are conjunct. The texture is almost entirely homophonic and rarely exceeds three parts. There is no melodic ornamentation in the minuet as Haydn wrote it, but galant-style decorations are added by the performer in the da capo (bars 45–64). The harmony is entirely diatonic, with six tonic chords, five dominant chords, and only two other types of chord (IV and VI). These define the tonality of A♭ major with absolute clarity. Finally, the binary structure is clearly delineated by the imperfect cadence at the end of the first section (bars 9–10) and the perfect cadence at the end of the minuet. See also *Rococo. EM 8.8.2.*

Style luthé (Fr.). An alternative term for *style brisé* (which originated in the broken style of early baroque lute pieces). See B1.

Subdominant. The fourth degree of a diatonic scale (B18, note 4). See *Scale degrees.*

Subdominant-7th chord (chord IV^7). In its complete form, a subdominant triad with the addition of the note a 7th above the root. A complete subdominant 7th in B♭ minor is shown in B78(iii) where it is identified by the symbol IV^7. It can be heard near the beginning of a sequence of secondary-7th chords in bar 3 of Brahms's intermezzo where it is presented as descending and ascending arpeggios above the root (E♭) in the left-hand part.

Subdominant triad (chord IV). A three-note chord consisting of the subdominant (the root) and notes a 3rd and a 5th above it. In the key of F major the subdominant triad consists of B♭ (the root), D♮ (the 3rd), and F♮ (the 5th). This is the chord heard in bar 34 of A59. See *Triad. EM 5.1.3.*

Subfinalis (Lat.). The note a tone below the final of a mode (A42).

Subito (sub.) (It.). Immediately. In bar 35 of B57 the performance direction 'pp subito' indicates a sudden dynamic change to *pianissimo*.

Subject. 1. The theme of a fugue (B9, bars 0–5). **2.** A theme or group of themes in the same key in sonata form. There are usually two such themes or groups of themes forming the first and second subjects of the exposition (B40, bars 1–18 and 26–48 respectively). *EM 4.5.1ff.*

Subjugalis (Lat.). A plagal mode. See A4 (Mode VIII), A5 (Mode IV), A8 (Mode II) and C57 (Mode VI).

Submediant. The sixth degree of a diatonic scale (B18, note 6). See *Scale degrees.*

Submediant-7th chord (chord VI^7). In its complete form, a submediant triad with the addition of the note a 7th above the root. A

Submediant triad

complete submediant 7th in B♭ minor is shown in B78(iii) where it is identified by the symbol VI^7. It can be heard towards the end of a sequence of secondary-7th chords in bar 4 of Brahms's intermezzo where it is presented as an arpeggio lacking the 5th of the chord (D♭).

Submediant triad (chord VI). A three-note chord consisting of the submediant (the root) and notes a 3rd and a 5th above it. In the key of D minor the submediant is B♭, so the submediant triad consists of B♭ (the root), D (the 3rd) and F (the 5th). This is the chord heard in open position on the second beat of bar 3 in A95. *EM 5.1.3.*

Subsemitonium (modi) (Lat.). In a mode, the note a semitone beneath the final (A20). In late medieval and renaissance polyphony the term applies to the sharpened seventh degree of a mode (B51, F♯).

Substitution chord. A complex chord that functions in the same way as the simple chord it replaces. C39(a) ends with a perfect cadence formed by chords V^7 and I in F major. In C39(b) a highly dissonant chromatic chord containing none of the notes of a dominant 7th is substituted for chord V^7, yet, because of its context, it functions in exactly the same way as the dominant chord in C39(a). Walton combines both chords in bar 12 of C38. *EM 5.7.2.*

Subtonic, subtonium (modi) (Lat.). The scale degree lying a step below the tonic, especially when it lies a tone below the final of a mode (A12, last bar). See *Leading note*, *Scale degrees* and *Subsemitonium*.

Suite. A collection of pieces intended to be performed together.

The baroque dance suite commonly contained an allemande (B17), a courante or corrente (A67), a sarabande (A88) and a gigue (A90). Between the last two of these dances there was often one or more French style *galanteries* such as the bourrée (A89) and gavotte (B18). These dances were usually in binary form and shared the same key apart from occasional dances in the tonic minor or tonic major. The dance suite was often prefaced with a preludial movement such as an *ouverture*.

The French *ordre* (a term coined by François Couperin in 1715) contained character pieces as well as traditional dances, and it is not certain that they were intended to be performed together as a suite. But Couperin's *Concerts Royaux* are similar to the traditional model outlined above. The fourth *concert*, for instance, contains a prelude, an allemande, two courantes, a sarabande, a rigaudon and a forlane (C32).

Later suites could consist of a series of extracts from an opera or ballet (C5, C6 and C31), or could be a set of pieces linked by an extramusical theme (C36, C37 and C41). Ravel's *Le tombeau de Couperin* (in both its piano and orchestral versions) is a neoclassical suite using the forms and styles of the classical French harpsichord composers. C33, for instance, is in the style of the forlane by Couperin (C32) and in the form of the rondeau by Jacquet de la Guerre (A84). *EM 8.7.3, 8.11.1, 8.11.5.*

Suivez (Fr.). *Attacca* (B4).

Sul A, sul C, sul D, sul E, sul G (Mac.). Performance directions requiring a string player to use a particular string even though it might be easier to use a string other than that specified. Instead of these terms a composer can indicate his intention by using a Roman numeral (I for the highest string, IV for the lowest). This is the case in bars 5 and 7 of C70 where the numeral IV requires the performer to play on the G string (the notes in these bars could be played on the D string, but this would not produce the particular timbre the composer wants). Although the Italian terms *sul la*, *sul do* etc are linguistically correct these terms are much less common than the macaronic terms at the head of this entry. French composers sometimes use terms such as *4e corde*, Spanish composers sometimes use terms such as *sobre el Sol*, and Germans often use terms such as *auf der G Saite* or just *G Saite*.

Sul ponticello (sul pont.) (It.). A performance instruction requiring a string player to bow as near to the bridge as possible (C72, bars 0 and 1). *EM 6.5.8.*

Sul tasto, sulla tastiera (It.). A performance instruction requiring a string player to bow or pluck over or near to the fingerboard (C68, bar 21). *EM 6.5.8.*

Suoni chiusi (It.). On a horn, stopped notes (C85, bars 24–25).

Superius (Lat.). The uppermost part of a polyphonic composition, labelled 'soprano (cantus)' in A52.

Syllabic style

Supertonic. The second degree of a diatonic scale (B18, note 2). See *Scale degrees*.

Supertonic-7th chord (chord II^7). In its complete form, a supertonic triad with the addition of the note a 7th above the root. A complete supertonic 7th in B♭ minor is shown in B78(iii) where it is identified by the symbol II^7. It can be heard at the end of a sequence of secondary-7th chords on the first beat of bar 5 in Brahms's intermezzo where it is presented as an arpeggio lacking the 5th of the chord (G♭).

Supertonic triad (chord II). A three-note chord consisting of the supertonic (root) and notes a 3rd and a 5th above it. In the key of F♯ minor the supertonic is G♯, so the supertonic triad consists of G♯ (the root), B♮ (the 3rd), and D (the 5th). This is the chord identified as II on the extra stave below bar 4 in B67. The chord is implied by Chopin's melody and bass: the C♯ is an accented passing note resolving onto the 3rd of the chord, and the 5th of the chord is absent (as is often the case for all types of triad – see bars 30–34 in B59 in which triads with and without 5ths alternate). A supertonic triad in first inversion is shown on the extra stave beneath bar 6 of B1, and the chord, articulated note by note, is heard throughout this bar of Bach's Aria. See *Triad*. *EM 5.1.3*.

Sur la touche (Fr.). On the fingerboard. 'Sur la touche' in bar 9 of C31 means 'bow near to or over the fingerboard'. *EM 6.5.8*.

Sur le chevalet (Fr.). *Sul ponticello* (bow at the bridge). See bars 0–1 of C72.

Suspended cymbal. A cymbal hung on a stand so that it can be played with a variety of beaters (C97, bars 7–8).

Suspension. A contrapuntal device in which a consonant note is repeated or sustained over a change of harmony so that it forms a dissonance with another part. The suspended part then resolves to a note that is consonant with the other parts (usually by step, and most often descending). In bar 20 of A24 a minim A♮ forms a consonant interval of a 6th with the C♮ below it, but when the tenor moves to B♭ it forms a dissonant 7th with the suspended alto part. Finally the alto resolves the suspension by moving down to a G♮ which forms another consonant 6th with the tenor. A decorated version of a 7–6 suspension can be heard in bar 24 of the same example.

A53 is a simplified version of the alto and tenor parts of bars 4–9 from the Kyrie by Palestrina shown in A52. It is entirely consonant. A54 shows the same passage decorated with suspensions that form dissonant 4ths with the bass. These are, for obvious reasons, called 4–3 suspensions. The same suspensions can be heard in the three-part polyphony of A55, but now they are somewhat disguised by Palestrina's decorations: the anticipation of the resolution of the first suspension (marked with an asterisk) and the quaver movement in the soprano part. These and other suspensions (marked 'sus.') can be heard in the context of Palestrina's four-part polyphony on track A52. *EM 4.3.6, 5.2*.

Sussurando (It.). Whispering (C97, trebles and harp in bars 65–67).

Sustaining pedal. The right-hand or damper pedal on a piano (B66, in which the abbreviation 'ped.' indicates the use of this pedal). It allows the pianist to sustain all the notes played while the pedal is depressed. See *Sostenuto pedal*.

Swell. A department of an organ that is enclosed in a box with louvres that can be adjusted by a foot pedal to produce graduated dynamics. The left-hand part of C55 is played on the swell organ. See *Récit 3*.

Swing rhythm, swung rhythm, swing quavers, swung eighths. The unequal performance of short notes that is characteristic of all styles of jazz. In C38 Walton notates these short notes as groups of dotted quavers plus semiquavers (which is pretty much what the performers on track C38 play). The degree of inequality of these short notes depends on the particular rhythmic groove of performers, who, in jazz, are governed by their own feel for rhythm rather than a composer's notation (if any). Although swing was a big-band style of the 1930s, swung rhythms (such as the uneven subdivision of the first crotchet of C20) date back to the beginning of the 20th century, and are particularly characteristic of ragtime. *EM 1.6.5*.

SWV. Abbreviation of *Schütz-Werke-Verzeichnis* (*Catalogue of Schütz's Works*), ed. W. Bittinger (Kassel, 1960). See A68.

Syllabic style. 1. A type of plainsong in which, generally speaking, each syllable is set to one note. Syllabic style is characteris-

Sympathetic strings

tic of plainsong psalmody in which the rule holds good for the reciting note, so the setting of the text in A6 is syllabic throughout. This is one of the three main categories of plainsong, the others being the neumatic style (A4) and the melismatic style (A5). *EM 8.4.1.* **2.** In polyphonic vocal music, syllabic style is most often found in the chordal textures of hymns or metrical psalms (A37).

Sympathetic strings. Strings that are not directly bowed or plucked but that are made to vibrate by those that are bowed or plucked, eg the extra strings on a viola d'amore (B5).

Sympathetic vibration. When a note is sounded near to a string that is free to vibrate, the vibrations of the sounded note can set up vibrations in the unplayed string, particularly when the sounded note is of the same pitch as the free string. Instruments such as the viola d'amore (B5) have a set of free strings that are not bowed but which vibrate sympathetically when the other strings are played.

At the start of C90 the pianist is required silently to depress all of the white notes from middle C to the G an octave and a 5th above it, thus releasing the dampers and allowing the strings to vibrate freely. When the performer plays the two-note chord below the bass stave it sets up sympathetic vibrations in the strings corresponding to the notes of the cluster chord. The cluster chord is renewed every time the pianist plays another two-note chord (as happens in bars 3, 6, 8, 9, 11 and 13). This provides a soft halo of sympathetic vibrations against which the marimba player articulates his solo. *EM 6.2, 8.11.9.*

Symphonia (Gk.). **1.** In the middle ages, a concord. In medieval terms all of the intervals and chords in A7 are concordant. **2.** In France from the 12th century onwards, an instrument capable of sounding two or more notes simultaneously, notably the hurdy-gurdy (A18). **3.** From the 17th century, an orchestral piece played before or within a larger composition such as an opera. In this sense the term was used synonymously with the term sinfonia (A64).

Symphonic. 1. Music for large orchestra, whether or not it comes from a symphony (B73). **2.** Music that exhibits the same sort of developmental processes that are often found in the classical symphony, whether or not it is written for a large orchestra (B50).

Symphonic band, concert band. Large ensembles of wind and percussion instruments devoted to concert performances (as distinct from marching performances). They are cultivated in nearly all American high schools and universities. A typical symphonic band includes a piccolo (C76, bars 9–11), flutes (C80), oboes (C78), cor anglais (C88, bars 3–5 and 9–10), E♭ clarinet (C10: although written for clarinet in D this part is usually played on an E♭ clarinet), B♭ or A clarinets (C79), alto clarinet, bass clarinets (C38), bassoons (C77), contrabassoon (C31), saxophones (C38, bar 9), cornets (C3), trumpets (C81), French horns (B59, bars 10–24), euphoniums (C37), trombones (C75, bars 16–17), tuba (C28, bars 1–7), double basses (C7) and assorted percussion, including bass drum (C42), side drum (C43), and cymbals (C47). To achieve proper balance each woodwind part is usually doubled by several instruments of the same type, and the exact instrumentation varies according to local circumstances. The repertoires of symphonic bands are as various as the instrumentation, ranging from transcriptions of classical orchestral scores to arrangements of military marches, jazz numbers and pop songs as well as newly composed items specifically written for concert bands.

Symphonic poem. A romantic work in one movement that is intended to portray extra-musical ideas in sound. The programme can be explicit (C10 is meant to represent the hanging of the eponymous hero and the flight of his soul to a villains' heaven), or it can subtly suggest images derived from an original literary source (C19 gives an impression of the shimmering heat of a summer's afternoon in dimly remembered antiquity symbolised in Mallarmé's poem). *EM 8.10.6.*

Symphonie (Fr.). Symphony. The title was used in all of the traditional senses, but was also used in the 19th century for multi-movement programmatic compositions such as the *Symphonie fantastique* by Berlioz (B63).

Symphonische Dichtung (Ger.). Liszt's term for symphonic poem (B73). Strauss preferred *Tondichtung* (tone poem).

Symphony. As most commonly understood, an independent orchestral work, usually abstract in conception and most often in four movements.

Haydn's Symphony No. 44 in E minor (1771) contains a fast opening movement, a minuet and trio, an Adagio, and a Presto (B21).

His *Oxford* Symphony (1789) begins with a slow introduction that prefaces the usual sonata-allegro. This is followed by a slow movement, a minuet and trio and a spirited Presto containing the fugato shown in B29.

Although called a 'symphonie', Berlioz's *Symphonie fantastique* (1830) can be seen as a string of five symphonic poems complete with the composer's own programme notes. His quotation from the medieval death-obsessed sequence 'Dies irae' (B62) with accompanying tolling bells (B63) is typical of a genre which, renamed 'tone poem', nearly supplanted the symphony in the late 19th century (C10).

Brahms's Symphony No. 2 (1877) maintains classical precedent in its four-movement pattern, but the usual minuet (or scherzo) is replaced by an Allegretto grazioso that is more like a romantic intermezzo (C1).

Tchaikovsky's Symphony No. 5 (1888) has four movements, but the first is prefaced by a motto theme that appears in every movement. This cyclic structure introduces a romantic element since it is well known that the motto theme was meant to represent inexorable and malign fate. Romantic, too, are the long lyrical melodies (C4) and the introduction of a balletic waltz as a replacement for the usual minuet or scherzo.

Programmatic elements are even more evident in Mahler's gargantuan symphonies (1888–1910), in which brass chorales and explosive timpani parts (C27), the distant sound of cowbells (C28) and the use of exotic instruments such as the mandolin (C29) evoke extramusical images. *EM 8.9.4, 8.10.7*.

Symphony orchestra. An instrumental ensemble of a size and composition that enable it to perform symphonies and other large-scale orchestral works. The term is most commonly used of orchestras capable of playing 19th- and 20th-century works such as Mahler's sixth symphony (C27 and C28) and Bartók's *Concerto for Orchestra* (C82). See *Chamber orchestra* and B21.

Syncopation. An alteration to the expected distribution of accents in metrical music. The effect can be momentary or can be extended to a limit that is determined by the listener's ability to hear an actual or imagined regular metrical pulse against which the syncopation is articulated. The following are among the most common types of syncopation: **a)** a temporary metrical dislocation caused by louder notes on what are normally weak beats (B38, bars 3–8, second violin and viola: f means loud, p means soft), **b)** offbeat accents caused by articulating notes between beats (B15, violins in bars 1–2 and trumpet in bars 5–6), **c)** weak-beat accents caused by tying notes from a weak to a strong beat (compare A53 with the syncopations in A54), **d)** a systematic disruption of the prevailing metre by a temporary imposition of a contrasting metrical pattern in the melody, harmony, or both (see *Hemiola* and A59(a), bars 25–27, and C1, bars 8–9). *EM 1.7.1, 1.7.2*.

Synthesised harpsichord. An electronic simulation of the timbres of a harpsichord. See *Sampling* and A87.

Synthesiser. An electronic instrument that can simulate the sounds of acoustic instruments, generate new sounds and process nearly all parameters of these sounds (A87). *EM 6.10*.

System. Two or more staves linked on the left-hand side by a vertical line and one or more braces. The music printed on all staves of a system is intended to be performed simultaneously. The three-stave systems of B58 contain the vocal part on one stave and the piano part on two braced staves.

T

T. Abbreviation of tenor (A30).

Tabor. A small medieval and renaissance drum with or without one or more snares (A35). See *Pipe and tabor*.

Tacet (Lat.). Be silent. The term is used in an instrumental part when a performer is required to remain silent for a whole movement or a significant part of a movement. 'Tacet al fine' in the piano part of C90 (bar 13) means that the pianist should remain silent until the end of the movement.

Tactus (Lat.). 15th- and 16th-century term for the beat or pulse. According to a 15th-century authority the speed of the tactus was about that of a normal heartbeat, say about 60–90 beats per minute. Although there is evidence that this was by no means always the case (tempo changes were not unknown in this period) a tactus within these limits suits much renaissance sacred polyphony (A28 and A29 are sung at about 63 minim beats per minute, and A52 at about 88 crotchet beats per minute). It should be noted that, although the tactus was represented by a semibreve in this period, modern editions use a minim or crotchet tactus (the type of note-value making no difference to the beat as the ear perceives it).

Tail. The vertical line added to a note-head. See *Stem* and the theme in B18.

Taille (Fr). Tenor. **1.** From the 16th century to the 18th century, a tenor voice (A23), though in printed music 'tenor' or 'ténor' were more common. **2.** In the same period, a tenor instrument. Hence Bach's *taille* or *taille de hautbois* (*d'hautbois*, *des hautbois*) meant a tenor oboe in F or oboe da caccia (B8), and *taille de violons* meant the viola (A38). **3.** In French organ music, a solo stop used in the middle of the texture. Hence *trompette en taille* and *cromorne en taille* (A94, in which the cantus firmus is played on pedal reed stops in tenor register). *EM 6.6.4.*

Take. A single, continuous recording of a passage of music. Because C97 was recorded live at a BBC Promenade Concert in the Royal Albert Hall, London, it was made in one take, but C96 was made up from two takes.

Takt (Ger.). **1.** Beat. **2.** Bar, measure. **3.** Metre, time. The beat in A14 is a dotted crotchet and there are two beats per bar so the metre is compound duple time.

Taktnote (Ger.). Semibreve. See *Note* and A17, bars 10–12.

Talea (Lat.). One statement of the repeating rhythmic pattern superimposed on an isorhythmic melody. Four rhythmically identical *taleae* are superimposed on a plainsong melody in the tenor of the Benedictus from Machaut's *Messe de Nostre Dame* (A20 and A21). *EM 1.13, 7.9.4.*

Talon (Fr.), **tallone** (It.), **Frosch** (Ger.). The part of the bow of a string instrument that the performer holds and that contains the mechanism for adjusting the tension of the hairs (the frog). 'Am Frosch', 'au talon' and 'al tallone' are all directions requiring the performer to use the section of the bow nearest the frog (C70, bar 1).

Tam-tam. A percussion instrument in the form of a large metal plate suspended in a frame and struck with any one of a variety of beaters to produce a sound of indefinite pitch (C48 and C53). *EM 6.8.3.*

Tambour (Fr.). **1.** Drum (C42–C45, C52 and C53). **2. Tambour de basque** (Fr.). Tambourine (C42 and C52). **3. Tambour militaire** (Fr.). Military snare drum (C45 and C52). **4. Tambour à corde** (Fr.). Lion's roar (C46 and C52). *EM 6.8.2.*

Tambourin (Fr.). **1.** In early music, a tabor (A35). **2.** An 18th-century French dance. **3.** A modern tambourine (C42 and C52).

Tambourine, tambourin (Fr.), **Tamburin** (Ger.), **tamburino, tamburo basco** (It.). A small single-headed drum with jingles mounted in the rim. It is usually held with one hand while the player taps the drumhead or rattles the whole instrument (C42 and C52). Among other techniques, the performer can rub a moistened thumb ('pouce' in French) over the skin (C53, bar 32). *EM 6.8.2.*

Tamburo (It.). **1.** Drum (C42–C45, C52 and

Tempo giusto

C53). **2. Tamburo basco** (It.). Tambourine (C42 and C52). **3. Tamburo di legno** (It.). Wood blocks (C51 and C53). **4. Tamburo grande** (It.). Bass drum (C42 and C52). **5. Tamburo militare** (It.). Military snare drum (C45 and C52). **6. Tamburo piccolo** (It.). Snare drum (C43 and C53). **7. Tamburo rullante** (It.). Tenor drum (C43 and C53).

Tangent. A metal blade attached to the far end of each key of a clavichord. It strikes a string and divides it, thus determining the pitch of the note. Because there is no intermediate machinery it is possible to wiggle the finger on the key to produce a vibrato-like effect known as a *Bebung* (B20).

Tanz (Ger.). Any sort of dance (B41–B44).

Tarantella (It.). A fast southern-Italian dance in compound time characterised by alternating parallel keys and a gradual increase in speed. The performance of the saltarello on A18 is so fast that it gives a pretty fair impression of a tarantella (though without any change of key or *accelerando*).

Tarole (Fr.). A high-pitched French side drum (C43 and C53).

Tastenmusik (Ger.). Keyboard music (A86, A87, A94, B1, B9–B14, B20, B25, B51–B56, B61, B74–B79 and C93).

Tastiera (It.). **1.** Keyboard. 'Musica per tastiera': keyboard music (A57 and A67). **2.** The fingerboard of a string instrument. 'Sulla tastiera' means the same as 'sul tasto' (C68, bar 21).

Tasto (It.). **1.** A single key of a keyboard. See *Tasto solo* and B5, bar 1. **2.** The fingerboard of a string instrument. See *Sul tasto* and C68, bar 21.

Tasto solo (It.). A performance direction in a basso continuo part indicating that the printed bass notes are to be played without any added harmony (B5).

Tb. Abbreviation of tuba (C28, bars 1–7).

Tba. Abbreviation of *tromba* (trumpet). See B36.

Te. The seventh degree of any major scale in the British system of tonic sol-fa. In A25 the fourth note of bar 3 is *te* in the key of D major.

Tedesca (It.). German, or in the German style. In the baroque era the term often referred to the slow, serious allemande in $\frac{4}{4}$

time (B17). In the late 18th and early 19th centuries it was associated with the fast, folky German dance or *Deutscher Tanz*. The latter type was usually notated in $\frac{3}{8}$ (B44) or $\frac{3}{4}$ time (as in Beethoven's 'Presto alla tedesca' in his Piano Sonata Op. 79).

Tema (It.). **1.** Theme (B76). **2.** Subject (B9).

Temperament. Adjustments to the tuning of acoustically pure intervals (such as those in the harmonic series played on C95) to allow music in most or all keys to be played without gross distortion of some intervals. All of the keyboard music recorded on the compact discs that accompany this dictionary was played on instruments tuned in equal temperament (in which every semitone is the same). A complete, equally tempered nine-octave scale of C major can be heard on A3.

Temple bowls. Vessels of various sizes and pitches that are made to resonate by rubbing the perimeter with rubber- or leather-covered sticks (C97, bars 53–68).

Tempo (It.). In metrical music, the speed of performance in terms of the rate of pulsation of the underlying beat. Tempo is not determined by printed note values. On the one hand it is possible for a theoretically long note-value to represent a fast beat (B55, in which there is just one dotted-minim beat per bar pulsating at the rate of 104 beats per minute). On the other hand a notionally short note-value can represent a very slow beat (B68, in which a quaver represents a beat pulsating at about half the rate of the dotted minim beat in B55). See *Tempo markings. EM 1.15*.

Tempo di menuetto (Mac.). At the speed of a minuet. Mozart's contemporaries would have understood this performance direction to mean a moderate tempo and a graceful style. In B41 the performers interpret such a tempo as about 76 crotchet beats per minute. See *Tempo markings*.

Tempo di trepak (Mac.). In the tempo of a trepak – a very fast Russian dance (C5). See *Tempo markings*.

Tempo giusto (It.). **1.** The correct tempo for the style of the piece. Thus Debussy's 'Allegro giusto' in C20 means 'at the correct tempo [for a cakewalk]'. **2.** A direction requiring performers to return to strict tempo or the original tempo. In this sense it

Tempo markings

can be synonymous with *a tempo* (C76, bars 5–6). See *Tempo markings*.

Tempo markings. Performance directions relating to the speed of the beat. These can be written in words that give an approximate guide to the composer's intention, or as a metronome mark (x = y, in which x is the note-value of the beat and y the number of beats per minute), which gives a more precise indication of what is required. But even when the latter system is used it has often been the case that composers performing their own music have taken a cavalier attitude to their own metronome marks. Furthermore it is often necessary to temper a composer's metronome mark according to the context of the performance. For instance, in a large resonant hall clarity might suffer if a fast metronome mark is slavishly obeyed. For a list of tempo marks see *EM 1.15*.

Tempo ordinario (It.). **1.** Common time, $\frac{4}{4}$ time (B32 and B31 respectively). **2.** At an ordinary speed – *moderato* (C70). See *Tempo markings*.

Tempo primo (It.). A performance direction requiring a return to the original tempo. The term is often abbreviated to 'Tempo I' (C71, bar 11). See *Tempo markings*.

Tempo rubato (It.). To be performed with a flexible approach to tempo, sometimes slowing down, sometimes speeding up, in accordance with the performer's perception of the style and mood of the music as it unfolds. Debussy uses this performance direction in the last movement of his String Quartet (C18(c)), but most romantic music is played rubato whether or not the composer asks for it (in B74 'molto rubato' is an editorial addition which accurately reflects the manner of performance). See *Tempo markings*.

Ten. (It.). Abbreviation of *tenuto* (B30, bars 2 and 4).

Teneramente (It.), **tendre, tendrement** (Fr.). Tenderly (B79).

Tenor. 1. The highest natural adult male voice. The typical range of a solo operatic tenor is shown on the folded insert. A counter-tenor may have a similar range, but the falsetto timbre of this type of voice contrasts strongly with that of a tenor (compare A12 with bars 8–16 of C73). **2.** In four-part textures, the third part down (whether sung or played). To distinguish between the four parts played by crumhorns on track A35 the uppermost part on the bass stave may be called the tenor voice or tenor part (the others being treble, alto and bass parts reading from the top down). **3.** In early medieval music, the part that sings the plainsong melody in polyphonic compositions. Although the lower part in A9 is sung by a bass voice it can still be referred to as a tenor because it holds (Lat., 'tenere') the plainsong melody above which the *vox organalis* weaves its florid counter-melody. Later the term was applied to the lowest part even when it was freely composed (A11). By the 15th century the third voice down in four-part polyphony was usually called the tenor whether or not it presented a cantus firmus (A27). *EM 8.5.1.*

Tenor clef. One of the moveable C clefs. It shows that middle C is represented by the second line down on the stave. The tenor clef is still in use for higher notes in cello, bassoon and trombone parts. See *C clefs* and A30. The tenor G clef is often used for vocal tenor parts. It can take several different forms, the most common of which are two treble clefs (𝄞𝄞) and a treble clef with a small 8 below it (𝄞). In all cases the tenor part is sung an octave lower than it would be with an unaltered treble clef. See A4, in which the first note is the G♮ a 4th below middle C.

Tenor drum. A double-headed drum of indefinite pitch, similar to a side drum but deeper and usually without snares (C43 and C52). *EM 6.8.2.*

Tenor guitar. A five-string guitar with a range falling between the *requinto* and the ordinary six-string guitar (C68).

Tenor Mass. A polyphonic setting of the Ordinary of the Mass with a cantus firmus in the tenor (A27, in which the cantus firmus is taken from the song shown in A26). *EM 8.6.1.*

Tenor tuba. The smallest and highest-pitched tuba commonly used in a symphony orchestra (C37).

Tenth. The interval of an octave plus a 3rd (A90, bars 11, 12, 16, 30 and 31). See *Compound intervals*.

Tenuto (ten.) (It.). Hold the note or chord thus marked for at least its full value (B30, bars 2 and 4).

Ternary form. A musical structure in three sections, the third being a repeat of the first with a contrasting section between (ABA). A26 shows the form at its simplest. The first and last sections begin and end on the final of the transposed dorian mode and the melody is confined to a range of a 5th (from the final to its dominant). The middle section (B) contrasts with the outer sections in its use of the top four pitches of the mode and in its cadence on the dominant. See *Character piece* (C2), *Da capo aria* (B15) and *Minuet and trio* (B25). *EM 7.5, 7.5.3.*

Terraced dynamics. Music, most often of the baroque era, in which dynamic levels change from loud to soft (and vice versa) without any other dynamic shading. The effect is particularly obvious on a harpsichord with two manuals (A84).

Tertial (tertian, tertiary) harmony. Harmony based on chords that are constructed from superimposed 3rds. At its simplest this manifests itself as triads in which two 3rds are combined (A59, bar 1). At its most complex it is manifested in chords of the 9th (C23) and 13th (C30, bars 2 and 6). *EM 5.8.2.*

Terz (Ger.). The interval of a 3rd (A52, bars 1 and 3).

Terzett (Ger.), **terzetto** (It.). A vocal work for three voices with or without accompaniment (A59 and A69).

Terzina (It.). Triplet (B18, Variation 3).

Tessitura (It.). The average range of an instrumental or (more often) vocal part, excluding occasional notes that lie outside this range. The complete range of the Angel's recitative in B16 is d^1–a^2, but the tessitura is $f\sharp^1$–g^2 (only the A in bar 3 is higher than this tessitura, and only the two D♯s in bar 6 are lower than it).

Testo (It.). Text. The term refers to narrative set as recitative in 17th-century Italian Passions and oratorios (A68).

Tetrachord. Four pitches. The term has a long history in musical theory but is now most often used to describe the two four-note segments into which a major scale can be divided (shown by brackets in A25). Their intervallic structure is identical (tone–tone–semitone in bars 1 and 3–4). *EM 3.1.*

Tetrad. A vertical sonority (chord) consisting of four different pitches. The term is commonly used of verticalisations of segments of a tone row (C40, bars 9–12 and C88, bar 1).

Teutsche (Ger.). Old spelling of *Deutsche* (German dance, B44).

Texture. The number of parts in a composition and the way they relate to each other.

The simplest texture, monophony, consists of one unaccompanied part (A4). By contrast the massive chords heard on track C86 contain as many as 15 parts. The three parts (tenor and two basses) heard in bars 1–5 of C92 relate to each other with complete unanimity in an absolute type of homophony that is sometimes described as homorhythmic. At the other extreme, in the three-part polyphony of A55 each voice part is almost entirely rhythmically independent of the other voices.

Most music inhabits a middle ground between these textural extremes. Thus in B34 the syncopated melody of the first violin is clearly independent of the three lower parts, but two of them (violin 2 and cello) are almost entirely homorhythmic, while the viola's subordinate role is to supply harmonic filling when required. The same example also shows how composers often vary their textures within a single movement (in fact this is one of the chief elements of Haydn's variation technique). Even within the first four bars of the theme itself (B32) the texture varies between two- and four-part homophony. The first variation (B33) contrasts the theme (violin 2) with a rhythmically independent counter-melody in a passage of two-part counterpoint. Finally, in Variation 4 (B35) the first violin is again dominant, but the subtle rhythms of the inner parts enliven what would otherwise be a less interesting chordal harmonisation of the theme. See also *Dynamics, Orchestration, Ornaments, Rhythm* and *Tessitura. EM 1.9, 4.4.1, 4.5, 4.5.6, 4.6, 6.11, 8.11.3.*

Thematic catalogue. An index of a composer's work, of a particular repertoire, or of a library. A thematic catalogue identifies each piece by quoting its opening notes. In the musical examples works by Bach, Haydn and Mozart are identified by references to the thematic catalogues of Schmieder (BWV), A86–B16, Hoboken (Hob.), B21–B36, and Köchel (K), B37–B50, respectively.

Thematic transformation

Thematic transformation. A compositional technique in which the pitches of a theme heard earlier in a work are retained (at least in outline), but other musical parameters (such as rhythm, tempo, accompaniment, key, dynamics and instrumentation) are changed. In C11, bars 1–3, the pitches of bar 2 of C10 are retained (an octave higher), but the tempo is much slower, the unequal rhythms have been converted to equal quavers, the dynamic level has been reduced, and the instrumentation has been changed from a solo clarinet in D to a complete section of violins. The technique was intended to unify the sections of a tone poem. See also C18. *EM 3.3, 3.4, 7.10.1, 8.10.6.*

Thematische Arbeit (Ger.). Thematic work. A compositional technique whereby a theme is developed by processes such as the extraction of its constituent motifs followed by manipulations of them in different melodic contexts. In B27 the four motifs of the first subject are identified by the letters a, b, c and d. Throughout the rest of the extract these letters are used to show how they have been altered (chiefly by intervallic augmentation and diminution) and reordered. Similar thematic work is evident in the melody shown in bars 17–23 of B68.

Theme. A musical idea, most often a melody, that plays an important structural role in a complete work, movement or substantial portion of a movement. The subject of a fugue (B14, bar 1) is thematic in this sense, but the term is used more often of longer melodies such as a subject in a sonata-form movement (B40, bars 1–14) or the theme of a set of variations (B32). *EM 3.2, 7.8, 7.8.1, 7.8.2.*

Theme and variations. See *Variations* and B32–B35. *EM 8.9.1.*

Themenaufstellung (Ger.). In sonata form, the exposition (B27 and B40, bars 1–51).

Theorbo. A large bass lute of the late 16th and 17th centuries. Usually it had six stopped courses to which seven or eight unstopped bass courses were added. This extension of its range made it an ideal member of a continuo group or the sole accompanying instrument for a solo song (A75). *EM 6.4.2.*

Thesis. See *Arsis and thesis* and the second note of A24.

Third. 1. See *Degree* and the third note of B18. **2.** See *Intervals* and C78. **3.** See *Triad* and A59, bar 1.

Third-inversion chord. A 7th, 9th or 13th chord with the 7th sounding in the bass. The dominant-7th chord of E major is shown on the extra stave below the first bar of B30. The 7th of the chord is A♮ and this is the note heard in the bass of the third-inversion chords heard on beat 3 of bars 1 and 3 of Haydn's Largo. A dominant 13th in third inversion can be heard on track C30, bar 6.

Thirteenth chord. See *Dominant chords* and C30, bar 2.

Thirty-second-note. Demisemiquaver (𝅘𝅥𝅰). See *Note* and B18, Variation 5, bar 7, beat 3.

Thirty-two-foot stop. A rank of organ pipes of which the longest measures approximately 32 feet. Music played on a 32-foot stop sounds two octaves lower than printed. The registration of the pedal part in A86 (stems down on the bass stave) includes a 32-foot reed stop sounding two octaves below the printed pitch.

Thorough bass. Basso continuo (A68). *EM 5.1.1.*

Three-eight time. A simple triple metre in which quaver beats are grouped in the repeating pattern strong–weak–weak (B78). In fast movements only one dotted crotchet beat per bar will be perceived (A90). It is indicated by the time signature $\frac{3}{8}$ (A86).

Three-four time. A simple triple metre in which crotchet beats are grouped in the repeating pattern strong–weak–weak. It is indicated by the time signature $\frac{3}{4}$ (C1 and C2).

Three-part counterpoint. A musical texture consisting of the combination of three rhythmically independent melodic strands (A24, bars 11–17). Entire movements can display this sort of texture (track A74).

Three-two time. A simple triple metre in which minim beats are grouped in the repeating pattern strong–weak–weak. (A28 and A29).

Threnody (Gk.). Lament (C95). See *Elegy*.

Through-composed. See *Durchkomponiert* and B57,

Tie, bind. A curved line joining two adjacent notes of the same pitch. The total value of the note in performance is the sum of the two notes thus conjoined. The advent of the tie coincided with the appearance of the barline, and ties are most often used nowadays across barlines in order to allow correct notation (A70, bars 5–8).

Tief (Ger.). Deep (-sounding). Mahler asks for 'tiefes Glockengelaute' (deep-sounding chiming bells) in his sixth symphony (C28, bars 19–23).

Tiento (Span.), **tento** (Port.). A Spanish or Portuguese composition for harp, keyboard or vihuela written in the 16th, 17th or early 18th century. The term embraces a wide variety of styles and genres including works that resemble the contemporary fantasia, ricercar (A57), prelude, or toccata.

Tierce (Fr.). **1.** The interval of a 3rd (A84, bar 10). **2.** An organ stop sounding a compound 10th above written pitch. It is an essential component of the *cornet* in French baroque music (A81).

Tierce-coulée en montant (Fr.). Couperin's term for an ascending three-note slide (A84, letter e in bar 12). See *Ornaments*.

Tierce de Picardie, tierce picarde (Fr.). A major 3rd in a tonic chord at the end of a section in the minor mode (A81, bar 14).

Timbales (Fr. and Span.). **1.** Timpani (C27). **2.** A pair of Latin American drums of different definite pitches (called *timbales cubaines* or *creoles* in French). They are played with thin wooden sticks on the skins, the rims and the metal shells.

Timbre. The tone-colour of an instrument or voice. This is determined by many factors, the most important of which is the relative strengths of the harmonics that go to make up a sound that is perceived as a single note of definite pitch. It is this complement of strong and weak harmonics that enables the ear to distinguish between two instruments playing the same note. For instance, the higher harmonics in sounds produced by a flute are weak compared with the same harmonics produced on a muted trumpet, so when they play the same pitch in the last bar of C35 it is possible to distinguish between them by their different timbres. *EM 6.1, 6.11, 8.10.6, 8.11.3.*

Timbres (Fr.). The snares on a drum. In C44 drums with and without snares can be heard.

Time. Metre. A12 is in simple triple metre or $\frac{3}{4}$ time. See also *Alla breve, Common time* and *Simple and compound time*.

Time signature. In metrical music, two vertically-aligned numbers most commonly appearing on the first stave of a movement (B7) and elsewhere whenever the metre changes (B6). In simple time the upper figure usually indicates the number of beats per bar, the lower figure the type of beat. Thus the time signature near the beginning of the first stave of A12 indicates three crotchet beats per bar (or three quarter-note beats per bar). In compound time, however, the upper figure only indicates the number of beats in slow tempi (B68, in which there are six quaver beats per bar, and C72, in which there are nine quaver beats per bar). In moderate or fast tempi the beat in compound time is a dotted note. Thus $\frac{3}{8}$ means one dotted-crotchet beat per bar (A90), $\frac{6}{8}$ means two dotted-crotchet beats per bar (A16), $\frac{9}{8}$ means three dotted-crotchet beats per bar, and $\frac{12}{8}$ means four dotted-crotchet beats per bar (B19). See also *Simple and compound time*.

Timpani (timp.). Bowl-shaped drums with membranes of skin or plastic. The tension of the membrane can be altered by adjusting screws around the perimeter or by adjusting a foot pedal, thus allowing the range of pitches shown on the folded insert (extended in both directions if unusually large or small drums are used).

In 18th-century music two timpani were the norm. These were usually tuned to the tonic and dominant and were used in conjunction with the brass to emphasise important cadences (B36, last seven bars). In the 19th century the tonal colours of timpani were more subtly exploited (B59, bars 26–30, and B60, bars 4–8).

Timpani are usually played with medium-hard sticks (C27). If hard wooden sticks are used the sound is drier (C36). In the 20th century chromatic timpani were introduced. These have a foot-pedal that allows instantaneous changes of pitch.

A roll on a single note is one of the most characteristic sounds of timpani (B36, bars 255–263), and a microtonal glissando roll is the most characteristic effect of chromatic timpani (C82, bars 68–69). *EM 6.8.1.*

Tiorba (It.). Theorbo (A75).

Tirade (Fr.), **tirata** (It.). An 18th-century

Toccata

ornament consisting of a rapid scalic run linking two principal melody notes. The *tirade* shown near the end of B20 links the melody note F (just before the pause) to the quaver A♭ at the end of the *tirade*. See *Ornaments*. *EM 3.10.2.*

Toccata. A keyboard composition originating in the 16th century and brought to maturity in the late baroque era, the toccata was designed to exhibit the virtuosity of a keyboard performer, and it often functioned as a prelude to a weightier movement such as a fugue. In the extract from Bach's Toccata and Fugue in F (A86), the performer's keyboard technique is tested in bars 8–16, and his pedal technique is tested in bars 17–20. Some toccatas included fugal passages such as those in Bach's Toccata in E minor, BWV 914 (B13). *EM 8.7.6.*

Tombeau (Fr.). Literally 'tomb', but as a musical term it refers to instrumental pieces written as a homage to a dead composer. *Tombeaux* were written by French baroque composers, but the term fell into disuse in the later 18th century. It was revived in the 20th century by Ravel in his neoclassical suite *Le Tombeau de Couperin*. A comparison of C32 with C33 reveals the full extent of Ravel's sympathy for the music of his eminent fellow countryman. But this is not mere pastiche, for Ravel's subtle use of mixed modes (see bars 1–4) and his delicately dissonant harmonic style suffuse his Forlane with a sense of nostalgia for the long-dead glories of France's *grand siècle*.

Ton (Fr.). A term with several meanings that only become clear in context. **1.** Pitch. 'Donner le ton': give the pitch. In the performance of plainsong it is usual for a cantor to sing the opening phrase to give the pitch for the choir (A4). **2.** Mode or key. 'Ton d'église': church mode (A5). **3.** Abbreviation of *ton entier*: the interval of a whole tone (C21). **4.** Note. 'Ton bouché': stopped note. **5.** A plainsong psalm tone (A8). **6.** The crook of a brass instrument. 'Ton de cor en Ut/Fa': horns crooked in C/F (B59).

Ton (Ger.). A term with several meanings, some of them the same as those of *ton* in French. **1.** Pitch. 'Ton angeben': to give the pitch (A4). **2.** Key or mode. 'Selbständige Tonart': authentic mode (A19). **3.** Whole tone. Abbreviation of *Ganzton* (C21). **4.** Note. 'Tonreihe': tone row (C40). **5.** Tone.

'Tondichtung': tone poem (C10 and C11). **6.** Timbre. 'Tonfarbe': tone colour (C35).

Tonal. Adjective describing music based on tonic-dominant polarity (B48 and B49) as distinct from modality (A4) and as opposed to atonality (C34).

Tonal answer. See *Real and tonal answers* and B14, bars 2–3.

Tonality. In western music, the relationships between seven pitch classes, and between them and a pre-eminent note (the tonic) in particular. These relationships can be expressed through any one of the 12 major and 12 minor scales. Thus in A16 the seven pitch classes of the melody can be arranged to form the scale of C major (shown on an extra stave). The tonality of this song is governed by a galaxy of relationships between the notes C, D, E, F, G, A and B, of which C is the principal pitch – the goal to which the melody strives and which finds eventual resolution in the final cadence (B–C). Similarly in A82 the individual pitches of the G-minor melody eventually resolve to the tonic. The same sort of relationships, somewhat modified, are heard in modal music (the *subfinalis* in A42 is drawn to the final in much the same way as the leading note is drawn to the tonic at the end of A16). *EM 2, 2.3.1, 2.5, 2.7, 5.7, 5.8, 8.11.1.*

Tonart (Ger.). Key. B48 is in the key of G major. B49 begins in the key of G major and ends in the key of D major.

Tondichtung (Ger.). Tone poem. See *Symphonic poem*, and C10 and C11.

Tone. 1. A sound of definite pitch (eg any of the notes played on A3). **2.** An interval encompassing two semitones (any two adjacent notes in the descending scale heard at the start of C21). **3.** The timbre of an instrument or voice (compare the tone-colours of the three instruments playing notes of the same pitch in the last bar of C35). **4.** The melodic formula of a psalm tone (A6). *EM 2.2.1.*

Tone cluster. See *Cluster chord* and C94, bars 1–2 and 8. *EM 8.11.9.*

Tone-colour. The characteristic sound of an instrument or voice as distinct from pitch. In the last bar of C35 it is tone-colour or timbre that chiefly distinguishes the sound of a flute from that of a trumpet or celesta, even though all three instruments play exactly the same note. Tone-colour is

Tonicisation

largely determined by the relative strengths of the harmonics (C95) present in the sound. Performers can modify the tone-colours of their instruments or voices for expressive purposes, but usually not to an extent that would make it difficult to identify what type of instrument or voice is being employed. *EM 3.7, 6.1, 6.3, 6.11.8.*

Tone poem. See *Symphonic poem* (C10 and C11). *EM 8.10.6.*

Tone row. In serial music, an ordering of non-repeating pitch classes (usually 12) used as the basis for a composition (C40, bars 0–7). *EM 2.7.1, 3.8, 4.6, 5.8.1.*

Tonfarbe (Ger.). Tone colour or timbre. The chief elements in C35 are the crystal clear contrasts and combinations of distinctive tone colours.

Tonguing. The technique by which wind instrumentalists articulate detached notes or the first notes of legato phrases. In passages of very fast notes double or triple tonguing may be used. Brass players achieve this by using the tongue to form the repeated consonants t-k, t-k etc (double tonguing), or t-k-t, t-k-t etc (triple tonguing). Both types are used in bars 27–34 of C97. See also *Flutter-tonguing* and C34, bass clarinet, bars 3–5.

Tonhöhe (Ger.). Pitch (see folded insert and A1–A3).

Tonic. The first degree of a diatonic scale and the note to which a melody tends to gravitate in tonal music. The first degree of the scale of F major is F itself, and this is the note from which the music departs in bar 1 of B40 and the note to which the music returns at the end of the movement. *EM 2.3.1.*

Tonic accent. An emphasis on a note caused by its high pitch in relation to other notes around it. The semiquavers in A87 are all of the same duration and dynamic level, but the first note of each group of eight semiquavers sounds accented from the start and throughout the extract because it is higher than any other note in each group. *EM 1.2, 1.3, 1.7.1.*

Tonic chord, tonic triad. A chord consisting of the tonic note and notes a 3rd and a perfect 5th above it. A59 begins with the tonic chord of F major repeated four times. B50 begins and ends on the tonic chord of D minor.

Tonic key. The key in which a movement begins and ends. The tonic key of B40 is F major. After the rapid modulations of the development (bars 52–71) the music can be said to return to the tonic key in bar 72.

Tonic major, tonic minor. See *Parallel key* and A96 (D minor), A97 (D major) and A98 (D minor).

Tonic pedal. See *Pedal* and the first two and a half bars of B5.

Tonic-7th chord (chord I^7). In its complete form, a tonic triad with the addition of the note a 7th above the root. The complete tonic 7th in B♭ minor is shown in B78(iii) where it is identified by the symbol I^7. It can be heard at the start of a sequence of secondary-7th chords in bar 2 of Brahms's intermezzo where it is presented as an arpeggio lacking the 5th of the chord (F).

Tonic sol-fa. A British system of notation designed to help singers to read at sight. It uses the syllables *doh, ray, me, fah, soh, lah* and *te* for the seven degrees of any major scale. Thus in C major these syllables correspond with the notes C, D, E, F, G, A and B, and in D major they correspond with the notes D, E, F♯, G, A, B and C♯ (A25). Relative minor scales begin and end on *lah* (with changes to the appropriate syllables to represent sharpened sixth and seventh degrees). If a modulation occurs the location of *doh* is changed to correspond with the new tonic. Adaptations of the system have been developed in many other countries including Germany (Tonika-Do) and Hungary (the Kodály system).

Tonic triad. A three-note chord on the first degree of a diatonic scale. The tonic triad of D minor (D, F and A) is heard spread out over several octaves in the second and last bars of B50. See *Tonic chord. EM 5.1.3.*

Tonicisation. The treatment of a chord other than the tonic as a new but fleeting tonic. This is usually brought about by the deployment of a secondary-dominant chord that resolves onto the tonicised chord. The dominant chord in bar 5 of B16 is tonicised by the secondary-dominant chord in bar 4 (V^6_5 of V), but the effect lasts only until the perfect cadence (bar 5) reaffirms the tonic key of D major. See also bars 5–7 of B67 in which chord IV of F♯ minor is tonicised by V^6_5 of IV. Again the effect is short-lived because IV is immediately followed by V^7 of F♯ minor. *EM 5.7.1.*

Tonika

Tonika (Ger.). Tonic. A91 begins and ends on the tonic of A major. See *Scale degrees*.

Tonkunst (Ger.). Music. See the entry on music and its associated music examples.

Tonleiter (Ger.). Scale (B18).

Tono (It. and Span.). **1.** Note, tone, pitch (see A3 and the folded insert). **2.** Key (B18 is in the key of G major). **3.** Mode (A4 is in Mode VIII). **4.** Whole tone (C21 begins with a descending whole-tone scale).

Tonsatz, Tonstück (Ger.). Composition. Among the complete compositions in Volume 2 are: A15 (medieval), A35 (renaissance), B15 (baroque), B40 (classical), B66 (romantic), C35 (20th-century).

Tonus (Lat.). **1.** Church mode, eg 'primus tonus' signifies Mode I (A40). **2.** A whole tone, eg the interval from the first to the second degree of Mode 1 (A40). **3.** Any of the simple melodic formulas to which the psalms and other liturgical texts are chanted (A6). **4.** Pitch. See A1–A3 and the folded insert.

Torculus (Lat.). A three-note neume. (A4).

Totenmesse (Ger.). Requiem Mass. B62 is an extract from a sequence sometimes sung in the Missa pro defunctis (Mass for the Dead).

Touch. 1. The manner in which a pianist or clavichordist varies the force exerted on the keys in order to produce the desired balance between parts or within chords. On a clavichord (not on a piano) it is also possible to produce a vibrato by altering the pressure on a key after the string has been set vibrating by the initial attack (B20). **2.** Those characteristics of a keyboard that affect the amount of finger-pressure required to sound a note.

Touche (Fr.). The fingerboard of a string instrument. 'Sur la touche' in bar 9 of C31 means 'bow near to or over the fingerboard'.

Tourdion, tordion (Fr.). In the 16th century, a lively triple-time dance described by contemporary authorities as a faster version of the galliard. Like the galliard it consisted of a number of repeated eight-bar phrases (the first of which is shown in A35). In the earliest extant sources it is paired with the *basse danse* (A36).

Tpt., Tr., Trp., Trpt. Abbreviations of trumpet (B36).

Tr. Abbreviation of trill (B66, bar 2).

Tr. picc. in Re. Abbreviation of *tromba piccola in Re* (little trumpet in D). Trumpets in D sound a tone above written pitch but the trumpet part in B15 is shown at sounding pitch.

Tranquillo (It.). Tranquil, quiet, calm, peaceful. All of these adjectives apply to C22.

Transcription. 1. A written or printed adaptation of a piece of music involving a change of medium. A32 is an instrumental transcription of a vocal work (A31). **2.** A translation of music written or printed in one notational system to another notational system. The first phrase of A4 is a modern transcription of the medieval neumatic notation shown on the extra stave. **3.** A written or printed score derived from a live performance or a recording (A16). Most of the scores in Volume 2 are transcriptions in one or more of the above senses of the term.

Transformation of themes. Thematic transformation (C18).

Transition. A passage linking two important sections of an extended composition. The function of the transition in the exposition of B40 (bars 18–25) is to effect a modulation from the tonic key of the first subject (bars 1–18) to the dominant key of the second subject (bars 26–48). *EM 7.7.1.*

Transitory modulation. A brief modulation to a key which is not confirmed by a decisive cadence. Bars 1–10 and 15–22 of B57 are firmly in the key of G major. Between these passages are four bars that modulate to A minor. But no sooner has the root-position tonic chord been sounded (on the first beat of bar 14) than the key of A minor is contradicted by the dominant 7th of G major and a return to another lengthy passage in that key. (An alternative method of analysing this passing reference to A minor is to regard all of the chords with accidentals as chromatic chords that simply colour the key of A minor – as shown by the chord symbols immediately beneath the chords on the extra stave.)

Transposing instruments. Instruments that are written at pitches other than their sounding pitches. In this dictionary all instruments are notated at sounding pitch. For instance, Strauss wrote the clarinet in D part of C10 a tone lower than the actual sounds represented in this example.

Triangle

Transposition. The rewriting of a passage of music at a different pitch-level. In B40 the C-major melody of bars 26–31 is transposed down a compound perfect 5th in bars 95–100, and the bass melody of bars 34–39 is transposed up a perfect 4th in bars 103–108.

Transverse flute. Any flute that is held horizontally and in which sound is generated by blowing across a hole. See *Flute* and *Piccolo* (C76, bars 1–5 and 9–11) and *Alto flute* (C87). *EM 6.6.4.*

Traps, trap set. See *Drum kit* and C38.

Traquenard (Fr.). A late 17th-century German version of the gavotte (B18).

Traverso (It.), **traversière** (Fr.), **Traversflöte** (Ger.). Transverse flute (C76, bars 1–5).

Trb. Abbreviation of trombone (A63).

Tre corde (It.). In piano music, a direction to release the left pedal so that all the strings are again free to vibrate when the keys are struck (C65, bars 12–16). See *Una corda* and B70.

Treble. 1. An unbroken boy's voice with a high range (C30). **2.** A high-pitched instrument (see *Soprano* and the recorder parts in A60). **3.** The highest-sounding part of a composition, whether for voice or instrument. In the four-part counterpoint of B2 the melody notated with upward-pointing stems on the upper stave could be described as a treble part.

Treble clef. See *Clef* and the symbol at the start of A25.

Tremblement (Fr.). A trill, one of the most important ornaments of French baroque music. There were many varieties. The *tremblement* shown at letter d in bars 8 and 24 of A84 is a short trill beginning, as was customary, on the upper note on the beat. Because it is approached from a note a step above the main note it involves a rapid repetition of the approach-note (B♮). Couperin called this a *tremblement détaché*. The *tremblement coulé en montant* is quite different in that it begins on the note a step below the main note (A84, letter f in bar 44). The *tremblement et pincé* is the same as Rameau's *double cadence* (letter f in bar 4 of B17). See *Ornaments* and *Trill*. *EM 3.10.2.*

Tremolando (It.). A performance direction indicating the use of tremolo. In C28 this performance direction has been added by the present author in order to avoid writing separate parts for the celesta (which plays block chords) and the violins (which continue with the tremolo shown by the strokes through the stems of the minims in bar 6). The direction in bar 15 is Mahler's own.

Tremolo (It.). **1.** The rapid and continuous repetition of a single note. In the early 17th century (when it was called a *trillo*) it was a common vocal ornament, often added at cadences even if the composer gave no indication that it should be used (A62). On string instruments a bowed tremolo is indicated by strokes through the stem of the note and it is achieved by rapid up-and-down bow strokes on a single note (B59, bars 25–35). On plucked string instruments a tremolo can be played by rapid strumming: it is a characteristic effect of the mandolin (C29). **2.** The rapid and continuous alternation of notes a 3rd or more apart. On string instruments this is known as a fingered tremolo. It can be heard in bars 4–9 of C69 where the first and second violins play *tremolandi* spanning the interval of a 3rd (both major and minor). *EM 3.10.2, 6.5.2.*

Trepak. A Russian Cossack dance in very fast duple time (C5). *EM 8.10.4.*

Très (Fr.). Very (eg 'très lent' in C19 means 'very slow'). See *Tempo markings*.

Trgl. Abbreviation of triangle (C47 and C54).

Triad. A chord of three pitches that can be arranged as two superimposed 3rds. There are four types of triad: **a)** a major triad consists of a major 3rd with a minor 3rd superimposed on it (A59, bars 1 and 2), **b)** a minor triad consists of a minor 3rd with a major 3rd superimposed on it (A35, bar 1), **c)** an augmented triad consists of two superimposed major 3rds (A♭–C and C–E in the first of the three augmented triads in bars 4, 6 and 8 of C21), **d)** a diminished triad consists of two superimposed minor 3rds (A♯–C♯ and C♯–E♮ in chord VII near the end of A73). See *Intervals*. *EM 5.3.*

Triadic. Adjective from 'triad' sometimes used to describe melodies that outline the notes of triads (B37, bars 20–26[1]).

Triangle, Triangel (Ger.), **triangolo** (It.). A metal percussion instrument shaped like a triangle open at one corner and played with a metal beater. Single notes and rolls can be heard on track C47. *EM 6.8.4.*

Trichord

Trichord. Any collection of three pitches but especially those derived from a tone row (A, B, C and D in C40).

Tricinium. In the 16th and 17th centuries, a composition for three instruments or voices (A59), but especially one written for didactic purposes.

Trill, Triller (Ger.). A melodic ornament consisting of a rapid alternation of two notes a step apart. An ocarina plays a very high-pitched trill throughout the first four bars of A18 (indicated by the conventional abbreviation *tr*). A trill in baroque music is often indicated by a short wavy line. In accordance with contemporary performance practice the two trills in B9 (bars 4 and 9) begin on the beat with the note a step above the printed note. The exact length of such trills is left to the discretion of the performer (both of the trills in B9 end on the fourth beat of the bar). Trills starting on the upper note remained the norm until the early 19th century (Chopin is known to have preferred this manner of performance, and this is the way the trills in B66 are played). In later styles trills usually begin on the printed note (C35, celesta, bar 3). Exceptions to these generalisations are numerous. In baroque music a vertical stroke through the left-hand end of a wavy line or a hook at the start (B1, bar 3, beat 2) indicate a trill that starts a step below the printed note (sometimes called a turned start or *Doppeltcadence*). Similarly trills can end with a two-note figure known as a *Nachschlag*. This turned ending can be shown by short notes (B11 and B76), by a vertical stroke through the end of a wavy line, or by a hook attached to the end of a wavy line. In A84 the symbol for this type of trill is shown in bar 8 (labelled d) and the same ornament is shown in written-out form in bar 24 (also labelled d and with the turn at the end marked x). See *Ornaments* and *Tremblement*. *EM 3.10.1, 3.10.2*.

Trillerkette (Ger.). A continuous series of trills (B36, bars 248–252).

Trillo (It.). In the 17th century, a vocal tremolo (A62), later a trill beginning on the upper note and on the beat (B9, bars 4 and 9). See *Ornaments. EM 3.10.1, 3.10.2.*

Trillo caprino (It.). Goat's trill. See *Bleat* and the *trillo* in A62.

Trio. 1. Music for three solo performers. B40 is a divertimento for three basset-horns. **2.** Music for a single soloist written throughout in three contrapuntal parts. The three contrapuntal strands in Bach's six Trio Sonatas for organ are played with the right hand on one manual, the left hand on another and the bass part played on the pedalboard. **3.** The middle section of the minuet–trio–minuet group that forms the third movement of many classical multi-movement compositions (B25). **4.** A term used as part of the name of an ensemble of three performers such as the Beaux Arts Trio.

Trio sonata. A baroque composition in several sections (later independent movements) written on three staves (hence trio sonata). The treble staves were for two equal high-pitched melody instruments (such as violins, recorders, flutes or oboes), while the bass stave contained a bass part for a low-pitched melody instrument (such as a bass viol, cello or bassoon). Whether or not this part was figured, it was expected that a fourth performer would improvise harmonic filling between these polarised parts on an instrument such as an organ or harpsichord.

By about 1650 two types of trio sonata had emerged in Italy. The *sonata da chiesa* (church sonata) was characterised by its serious style (including fugal sections or movements), often in the pattern slow–fast–slow–fast. It is probable that these movements were intended to replace items of the Proper of the Mass and the antiphons at Vespers. The *sonata da camera* (chamber sonata), like the contemporary suite or partita, contained binary-form dance movements such as the *allemanda*, *corrente*, *sarabanda* and *giga*. There was, however, no absolute rule. On the one hand, it was common for a chamber sonata to begin with a serious preludial movement, and on the other many church sonatas end with a fast triple-time or compound-time movement in the style of a gigue. A73 is just such a cross-over movement. Although constituting the last movement of one of Corelli's church sonatas, its binary form and gigue-like style suggest that it would be equally at home in a chamber sonata (the fugal textures of this movement were common to most gigues of the period). *EM 8.7.4.*

Triole (Ger.), **triolet** (Fr.). Triplet (B18, Variation 3).

Tripartite. An adjective describing any composition that falls into three distinct sections, such as the da capo aria (B15) and the minuet–trio–minuet form of classical genres (B25).

Triple-croche (Fr.). Demisemiquaver, thirty-second-note (B18, Variation 5, bar 7, beat 3). See *Note*.

Triple harp. A chromatic harp with three parallel ranks of strings. It is a development of Monteverdi's double harp (A66) and a forerunner of the modern double-action harp (C35). It was popular in Italy in the 17th century and is still in use in Wales.

Triple metre, triple time. Any metre of repeating strong–weak–weak patterns (A12).

Triple stopping. The performance of three-note chords on a bowed string instrument. See *Stopping* and A88, bar 3.

Triple time. See *Triple metre* and A12.

Triple tonguing. See *Tonguing* and C97, bars 27–34.

Triplet. A group of three notes of equal length played in the time of two notes of the same time-value (B18, Variation 3). *EM 1.8.*

Triplum (Lat.). In medieval music a third polyphonic part added above the tenor. On track A19 the *triplum* is sung by an alto.

Tristan chord. The first chord of the Prelude to the first act of Wagner's opera *Tristan und Isolde* (C68). The *Tristan* chord has assumed universal importance as a paradigm of chords that are so dissonant and chromatic that their tonal function is ambiguous. Hence they can be interpreted as harbingers of the non-functional chords that form atonal progression in expressionist music of the early 20th century (C34 for example). B70–B72 suggest the historical context of the *Tristan* chord. B70 begins with a progression which is almost identical to that in bars 2–3 of B71. Liszt's progression is clearly tonal: the dominant minor 9th of A resolves to the dominant 7th (decorated with a telling chromatic accented passing note), and this in turn resolves to the tonic chord of A (major, then minor). B71 differs from B70 in two important respects. Firstly Liszt's D♮ is changed to D♯, thus increasing the dissonant effect. Secondly the dominant 7th (decorated with the same Lisztian chromatic accented passing note) remains unresolved. Instead Wagner repeats the progression in sequence (C68, bars 6–7). B72 is closely related to B71 by virtue of its almost identical melody, but the progression of chords notated as diminished 7ths and French 6ths derives from a 12-tone row (shown in C40) which, by its very nature, robs the music of any clearly defined tonality. Thus Janus-faced, the *Tristan* chord simultaneously refers back to Lisztian tonality and foreshadows Hauer's atonality. In view of the fact that the tonal tensions apparent in B68 are resolved by clear A-major tonality at the end of the version of the Prelude that Wagner himself made for concert performances there are those who hear the *Tristan* chord as a chromatic dissonance in the key of A. On the contrary there are those who describe the chord as a half-diminished 7th (F–G♯–B–D♯ = F–A♭–C♭–E♭), the tonal function of which is quite obscure. Between these two extremes there are many equally tenable interpretations of this ambiguous chord. See also B67, bars 7–9. *EM 2.7ff, 5.7.5.*

Tritone. An interval spanning three tones (C96, bars 1–28). See *Diabolus in musica* and *Intervals. EM 2.4.3, 5.2, 8.10.1, 8.11.11.*

Tromba (It.). Trumpet (B15).

Tromba piccola (It.). Piccolo trumpet (B15).

Trombone. A brass instrument with a slide that can be adjusted to any one of seven positions. By altering the embouchure the player can produce a harmonic series in each of these positions, thus allowing the performance of a wide chromatic range of notes (see the folded insert). The instrument has, from earliest times, been associated with solemn rituals in church and on the stage. In A62 two trombones are used, one to double the voice, the other to provide the bass. At this point Speranza (Hope) is declaiming the words of Dante that are supposed to be written above the portal of hell: 'Abandon hope all you who enter here'. A trombone also accompanies the recitative of Caronte (the boatman who ferries souls to Hades) in A63. The slide enables trombonists to play glissandi such as those heard at the end of C75. *EM 6.7.3.*

Trommel (Ger.). Drum (C27 (timpani), C42–C46, C52, C53 and C74).

Trommelbass (Ger.). In the 18th century, an often-repeated single pitch in the bass.

Apart from the cadences a G♮ is repeated beneath the melody shown in B28. Cellos and basses play a very loud E♭ *Trommelbass* in bars 13–20 of B36.

Tromp. en Ut. Abbreviation of *trompette en Ut* (trumpet in C). Bartók specifies trumpets in C in his *Concerto for Orchestra* (C81 and C82, bars 14–57).

Trompete (Ger.), **Trompette** (Fr.). Trumpet (B36).

Trompette piccolo (Fr.). Piccolo trumpet (B15).

Trope (from the Lat. *tropus*). In the tenth to the 12th centuries: **1.** Texts added to an existing plainsong melisma such as the jubilus of an Alleluia (A5). See *Sequence* 3. **2.** Newly composed melodies and texts added to existing chants such as an introit (A4). These could be sung before or after the original chant, or they could be interpolated between phrases of it. **3.** Untexted melismas added to an existing plainsong melody. **4.** In Josef Hauer's 12-tone technique, the division of a row into two hexachords, the contents of which may be played in any order. This principle is at work in C40. As first presented the first hexachord (A+B) is melodically inverted to become the second hexachord (C+D). The chords at the end of the extract are formed by reordering the contents of both hexachords to form ascending chromatic scales then dividing both of them into two trichords, one for each of the four parts that make up the four chords. The term has been adopted by 20th-century theorists in their analyses of works by more famous composers such as Schoenberg.

Trop (Fr.), **troppo** (It.). Too much. The phrase 'non troppo' (not too much) qualifies 'andante' (moderately slow) at the beginning of B78. See *Tempo markings*.

Troubadours, trouvères. Poet-musicians of the late 11th to 13th centuries, the troubadours (m.) and trobairitz (f.) writing of courtly love in Occitan in southern France and the trouvères writing on similar subjects in Old French in northern France. Although about 2,500 troubadour poems have survived there are fewer than 300 extant melodies. Many more trouvère melodies have survived and from these and later sources a clear picture of the medieval *formes fixes* emerges – the ballade (A12), virelai (A22) and rondeau (A23). See *Minnesinger* and *Minstrel*.

Trumpet. The principal treble brass instrument of the modern symphony orchestra. The approximate range covered by a modern trumpet in B♭ is shown on the folded insert. The incisive tones of a pair of trumpets in C can be heard in bars 14–57 of C82 and the quite different timbres of a pair of muted trumpets can be heard in C81. The natural trumpet of the baroque era had no valves and so could only play the notes of the harmonic series. To compensate, virtuoso baroque trumpeters specialised in playing in the highest (clarino) register where a complete scale could be produced (B15, bars 79–80). Less able trumpeters had to be content with the lower *principale* register exemplified in bars 15–22 of B15. *EM 6.7.2.*

T.s. Abbreviation of *tasto solo* (B5, basso continuo, bar 1).

T-Tam. Abbreviation of tam-tam (C48 and C54).

Tuba. A large brass instrument that provides the bass for the orchestral brass choir. Three sizes are commonly used and the folded insert shows the approximate range of the bass tuba in F. A solo tuba can be heard at the start of C28 (its solo resumes in bars 5–7), and a tenor tuba solo can be heard on C37. *EM 6.7.3.*

Tubular bells. Metal tubes mounted in a rack and covering a chromatic range of up to two octaves (C97, bars 36–38). *EM 6.8.4.*

Tune. 1. A melody. The term usually refers to popular, catchy melodies such as those heard on tracks C38 and C73. **2.** To adjust the basic pitch of an instrument, usually to a^1 at 440 Hz (A1). *EM 3.1.*

Tuning. The act of adjusting the tension of strings or membranes, or adjusting the lengths of pipes to bring them into agreement with predetermined pitches. In a modern orchestra the predetermined pitch is usually given by an oboist playing a^1 at 440 Hz (see A1 and the folded insert). From this pitch other performers adjust their instruments so that they agree with the oboe (or so that pitches one or two octaves below are set at 220 Hz or 110 Hz respectively). String players then adjust the other three or four strings in perfect 4ths or 5ths to agree with the tuning of their A strings. The effect of perfect 5ths based on the standard pitch of A=440 can be heard in bars 16–26 of B73 (where the uppermost parts are played on the open strings of all the violins of a large symphony orchestra). Tuning to other standard pitches is not uncommon. Many modern ensembles specialising in the performance of baroque music tune a^1 at about 415 Hz (approximately a semitone lower than normal 21st-century pitch). Thus in A88 the sarabande in D minor (shown in (i)) actually sounds in C♯ minor (ii) when played on a violin tuned to A=415 Hz.

Turba (Lat.). Crowd. *Turbae* in Passion music are settings of the crowd's interjections recorded in Gospel narratives, eg 'Not this man, but Barabbas!' (B4(b)).

Turkish music. See *Janissary music* and B37.

Turn. A four-note ornament comprising the note a step above the written note, the written note, the note a step below the written note and the written note again. In A84 the conventional symbol for a turn is shown in bar 1 (letter b), and the same turn is shown written out in bar 17 (also at letter b). In an inverted turn (∞, ⌬ or ⌬) the order of notes described above is reversed. See *Ornaments*. *EM 3.10.2, 3.10.3.*

Tutti (It.). All, everyone, the whole ensemble or orchestra. The passages marked 'tutti' in B19 are played by the full string band (as opposed to the passages marked 'soli' which are played by a group of solo strings).

Twelfth. 1. The interval of an octave and a 5th (B77, bar 2, first two notes in the right hand part). **2.** An organ stop sounding an octave and a 5th above eight-foot foundation pitch. It is one of the constituent ranks of the cornet that adds brilliance to the timbre of the organ recorded on A81.

Twelve-eight time. A compound quadruple metre in which four dotted-crotchet beats form the repeating pattern strong–weak–strong–weak (possibly with the first strong beat being more accented than the second strong beat). It is indicated by the time signature $\frac{12}{8}$. In very fast $\frac{12}{8}$ time only two dotted-minim beats are readily perceived (A18) while in slower tempi (B19) it is possible to perceive the way in which each dotted-crotchet beat divides into the characteristic dotted rhythm heard throughout this piece (marked x in bar 1).

Twelve-note row, twelve-tone row. A set of 12 different non-repeating pitch classes used as a basis for composition in serial music (C40, bars 0–7). See *Serial music* and C88. *EM 3.8.*

Two-foot stop. A rank of organ pipes of which the longest measures approximately two feet. Music performed on a two-foot stop sounds two octaves above printed pitch. The registration of A93 includes a two-foot flue stop that adds brilliance to the basic eight-foot tone. The highest notes of A3 are played on a two-foot stop.

Two-four time. A simple duple metre in which two crotchet beats form the repeating pattern stong–weak. It is indicated by the time signature $\frac{2}{4}$ immediately after the first clef or first key signature (B15).

Two-part counterpoint. A musical texture consisting of the combination of two rhythmically independent melodic strands. Entire compositions can display this sort of texture (see *Invention* and C93). The term should not be confused with double counterpoint. For a wide variety of two-part counterpoint see also A10, A11, A16, A24 (bars 17–36), A28, A29, A84, A89, A92, A93, B22–B24, B33, B77, C58, C63 and C64 (bars 4–11). *EM 4.1, 4.2.*

Two-two time. A simple duple metre in which two minim beats form the repeating pattern strong–weak. It is indicated by the time signature $\frac{2}{2}$ immediately after the first clef (B18).

Tympani. Eccentric spelling of the Italian word 'timpani' (C27).

U

Übergang, Überleitung (Ger.). In sonata forms, a transition (B40, bars 18–25).

Übung (Ger.). Study. B1, B2, B10, B11 and B12 are taken from a movement in the second volume of Bach's *Clavier-Übung* (*Keyboard Study*). Bach's aim was not only to provide material for keyboard practice, but to furnish examples of most styles, genres and compositional techniques of the baroque era. In the *Goldberg Variations* he combines a wide variety of baroque styles with canonic techniques, and in the Gigue from the Partita BWV 829 he combines the style of this familiar baroque dance with the techniques of double fugue.

Umfang (Ger.). The range or compass of a voice or instrument (see the folded insert).

Umkehrung (Ger.). Inversion (C64, x and xI).

Un, un', una, uno (It.). A (the indefinite article). Towards the end of C82 the direction 'Un poco meno mosso' means 'a little less fast' (a little slower).

Una corda (It.). One string. When the left-hand pedal of a grand piano is depressed the hammers move sideways so that only one (or two) of the two (or three) strings of the same pitch are struck. The use of the 'soft pedal' not only reduces the volume, it changes the timbre of the instrument (compare bar 1 of B70 with bars 2 and 3). 'Tre corde' (three strings) countermands 'una corda' (C65) even though there are fewer than three strings at each pitch in the middle and low registers of a modern piano. The same terms apply to cheap upright pianos even though the *una corda* pedal operates a mechanism that moves a piece of felt between the hammers and strings.

Underlay. In the notation of vocal music, the manner in which syllables or words are laid under the notes of a melody. In modern performing editions this is usually explicit, but in music written or printed before about 1600 it is often the case that only the first few words of the text are shown in some or all of the parts (A33, bars 23–31, alto and tenor parts).

Unending melody, unendliche Melodie (Ger.). Wagner's term for a melody that avoids formulaic cadences and regular phrasing. Instead it relies on subtle manipulations and combinations of a number of motifs over a long timespan. Bars 17–24 of B68 show the beginning of an unending melody of this kind. *EM 3.4.*

Unessential note. A melodic decoration not belonging to the chord against which it is heard. In bar 6 of A30 the notes labelled 'pn' do not belong to the chord of G major and the notes labelled 'en' and 'apn' do not belong to the chord of C major.

Unison, unisono (It.) **(unis.).** Two or more voices or instruments (or both) singing or playing the same melody at the same pitch. Unison male voices sing bars 12–22 of A26. However, the same term is generally used for females and males singing in octaves (bars 1–11 of the same example) and for boys and men singing in octaves (bars 1–4 of A25), but orchestral textures in which a melody is doubled at the octave (above or below or both) are not usually described as being in unison (see bars 1–8 of B59). *EM 2.1.*

Unmeasured music. See *Measured and unmeasured music*, and compare A4–A9 (unmeasured) with A10–A11 (measured).

Unprepared and unresolved discords. See *Preparation* and *Resolution*. The appoggiatura is one of the most common types of unprepared discord (B68, bar 17). In the same example the dissonant 7th in each of the dominant chords at the end of each of the first three phrases remains unresolved (potential resolutions are shown on the extra staves to the right of each system). See also A81, bar 3, and B31, bars 4–5.

Unstopped notes. See *Stopped notes*.

Upbeat. A weak beat immediately before the first downbeat. See *Anacrusis* and A24 (in which the first note is an upbeat and the second a downbeat).

Upper auxiliary. See *Auxiliary note* and the semiquaver D♯ in the first beat of B19. *EM 4.3.4.*

Upper mordent. A melodic ornament consisting of the printed note, the note above it and the printed note again (B25, bars 56, 58 and 62). The upper mordent is sometimes called an inverted mordent. See *Mordent* and *Ornaments*. *EM 3.10, 3.10.1, 3.10.2, 3.10.3.*

Upright piano. See *Pianoforte* and C73.

Ut (Fr.). C♮. See *C*, the diagram of a keyboard on the folded insert and A1.

V

Va., Vla.. Abbreviations of viola (A38).

Vagrant harmonies. Schoenberg's term for ambiguous chords, the functions of which change according to context. He points out, for instance, that in terms of absolute pitch there are only three possible diminished-7th chords: G–B♭–C♯–E, G♯–B–D–F (B50, bars 93–94) and A–C–E♭–F♯ (B59, bars 26–29), but that each of them can be transformed by the context in which they are found to act as dominants in four different keys. Thus in B20 the diminished-7th chords in the second system are dominants in E minor (a key firmly established in the first system). Yet the same diminished-7th chord (with D♯ notated as E♭) is transformed in the fourth system to become a dominant in G minor (a key confirmed by the resolution of the diminished 7th to the tonic chord of G minor at the end of the system). Perhaps the most ambiguous of vagrant harmonies is the *Tristan* chord. In of B68 there are just three cello notes before it, so no key has been firmly established before it is sounded, but at the end of the phrase it resolves to V^7 of A minor. There are those who would agree with the implicit analysis of this vagrant chord shown in B68, but there are others who hear much more ambiguous tonal relationships, likening the *Tristan* chord to II^7 in a minor key (a chromatically altered supertonic 7th in a major key). Indeed the sound of this so-called half-diminished 7th is so memorable that Debussy is able to satirise Wagner's solemn chromatic idiom by quoting it in the decidedly unsolemn context of a piece in ragtime style. The same absolute pitches as Wagner used at the start of *Tristan* are replicated but with enharmonic alterations (F–G♯–B–D♯ = F–A♭–C♭–E♭) in bars 10–11 of B20 (later on in the cakewalk Debussy's parody becomes even more obvious). When vagrant harmonies such as these form a progression of unresolved discords they lack any sense of tonal direction.

Valse (Fr.). Waltz (C2).

Valve horn, valve trumpet. Instruments with valves that allow the performance of a full chromatic range of notes (C85, bars 8–23) as opposed to a natural instrument that, without hand stopping, is only capable of playing notes from a single harmonic series (C84 is played without using valves so only the notes of a harmonic series on F can be played). The same principles apply to the trumpet. The valveless natural trumpet used on track B15 is confined to the notes of the tonic triad in mid-register (bars 15–22) but can play a complete diatonic scale in high register (bars 79–80). With modern piston valves, however, all 12 chromatic notes can be played in all registers (C81). *EM 6.7.2.*

Vamp. A simple improvised accompaniment for a vocal or instrumental solo in the style shown in the orchestral reduction of C73. The direction 'vamp till ready' means that the accompanist should improvise such simple oom-pah harmonies until the singer or instrumentalist is ready to begin.

Variations, theme and variations. A musical structure in which a theme is repeated, each time with alterations to one or more of its original elements.

In the 16th century the theme was often a popular song, or a formulaic bass that could itself be varied. See *Diferencias*, *Romanesca* and A34.

In the 17th century the theme was often a basso ostinato that remained unchanged throughout (though it was sometimes transposed) while the melody unfolded above it. See *Ground* and A75.

In the 17th and early 18th centuries 'divisions' were variations in which the bass, the melody or both were divided into running passages of shorter notes. See B18.

In the late baroque era the chaconne and passacaglia were continuous variations based on a short harmonic progression, a stereotyped bass melody or both. See A95–A98.

In the late 18th and 19th centuries it was common to use a more extended theme, any element of which could be altered in the ensuing set of variations. B32 shows the opening bars of an extended theme that has come to be known as 'The Emperor's Hymn' (which was written by Haydn himself). In the first variation (B33) the melody is played unaltered by the second violin against a new counter-melody played by the

Varsovienne

first violin. In the second variation (B34) the theme is played by the cellist with the second violin playing mostly in 3rds or 6ths above. Meanwhile the first violin plays a syncopated counter-melody and the viola provides essential bass notes. In the fourth variation (B35) the melody returns to the first violin part while the other three instruments provide a new chromatic harmonisation. This set of variations forms one movement of a string quartet, but in the classical and romantic periods self-standing variation sets became longer and more complex. Brahms's Op. 24 is a set of 25 variations and a fugue based on the binary-form theme by Handel shown in B76. In the 16th variation (B77) Brahms retains only the bare outlines of Handel's harmonic progression (I–V in the first four bars, V–I in the last four bars) but makes extensive use of Handel's turn motif in his virtuosic two-part counterpoint. *EM 3.2, 4.4.7, 8.6.3, 8.7.7.*

Varsovienne (Fr.). A Parisian dance of the mid-19th century named after Warsaw and partaking of characteristic features of the slow mazurka (B65) and the faster waltz (C2).

Vc., vlc. Abbreviations of violoncello (A90). See *Cello*.

Veloce (It.). Swift, quick, rapid. All of these adjectives accurately describe C5. See *Tempo markings*.

Vengeance aria. In the 18th and 19th centuries, an operatic song in which the singer gives vent to feelings of anger about a real or supposed affront and expresses a determination to seek revenge. B37 is a buffo vengeance aria. B50 is in the style of an opera seria vengeance aria.

Vent (Fr.). Wind. 'Instruments à vent' are wind instruments (C27).

Ventilhorn (Ger.). Valve horn (C85, bars 8–25).

Veränderungen (Ger.). Variations. Bach's original title for his *Goldberg* Variations (B1 and B2) is 'Aria mit verschiedenen Veränderungen' ('Aria with sundry variations').

Vergrösserung (Ger.). Augmentation (B14, bars 14–16).

Verkleinerung (Ger.). Diminution (C34, bars 1–2, piano, left-hand part).

Verse, verse part. A solo voice in a verse anthem (A61).

Verse, versus (Lat.). **1.** A line of poetry or a sentence of a psalm. There are eight verses in the stanza of poetry printed at the foot of A23, and A6 is a setting of verse 31 from Psalm 104. **2.** In plainsong, the verse or verses from the psalms in the introit (A4), gradual or alleluia (A5).

Verse anthem. An English anthem for solo vocalists (verse parts) and choir accompanied by organ alone or by a consort of viols (with or without organ). The verse anthem grew out of the metrical psalm (A37) and the Elizabethan consort song (A60). A61 is an extract from a typical example of the genre in which imitative viols are heard on their own, then doubling the entries of solo alto, bass then tenor voices (bars 2, 4 and 5 respectively). After a number of overlapping points of imitation this section of Gibbons's verse anthem ends with a homophonic passage for the whole choir and consort of viols (bars 22–27). A typical verse anthem contains several sections for soloists answered by full choir. *EM 8.6.2.*

Verset. A short organ piece that replaced a verse of a liturgical text from about 1400 to 1903 (when liturgical reforms did away with the practice). Organ versets alternated with plainsong in the Ordinary of the Mass and in items of the Divine Office such as the Magnificat. The offertory was often omitted altogether and replaced by a more extended organ solo (A81). *EM 8.7.2.*

Versetto (It.). Diminution of verset (A81)

Versicle. A short text sung by a priest or cantor in Christian liturgies. This is answered by a response sung by the choir and/or congregation (A8).

Versillo (Span.). Verset (A81).

Vertical sonority. A collection of pitches sounded simultaneously. In modernist music the term is preferred to 'chord' because the latter is thought to imply tertian harmony (C90, any of the chords formed where there is a vertical pecked line).

Verticalisation, verticalization. The performance of adjacent pitches of a note row as chords. The first three chords of C88 are verticalisations of the solo tenor part in bars 7–9 (chord 1 derives from the four pitches sung to the syllables '-tum meum, et'; chord

2 from 'fluant aro-'; chord 3 from '-mata illius'). *EM 5.8.1.*

Verzierungen (Ger.). Ornaments. See *Ornaments* and associated music examples.

Vespers. One of the services of the Divine Office, it is sung at twilight and usually includes psalms (A6), antiphons (A4), a hymn (A49), the Magnificat and the acclamation, 'Benedicamus Domino' (A8).

Vessel flute. A flute with a body in the shape of a distorted egg (rather than the usual tubular shape of most flutes). The ocarina is probably the most familiar type of vessel flute (A18).

Vibraphone. A tuned percussion instrument with a set of metal bars arranged like a piano keyboard. These are struck with any of a variety of beaters. Under the bars are resonating tubes. At the top of each one is an electrically driven fan that, when switched on, produces the characteristic vibrato often heard in pop and modern jazz. On C87 the vibraphone is played with hard sticks and without vibrato. The range of a typical vibraphone is shown on the folded insert. *EM 6.8.7.*

Vibrato (It.). An undulating sound produced on string instruments by moving a finger that is stopping a string rapidly to and fro (C18(c)). In the performance of early music little or no vibrato is used (A16). Woodwind and brass instruments and the clavichord can also produce vibrato (B20, the note marked 'Bebung'). A controlled use of vocal vibrato can be hear in bars 29–35 of C96. See *Ornaments. EM 3.10.2, 6.5.12.*

Vielle (Fr.). Any of a variety of medieval bowed string instruments including the fiddle and *vielle à roue* or hurdy-gurdy (A13 and A18). *EM 6.4.3.*

Vielle à roue (Fr.). Hurdy-gurdy (A18).

Viennese Classical School. A group of composers working in Vienna in the late 18th century and the early 19th century, notably Haydn (B26–B36), Mozart (B37–B50) and Beethoven (B51–B55). *EM 8.9.*

Viertel, Viertelnote (Ger.). Crotchet, quarter-note (B18, theme). See *Note.*

Viertelton (Ger.). Quarter-tone (indicated by arrows in C70, bars 6, 8 and 9).

Vierundsechzigstel, Vierundsechzigstelnote (Ger.). Hemidemisemiquaver, sixty-fourth-note (B18, Variation 5, the last six notes of bar 7). See *Note.*

Vif (Fr.). Fast, lively. The direction 'Assez vif et bien rythmé' at the head of C17 means 'quite fast and very rhythmical'. See *Tempo markings.*

Vihuela (Span.). A Spanish plucked string instrument of the 15th and 16th centuries, it was played like a guitar but belonged to the viol family. There were varieties that were bowed like a viol, but, used without qualification, the name is taken to mean the *vihuela de mano* which was plucked with the fingers (A34). *EM 6.4.2.*

Viol. Any of a family of bowed and fretted string instruments tuned like lutes and popular both as solo and accompanimental instruments throughout the 16th and 17th centuries. A consort of viols can be heard accompanying the voices in a verse anthem on A61. This particular consort comprises a treble viol, a tenor viol, two bass viols and a violone (contrabass or double-bass viol). For the contrabass viol see A36. *EM 6.4.3.*

Viola. The second smallest member of the modern bowed string family, pitched a 5th lower than the violin. Its range is shown on the folded insert. Its most characteristic register can be heard on track A38 and a section of violas plays Tallis's theme in A39. *EM 6.4.1.*

Viola clef. A term sometimes used for the alto C clef. See *C clefs* and the symbol at the start of the stave in A38(b).

Viola d'amore. A 17th- and 18th-century instrument about the same size as a viola but with a distinctly different timbre due in part to the seven unbowed strings that vibrate in sympathy with the seven bowed strings. A pair of solo viole d'amore can be heard on track B5. *EM 6.4.3.*

Viola da braccio (It.). In the 16th and 17th centuries, any instrument of the violin family held on the arm (upper parts of A64). *EM 6.4.3.*

Viola da gamba (It.), **viole** (Fr.). In the 16th and 17th centuries, any member of the viol family that was held in an upright position on the lap or between the legs. See *Viol* and A61. *EM 6.4.3.*

Violento (It.). Violent (C97, bar 9).

Violin, violino (It.), **violon** (Fr.). The small-

Violoncelle

est of the modern bowed string instruments, it has wide range (shown on the folded insert) and great flexibility and agility (A95–A98). Its four strings are tuned in 5ths (g, d^1, a^1 and e^2) and these open strings can be heard clearly in bars 16–26 of B73. *EM 6.4.1.*

Violoncelle (Fr.), **violoncello** (It.). Cello (A90).

Violone (It.). A name for a large bowed string instrument. It has changed its meaning since it was first used in the 16th century to designate any member of the viol family of instruments. Nowadays it usually refers to the contrabass viol, the direct ancestor of the modern double bass (A36, bars 9–16).

Virelai (Fr.). One of the medieval French *formes fixes* with a musical structure ABBAA (repeated for each of the poetic stanzas). The most famous are the virelais of Machaut (A22). *EM 7.9.2, 8.4.2.*

Virginal, virginals. A small, one-manual harpsichord with one set of strings. Dating from the late 15th century virginals were probably more numerous than harpsichords throughout the 16th and 17th centuries. They differ from the spinet (A67) in construction but not in sound (the voicing of individual instruments being a more important factor determining the timbres of such instruments). Indeed the virginal and spinet had the same name in some continental countries (*épinette* in France, *spinett* in Flanders and *spinetta* in Italy). In England the word 'virginals' and the phrase 'pair of virginals' refer to a single instrument.

Virtuoso. A performer of outstanding technical brilliance. Music that requires such a performer is sometimes described as 'virtuosic' (C90, the marimba part).

Vite (Fr.). Fast. Compare *Vif* (C12) and *Gaiement* (C32). See *Tempo markings*.

Vivace (It.). Lively, brisk. 'Molto vivace' at the head of C9 means 'very lively' and, in this context, 'very fast'. See *Tempo markings*.

Vivo (It.). Alive, quick, spirited. All of these adjectives accurately describe B37. See *Tempo markings*.

Vl., vln, viol. Abbreviations of violin, *violín* (Span.), *violino* (It.) and violon (Fr.).

Vla. Abbreviation of viola.

Vlc. Abbreviation of violoncello (cello) and violoncelo or violonchelo (Span.) and violoncelle (Fr. and Ger.).

Vocalisation, vocalise. A vocalisation is a passage sung to vowel sounds (C91). Singers often warm up before a concert by vocalising scales, arpeggios and other exercises – a practice that is wonderfully parodied in Mozart's Queen of the Night aria (B50, bars 24–32, 35–43 and 74–79). A vocalise is a complete composition without text.

Voce (It.). **1.** Voice (A22). **2.** Part, whether vocal or instrumental (eg the two canonic parts of A92).

Voice. 1. A vocal or instrumental part. A27 can be described as a four-voice composition despite it being sung by a chamber choir with more than one voice to each part. B10 can be described as a three-voice fugal exposition despite there being no singing at all. **2.** The human instrument for speaking (C38) and singing (C40). Singing voices are classified according to sex, range, timbre and, in some cases, technical ability. The most important types of voice (starting with the highest and finishing with the lowest) are: coloratura soprano (B50), soprano (the Angel in B16), treble (the uppermost vocal part in C30), mezzo-soprano (A60), contralto (A22), countertenor (A12), tenor (B57), baritone (B58), bass-baritone (B5), bass (A63).

Voice exchange. The exchange of musical phrases between voices or instruments in medieval music. In the *pes* of A15 the two-bar phrase x is sung by voice 1 (bars 1–2) then immediately repeated by voice 2 (bars 3–4). Simultaneously the two-bar phrase y is sung by voice 2 (bars 1–2) then immediately repeated by voice 1 (bars 3–4). This swapping of phrases continues throughout the entire track. The more appropriate term 'phrase exchange' has been suggested but not widely accepted. *EM 4.4.6.*

Voice leading. The conduct of individual parts in homophonic or contrapuntal textures. In the three-voice homophony of A19 the voice leading of the bass part in bar 6 (a leap of a 3rd to the only chromatically inflected note in this section of the Agnus Dei) would lead one to expect a stepwise descent – an expectation which is fulfilled in the next bar. This voice leading complements the voice leading of the alto and tenor, both of them moving up in contrary motion with the descending bass.

Voicing. The adjustment of the tonal qualities of keyboard instruments. Compare the mellow sound of the two- and three-part textures played on B10–B12 with the brilliant sound of the same sort of textures played on a differently voiced harpsichord, B17. The term is also used for the manner in which individual components of a chord are emphasised. On track B56 the uppermost note of every chord is played more loudly than any of the other parts to give the impression of a cantabile melody with chordal accompaniment.

Voix (Fr.). Voice or voices. See A22 and A23 (contralto and tenor voices respectively) and B10 (a three-voice fugal exposition).

Voix céleste (Fr.). See *Céleste* and A55.

Volta (It.). **1.** Time (ie instance). In bar 5 of C76 the direction 'più volte ad libitum' means that the flautist is allowed to repeat the bracketed notes as many times as desired. **2.** 'Prima volta' and 'seconda volta' mean 'first time' and 'second time' respectively. The term is most commonly used in connection with a section that is to be repeated but with a different ending. In C5 bars 7–8 are played at the end of the first phrase (*prima volta*), then bars 1–6 are repeated, but this time the phrase ends with bars 15–16 (*seconda volta*). First- and second-time bars are also used at the ends of the next eight-bar phrases (bars 39–40 and 47–48 respectively).

Volta (It.), **volte** (Fr. and Ger.). A dance known to Shakespeare as 'lavolta', it was described by Arbeau in 1588 as similar to the galliard (A35).

Volume. Loudness. For extremes of volume compare bars 48–50 and 51–68 of C97. See *Acoustics* and *Intensity*.

Voluntary. An organ piece played before or after a church service, particularly services of the established Church of England. Voluntaries can be composed or improvised. The earliest extant voluntary dates from about 1560 and is in the contrapuntal style of the contemporary continental ricercar (A57, a composition which is likely to have served a similar preludial function in a Roman Catholic service).

Vorschlag (Ger.). **1.** Appoggiatura (B69(b)). **2.** Grace note (see the notes in small print in B1, bar 2). See *Ornaments*.

Vorspiel (Ger.). A prelude, or, since the mid-19th century, an overture (B68).

Vorzeichen (Ger.). Accidental (B68, bar 2, G♯ and D♯)

Vorzeichnung (Ger.). Key signature (B67, the three sharp signs after the clefs).

Votive Mass, votive antiphon. A mass setting or antiphon intended for a special occasion (such as the Mass for the Dead, B62) or special devotion (such as a Mass dedicated to the Blessed Virgin Mary, A21).

Vox (Lat.). Voice. See *Vox principalis* and A9.

Vox coelestis (Lat.). See *Céleste* and C55.

Vox organalis (Lat.). A part added to a plainsong melody in organum (A9). *EM 8.5.1.*

Vox principalis (Lat.). The plainsong cantus firmus in organum (A9). *EM 8.5.1.*

Vuota, vuoto (It.). Empty, vacant. In music the term applies to: **1.** Notes played on an unstopped ('empty') string. These can be indicated by placing a circle above the notes in question (A98, bar 2). **2.** A general pause (B59, bar 8, beat 4).

W

W., Wq. Abbreviations of Wotquenne, the author of a thematic catalogue of the works of C. P. E. Bach (B20).

Wait, waits. A civic or domestic watchman who played a horn or shawm as a signal. City waits were groups of watchmen who diversified into bands playing a variety of instruments. A60 is played by the Waits of the City of York.

Waldhorn (Ger.). Literally 'forest horn' and therefore a hunting horn and therefore a natural horn (like those that inhabit the forest glades in *Der Freischütz* – B59, bars 10–24).

Walking bass. A bass part moving steadily throughout a piece (or a substantial passage in a piece), mostly in notes of the same time-value and mostly in conjunct motion (A89, bars 1–8).

Waltz, vals (Span.), **valse** (Fr.), **Waltzer** (Ger.). A triple-time dance of the 19th century that originated in the late 18th-century *Ländler* and *Deutsche* (B44). By the middle of the century the waltz had become the most popular ballroom dance throughout Europe. It was characterised by an on-beat accompaniment in which the lowest note (often the root of the chord) was sounded on the first beat of the bar followed by upper notes of the chord on beats two and three (C2). *EM 8.10.4.*

Weihnachtsmusik (Ger.). Christmas music. See A25, A44, A60, A68, A69, A91, A94, B15, B16.

Whip. Two flat pieces of wood hinged together at one end. When slapped together they produce a loud report like the cracking of a whip (C46 and C52). *EM 6.8.5.*

Whole consort. In 16th- and 17th-century England, an ensemble of solo instruments all of the same family. The whole consort heard on A61 comprises a treble viol, a tenor viol, two bass viols and a violone (double-bass viol).

Whole-note. Semibreve (o). See *Note* and the last bar of A52.

Whole tone. An interval of two semitones. The interval between the first and second degrees of a major scale is a whole tone (A25, the interval between *doh* and *ray*).

Whole-tone scale. A scale in which there is a tone between all adjacent notes. C21 opens with a complete whole-tone scale (G♯ down to A♭/G♯). The whole extract is built from the six pitch classes shown in the whole-tone scale printed above the first system of C21. Because there are no semitones there can be no hierachy of notes such as there is in a major or minor scale, so the establishment of tonality is all but impossible (though Debussy does give B♭ a sort of pre-eminence by the simple expedient of repeating it throughout the extract as a pedal). The only type of triad that can be constructed from the notes of a whole-tone scale are the augmented triads shown in bars 4, 6 and 8: these do nothing to help establish any tonal centre, in fact they detract from the anchoring effect of the pedal. *EM 2.7.2, 2.8, 5.3.2, 8.11.2.*

Wind band, wind section. A generic term for ensembles of wind instruments (with or without percussion) ranging from the 16th-century whole consort of loud winds (A33) and 18th-century *Harmoniemusik* (B40) to complete symphonic sections of woodwind and brass instruments (C27). The term encompasses military bands and symphonic bands but not brass bands.

Wind instruments. See *Brass instruments* and *Woodwind instruments*. Chords for varying combinations of wind instruments can be heard on C86.

Wind-cap instruments. Wind instruments in which a double reed is enclosed in a cap and so is not directly activated by the player's lips. The crumhorn is such an instrument (A35).

Wirbeltrommel (Ger.). Tenor drum (C43 and C53).

Wood blocks. Solid rectangular pieces of hardwood, partially hollowed out and usually beaten with rubber or plastic mallets (C51 and C53). There are several varieties including Chinese blocks. See *Percussion instruments. EM 6.8.5.*

Woodwind instruments. A group of wind

instruments that were originally made of wood and in which sound is generated by directing the player's breath at a sharp edge (directly in transverse flutes, indirectly in recorders), or by the vibrations of a single reed (clarinets) or double reed (oboes and bassoons). Examples include alto flute (C87), bass clarinet (C38), basset-horn (B40), bassoon (C77), clarinet (C79, in A, and C10, in D), contrabassoon (C31), cor anglais (C88, bars 3–5 and 9–10), crumhorn (A35), curtal (A60), flute (C76, bars 1–5), oboe (C78), oboe d'amore (B8), oboe da caccia (B8), piccolo (C76, bars 9–11), *Rauschpfeife* (A32), recorder (A60), saxophone (C38), shawm (A32).

Sustained woodwind chords can be heard on track C86 (the instrumentation in bar 3 includes flutes, oboes, a cor anglais, a bass clarinet, an alto saxophone, bassoons and contrabassoon).

Word-painting. The use of special musical effects to illustrate the meaning of particular words. In A31 the words 'de tous cotés' (on every side) are represented by the alternation of female and male voices. *EM 8.6.3.*

X

Xylophone (Eng. and Fr.), **Xylophon** (Ger.), **Xilofono** (It.). A tuned percussion instrument with a set of wooden bars arranged like a piano keyboard. These are struck with beaters and the resultant sound is amplified by tubular resonators beneath the keys. The approximate range of a modern xylophone is shown on the folded insert and a solo can be heard on track C8. *EM 6.8.7.*

Xylorimba, xylomarimba, marimba-xylophone. A xylophone (C8) with an extended range covering those of the xylophone and marimba (C90).

Z

Z. Abbreviation of F. B. Zimmerman's *Henry Purcell, 1659–1695: An Analytic Catalogue of his Music* (London, 1963). See A75–A80.

Zahl (pl. **Zähle**) (Ger.). The beats that can be counted in a bar (*zählen* means 'to count'). See *Tempo* and the three crotchet beats in A33, bar 1.

Zampogna (It.). Bagpipes with double reeds in all pipes and two chanters (A17).

Zanfonía (Span.). Hurdy-gurdy (A18).

Zarabanda (Span.). Sarabande (A88).

Zart (Ger.). Tender, delicate, soft, subdued. The performance direction at the head of C35 means 'very peaceful and delicate'.

Zauberoper (Ger.). Magic opera, a type of musical drama popular in Vienna in the late 18th century and the early 19th century. It was a cross between a pantomime and a fairy story that included spoken dialogue and songs. Mozart's *Die Zauberflöte* is a *Zauberoper* which, as B50 shows, transcended the normal musical limitations of the genre. *EM 8.9.5.*

Zimbalon (Ger.). Cimbalom (C41).

Zink (Ger.). Cornett (A58).

Zither. 1. A generic term for a category of string instruments including the cimbalom (C41), clavichord (B20), harpsichord (B17) and piano (C65). **2.** An Alpine folk instrument which, in its most familiar form. is box-shaped with four or five melody strings and 30 to 40 unstopped accompanimental strings stretched over a resonator. The player stops the melody strings with one hand and plucks the strings with a plectrum held in the other hand.

Zu 2, zu 3 (Ger.). **1.** Two or three instruments playing in unison (C82, bar 9 where 'a 2' = 'zu 2'). **2.** A section of instruments divided into two or three parts (C28, bar 6). See *A 2.*

Zukunftsmusik (Ger.). Music of the future, a nickname applied to the music of Wagner by contemporaries such as Spohr (B68). In fact some of Liszt's music is at least as futuristic as Wagner's (eg the quintal harmony of B73 and the quasi-atonal style of B74). *EM 8.10ff.*

Zweiunddreissigstel, Zweiunddreissigstelnote (Ger.). Demisemiquaver, thirty-second-note (B18, Variation 5, bar 7). See *Note*.

Zyklus (Ger.). Cycle. A *Liederzyklus* is a song cycle (such as Schubert's *Die schöne Müllerin* from which B57 is taken).

Elements of music

1:
Rhythm, metre and tempo

This chapter deals with those elements of music that have to do with the durations of notes, the patterns the listener notices in a couple of bars (rhythm) and the successions of strong and weak beats or pulses generated by these patterns (metre), and the speed of these beats (tempo). In order to understand the chapter it is also necessary to understand the terms for note-values (semibreve or whole-note, minim or half-note, crotchet or quarter-note, quaver or eighth-note, semiquaver or sixteenth-note, demisemiquaver or thirty-second-note and hemidemisemiquaver or sixty-fourth-note in descending order of magnitude). All of these terms can be found among the alphabetic entries in pages 1 to 188 of this volume. An immediate impression of how note-values relate to each other can be gained by listening to A17 (semibreves in the shawm part of bars 10–12 and minims in bar 13) and B18 (for all other note-values listed above).

1.1 Rhythm

A rhythm is a group of two or more sounds which form a pattern in time principally determined by their relative durations and loudness. Music cannot exist without rhythm. Even when the duration and loudness of a series of notes remains constant, the listener will still perceive a rhythmic pattern. This is evident in A87. The performance has been generated by a computer so that every note has exactly the same duration and dynamic level (such uniformity is very rare in live performances where there will usually be subtle differences in the lengths of notes). At the other extreme is music in which the rhythms are so complex or so free that they are impossible to notate with any degree of accuracy. In the plainsong on A4 it is obvious that notes with a dot after them are longer than most of the other notes in this introit, but the only way of accurately indicating their lengths would be to time them exactly with a stopwatch. This, of course, would be a futile exercise, since the rhythmic effect is one of the utmost flexibility, and no two performances will be rhythmically identical.

1.2 Accents

Accents or stresses are frequently caused by longer durations of notes These **agogic accents** are apparent in B10 where the first note is very short and the second much longer.

Another way in which a note can be accented is by increased loudness. Such **dynamic accents** can be heard clearly in the extract from a minuet by Mozart on B38. Those notes marked *f* ('forte', meaning loud) have dynamic accents while those marked *p* ('piano', meaning soft) are relatively unaccented.

A third type of accent often occurs when a note is higher or lower in pitch than most of the other notes in a melody or figuration, especially when that note is approached by a leap. This **tonic accent** will usually be felt more strongly on notes of high pitch than on notes of low pitch. In A87

Elements of music

there are strong tonic accents on the highest notes of the first and third groups of semiquavers and weaker tonic accents on the lowest notes of the second and fourth groups.

1.3 Metre

All of these **tonic accents** in A87 come on the first note of each group of four semiquavers, so implying a regular underlying crotchet pulse, while the alternating high and low tonic accents create a feeling of alternate strong and weak **beats**. In A87 these are marked – or – (strong) and u (weak). Thus the pattern strong–weak, strong–weak, strong–weak (like trochaic feet in poetry) is soon established.

In many types of music, harmony can also help determine metre. Whenever a new chord is used it tends to accentuate the beat at the point of change. In Bach's prelude the rate of change of the chords (the **harmonic rhythm**) is quite regular. A87 shows how the first four groups of semiquavers outline a chord consisting of the notes C, E♭ and G (reading from the bass up). The next four groups of semiquavers change to outline a different chord (C, F and A♭). The third set of four groups of semiquavers changes to outline a dissonant chord (C, F, A♭ and B♮), while the next group returns to the chord heard at the beginning of the Prelude. These chords are separated from each other by vertical lines which divide the music into bars, each containing four pulses of alternate strong and weak beats. So over and above the alternate strong and weak tonic accents there is an even stronger accent on the very first note of each bar caused by the change of harmony. Thus a pattern of accented beats or pulses emerges in this order: very strong (–), weak (u), strong (–), weak (u), and this pattern is repeated in every bar of A87. Because the repeating metrical pattern is of four beats' length the metre it establishes is known as **quadruple time** (indicated by the time signature $\frac{4}{4}$ in A87). It is sometimes impossible to tell by ear alone whether music has been notated in **duple time** (two beats per bar) or quadruple time because the metrical effect is often identical, but in this case the harmonic rhythm clearly establishes quadruple rather than duple metre.

1.4 Simple and compound metres

When the **beat** normally divides into two, four or eight shorter notes (or their equivalents), the music is said to be in **simple time**. In Bach's Prelude in C minor (A87) every beat divides into a group of four fast notes (semiquavers) and there are four beats in every bar, so the music can be described as being in simple quadruple time. In the minuet from Mozart's opera *Don Giovanni* (B41) the beats often divide into groups of two shorter notes (quavers) and there are three beats in every bar, so the music is in simple triple time (indicated by the time signature $\frac{3}{4}$ in B41).

These simple metres contrast sharply with compound metres. Here the beat normally divides into three, six or twelve shorter notes (or their equivalents), the beat itself being a dotted note of some sort. In the first extract from the sonata by Corelli on A70 the fastest notes (the quavers) are grouped in threes, each group being of the same duration as the dotted crotchet beat. The beats themselves are alternately strong and weak, so the music is said to be in compound duple time (indicated by the time signature $\frac{6}{8}$). Of course many other rhythms are possible in **compound**

1: Rhythm, metre and tempo

time, some of which can be heard in the other extracts from the sonata (A71–A74). But no matter how complicated the rhythms of the individual melodies are, the underlying characteristic swing of compound time prevails throughout all of these tracks.

1.5 Complex metres

Duple time and triple time (whether simple or compound) are the basic metres from which more complex metres can be constructed. In the first movement of Holst's *Planets* Suite (C36) five-beat bars are constructed from alternating triple time and duple time ($\underline{1}$ 2 3 $\underline{4}$ 5 – indicated by the time signature $\frac{5}{4}$). The accented first beat is emphasised by a triplet of quavers, and the accented fourth beat is emphasised by a group of two quavers. In the 'Dance in Bulgarian Rhythm No. 6' from Bartók's *Mikrokosmos* (C66) very fast quavers are grouped in repeating patterns of 3+3+2 ($\underline{1}$ 2 3 $\underline{4}$ 5 6 $\underline{7}$ 8 – like two bars of triple time joined to one bar of duple time). Such systematic use of asymmetric groupings of short notes within each bar is sometimes called additive metre (or **additive rhythm** when this asymmetry is only used for a few bars).

1.6 Characteristic rhythms

There are innumerable different types of rhythm in both simple and compound metres, but there are some which are so characteristic that they merit special attention.

1.6.1 Dotted rhythms

Some groups of long and short notes are called dotted rhythms because they are notated with a dot after one of the notes in the rhythmic group. This has the effect of making that note half as long again as it would be without the dot. In order to fit within the beat the other note of the pair has to be much shorter than the dotted note, for instance a quaver after a dotted crotchet, or a semiquaver after a dotted quaver. In both of these dotted rhythms the ratio of the longer to the shorter note is 3:1. Dotted rhythms of both of these types can be heard in the opening bars of the overture to Purcell's opera *Dido and Aeneas* (x and y in A76).

1.6.2 Double-dotted rhythms

Although A76 shows what Purcell wrote, contemporary performance practice decreed that, in this stylistic context, the second note of dotted-crotchet–quaver groups should be played shorter than written. Consequently the first note has to be longer. One way of achieving this is **overdotting**, in which the performer effectively adds a second dot to make the crotchet not half as long again but three quarters as long again as without the dots. A comparison of x in A76, with x^1 in A77 will reveal that the ratio of the duration of the longer to the shorter notes is 3:1 in the performance on A76 and 7:1 in the performance on A77. From the late 17th century onwards there are isolated instances of composers explicitly using double dotting, but most used single dots and relied on accepted conventions to achieve this rhythmic effect in appropriate contexts.

An alternative way of shortening the second note of a dotted rhythm is to replace the second of the two dots with a silence (indicated by a semiquaver rest in x^2 of A78). This ***silence d'articulation*** imparts an

Elements of music

even more forceful and jerky rhythmic effect than over-dotting, as A78 reveals.

1.6.3 Reversed dotting

Sometimes the dotted note and the shorter note are reversed so that the shorter note falls on the beat. This sort of rhythm is known as a **Scotch snap** (because it is a feature of some Scottish folk music) or a **Lombard rhythm** (because it features in much 17th-century northern-Italian music). After the three double-dotted groups of A79 there are two Scotch snaps (marked z) which can be clearly heard at the end of the corresponding track.

The whole overture to *Dido and Aeneas* is recorded on A80. In the slow section with which it begins normal dotted rhythms (dotted quaver plus semiquaver), over-dotted rhythms (double-dotted crotchet plus semiquaver) and Lombard rhythms (semiquaver plus dotted quaver) can be distinguished in all four string parts. A80 is a skeleton score of the whole movement.

Lombard rhythms are a striking feature of Hungarian folk music and are prominent in the folk-influenced styles of Bartók and Kodály. They can be heard in bars 1–2, 7–8 and 10 of C41 (where they are identified by horizontal brackets).

1.6.4 *Notes inégales*

In much late 17th- and early 18th-century French or French-style music it was customary in some contexts to play a written pair of even quavers (***croches égales***) unevenly as a long note followed by a shorter note (or vice versa in Lombard rhythms). The conventions governing the use of such ***notes inégales*** are too complex to consider here. Much depended (and still depends) upon the judgement of the individual performer. In bars 38–39 of A84 de la Guerre wrote even quavers, but when these bars are repeated (bars 42–43) the harpsichordist plays the same melody unevenly. The recording of this rondeau was made specially to demonstrate certain features (such as *notes inégales*). In a normal performance the principles of inequality would be observed consistently throughout the piece. This is the case in the performance of an allemande by Rameau recorded on B17. Here every semiquaver group that moves by step is played unequally, with ***notes égales*** (even semiquavers) being reserved for passages such as bars 22–23.

1.6.5 Jazz quavers

The same sort of principles apply in the performance of jazz quavers where short notes may be '**swung**' (played unevenly) to a greater or lesser extent depending upon the style of jazz, its prevailing mood and the good taste of the performer. Twentieth-century composers of art music sometimes wrote such swung rhythms, often as a deliberate parody of jazz styles. This is the case in C38.

1.7 Metrical disruptions

When normally unaccented beats are stressed, or when off-beat notes are accented the smooth flow of weak- and strong-beat patterns can be disturbed by the phenomena described below.

1:: Rhythm, metre and tempo

1.7.1 Syncopation

When the normal metrical pattern of strong and weak beats is disturbed by off-beat accents, or by accents on weak beats, the music is said to be syncopated. It can happen by simply applying a **dynamic accent** to a beat of the bar that would normally be unaccented. This is the case in bars 3–8 of B38, in which Mozart's alternating dynamic marks introduce **accents** on the normally unstressed second and third beats of the bar. The syncopation in this passage contrasts strongly with the rest of the extract (which contains no syncopation at all). An example of isolated syncopation occurs in the fourth bar of C38 where a loud stroke on the rim of the snare drum falls on the normally weak fourth beat of the bar. A similar effect is produced in bar 6 where the bass clarinettist begins a phrase with a dynamic accent on the normally unstressed second beat of the bar. In this case the syncopated effect is strengthened by an **agogic accent** (caused by the preceding rest and the length of the accented note) and a **tonic accent** (caused by the high pitch of this note in relation to the notes which precede it).

Another type of syncopation occurs when a note is strongly articulated off the beat. This happens in the first extract from the first movement of Beethoven's Piano Sonata Op. 10 No. 2 (B51) in which the last quavers of bars 2–6 (marked sf) are accented. The same effect can be heard in bar 4 of Debussy's 'Golliwogg's Cakewalk' (C20) in which a chord is articulated off the beat with a strong dynamic accent (similarly in bars 12 and 24). The cakewalk is a type of **ragtime** dance that was characterised by another type of syncopated rhythm which occurs within a single beat. This is marked x at the start of C20 and it dominates the whole of the extract.

Syncopation can occur more subtly when a relatively long note is sustained from an off-beat to the following strong beat, even though there is no dynamic accent. This is the case in B52, where the notes marked with a cross are syncopated. In B53 syncopations are particularly obvious on the notes marked sf since they combine the articulation of off-beat notes with dynamic accents (sf = *sforzando*, a sudden strong dynamic accent).

When two or more contrapuntal parts are syncopated at different points the rhythmic effect can be delightfully complex. In the last phrase of each verse of A24 (bars 33^3–36) the syncopated off-beat notes marked with asterisks are particularly prominent after the straightforward triple metre of the rest of the verse.

1.7.2 Hemiola

A special type of **syncopation** called a hemiola was common in the baroque era, especially at cadences. It occurs when music in a compound duple metre (such as $^6_8$ time) is interrupted by a bar of simple triple time (such as $^3_4$ time). Thus the accentuation of the quavers changes from <u>1</u> 2 3 <u>4</u> 5 6 to <u>1</u> 2 <u>3</u> 4 <u>5</u> 6. A hemiola of this sort can be heard at the end of A71: the brackets in the corresponding example show how the metre effectively changes from compound duple time to simple triple time, and the extra stave shows an alternative method of notating the hemiola in both treble and bass parts. The same effect can be heard in bars 8–9 of C1, but this time the music is notated in simple triple metre, the hemiola being effectively three bars of $^2_4$ time superimposed on the surrounding $^3_4$ time.

Elements of music

1.8 Triplets and duplets

In **simple time** the beat usually divides into groups of two, four or eight shorter notes. Sometimes, however, the beat, or a subdivision of the beat, may be divided into groups of three notes which are all shortened to fit into the time usually taken by two notes of the same type (for instance, a group of three 'short' semiquavers played in the time of two 'normal' semiquavers). These triplets can be seen in bars 5, 6 and 8 of B54, each of them fitted into the time taken by two of the 'normal' semiquavers in the first four bars.

In **compound time** the beat usually divides into groups of three, six or twelve shorter notes. The beat may be divided into groups of two notes, each lengthened to fit into the time normally taken by three notes of the same type (for instance, two 'long' quavers played in the time of three 'normal' quavers). These duplets can be heard in the extract from Tchaikovsky's fifth symphony on C4. Throbbing strings play 'normal' three-quaver groups in compound quadruple metre ($\frac{12}{8}$ time) against which the duplets of bars 4–5 can be clearly distinguished.

It should be noted here that the beat can divide into more complex groups such as the **quintuplets** and the sextuplets in simple time in bars 2–4 of B64 or the **quadruplet** in compound time in bar 4 of C90.

1.9 Polyrhythms

As well as illustrating duplets, bars 4–5 of C4 also illustrate polyrhythm, the superimposition of two or more conflicting rhythms (in this case groups of three quavers in compound time in the strings against the duplets of the oboe and horn solos). A more complex example of a polyrhythmic **texture** occurs at the start of the second movement of Debussy's string quartet. C12 consists of a two-bar ostinato in $\frac{6}{8}$ time played on the viola. In the third bar it is joined by the second violin playing a simple one-bar ostinato of even quavers. A third ostinato of pizzicato chords and duplets is played by the cello on C13. Finally the first violin plays a melody which consists of two four-bar phrases containing more duplets (C14). When the ostinati of the second violin and cello are played together (C15) rhythmic conflict can be heard on the second beat of every one of the four bars. Similar rhythmic conflicts can be heard when the two phrases of the first violin are combined with the viola ostinato (C16). When all four instruments play simultaneously (C17) each of them contributes its own distinctive rhythms to a complex polyrhythmic texture.

1.10 Cross-rhythms

Some musicians use the term cross-rhythm in a broad sense to cover all types of **polyrhythm**, including the types of rhythmic conflict described in the previous paragraph. However, most reserve this term for rhythmic displacements which contradict the normal accentuation of the prevailing metre of the music. In this sense the most familiar type of cross-rhythm is the hemiola (see 1.7.2) in which simple triple time displaces compound duple time for a bar or two (as happens in the cadence at the end of A71). Bars 21–24 and 29–31 of C2 show similar short-lived cross-rhythmic passages in which groups of three quavers (not triplets) conflict with the triple metre of most of the rest of the waltz.

1: Rhythm, metre and tempo

1.10.1 Complex cross-rhythms

More complex examples of cross-rhythms are common in nineteenth-century music. B79 shows a passage from an intermezzo by Brahms in which the chords in bars 1–20 are shown in simplified form. Brahms wrote the whole piece in simple triple metre ($\frac{3}{4}$ time), and this is what is heard in the first eight bars of B79. But from bar 8 Brahms begins to phrase his melody across the barlines. The beginning of each of these phrase marks coincides with a change of chord and together they bring about the series of metrical changes shown on the lower staves in bars 8–15. Even after triple time has been regained (bars 17–20) the way the harmony changes in bar 21 brings about another metrical disturbance in which a bar of compound duple time effectively replaces triple time. Similar cross-rhythms occur in bars 30–37. In these bars Brahms' notation is unaltered, but time signatures beneath the staves show that the cross-rhythms that were heard in bars 9–17 can also be heard in these bars.

1.10.2 Cross-phrasing

In bars 8–15 and 30–37 of B79 Brahms draws his phrase marks across the barlines and this cross-phrasing coincides with harmonic rhythms that create cross-rhythms (see 1.10.1). But even without obvious chord changes cross-phrasing can create cross-rhythm. From the end of bar 8 of C64 the phrase marks of the right-hand part cross the barlines so that the quavers are phrased first in a group of four notes, then in three groups of three notes. These three-note phrases are particularly noticeable because each group consists of the same three pitches, thus forming a short ostinato pattern which runs against the metre of the rest of this extract. In the left-hand part of bars 9–10 there is a different ostinato, this time consisting of four quavers phrased across the barlines. Heard together the two sets of cross-phrasing (one effectively in $\frac{3}{8}$ time, the other in $\frac{2}{4}$) conflict with each other as well as with the metre of the whole extract.

1.11 Polymetre

Perhaps the most complex type of rhythmic combination is polymetre. This, as the name suggests, is the superimposition of two or more layers of music, each layer being in a different metre. It can be found quite frequently in twentieth-century music, but one of the most complex yet clear examples occurs in Mozart's opera *Don Giovanni*. At a ball in a stately home there are bands in three rooms, each providing music for a different dance. In the ballroom at the front of the stage the first band plays a minuet in fairly slow $\frac{3}{4}$ time (B41 and B42). In a back room letting off the ballroom a second orchestra plays a country dance. The speed of the pulse is the same as that of the minuet, but the metre is $\frac{2}{4}$ time (B43). When, as happens in the opera, these two dances are combined, three bars of the country dance are played in the time of two bars of the minuet. Thus the strong beats coincide at the start, but then the strong first beat of the second bar of the country dance falls on the weak third beat of the minuet, while the strong first beat of the third bar of the country dance falls on the weak second beat of the minuet. This can be represented diagrammatically:

    Minuet: <u>1</u> 2 3 <u>1</u> 2 3 <u>1</u> 2 3
    Country dance: <u>1</u> 2 <u>1</u> 2 <u>1</u> 2

Elements of music

In another back room letting off the ballroom a third orchestra plays a *Deutsche* or German dance in fast $\frac{3}{8}$ time (B44). When all three dances are combined (B45) every beat of the minuet and country dance equals one bar of the German dance, thus creating rhythmic conflict between the simple-time two-quaver groups of the minuet and country dances and the compound-time groups of the German dance.

1.12 Rhythmic modes

The six rhythmic modes represent the most important development in musical **notation** in the second half of the twelfth century. They enabled thirteenth-century composers to set down precise note-values in six rhythmic patterns by using just two types of note, the **long** and the **breve** (shown beneath bars 7–10 and 19–20 in A13). The precise duration of each of these notes was determined by its position in one of the rhythmic patterns that constituted a **mode**. Thus in Mode 6 (shown at the foot of A10) a pattern of three breves meant three equal short notes (usually rendered as a group of three quavers in compound time in modern notation), but in Mode 3 (a long and two breves) the second breve is twice as long as the first breve (as shown in modern notation at the foot of A10). Most authorities agree that there is an underlying compound duple metre in thirteenth-century music that is best represented in $\frac{6}{8}$ time because the underlying beat divides into three shorter notes (Mode 6) or two unequal shorter notes that together last as long as the three shorter notes (Mode 3). Another method of representing modal rhythms in modern notation is shown in A19. Here the long is represented by a dotted minim in simple triple time (instead of the dotted crotchet used in A10), with the short and long breve represented by a crotchet and a minim respectively (instead of the quaver and crotchet used in A10). But whatever modern notational system is used, the most significant aspect of modal rhythm for the listener is the fact that the repeating rhythmic patterns of the modes strongly influenced the style of music of the **Ars Antiqua**. They provided a metrical and rhythmic framework that ensured musical coherence. But coherence was achieved at the expense of variety. If the dancing rhythms of A10 were to be extended to twice the length of this clausula the constant repetitions of Mode 3 and Mode 6 rhythms would become unbearably monotonous. It was perhaps for this reason that composers in the next century sought and found more flexible and varied rhythmic styles.

1.13 Isorhythm

The late medieval technique of isorhythm is different from all of the other rhythms that have been discussed in this chapter in that, because it extends over such a long time-scale, it is difficult to perceive by ear alone. It also differs in being a structural device which enabled composers to write extended polyphonic movements. The technique involved the superimposition of a repeating rhythmic pattern called a **talea** on the melodic line of one or more voice parts. Most commonly isorhythm was applied to a **cantus prius factus** (a pre-existing melody, such as a monophonic chant). This was sung as a **cantus firmus** in the tenor part with the predetermined note-values of the *talea* repeated as often as necessary. In the Benedictus from Machaut's *Messe de Nostre Dame* (A21) the *cantus prius factus* is the plainsong Benedictus shown in A20. With the exception of only one note, every pitch in the plainsong melody is replicated in Machaut's isorhythmic tenor part (shown beneath the plainsong). Talea I is exactly the same as Talea II because of the repeat in the original plainsong melody. In A21 the tenor part can be distinguished from the bass part by the direction of the stems (pointing upwards for tenors and downwards for basses) and by the lines joining the notes of the *cantus firmus*.

1.14 Articulation

Any of the rhythms discussed so far can be modified by the way in which individual notes are articulated (the manner in which they are attacked and quitted). The two most obvious types of articulation are illustrated in B41. The melody of this minuet features two prominent motifs, the first consisting of repeated notes (x), the second a dotted rhythm (y). The repeated notes are always played in a very detached manner (**staccato**) and these contrast with the smooth performance of the dotted rhythms (**legato**). When either of these types of articulation is required the abbreviations 'stacc.' or 'leg.' might be printed in the music; alternatively dots above or below the notes may be used to indicate staccato articulation, and **slurs** (curved lines) may be used above or below notes which are to be played legato.

1.15 Tempo

The final rhythmic consideration is the speed or tempo of the music. This has very little to do with the type of note-values used to represent various rhythms since a quaver can be used to represent a slow **beat** (B68), and a minim can represent a fast beat (B21). So tempo is determined by the speed of the beat, not the particular note-value the composer chooses to represent it. An objective measurement of tempo is the number of beats per minute. Since the invention of the metronome early in the nineteenth century composers have been able to show the precise tempo they require. For instance, at the start of C64 Bartók's metronome mark indicates that he intends there to be 96 crotchet beats per minute. But metronome marks were not an option for composers working before the nineteenth century and many later composers chose not to make use of them. Instead the speed of the music was often approximately indicated by tempo marks, generally in Italian but sometimes in the native language of the composer. Some of the more common ones are given below, but it should be noted that the meaning of Italian tempo marks varies from one historical period to another. Indeed, some early composers used these terms to indicate the style of the music rather than just its tempo.

Elements of music

Tempo markings

The following are some of the most common tempo marks arranged in ascending order of **tempo** (but note that some of them indicate style as well as speed, and some would dispute the order given here):

Grave	solemnly	A81
Lento	slow	C85
Adagio	slow	B5
Larghetto	fairly slow, broadly	A39
Andante	slowly moving	B19
Andantino	moderately slow	B67
Moderato	moderate	B66
Allegretto	moderately fast	B38
Allegro	fast, joyful	C60
Presto	very fast	B28

Terms like these can be moderated by words such as:

Assai	much or rather	B30 (Largo assai)
		B50 (Allegro assai)
Giusto	right or precise	C20 (Allegro giusto)
Molto	very	C9 (Molto vivace)
Non troppo	not too much	B78 (Andante non troppo)
Più	more	B79, bar 38 (più lento)
Poco	a little	B32 (Poco adagio cantabile)
		C2 (Poco allegro)
Quasi	almost	B73 (Allegro vivace, quasi Presto)
Vivace	vivacious	B37 (Allegro vivace)

Tempi can also be indicated by reference to types of dance that the composer thinks might already be familiar:

Tempo di menuetto	at the speed of a minuet B41
Tempo di trepak	at the speed of a trepak C5

Tempo markings are sometimes allied to an expression marking that can influence the performer in choosing an appropriate tempo, for instance:

Amoroso	amorous	C29 (Andante amoroso)
Appassionato	passionate	C85, bar 8 (Andante appassionato)
Grazioso	graceful	C1 (Allegretto grazioso)
Scherzando	jokingly	C77 (Allegretto scherzando)
Teneramente	tenderly	B79 (Andante teneramente)

1: Rhythm, metre and tempo

Tempo markings (contd)

Performance markings indicating changes of tempo include:

Accelerando (accel.)	getting faster	C82, bars 1–8
Allargando (allarg.)	becoming slower (and louder)	C97, bars 15
A tempo (Tempo I)	original tempo	B67, bar 8
Calando	becoming slower (and softer)	C59, bars 23–24
Meno mosso	slower	C82, bar 69
Rallentando (rall.)	gradually slowing down	C85, bar 24
Ritardando (ritard.)	gradually slowing down	C96, bars 33–35
Ritenuto (rit.)	immediately slowing down	B67, bar 7
Rubato	flexible rhythm and tempo	C41 (Andante, poco rubato)
Slentando	slowing down	B65, bars 40–43
Stretto	getting faster	B65, bars 29–32

Any of the above tempo directions could, of course, be expressed in languages other than Italian. Purcell uses English (A80). French and German composers are more likely to use their own languages. The following are among the most common tempo markings to be found in French scores:

Animé	animated, moderately fast	C18(a)
Gaiement	lively	C32
Lent	slow	C19
Modéré	moderate	C31
Mouvement de valse	waltz tempo	C31
Retenu	immediately slowing down	C19
Vif	fast, lively	C18(b)

These tempo markings may be modified by:

Assez	rather	C18(b) (Assez vif)
Bien	very (in this context)	C12 (bien rythmé)
Extrèmement	extremely, exceedingly	C55 (Extrèmement lent)
Très	very	C19 (Très lent)

The following are among the most common tempo markings to be found in German scores:

Gemächlich	comfortably slow	C17
Langsam (Sehr langsam)	slow (very slow)	B58
Mässig	moderate, moderately	B57
Ruhig	peaceful, and therefore slow	C35
Schwer	heavy, ponderous	C27

Any of these tempi can be modified by:
a) gradually speeding up ('accelerando' or 'accel.', as in bar 1 of C82)
b) gradually slowing down ('rallentando' or 'rall.', 'ritardando' or 'rit.', as in bars 5–7 of B75)
c) a sequential combination of both at the discretion of the performer ('rubato', C40)
d) a temporary suspension of the pulse when the music pauses on a sustained note (C76, bar 5) or on a rest (B68, bars 11, 13 and 14).

When the original tempo is to be resumed after a change of speed the music is marked 'A tempo' or 'Tempo I' (C76, end of bar 5).

2:
Tonality, modality and atonality

Tonality is the manner in which a limited number of pitch classes relate to each other, particularly the manner in which a pre-eminent pitch (called the tonic or final) relates to all other pitches heard in a passage of music.

In its narrowest sense tonality refers to music that employs seven pitch classes that can be arranged to form a diatonic scale such as that outlined by Handel's theme at the start of B18. In this case the tonic is G♮, the note on which the scale begins (1) and ends (8). G is also the pitch on which Variation 5 begins and ends. Because of the pre-eminence of this pitch the music is said to be in the key of G major.

A82 shows another melody in which G is again the tonic, but here the relationships between this pitch and the other six pitches are not the same as they are in Handel's gavotte (because both E and B have been flattened by a semitone). Instead of major tonality (B18), minor tonality prevails in A82 so the melody is said to be in the key of G minor. The fact that A84 begins in G minor does not preclude the possibility of a change of tonality. This what happens in bar 11 where major tonality based on B♭ is established. Nevertheless G minor is clearly the principal tonal centre of the gavotte, and, as expected, the whole piece ends in this key.

Major/minor tonality of the types described above dominated western music from the late seventeenth century to the early twentieth century (and, in some styles, through to the present day). For music of this period the term tonality is sometimes used synonymously with key (one may speak of the G-major tonality of B18 and the G-minor tonality of A82). But similar principles underlie the earliest western music, especially the Gregorian chant of the western Catholic Church. Like A84 and B18 the melody of A4 is clearly dominated by a pre-eminent G♮. Phrase 1 (*Ad te levavi*) and 11 (*non confundentur*) begin and end on this pitch. Phrases 2 (*animam meam*), 8 (*inimici mei*), 10 (*qui te exspectant*) and 12 (*Vias tuas, Domine, demonstra mihi*) begin on G. Phrases 5 (*non erubescam*), 7 (*irrideant me*) and 9 (*etenim universi*) end on G. Finally, the whole introit comes to rest on this pitch. In modal music of this type the pre-eminent pitch on which the plainsong ends is called the final (or *finalis*), but it clearly relates to the other six pitch classes in much the same way as the tonic does in later musical styles. The same is true of most modal melodies, and it is for this reason that modality is discussed alongside tonality in this chapter.

Melodies with fewer pitch classes than the major, minor or modal music discussed above can also suggest tonal centres, but they are usually more ambiguous. Thus the same collection of five pitch classes (G, A, B, D and E) suggests G major in C60 and a modal E minor in C61. The impression of music with two potential tonal centres is stronger when these phrases are heard in the context of the first 8 bars of C63. In fact this tonal ambiguity is only resolved when the music comes to rest on an E in the last bar.

Music ranging from the tonally ambiguous pentatonicism of C63 to the absolute atonality of C40 form important strands in this chapter, but to understand tonality, modality and atonality properly it will first be necessary to study a number of the more basic elements of music.

2: Tonality, modality and atonality

2.1 Pitch

When men and women sing the same tune together they are most often singing each note of that tune an **octave** apart. This can be heard in the first 11 bars of A26 (in the corresponding example note that the figure 8 beneath the treble clefs indicates that the male voices are singing an octave below the females). Even when a melody is marked '**unison** voices' (A14) a choir of mixed voices will actually sing the melody in octaves. This equivalence of notes an octave apart is so universally recognised that notes one or more octaves apart are designated by the same letter name: notes with the same letter name are said to belong to the same pitch class.

On the other hand, notes that really do have the same absolute pitch can be notated differently. For example C♭ and B♮ are **enharmonic** notations of the same pitch, as are D♭ and C♯ (see the boxes labelled 'chord 1' and 'chord 2' on the extra stave beneath bar 1 of C88). Such octave and enharmonic equivalence will be taken for granted throughout this chapter. It should be noted, however, that these remarks only apply to the modern western system of tuning, in which all semitones are exactly the same. This is the type of tuning, known as **equal temperament**, which is now almost universally used on modern keyboard instruments. There are other older types of tuning in which enharmonic notes are not exactly the same, but today these are only used by ensembles that include keyboards predating equal temperament (or reproductions of such instruments), or in contemporary microtonal music using effects such as the quarter tones in bars 6 and 8–10 of C70.

2.2 Intervals

An interval is the distance between two pitches. A **melodic interval** is formed between two notes of different pitch sounded successively, and a **harmonic interval** is formed between two notes of different pitch sounded simultaneously. Intervals can be described very precisely. For example, if the interval of an octave at the start of A26 were to be played on two organ pipes, the lower note would require a pipe twice as long as that needed for the upper note. Similarly the open A string of a violin vibrating along its whole length will sound an octave lower than the same string stopped so that only half of it vibrates. These principles apply to all instruments capable of producing precise pitches. Thus the relationship of the two notes which form the interval of an octave can be designated by the ratio 2:1. Although all musical intervals can be identified by mathematical ratios, musicians identify them by a range of terms that tell more about the musical function of each interval than can be expressed by numbers.

2.2.1 Tones and semitones

An octave divides into 12 equal semitones. These are the smallest intervals used in most western music and correspond with any two adjacent notes on a keyboard (including both 'black' and 'white' notes). The interval between the two notes forming a pair of notes labelled x in bars 8–25 of C85 is a semitone.

Intervals greater than a semitone can be computed by counting the number of semitones between the two notes of each interval. Thus if C–D♭ is a semitone then C–D♮ is a tone (that is, two superimposed semitones,

Elements of music

C–D♭ and D♭–D♮). The musical effect of tones may be judged by listening to C21 in which the interval between each successive melody note is a tone.

2.2.2 Perfect intervals

These bare-sounding intervals are those which were first used to form chords. In bars 1–10 of A26 female and male voices are singing in octaves. It is perhaps because the sound of these octaves is so agreeable that these intervals became known as **perfect octaves**. To medieval ears the sound of **perfect 5ths and 4ths** were similarly agreeable (or, in technical terms, consonant). In A7(a) the melody of the first phrase of A6 is sung by two voices a perfect 5th apart, so forming a succession of two-note chords. In A7(b) the second phrase of A6 is again sung in perfect 5ths (by the two inner parts), but this time both voices are doubled at the octave (the *vox principalis* at the octave below, the *vox organalis* at the octave above). The result is a succession of **chords** containing not only perfect octaves and 5ths, but also perfect 4ths (between the two voices on the treble stave and also between the two voices on the bass stave). These perfect intervals were still regarded as the most agreeably consonant of intervals in the early thirteenth century, as A10 shows. In this clausula there is a perfect interval at the beginning of every bar except the last (and the dissonant effect here soon dissipates as the upper part moves up to form a perfect octave with the lower voice).

The effect of these perfect intervals in a melodic context can be heard on track A26 (identified in the corresponding music example).

2.2.3 Major and minor intervals

Major and **minor 2nds** are, for our present purposes, the same as tones and semitones respectively. They have been discussed in 2.2.1 above. To a greater or lesser extent musical contexts will modify the effect of all intervals, but when one type of interval is repeated several times within a short passage it tends to assert its individual character quite clearly. This is evident when the opening bars of Palestrina's Kyrie (A52) are compared with the extract from Brahms' Op. 5 sonata (B75). In the Kyrie the **minor 3rds** at the start of all four vocal parts set the mood for the rest of the extract. In the sonata, **major 3rds** (F and D♭) at the ends of all three phrases help determine the peaceful mood of the whole extract.

The languishing mood of the prelude to Wagner's *Tristan und Isolde* (B68) is established in the first few notes by the rising interval of a minor 6th. This creates tension which seeks the **resolution** which comes when the upper note of the interval (F♮) resolves down a semitone to E♮. Normally a rising **major 6th** would not create as much tension or need for resolution as a rising **minor 7th**. But in the chromatic context of B68 the rising major 6ths at the start of the second and third phrases (bars 4–5 and 8–9) have exactly the same effect as the rising **minor 6th** at the start of the first phrase. In C4 falling major 6ths can be heard at the start of the oboe melody (bars 2 and 3) and in the clarinet solo (bar 7) and bassoon solo (bar 8). A prominent falling minor 6th can be heard in the vocal part of A75 (bars 9–10).

To an even greater extent than a minor 6th, a minor 7th demands a downward resolution, but a **major 7th** seeks resolution by moving up to a consonant note. This is the case in Bach's gigue from his third cello suite

2: Tonality, modality and atonality

(A90). In bars 25 and 27 the F♯s at the top of both minor 7ths resolve down to the E♮s on the second beat of the bar. In the next two bars the F♯s at the top of both major 7ths resolve up to G♮s. A prominent falling minor 7th can be heard at the start of the vocal part of Purcell's song *O Solitude* (A75).

2.2.4 Tritone

The tritone, known as ***diabolus in musica*** (the devil in music), was an interval which was scrupulously avoided in medieval and renaissance vocal melodies because among other things it is so difficult to sing. But in later music it was frequently used for its bitter-sweet effect (A75, bars 7–8). As its name implies the tritone spans an interval of three tones and comes in two main varieties, the **augmented 4th** and the **diminished 5th**. In isolation the only difference between the two is the way they are notated, but in context they behave differently. As a chord or part of a chord the augmented 4th tends to resolve outwards, the top note rising as the lower note falls to a consonance. The effect can be heard in bars 38–39 of B40, in which the augmented 4ths are marked T (for tritone), and the resolutions to consonant minor 6ths are marked R (for resolution).

The second type of tritone, the diminished 5th, tends to resolve inwards, the lower note rising as the upper note falls to form a concord. At the end of the first bar of B5 the two viole d'amore form the interval of a diminished 5th (T) that is held over the barline before the A♭ resolves down a semitone and the D♮ resolves up a semitone to form a concordant major 3rd (R). At the end of the aria the same notes are played by the viole d'amore, but this time the intervals are inverted to form an augmented 4th (T) resolving to a minor 6th (R).

2.2.5 Augmented 2nd and minor 3rd

As with the two versions of the tritone there is no difference in the sound of a minor 3rd and an augmented 2nd when they are played in isolation. The same is true of the major 3rd/diminished 4th, major 6th/diminished 7th, and the augmented 6th/minor 7th. But when they are played in context they differ from each other to an even greater degree than do the two types of tritone. The different notation of these chords has something to do with the logic of written music, but on a deeper level it has more to do with the way intervals function as sounds in the context of particular melodies or chords.

The minor 3rds (C–A–C or F–D–F) at the beginning of each vocal part in Palestrina's *Missa Iste confessor* (A52) sound completely different from the oft-repeated augmented 2nds (F–G♯) in Bartók's *Romanian Dance* No. 3 (C56). Both intervals span three semitones, yet they sound completely different because the minor 3rds are heard in the context of modal melodies, whereas the augmented 2nds are heard in the context of a segment of a Gypsy scale on D.

2.2.6 Major 3rd and diminished 4th

The major 3rd and diminished 4th both span four semitones, yet the major 3rds at the ends of all three phrases of B75 sound quite different from the diminished 4th at the end of A79. The reason is that the major 3rds in Brahms's sonata are heard in the context of music based on a major scale, while the diminished 4th in Purcell's overture is heard in the context of music based on a minor scale.

Elements of music

2.2.7 Augmented 6th and minor 7th

The augmented 6th and minor 7th both span ten semitones. In context a minor 7th forms a dissonance which sounds as though it needs to resolve to a consonance. The first two vocal notes in B5 form a minor 7th which is resolved when the A♭ falls to the G♮. This minor 7th contrasts strongly with the augmented 6ths in B9, which, though spanning the same interval of ten semitones as the minor 7th, resolve outwards: the C♮ falling a semitone to B♮, and the A♯ rising a semitone to B♮ in bars 2–3 (similarly in bars 7–8). The resolution of this interval to a perfect octave clinches the expanding intervals of the wedge-shaped subject from which this fugue derives its nickname, the 'Wedge Fugue'.

2.2.8 Major 6th and diminished 7th

Both of these intervals span nine semitones, but in context they sound quite different from each other. The repeated major 6ths in Bartók's piano piece in C62 need no resolution, but the diminished 7ths in bar 2 of A96 beg for the resolution that comes in the next bar (E♭ resolving down a semitone to D♮, and F♯ resolving up a semitone to G♮).

As with all the other pairs of intervals discussed in 2.2.4–2.2.7, the way these two intervals behave is both a result of and an influence on their context. On the one hand the role of the major 6ths in the extract from the piano piece is passive – they initiate no change of key or mood. On the other hand the diminished 7ths in A96 are dramatic in themselves (because they are dissonant), and in the context of the whole piece they initiate radical changes to the harmonic scheme that is the very core of the chaconne (compare A96 with the theme heard at the start of A95).

2.2.9 Compound intervals

Compound intervals are those that span more than an octave. A compound major 2nd is the same as a major 9th (14 semitones), a compound minor 3rd is the same as a minor 10th (15 semitones), a compound perfect 4th is equivalent to a perfect 11th (17 semitones), and so on. As two-note chords, compound intervals behave in almost the same ways as simple intervals. For example, the perfect 5th between the theorbo and soprano on the first beat of bar 4 of Purcell's song *O Solitude* (A75) functions in exactly the same way as the compound perfect 5th on the second beat of the bar. However, compound melodic intervals sound much more athletic than simple intervals, as a comparison of the intervals in bars 21–22 of A90 with those in bars 30–31 will reveal. In the first set of bars the intervals are major 2nds, major 3rds and perfect 4ths. In the second passage the intervals are compound major 2nds (or major 9ths), compound major 3rds (or major 10ths) and a compound perfect 4th (or perfect 11th).

2.3 Scales and tonality

Scales are theoretical constructs derived from the common practice of composers working within a given style. Nevertheless it is true that most composers are fairly consistent in their use of collections of notes which can be arranged into series corresponding with one or more types of scale. It is also true that the types of scale used and the extent to which the composer limits himself to their constituent notes (or deviates from them) are among the most important factors determining the styles of most types of music.

2: Tonality, modality and atonality

2.3.1 Music in major keys

Listening to B38 one cannot fail to notice how the whole phrase seems to gravitate towards the last note. If the recording is cut short at any point before this note it will be evident that the music has not reached its goal: only with the arrival of the G♮ at the end of the extract is there a sense of completion. This is the essence of **tonality**. It is a hierarchy of pitches which, to greater or lesser extents, are attracted towards one particular note called the **tonic**. Any note can be endowed with the attractive power of a tonic provided the composer limits himself to certain pitches arranged in particular orders. In this case Mozart has selected G♮ as the tonic. He has empowered this note by limiting his melody to just seven pitches which stand in a particular relationship to each other and to the tonic. At the end of B38 an extra stave shows how these seven pitches can be arranged in an ascending series known as a **scale**, the last note of which repeats the tonic an octave higher than the first note. This is one of 12 major scales based on the 12 possible pitch classes of most western music (see 2.1). Because the tonic is G this is known as the scale of G major. It shares with all other major scales a structure which can be defined by the intervals between each successive degree of the scale. In a **major scale** these intervals will always come in the order of tone–tone–semitone–tone–tone–tone–semitone, reading up from the lower tonic.

The same phenomenon is apparent when listening to the soprano solo on A91. This melody divides into eight phrases identified by the letters AABCBCDE. All eight sound incomplete apart from the last one which ends with a long-sustained tonic note, this time an A♮. Again there are only seven different pitch classes. These can be arranged in an ascending series of pitches in which the intervals between successive notes are exactly the same as those in the scale of G major. This is the scale of A major shown at the end of A91. Similarly every note of every part in the extracts from Janequin's chanson (A31) and the anonymous pavan (A32) belong to a major scale with C as its tonic. Because all of these pieces are based on scales with the same intervallic structures they are all in major keys, even though the scales start on different pitches. More specifically Mozart's quartet is in the key of G major, the soprano solo is in the key of A major, and the chanson and pavan are both in the key of C major.

2.3.2 Diatonic and chromatic music

All of the music discussed in 2.3.1 is **diatonic**. This means that only the notes of the **scale** that defines the key of the music have been used in each example. It is possible, however, to introduce notes which are foreign to a diatonic scale without disturbing its tonality. B38 is an extract from a minuet by Mozart. The first part of this extract (bars 1–12 in B38) sounds quite different from the second part (bars 12–19). This has something to do with the syncopations which are so evident in the first section and which are absent in the second section. But an equally obvious contrast is created by the **chromatic** notes which are such a feature of the first section compared with the diatonicism of the second section. B39 shows four melodic fragments taken from B38 arranged to show how they cover all 12 possible pitches used in western music. Placed in ascending order they form a chromatic scale in which the intervals between adjacent notes are all semitones. The same example also shows the G-major scale that

Elements of music

determines the G-major tonality of the music (semibreves), and the chromatic notes that add colour to the music (crotchets). With the exception of the last two notes, diatonic semibreves and chromatic crotchets alternate in the ascending chromatic scale, and this is true of motifs a and b (which between them cover ten of the 12 possible pitches of a complete chromatic scale). In context (B38) these chromatic notes sound like passing decorations between the diatonic notes (they are, in fact, called **chromatic passing notes**). With just one exception (the E♭ at the start of motif d) all of the motifs begin and end on diatonic notes of the scale of G major. It is for these reasons (among others) that, despite the number of chromatic notes heard in this section, it is just as firmly rooted in the key of G major as is the second section (in which the melody uses only notes belonging to the scale of G major).

2.3.3 Music in minor keys

A comparison of the melody of bars 12–19 of Mozart's minuet (B38) with the melody of the first eight bars of Jacquet de la Guerre's rondeau (A84) will show that the two inhabit very different sound worlds. A82, in which a scale has been derived from the first phrase of the music, shows why this is so. Although the scale is shown in its descending form (because the melody descends), it will be seen that the intervals between the degrees of this minor scale differ markedly from the major scale of B38, even though both scales begin and end on a G♮:

Ascending major scale in B38:
tone–tone–semitone–tone–tone–tone–semitone
Minor scale in A82 rearranged in ascending order:
tone–semitone–tone–tone–semitone–augmented 2nd–semitone

The semitones of the minor scale are differently distributed, and a new interval is introduced, the **augmented 2nd** (shown by a square bracket). The interval of an augmented 2nd characterises this particular minor scale, called the **harmonic minor**.

In fact augmented 2nds are usually avoided in melodies written before 1900 (except for oriental effects): notice that F♯ and E♭ are never used consecutively in Jacquet de la Guerre's melody (A82), whereas they are used repeatedly in the violin part of Bartók's *Romanian Dance* No. 3 (C56). In the decorated melody of bars 37–41 from the rondeau (A83) the augmented 2nd is avoided by raising the sixth degree of the scale a semitone to E♮ when the melody ascends, and by lowering the seventh degree a semitone when it descends. Observing this common practice theorists derived the **melodic minor scale** from melodies of this sort of music. Although the scale has two forms, one ascending and one descending (the latter also known as the **natural minor scale** or **aeolian mode**), composers often reverse the expected order of notes in the melodic minor (as Jacquet de la Guerre does when she uses E♭ and F♯ ascending in the second bar of 83). The fact that there are three versions of the minor scale (harmonic, ascending melodic and descending melodic) reflects the difficulty of reducing the actual practice of composers to neat systems.

2.4 Modality

Nowhere is the practice of composers more difficult to reduce to scalic systems than in the case of the **church modes**, the scales which predated

2: Tonality, modality and atonality

the major/minor system described in the previous section. Initially theorists of the medieval and renaissance eras admitted just eight modes divided into two categories, authentic (Modes I, III, V and VII) and plagal (Modes II, IV, VI and VIII).

2.4.1 Authentic modes

Mode I (the **dorian mode**) can be reproduced by playing a scale on the white notes of a keyboard starting and ending on D (the tonic or final of the mode). It differs from a natural minor scale (see 2.3.3) in having a raised sixth degree so that the upper semitone occurs between the sixth and seventh degrees instead of the fifth and sixth degrees. Compare A40 (dorian mode) with A42 (which has the same interval structure as the natural minor scale shown in A83 but starts on a different tonic note).

Mode III (the **phrygian mode**), can be reproduced by playing a scale on the white notes of a keyboard starting and ending on E (the final of the mode). This mode differs from a natural minor scale in having a rather startling flattened second degree so that the lower semitone occurs between the first and second degrees instead of the third and fourth degrees. Compare the natural minor scale shown in A42 with Tallis's *Third Mode Melody* and the phrygian scale shown at the end of it (A37). Just as major and minor scales can begin on any note (see 2.3.1 and 2.3.3), so modes can be transposed. This is the case in Vaughan Williams's *Fantasia on a Theme by Thomas Tallis* (A39), in which the original theme has been transposed so that its final is G rather than E (violas, bars 2–18). A38 contains the last four bars of this transposed melody and shows how Mode III on G can be derived from this viola phrase.

Mode V (the **lydian mode**) can be reproduced by playing a scale on the white notes of a keyboard starting and ending on F (the final of the mode). This mode differs from a major scale in having a characteristic sharpened fourth degree so that the lower semitone comes between the fourth and fifth degrees instead of the third and fourth degrees (compare the F-major tonality of A18 with the lydian modality of A19). All but one of the notes of the Agnus Dei shown in A19 belong to the lydian scale shown beneath it. The exception is the B♭ in bar 6. This alteration of the fourth degree of Mode V is common in plainsong melodies (as in the setting of the last syllable of 'Hosanna' in A20) and in medieval polyphony (as in bar 11 of A21).

Mode VII (the **mixolydian mode**) can be reproduced by playing a scale on the white notes of a keyboard beginning and ending on G (the final of the mode). This mode differs from a major scale in having a characteristic flattened seventh degree so that the upper semitone comes between the sixth and seventh degrees instead of the seventh and eighth degrees. Compare the G-major scale shown in B38 with the tenor part of Obrecht's Kyrie and the mixolydian mode shown in A28.

In 1547 a Swiss monk called Glareanus proposed the addition of some new modes in order to account for music that obviously did not correspond with any of the church modes. In their authentic forms he called them the **aeolian mode** and the **ionian mode**. The aeolian mode is the same as the **natural minor scale** (or descending melodic minor) shown in A83 and discussed in 2.3.3. In fact music in this mode had been commonplace for centuries (see A12). The ionian mode is the same as the **major scale** shown in B38 and discussed in 2.3.1 above. Like aeolian

Elements of music

modality, music in the ionian mode (or, as we would say nowadays, music in major keys) had been commonplace for centuries (see A14, which is, to all intents and purposes, in the key of D major).

2.4.2 Plagal modes

Modes II, IV, VI and VIII are plagal versions of authentic modes I, III, V and VII discussed above (2.4.1). They differ in that their melodic **ranges** are lower than their authentic partners, but they have the same **final** (tonic).

A8 shows a plainsong acclamation which covers a pitch-range (or **ambitus**) from A to A, but the melody begins on D and all three phrases end on this note. Thus it shares the same final as A40 (Mode I), but has a range which is exactly a perfect 4th below the hymn. This is Mode II, the plagal form of Mode I, otherwise known as the **hypodorian mode**. It is possible that the ranges of authentic and plagal modes reflect the natural ranges of tenor and bass voices, and it is certainly true that many polyphonic compositions have voice ranges which stand in this relationship one to another (A44).

Mode IV (the **hypophrygian mode**) has the same final (tonic) as Mode III (see A37), but the ranges of melodies in this mode are lower than the ranges of melodies in the authentic mode. Theoretically this range (or ambitus) was pitched a 4th below the authentic mode (A5(i)), but in practice the ambitus could be slightly different (A5(ii)). Note that, although the alleluia shown in A5 begins on D (and other phrases begin on A and C), the **mode** is determined by the note on which principal sections of the plainsong end (E at the end of the alleluia and at the end of the verse).

Mode VI (the **hypolydian mode**) has the same final (tonic) as Mode V (see A19) but, as with all plagal modes, its range is different. If the lydian mode were transposed to A it would consist of the notes A–B–C♯–D♯–E–F♯–G♯–A. But in its plagal form its range would be a 4th lower (E–E). This is the case in the 'Midsummer Night Song' shown in C57, a melody that begins and ends on A, but which has a range from E to E an octave above.

The plainsong hymn *Iste confessor* (A49) begins and ends on G, and all three phrases end on this note, the final of Mode VII. But unlike the mixolydian tenor in A52 the ambitus (range) is C to C. This is Mode VIII, otherwise known as the **hypomixolydian mode**.

Glareanus's authentic aeolian and ionian modes (see the last paragraph of 2.4.1) had their plagal counterparts in his **hypoaeolian** and **hypoionian modes**. The hypoaeolian melody in bars 7–11 of B61 has G♮ as its tonic, but its range extends from dominant to dominant (d^1 to d^2). Similarly the hypoionian melody of A13 has D♮ as its tonic (all phrases ending with a closed cadence end on this note, and the same note is heard as a sustained bass note throughout most of the piece), but its range extends from dominant to dominant (a to a^1).

Figure 2.4.2 sums up Glareanus's modal theory. White notes are the finals of each mode, black notes show the theoretical ranges of melodies in these modes. It must be stressed, however, that the actual modal practices of musicians diverged from this neat scheme in numerous details, and that modes 1–8 shown in the chart are simplifications of the eight church modes as understood by medieval theoreticians. As a rough guide to modal theory figure 2.4.2 might prove about as useful as a book of scales is to a student aspiring to play a romantic concerto: nothing can replace the sound of the real modal music discussed earlier in this section.

2: Tonality, modality and atonality

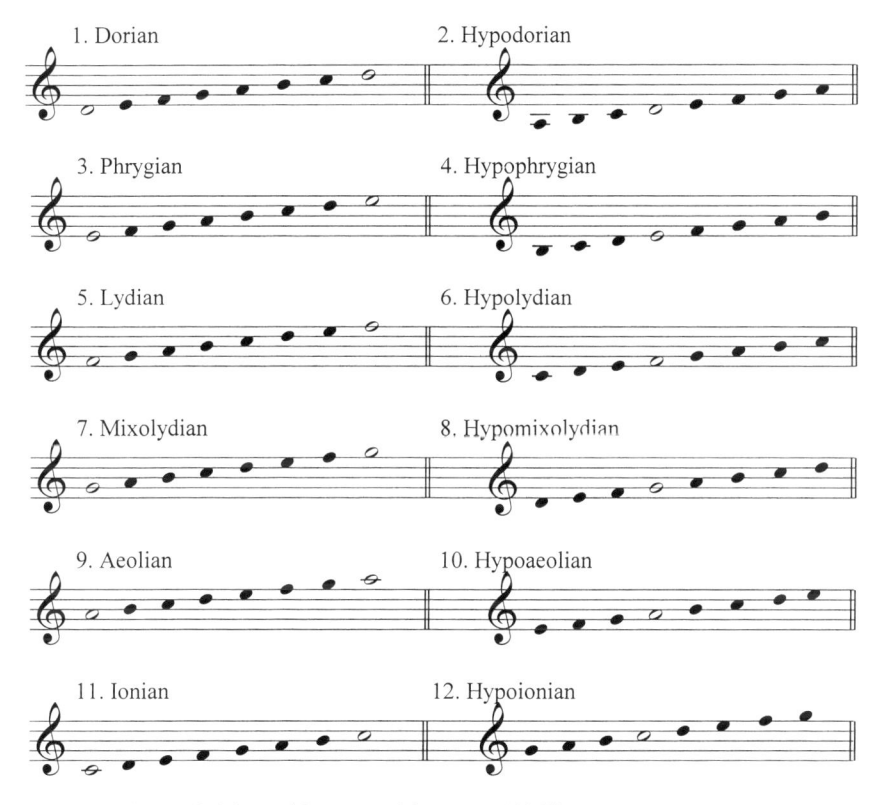

Figure 2.4.2 The 12 modes of Glareanus (1547)

2.4.3 Chromatic alteration of modes

In practice the modes described in 2.4.1 and 2.4.2 were often modified by **chromatic** inflexions. These were introduced to avoid outlining the interval of a **tritone**. This is the case in the Benedictus from Mass XVII (A20). In the plainsong the fourth degree of Mode V occurs only twice. Both times it is flattened to avoid the tritone outlined between the final (F♮) and the fourth degree of Mode V (B♮). To modern ears this has the effect of changing lydian-mode music to music in F major. Interestingly the isorhythmic tenor which Machaut fashioned from the plainsong (A20 and A21) retains the B♮ of Mode V for the most part, introducing a B♭ just once (bar 24 in both examples).

Equally common is the sharpening of the seventh degree of the mode when it rises to the final, particularly at a **cadence**. A49 shows a plainsong hymn in Mode VIII (the plagal form of the mixolydian mode). This hymn was used by Palestrina as the basis for his paraphrase mass *Iste confessor*. A50 and A51 show how the composer has fashioned a decorated melody from the second phrase of the hymn. Among the changes he has made his introduction of the sharpened seventh degree of the scale (F♯) between the repeated notes at the end is particularly striking. By this means he

Elements of music

effectively changes mixolydian modality to ionian modality, or major tonality, at this cadence. In other parts of this Kyrie (A52) similar chromatic alterations can be heard.

Modal melodies can cadence on degrees of the scale other than the final. The *Agincourt Song* (A24) is in the dorian mode with very obvious cadences on the final at the end of both burdens (bars 8 and 17). But there are subsidiary cadences on the fifth degree of the mode (bars 4 and 21), and on the third degree (bars 10, 13 and 29). The cadence on the fourth degree of the mode at the end of the verse (bar 36) introduces a new chromatic alteration. The F♯ simultaneously avoids a tritone with the B♭ in the tenor part, and strengthens the cadential effect by turning the third degree of the mode into a leading note. When two voices cadence on the final and the dominant (as they do in bars 8 and 17) it was common practice in the fifteenth century to chromatically alter the approach to both notes by sharpening the fourth degree of the mode as well as the seventh. The simple cadence at the end of the first burden is known as a **double-leading-note cadence** (because both the C♯ and the G♯ sound like leading notes). An alternative name for this sort of cadence is less satisfactory. The **lydian cadence** is so called because the fourth degree of the mode in its altered form (G♯ in bar 7 of A24) is a tritone above the final, like the unaltered fourth degree of the lydian mode (B♭ in A19).

The double leading-note cadence can be heard in many compositions of the fourteenth-century Ars Nova, including the works of Machaut (for example, bars 24–25 of A21). The more complex cadence in bars 16–17 of A24 is known as a **Burgundian cadence** because it is characteristic of the styles of fifteenth-century composers such as Dufay, Binchois and Busnoys, all of whom were associated with the court of the duke of Burgundy. The Burgundian cadence has the same sharpened fourth and seventh degrees of the mode as the double leading-note cadence (G♯ and C♯ in bars 7 and 16), but differs from it in overshooting the leading notes (F♯ and B♭ in bar 16) before resolution to the dominant and final of the mode (A♭ and D♭ in bar 17).

The increasing use of such chromatic alterations (collectively known as ***musica ficta***) throughout the renaissance eventually so modified the theoretical modes that by the middle of the seventeenth century they were largely superseded by the major/minor key system.

2.4.4 Modality in the nineteenth and twentieth centuries

Modality never completely died out, despite the pre-eminence of the major/minor tonal system in the baroque, classical and romantic eras. Indeed some late nineteenth- and twentieth-century composers deliberately resorted to modality as an expressive resource. This is particularly true of those late nineteenth-century **nationalist** composers who used flattened sevenths to suggest the modality of the native folk music of their homelands. Despite being a waltz (perhaps the most characteristic dance of the nineteenth century) and using romantic harmonic progressions, the melodies of the flanking sections of C2 are in the authentic aeolian mode transposed to E (as the scale on the extra stave shows).

Twentieth-century composers of **neoclassical** music also resorted to modality to create antique effects. The Forlane from Ravel's homage to

Couperin (C33) is a nostalgic recreation of a courtly dance of the seventeenth and eighteenth centuries. The extract from Couperin's Forlane shown in C32 contains a passage (bars 10–22) which was anachronistic even when it was written (c.1714) since it is in the aeolian mode on E throughout. Ravel's modality is more complex, as bars 1–9 of C33 show. This subtle mixing of modes is not at all uncommon in certain styles of twentieth-century music (see C41 and C82).

2.5 Modulation

Modulation is a process in which notes foreign to a given key are introduced and thus change the **tonality** of the music so that a new **key** becomes established. Clear evidence of the origins of modulation is to be found in renaissance music. In 2.4.3 it was shown that the addition of an F♯ to a mixolydian melody (A49) briefly changed the mode to a major key (G major in A51).

In the sixteenth century it was common for composers to use **chromatic alterations** to form intermediate **cadences** on almost any of the degrees of the mode. In Palestrina's Kyrie (A52) there are two cadences on D, the fifth degree of Mode VIII, as well as the expected cadence on the final of the mode at the end. Chromatic alteration of the sixth and seventh degrees of Mode VIII (B♭ and C♯ respectively) in bars 4 and 6–7 help form what are in effect perfect cadences in D minor. Similarly the sharpened seventh degree (F♯) in bars 13–14 helps form a perfect cadence in what is, in effect, the key of G major. Of course, these are not modulations in the full sense of the word since the key of D minor is hardly established before the cadences are contradicted by a return to modality. However, they do show the sort of processes which led to the possibility of modulation once the major/minor tonal system became fully established.

When in the seventeenth century tonality began to replace modality, composers realised what an important structural device such changes of key could be. Thus, instead of brief cadences on various degrees of the mode, composers now deliberately set out to cancel the original tonal centre by consistently altering one or more of the notes of the original key and substituting notes of another key. Procedures of this type can be heard in the rondeau by Jacquet de la Guerre on A84. The first eight bars (identified by the letter A) clearly remain in the key of G minor (called the tonic key or home key because the piece begins and ends in G minor). Then in section B the music modulates to a major key (B♭, the relative major of the tonic key of G minor). B♭ major is confirmed by the cadence in this key in bars 12–13. The music returns to the original key of G minor for the repeat of section A (bars 17–25). There are more modulations in section C, where the music passes through F major (with a perfect cadence in this key at bars 28–29) and D minor (with a perfect cadence in this key in bars 32–33). The varied repeats of A (A1 and A2) are both in the original key of G minor. The whole piece is a rondeau, a form in which a refrain (section A) alternates with contrasting *couplets* (sections B and C) making an overall structure which can be represented as ABACA1A2. But the melodies of the *couplets* (sections B and C) are not very clearly distinguishable from each other or from the refrain: what does distinguish them are the modulations to related keys, with the G-minor tonality of the refrains clearly contrasting with the related keys of the *couplets*.

Elements of music

2.6 Bitonality and polytonality

In the twentieth century several composers produced remarkable effects by combining two **keys** simultaneously. Such bitonality can be heard clearly throughout Bartók's 'Melody against Double Notes', a study from Volume 3 of *Mikrokosmos* (C59). The right-hand part (on the upper stave) uses the first five degrees of the scale of F♯ major, reinforcing this key by repeatedly dwelling on a two-note chord consisting of the tonic and dominant (bars 2, 4, 7 and, most importantly, bar 15). Simultaneously the left-hand part uses the first five degrees of the scale of D minor, reinforcing this key by repeatedly dwelling on the dominant (bars 1-2, 3-4 and 11) and by ending on a two-note chord consisting of the tonic and dominant. Bartók's piece sounds hazy rather than aggressive, and when the final cadence arrives the two perfect 5ths of F♯ major and D minor form a 7th chord which sounds like a resolution of the tension generated by the previous bitonal conflict.

Polytonality obviously includes bitonality, but it is not a very useful term since the simultaneous use of more than two tonalities is extremely rare.

2.7 Tonality and atonality

Another strand of twentieth-century music led to compositions based on the **chromatic scale**, with every one of the 12 possible pitches given equal importance so that none could exert a gravitational pull on the others (as the tonic does in tonal music). B39 shows that bars 3–9 of the minuet by Mozart on B38 contain all 12 chromatic degrees. Nevertheless this use of notes not contained in the diatonic scale of G major fails to undermine that tonal centre: we simply await the confirmation of the tonic key of G major which comes with the perfect cadence in bars 11–12. Such use of chromaticism had been an expressive resource from the sixteenth century onwards. But in the latter half of the nineteenth century, music was often so saturated with chromaticism that it was difficult to ascribe a **key** to many an extended passage of otherwise tonal music. The most famous example of such tonality-challenging chromaticism in the romantic era is the opening of Wagner's *Tristan und Isolde*. Like B39, bars 1–7 of B68 contain all 12 chromatic pitches (as shown in B68(i)). Yet despite this chromaticism the assault on tonality does not destroy it, because some notes and chords are given a prominence which ensures that tonality is never completely abandoned.

However at the beginning of the twentieth century composers began to explore the possibilities of music that totally relinquished tonality. What they wrote could be very expressive, but having kicked away the prop of tonality they faced the problem of finding alternative means of articulating musical structures. In the meantime they relied on the cohesive force of a text (C34) or wrote very short pieces in which timbre and texture were the most important elements (C35).

2.7.1 Serial music

Having decided that nothing remained to be achieved in tonal music after the extreme chromaticism of Wagner's *Tristan*, Hauer (and more famously Schoenberg) devised serial technique as a way of structuring music in the absence of keys. In C40 Hauer has arranged his melody in a series of four cells (A, B, C and D), each contributing three notes to the chromatic scale

2: Tonality, modality and atonality

shown beneath bars 0–7. In the piano part none of these notes is repeated until all of the chromatic degrees have been heard (the repetitions of C♯ and G♯ in the vocal part merely take care of the two syllables of 'hangen' and 'Rosen'). The avoidance of repetition ensures that none of the chromatic degrees can assume more importance than any other (and thereby begin to suggest a tonal centre). These 12 notes constitute a **tone row**: a series of all 12 chromatic degrees which forms the basic material of a composition using serial techniques (otherwise known as 12-tone or **dodecaphonic** techniques). Once having established a particular row the composer could manipulate it throughout the composition. One such manipulation can be seen in bars 9–12 of C40, where the four cells of Hauer's row are repeated, this time in the form of chords rather than as a melody. It is in these bars that the composer's indebtedness to Wagnerian chromaticism is acknowledged by a direct quotation from *Tristan* (compare motif x in the vocal part of bars 8–12 of C40 with the same motif in the oboe part at the start of B68). The difference between the two composers becomes apparent when B71 is compared with B72. The first, though very chromatic, forms an imperfect cadence in A minor, the key that Wagner establishes quite clearly in the cadence heard in bars 16–17 of B68 (shown in simplified forms in B69). But Hauer's use of serial technique prevents him from establishing any form of tonality since his chords are the result of the combination of segments of a tone row that makes no concessions to tonality.

2.7.2 Whole-tone scale

The whole-tone scale is one of a number of artificial scales invented by nineteenth- and twentieth-century composers to add colour to their tonal music or even to deny tonality altogether. It is a six-note scale, in which the interval between any two adjacent notes is a tone. Like the chromatic scale all of the pitches are of equal importance and, lacking a note which creates a gravitational field (like the tonic in diatonic music), it too is atonal. The use of this scale is most famously associated with Debussy. Many of his works contain whole-tone passages, but his piano prelude 'Voiles' is the only piece of his which is based on a whole-tone scale almost throughout. C21 shows how the notes of a whole-tone scale can be derived from the first few bars of the prelude. One way in which a rather ambiguous tonal centre can be generated even in this sort of music is by repeating one of the pitches of the scale. In 'Voiles' Debussy manages to suggest B♭ major (or minor) by repeating this pitch as a pedal in almost every bar of the extract. It is precisely this atonal/tonal ambiguity upon which Debussy plays in his evocation of sails reflected in water.

2.7.3 Octatonic scale

The octatonic scale consists of eight pitches arranged so that semitones alternate with tones. In common with the chromatic and whole-tone scales discussed in 2.7, 2.7.1 and 2.7.2 an octatonic scale cannot of itself suggest a tonal centre. This is apparent in C64 in which the passage of music enclosed in a box is no more tonal than the rest of this extract. As in many areas of twentieth-century music, Stravinsky was a pioneer in the use of this scale. In C88 some of the notes in bars 5–7 have been enclosed in a box. If these are arranged in ascending pitch order an octatonic scale on A is formed. This is shown on the extra stave below bar 6, with the alternating semitones and tones shown by pointed and rounded slurs respectively. It has to be admitted that such octatonic music stands at the extreme limit of what can be discerned by ear alone. Nevertheless Stravinsky's use of the scale gives his music a characteristic flavour throughout 'Surge, aquilo' because six consecutive notes of his tone row (and all of its permutations) belong to a six-note segment of an octatonic scale (see figure (i) printed beneath C88).

2.8 Modes of limited transposition

Both the **whole-tone scale** and the **octatonic scale** are included in Messiaen's collection of modes of limited transposition (scales which can only be transposed a limited number of times before transposition results in a repetition of the original collection of pitches). These modes have nothing to do with the church modes discussed in 2.4. The first five chords of 'Prière du Christ montant vers son Père' (C55) are derived from the composer's seventh mode of limited transposition. This consists of two superimposed six-note scale segments, each of which forms intervals of three consecutive semitones followed by a tone and a semitone between adjacent notes (as shown by the square brackets above and below the modal scale printed beneath the extract). Messiaen's first chord consists of notes 1, 3, 6, 8 and 10 of the mode. Similarly, each of the following four chords employ different five-note collections derived from the mode (as shown on the extra stave below the first bar of Messiaen's music). The particular **atonal** flavour of this music becomes strikingly apparent when compared with the sustained chords in bars 2–4, 7–8 and 10. The chord utilises the same pitches as the dominant-7th chord in bar 3 of Mozart's very tonal minuet (B41), but here there is no resolution to a tonic chord of G major. Instead it is used as a pungent tonal colour rather than as a key-defining element of a tonal progression. This is true of the final chord of the extract. It begins to sound like a tonic chord simply because it is sustained for such a long time. Nothing in the music that comes before even vaguely hints at C major as a possible tonal goal. Messiaen's music often seems to hover like this in a seemingly timeless world of sound on the very borders of tonality and atonality.

2.9 Pentatonic music

Just as the notes of a chromatic scale can be used tonally or atonally, so a wide variety of five-tone scales can be used to suggest or deny a tonal centre. It was the tonal ambiguity (or even atonality) of such scales that appealed to many of those composers who did not wish to follow Schoenberg's quest for a completely radical solution to the tonal problems Wagner had bequeathed to the twentieth century.

2.9.1 Gapped scales

For more than a century the influence of non-western music has been very evident in much European and American art music. The influence of Indonesian music is particularly apparent in Bartók's piano study 'From the Island of Bali' (C64). It begins with a passage in octaves that includes an atonal pentatonic scale (bars 3–4). The rest of the music on this track is based upon transposed segments of the scale. Such scales are known as gapped scales because of the large intervals between some of their pitches (in this case a perfect 4th between C♮ and F♯). This is the sort of scale used in tuning the gongs of a gamelan orchestra (though western tempered scales can only approximate to the actual pitches used in Indonesian music). It will be immediately obvious from the sound alone that this type of pentatonic music is as atonal as Hauer's chromatic song or Debussy's whole-tone prelude.

2.9.2 Anhemitonic pentatonicism

Another and more familiar type of pentatonic scale is tonally ambiguous rather than atonal. This is the familiar scale which can be produced by playing the black notes on a keyboard instrument (but these notes can be transposed to start on any other chromatic degree, as can major and minor scales). Because this particular pentatonic scale contains no semitones it is sometimes called an anhemitonic scale. The lack of semitones deprives it of the tonal pull of the seventh degree to the tonic which is apparent in major or minor scales. There are, however, two notes in this sort of pentatonic scale which exert more gravitational force than the other three (though this force is not nearly as strong as that of the tonic in a major or minor scale). Bars 1–9 of C63 make use of a **pentachord** containing the pitches G, A, B, D and E. Heard in isolation these pitches in the left-hand part of bars 1–4 (C60) form melodic units that suggest the key of G major (simply because the passage ends on G). But if the left-hand part of bars 5–8 is detached from its context (C61) the tonal centre seems to have shifted to E minor. In the left-hand part of bars 9–19 (C62) Bartók introduces a new pentachord containing the pitches D, E, F♯, A and B. Heard in isolation this passage strongly suggests the key of D major (because the pitches of its tonic triad – D, F♯ and A – are given such prominence). Heard in context the G-major tonality of bars 1–4, the E-minor tonality of bars 5–8 and the D-major tonality of bars 9–19 seems to be confirmed, but it is not until the very last chord that the tonal ambiguity of Bartók's pentatonicism is clarified by an E-minor triad with an added 7th.

3:
Melody, figuration and ornamentation

When defined pitches are combined with rhythmic patterns to form a coherent succession of sounds, **melody** emerges. It is obvious that melody is dependent upon **rhythm**, since it is impossible to have a succession of pitches without those pitches having durations that can be related one to another. This is true even when the relationships between the durations of notes in a succession of pitches is so complex or so free that it cannot adequately be represented in modern western musical notation (for example, the plainsong on A5). In addition to rhythm and pitch most western music is also dependent upon tonality or modality as a cohesive force (see Chapter 2).

3.1 Tune

Melody is a generic term that encompasses several cognate types of music. The most obvious of these is tune, a melody which is sufficiently simple and complete in itself that it can easily be memorised. The melodies of simple carols are of this type. A25 is an apparently simple tune that is unified by four-note segments of a scale known as **tetrachords**. The first phrase (bars 1–4) begins with the first tetrachord of D major. This is answered in bar 3 by the second tetrachord of the same scale. The longer second phrase (bars 5–10) begins with a disguised descending version of the second tetrachord (identified by the beam joining the upward-pointing stems). The first tetrachord reappears in bar 8 (lower stave) and the whole tune is rounded off with a varied repetition of bars 1–2 (now ending firmly on the tonic). Apparently simple tunes are nearly always unified by direct and varied repetitions of this sort.

In dulci jubilo (A91) is a carol in which the same principles are apparent on a larger scale. Only three rhythmic durations are used (apart from the last note) and both the metre ($\frac{3}{4}$ time) and the tonality (A major) remain constant throughout. Just as the text divides into lines defined by end-rhymes, so the tune falls into eight four-bar **phrases** defined by cadential melismas and melodic repetitions. The diagram below shows how musical features reinforce the simple rhyme scheme.

A91 Carol: In dulci jubilo		
End-rhymes	**Text**	**Musical phrases**
A	In dulci jubilo	A (melisma ends on E, the dominant)
A	Nun singet und seit froh!	A (melisma ends on E, the dominant)
B	Unser Herzens Wonner	B (melisma ends on A, the tonic)
A	Liegt in praesepio	C (melisma ends on C♯, the mediant)
B	Und leuchtet als die Sonne	B (melisma ends on A, the tonic)
A	Matris in gremio	C (melisma ends on C♯, the mediant)
A	Alpha es et O,	D (melisma ends on E, the dominant)
A	Alpha es et O.	E (ends without a melisma on the tonic)

3: Melody, figuration and ornamentation

Further memorability stems from the use of the same three-note **motif** (x) at the end of the first two phrases and at the beginning of the two phrases identified by the letter B. More subtly another three-note motif spanning a 3rd (y) reappears in varied forms in most of the subsequent phrases. At the beginning and end of phrase C the rising 3rd is filled in with a passing note (y^1 and y^2). At the start of phrase D motif y2 is extended and transposed down a 3rd (y^3). Finally, at the start of phrase E motif y3 is inverted to become a motif (y^4) that leads conclusively to the long tonic note with which the tune ends. This may seem a very complicated analysis of a simple tune, but it does show some of the features which contribute to that simple memorability. Of course, it is highly unlikely that the anonymous fourteenth-century composer consciously resorted to motivic manipulation, just as twenty-first-century carol singers are unlikely to be aware of it. Nevertheless it is this motivic saturation which brings about the very evident melodic cohesion of this delightful tune.

3.2 Theme

Themes differ from self-sufficient tunes such as the carols shown in A25 and A91 in that they form part of a larger musical structure. In the form known as theme and **variations** the melody heard at the start might indeed be as self-sufficient as a simple carol tune (B76). More often, however, a theme is used like a proposition at the start of an extended discussion. Just as a logical proposition may be developed alongside other related propositions in an ensuing argument, so the theme at the start of a piece in sonata form (B40, bars 1–14) may be developed in conjunction with other musical materials in the rest of the movement.

3.2.1 Periodic phrasing in a classical theme

B28 shows a complete theme in G major from the finale of Haydn's *Oxford* Symphony. The **antecedent** of this melody (stave 1) ends on the dominant (as though asking a question), while the **consequent** (stave 2) is an exact repeat of the antecedent up to bar 15 where there is a new cadence ending on the tonic (as though answering the question posed by the antecedent). Although the theme sounds complete in itself (by no means do all classical themes sound so complete), it is better adapted than the tunes discussed in 3.1 for use in musical arguments such as that shown in B29.

3.2.2 Monothematic elaboration of a theme

In some cases a lengthy section or even an extended movement might consist solely of an argument based upon just one theme proposed at the start. This is the case in the first movement of Haydn's String Quartet Op. 42. B27 is a skeleton score in which only the principal melodic lines of the first section are shown. The theme upon which the whole movement is built is played by the first violin in the first eight bars. Brackets above the stave show that it is constructed from four short **motifs** (a, b, c and d), each of which is repeated. Motifs b and d are each repeated at a different pitch. The repetition of b is a transposition, while the repetition of d in bar 7 constitutes a tiny sequence. The melodic outlines of motifs a and c are subtly changed when they are repeated. This is achieved by augmenting the first two intervals of motif a (the perfect 4th becoming a perfect 5th,

Elements of music

and the minor 6th becoming a minor 7th in motif a^1), and by diminishing the interval of a perfect 5th outlined by motif c to the diminished 5th outlined by motif c^1. The rest of B42 has been annotated to show how practically every note derives from one of these four motifs (superscript numbers indicate modifications of the motifs). When listening to the whole section it is worth noticing that:

1) in the passage marked 'transition' motifs a and b are shared between the viola (vla) and first violin (vln 1) in a typical passage of Haydnesque dialogue
2) in the passage marked 'IIa' the last note of motif c is repeated in motif c^2, while motif c^3 (although different in rhythm and outlining a perfect 4th instead of a perfect 5th) is clearly related to c^2 in that it too forms part of a falling scale ending on a repeated note
3) these motifs are treated canonically in bars 13–16 (see B26)
4) in the passage marked IIb, motif a is treated in imitation between the cello and second violin, then versions of the semiquavers from this motif are detached (n) and used in sequence (n^1), followed by just the first two of these semiquavers (p) (such use of ever-smaller parts of a theme or motif is known as **fragmentation**)
5) finally, in the passage marked 'codetta', motif d is heard in inversion and rhythmic diminution (d^2), and this is followed by a staccato version of the descending scalic motif (c^7). All of this is repeated in varied forms in bars 36–38.

Listening to the whole movement again it will be noticed that one or other of motifs a, b, c and d crops up in almost every bar. When a whole movement is thus based upon just one theme it is said to be **monothematic**.

3.3 Thematic transformation

In the nineteenth century a new form of thematic manipulation was introduced which depended not on motivic development of parts of the original theme but on the repetition of the pitches of the whole of the original theme with different rhythms. Sometimes such thematic transformation (or thematic metamorphosis) would be further distinguished by altering the metre, tempo or tonality of the original theme. Further alterations could involve new harmonies and, in programme symphonies, symphonic poems or tone poems, new orchestration. In multi-movement works thematic transformation can be used as a means of unifying the otherwise contrasted musical materials of each movement. This is true of Debussy's string quartet. C18(a) shows the composer's original theme at the start of the first movement. It is in a modal G minor, and fast simple quadruple metre. Near the start of the second movement (C18(b)) the theme is transformed by the new tempo and metre (compound duple time), and by other rhythmic changes. In context (C17) it is also evident that the phrygian modality of the original theme has given way to a chromatically altered G-major tonality in which the transformed theme is used as an ostinato. In the last movement the theme is again in $\frac{4}{4}$ time, but all of the notes have been rhythmically **augmented** and some are now syncopated (C18(c)).

3.4 Leitmotif and unending melody

The use of **thematic transformation** as a unifying device in large-scale compositions is similar to Wagner's use of leitmotifs in his later operas.

3: Melody, figuration and ornamentation

They differ from themes used in cyclic compositions (such as the quartet discussed in 3.3) in being but a fragment of a melody (supposedly representing an object, person or mood). Two such leitmotifs are combined at the beginning of B68. The first (sometimes called 'Tristan's Motif') consists of a rising 6th followed by a semitonal descent to a D♯ (the first four notes in B68, also identified as leitmotif 1 in B68(ii)). The second (said to represent Isolde or 'Desire') is the rising chromatic motif identified as leitmotif 2 in B68(ii)). But Wagner's aim in his use of leitmotifs is not simply to provide the musical equivalent of flash cards. Even within the first 17 bars of the prelude he has begun to manipulate these two motifs in order to increase the tension as he approaches his first climactic cadence (bars 16–17). In bars 4–7 he transposes the first four bars up a 3rd. In bars 8–11 he transposes the music up another 3rd and screws up the tension by adding a note to the semitonal descent of leitmotif 1, thus delaying the expected repeat of leimotif 2. When the second leitmotif does return (bars 10–11) it too is given one new note (D♯). Then a process of **fragmentation** begins. In bars 12–13 only leitmotif 2 is heard, its last two notes echoed in the next two bars. Finally, in bars 16–17, the rhythm of the second leitmotif is changed and another note added – the climactic appoggiatura that delays the resolution of the leading note (G♯) to the tonic (A♮).

Wagner's most subtle and purely musical way of treating leitmotifs is apparent in his concept of unending melody. B68 ends with a prominent cello melody (later transferred to the violins) which is shown in bars 17–23 of B68. This melody begins with a third leitmotif (identified as leitmotif 3 in B68(ii)) which has been called the 'Glance Motif' (a representation of that moment when the two protagonists' eyes first meet in loving recognition of each other's need). This tiny but very memorable fragment of melody (z in bars 17–18) contains within itself two even smaller motifs. The first (a) is a three-note motif characterised by its rhythm and conjunct (stepwise) movement. The second (b) is a two-note motif characterised by the on-beat discord which it forms with the accompaniment and by the leap of a 7th. Over many bars these motifs mutate and link together so as to form a melody which, in the opera, does indeed often seem endless. When the Glance Motif is repeated in varied form (z^1) motif a is repeated a 3rd higher, but in motif b^1 the dissonance resolves down a tone instead of a 7th. In the third statement of the Glance Motif (z^2) the rhythm of motif a is changed by being tied to z^1, and the falling 7th of motif b is inverted to become the rising 7th of b^2. Motif b^2 is then tied over to the first of two inversions of a (a^2 in bars 20 and 21). In the second half of bar 21 the rhythm of the original motif is retained in a^3 but the last note is inflected upwards. Bar 22 begins with the dissonant motif b^1 (also heard in the second half of this bar), followed by a rhythmic **diminution** (b^3) of the rising 7th heard earlier in bar 20. The rhythm of the weak-beat semiquavers is retained in motif b^4, then the appoggiatura motif (b^1) returns as the music approaches the second cadence of the prelude (bar 24).

3.5 Recitative, arioso and aria

If a simple tune like A25 lies at one end of the spectrum of melody types, **recitatives** like those shown in A62 and A63 must lie at the opposite end. Monteverdi's avowed intention in writing this music was to represent the

Elements of music

verbal accentuation of Italian with as little distortion as possible, and to stir his audience to a sympathetic understanding of the emotions of the protagonists at this point in the drama. If this meant singing on a monotone the better to focus on the fateful words 'Abandon all hope, you who enter here' (A62), then so be it. If it meant that the solemn trombone part should grotesquely follow the minatory bass voice of Charon like a dog on a lead (A63), then the composer's object had been achieved. In recitative the text is the master of the music to such an extent that musical metre gives way to poetic metre, and musical beauty gives way to the need for dramatic representation.

In the dry recitatives of later baroque vocal works the melody was often purely functional, following the rhythm of the words, but not attempting to express their emotional significance as Monteverdi had done (A68). Yet the most urgent emotions could be expressed through the melodic lines of **recitativo secco**, as B4 shows. Pilate has offered to release Jesus, but the crowd shout for the release of Barabbas instead. Bach sets the keyword ('cried out') of the Evangelist's narration at the extreme upper limit of the tenor's voice, from which point the melody tumbles down an octave to link directly with the ensuing cries of the rabble. Even more dramatically in B4(c) the shocked Evangelist enters on his highest note as he pronounces the name of the murderer who is to be released in Jesus's stead, and the word that translates as murderer ('Mörder') is sung to a tritone (known from medieval times as the *diabolus in musica*). The lashing rhythms of Bach's setting of 'geisselte ihn' (flogged him) are matched by the angular melody of the continuo part.

Sometimes the functional melodic lines of *recitativo secco* flower into the more song-like and metrical melodies of **arioso**. This is the case in B7, where at bar 7 the syllabic setting of bars 1–6 gives way to an arioso (bars 7–16) in which the sequential and melismatic melody is at least as important as the text. Some ariosos are independent movements (B5) that are distinguishable from **arias** (B15) only by their relative brevity. In both the focus of attention is most certainly on the melody rather than the text. As such the late baroque aria stands at the opposite pole to the early baroque recitative.

3.6 Recitation

In emotional terms it is but one step from Bach's extreme melodic expressiveness (B4(c)) to the expressionist recitation of Schoenberg's **Sprechstimme** (C34). Bach's vocal and bass melodies convey barbarity while Schoenberg's recitation plumbs pathological depths of the psyche where 'Huge black wings obscure the sunlight' ('Nacht'). But though they share the same emotional intensity the melodic techniques could not be more opposed. Where Bach requires precise pitches of his singer, Schoenberg asks for half-speech, half-song, in which pitches are touched upon before the vocalist slides to the next note. Where Bach's vocal and instrumental melodies, no matter how angular, are governed by the restraining influence of tonality, Schoenberg's atonal melodies are governed only by the self-imposed limitations of motifs x and y and their derivatives. Motif x is the three-note figure first heard in the piano bass in bar 1. It consists of rising and falling minor and major 3rds. The first derivatives are heard in the bass clarinet in which part the intervals of x are retained but in notes a quarter of the length of the original motif (double diminution). Motif y is a two-note figure of a rising 7th heard in the same bar played on the cello, then in the next bar on the bass clarinet. The melodic line that emerges in the first two bars of the bass clarinet part is atonal, angular and disjointed (and so unlike Bach's recitative, but quite typical of early twentieth-century expressionist music). In bars 7–8 motif x is changed by displacing the last note by an octave (cello and bass clarinet). The melodies that emerge from immediate repetitions of this derivative in the same part are continuous but still atonal and angular. In the piano part in bars 12–13 another continuous melodic line is forged from the alternation of the diminished version of x and its inversion (x^2). The melody that emerges from this process is again atonal, containing all twelve possible chromatic tones (and the same applies to the mirror image of this melody in the left-hand piano part). This sort of motivic saturation is technically similar to Wagner's unending melody in B68 but without any hint of tonality.

3.7 Klangfarbenmelodie

At about the same time as Schoenberg was writing *Pierrot Lunaire* (1912) his pupil Webern was composing his *Five Pieces for Orchestra* Op. 10. The first of these is recorded on C35. Listening to it one cannot help noticing the constantly changing instrumental **colours**. The individual notes of the seven-note melody with which it starts are played on a muted trumpet with harp, a celesta with viola and harp harmonics, flutter-tongued flute and harp, then three glockenspiel notes, and a celesta trill in bar 3. This is a *Klangfarbenmelodie* or melody of **tone colours** (*Klang* = tone, *Farben* = colours, and *Melodie* = melody). In the last bar the concept of *Klangfarbenmelodie* is reduced to its bare essentials since there is no change of pitch or duration, simply four changes of instrumental colour.

3.8 Serial melody

One of the problems with **atonal** music such as Webern's orchestral piece (C35) was that without the possibility of a structural use of tonality it became very difficult to construct large-scale movements. The answer for many twentieth-century composers was **dodecaphony** or serialism. This technique relied on a consistent use of a pre-determined **series** of all twelve chromatic notes to give extended movements some coherence. Such a series (or **tone row**) is evident in the first seven bars of the song by Hauer on C40 (see 2.7.1). It is nearer to conventional ideas of melody than Schoenberg's vocal and instrumental part in 'Nacht' (C34). This is because the twelve pitches of Hauer's row are grouped in four melodic **cells**, each containing one tone and one semitone between consecutive notes. In C40 these cells are identified by brackets beneath the piano bass part, and tones and semitones are shown by straight and pointed brackets above the vocal part.

In fact the simplicity of Hauer's serial melody is atypical of **twelve-tone** melodic style, in terms of both its undifferentiated rhythms and its largely conjunct motion. The tenor melody in C88 better reflects dodecaphonic melodic styles in the twentieth century (except for an idiosyncratic twist that is more characteristic of Stravinskian style than it is typical of serial music). Firstly the large intervals in bars 2–3 are similar to Schoenberg's vocal style (C34), not to Hauer's. The melody begins with a semitone followed by a leap of a minor 7th (between 'surge' and 'aquilo'), the setting of the second word outlines a diminished octave between the first and last syllables, and bar 3 begins with another leap of a minor 7th. The setting of 'veni' introduces the idiosyncratic twist mentioned above. The oscillation between E♭ and D♭ is an almost Italianate ornamentation of the seventh and eighth notes of the tone row (compare this with the *ribattuta* shown in A62) that is characteristic not only of the melodic writing in this movement (tenor, bar 6, and cor anglais, bar 10) but of Stravinsky's music throughout his life (he called it his 'lifelong affliction'). All of the melodic lines in C88 are serial, as the extra staves and letters show (see (i), (ii), (iii) and (iv) following C88 for an explanation of these letters).

3.9 Figuration

Do the continuous semiquavers of Bach's Prelude in C minor (A87) constitute a **melody**? They are certainly 'defined pitches combined with rhythmic patterns to form a coherent succession of sounds', yet most people would not describe them as being melodious. The whole of this track is built from varied forms of the first eight semiquavers of the movement. But clearly these semiquavers are not tuneful (like the carol in A25), lyrical (like Tchaikovsky's oboe melody in C4), or thematic (like the first eight bars of the violin part of the string quartet by Haydn in B27). Such an ornamental pattern as that formed by the first eight notes of the prelude is known as a **figure**, and the whole passage which derives from it is called figuration. The process of manipulating a figure to form continuous figuration is sometimes called ***Fortspinnung*** (German for 'spinning out'), a technique which was particularly favoured in the late baroque era, but which reappears in different forms throughout the nineteenth and twentieth centuries (for instance, the right-hand part throughout B66).

Figuration may also appear in a more subservient role as part of a larger musical concept. This is the case in bar 18 of B27, where the passage marked x is scalic figuration which has nothing to do with the main thematic argument of the movement. It simply serves to link the development of motif c (bars 13–17) with the cadence figure (y). In other works figuration may be of paramount importance. In romantic lieder the piano accompaniment was often as expressive as the vocal part. Schubert's song cycle *Die schöne Müllerin* tells of a young man leaving home to find something of great importance which he cannot yet identify. He encounters a little stream which he decides to follow. At this stage of his journey the joyous optimism of youth is reflected in the babbling brook. Schubert evokes both scene and sentiment in the piano's rushing sextuplet figuration (the brook) and the striding bass (the youth's resolute step), both of which run throughout the entire song.

3.10 Ornaments and ornamentation

Ornaments are melodic decorations that embellish a simple melodic outline. They may be improvised, indicated by conventional signs placed above or alongside certain notes by the composer, or written out in full.

Improvised ornamentation seems to have been practised from earliest times, especially in oral traditions. Since this sort of ornamentation was not written down reliance has to be placed on contemporary verbal

3: Melody, figuration and ornamentation

descriptions and recordings or transcriptions in staff notation of the music of societies that still had living oral traditions in more recent times. One such living oral tradition in Europe is the huge corpus of melodies played on bagpipes throughout Europe. The ornamentation of these tunes is often so complex that it cannot be rendered in staff notation with complete accuracy. A17 shows a melody played on a (reproduction) medieval bagpipe. (Note that this is a modern realisation reproducing late twentieth-century ideas both about choice of instruments and about the way in which they should be played in this anonymous fourteenth-century work.) The melody is here decorated with ornaments represented by **grace notes** (printed small) and the sign for an **upper mordent** (the wavy line in bar 3). These give a vague impression of what is played, but in bar 7 the ornament is simple enough to be transcribed as a group of four semiquavers.

The rapid alternation of two notes a step apart played on an ocarina throughout A18 is a less ambiguous ornament called a **trill**. (As before, the instrumentation here reflects modern taste and cannot be regarded as an uncomplicated witness to medieval practice, about which academic opinion continues to develop.) It can be accurately represented in a transcription by the abbreviation *tr* and a wavy line. Conventional signs like this were unknown in the fourteenth century, but are common in more recent music. They can, however, pose their own problems. In one period, for instance, trills might begin with the upper of the two alternating notes, but in a later period they might begin with the written melody note. Again, a trill might simply stop on the written note or might include the note a step below the written note immediately before ending on the written note itself. Sometimes these variants are represented with additional or different conventional signs, but consistency of usage is not guaranteed. Still further confusion is added by the fact that different composers often used the same sign for different ornaments (or different terms for the same ornament). So whatever signs are used they have to be interpreted according to the stylistic norms of particular periods or even of particular composers.

Written-out ornaments, such as the flurries of short notes that decorate the cadences in A56 (bars 6 and 16–17), give a clearer indication of a composer's intentions. But even when all the pitches of elaborate ornaments like these are written out, the precise durations of the ornamental notes are sometimes left to the performer's discretion and artistry. In B64 the triplets in bar 7 are clear enough, but the **arabesque** in bar 8 has to be performed according to the pianist's understanding of nineteenth-century style.

It is for these reasons that ornaments are discussed below in the context of specific compositions.

3.10.1 Improvised ornamentation

From the sixteenth to the eighteenth century it was common for performers to **embellish** melodies with a variety of improvised ornaments, particularly when a passage of music was repeated. Collectively all types of extensive ornamentation of this sort are called **diminutions** or **divisions** (the latter term referring in its narrowest sense to seventeenth- and eighteenth-century English variations upon a ground). A34 consists of two variations from a set of *diferencias* (a term that could mean the technique of variation or the variation form as a whole). They are based on the melody *Guárdame las vacas* (the first phrase of which is shown on the extra stave above the first variation) and the romanesca shown on the extra stave above the bass of the second variation. In the first bar of Variation 1 the first crotchet of the song is divided into two quavers, while in the fourth bar the dotted crotchet is divided into six semiquavers (the pecked line shows that the original melody note is still present in this division). Only the bass part of the second variation is printed. It shows how the falling 4ths of the romanesca bass are filled in with passing notes, a common feature of both diminutions in general and divisions in particular.

A65 shows a couple of phrases from an aria by Monteverdi. The next example shows the same melody embellished with a continuous stream of diminutions that, quite exceptionally, were written out by the composer, probably as a model for the sort of ornamentation he expected of the performer in this type of composition. In Italy such diminutions, whether improvised or written out, were known as ***fioriture*** (literally, 'flowering'), or, more specifically in early seventeenth-century Italian vocal music, ***gorgie***. A particular feature of such early seventeenth-century ornamentation was the ***trillo*** – rapid repetitions of the same note that some call a Monteverdi **trill**. The composer himself wrote out the *trillo* in bar 4 of A65, but this ornament was a common embellishment of cadences in vocal music of the time even when not written out. This is the case in A62, in which the ornaments in bar 3 are a transcription of what is sung (in the original score this bar contains just two minims in the vocal part).

Later the same term was applied in Italy to what is now known as a **trill** (a rapid alternation of two notes a step apart). These too were improvised at cadences, even when the composer left no indication that they were appropriate. The conventional sign in bar 12 of A75 represents a short **shake** (the English term for a trill in this period) beginning on C♯. Although this English sign for a trill does not appear in the original score a shake of this sort would normally be improvised at a cadence in the manner illustrated by the singer on this track. Similarly there is no indication of a shake in bar 12 of Purcell's score of A80, but a trill is performed here and in the final cadence (where Purcell *did* indicate that he required it). Here, as in many modern editions, the shakes are represented by the modern abbreviation *tr* (*tr*).

In baroque music in slow tempi it was customary to change a repeated note at the end of a phrase to an **appoggiatura** resolving onto the second written note. The discord it created could have a strongly emotive effect. In bar 7 of B5 the two F♯s that Bach wrote (shown on the extra stave) are interpreted as a dissonant G (forming a 7th with the bass) resolving to Bach's F♯ on the word 'Schmerzen' (suffering). A similar improvised appoggiatura can be heard in bar 11 (again with Bach's original notation shown on an extra stave). In bar 7 of B16 the soprano decorates a single note with an appoggiatura (E♮).

It was common baroque practice to introduce improvised ornamentation into repeated passages, particularly in the repeat of the first part of a **da capo aria**. In B15 appoggiaturas similar to those discussed in the last paragraph can be heard when bars 20, 30 and 34 are repeated (and in the repeat of bar 32 the appoggiatura is itself decorated). In this aria all of the added ornaments are shown on the extra staves (D.C. = da capo).

The practice of introducing improvised ornaments into a repeated passage continued well into the classical period. In B25 a comparison of bars 1–20 (Haydn's original notation) and 45–64 (a transcription of the embellished repeat on track B25) shows how lavish such improvised ornamentation could be. The ornaments include the following:

(a) The *Mordant* (German spelling of mordent) is a **lower mordent** consisting of the written note, the note a step below it and the written note again. In this period it could be played before the beat (compare Haydn's unembellished music in bars 3, 5, 7 and 17 with the lower mordents introduced by the performer in bars 47, 49, 51 and 61).

(b) The ***Nachschlag*** (which, in one of its manifestations, is the same as the English **springer**) is an unaccented decoration that leaves an essential note by step and returns to the next essential note by a leap in the opposite direction and so is similar to a written-out *échappée* (compare bars 8 and 52).

(c) The ***Schneller*** is an **upper mordent**, which, in this period, could be played on the beat in the baroque manner (compare bars 12 and 56) or before the beat as was customary in later styles (compare bars 4, 14 and 18 with bars 48, 58 and 62).

(d) The ***Schleifer*** or **slide** is an on-beat run of two conjunct notes leading to the main melody note (compare bars 16 and 60).

3.10.2 Ornaments represented by conventional signs

The ornaments represented by Jacquet de la Guerre's conventional signs in the first 16 bars of A84 are printed in fully notated form in bars 17–25.

(a) The ***pincé*** in bar 1 of A84 in this context is a **lower mordent** (in other contexts the term *pincé* could mean vibrato). It consists of the written note, the note a step below it and the written note again. In 1713 Couperin called the same ornament a *pincé simple* (C32, bars 2, 3, 6, 7 and so on), and in 1720 or thereabouts Bach called it a *Mordant* (B1, bar 1).

(b) The ***cadence*** or ***doublé*** in bar 1 of A84 is a **turn** (though *cadence* could also mean a trill). It consists of the note above the written note, the written note itself, the note a step below the written note, and the written note again. Bach used the same French term (*cadence*) for the turn. An example can be heard at the end of bar 6 in B1. Turns are often articulated between principal melody notes. In B32 the turn in bar 3 is played as a group of four demisemiquavers (so changing the A♮ into a quaver).

(c) The short ***tremblement*** in bar 5 of A84 is an **upper mordent**, an ornament consisting of an alternation of the note above the written note (sounded on the beat) and the written note. In other contexts the same sign could indicate a longer **trill** (whether or not there are a few extra wiggles added to the wavy line of the conventional symbol). This is the case in bar 4 and bar 9 of B9 where a short wavy line is interpreted as a long trill (which Bach called a ***trillo***) ending on the fourth beat of the bar. The sign was still in use in the twentieth century, but it usually meant an ornament beginning with the written

Elements of music

note, the note a step above it, and the written note again. Unlike its baroque counterpart the ornamental notes were played before the written note (as in C56).

(d) The hook at the end of the wavy line in bar 8 of A84 indicates a *tremblement et pincé* or **double cadence** in which a trill ends with a turn (x in bar 24). In C32 the same compound ornament is represented by a wavy line with two grace notes (bars 11 and 13).

(e) The *coulé sur une tierce* shown in bar 12 of A84 is written out in full. It is the same as the **slide** discussed in 3.10.1, and could be represented by a variety of symbols, including that shown on the extra stave above this bar.

(f) The *tremblement coulé* with a hook pointing down in bar 44 of A84 and the similar ornament with a hook pointing up in bar 3 of B1 both indicate a trill beginning with a turn. The first starts on the lower note (as shown on the extra stave at the end of A84) and is sometimes called an **ascending trill**. The second begins on the upper note and is sometimes called a **descending trill**. Bach called both a *Doppelt cadence*.

(g) A vertical wavy line in front of a chord indicates that it should be rolled upwards as an **arpeggio**. In French sources this is sometimes confirmed by a little hook at the bottom of the wavy line (A84, bar 45) forming a symbol and ornament known as an *arpègement en montant*. The less common *arpègement en descendant* (a downwards arpeggiation) can be indicated by an arrowhead pointing down, a hook at the top of a wavy line, or by a stoke through the stem of the chord (as shown in bar 3 of B17).

An **appoggiatura** is an accented single-note ornament a step above or below the principal melodic note onto which it resolves. The most usual sign for it is the note itself written as a small **grace note**. Usually these are sounded on the beat (or a relatively strong off-beat) and they shorten the note they embellish. The exact length of an appoggiatura is left to the good taste of the performer (informed by what is known of the performance practices of the period). Thus the first semiquaver grace note in bar 2 of B1 is played as a semiquaver, but the second is played as a quaver (as shown in the rhythm above the stave). The quaver appoggiatura in bar 4 is played as an on-beat quaver (thus reducing the length of the note it decorates to a dotted crotchet). In B5 Bach's signs for appoggiaturas are shown on extra staves above bars 4, 9, 14 and 16, with the singer's interpretation of them in the vocal part below. In other works Bach used an upright arc before a note-head as a symbol for an appoggiatura and used the French term *accent* for such signs.

B17 illustrates several late baroque French ornaments (written-out versions are shown on the extra staves beneath bars 1–4).

(a) The allemande begins with a lower mordent (discussed above). In his *Explication des signes d'agrément* Rameau shows this *pincé* as a short trill, an ornament Couperin called a *pincé double* (to leave no room for doubt the same composer called the mordent a *pincé simple*). But there is clearly insufficient time in the first bar of B17 to execute a trill before the melody enters.

(b) The ornament symbolised by the upright arc in front of the F♮ in bar 1 represents an appoggiatura variously called a *port de voix*, a *coulé*

3: Melody, figuration and ornamentation

or a ***chute*** (or ***cheute***) in France, and a **backfall** (when resolving down) or **forefall** (when resolving up) in England.
(c) At the beginning of bar 3 an *arpègement en descendant* (a descending arpeggiation indicated by the stroke through the stem of the chord) is combined with another *port de voix* (the appoggiatura G♯ resolving up to A♮).
(d) A more elaborate version of the *port de voix* is indicated by the arcs on either side of the minim in bar 3 ('pincé et port de voix' in Rameau's *Explication*).
(e) The *doublé* in the first beat of bar 4 is a turn indicated by the familiar sign above the semiquaver F♯.
(f) On the second beat of bar 4 the *double cadence* consists of a short trill with a turned ending (indicated by a pair grace notes here, but elsewhere indicated by a hook on the end of the wavy line).

As well as a wealth of ornamentation the unequal performance of most of the printed semiquavers is immediately striking. Such **notes inégales** (shown as they are performed on the extra stave below bar 1) are sometimes regarded as a type of ornamentation, but in this dictionary they are discussed as rhythmic alterations (see 1.6.4).

The ***Bebung*** is a type of **vibrato** that can be performed on the **clavichord** and no other keyboard instrument. This is because there is continuing contact between one end of the key mechanism and the string, and thus the performer's finger can continue to affect the strings sound even after striking the key. So by waggling the finger the performer can induce a waggling movement of the tangent that produces a fluctuation of pitch like vibrato on a violin. The conventional sign is a number of dots with a slur (shown at the end of the first system of B20). The same sign can also indicate tremolo in early music and, in later periods, semi-staccato. As with most signs with more than one meaning the context will usually reveal what the composer meant. In the same example (B20) a ***tirade*** is shown in the penultimate system. This rapid scale linking two principal melody notes is sometimes improvised, but here Bach writes it out in full.

The **tremolo** proper is a rapid repetition of the same note. It is a characteristic feature of mandolin technique designed to substitute for a sustained note that is impossible on this instrument. It is usually indicated by two or three strokes through the stem of the note that is to be embellished in this way (C29, bars 8, 10 and 12).

The **acciaccatura** or crushed note is described in seventeenth- and early eighteenth-century sources as a note a step away from the principal melody note it decorates that is sounded with it then immediately released. As such it could be called a simultaneous appoggiatura. This method of performance is possible on keyboard instruments, but in reality the realisation of what most musicians now call an acciaccatura (and which scholars prefer to call a short appoggiatura) depends on the style and speed of the music. The acciaccatura as a simultaneous or short appoggiatura is now represented by a grace note with a stroke through the stem and flag. In bars 27–28 a melodic fragment without ornaments can be heard. The same fragment is heard in the next two bars with acciaccaturas played immediately before the notes they decorate. These 'short appoggiaturas' can then be compared with a 'real appoggiatura' at the end of bar 32, where the A♮ and G♯ are played as even semiquavers. On melody

Elements of music

instruments acciaccaturas are almost always played in this manner (simultaneous performance often being impossible). In fast tempi acciaccaturas are performed as fast as the instrument allows (as the first 15 bars of B73 demonstrate), but in slower tempi they can be quite languorous (C1, bar 1). C1 also shows how other grace notes can be performed in a similar manner to acciaccaturas (bar 2). In B65 acciaccaturas can heard in bars 9 and 11 while similar rapidly executed grace notes are evident in bars 8 and 15, and there are many more examples of both types of ornament in the remainder of the extract.

A **glissando** is a modern, extended version of the slide that can be either a sweeping performance of a series of discrete pitches or a microtonal slide in which no discrete pitches can be heard. The latter is called **portamento**, particularly when performed on bowed string instruments or sung (as at the end of C96). The conventional symbol in instrumental music is a solid straight line between the outermost notes of the glissando (with or without the abbreviation 'gliss.'). The first type of glissando is a characteristic technique of harp playing. In C27 the harpist sweeps up three octaves of a G-major scale (indicated by the words 'G dur') from dominant to dominant. In C81 the first harp sweeps up and down the whole-tone scale shown in the first beat of the extract (the second harp part is not shown in the printed music). In C71 pizzicato glissandi are performed in bars 7, 9 (particularly clear) and bars 10–13 by plucking the string then sliding a finger of the left hand up or down it. At the end of C75 trombones play glissandi by drawing the slide from the fully extended position (B♮ and E♮ on the bass and tenor trombone respectively) to the fully closed position (F♮ and B♭). In bars 68–69 of B82 a glissando is performed on a chromatic kettle drum by rolling and simultaneously changing the tension of the membrane by gradually adjusting the position of the foot-pedal. At the end of C90 a double glissando is performed on the white and black notes of a marimba.

3.10.3 Written-out ornamentation

Over the centuries there has been an evolution from improvised ornamentation to ornamentation represented by symbols of ever-increasing complexity, then to fully notated ornamentation. The last two stages are neatly encapsulated in the first bar of B76, where a trill is represented by the abbreviation *tr* (*tr*), but the four-semiquaver figure in the next beat is a written-out **turn**. Similarly in bars 1, 4, 5 and 8 of C32 Couperin uses a conventional sign to represent an **upper mordent** (leaving its precise realisation to the knowledge and good taste of the performer), whereas in C32 the upper mordents are written out using **grace notes**.

On a much larger scale **diminutions** that were originally improvised were later fully notated. Where in the seventeenth century English viol players improvised **divisions** upon a ground, in the eighteenth century Handel notated similar ornamentation in full. This is shown in B18, in which a theme in crotchets is successively divided into quavers (Variation 1), triplet quavers (Variation 3) and semiquavers (Variation 5). Similarly where Monteverdi usually leaves the ornamentation of a primitive melodic phrase such as A65 to the singer Mozart writes out elaborate **roulades** (such as those in B50) in full.

In the nineteenth century composers notated ever-more complex ornamental figures such as the quintuplet groups in B64. Yet even in romantic styles composers were prepared to allow the performer some degree of discretion, as the **arabesque** in the same example shows. Every pitch is carefully notated, but it is clear that the precise rhythm of this extended ornament is not meant to fit with mathematical precision against the metrically notated left-hand part.

More recently there has been a move back towards the interpretative liberties composers once allowed performers. After the attention to every last ornamental detail that is a hallmark of the scores of twentieth-century avant-garde composers such as Boulez (C87), composers at the end of the century again realised the excitement of re-creation in performances in which details of ornamentation were left in the hands of performers. In C97 strings and woodwind players are given graphic representations of the sort of ornamentation the composer required to decorate the simple brass parts (bars 23–25). Similarly, percussionists are free to decorate the massive orchestral tuttis in bars 36–38, 42–44 and 48–51 with rhythmically free tintinnabulations that would lose spontaneity if precisely notated.

4: Counterpoint

Counterpoint is the sounding together of two or more melodic lines, each of them having a measure of independence. The word derives from the Latin 'punctus contra punctum' which means 'note against note'. In this original sense the parallel organum shown in A7 could be regarded as contrapuntal or polyphonic (as distinct from monophonic music such as the plainsong shown in A8). To modern ears, however, parallel organum sounds more like a succession of chords (because none of the parts is independent of the others). Consequently the term **counterpoint** is usually reserved for music in which each melody can be distinguished from those sounding against it by its pitch contour or rhythm (or both).

4.1 Contrapuntal motion

The refrain from Jacquet de la Guerre's rondeau (A85) is an example of note-against-note counterpoint in which the two melodies can easily be distinguished from each other. Unlike the parallel organum of A7 the pitch contours of these two parts are quite different. In the organum all of the parts move in the same direction and by the same intervals (parallel motion), but in the rondeau the movement of the two parts in relation to each other is much more complex. To be sure, parallel motion is heard in the passages marked with the letter p (parallel 6ths in bars 1–2 and 5, parallel 3rds in bars 2–4 and 6–7), but these passages are mixed with:

(i) **contrary motion** (c) in which the parts move in opposite directions to each other (as in bar 4)
(ii) **similar motion** (s) in which the parts move in the same direction, but with changing intervals between them (as in bar 2)
(iii) **oblique motion** (o) in which one part remains on the same note while the other moves towards or away from it (as in bar 8).

So despite the two melodies having almost identical rhythms the music is perceived as **two-part counterpoint** rather than a procession of two-note chords.

4.2 Two-part counterpoint

When the melodies of a contrapuntal texture are rhythmically independent of one another it is much easier to distinguish the individual parts. Thus the quaver figures sounding against crotchets in bars 5 and 8 of A85 add to the differentiation which is engendered by the contrary motion at these points. With its original ornamentation (A84, bars 1–17) the left- and right-hand parts of the refrain become quite distinct from each other. But the rhythmic complexity of the ornamentation gives the upper part a prominence which changes the balance of the texture from the equal-voice counterpoint of A85 to a texture in which a principal melodic line is supported by a simpler bass part. This is true of the first twelve bars of the bourrée from Bach's Lute Suite in E minor (A89), in which quaver figures in the upper part are frequently sounded against crotchets in the lower part, thus giving the treble pre-eminence over the bass. In the last phrase, however (bars 20–24), both of the parts have quaver figures and become equal partners in a truly contrapuntal two-voice texture. In many contrapuntal compositions there will be similar variations of **texture**, with first one part then another being highlighted as well as passages where the parts are of equal importance (C93).

4.3 Melodic decoration in two-part counterpoint

In its undecorated version nearly every note of the refrain of Jacquet de la Guerre's rondeau (A85) belongs to a chord which helps define the key of G minor. For instance, the four notes sounding in the first minim beat of bar 2 are all notes of the tonic chord of G minor (G, B♭ and D) and the same is true of the first minim beat of bar 3. Since they belong to the basic harmonic framework of the music all these notes are known as **essential notes** (or harmony notes). In Jacquet de la Guerre's decorated version of the refrain (A84, bars 33–41) a number of different types of melodic decoration are introduced (in addition to the ornaments indicated by conventional signs that the composer has retained). In this section of the rondeau crosses indicate notes from the original refrain and numbers identify examples of the five different types of melodic decoration Jacquet de la Guerre has added.

4.3.1 Passing note or passing tone

This unaccented decoration links two essential notes a 3rd apart. In the bass part of bar 33 of A84 the D♮ on the second crotchet and the B♭ on the third crotchet both belong to the two-part chords at this point, while the passing note C fills the gap of a 3rd between them. Although a passing note is usually dissonant, the fact that it is off the beat disguises the clashing sound. In this case the passing note (1) forms a dissonant major 9th with the D♮ in the upper part, but aurally the effect is entirely concordant.

4.3.2 Accented passing note or accented passing tone

This melodic decoration is the same as a passing note, but it falls on the beat, so the dissonant effect is often quite pronounced (because it is usually dissonant and is articulated at the same time as the note with which it clashes). In bar 35 of A84 the note identified by the figure 2 is an accented passing note which forms a dissonant diminished 4th with the bass F♯.

4.3.3 Essential note or harmony note

The name of this melodic decoration is almost self-explanatory. It refers to a note that belongs to the harmony against which it sounds. At the start of bar 36 of A84 the implied harmony is a chord of G minor (G, B♭ and D). The note that de la Guerre has added to her original refrain at this point (3) is one of the notes of that chord (compare the first beats of bars 4 and 36).

4.3.4 Auxiliary note or neighboring tone

This unaccented decoration comes between two harmony notes of the same pitch and is a step above or below them. The E♭ (4) in bar 37 of A84 is called an **upper auxiliary** since it is a step above the harmony notes on either side of it. **Lower auxiliaries** are equally common: there is a pair of them (quaver C and quaver A) at the end of bar 26 in the same example.

Elements of music

The auxiliaries in the verse of A24 (marked with crosses in bars 19 and 23) are strikingly dissonant because they are articulated against a moving tenor part, forming intervals of a minor 7th (B♭ against C) and a major 9th (E against D).

4.3.5 Appoggiatura

This accented dissonant decoration is approached by a leap and resolved by step (most often descending). In bar 39 of A84 the E♭ (5) is approached by a leap of a 3rd, forms a dissonant 4th with the bass, and resolves down a step to a concordant D.

4.3.6 Suspension or retardation

Like the appoggiatura the suspension is a dissonant note which resolves by step (though sometimes the resolution is itself ornamented). It differs from the appoggiatura in that the dissonance is softened by **preparation**. This means that the note which forms the **dissonance** is sounded as a **consonance** immediately before the suspension. It is relatively easy to hear the suspensions in the two-part texture of the verses of the A24. In bar 20 the three elements of a suspension happen on consecutive beats. The minim A sounds as a consonance against the tenor C a 6th below it: this is the preparation. On the second beat the tenor moves to a B♭ forming a dissonant 7th with the suspended minim A. Finally the alto resolves down to a crotchet G so forming a consonant 6th with the tenor. The same type of suspension can be heard transposed down a 5th in bar 32. In the decorated version of it in bar 24 the note of **resolution** is anticipated by the quaver C♯.

It is harder to hear suspensions when more than two parts are involved. In the Kyrie from Palestrina's *Missa Iste confessor* (A52) there are six suspensions (marked 'sus.'), all of them prepared on a weak beat, sounded on a strong beat and resolved on the next weak beat (this was standard practice from the sixteenth century onwards). In order to help identify those in bars 6 and 7 two simplified versions of the alto and tenor parts of bars 4–9 are sung on A53 and A54. In the first version (A53) Palestrina's alto and tenor parts have been reduced to two contrapuntal parts which form consonant harmonic intervals throughout. In the second version (A54) three of these intervals have been altered by lengthening the values of three notes of the tenor part, thus delaying movement to the next consonant interval. In bar 6 the alto's E♮ forms a consonant major 3rd with the tenor C♮: this is the preparation. On the next beat the tenor moves to B♭ while the alto remains on E♮, thus forming a dissonant augmented 4th between the two parts: this is the suspension. On the fourth beat the alto falls a tone to form a consonant major 3rd with the tenor: this is the resolution. The same process is repeated at a lower pitch starting on the last beat of bar six (the alto's D♮ being both a resolution of the suspension immediately before it and a preparation for the suspension on the first beat of bar 7). Having identified these suspensions in two-part textures it ought now to be easier to identify them when they are heard in the three-part texture of A55, noting that the resolution of the suspension in bar 6 is decorated with an **anticipation** (marked with an asterisk) and that the resolution is disguised by the accented passing note in the soprano part. Despite being part of a four-voice texture, the suspensions in bar 13 of the original Kyrie (A52) are easier to hear because there is less contrapuntal movement and they occur in the soprano part.

4.3.7 Cambiata, nota cambiata or changing note
This unaccented dissonant decoration leaves a consonant note by step and proceeds to another consonant note by a **leap** of a 3rd. In A47 the dotted crotchet A♭ in the bass part is consonant with the dotted crotchet E♭ and the crotchet C in the soprano part (the quaver D♭ being a passing note). The bass then moves by step to the cambiata (labelled x) which forms a dissonant 4th with the soprano. It then leaves the cambiata by leaping a 3rd to the crotchet E♭ which forms a consonant perfect 5th with the soprano B♭. The same cambiata can be heard in a three-voice texture on A48 and in its original four-voice texture at the end of A46.

The term cambiata can also refer to complete three-note figures such as the bracketed notes in bar 2 of A47, or to four- or five-note figures such as those shown in bars 1–3 of A61. However, the English term 'changing note' is reserved for the single dissonant note (x in A47 and A48).

4.3.8 Échappée, escape note or escape tone
The *échappée* is an unaccented dissonance which is approached by step and quitted by a leap in the opposite direction. The last notes of the alto part in bars 11 and 14 of A24 are escape notes (marked with crosses). In both cases they form the dissonant interval of a 7th with the second tenor part before the alto leaps down a 3rd to a note which forms the consonant interval of a 6th with the second tenor at the beginning of the next bar. Similarly, in the first bar of A97 the first note of the upper part (F♯) forms a consonant 3rd with the lower part. The upper part then moves up a step to the *échappée* (G♮) which forms a dissonant perfect 4th with the lower part. Finally the upper part leaps down a 3rd to an E♮ which forms a consonant 3rd with the C♯ in the lower part.

4.3.9 Anticipation
This unaccented decoration is frequently found in the most important **cadences** of baroque music, such as the bourrée from Bach's Lute Suite in E minor (A89). In all four principal cadences of this dance (bars 7–8, 11–12, 15–16 and 23–24) there is an anticipation (each marked with an asterisk). Each one of these quavers forms a dissonant perfect 4th with the bass, and each of them anticipates the same note sounded as a consonant perfect octave in the following bar.

4.4 Contrapuntal techniques
In order to clarify complex contrapuntal textures composers developed a battery of compositional techniques which also offered intellectual stimulation to listeners and performers alike. Any of these techniques can be so pervasive that a whole movement might be named after the technique. For instance, fugal technique can be so dominant that the composer might entitle his work 'Fuga' or 'Fugue' (as is the case with Bach's Fugue in C minor on B14). Equally, any one or more of the techniques can be used in the context of a movement in which they are of secondary importance in the larger design, as is the case with the fugato in the sonata-form structure of the finale of Haydn's *Oxford* Symphony (B29).

Elements of music

4.4.1 Imitation

Imitation is a contrapuntal technique in which a **melody** or **motif** in one part is repeated more or less exactly in another part, the repetition being heard against the continuing melody of the first part. In bars 13–16 of the Andante from Haydn's String Quartet Op. 42 (B26) the first violin (the contrapuntal *dux*, or leader) enters with a one-bar motif which is imitated by the same motif at a lower pitch played by the second violin (the contrapuntal *comes*, or follower). Meanwhile the first violin continues its melody, thus forming two-part counterpoint with the second violin. The same process is repeated in the next two bars.

In true imitation there is enough of an overlap between the parts to create a contrapuntal **texture** between the melodic continuation of the *dux* and the repetition of the original melody or motif in the *comes* (as in B26). However, the term is often used loosely of textures where overlap is minimal. This is the case in bars 23–26 of B27 where *dux* (cello) and *comes* (violin) overlap by only one note (for instance, F♮ and D♮ in beat 1 of bar 24).

4.4.2 Point of imitation

Listening to the two passages discussed in 4.4.1 in context on B27 it becomes apparent that the other two instruments play subservient roles in the whole texture. Of course, it is possible for imitation to spread to all parts of a contrapuntal texture, as happens in the Kyrie of Palestrina's *Missa Iste confessor* (A52). The tenor sets off singing the first six notes of phrase 2 of the plainsong hymn shown in A50. This motif is imitated in turn by the bass, the soprano and the alto, but each is subtly varied. For instance, the bass sings just the first five notes of the plainsong phrase before continuing with a free part (a part that is unrelated to the original hymn), and the fourth and fifth notes are longer than the corresponding notes in the tenor part. Similarly, when the motif reappears in bars 7 (bass), 9 (soprano) and 10 (alto) the first note is shortened to a crotchet. A passage of music such as this in which imitation of just one motif is so pervasive is known as a point of imitation.

4.4.3 Pervasive imitation

In order to construct longer musical paragraphs than the Kyrie discussed above (4.4.2) composers of the late renaissance wrote a distinctive motif for each phrase of the text, used each motif for a **point of imitation**, and contrapuntally overlapped each point of imitation with the next. The technique is exemplified in the first 22 bars of A61. The first point of imitation is played by viols. The motif is a dotted figure rising a 3rd or a 5th to a cambiata (heard twice in the uppermost part, and replaced with a scalic figure in the lowest part). When the verse alto reaches his cadence in bar 4 the second point of imitation (built on the falling figure at the start of 'Christ Jesus made a sacrifice for sin') begins while the first viol continues its melody. Similarly, the end of the tenor phrase 'for sin' in bar 9 overlaps the start of the third point of imitation (beginning with the alto phrase 'the earth quakes'). In the same way the end of point 3 (tenor, bar 11) overlaps the start of point 4 (alto, 'the sun is darkened'), the end of point 4 overlaps the beginning of point 5 in bar 13, and the end of point 5 overlaps the beginning of point 6 (by one beat) in bar 18. In this way Gibbons has constructed a seamless passage of imitative counterpoint lasting 22 bars (it comes to an end when the full choir enters in five-part homophony at the end of bar 22).

4.4.4 Canon

Canon is a strict form of imitation in which the melodies of the **dux** (the contrapuntal leader) and the **comes** (the contrapuntal follower) are usually exactly the same. This is the case in the passage enclosed in a box in C64. Because the *comes* is pitched a compound 6th below the *dux* and because there are just two contrapuntal parts with the same melody it can be described as a **canon 2 in 1** at the 6th below.

In bars 6–8 of the same example there is a **canon by inversion**. In this passage it is quite clear that the falling pattern of a semitone, perfect 4th and another semitone in the *dux* (x^1 in bars 6–7) is mirrored by the rising pattern using the same intervals in the *comes* (x in bar 7). All of the remaining intervals of the *dux* (bars 6–8^3) are inverted in the *comes* (bars 7–9^1). For a more extended example of canon by inversion see bars 34–41 of C82.

Bach's Chorale Prelude BWV 608 is based on the famous carol tune *In dulci jubilo* (A91) which Bach used as a cantus firmus in his organ chorale (A94). The cantus firmus is itself treated as a canon 2 in 1 at the octave (A92). Between and beneath these canonic parts Bach added two other parts which are also in canon at the octave (A93). The melodies of these two canons are quite different from each other, so it is easy to follow their progress when they are combined in the performance of the complete chorale prelude on track A94 (the first 16 bars of which are shown in the corresponding printed example). A four-part composition such as this which combines two canons simultaneously is known as a canon 4 in 2 (the first number always designating the number of parts, the second the number of canonic melodies).

Canonic writing is often employed as an integral part of large-scale movements, particularly as a way of intensifying the prevailing mood. This is the case in the finale of Haydn's *Trauersinfonie*, an extract from which can be heard on track B21. The movement begins with a fast, relentless eight-bar melody in bare octaves that falls into two four-bar phrases (a and b). From this point onwards the texture becomes more complex. A repeat of phrase a played by violins in 6ths (bars 8–12) is followed by an extension of phrase b in two-part counterpoint with a new melody (c). In the tutti starting at bar 19 theme a is extended by sequential repetition (shown by the pecked line) and the passage ends with an imperfect cadence in bars 27–28. It is at this point that Haydn treats a version of phrase b canonically between first violins and cellos and double basses (b^2). Apart from the very first note this is a canon at the 7th below, or, more precisely, a canon at the compound 7th below. The canon can be heard in isolation on B22 (the pecked lines in B21 and B22 indicate non-canonic melodic continuations). Combined with this canon there is another based on a new theme (identified by the letter d in the viola and violin 2 parts of bars 29–37). This canon at the 4th above can be heard in isolation on B23 (the dotted lines again indicating non-canonic continuations). When the two canons are combined (B21, bars 28–34) the result is a canon 4 in 2 as in *In dulci jubilo*, but this one is heard in the context of a symphonic finale.

Elements of music

4.4.5 Contrapuntal inversion and invertible counterpoint

In Haydn's canonic writing in bars 28–34 of B21 it will be seen that violin 1 and cello play phrase b^2 in **canon** while the second violin and viola play phrase d in canon. In bars 37–42 the distribution of the phrases is reversed so that the outer parts now play phrase d in canon while the inner parts play phrase b^2 in canon. This example of contrapuntal inversion is easier to understand if just two strands of the contrapuntal textures of both passages are extracted as shown in B24. In the first passage (bars 1–5 of B24) phrase d sounds above phrase b^2, but in the second passage (bars 5–9 of B24) phrase d sounds below phrase b^2.

Invertible or **double counterpoint** is a type of counterpoint so written that it allows melodies to change places, the upper part becoming the lower part and vice versa. Contrapuntal inversion refers to the process of **inversion**. In B24 contrapuntal inversion is achieved by the simple expedient of transposing both parts by an octave. Similar counterpoint for three or four voices is called triple or **quadruple counterpoint**, and it is this last type of invertible counterpoint which is heard in the complete performance of the first 59 bars of Haydn's finale (B21).

4.4.6 Round and voice exchange

Near the end of A94 the ***dux*** (or leader) ends two bars before the ***comes*** (or follower), so Bach has to fill in the end of the uppermost part with a freely composed melody in order that the two parts should end together. This is not necessary in the special type of **canon** known as a round, the melody of which allows each voice to return immediately to the beginning and repeat the tune as often the singers desire. Because this process can theoretically last forever the round is sometimes classed as an infinite or perpetual canon. One of the finest examples of the genre is a medieval English round known as the Summer Canon or Reading Rota ('rota' being the Latin for round). It has two texts, one a secular English poem celebrating the coming of summer, the other a Latin hymn. The hymn is sung in unison on A14, and the round itself is sung with the English text on A15. It begins with a four-bar ostinato ('Sing cuccu nu sing cuccu') which is sung by two bass voices throughout the whole round. The manuscript calls this the ***pes*** (foot), presumably because it is written beneath the canonic melody of the round. It features in miniature the medieval contrapuntal technique of voice exchange, in which a phrase sung by one voice is sung by another while the first voice sings the phrase that the second voice has just completed. This is shown by the letters x and y above each two-bar phrase of the *pes* in A15, bars 1–8. Also heard throughout the whole rota is a **bourdon** (drone) played on a sinfony (hurdy-gurdy). Above the *pes* the canonic voices enter at two-bar intervals, each of them singing a melody identical with that sung on A14. When the first voice to enter reaches the end of bar 30 he immediately returns to the sign at the start of bar 7 and repeats the melody. Similarly, when the second, third and fourth voices reach the end of bars 32, 34 and 36 respectively, they return to the appropriate sign in bars 9–13. The recording fades out towards the end of the first repeat.

4.4.7 Quodlibet

In a quodlibet (the Latin name means 'as you like it') as many well-known tunes can be combined successively or contrapuntally as the composer wishes. The light-hearted nature of the genre is conveyed by the names of the types of quodlibet which were popular in sixteenth-century France and Spain – the *fricassée* (which the *Oxford English Dictionary* charmingly defines as 'a ragout of small animals or birds cut in pieces') and the *ensalada* (a Spanish salad). The last of Bach's *Goldberg Variations* (B2) is a quodlibet in which the harmonic progression common to all of the **variations** (shown between B1 and B2) is combined with two popular songs (sung on B3). The words suggest less sophisticated cuisine than the *fricassée* and *ensalada*: 'I have been so long away from you' and 'Cabbages and turnips have driven me away'. Apart from an added passing note Bach sticks rigidly to the bass of the harmonic progression. Above this the first popular song is heard in the tenor register imitated a bar later in the uppermost part. The second popular song is contrapuntally combined with the first, the end of it overlapping with another statement in the uppermost part (the two melodies are identified by encircled numbers in B2 and B3).

4.5 Fugue

Fugue is one of a number of musical terms that have changed their meaning over the ages. In medieval times 'fuga' meant **canon** (see 4.4.4 above), and in the renaissance the same term meant **imitation** (see 4.4.1, 4.4.2 and 4.4.3 above). From the seventeenth century onwards it applied to movements which were based upon a single melodic idea (very rarely more than one) which was heard successively in all voices of a consistently contrapuntal and largely imitative **texture**. This is as far as one can go in formulating a definition of fugue that will hold good for the almost infinite variety of movements bearing this title. Nevertheless there are a number of structures, techniques and textures that are particularly associated with fugal writing. Most of them can be illustrated by reference to Bach's Fugue in C minor from Book 2 of *The Well-Tempered Clavier*. In B14(a) this fugue is printed and performed in skeletal form to reveal its underlying structure (discussed in 4.5.1–4.5.7 below). On track B14(b) the fugue is performed as Bach wrote it.

4.5.1 Fugal exposition

At the start of a majority of fugues a distinctive melodic idea or **motif** is heard in one part, usually unaccompanied. This is the **subject**: in B14 it is a one-bar phrase first heard in the alto part. The subject is then imitated at a different pitch (usually a perfect 4th or a perfect 5th away from the subject). This is the **answer**: in B14 it is shown in the soprano part of bars 2–3[1]. Meanwhile the melodic line of the part that began the fugue continues so as to form a **counter-subject** sounding against the answer: in B14 it is shown in the alto part of bars 2–3[1]. Sometimes a short passage of free counterpoint is introduced between entries of the subject, either to help focus attention on the next entry, or to effect a **modulation** back to the tonic, or both. This is confusingly called a **codetta** (it has nothing to do with the codetta at the end of the exposition of a movement in sonata form). In Bach's fugue the codetta effects a modulation from the G-minor tonality of the answer back to the tonic key of C minor (soprano and alto parts, bars 3–4[1]). The next part to enter states the subject at its original pitch (or an octave above or below the original pitch). In B14 this entry of the subject is heard in the bass part of bars 4–5[1]. Meanwhile the part which presented the answer continues with the counter-subject (soprano, bars 4–5^1), and the part which began the fugue continues with a free contrapuntal melody (the inner part in the same bars).

In some fugues the counter-subject has the same melodic outline whenever it appears in combination with the subject or answer. When this is the case it is described as a regular counter-subject. In B14 the counter-subject heard in bars 2–3^1 is the same as the counter-subject heard in bars 4–5^1. They contain the same figure falling from the dominant to the tonic (G minor in bars 2–3^1 and C minor in bars 4–5^1). However, for the rest of the fugue Bach abandons this counter-subject in favour of free counterpoint. A fugal exposition is complete once all voices have stated the subject or answer. In B14 that point is reached when the bass part completes the subject (the E♭ at the beginning of bar 5).

4.5.2 Real and tonal answers in fugal expositions

When every note of a fugal **answer** remains at a fixed interval above or below the subject the answer is said to be real. This is the case with the real answer shown B9. It is pitched a perfect 5th higher than the subject, but is otherwise an exact copy of it. Some fugal subjects will not allow exact replication at a different pitch without initiating an unwanted modulation. To avoid this problem one of the intervals of the subject is altered to form what is known as a tonal answer. In B14 the descending 3rd with which the subject began becomes a descending second in the tonal answer, the remainder of the answer being an exact replica of the **subject** pitched a perfect 5th higher.

4.5.3 Fugal episodes

Most fugues contain passages in which the complete **subject** or **answer** is not heard. These passages are called **episodes**. They may be based on motifs from the subject or **counter-subject**, or they may introduce new material. Bach's first episode (bar 5 to the first quaver of bar 7 in B14) includes both. A new scalic figure (z) is melodically inverted in the next bar (z^1), the latter accompanied by versions of motif x from the start of the fugue subject.

4.5.4 Counter-exposition

Some fugues contain a counter-exposition in which all of the contrapuntal parts restate the **subject** or **answer** at the original pitches but in a different order. In most fugues containing a counter-exposition it follows on directly from the exposition proper. In B14 it is separated from the exposition by the first **episode**. As is usually the case both the order in which the voices enter and the order in which the subject and answer appear are changed in this counter-exposition. In the **exposition** the voices enter in the order alto (subject) – soprano (answer) – bass (subject). In the counter-exposition they enter in the order bass (answer, bars 7–8^1) – soprano (subject, bars 8–9^1) – alto (answer, bars 10–11^1). Both the answer and the subject are slightly modified (the former avoiding a modulation to G minor by changing the B♭ of the tonal answer to a B♮, the latter by the introduction of dotted rhythms). As in the exposition a bar of free counterpoint (codetta in the exposition, episode 2 in the counter-exposition) separates the second entry from the third.

4: Counterpoint

4.5.5 Middle entries

In most fugues the central section passes through a number of different keys. Entries of the **subject** or **answer** in keys other than the tonic and dominant in this central section are therefore known as middle entries. In this fugue there is only one. It is heard in the subdominant key of F minor in the bass part (bars 11^3–12^3). This middle entry is followed by a third episode (bars 12^3–14^1) which, with the help of motifs y and x in the bass, brings the first section of the fugue to an end with a perfect cadence in the dominant key of G minor.

4.5.6 Stretto, augmentation and inversion

The second section of Bach's Fugue in C minor (B14) begins with an entry of the **subject** in its original form (soprano, bars 14–15). Almost immediately it is joined by the alto part which presents the same subject in **augmentation** (every note of the subject is doubled in length so it extends over two bars instead of one). The last six notes of the augmented subject are then combined with a free **inversion** of the **answer** (nearly all of the intervals of the original answer are retained, but they all move in the opposite direction). When entries of the subject are telescoped so they overlap each other in this way they are said to be in **stretto**. Frequently composers will give an impression of stretto by imitating just the start of the subject. A stretto in which the whole subject is heard in all participating parts is known as a **stretto maestrale**, and it is this type of stretto which Bach exploits in bars 16–18^1, where all three contrapuntal voices present the complete subject or answer, overlapping each other at two-beat intervals.

In the first eighteen bars of the fugue no more than three contrapuntal parts can be heard at any one time. At bar 19 the **texture** dramatically increases to four voices with the entry of the augmented subject in the bass. A majority of fugues (particularly those for ensembles of voices or instruments) strictly maintain the same number of parts throughout the fugue (using rests when the texture is reduced). But, as with most generalisations about fugue, the exceptions are so numerous that they do more than simply prove the rule. Bach's four-part texture is maintained above the answer in its inverted and original forms (bars 21–23^1), and the second section of the fugue ends with another version of motif x forming the bass of a definitive perfect cadence in the tonic key (bar 23).

4.5.7 Fugal coda or closing section

A variety of definitions of the concluding bars of a fugue are to be found in textbooks, but since none of them applies to all fugues it is probably best to examine each fugue as a unique entity. In the Fugue in C minor from Book 2 of Bach's *Well-Tempered Clavier* (B14) there are three very conclusive cadences. The first, in bars 13–14, is a perfect cadence in the dominant key of G minor. The second, in bar 23, is a perfect cadence in the tonic key of C minor, and it replicates the bass and syncopated figuration of the first cadence. These two cadences mark the ends of the first and second sections of a binary-form structure. (The third perfect cadence is heard at the end of the whole fugue.) By no means do all fugues exhibit such clear-cut binary form, and in other fugues it might be better to describe the passage which begins with the final statement of the **subject**

Elements of music

in its original form and original key as a closing section. But here bars 23³–28 form a coda to the binary structure of bars 1–23 and they conform to the concept of a fugal coda.

It begins at the end of bar 23 with very close **stretti** between the upper two parts (only one beat now separates one entry from the next where before there had been gaps of two or four beats). In bars 1–22 statements of the subject or **answer** begin after the first or third beats of each bar so that the fourth note always falls on a strong beat. But in the soprano part the answer enters after the fourth beat of bar 23, and the subject enters at the same point in bar 24. This displaces the first accent from the fourth note of each entry to the second note (B♮ at the start of bar 24 and A♭ at the start of bar 25). Meanwhile entries in the alto part start after the third beat of bar 23 and the first beat of bar 25. Fugal entries that occur alternately on or just after both weak and strong beats are said to be made *per arsin et thesin*.

In bar 26 the bass part enters with what sounds like a free inversion of the subject, but after five notes it breaks into non-thematic semiquavers (compare this entry with the free inversion of the answer in bars 15–16¹). Such incomplete statements of the subject or answer are known as **false entries**.

4.5.8 Double fugue

Double and **triple fugues** have two and three subjects respectively. Genuine triple fugues are so rare that they need not be illustrated here (readers who wish to pursue the matter are referred to the Fugue in F♯ minor in the second book of *The Well-Tempered Clavier*, BWV 883). There are two types of double fugue. In the first type the two subjects and their answers are heard together from the outset (as shown in B13). In this *fughetta* (a short fugal movement) the two subjects always appear together, with the other parts providing free contrapuntal lines (as the inner voices do in bars 3⁴–6). Only the fugal exposition is recorded on B13, but it is long enough to indicate that this type of double fugue with its paired entries could equally well be described as a fugue with a regular counter-subject. In fact the only way to distinguish it from a normal fugue is the appearance of the counter-subject (alias second subject) combined with the 'real' subject right from the start of the fugue.

The second type of double fugue is quite distinct from the type of double fugue described above. The first subject is treated imitatively in all of the contrapuntal parts so as to form a normal fugal exposition, such as that to be heard at the start of the gigue from Bach's Partita in G major (B10). Ideas from this first exposition might then be developed in any of the ways discussed above (4.5.3–4.5.6). In the same way, the second subject is used to form another fugal exposition, such as that recorded on B11. This might then be followed by the same sort of development as followed the first exposition. Finally the two subjects are contrapuntally combined in the manner shown in B12 (the two subjects can be identified quite easily on the corresponding track because they are in the outer parts).

4.5.9 Fugato

A fugal passage sometimes occurs as part of a larger formal design, particularly in the development section of movements in sonata form, and

4: Counterpoint

it is often thematically linked with the rest of the movement. Such a passage is called a fugato. The treatment of the subject and counter-subject is often freer than is the case in a completely independent fugue (such as that recorded on B14). This is true of the fugato in the finale of Haydn's *Oxford* Symphony. B28 shows the periodically phrased first-subject theme heard at the beginning of the movement. The fugato (B29) begins with a four-bar subject which is substantially the same as the first four bars of B28. It is accompanied by a regular **counter-subject** characterised by a falling chromatic scale. In bars 5–9 there is free counterpoint in which motif x from the first subject (B28) is treated imitatively. In an independent fugue one would call this passage a codetta (see 4.5.1). The answer (bars 9–13) is contrapuntally inverted with the counter-subject (the former now above the latter). After another, shorter passage of free counterpoint the final entry of the exposition of this three-voice fugato is heard in bars 15–19, again with the regular counter-subject. The end of this entry is also the end of a fugal exposition which has followed the usual tonal scheme (the tonic key of E minor for the subject and the dominant key of B minor for the answer). However, the two entries that follow (bars 21–25 and 28–30) do not follow normal fugal practice. The first could be described as a **redundant entry** (since all three contrapuntal parts have already stated the subject or answer) were it not for the fact that it is in the 'wrong' key (A minor instead of E minor or B minor). The second of these entries peters out after a couple of bars (and could therefore be described as a **false entry**). In fact the whole fugato peters out at this point as Haydn abandons counterpoint for the dramatic homophony of bars 38–48. Right at the end of the track (bars 48–54) the second subject of the sonata-form exposition returns in C major. Since the tonic key of the whole movement is G major this is a false recapitulation (there are 38 bars of the development to go before the 'real' recapitulation begins in the 'right' key). Thus it is that the mock-heroics of this fugato are completely integrated with the jovial mood of the whole finale.

For a modern example of fugato integrated into an extended movement see bars 14–41 of C82.

4.6 Serial counterpoint

The texture of the second movement of Stravinsky's *Canticum sacrum* (C88) is, like much twentieth-century **serial music**, extremely contrapuntal. Unlike earlier polyphony it does not rely upon tonal tensions generated between contrapuntal parts, nor does it rely on a structured use of consonance and dissonance. Indeed, such a concept has no meaning in music in which any combination of notes may form acceptable chords provided they are products of serial manipulation. Instead the music relies upon a preconceived **tone row** or **series** to achieve coherence. Stravinsky's row in its original form (the **prime order**) can be clearly heard in the first three bars of the vocal part of C88. It includes all twelve chromatic tones, some of which are repeated in the oscillation between the seventh and eighth notes of the row (E♭ and D♭), and the simple repetition of the eleventh note (B♮). This prime order (P) is represented in its simplest form on the extra stave below these three bars (C88), and is also shown at (i) following C88. Against the tenor melody a counter-melody is

Elements of music

heard on a cor anglais, a flute and a harp. This consists of the row in **retrograde inversion** (a melodically inverted version of the prime order played backwards). Figure (ii), which follows C88, shows the retrograde row, the notes of which correspond with those in the three chords at the beginning of the movement and with the tenor part starting on the fourth note of bar 7 (C88) up to the end of the extract. C88(iii) shows the retrograde inversion, in which every ascending interval of C88(ii) becomes a descending interval encompassing exactly the same number of semitones as the corresponding interval in the retrograde row (as the brackets above and below C88(ii) and C88(iii) show). There are two-note oscillations in both of these rows (between D♭ and E♭ in the vocal part of bars 8–9 of C88, and between G♮ and F♯ in the cor anglais part of bars 3–4). The retrograde inversion (RI) is shown in its simplest form on the second extra stave below bars 3–5 of C88. The rest of the extract consists of the first six notes (**hexachord**) of the **retrograde order** (R 1–6, tenor, bars 5–6) overlapped with the first hexachord of the sixth transposition of the retrograde inversion (RI_6 1–6, tenor, bars 6–7). C88(iv) shows this transposed hexachord (pitched six semitones above the first six notes of C88(iii)). This hexachord in turn overlaps the first note of another complete statement of the retrograde order (tenor, bars 7–10). The pitches of the retrograde order in the tenor are canonically imitated by the harp and flute (with the last two notes pre-echoed in the oscillations between G♮ and A♭ in the cor anglais part).

Thus serial counterpoint forsakes most of the contrapuntal conventions and techniques of tonal counterpoint. Instead order is imposed by the interaction of melodies which all derive their pitch outlines from a single predetermined series of twelve notes. In 'Surge, aquilo' it is relatively easy to hear the compositional processes in the tenor part, but very difficult to identify the rows in the instrumental parts (because of the changes from one instrument to another, and the **octave displacements** of individual notes). It is all too easy to examine twelve-tone music with a magnifying glass, as though the essence of the music could be revealed by serial analysis. It is as well to stand back and listen to the whole effect and, with this piece, ask how well these translucent contrapuntal **textures** help us to appreciate the beauty of the text:

'Awake, O north wind, and come thou south;
Blow upon my garden, that the spices thereof may flow out.'

5:
Harmony

Harmony is the simultaneous combination of sounds to form a succession of **chords**. Harmony is an unavoidable by-product of counterpoint (Chapter 4), since the sounding together of melodies cannot fail to produce a series of chords. This is evident in A15 where the contrapuntal combination of two melodic fragments x and y (bars 1–8) results in the series of two-note chords shown on the extra stave. In the same example the four contrapuntal strands sounding together in bars 15–18 produce the succession of chords shown on the extra stave beneath these bars. Conversely, the four chords at the end of the extract from a song by Hauer shown in C40 can be heard as four separate semitonal melodic fragments (A, B, C and D) derived from the melody of the first seven bars. So harmony is music heard as successive vertical combinations of sounds, while counterpoint is music heard horizontally as combinations of melodies. Harmony and counterpoint contribute to the texture of most types of music in which two or more pitches are sounded simultaneously, but often one of these two elements will feature more strongly than the other. This is true even in music that at first hearing seems to be just a series of chords, such as A35. Closer listening to this music will reveal that the bass part is just as melodic as the soprano. Although the two inner parts are subordinate to the outer parts, playing or singing them individually will reveal that both of them are melodies (albeit somewhat primitive). Only in extreme cases like C86 is the element of counterpoint totally absent.

5.1 Chord symbols

This section describes three systems of symbols commonly used to identify types of chord. The first two tell the performer what sorts of chord to improvise at more or less precise points in a composition. Baroque figuring (5.1.1) is always associated with a written-out bass part. Above it the performer improvises harmonies in accordance with a series of figures (or in accordance with contemporary performance practice in passages where no figures are shown). Letter-name chord symbols (5.1.2) are usually shown under a melody, the precise configuration of the bass part being left to the performer. Unlike figuring and letter-name symbols, Roman numerals (5.1.3) show how chords that are already fully notated function in relation to the prevailing key. Rather than showing what chords should be improvised, they are analytical tools that help explain the inner logic of tonal music. All three systems are used in the music examples, the choice being determined by the type of music and the definition the symbols help to illustrate. Thus, for instance, Roman numerals would make no sense in non-tonal music, but, in certain circumstances, one of the other systems could aid understanding.

5.1.1 Figuring

Arabic numerals beneath bass notes show the intervals formed between the bass and the chord-notes above it. In its fully developed form this system of figuring (**figured bass** or **thorough bass**) was used in baroque music as a type of shorthand showing keyboard instrumentalists (or performers playing any of a range of plucked instruments) what sort of chords to improvise above the written-out bass part. In the first four bars of the recitative by Bach shown in B16 there are two or three figures under each bass note in the first three bars. The two figures in bar 1 indicate that the organist should play notes a 6th and a 3rd above the bass C♯. The transcription from the recording shows that the organist plays an A♮ a 6th above the C♯ and an E♮ a 10th above it. A 10th is a compound 3rd (an octave plus a 3rd) and it is implicit in figuring that any interval indicated by a figure can be augmented by one or more octaves. The process by which the organist translates the figured bass into improvised chords is known as **realisation**.

The figuring beneath the first bass note of bar 2 indicates that the notes A (a 5th above the bass D♯) and F♯ (a 3rd above the bass) should be played. There is no need to indicate that the 3rd should be sharpened since the key signature at the start of each stave (F♯ and C♯ in this example) affects chords derived from the figuring as well as notes on the stave. In the same way the second chord of bar 2 shows that notes a 6th and a 3rd above the bass note should be included in the improvised chord, and again an accidental is not required because C♯ is included in the key signature. The figuring under the first chord in bar 3 indicates a four-note discord consisting of the bass C♯ and notes a 6th (A♮) a 5th (G♮) and a 3rd (E♮) above it.

In the first three bars of the recitative the figures shown in brackets would not normally be shown because an unwritten convention decrees that an unfigured bass note implies a $\substack{5\\3}$ chord, that the figure 6 implies a $\substack{6\\3}$ chord and so on.

As well as a type of shorthand for the performer, figuring also indicates whether a chord is a simple triad (see 5.2.1), or a dissonant chord such as a 7th (see 5.4.3), and whether it is in root position or inverted (see 5.2.3, 5.4.1, 5.4.2 and 5.4.4). The system has the disadvantage that it does not relate chords to the prevailing key in the way that the Roman numerals in the rest of the recitative do.

5.1.2 Letter-name chord symbols

Like figuring, guitar chord symbols tell the performer what sort of chords to improvise, but instead of figures a letter shows the type of chord that is to be improvised. A single capital letter is taken to mean a root-position major triad, as with the letter F under the first chord of C86. A lower-case letter m (or abbreviation such as 'min.') after a capital letter indicates a root-position minor triad, as with the letters 'Dm' under the fifth chord of the same example. A degree sign or the abbreviation 'dim.' means a diminished chord, as with the symbols under the first chord of B20. A plus sign means an augmented triad, as with the symbols under the chords in bar 6 of C21. (For an explanation of major, minor, diminished and augmented triads see 5.3.2.)

Inverted triads (5.3.3) are shown by the letter-name of the bass note beneath an oblique slash. Thus the first chord symbol in A87 indicates an F-minor chord with the 5th (C♮) sounded in the bass (an F-minor chord in second inversion). Like figuring, letter-name chord symbols are not related to a specific key.

5.1.3 Roman numerals

Roman numerals indicate particular triads in particular keys, each numeral corresponding with a degree of a diatonic scale.

- I = **tonic triad** (A95, bar 1)
- II = **supertonic triad** (B67, bar 4)
- III = **mediant triad** (A81, bar 13)
- IV = **subdominant triad** (A95, bar 3)
- V = **dominant triad** (A95, bar 7)
- VI = **submediant triad** (A95, bar 2)
- VII = **leading-note triad** (A95, bar 3).

When combined with figuring, Roman numerals precisely identify the type of chord, its relationship to the prevailing key and whether it is in root position or one of the possible inversions. For instance the second chord in bar 7 of A91 is identified as the tonic chord of E major by the Roman numeral I, while I^6 under the first chord in this bar identifies it as the same chord in first inversion. Similarly I^6 in bar 20 identifies this chord as the tonic chord of F♯ minor in first inversion, while I^6_4 identifies the second chord as the tonic chord of F♯ minor in second inversion. On the extra stave beneath bars 10–12 in the same example the dominant chord of F♯ minor is shown with a 7th added above the bass. This dominant-7th chord is identified by the roman numeral V (identifying a triad on the fifth degree of the scale of F♯ minor) plus an Arabic figure 7 (identifying the added 7th). The next two chords contain the same four notes (C♯, E♯, G♯ and B) arranged in a different way so that in the first of them the 7th of the original chord is the lowest note and in the second the 5th of the chord is the lowest note. Since these two chords contain the three notes that form the dominant triad of F♯ minor (C♯, E♯ and G♯) the Roman numeral V is still used. Added to this are three figures that indicate the intervals formed between the lowest note and the other three notes of these inversions of the dominant-7th chord.

Because of the possibility of confusing figuring with the names of the component notes of a chord (root, third, fifth, seventh and so on) an alternative system of Roman numerals combined with lower-case letters is widely used, the letters standing for inversions. The letter a indicates a root-position chord (though like $^5_3$ it is rarely used) while the letters b and c indicate first- and second-inversion chords respectively. For chords containing more than three notes a superscript Arabic numeral is placed between the roman numeral and the lower case letter. The two systems are shown one above the other below the first four bars of A95. For root-position chords there is no difference between the two systems, but for inverted chords they diverge. Roman numerals with figuring is the system used throughout this book because it combines the best features of both methods and is compatible with figured basses found in many baroque scores. The meanings of these symbols in terms of aural phenomena is explored in the rest of the chapter, but the following concordance might be useful for those who are already familiar with one or other of the systems.

- I (in both systems) = root-position tonic triad
- V^7 (in both systems) = root-position dominant 7th chord
- I^6 or Ib = first-inversion tonic triad
- I^6_4 or Ic = second-inversion tonic chord

Elements of music

V_5^6 or V⁷b = first-inversion dominant-7th chord
V_3^4 or V⁷c = second-inversion dominant-7th chord
V_2^4 or V⁷d = third-inversion dominant-7th chord.

The two systems apply in similar ways to chords built on other degrees of diatonic scales.

5.2 Consonance and dissonance

Chords of two or more notes that sound relatively stable are described as being **consonant**, and those which sound relatively unstable are described as **dissonant**. Instability engenders movement (an unstable house is likely to fall down). Similarly, dissonant chords generate a feeling of instability which only resolves when one or more of the constituent notes moves to the relative stability of a consonance. There are many mathematical and psychological theories that attempt to explain these phenomena. Pythagoras discovered that, other things being equal, a vibrating string that is twice as long as another vibrating string will sound a **perfect octave** lower than the shorter string. So a two-note chord forming an octave can be produced by any two strings (or pipes) which differ in length by the ratio 2:1. Similarly a **perfect 5th** can be produced by a difference in length in the ratio 3:2, a **perfect 4th** by a ratio of 4:3, a **major 3rd** by a ratio of 5:4 and so on in gradually increasing mathematical complexity as the intervals move from consonance to dissonance. These intervals occur naturally in a **harmonic series** (C95). The notes of the harmonic series are the only ones which 'natural' brass instruments can play without some distortion (the slide on a trombone and valves on other brass instruments make it possible to play a full chromatic range of notes). Additionally notes of the harmonic series are present to a greater or lesser degree in all but electronically generated sounds. So perfect octaves, perfect 5ths, perfect 4ths and 3rds are essential and unavoidable elements of the texture of nearly all types of music (the higher, more dissonant **partials** are usually not as loud as the lower ones that form consonant intervals).

Such theories correspond with subjective experience of consonance and dissonance. The harmonic interval of a perfect octave is universally regarded as being **concordant**. Thus one hardly notices when members of a mixed congregation sing a hymn tune an octave apart from one another (the effect can be heard in the first 11 bars of A26). There can be no doubt that the earliest extant Christian chants would often have been sung in this way, with the unbroken voices of novices sounding an octave above older monks. In later, more complex styles it is evident that the perfect octave was always regarded as being completely consonant: the first phrase of the fifteenth-century Kyrie shown in A28 begins and ends with this entirely stable interval. Asked to describe the effect of the end of this phrase a layman might say that 'the music comes to rest at the end of the phrase'. The notion of the stability of the perfect octave is obviously implicit in such descriptions.

The second of Pythagoras' intervals, the perfect 5th, was the next interval to be accepted as consonant in early polyphony (as A7(a) shows). The second burden of A24 (bars 8–17) begins and ends with this harmonic interval sung by two tenors. It will be seen that this three-note chord contains a perfect octave and a perfect 4th as well as a perfect 5th. The perfect 4th was another of Pythagoras' perfect intervals and it was accepted as a concord as early as the tenth century (as A7(b) shows).

5: Harmony

By the sixteenth century the major 3rd (Pythagoras's fourth most complex interval) was thought to be concordant enough to be used in the final, stable-sounding chord of a composition. The last chord of A33 shows that, if a 3rd or compound 3rd above the bass is included in a chord in which the bass note is doubled an octave above, the interval of a 6th will be formed between the upper parts. So acceptance of the 6th as a consonant interval followed naturally from acceptance of the 3rd. To modern ears these two intervals sound more mellifluous than austere perfect intervals. Pieces such as Janequin's chanson *La Bataille* (A31) show that this was probably the view of composers of secular music as early as the beginning of the sixteenth century. Of the thirty four intervals formed between the soprano and alto on the treble stave of A31, no fewer than twenty are 3rds, ten are 6ths and only four are perfect intervals.

Generally speaking 3rds, perfect 4ths and 5ths, 6ths and perfect octaves, were regarded as consonant, relative to the dissonant, unstable intervals of the 2nd, **tritone** (**augmented 4th** or **diminished 5th**) and 7th from the beginning of the fifteenth century to the end of the nineteenth century. Some historians maintain that tolerance of dissonance increased with the development of western harmony. As a broad generalisation there is some truth in this observation, but there are so many exceptions (such as the high level of dissonance in the Benedictus from Machaut's *Messe de Nostre Dame* shown in A21) that it is better to turn to the music itself for confirmation.

A53 is a simplified version of the alto and tenor parts of bars 4–9 from the Kyrie of Palestrina's *Missa Iste confessor*. All of the consonant intervals discussed above are used in this passage (with the sole exception of the perfect 5th). There is just one discord – the tritone B–F on the second beat of the last bar. But the B♮ is a **passing note** that, in this context, hardly registers as a discord (because it sounds on a weak beat and is part of a melodic line that moves smoothly from a concordant 6th to an equally concordant 3rd). In another simplified version (A54) of the same passage a tritone on a strong beat is introduced on the third beat of the second complete bar. This really does sound dissonant, but Palestrina mitigates the effect by sounding the E♮ as a concordant 3rd against the tenor on the second beat of the bar and by allowing the alto to fall a step to another concordant 3rd above the tenor on the last beat of the bar. This whole formula, consisting of **preparation** (beat 2), **suspension** (beat 3) and **resolution** (beat 4) is often called a suspension, though the term ought strictly to be limited to the actual point of dissonance.

The figure of a pair of tied notes resolving down by step is replicated in the alto part from the fourth beat of the second complete bar to the second beat of the next bar. Many will feel that the perfect 4th at the start of the third complete bar is as dissonant as the tritone in the second complete bar. Palestrina would have agreed for, although the perfect 4th was regarded as a concord in earlier and later periods, it was considered to be dissonant in the renaissance when it was formed between the lowest-sounding part and any part above it. When it was formed between any of the upper parts it was considered to be consonant – as with the 4ths between the alto and the first tenor in the chords labelled $^6_3$ in bars 5–7 of A24. So, since the tenor is the lowest-sounding part at the start of bar 3 in A54, Palestrina prepares and resolves the dissonant 4th in a similar manner to the previous suspension.

Elements of music

The ambiguous status of the perfect 4th vis-à-vis consonance and dissonance becomes even more complex in a very characteristic cadence formula of the sixteenth and early seventeenth centuries. In this formula a 4th between the lowest part and an upper part is treated as though it were consonant, provided certain constraints are observed. A47 shows the soprano and bass parts at the end of the Kyrie from Victoria's *Missa O quam gloriosum*. Here a **consonant 4th** (marked with an asterisk) is heard in its most basic form. As in all such cadences the consonant 4th is approached by step, articulated on a weak beat and resolved on the next weak beat. When the tenor part is added to this passage (A48) two further dissonances appear. Both are suspensions, and both form the interval of a minor 7th (indicated by vertical brackets). Thus in relation to the suspensions on either side of it the consonant 4th does indeed sound relatively consonant.

This concept of the relativity of consonance and dissonance runs throughout the history of harmony. An interval that sounds very dissonant in one style might well sound completely consonant in a different context. Indeed the extent to which dissonance is tolerated is one of the determining features of style.

5.3 Triads

Since the fifteenth century the commonest chords used in most styles of European music have consisted of combinations of the consonant intervals described in the previous section (5.2). Of these the most basic has been a type of chord consisting of two superimposed 3rds known as a triad. The setting of the words 'Though Philomela' at the start of A59 consists of repetitions of a triad containing the notes F, A and C (the superimposed 3rds are shown by vertical brackets).

5.3.1 Root-position triads and common chords

Triads can be formed on any degree of a modal or tonal scale. Those shown in A59(c) are based on the notes of the mixolydian mode on F (F–G–A–B♭–C–D–E♭–F). Apart from the bracketed chord, each of them consists of a bass note (known as the **root**) plus a 3rd and a 5th above it (labelled R, 3, 5 in the first chord). All chords in which the **intervals** between the lowest-sounding note and any notes above it are a 3rd (or a compound 3rd), a 5th (or a compound 5th) and (possibly) an octave are known as root-position triads. In bars 30–34 of A59(b), complete root-position triads are sung on the first beat of each bar. They are built on the descending mixolydian mode and are identified by Roman numerals according to the degree of the scale upon which they are built. Thus the triad on the first beat of bar 30 is based on the first degree of the mode (tenor F), so it is known as chord I. Similarly the triads on the first beats of bars 32, 33 and 34 are based on the sixth, fifth and fourth degrees of the mode (D, C and B♭ in the tenor part), so they are known as chords VI, V and IV respectively. Both sections of Morley's complete ballett begin and end in F major, but modality is evident in his use of the flat seventh degree of F major (E♭) and the triad built on it (♭VII in bar 31).

On the last beats of bars 30–33 chords are built successively on the fourth, fifth, second and first degrees of the scale. They differ from the triads on the first beats of the same bars in that the 5th is omitted and the root is doubled. Nevertheless, when heard in the context of a complete harmonic progression they function in the same way as complete triads.

When triads are expanded to become four-note chords it is obvious that at least one of the notes will have to be **doubled**. This is the case in the first two bars of A30 where the bass note of every one of these root-position triads is doubled at the octave. Theoretically the three pitch classes of a triad can be doubled as often as desired. The effect is a thickening of the texture rather than a change in the type of chord. This is evident in A64 in which all of the chords except those with the figure 6 beneath them are in root position. The bass part of all of these chords is doubled at the octave below and, in the first bar, at the octave above. An extreme case of doubling notes of a triad is shown in C86. Britten's first chord is the same F-major triad as the first chord of A59 except that it is in seven parts instead of three. Britten's next chord is a simple A-major triad (A, C♯ and E) arranged as a massive 14-part chord.

5.3.2 Major, minor, diminished and augmented triads

All types of triad consist of two superimposed 3rds (possibly with one or more of its constituent pitches doubled at the octave). A major triad consists of a major 3rd with a minor 3rd superimposed on it (A59, bars 1–2). A minor triad consists of a minor 3rd with a major 3rd superimposed on it (A35, bar 1). In both cases the interval between the outer notes is a perfect 5th. A diminished triad consists of two superimposed minor 3rds, and the interval between the outer notes is a diminished 5th (A59(c)). An augmented triad consists of two superimposed major 3rds, and the interval between the outer notes is an augmented 5th (C21).

In the extract from *Billy Budd* (C86) only major and minor triads are used (the latter indicated by the letter m after the letter that identifies the root of the chord). In Britain these simple major and minor triads are known as **common chords**. In America the term is restricted to major triads.

Because the root-position diminished triad contains a very prominent diminished 5th (or tritone) between the bass and an upper part it is rarely used. A diatonic triad on the leading note (chord VII) is a familiar example. It is shown at the end of A59(c) in the key of F major, but although Morley makes use of the leading note (E♮) in chord V (A59(b), bar 31) he completely avoids the diminished triad which can be constructed on it. Instead he uses a major triad on the flattened leading note, a characteristically modal sound also heard in bar 31. A diminished triad on the leading note is sometimes used in later styles when it resolves to the tonic triad. This is the case in bars 3–4 of A95 in which chord VII in D minor resolves to chord I.

The augmented triad commonly occurs in music based on a **whole-tone scale**. Ascending augmented triads can be heard three times in the extract from Debussy's 'Voiles' shown in C21. The whole of this extract derives from the whole-tone scale at the start. Only two triads can be constructed from the whole-tone scale: they are both augmented triads and are shown on the extra stave above bar 4. Debussy's third augmented triad consists of the same pitches as the first and the intervals are same (two major 3rds making an augmented 5th between the outer parts).

5.3.3 Inverted triads

Chords are said to be **inverted** when a note other than the root is sounded in the bass (the lowest-sounding note). Two inversions of a triad are

Elements of music

possible: in a **first-inversion triad** the third of the **root-position chord** is sounded in the bass. In a **second-inversion triad** the 5th of the root-position chord is sounded in the bass.

In fourteenth-century England an improvisatory technique known as **faburden** produced streams of first-inversion triads. The effect in miniature can be heard in the first burden of A24 in which there are four first-inversion chords in bars 5–7. These are identified by the figures $^6_3$, the upper figure showing the interval of a 6th between the lowest and highest notes, the lower figure referring to the interval of a 3rd between the two tenor parts (an alternative name for a first-inversion triad is a **six-three chord**). As with root-position triads any of the notes of a first-inversion chord can be doubled.

The extra stave labelled y below A39 shows the three first-inversion chords Vaughan Williams uses in the extract from his *Fantasia on a Theme by Thomas Tallis*. These are placed immediately below the root-position triads to which they are related (x) to show how the third of the root-position triads becomes the lowest-sounding note in the three first-inversion chords. First-inversion G-minor triads can be heard as four-part chords in the context of the composer's phrygian harmony in bars 3 and 7 (where first-inversion chords immediately follow the root-position triads to which they are related). First-inversion A♭-major triads occur in bars 13 and 15, and there is an F-minor triad in first inversion on the second beat of bar 17.

While root-position **diminished triads** are very rarely used (see 5.3.1 and chord VII in bar 3 of A95) they occur frequently in first inversion. In B16 the last chord of the second bar is a first inversion of the root-position diminished triad identified as chord VII in bar 3 of A95. The third of the chord (E♮) is played by the cello and double bass, the 5th of the chord (G♮) is played by upper strings, and the root of the chord (C♯) is sung by the soprano. Another first-inversion diminished triad occurs on the third and fourth beats of bar 6. This chord derives from the root-position diminished triad on the seventh degree of the scale of B minor in which the root is A♯, the third is C♯ and the fifth is E♮.

In tonal music the **augmented triad** in first inversion which is most frequently encountered is that based on the third degree of a minor scale. The root-position augmented triad in the key of C minor is shown on the extra stave to the left of bar 13 of A81. Couperin uses it in first inversion in the last beat of bar 13. The effect is particularly pungent in this context because the E♭ in chord III^6 forms a telling false relation with the *tierce de Picardie* (E♮) in the tonic chord with which the extract ends.

A second-inversion triad is formed when the 5th of the triad is the lowest-sounding note of the chord. The extra stave beneath bar 10 of the extract from Schubert's 'Der Doppelgänger' (B58) shows that the intervals between the bass note of a second-inversion triad and any notes above it are a 4th (E–A in this A-minor chord) and a 6th (E–C in the same chord). An alternative name for a second-inversion triad is a **six–four chord**. Because a 4th from the bass was for centuries regarded as a dissonance, second-inversion triads are less common and more striking than root-position and first-inversion triads. When listening to B58 there can be no mistaking Schubert's second-inversion tonic chord (I$^6_4$) since it initiates a return to the tonic key of A minor, and forms the dynamic and emotional climax of the whole song.

5: Harmony

Second-inversion triads just before the end of a phrase are characteristic of classical music. The first chord of B46(i) is a good example. The same chord can be heard in B46(ii) and, in its original context, at the end of B41 (bar 15, beat 2).

5.4 Cadences

Cadences can occur in a purely melodic context, as in the antecedent phrase ending on the dominant and its consequent ending on the tonic in bars 8 and 16 of B28. These cadences function in a manner analogous to punctuation marks in English, the first like a comma at the end of a phrase or clause, and the second like a full stop at the end of a sentence. The effect can be considerably enhanced by the addition of chords which confirm or alter the implied tonality of the melody.

5.4.1 Perfect and imperfect cadences

In harmonic terms the musical equivalent of a full stop is the perfect cadence (otherwise known as an **authentic cadence**, **full cadence** or **full close**). This consists of a triad on the fifth degree of a major or minor scale (the dominant chord or chord V) followed by a triad on the first degree (the tonic chord or chord I). Two isolated perfect cadences in G major are shown in B46, both of them preceded by the second-inversion triads discussed in 5.3.3 above. The perfect cadence at the end of the first four-bar phrase of Mozart's minuet can be heard in simplified form in B48. In B49 the same perfect cadence (bars 3–4) is followed by a perfect cadence in the dominant key of D major at the end of the second four-bar phrase (bars 7–8). The original and somewhat more elaborate versions of all of these cadences can be heard in B41 in bars 3–4 (related to B48), bars 7–8 (related to the last two bars of B49) and bars 15–16 (related to B46). Perfect cadences in the key of A major are played on an organ in bars 11–12 and 14–15 of B6. The organist plays Bach's harmonisation of the whole of the last phrase ('auf Erd' ist nicht seins gleichen') at the end of which another perfect cadence can be heard, this time in the tonic key of D major.

When chords V and I are reversed at the end of a phrase an imperfect cadence (also called a **half cadence** or **half close**) is formed. This may be likened to a comma that suggests a caesura in a line of poetry. The effect can be heard in bar 16 of B6, in which the imperfect cadence in E minor mirrors the effect of the comma at the end of the phrase 'sein grausam Rüstung ist'. In both Luther's text and Bach's harmony one feels that a slight break is needed here before the sense of the text and the music is completed by the final phrase (the end of which is marked by Luther's full stop and Bach's perfect cadence). The imperfect cadence at the end of the first phrase of B25 (bars 9–10) is similarly made up of chords I and V, this time in the key of A♭ major.

Imperfect cadences can be formed with almost any chord proceeding to the dominant triad (chord V). In bar 2 of A30 chord IV (the triad on the fourth degree of the scale) in the key of C major forms an imperfect cadence with chord V (after which there is an obvious caesura before the next phrase that ends with a perfect cadence in the same key). At the end of the first four-bar phrase of B1 and B2 imperfect cadences in the key of G major are formed by chords VI and V (as shown on the extra stave between these two examples).

Elements of music

All of the cadences discussed thus far have been **radical cadences** – cadences in which both chords are in root position. It is possible to form less conclusive cadences in which one or both of the two chords forming the cadence are inverted. In the cadence in bars 27–28 of A91 the second of the two chords is inverted (V^6 instead of V). The aural effect of such an **inverted cadence** is less conclusive than a radical cadence (compare the sound of this cadence with the last cadence in this example). The **medial cadence** is a special type of inverted cadence in which the first of the two chords is inverted. An example occurs in bars 12–13 of A91. The four chords in these two bars establish the key of F♯ minor. The dominant triad in this key consists of the notes C♯ (root), E♯ (third) and G♯ (fifth). On the last beat of bar 12 this chord appears in its second inversion (that is to say with the 5th of the chord sounding in the bass). It resolves in the usual way on to the tonic chord of F♯ minor on the first beat of bar 13. Because it ends on a root-position chord the medial cadence sounds more conclusive than an inverted cadence that ends on an inverted triad (compare bars 12–13 with bars 27–28).

5.4.2 Phrygian cadence

The cadence heard in bars 23–24 of A91 is a special type of **medial cadence** (see 5.4.1 above) consisting of chords IV^6 and V in a minor key. It is known as a phrygian cadence from its origin as a harmonisation of a bass part moving from the second to the first degree of the phrygian mode (A37, bars 2–3). In his *Fantasia* on Tallis's melody (A39) Vaughan Williams retains the phrygian modality of the Tudor composer (transposed to G) and uses phrygian cadences in bars 3–4 and 7–8. The phrygian cadence continued to be used long after the establishment of major/minor tonality. An example can be found at the end of the *turba* in B4 where chords IV^6–V in D minor (bar 5) create a sense of expectancy for the ensuing dramatic recitative. In the romantic era phrygian cadences were sometimes decorated. This is the case in bars 38–39 of B57 where chords IV^6–V in E minor are decorated with a chromatic passing note (A♯) between the two cadential chords.

5.4.3 Plagal cadence

When 'Amen' is sung at the end of a hymn the accompanying chords are most frequently IV and I. For this reason the plagal cadence is sometimes referred to as an **amen cadence**. Plagal cadences occur frequently in modal music. A striking example is the cadence at the end of A39 where the effect of the cadence is enhanced by a passing note (A♮) that links the cadential chords and leads up to a *tierce de Picardie* (the whole *Fantasia* ends with the same cadence lavishly scored for two string orchestras and a solo string quartet). The two plagal cadences in Bach's harmonisation of *In dulci jubilo* (bars 3–4 and 32–33 of A91) are less obvious because of the florid melodies of the lower parts. In the first of them a tonic chord in root position (I) is followed by chord IV slightly disguised by an accented passing note in the bass (E♮ resolving onto the root of chord IV). In the final cadence chord IV is decorated with auxiliary notes in 3rds in the minor parts. As with perfect and imperfect cadences (5.4.1) one or both chords of a plagal cadence may be inverted. This is the case in the final cadence of B58 in which chord IV of A minor is heard in second inversion (IV^6_4) resolving to the tonic chord with a *tierce de Picardie*.

5.4.4 Interrupted cadence

The interrupted cadence (otherwise known as a **deceptive cadence** or **false cadence**) defeats the expectation of a tonic chord after the dominant has been heard just before the end of a phrase. The leading note still most frequently fulfils its destiny in rising to the tonic, but the chord in which this note is heard is unexpected. Romantic composers often made use of this type of cadence in order to maintain tonal tension. B69(a) shows an interrupted cadence in its most common form – chords V and VI (in this case in the key of A minor). In B69(b) a fourth part played by the first violin has been added to the same interrupted cadence. The chromaticism and dissonance which this extra part brings to the cadence increases the tonal tension but does not alter the underlying cadential progression. In both cases the ear expects the tonic chord of A minor, but instead hears a major chord on the submediant. The full impact of this cadence can be appreciated by listening to the first 17 bars of Wagner's prelude to *Tristan und Isolde* (B68).

There are many other chords that can be used after chord V to form an interrupted cadence. A different diatonic chord can replace chord VI. In bars 21–22 of B79 Brahms uses chords V and IV. Alternatively a chromatic chord can be used, often to great effect. In A86 Bach dramatically 'resolves' the dominant chord of F major (bar 7) on to the dominant chord of G♭ major (bar 8).

5.4.5 Masculine and feminine cadences

All of the cadences discussed so far have ended on a strong beat. They are known as masculine cadences. Feminine cadences end on a weak beat and are particularly characteristic of late eighteenth-century music. In the first movement of Mozart's Divertimento KA229 (K439b) (B40) a perfect cadence (V–I in C major) can be heard in bars 10 and 81. They differ from all other perfect cadences in this movement in that the dominant chord is heard on the strong beat and the tonic chord on the weak third beat of the bar. The difference between these two types of cadence will be apparent if the first 14 bars of the movement are played, since the feminine cadence of bar 10 is followed by a masculine cadence only four bars later. A variant of this cadence in which the tonic note in the bass is sounded against the dominant chord is characteristic of late eighteenth-century styles. In bar 4 of B41 the cello plays the tonic note of G major on the strong beat. Above this the dominant triad forms discords with the G that are resolved on the second beat of the bar. B30 and B31 both end with cadences of this type.

5.4.6 Medieval and early renaissance cadences

The most characteristic cadence in early polyphony is formed by the interval of a 6th expanding by step to form an octave on the final (tonic of the mode). This type of cadence can be heard clearly in the two-part textures of A28 and A29. In the final cadence of both of these extracts the alto F♯ forms a 6th with the tenor A, then the tenor moves up a step to the final of Mode VII (G♮) while the tenor moves down a step to the lower final. The same sort of cadence can be heard in the three-voice texture of A19 in which the alto E♮ in bar 8 forms a 6th with the bass G♮. The parts then move in contrary motion to the final of Mode V (F♮). These cadences are clearly

Elements of music

related to the **phrygian cadences** described in 5.4.2. The only significant difference between them is that the bass falls a tone in A19, A28 and A29, whereas the bass falls a semitone in the phrygian cadence at the end of the first phrase of A37. The three medieval cadences discussed in the next three sections are all variants of the cadences discussed in this paragraph.

5.4.7 Double-leading-note cadence

In polyphonic music in the dorian and mixolydian modes the seventh degree of the scale was normally sharpened according to the conventions of ***musica ficta***. This can be heard in the alto part in the cadence at the end of the first burden of A24 (bar 7, where the modal C♮ is raised a semitone to C♯). When an inner voice in this sort of cadence sings the fifth of the mode in the last chord it was common in the middle ages for it to be preceded by the sharpened fourth degree of the modal scale. This is evident in the first tenor part of bars 7–8, where the sharpened fourth degree (G♯) rises a semitone to the fifth degree (A♮). To ears not attuned to medieval music the double-leading-note cadence can sound very odd. This has much to do with the way we tend to listen to music as a series of chords compared to the experience of those who sing the music as one strand in a contrapuntal texture. It would be as natural for the first tenor improvising a faburden to alter his penultimate note chromatically as it would for the alto to raise the seventh degree of the mode by a semitone. Compare the chromatic alterations of this cadence with the cadence at the end of A19, where no chromatic alterations are necessary because the intervals from both the fourth to the fifth (B–C) and the seventh to the eighth degrees of the mode (E–F) are already semitones in the lydian mode. It is because a double-leading-note cadence can occur naturally (that is to say without any chromatic alteration) in Mode V that it is sometimes called a lydian cadence. There are four of these cadences buried in Machaut's lydian polyphony in A21. In each case the cadence is shown in simplified form on an extra stave below the composer's music. In bars 6–7 the progression from B♮ to C is interrupted by an *échappée* (A♮), but in the other three cadences the 'leading notes' make straight for their goals (as shown by the arrows).

5.4.8 Landini cadence

This type of cadence is named after Francesco Landini (c.1325–97), in whose compositions it frequently occurs (though it soon became common property throughout Europe). Its most characteristic feature is the interpolation of the sixth degree of the mode between the sharpened seventh and the final. A Landini cadence can be heard in bars 24–25 of A24. The music is in the hypodorian mode and, as was usual in a phrase cadencing on the final, the seventh degree (C♮) is sharpened (C♯). But, instead of this note immediately resolving to the final, the sixth degree of the mode (B♮) is interpolated between them.

5.4.9 Burgundian cadence

This crossbreed between the double-leading-note cadence and the Landini cadence is named after Burgundian composers of the fifteenth century, and is most characteristic of the secular polyphony of the period. The two leading notes of the cadence described in 5.4.7 are combined with the fall of a tone from the chromatically altered note described in 5.4.8. The result is the sort of cadence heard at the end of the second burden of A24 (bars 16–17). This is the final cadence of the whole song, so of course it cadences on D♮, the final of the prevailing dorian mode. The leading note is C♯ (bar 16), but before the alto part reaches its goal (D♮) it drops a tone to the sixth degree of the mode (B♮). Likewise the G♯ in the first tenor part drops a tone to an F♯ before reaching its goal (A♮, the 5th of the final chord, and the fifth degree of the mode).

5.5 Diatonic harmony

Harmony in which all of the chords are constructed from notes of the scale of the prevailing key is said to be diatonic. All of the chords in B25 are diatonic chords in the key of A♭ major.

5.5.1 Primary triads in root position and first inversion

As well as marking off one phrase of music from another, most of the cadences discussed in 5.4.1–5.4.5 serve to confirm the prevailing key of a passage of tonal music. Consequently the chords which most clearly establish tonality are those which occur most frequently in perfect, imperfect and plagal cadences, namely the primary triads, I, IV and V and their inversions. Haydn's minuet (B25) is entirely dominated by these chords.

In the first phrase (bars 1–10 of B25) chord I in root position or first inversion is heard in bars 1, 3, 5, 7, 8 and 9, chord IV in bar 6, and chord V in bar 10. In fact nearly all of the other chords are variants of chord V in which a 7th above the root is added to the basic triad (as shown on the extra stave below bar 2). The only exception is chord VI in bar 7. Since the second half of the minuet (bars 11–20) is the same as the first half played backwards it follows that the whole minuet is dominated by chords I, IV, V (or V^7) and their inversions. The same is true of the trio (though not shown in the printed extract the accompanying harmony is played in the recording). Although it is unusual for a complete movement in classical style to remain in the same key, it is by no means unusual for classical composers to restrict their harmonic vocabulary to the primary triads, the dominant 7th and their inversions.

5.5.2 Cadential six–four chord (I^6_4 or Ic)

One of the most common chords used by classical composers in the approach to a perfect cadence is the tonic chord in **second inversion**. The 5th of the chord is heard in the bass, and the intervals from the bass to the other components of the chord are a 6th and a 4th (hence '**six–four chord**'). The first chord of B46(i) is the tonic six–four chord of G major. The 5th of the root-position triad (D♮) is in the bass (doubled an octave above in the viola part), and the violins play the root and 3rd of the chord. Since the interval between the bass and the root is a 4th (regarded as a dissonance when sounding between the bass and an upper part until the end of the eighteenth century) the cadential six–four nearly always resolves down to chord V. In fact it is often regarded not as a chord in its own right but as a decoration of the dominant chord on to which it resolves. The same cadential six–four can be heard preceded by chord IV in B46(b), and in its proper Mozartian context in the final cadence of B41.

Elements of music

5.5.3 Dominant-7th chord (V⁷)

On the extra stave below bars 1–10 of B25 Haydn's harmonic progression is shown in simplified form. In bars 2 and 4 it will be seen that another 3rd has been added above the superimposed 3rds of the triad on the dominant of A♭ major to form chord V⁷ (the dominant-7th chord). The chord consists of the root (E♭), a 3rd above it (G♮), a 5th above it (B♭) and a 7th above it (D♭). The dissonant 7th creates tonal tension which enhances the tendency of chord V to resolve to chord I. The tension inherent in the leading note (G♮ is resolved when it moves up to the tonic A♭, the root of chord I), while the dissonance is resolved when the 7th (D♭) moves down to the mediant (C♮, the 3rd of chord I). The arrows show the way these notes resolve in bars 4–5, but the bland context makes it difficult fully to appreciate the tonal tension which can be generated by the dominant-7th chord. This is much more obvious in the extracts from a polonaise by Chopin shown in B64. The second extract (b) begins with the left-hand part of bars 7–8 from B64(a). This consists of a broken version of chord V⁷ in the key of G major. After a pause the tensions of the dominant 7th are resolved in an arpeggiated tonic chord and another perfect cadence. In bars 7–8 of B64(a) the same dominant-7th chords are embellished with an elaborate arabesque, but despite its extreme chromaticism the accompanying diatonic chords ensure that the key of G major is never in doubt.

5.5.4 Inversions of the dominant 7th: V^6_5 (V⁷b), V^4_3 (V⁷c), and V^4_2 (V⁷d)

Like ordinary triads the dominant-7th chord can be inverted. In its first inversion the 3rd of the chord is heard in the bass with the other chord-notes ranged above it to form intervals of a 6th, a 5th and a 3rd: hence V^6_5 (the 3rd being implied). On the extra stave below bar 2 of B25 the dominant 7th of A♭ major is shown in root position. In bar 8 the same pitches are rearranged so that the 3rd of the chord sounds in the bass with the other components of the chord forming a 6th (E♭), a 5th (D♭) and a 3rd (B♭) above it. The same chord in a different spacing occurs in the second bar of B30, where another extra stave shows the derivation of V^6_5 from V⁷ and arrows show its resolution to chord I.

A modulation from the tonic key of E major to the dominant key of B major begins in bar 5 of B30 and it is in this key that a second-inversion dominant-7th chord is heard at the start of bar 6. The dominant-7th chord of B major in root position consists of the pitches F♯ (root), A♯ (third), C♯ (fifth) and E♮ (seventh). All of these notes are present in the first chord of bar 6 but, in common with all other second-inversion dominant-7th chords, the 5th of the chord (C♯) is in the bass. As expected, this dominant chord resolves to chord I of B major on the last beat of the bar.

In the third inversion of a dominant-7th chord the 7th is heard in the bass. An example occurs on the third beat of bar 1 in B30. Its derivation from the root-position dominant 7th of E major printed beneath it is clear: the 7th of the chord (A♮) is the highest note of chord V⁷ and the lowest note of V^4_2 while the tonic triad in V⁷ is moved up an octave to form the upper notes of V^4_2.

Second and third inversions of chord V⁷ can be heard in the key of F♯ minor in bar 12 of A91. The dominant-7th chord of F♯ minor is shown on an extra stave. The top note of this chord is the 7th and it is this note that is heard in the bass of Bach's chord at the start of bar 12. This is the third inversion of the dominant 7th in which the intervals formed between the bass and the other components of the chord sounding above it are a 2nd (C♯), a 4th (E♯) and a 6th (G♯) – hence V$^4_2$ (the 6th being implied). In fact Bach omits the G♯ from his chord and doubles the root instead. The omission of one or more of the theoretical components of a chord is common practice in all sorts of harmonic contexts. The third chord of bar 12 provides another example, for it is only when one views both of the quavers as being part of this second-inversion dominant-7th that all components of the chord can be considered to be present.

5.5.5 Chords of dominant function: VII^6 (VIIb) and III^6 (IIIb)

Any chord which contains the leading note can, and often does, behave in the same way as an unambiguous **dominant chord**. If the root of a complete dominant-7th chord is removed, what remains is a triad on the leading note (chord VII, as shown in the third complete bar of A95). This **diminished triad** is rarely heard in root position (because of the tritone between the root and 5th), but in first inversion it is frequently used as a substitute for a dominant-7th chord. Despite not containing the dominant note, its dominant function cannot be mistaken in progressions such as that at the end of the development in the finale of Mozart's Divertimento KA229 (K439b) (B40). After a passage in B♭ major (bars 56–59) the tonality of the development becomes unclear, but in bars 66–68 the key of D minor is briefly established. This momentary tonal stability is undone by the chords in bars 69–70, but chords VII^6 and I in bars 71–72 re-establish the key of F major as convincingly as complete dominant-7th and tonic chords would have done. This principle of strongly dominant function in chords which lack the dominant note itself holds good for a whole range of chords (chromatic as well as diatonic) which derive from chord V.

Chord III^6, though containing the leading note, is rarely used as a dominant chord in major keys because it lacks the dissonant intervals which drive dominant dissonances towards resolution on the tonic chord. An exception is the loud chord at the end of bar 4 in Debussy's 'Golliwogg's Cakewalk' (C20). Coming at the end of the introduction and followed by a bar of silence, its dominant function as a curtain raiser for the ensuing E♭-major ragtime bass is obvious. However, in the minor chord III is a dissonant-sounding **augmented triad**. It is shown in root position on the third degree of the scale of C minor at the end of A81. The acidic augmented 5th that gives the triad its name is formed between the outer parts (E♭ and B♮), but in first inversion the effect of this interval is somewhat mollified by being tucked away in the inner parts, and its dominant function becomes more obvious because the dominant note is in the bass (bar 13, beat 4). This is the chord that Couperin uses to form a perfect cadence at the end of A81.

5.5.6 Higher dominant dissonances

Although the dominant-7th chord was originally viewed as dissonant, from the eighteenth century on it was treated with great freedom. No preparation of the 7th was necessary, though most often it resolved down a step to a consonant note. By this time composers had begun to use a variety of **dominant chords** which, unlike the dominant 7th, can still sound dissonant to us today. These chords derive from the triad on the dominant, but extra 3rds are added above the 7th to form a 9th, 11th or 13th above the root.

Elements of music

5.5.7 Dominant major 9ths (V^9 or VII^7) and minor 9ths ($V^{\flat 9}$ or $VII^{\flat 7}$)

The first dissonant chord played by the cello in C38 is the **dominant-major-9th chord** of F major heard at the start of bar 5. The complete five-note chord consists of the dominant (C♮) plus a 3rd (E♮), a 5th (G♮), a 7th (B♭) and a 9th (D♮) above the root (as shown on the extra stave beneath bar 5). The cello only has four strings, so one of these notes must be left out. Walton omits the 7th.

More frequently it is the root which is omitted. This is the case in the third bar of B56. Below the first beat of bar 3 a complete dominant major 9th in the key of D major is shown, but the chord Schubert uses lacks the root (A♮). There is more than one way of hearing this chord. The 9th itself (B♮) can be regarded as being an appoggiatura resolving down to the root of chord V^6_5 (similarly the B♮s in bars 1 and 5 can be regarded as appoggiaturas resolving to the 5th of chord I). As a chord in its own right this rootless dominant major 9th is sometimes called a **half-diminished 7th**, but this is a particularly unhelpful term since it does not recognise the dominant function of the chord, nor is the minor 7th which this chord contains in any sense whatsoever a diminished 7th. The only diminished interval is the 5th between the C♯ and the G♮ (shown in the chord on the extra stave below bar 4). The same two chords that Schubert uses (VII^7 resolving to V^6_5) can be heard in the key of C major in bar 8 of C30.

It is possible to omit two notes from the complete dominant major 9th chord and, provided the 9th and the all-important leading note is present, it still functions as an unambiguous dominant dissonance. This is the case in bar 4 of B30 where the chord consists of just the 3rd (D♯), 7th (A♮) and major 9th of V^9 in E major. Alternatively this chord could be described as VII^7 with no 3rd and a doubled 5th (as shown on the extra stave). Whichever symbol is used the leading note rises to the tonic as the dissonances resolve down to the 5th and 3rd of chord I (as shown by the arrows). The relative levels of dissonance of a dominant major 9th and a dominant 7th may be judged by comparing the sound of the chords in bars 2 and 4 of this example: VII^7 sounds more dissonant than V^6_5 because it contains two discords – a tritone between D♯ and A, and a minor 7th between D♯ and C♯ (as against the single discord in V^6_5).

In minor keys a similar addition of a minor 9th above the root of a dominant 7th chord produces the chord of the **dominant minor 9th** (using the harmonic minor scale). In its complete form it can be heard in bars 9 and 11 of B65. The key is C♯ minor, and the chords on the extra stave below these bars show this five-note dominant chord in close position. The dissonant effect of the second of these two chords is particularly apparent as it is the last full chord before a series of descending 3rds in the right hand wind their way down to a resolution of $V^{\flat 9}$ on to the tonic chord at the start of bar 13.

The dominant-minor-9th chord is most often heard without its root. The complete chord in the key of C minor is shown below bar 9 of A81. Couperin's chord lacks the root (G♮) and so could be described as $VII^{\flat 7}$. It resolves, as expected, on to chord I. In C minor this is a diatonic chord, but in major keys the incomplete dominant-minor-9th chord (or $VII^{\flat 7}$) is a chromatic chord. This is evident in bar 5 of B31 where the minor 9th (C♮) is foreign to the key of E major. As expected, this chord, like Couperin's, resolves to the tonic chord in bar 6.

Both of these chords are known as **diminished 7ths** because the interval between the 3rd (D♯ in bar 5 of B31) and minor 9th (C♮ in the same bar) is a diminished 7th. However, it should be noted that the term can be used to describe any chord built from superimposed minor 3rds (or their enharmonic equivalents), and it tells us nothing about the way these chords function in particular keys. From the late seventeenth century onwards diminished 7ths have been valued for their dramatic effect. Their potency is amply exploited in the following examples drawn from a range of historical style-periods:

A81, bars 8 and 9 (mid-baroque solemnity)
A88, bar 2, beat 1 (late baroque drama)
B31, bars 4 and 5 (classical pathos)
B50, bars 93–94 (classical drama)
B60, bars 4–9 (romantic melodrama)
B70, bar 1, beats 1–2 (romantic pathos).

5.5.8 Dominant-11th chord (V^{11})

When another 3rd is piled on top of a dominant 9th to make a dominant 11th, the added note turns out to be the tonic. Because this jars harshly with the essential leading note (effectively pre-empting its resolution to the tonic), the dominant 11th is rarely used as a chord in its own right. The dominant 11th of A major is shown in the extra stave below bar 5 in A70. In this and the following bar the chord is not an independent entity; it is simply a dominant chord sounding against an inverted pedal in the violins.

The dominant 11th in bar 12 of B58 might seem to be more independent, but in this case the 11th (A♮) is really no more than a suspension (prepared in the previous bar) which resolves to the leading note in chord V^7 in the next bar.

5.5.9 Dominant-13th chord (V^{13})

The complete dominant 13th is a chord of seven notes, three of which clash with the root (the 7th, 9th, and 13th). This chord is shown in the key of C major under the second bar of Stanford's Magnificat (C30). In fact composers rarely make use of more than four pitches from the complete dominant 13th: the root, 3rd, 7th and 13th (G, B, F and E on the word 'soul'). The same applies to the dominant 13th in minor keys. The second phrase of the Magnificat ('and my spirit hath rejoiced') begins in D minor, in which key another dominant 13th is heard at the start of bar 6. The complete chord is shown on the extra stave below this bar, but again Stanford only uses the root, 3rd, 7th and 13th, the last of these sounding in the bass. In both chords the 13th is prepared (organ E♭ in bar 1, soprano F♮ in bar 5) and resolved (organ D♮ in bar 2, soprano E♮ in bar 6), so it is possible to view them as dominant 7ths with suspensions. Similarly, the dominant 13th in D major heard in the sixth bar of Schubert's Andante (B56) could be viewed as chord V^7 with an appoggiatura (F♯) resolving to the 5th of chord V^7.

There is little ambiguity about the dominant-13th chords heard in the perfect cadences at the end of B75 and C20. In both cases the 13th (F♮ in Brahms's sonata, and D♮ in Debussy's 'Golliwogg's Cakewalk') is heard in the uppermost part, and in both cases it is neither prepared nor resolved by step.

Elements of music

Debussy's chord is the most complete dominant 13th discussed here, containing three dissonances – the 7th (E♭), the 9th (G♮) and the 13th itself (D♮) in addition to the all-important leading note (A♮).

When the dominant 13th is reduced to a three-note chord the component pitches are usually those which form a first inversion of the triad on the mediant: chord III^6 (see 5.5.5). The complete dominant 13th of E♭ major is shown on the extra stave below bar 5 of C20, and it will be seen that the root, 3rd and 13th (printed as semibreves) are the same notes as those used by Debussy at the end of bar 4. Similarly, the semibreves in the complete dominant 13th of F♯ minor shown below bar 2 of B67 form the dissonant-sounding minor version of chord III^6 heard on the third beat of bar 2.

5.5.10 Secondary-7th chords (non-dominant 7th chords)

Secondary-7th chords, consisting of a root, with notes a 3rd, 5th and 7th above it, may be formed on any degree of the scale save the dominant (hence the alternative name, non-dominant 7th). Root-position secondary-7th chords on every degree of the natural minor scale of B♭ minor can be heard in B78. They are shown in close position in B78(iii). Under Brahms's broken chords and chromatic decorations the lowest notes of the left hand (stems up) clearly delineate the bass of a harmonic sequence that starts on the third beat of bar 2 and ends on the first beat of bar 5. Every one of the broken chords above these bass notes is a secondary 7th in root position (as shown in B78(i)): they are shown in close position on an extra stave beneath every system of the score with brackets that identify the 7ths in each chord. In the second complete bar it will be seen that the 7th in the tonic chord (A♭ in chord I^7) is simply added to the triad without preparation, but the harmonic reduction also shows that Brahms's figuration contains preparations and resolutions of all the other 7ths. For instance, the dissonant F♮ at the top of chord VI^7 (bar 4) is prepared as the consonant third of chord III^7 and it is resolved to the consonant E♭ of chord II^7 at the start of bar 5.

Brahms's harmonic sequence (bar 2^3–5^1) is a special type known as a **circle of 5ths**. It takes its name from a diagrammatic representation of the twelve chromatic tones arranged in perfect 5ths around a circle (B78(ii)). Starting with the C♮ at the top of the circle and reading clockwise the notes ascend by perfect 5ths until all of the chromatic notes have been covered and the circle returns to the note with which it started (C♮). Reading anticlockwise the notes descend in perfect 5ths with the same outcome. Brahms uses a segment of this circle of 5ths starting with a B♭ and reaching G♭ at chord VI^7. It is impractical literally to descend in perfect 5ths throughout this segment of the cycle (there are not enough notes on the piano), so Brahms alternates falling 5ths (B♭–E♭, A♭–D♭ and G♭–C, indicated by brackets above B78(i)) with rising 4ths (E♭–A♭ and D♭–G♭, indicated by brackets below B78(i)). This achieves the same harmonic effect as a continuous descent in 5ths, but it is achieved within a much narrower compass. The interval between the roots of chords VI^7 and II^7 (G♭–C♮ in bars 4–5) is a diminished 5th, thus avoiding the chromatic C♭ which another perfect 5th would have entailed.

5.5.11 Added-note chords

Another type of non-dominant dissonance appears in Debussy's

'Golliwogg's Cakewalk' (C20). In bars 6–9 an F♮ is added to the tonic chord of E♭ major. It is quite different from any of the dissonant chords already considered because those dissonances were the result of piling 3rds one upon another, whereas in this chord a note a tone above the root is added. The **added 2nd** does not alter the clear tonic function of the chord, it simply adds colour.

This is true of the much commoner chord of the **added 6th**. Chopin's Prelude in F major (B66) is coloured throughout by these chords. In the first four bars the semiquaver figuration contains a major 6th (D♮) that colours the tonic chord (bar 1) and its second inversion (bar 2). The remainder of the right-hand part is not shown, but the harmonic progressions of the rest of the prelude can be followed in the left-hand part and in the harmonic reduction given on the extra staves below it. Bars $5-8^1$ are a transposed repeat of bars $1-4^1$. A four-bar link contains an added 6th on the subdominant triad (bar 13) and an added 6th as well as a suspension on a second-inversion tonic triad (bars 15–16). Finally the first phrase is repeated with a flat 7th added to the final chord (which, like the added 6ths, simply adds a touch of non-functional colour to what is clearly the tonic chord).

In bars 3–4 of C23 the B-major triad that runs through both bars acquires an added 2nd (C♯) and an added 6th (G♯). More added-note chords can be heard in C25 and C26.

5.6 Modulation and pivot chords

Modulation is the process of tonal change by means of which one key is relinquished and a new one established. In the simplified extract from a minuet by Mozart shown in B49 modulation is achieved by the use of a pivot chord (a chord that is common to the key before the modulation and the new key established after the modulation). In bar 4 the pivot chord (a G-major triad) is common to G major (in which it is the tonic chord) and D major (in which it is the subdominant chord). The dual allegiance of this G-major triad allows it to function simultaneously as the tonic chord in the perfect cadence of bars 3–4, and as an approach chord to the dominant-7th chord of the new key of D major that follows it (bar 5). The music moves into D major when V^7 resolves to I in bar 6, after which it is fully confirmed by the perfect cadence in bars 7–8.

This modulation is shown in its original form in bars 1–8 of B41. The return to G major is accomplished by adding a C♮ to the D-major chord, thus turning the tonic chord of D major (bar 8) into the dominant 7th of G major (bar 9).

5.7 Chromatic harmony

A chromatic chord contains at least one note which is foreign to the scale of the prevailing key of a passage of music. There is a complete spectrum between absolutely diatonic harmony, in which every chord derives from notes of the scale of the prevailing key, and harmony in which most of the chords have been chromatically inflected. The difference between these two extremes may be judged by comparing the harmony of B25 with the chords at the start of B68. The Menuetto is entirely diatonic. The prelude is so chromatic that the tonic key of A minor is often obscured.

Extreme melodic chromaticism can decorate a firmly diatonic harmonic

Elements of music

progression without disturbing the **tonality**. B64(a) begins with four bars in the key of A♭ major, clearly defined by chords V^7 and I. After the double bar the chord progression of bars 1–4 is repeated a semitone lower. In the first two of these bars the melody is also repeated, but in bars 7–8 florid and extremely chromatic figuration replaces the original diatonic melody of bars 3–4. Nevertheless, the dominant-7th chords that underpin this chromatic figuration ensure that there is never any doubt about the G-major tonality that is confirmed by the perfect cadence in this key in bars 9–10. In fact if the chromatic figuration is removed (as it is in B64(b)) the key of G major is no clearer than it was with the chromatic figuration.

When the situation is reversed chromatic harmony can undermine the tonality of a diatonic melody. In B65 the melody in bars 5–26 sticks rigidly to the natural minor scale on C♯ (shown on the extra stave above bars 11–12). In bars 5–11 Chopin harmonises the melody with the tonic and dominant chords of C♯ minor (the latter sometimes over a double pedal that reinforces this key). But when the melody begins to repeat at bar 13 he reharmonises the melody in E major and stays in this key throughout bars 17–20. In bar 21 he introduces a D-major chord that is chromatic in both C♯ minor and E major. This chromatic chord then alternates with V^7–I of C♯ minor in a tonal tug-of-war that seriously undermines the diatonic melody.

When a harmonic progression contains all twelve chromatic degrees with none having pre-eminence over the others all sense of tonality can be lost. This is as true of Chopin's stream of 'dominant 7ths' in bars 33–36 of B65 as it is of Hauer's serial chords at the end of C40 (in both cases all twelve chromatic notes are heard in just four successive chords). In fact Chopin's extreme chromaticism in bars 33–36 seems to be the logical outcome of the battering his C♯-minor melody received from the repeated chromatic D-major chords in bars 21–27. It is as though the melody has succumbed to chromaticism and gives up the fight in its chromatic slither from C♯ to F♯ in bars 33–36. It is significant that not a single dominant chord of C♯ minor is heard in the last 11 bars of the mazurka: the music just collapses wearily from tonally ambiguous half-diminished 7ths to the final chord of C♯ minor.

5.7.1 Secondary-dominant chords

Just as the tonic chord (I) has a dominant chord (V) which is closely related to it, so diatonic triads on other degrees of the scale can have their own attendant dominant chords known as secondary dominants (or **applied dominants**). The way in which these chromatic chords relate to diatonic triads can be likened to the way satellites relate to planets in a solar system. Just as the sun exerts a gravitational force on the planets, so the tonic chord exerts an attractive tonal force on other diatonic chords (the arrows in Figure 5.7.1a show some of the most important tonal forces in an imagined musical solar system). Five of the six non-dominant triads can have attendant satellites in the shape of chromatic dominant chords which, when they resolve to their parent chords, turn these diatonic triads into temporary tonic chords in a process known as **tonicisation**. (Chord VII cannot normally have its own secondary dominant because it is a diminished triad incapable of tonicisation.) There need be no modulation, since the tonicised chord can return to its role as a diatonic chord related to the real tonic as soon as the

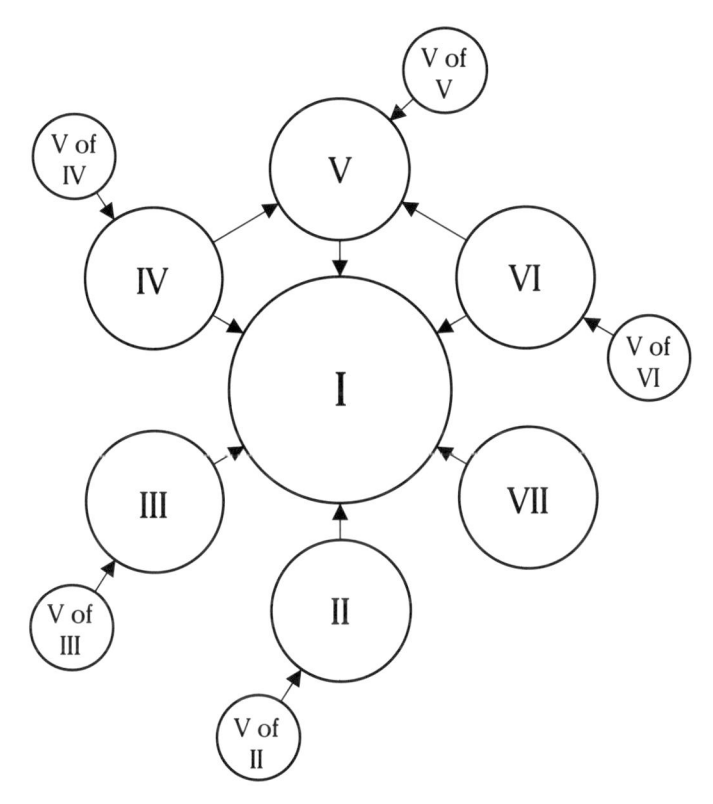

Figure 5.7.1a

effect of the chromaticism introduced by the secondary dominant has been cancelled out by a diatonic chord progression.

Figure 5.7.1b represents the tonal progression in bars 4–5 of B16 which essentially moves from chord I of D major to chord V then back to chord I. The dominant triad of D major consists of the notes A, C♯ and E. To tonicise this triad it must be preceded by its own dominant, the dominant of A major. This is a triad on the fifth degree of the scale of A major: E, G♯ and B. To this can be added a minor 7th above the root (D♮) which turns the triad into the dominant 7th of A major. If this dominant 7th is inverted so that the third (G♯) is sounding in the bass, the result will be the first-inversion dominant-7th chord shown on the third beat of bar 4 in B16 (the 7th of the chord is the semibreve D that is sustained throughout the bar). In the normal way of things the temporary leading note (G♯) ought to rise a semitone to the temporary tonic (A♮) and the dissonant 7th (D♮) should resolve down a semitone to C♯. This is precisely what happens in bar 5, beat 2 – the A-major chord has been tonicised by its own secondary dominant, V^6_5 of V. But the effect is momentary, for the perfect cadence which this fleetingly tonicised chord forms with chord I immediately cancels out the chromatic G♯ (notice that the soprano sings a G♮ immediately after the perfect cadence). Indeed, in the context of the whole

Elements of music

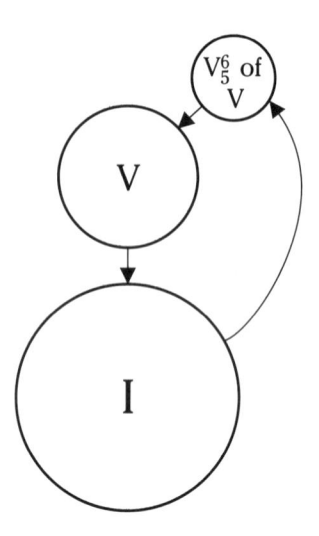

Figure 5.7.1b

recitative the G♮ hardly affects the D-major tonality of bars 1–5.

This is not the case with the next chord (bar 6, beat 3), for here the introduction of an A♮ precipitates a modulation to B minor that is confirmed by the perfect cadence at the end of the recitative. Thus, as with any chord in a tonal context, dominant chords can be understood only by taking account of the tonality before it is sounded and by listening to what happens after it has been articulated. The dominant chords in bars 4 and 6 are both chromatic in terms of the key of D major. However, the secondary dominant in bar 4 remains a chromatic intruder because the D-major tonality has never been threatened, whereas the dominant chord in bars 6–7 is the first chord in a progression that leads to the establishment of a new key, B minor. The principle of tonicisation applies to all of the chromatic progressions discussed in the following paragraphs (with the sole exception of the irregularly resolving secondary dominant in B31).

Figure 5.7.1c is a diagrammatic representation of the harmonic progression heard in bars 3–6 of B67. The key of F♯ minor is firmly established by dominant chords that resolve to the tonic chord in bars 1–3 of this nocturne. The outward journey from chord I to chord IV via its satellite (V^7 of IV) and the return to chord I via chord II and a diatonic dominant 7th is shown in simplified form on the extra stave beneath bars 3–6. The whole progression is repeated in bars 5–7 with subtle melodic and harmonic variations (notably the use of the first inversion of V^7 of V in the second half of bar 5).

Figure 5.7.1d is a diagrammatic representation of bars 3–5 of B75. The key of D♭ major is firmly established by the diatonic harmony of the first three bars. The harmonic round trip this time involves the rootless dominant-minor-9th chord (D♮, F♮, A♭ and C♭ at the start of bar 4) of the supertonic (E♭, G♭ and B♭). The omitted root (B♭) of the secondary dominant chord is shown as a stemless black note on the extra stave

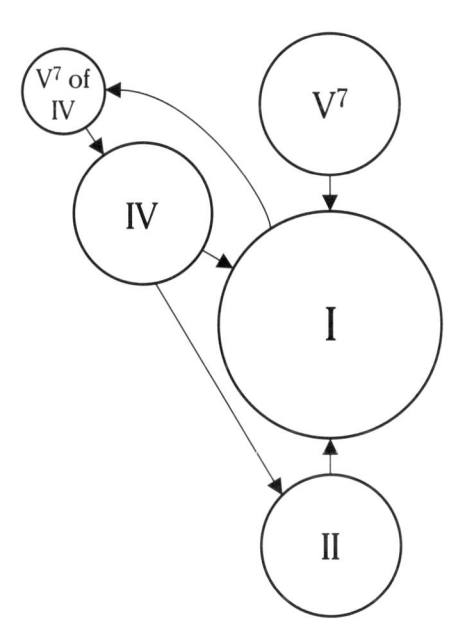

Figure 5.7.1c

below bar 4. The remaining four notes form a diminished-7th chord that resolves to chord II, the dissonant 7th and minor 9th both falling a semitone, and the temporary leading note (D♮) rising to the root of chord II. Immediately after the tonicisation of chord II the key of D♭ major is reasserted by the diatonic dominant and tonic chords (V^{13} and I^6) and fully confirmed by the perfect cadence in the last two bars. Brahms's progression is slightly complicated by the dominant pedal (the oft-repeated A♭) which runs throughout the extract.

Figure 5.7.1e shows the way a rootless dominant major 9th (V^9 of V alias VII^7 of V) can act like a satellite of a real dominant-7th chord. C1 is in the key of G major. In this key the dominant triad consists of the notes D, F♯ and A. The secondary dominant of this triad is A (root), C♯ (3rd) and E♮ (5th) to which can be added a 7th (G♮) and a major 9th (B♮). This secondary-dominant chord (without its root) lasts from the third beat of bar 17 to the first beat of bar 19. Brahms does not directly resolve V^9 of V to chord V itself. Instead the two chords are separated by chord I^6_4, but since this chord can be regarded as a decoration of the dominant chord (see 5.5.2) it makes no difference to the way in which the secondary-dominant and diatonic-dominant chords relate to each other.

Figure 5.7.1e also shows that minor-9th chords can replace major-9th chords both as secondary dominants and as dominant chords of the prevailing key. B31 is in the key of E major throughout, but it contains two chromatic chords. The first is a diminished-7th chord derived from a major triad on the supertonic of E major (the F♯ shown as a stemless black note on the extra stave below bar 4). Instead of resolving onto chord V (as shown on the extra stave) it moves to another diminished 7th, this one

Elements of music

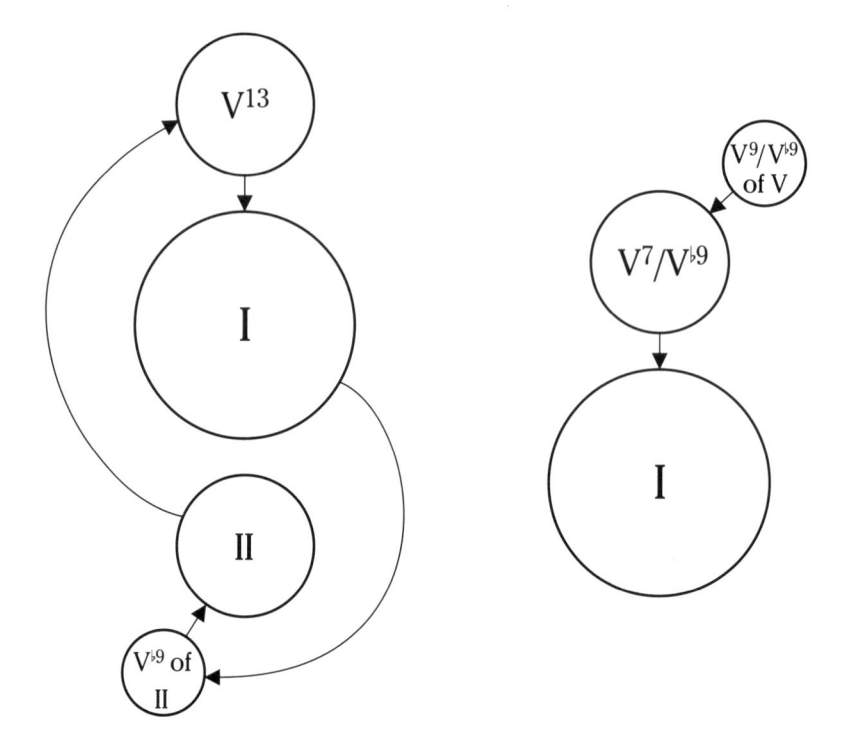

Figure 5.7.1d

Figure 5.7.1e

deriving from the dominant triad itself (the C♮ in this chord is a chromatic 'borrowing' from the tonic minor key). This movement from one chromatic discord to another is known as an **irregular resolution** (irregular because the expected resolution of the secondary dominant to a tonicised diatonic triad never happens).

$V^{♭9}$ of V (or $VII^{♭7}$ of V) sometimes appears just before the final cadence. This dramatic chromatic interloper makes its presence felt in the penultimate bar of B14. The chords on the extra stave below bar 27 show how the dissonant minor 9th (E♭) and 7th (C♮) resolve down a step to the 5th and 3rd of chord V as the leading note rises a semitone to the root of the dominant triad. There is no real tonicisation here because Bach adds an F♮ (the 7th of chord V^7) to his penultimate chord, and this note immediately cancels the effect of the chromatic F♯ heard in the secondary dominant.

5.7.2 Substitution chords

In jazz, and in art music influenced by jazz idioms, even more complex dominant discords are common. The first of the two chords in the final cadence of Walton's 'Popular Song' (C38) is a very dissonant dominant chord in the key of F major. In addition to the root (C♮), 3rd (E♮) and minor 13th (notated as a G♯), it contains both a minor 7th (B♭) and a major 7th (B♮), both a minor 9th (D♭) and a major 9th (D♮). These components of Walton's dominant chord are labelled in the penultimate chord of C38 and in the chord printed on the extra staves beneath it (where the chord is arranged as superimposed major and minor 3rds). If just the lower parts of the last two chords are played (C39(a)) a simple perfect cadence is heard. If just the upper parts are played (C39(b)) a perfect cadence will still be heard despite the fact that the penultimate chord contains none of the normally indispensable notes of a dominant chord (notably there is no root, 3rd or 7th). The fact is that the key of F major has been so thoroughly established by this stage that the ear hears what it wants to hear, accepting the chromatic dissonance as a functional equivalent of a dominant 7th in the final perfect cadence. Appropriately this sort of dissonant chromatic chord which functions like another more common chord is known as a substitution chord. Thus a simpler description of Walton's final dominant dissonance would be that it consists of a dominant 7th surmounted by a chromatic substitution chord.

5.7.3 Neapolitan chords

The Neapolitan 6th is a first-inversion major triad on the flattened supertonic. It is a chord of subdominant function which is most often heard in minor keys at the approach to a cadence. The chords on the extra stave below bars 22–25 of B65 illustrate this definition. In this passage the music is in C♯ minor (defined by dominant-7th and tonic chords in bars 22 and 24). The supertonic of this key is D♯: the flattened supertonic is therefore D♮. A major triad on this note consists of the notes D♮, F♯ and A♮. This D-major triad (♭II) is shown on the extra stave below bar 23 together with its first inversion, the Neapolitan 6th (N^6) of C♯ minor. It is immediately followed by a perfect cadence in C♯ minor, the Neapolitan 6th acting like a chromatically altered version of chord II^6 (F♯, A♮ and D♮ instead of F♯, A♮ and D♯). This is how Chopin makes use of the Neapolitan 6th in bars 25 and 27, its last appearance being particularly telling since it is spread over nearly five octaves and followed by a dramatic silence.

In B50 Mozart unleashes the full dramatic potential of the Neapolitan-6th chord. The Queen of the Night's coloratura in bars 69–79 is firmly in the key of D minor. Suddenly she ascends through the notes of an E♭-major triad and is accompanied by the Neapolitan 6th of D minor which resolves to chord V in bar 82 (via a very brief secondary dominant at the end of bar 81). Even more dramatic is the Neapolitan enclave in bars 90–92 where the Neapolitan 6th is reinforced by its own dominant (V^4_2 of E♭ major).

The effect of a Neapolitan 6th is startling when heard in the context of music in a major key. The passage at the end of Bach's Toccata BWV 540 (A86) begins with dominant harmony in F major followed by transitory modulations to unrelated keys. In bars 14–16 the first-inversion chord of G♭ major is the Neapolitan 6th of the tonic key of F major. It is followed by a return to dominant harmony in bars 17–20 and a perfect cadence in F major in the last two bars.

Sometimes the triad on the flattened supertonic is heard in root position. A disquieting use of this root position Neapolitan chord can be heard in bar 17 of B58. From the climax of the song in bar 10 to the end the music is in the key of A minor, in which key a root-position chord of B♭ major (bar 17) is, to say the least, extremely unusual.

Equally romantic is the second-inversion Neapolitan chord heard in bars 33–34 of B59. It arrives at the climax of a chromatic harmonic progression

Elements of music

in the key of C minor, in which context it functions like a subdominant chord resolving to dominant harmony in the last two bars.

5.7.4 Augmented-6th chords

There are three varieties of chords based on the interval of an augmented 6th on the flattened submediant. The simplest, known as an **Italian 6th**, is a three-note chord consisting of the flat submediant together with notes a major 3rd and augmented 6th above it (C♮, E♮ and A♯ in the key of E major or minor). It is easy to understand this chord as a chromatic variant of chord IV^6 in the minor, particularly when it is heard in the context of a phrygian cadence (see 5.4.2). On the lower of the two extra staves below bars 38–39 of B57 a phrygian cadence is formed by chords IV^6 and V in E minor. On the stave above a chromatic passing note (A♯) is inserted between the uppermost notes of the chords. This changes chord IV^6 into an Italian 6th that resolves onto chord V in the next bar. This cadence is repeated in bars 39–40 and 40–41, this time with the Italian 6ths functioning as autonomous chords (rather than as by-products of a chromatic melody). In all three cadences the root (C♮) resolves down a semitone to the dominant, and the augmented 6th (A♯) resolves up a semitone to the same degree of the scale (as do all normally resolving augmented-6th chords).

The **German 6th** is the same as the Italian 6th except that a note a perfect 5th above the root is added. The Largo from Haydn's quartet Op. 74 No. 3 (B30) begins in the key of E major but modulates to B major in bar 6. In this key the flattened submediant is G♮. A German 6th on this root consists of a G♮ (the root), a B♮ (the 3rd), a D♮ (the 5th) and E♯ (an augmented 6th above the root). This is the fortissimo chord heard in bar 8. Like the Italian 6th the root resolves down a semitone (G♮–F♯ in the cello), and the augmented 6th resolves up a semitone (E♯–F♯ in the first violin). As is so often the case in classical music this augmented 6th resolves onto a cadential six–four (see 5.5.2) which in turn resolves to the dominant 7th followed by a feminine cadence. The effect of a German 6th in a major key is much more dramatic than its effect in a minor key because it contains three chromatic notes. In addition to the sharpening of the subdominant (the augmented 6th), the submediant (root) and mediant (3rd) are both flattened in major keys.

A chord of the augmented 6th can be used to effect a modulation. The extract from Schubert's 'Der Doppelgänger' (B58) begins in A minor then rises chromatically to reach the remote key of C♯ minor at bar 5 (a key confirmed by the alternating dominant and tonic chords that follow the C♯-minor chord). The return to A minor is achieved by using two chords with one note in common, but which are otherwise unrelated (the common note is the B♯ in bar 8, the enharmonic equivalent of the C♮ in bar 9). The first of these chords is the dominant triad of C♯ minor (bar 8), the second a German 6th in the tonic key of A minor. It is the use of this augmented 6th which makes the precipitate return to A minor possible and which, more than any other element, justifies Schubert in his unusual use of the extreme dynamic mark *fff* as the German 6th resolves with fateful inevitability to the cadential six–four of the tonic key of A minor.

In the **French 6th** an augmented 4th above the root is added to the three basic notes of an Italian 6th. In A major or minor the flattened submediant is F♮. An Italian 6th on this key therefore consists of an F♮ (the root), an A♮

(the 3rd) and a D♯ (the augmented 6th). To form a French 6th a B♮, an augmented 4th above the root, needs to be added. This is the chord heard in the last two beats of bar 7 of Chopin's Nocturne in F♯ minor (B67). This French 6th is shown as a block chord on an extra stave on which the delayed resolution to chord V^7 is also shown.

5.7.5 Tristan chord

The first chord heard in the prelude to Wagner's opera *Tristan und Isolde* (B68) is a dissonance which became notorious because of its ambiguous tonality. Yet this '*Tristan* chord' functions in much the same way as the French 6th in bar 7 of Chopin's Nocturne in F♯ minor (see the last paragraph of 5.7.4 and the extra staves below B67). In fact the pitches of three of the four chord-notes are the same. The A♮ of Chopin's chord is replaced by a G♯ in the Tristan chord, but this turns out to be an appoggiatura when it resolves to an A♮ at the end of the bar (at which point the *Tristan* chord becomes a **French 6th**). Both chords resolve to the same dominant 7th, but Wagner's chord is decorated with a chromatic passing note (A♯) which soon resolves on to the 5th of chord V^7. But whereas the A-major tonality of the nocturne is clinched by a perfect cadence there is no resolution of Wagner's dominant 7th.

Fourteen years before the completion of *Tristan* Wagner's friend Liszt wrote the cadence shown in B70. A comparison of this cadence with Wagner's famous progression (B71) reveals that, apart from Liszt's resolution of the dominant 7th to the tonic chord of A major, they are almost identical. So another, and equally valid, way of hearing the opening bars of *Tristan* is to view the *Tristan* chord as the dominant minor 9th of A minor with an appoggiatura (D♯) resolving to the seventh (D♮) of V^7 of A minor. Viewed in the light of the source of Wagner's harmony and melody (B70) the *Tristan* chord is a very intense dominant dissonance resolving to a much less acute dominant dissonance.

What happens after the first two chords of the prelude to *Tristan* is probably more important than the chords themselves. In both Chopin (B67, bars 7–9) and Liszt (B70, bars 1–2) the dominant 7th after the French 6th resolves to a chord of A major, but Wagner's dominant 7th remains unresolved. Instead a long silence intervenes between this first phrase (B68, first system) and its sequential repeat (second system), and there is another long silence before a variant of the first phrase is heard in bar 8–11 (third system). Every one of these phrases ends on a dominant 7th. In less ambiguous tonality these would resolve to the chords shown in the column of resolutions to the right of Wagner's music. These are all diatonic chords of the key of A minor, so the dominant 7ths could be heard as unresolved secondary dominants leading to the massive interrupted cadence of bars 16–17. The goal of the tonic chord of A major is only reached after another seven bars of chromatic harmony, but the perfect cadence in this key is less than conclusive. Indeed there are those who hear the A-major chord in bar 24 as a subdominant in the key of E major, a tonality that dominates the ensuing bars (not shown in B68).

Before *Tristan und Isolde* was staged Wagner wrote a version of the prelude that he intended for concert performance. It differs from the operatic version in that, instead of ending inconclusively on the dominant of C minor (the key as the curtain rises on the first scene), it ends conclusively with a 25-bar coda in A major. Despite the fact that Wagner clearly thought his concert prelude to be in A minor/major (parallel keys were treated as simple colourings of the same tonal centre in the late nineteenth century), there are many other analyses of the *Tristan* chord. With some justification it is sometimes described as a half-diminished 7th (respelling G♯ as A♭, B as C♭ and D♯ as E♭), for it appears as such at the greatest climax of the prelude. This is not surprising for, as B68(i) shows, Wagner uses all twelve chromatic degrees in the two **leitmotifs** heard in the first seven bars. What is indisputable is the fact that the lack of conclusive resolution of these chromatic discords creates an almost unbearable tension that mirrors the as yet unfulfilled desires of the fated lovers.

5.8 Non-functional harmony

Nearly all of the harmony discussed in this chapter so far has been functional. To a greater or lesser extent, chords have helped define **tonality** and have interacted dynamically to form harmonic progressions which are directed towards a tonal goal, such as a perfect cadence in the tonic key. Even the extreme chromaticism of *Tristan und Isolde* is potent precisely because there are tonal centres towards which Wagner's harmonic progressions can struggle (B68 begins in A minor and ends with a perfect cadence in A major).

More than 60 years after the first performance of *Tristan* Josef Hauer composed a set of lieder with texts by Hölderlin, one of which contains exactly the same rising chromatic melody used by Liszt and Wagner (B70, B71 and B72 respectively). After a tonally ambiguous chord, a diminished 7th, Hauer uses an inversion of a French 6th (C♮–E♮–F♯–A♯ in root position). The third chord would also be a French 6th if the F♮ and B♮ were enharmonically notated as E♯ and A×. But these 'French 6ths' do not function as such: they simply slide up chromatically to reach another diminished-7th chord. In Hauer's progression it is impossible to detect any sense of tonality because the chords completely lack functional direction. They have been derived from the superimposition of four three-note cells from the tone row shown in the first eight bars of C40. This **atonal** music illustrates one of many twentieth-century styles in which chords follow each other in non-functional harmonic progressions that lack the tonal drive of earlier music.

5.8.1 Serial harmony

Using a similar technique to Hauer, Stravinsky, in C88, derives the three introductory chords of 'Surge, aquilo' from the **tone row** sung by the tenor in bars 2–4 (the **prime order**, labelled P on the extra stave immediately beneath these bars). These chords are **verticalisations** of the **retrograde order** of the tenor's row (shown on the extra stave beneath bar 1 with enharmonic notations shown in boxes). Thus the first chord consists of the last four notes of the tenor's prime order, the second chord uses notes 8, 7, 6 and 5, and the third chord uses the remaining four notes of the row. The composition of these three highly dissonant four-part chords is entirely determined by Stravinsky's permutation of a series of notes which includes all 12 chromatic notes, so it is not surprising that they have no tonal function. Instead we perceive them as completely discrete harmonic entities unrelated to any key. It is Stravinsky's deliberate avoidance of goal-directed functional harmony which, more than any other factor, renders this music completely **atonal**.

5: Harmony

5.8.2 Quartal and quintal harmony

At the dawn of polyphony, perfect octaves, 5ths and 4ths were the only intervals regarded as being consonant, and the only chords that were used were those based on these intervals. A7 shows that the chords themselves were formed by combining the same plainsong melody sung simultaneously at two or more pitch-levels. The result was parallel octaves (now hardly recognised as chords), parallel 5ths, parallel 4ths, or a combination of these intervals. This type of quintal and quartal harmony was resurrected in the early twentieth century, notably in Debussy's impression of the legendary sunken cathedral of Ys appearing from the mist (C22). But when Debussy superimposes one perfect 5th on another (C23, left-hand crotchets) the result is a series of dissonant-9th chords.

Liszt used such quintal harmony more systematically to suggest a diabolical atmosphere at the start of his *Mephisto Waltz* No.1 (B73). Here, instead of the concordant combination of octaves, 5ths and 4ths heard in the **composite organum** of A7(b), perfect 5ths are superimposed in the same way as they are in C23. But here there are two such chords piled on top of each other (each indicated by a vertical bracket in bar 19). The result is the extremely dissonant six-part chord heard throughout bars 17–21.

In much the same way twentieth-century composers have employed quartal harmony as an alternative to the **tertian harmony** of earlier tonal music. Throughout C65 Bartók uses chords built out of perfect 4ths (and most of the melodic motives are also constructed out of perfect 4ths). At the start of the extract notes a perfect 4th apart are superimposed to form a six-part discord like that produced by superimposed 5ths in the *Mephisto Waltz*. This 4th chord, slightly varied, is twice repeated at lower pitches. These quasi-sequential bars lack any sense of tonality, but from bar 7 the music begins to revolve around an E♭ (in the pianissimo bars the chords with accidentals are heard as auxiliaries to the quartal chords containing an E♭). This tonal centre is confirmed in the last four bars by the reiteration of E♭ as an inner pedal. Thus, although the quartal harmony is itself non-functional, the use of a pedal can establish a tonal centre.

5.8.3 Chord streams

Debussy's 'La Cathédrale engloutie' exemplifies his impressionistic use of chord streams and **added-note harmony**. C23 begins with a passage in which superimposed 5ths produce a stream of parallel 9th chords. In C24 3rds are added to organum-like parallel 5ths to form a stream of unsullied triads. C25 includes a stream of chords notated as dominant 7ths, but any suggestion of tonal function is absent as they slip down part of a whole-tone scale (Chopin's chromatically descending 'dominant 7ths' in bars 33–36 of B65 are equally atonal). The last extract from 'La Cathédrale engloutie' (C26) begins with quartal harmony (superimposed perfect 4ths form 7th chords sliding upwards in parallel motion), and it ends with a couple of added-2nd chords as the cathedral disappears into the mists from which it arose.

It is but a short step from the non-functional parallel 'dominant 7ths' of Chopin and Debussy to the equally non-functional 'dominant 7ths' in bars 2–4, 7–8 and 10 of Messiaen's 'Prière du Christ montant vers son Père'

(C55). None of these resolves; even the last one simply shifts to an unrelated chord of C major (which the ear accepts as a tonic chord simply because it lasts so long). The atonal streams of dissonant chords which precede the 'dominant 7ths' derive from Messiaen's seventh mode of limited transposition (shown on the stave beneath the organ score). The first chord is made up of notes 1, 3, 6, 8 and 10 of the mode. The chords in the first complete bar are similarly derived from the five-note modal collections shown beneath each one of them. Just as Debussy's stream of 'dominant 7ths' moves down a segment of a whole-tone scale, so Messiaen's discords move up a segment of his mode (the pedal part of the first five chords corresponds with the first five pitches of the scale shown at the foot of the score). Thus Debussy's mythical impression of a resurgent cathedral becomes Messiaen's mystical vision of the Ascension of Christ, both expressed in one or other of the non-functional harmonic languages of the twentieth century.

6:
Timbre and texture

This chapter is concerned with those elements of music that first strike the listener – the tone-colours of instruments and voices, and the way they are combined to form an aural picture. Although metaphors such as tone-colour are often used to describe these superficial musical events, the elements of timbre and texture are impossible to understand without living sound. It is as pointless to describe the chalumeau register of the clarinet as a dark oily sound for someone who has never heard it as it is to describe purple as a deep, sombre colour for someone who is colour-blind. The intellect can grasp the principles of contrapuntal inversion, but the sound of a clarinet playing a melody in its lowest octave just is: one can identify the sound only by hearing it.

6.1 Timbre

Timbre is to the ear what colour is to the eye. Just as blue paint remains blue whether the artist uses it to delineate a small triangle or a large square, so the distinctive **tone-colour** or timbre of a flute remains flute-like whether the instrumentalist plays a legato melody (C76, bars 1–5) or detached notes (C76, scale at the end of bar 5). Conversely, the sensuous appreciation of two otherwise identical triangles differs according to the colours the artist chooses: for example, a deep purple triangle might appear more threatening than an identical triangle painted sky blue. In the same way the sensuous effect of otherwise identical notes will differ according to the timbres of the instruments playing them. This can be heard in bars 14 and 15 of B68. In the first of these bars violins in octaves play the notes E♯ and F♯. In the second, woodwind instruments in octaves play the same notes an octave higher. The contrasting sound of the two bars has more to do with the contrasting timbres of the two groups of instruments than it has to do with the octave displacement and higher dynamic level of the second pair of notes.

6.2 Harmonic series

Most sounds of definite pitch produced by instruments or voices are made up of a **fundamental** (the pitch printed in a score) together with several other higher pitches called **harmonics**. These cannot normally be individually distinguished: for instance, the sustained cello note heard in bars 7–10 of C95 is an amalgam of the printed C♮ plus the pitches shown in the harmonic series beneath the last stave of the *Élégie*. No matter what the pitch of the fundamental is, harmonics always form the intervals shown in the last four bars of this example. If, for instance, the fundamental (first harmonic) is F_1 (as it is in the harmonic series shown in C84) then the second harmonic will be F (an octave higher than the fundamental), the third harmonic will be c (a 5th above the second harmonic), the fourth harmonic will be f (a 4th above the third harmonic) and so on.

A simple experiment with a piano will allow these harmonics to be heard individually. Piano sound is generated by hitting the strings with the felt-

Elements of music

covered hammers that can be seen beneath the strings in a grand piano and in front of the strings in an upright piano. The impact of these hammers causes the strings to vibrate. The number of times each one vibrates along its full length each second determines the **pitch** of the fundamental – slow vibrations for low notes, faster vibrations for high notes. If a note of the same pitch as a stretched string is sounded close to it the string will be set vibrating sympathetically. In order to avoid unwanted **sympathetic vibration** every piano string is provided with a damper that is released just before the hammer hits the string. As soon as the key is released the damper re-engages with the string and suppresses its vibrations almost immediately. To demonstrate the phenomenon of sympathetic vibration one can gently depress any key so that the hammer mechanism is not activated but the damper is lifted from the string. If one then sings or plays a note of the same pitch as the undamped string loudly and in close proximity to it, the string will begin to vibrate and keep sounding until the key is released or vibrations have died away naturally. If the keys corresponding to harmonics 4–6 on the extra stave at the end of C95 (c^1, e^1 and g^1) are gently depressed in the same way, and the fundamental (C) is struck loudly and immediately released, the ghostly sound of a C major triad will be heard. This chord has been produced by the harmonics of the fundamental setting the undamped strings vibrating. The relative loudness of the individual notes of the 'ghost chord' (and of all the other harmonics) is one of the chief factors determining the timbre of a particular piano. Peter Maxwell Davies makes use of the phenomenon of sympathetic vibration in the first 13 bars of C90 in which the pianist silently depresses all of the white notes from c^1 to g^2 and keeps them depressed while playing detached notes in the lowest range of the piano. The harmonics of the bass notes cause the undamped strings to vibrate sympathetically, thus providing the shimmering sustained cluster chord that accompanies the marimba solo.

The way in which stretched strings vibrate is quite complex. As well as the whole length of the string vibrating like this (Figure 6.2a):

it simultaneously vibrates in halves, like this (Figure 6.2b):

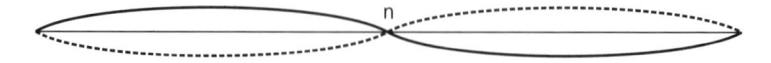

in thirds, like this (Figure 6.2c):

in quarters, like this (Figure 6.2d):

and so on. The points at which these oscillations change direction are called **nodes** (labelled n in the diagrams above). This is of more than theoretical interest because if the string is touched lightly at one of these nodal points one or more of the **modes of vibration** will be suppressed and a higher harmonic will be heard. The cellist demonstrates this in her performance of the *Élégie* (C95). After playing the fundamental or first harmonic (Figure 6.2a) on the open C string (bars 7–11[1]), the second note of bar 11 is produced by bowing the same string while lightly touching it halfway along its length (Figure 6.2b). The result is a ghostly sound in which the fundamental has been suppressed and the pitch heard (c) corresponds with the second harmonic shown on the extra stave at the foot of C95. The next note played by the cellist is produced by bowing the C string while touching it lightly at one of the nodes shown in Figure 6.2c, thus suppressing the first two harmonics to reveal the third harmonic (g in bar 11). Similarly bowing the C string while touching the string lightly at one of the nodal points shown in Figure 6.2d produces a pitch corresponding with the fourth harmonic (the middle C in bar 11). As higher and higher harmonics are played so the sound becomes purer and more flute-like (because the harmonic contents of the notes are successively reduced). So it is the presence of these harmonics which makes the first note the cellist plays sound so rich in tone-colour.

6.3 Tone-colours

The timbre of a flute is purer than the penetrating reedy timbre of an oboe (compare the flute and oboe melodies in bars 10–14 of C1), while the timbre of a horn sounds much fatter than that of an oboe (compare their melodies in C4). The reason why the tone-colours of these instruments sound so different is that the relative dynamic levels of the **harmonics** which are sounding at the same time as the **fundamental** are different. In the case of the flute the harmonics are relatively weak in relation to the fundamental, while the oboe tone is rich in harmonics. There are many other factors that affect the tonal qualities of an instrument, such as competence of the performer, but the harmonic profile of an instrument is the chief determinant of tone-colour when an instrument is played in a normal manner.

6.4 Bowed and plucked string instruments

This section illustrates the tone-colours of string instruments in common use from the eighteenth century to the present day. String instruments that are now only used in authentic performances of ancient music are discussed and illustrated in sections 6.4.2 and 6.4.3.

6.4.1 Orchestral string instruments

The string section of a symphony orchestra normally comprises five sections: violins 1 and 2, violas, cellos and double basses. All of them can be bowed or plucked (see 6.5.4), and all have four strings tuned in perfect 5ths

Elements of music

(except for the double bass which is tuned in perfect 4ths and can have a fifth string allowing the performance of notes as low as bottom C on the piano). The lowest note that can be played on a string instrument is determined by the pitch of the lowest-sounding string. The highest note is determined by the performer's competence. The ranges of these instruments are shown on the folded insert:

a) **Violin**
   Violin solo: A88, A95–98 (baroque violin), C18, C97 (bars 53–65)
   Violin duo: C58
   Violin section: B59, bars 3–4 and 7–8 (unison), C6 (octaves)
b) **Viola**
   Viola solo: A38, C72 (bars 6–8), C87
   Viola section: A39 (the complete melody throughout)
c) **Cello**
   Cello solo: A90, C69, C95
   Cello continuo: B4
   Cello section: B59 (bars 27–36), B68 (bars 0–1, 4–5, 8–9, 17–22)
d) **Double bass**
   Double bass solo: C7
   Double bass continuo: B16 (sounding an octave below the cello)
   Double bass section: B59, bars 1–2 and 5–6 (arco), C3 (pizzicato)

6.4.2 Ancient plucked string instruments

The **citole** is a fretted plucked string instrument of the cittern family that was popular in the thirteenth and early fourteenth centuries. It was used as an accompanimental and as a solo instrument (A13).

The **vihuela** was one of the most important instruments of medieval and renaissance Spain. There were three varieties – those that were bowed, those that were plucked with a quill, and those that were plucked with the fingers. It was the last of these which was chiefly cultivated in the late renaissance and which has been revived in the twentieth century. It has frets (ridges set at 90 degrees to the strings) and six or seven courses of strings. Although a member of the viol family, it looks and sounds more like a guitar. Its repertoire is extensive, and includes *diferencias* (variations) such as those in A34 (which shows the theme together with the bass of the first variation).

The **lute** is plucked like a guitar, and like a guitar it has frets. In its most familiar form it has six courses of unison strings. The sound is quieter than that of the guitar and more plaintive than that of the vihuela. It was one of the most popular instruments of the late renaissance and baroque eras, and was used as a solo instrument (A89), as an accompanying instrument in solo songs and as a continuo instrument. In B5 a lute is entrusted with an important obbligato solo in a baroque aria.

The **theorbo** is a large bass lute that became popular in the seventeenth century as a suitable instrument to realise a basso continuo, since it could encompass both the bass part and the improvised harmonic filling required in music of the *seconda prattica*. It can be heard in an accompanimental role in A75, where the lowest strings are used for the ground while the higher strings are used to realise the implied harmony of the bass. In the seventeenth century the theorbo and the **chitarrone** (A65) were identical instruments.

6.4.3 Ancient bowed string instruments

In the middle ages **fiddle** was a generic term for almost any type of bowed string instrument including the vielle (A18). **Vielle** could also refer to a wide range of bowed string instruments, but often it meant the **hurdy-gurdy**, an instrument in which a set of melody and drone strings are bowed mechanically by turning a crank connected to a rosined wheel. Melodies (such as that in bars 10–18 of A13) are played by means of keys attached to tangents that stop the strings. There are many alternative names for the hurdy-gurdy, the earliest being the Latin term *organistrum* (depicted in twelfth-century sources as a large two-man instrument); another is 'symphonia' (a later one-man instrument). The English **sinfony** is the same instrument (though only its drone strings are heard in A15), and the French *vielle à roue* survived into the eighteenth century, when playing pastoral games and music became such a feature of aristocratic entertainment.

The **rebec** is a bowed string instrument of Arabic origin that was introduced into Europe in the middle ages and which remained popular until the sixteenth century. In its commonest form it has three strings tuned in 5ths like the three lowest strings of a violin. A duet for two rebecs is shown in A16.

During the course of the sixteenth century most of these bowed string instruments were superseded by instruments of the **viol** family, particularly in the performance of solo and ensemble art music. They were soft-toned fretted instruments held on the lap or between the legs: hence **viola da gamba** ('leg viol'). Most had six strings and the bow was held with an underhand grip. They were made in a variety of sizes ranging from the high treble (an eighteenth-century French addition to the family) to the contrabass or violone. The latter can be heard providing a solo bass part to the *basse danse* shown in A36, and in the string ensemble shown in A64 it doubles a bass viola da gamba at the octave below. Consorts of viols, most often consisting of treble, tenor and bass instruments, were particularly popular in late sixteenth- and seventeenth-century England, both as secular chamber ensembles and as accompanimental groups for the verse anthem (A61).

The viola da gamba should not be confused with the sixteenth- and seventeenth-century **viola da braccio** ('arm viol'), a bowed string instrument of the violin family that was played on the arm. Two of these instruments play the uppermost parts of the Sinfonia shown in A64. Nor should either of these instruments by confused with the **viola d'amore**, a late seventeenth- and eighteenth-century bowed string instrument about the same size as a viola but with the body of a lute. Typically it has seven gut strings that are bowed and a set of unbowed strings that vibrate in sympathy with them. A pair of viole d'amore can be heard playing obbligato parts in the arioso shown in B5.

6.4.4 Harp

The harp dates back to 2600 BC or earlier and, although the earliest music known to be written specifically for it only dates back to the sixteenth century, it is known that it was widely used as a solo and accompanimental instrument in the middle ages (A12). In early baroque ensembles harps were used as **continuo** instruments (they are specifically mentioned in the list of instruments used for the first performance of Monteverdi's opera *Orfeo* in 1607). In A65 a continuo harp joins a ceterone in supplying a simple arpeggiated accompaniment for the tenor. In Monteverdi's own ornamented version of the same phrase (A66) there are florid solos for a double harp (an instrument with two rows of strings, one diatonic, the other containing some chromatic pitches). From the early nineteenth century onwards double-action harps were increasingly used as orchestral instruments, especially in opera and ballet scores. These have 47 strings covering the range shown on the folded insert. Foot pedals allow the strings to be instantly retuned, so permitting the performance of music in any key. In C6 sweeping arpeggios between each melodic phrase cover a large part of this range. One of the most characteristic sounds of the harp is the glissando. In C27 two double-action harps sweep up three octaves of a G-major scale ('G dur' is German for G major and is a performance mark directing the harpists to preset this scale using the foot pedals described above). Harp harmonics can be heard unaccompanied in bars 10–11 of C35 and in an orchestral context in C19.

6.4.5 Guitar

The history of the guitar can be traced back almost as far as that of the harp, but the modern six-string fretted instrument (the range of which is shown on the folded insert) originated in Italy in the mid eighteenth century. The guitar is capable of a wide variety of tone-colours, but two playing techniques produce sounds that are particularly associated with the instrument. The first is the strumming technique known as **rasgueado** (or **rasgado**) that can be heard in the first 17 bars of C83. The second is the classical finger-picking technique known as **punteado**. This can be heard in bars 19–26 of C83. Normally the lowest string of the guitar is tuned to the E♮ on the first ledger line below the bass stave. To achieve the massive six-part chords in bars 13–15 the sixth string is tuned down to a D♮ (a technique known as *scordatura* that is equally applicable to other string instruments).

6.4.6 Mandolin

A plucked string instrument dating from the sixteenth century, but in its modern form originating in Italy in the mid eighteenth century, the mandolin has four strings tuned to the same pitches as the violin. It is played with a plectrum and its most characteristic sound is a tremolo that allows its quickly decaying sound to be extended when long notes are written for it. Single notes can be plucked individually in faster melodies. Both types of performance are evident in bars 5–12 of C29. Mahler wrote minims in bars 8, 10 and 12, but it has become standard practice to use tremolo for these notes. The mandolin is associated with serenades and has been used orchestrally by several nineteenth- and twentieth-century composers to add amorous colour to their scores.

6.5 Special string effects

There are many other ways by which special performance techniques can alter the timbres of string instruments. The most audible of these are described in the following paragraphs.

6: Timbre and texture

6.5.1 String harmonics

It has already been seen (6.2) that some of the harmonic content of notes played on string instruments can be reduced by removing the fundamental (the lowest-sounding harmonic) so that the natural tone-colour changes to a more flute-like sound. From the early nineteenth century onwards composers took advantage of this addition to the orchestral palette. In the third of Bartók's *Romanian Dances* (C56) the violinist plays harmonics throughout the extract. Another striking use of harmonics can be heard at the start of the second movement of Stravinsky's *Canticum sacrum* (C88) where three solo double basses play harmonics in a register usually reserved for the upper strings. Unaccompanied harp harmonics can be heard in bars 10–11 of C35 and at the end of Debussy's *Prélude à L'Après-midi d'un faune* (C19).

6.5.2 Tremolo

There are two types of string tremolo. The violin and viola accompaniment to the cello melody in bars 25–35 of B59 consists of rapid repetitions of the same note produced by very fast up-bows and down-bows, the fingers of the left hand (which help determine the pitch of the note) remaining stationary until a change of chord. This bowed tremolo is indicated by sloping lines drawn through the stems of the minims. In the last five bars of B60 the bowed tremolo contributes much to the gothic horror of this operatic melodrama. Bowed tremolo for solo instruments can be heard at the start of C72, where the strings are bowed near to the bridge (*sul ponticello*), the combination of the two techniques at a low dynamic level giving a particularly eerie effect.

A fingered tremolo consists of a rapid alternation of two pitches more than a tone apart (the alternation of pitches a semitone or tone apart being a trill). It is achieved by alternating between two notes on the same string while bowing in the normal way. Both violins use this technique in C69 (first violin indicated by upward stems, second violin by stems pointing down). It will be seen that the notation for a fingered tremolo differs from that for a bowed tremolo in that the two notes in C69 are beamed together (bar 4) or sloping lines are drawn between them (bar 5). Fingered tremolo for orchestral cello and bass sections can be heard at the end of C31.

6.5.3 Arpeggiando

Bow strokes across the strings produce the successive sounds of an arpeggio rather than the simultaneous articulation of notes in a chord. In baroque solo string music, block chords are often notated with the instruction 'arpeggio', the precise nature of the arpeggiation being left to the discretion of the performer. The lower stave of A96 shows what Bach actually wrote, while the upper stave shows the violinist's realisation of the composer's notation.

6.5.4 Pizzicato

Plucking the strings is the most common way of changing the sound of instruments that are normally bowed. This method of performance is indicated by the direction 'pizzicato' (or 'pizz.'), and 'arco' indicates a return to normal bowing. The contrast between bowed and plucked string

Elements of music

instruments can be heard in C12 where the viola is played with the bow while the violinist plucks the strings. Arpeggiated pizzicato chords are normally played in ascending order. This is the case in the last two bars of C72 where the violins sustain bare 5ths against arpeggiated pizzicato chords on the cello. Pizzicato chords for a full orchestral string section can be heard throughout C6.

6.5.5 Alla chitarra, quasi chitarra
These directions indicate that the performer is to lay aside his bow and strum up and down across all of the strings in the same way as the guitarist strums chords in the opening bars of C83. The technique is used by the viola player in C69 where its use is indicated by the bracketed arrows and the direction 'pizz.' (plucked).

6.5.6 Snap pizzicato
This rather alarming sound is produced by plucking a string vigorously so that it bounces off the fingerboard with a percussive crack. Mahler was the first to use snap pizzicato, but Bartók invented the symbol (a circle with a vertical line through the top) which can be seen, and its effect heard, in bars 1 and 5 of C71.

6.5.7 Glissando
Instead of moving cleanly from one note to the next a glissando (or **portamento**) requires the performer to slide between two notes. It is indicated by a straight line between them (with or without the instruction 'gliss.'). The effect can be heard in C69 when the cellist sweeps up from the repeated notes at the start to a harmonic (indicated by a circle above the grace note).

6.5.8 Sul ponticello
The normal position for bowing is halfway between the bridge and the end of the fingerboard nearest the bridge. The direction 'sul ponticello' (or 'sul pont.') means that the strings should be bowed as close as possible to the bridge. This produces the ghostly sound heard in the opening bars of C72. The direction 'ord.' between and after the two *sul ponticello* passages is an abbreviation for 'ordinario', a performance direction indicating the resumption of normal bowing. In C34 *sul ponticello* ('am Steg' in German) is combined with bowed tremolo in bars 2–6.

6.5.9 Sul tasto, sulla tastiera, sur la touche
These directions indicate that the player is to bow over the fingerboard. This produces timbres that are less rich in harmonics than the sounds produced by bowing in the normal position (C31, bars 9–10). The direction 'flautando' (flute-like tone) is often realised by using this bowing position.

6.5.10 Bariolage
The technique of playing alternate notes on open and stopped strings known as *bariolage* causes subtle contrasts of timbre between notes of the same or different pitches. The effect can be heard in bars 2–13 of A98 where notes on the open A string (indicated by circles in bars 2–3) contrast with stopped notes played on the D and G strings.

6.5.11 Col legno

The use of a reversed bow so that the wood (*legno*) of the bow bounces off the strings produces a brittle timbre quite unlike that of bowed or plucked strings. The whole string section is directed to play in this way throughout C36. In C74 the menacing approach of German forces is represented by an insistent snare-drum figure which accompanies a parody of a military march tune. The grotesque nature of Shostakovich's melody is enhanced by the simultaneous use of three string effects at the same pitch. The first violins play the melody in the normal way (arco, but very staccato), the second violins play the same melody *col legno*, and the violas play it pizzicato.

6.5.12 Vibrato

A fluctuation of pitch caused by a rocking motion of the finger stopping a string increasingly became a normal mode of performance in the nineteenth century. It is now so common that modern composers are compelled to write 'non vibrato' when it is not required. Although its use dates back to the sixteenth century, it was regarded as a kind of optional ornament in early music. Generally speaking, authentic performances of early string music are characterised by little or no vibrato (A88), while performances of romantic or twentieth-century music are generally marked by a degree of vibrato determined by the character of the music (in C18(a) there is some vibrato, in C18(b) there is almost none, in C18(c) there is pronounced vibrato).

6.5.13 Mutes

Without resorting to any special performance techniques the timbre of bowed string instruments can, like that of many other instruments, be radically altered by the use of a mute. For string instruments this is a clip or similar device placed on the bridge that reduces the resonance of the instrument. The change of timbre is obvious in the last few bars of Bartók's String Quartet No. 6 (C72), where a solo for unmuted viola (bars 6–8) is followed by the muted sound of the two violins in the next bar.

6.5.14 Scordatura

Scordatura is the detuning of one or, more rarely, more than one string from its normal pitch. In most cases this is done to allow the performance of notes that cannot be played with normal tuning, but the difference in timbre of the detuned string from the others is so slight that it will not be apparent to most listeners. A special case is the opening bars of C83, where the massive six-part guitar chords in bars 13–15 can only be performed with the lowest string tuned to D (a tone below the normal pitch of this string).

6.6 Timbres and special effects of woodwind instruments

There is much greater variety in the timbres of woodwind instruments than in the more uniform tone-colours of string families such as a consort of viols or the string section of a modern symphony orchestra. But woodwind instruments are less susceptible than strings to changes of timbre brought about by special performance techniques. Only the most common of them are discussed below.

Elements of music

6.6.1 Flute family

The range of the flute is shown on the folded insert. Above the first octave all notes are harmonics, but it is possible to alter the timbre of a given pitch by using a different harmonic to that normally used (by using non-standard fingering and a different embouchure). It is these modified timbres that can be heard when a flautist plays harmonics indicated by the conventional symbol of a circle above the note (as shown in bar 4 of C88). **Flutter-tonguing** is the woodwind equivalent of a bowed tremolo. It is performed by blowing while holding the tongue as though rolling the letter r and maintaining the appropriate fingering and embouchure for the designated pitch. It is usually indicated by the German term 'flatterzunge' or its abbreviations 'flatterz.' or 'flz.' together with strokes through the affected notes (C35, bars 1 and 8–9).

The **piccolo** is a half-size flute with the range shown on the folded insert. The timbres of the flute and piccolo at low dynamic levels can be compared in C76. When playing loudly in the upper part of its range the piccolo can be heard above a loud orchestral tutti (B37, bars 1–19).

The **alto flute** extends the range of the flute family down to the G a 4th below middle C. Its full range can be heard in C87.

6.6.2 Double-reed woodwind instruments

Double-reed instruments have a more penetrating timbre than any other woodwind instrument with the exception of the piccolo in its highest register. The **oboe** is the treble instrument of the orchestral double-reed family, having a range of nearly three octaves (see the folded insert). C1 begins with an oboe solo, there is a duet for horn and oboe in C4 and a pair of oboes is featured in C78.

Like the oboe the **bassoon** is a standard member of the modern symphony orchestra. It provides the bass of the woodwind section in most scores, having a range of about three octaves (see the folded insert). A bassoon solo in the instrument's extreme upper register can be heard in bars 7–9 of C76, a solo in mid-register can be heard in bars 7–8 of C4, and a pair of bassoons are featured in C77.

The **cor anglais** or **English horn** is neither English nor a horn. This is an important point because 'cor' (an abbreviation of *cor à pistons*) is French for 'horn' and it is a common error to misread abbreviations of cor anglais (such as 'cor' and 'cor a.') as references to the French horn. One of the ways of avoiding such confusion is to remember that a cor anglais part will almost always appear in an orchestral score on a stave immediately beneath its nearest relative, the oboe. It has a range a 5th lower than that of the oboe (see the folded insert) and its music is usually printed a perfect 5th above sounding pitch (though, as with all transposing instruments, its music is printed at sounding pitch in Volume 2). It is not a regular member of a symphony orchestra, but as an auxiliary instrument its plaintive nasal sound has been prized by composers since the middle of the nineteenth century. It can be heard in a duet with a tenor voice in bars 3–4 of C88. Its range makes it a suitable substitute for the **oboe da caccia** in baroque music (see 6.9.4).

The largest and lowest of the double-reed family is the **contrabassoon** or **double bassoon**. It has a range pitched an octave below the bassoon (see the folded insert). Ravel explores its lowest register in C31.

6: Timbre and texture

6.6.3 Single-reed woodwind instruments

There are at least half a dozen types of **clarinet** ranging from the clarinet in E♭ (the highest pitched, with a tube-length of 14 inches) to the contrabass clarinet in B♭ (the lowest pitched, with a tube-length of nearly nine feet). The most commonly used are the clarinets in B♭ and A, both of them transposing instruments sounding a tone and a minor 3rd lower than printed respectively (though, as with all transposing instruments, they are notated at sounding pitch in Volume 2). These instruments have a wider range of pitch (see the folded insert) and tone-colour than any other wind instrument, and are at least as agile as the flute. This agility is heard to good advantage in the solo for clarinet in B♭ starting at bar 2 of C75 and in the trill and descending chromatic scale (in bars 12–15) which are such a vital part of Bartók's uncanny representation of derisory laughter. A pair of clarinets are heard playing acidic parallel 7ths in C79, but the instrument is equally capable of lyricism (as the solo for clarinet in A in the second phrase of B68 demonstrates). Its lowest range, known as the **chalumeau register**, has a rich oily sound which Weber exploits in his overture to *Der Freischütz* (B59, bars 24–36).

At the opposite end of the pitch spectrum the shrieking wail of a small clarinet in E♭ playing at the top of its register graphically illustrates the death of Till Eulenspiegel in C10. (Strauss specifies the slightly larger clarinet in D, but this instrument is almost defunct, and its parts are usually played on the smallest of the modern orchestral clarinet family.)

The **bass clarinet** in B♭ is a transposing instrument normally sounding a major 9th/minor 10th lower than written pitch (though, like all other transposing instruments, its parts are printed at sounding pitch in Volume 2). Thus, rather confusingly, the lowest of the single-reed instruments commonly found in large symphony orchestras is usually notated in the treble clef (though Russians and some other composers prefer the bass clef). The bass clarinet in B♭ has a range of over three octaves (see the folded insert), most of it covered in bars 7–8 of C34 (in which flutter-tonguing can be heard in bars 3–5). A solo of an entirely different character can be heard in the first eight bars of C38.

Although the **saxophone** is a single-reed instrument its timbre is quite different from all other members of this family of instruments because its body is made of metal. It is strongly associated with jazz and popular music, hence Walton's use of it in *Façade* (C38, bar 9).

6.6.4 Ancient woodwind instruments

The sound of **transverse flutes** (6.6.1) is generated by blowing across a hole (in the same way that a note can be produced by blowing across the top of a milk bottle). The **recorder** family differs from them in that the sound is generated by blowing through a mouthpiece which directs the jet of air across a sharp edge, thus obviating the need for changes of embouchure. The dynamic range of this type of flute is too narrow for it to be a regular member of the modern symphony orchestra, but it was used by Bach in chamber ensembles as frequently as the transverse flute, and concertos were written for it in the baroque era, notably by Vivaldi. Recorders can be as agile as transverse flutes (A69) and are also capable of long sustained melodies (A60). The **gemshorn** is a type of medieval and early renaissance recorder originally made from the horn of a chamois (A36).

Elements of music

In medieval and renaissance Europe double-reed instruments were popular for outdoor entertainment and dancing because of their incisive timbre and relative loudness compared with strings and flutes. **Bagpipes** have been common from Roman times to the present day and in almost every corner of the globe. The 'bag' is a reservoir of pressurised air supplied by the player's lungs via a pipe, or by a pair of bellows operated by the player's arm. Air is fed through a double reed enclosed in a cylinder at the top of the **chanter**, which has holes that allow the player to perform a range of pitches. In addition to the chanter there are usually one or more drone pipes of fixed pitches. In the bagpipe music shown in A17 there is a drone that sounds a low F♮ throughout. The melody played on the chanter is characterised by the sort of grace notes that are typical of bagpipe music of every age and style.

The **shawm** is a double-reed instrument that was an ancestor of the oboe, but it had a more penetrating, nasal timbre that is evident in its duet with bagpipes shown in A17. It was the most prominent outdoor woodwind instrument from the late thirteenth to the seventeenth century. There were seven sizes giving a total range of C–e^3, thus making the shawm family capable of playing most contemporary instrumental ensemble music. Four of them can be heard playing the pavan shown in A32. The *rauschpfeife* shown in this score is a sixteenth-century German shawm. Various other names were given to members of the shawm family such as the bombarde and pommer (both large shawms).

The **crumhorn** is a double-reed wind-cap instrument that differs from the shawm in construction, and in its less strident timbre. Like the shawm it was made in a range of sizes that covered a compass extending from B♭$_1$ to d^2. It was popular in the sixteenth and early seventeenth centuries both as a solo instrument and in consorts such as that heard in the galliard shown in A35.

The English **curtal** and the German ***dulzian*** of the sixteenth and seventeenth centuries were double-reed instruments made in a variety of sizes of which the bass instrument was the most important (A60). It was used as a substitute for the **pommer** and was a precursor of the modern bassoon.

The baroque **oboe d'amore** is somewhat larger than the modern oboe (it is pitched a 3rd lower) and has a more muted timbre. In the fifth movement of Bach's Cantata No. 80 (B8) the first oboe d'amore is doubled by first violins throughout most of the passage from bar 4 to the end of the extract, but its reedy timbre can still be heard, especially in those passages where it is independent of the violins (bars 7–9 and 17–19). In the same movement 'taille' is short for ***taille des hautbois*** (French for tenor oboe). This is the instrument more familiarly known as the **oboe da caccia**, the precursor of the modern cor anglais and, like the cor anglais, pitched a 5th lower than the oboe. Its plaintive timbre can be heard in bars 3–4 of B8.

The **basset-horn** is a single-reed woodwind instrument pitched a 3rd lower than the modern clarinets in B♭ and A to which it is related. It might now be extinct were it not for the fact that Mozart wrote such wonderful music for it in his Requiem Mass. An ensemble of three basset-horns can be heard in B40. (The question of the instrument for which his clarinet quintet and clarinet concerto were written is still vexed, but it is now usually referred to as a 'basset-clarinet' – an instrument closely related to the basset-horn.)

6.7 Timbres and special effects of brass instruments

In the baroque era brass instruments were used in instrumental ensembles on an ad hoc basis for special occasions – trombones for solemnity (A62) and trumpets for festivity (B15). In early classical music the wind section of an orchestra often comprised just five or six players – two oboes, one or two bassoons and two horns (all of them clearly audible in the tutti starting at bar 19 in B21). By the late eighteenth century a pair of trumpets was added, especially in opera orchestras (B50), as well as a chorus of trombones (Mozart uses three of them to great effect in the overture and priests' music in *Die Zauberflöte*). In a modern symphony orchestra the core of the brass section usually includes at least four horns, two trumpets, three trombones and a tuba (listed here in normal score order). This is the brass section that Liszt employs in his *Mephisto Waltz* No. 1 of 1860, and all of these instruments contribute to the climax heard in bars 57–58 of B73. To this core, late romantic composers added any number of additional or alternative instruments (a pair of cornets for local colour in C3, six trumpets for awesome power in C27 and a solo tenor tuba in C37). Despite dire warnings about impending extinction, symphony and opera orchestras in the second half of the twentieth century still included full brass sections (Britten and MacMillan both employ four horns, four trumpets, three trombones and a tuba in C86 and C97 respectively).

6.7.1 Horns

When reference is made to a horn and the noun is unqualified the instrument is taken to be the **French horn** (as opposed to, say, the alpenhorn). The first type of horn to be used in instrumental ensembles was the **natural horn**, an instrument normally capable of playing only the pitches of the harmonic series derived from a fundamental determined by the length of its tubing. Thus a natural horn in F can theoretically play the notes shown on the stave beneath Britten's Prologue shown in C84 (the fundamental and the highest **harmonics** are rarely used). In this music Britten makes use of harmonics 4 and 6–13. It is possible to inflect this limited range of pitches by a semitone by pushing the hand further up the bell of the instrument to produce **stopped notes**, but, as the last two bars of C85 demonstrate, this is only achieved at the expense of a dramatic change in the timbre of the instrument. Eighteenth-century horn players managed to overcome the problem, but the range of notes the horn could produce was still limited. It is obvious that the contribution that a natural horn in F can make to music in E♭ major is minimal, so early horn players used extra lengths of tubing (called **crooks**) that could be inserted into the instrument. By altering the total length of the horn's tubing these altered the fundamental of the instrument. Thus to play B36 (which is in the key of E♭ major) horn players added a crook that changed the fundamental pitch of their instruments to E♭, thus allowing them to play the range of pitches shown in the two lowest parts of bars 38–43 of B36.

Sometimes horns were crooked to different fundamental pitches in the same work. The horn parts heard in the tutti of B21 (bars 19–59) are crooked in E and G. Between them these two horns can supply a whole range of notes in the E-minor tonality at the start of the tutti and the G-major tonality towards the end of the extract. Weber solves a similar problem in B59 by using four horns, two of them crooked in F and two in C. This enables him to write duets in C major (bars 10–13) and F major (bars 14–15) and complete four-part harmony in C major and F major (bars 18–25).

The need for such stratagems ceased with the invention of valves in the early nineteenth century. These instantaneously changed the fundamental pitch of the horn, so allowing the complete chromatic range of pitches heard in C85 (bars 8–25). As with all modern brass instruments a mute can be inserted into the bell of the instrument to produce a timbre that is quite distinct from hand stopping, as the opening bars of C19 demonstrate.

6.7.2 Trumpets

The problems associated with natural horns apply with equal force to **natural trumpets**. In the baroque era a virtuoso style of clarino trumpeting made use of the highest harmonics of the natural trumpet. In this register the overtones are close together, so allowing the performance of a scale of pitches like that shown in bars 79–80 of B15. Less able players specialised in the **principale register**, which, being lower than the clarino parts, most often consisted of arpeggios such as those shown in bars 15–22 of B15.

Clarino trumpeting died out in the eighteenth century as baroque styles gave way to classicism. Various attempts were made to adapt the trumpet to allow it to play a full chromatic range. The most successful of these was the keyed trumpet featured in B36. The key mechanism allowed dexterity and ornamentation (bars 85–91) and chromaticism (bars 92–96) but the highest notes of the clarino register are not used.

Keyed trumpets were rendered obsolete when **valve trumpets** were introduced in the second decade of the nineteenth century. The trumpet most commonly used in orchestras of the nineteenth, twentieth and twenty-first centuries is the valve trumpet in B♭ though trumpets in other keys are still specified (see the folded insert). The enormous dynamic and timbral range of the modern trumpet may be judged by comparing the overwhelming six-part chord played on F and B♭ trumpets in C27 with the delicate sounds of a muted trumpet in C35. A completely different tone-colour is heard when muted trumpets are played loudly. In the 'Intermezzo interrotto' from his *Concerto for Orchestra* Bartók uses two muted trumpets playing trills a tone apart in bar 10 of C75. The effect is (and is meant to be) sardonically humorous. Yet another timbre is heard in C81, where a pair of muted trumpets play parallel 2nds moderately loudly. C97 begins with a chord for four muted trumpets that rises from soft to very loud within a couple of seconds, and in the ensuing bars their detached fortissimo chords sound almost as percussive as the brake drums with which they are coupled. Without mutes trumpets can cut through an orchestral tutti with ease (C82, bars 14–67). All of these passages are a far cry from the conventional fanfares of C37.

6.7.3 Trombones and tubas

The **trombone** (see the folded insert) has a long history as a ceremonial instrument, particularly for solemn liturgies or sombre operatic scenes (see also 6.7.5). Having a slide that can instantaneously alter the pitch of the fundamental means that, unlike horns and trumpets, trombones have always

6: Timbre and texture

had a complete chromatic range of notes. Both of these aspects of the trombone are illustrated in the sombre scene from Monteverdi's *Orfeo*, where the eponymous hero approaches the gates of Hades (A62 and A63). Similarly, in the Wolf's Glen scene from *Der Freischütz* Weber reserves his trombones for the point at which the Devil (Samiel) actually appears (last chord of B60). The range of dynamics and timbres of the instrument may be judged by comparing this C-minor chord with the delicate muted-trombone chords heard in bars 6–7 of C35 and the comic glissandi heard in the last two bars of C75 (the trombone is the only brass instrument capable of a true glissando).

The chief role of the **tuba** (see the folded insert) in much orchestral music is to provide a firm bass line to a passage for full orchestra or a passage for the full wind band. This is the case in the first four bars of C27 where a tuba and contrabassoon are powerful enough to support fourteen other wind instruments. Tuba solos are relatively rare, but those in the opening bars of C28 and in bars 5–7 allow the rounded timbres of the tuba to be distinctly heard.

6.7.4 Brass-band instruments

Although the **cornet** is a descendent of the post horn it has evolved to become very like a trumpet. Nowadays it is associated with brilliant solos in brass bands, but it was often specified in nineteenth-century French scores. It remains a popular instrument in carnival bands in southern Europe, and it is for this reason that Tchaikovsky features a pair of them in his *Capriccio italien* (C3), in which the timbres of the cornet and trumpet can easily be compared. It will be noticed that the cornet players use vibrato (which is very common in brass bands) whereas the trumpeters play with 'straight' tone. This does not have to be the case, but Tchaikovsky's (tongue-in-cheek?) direction 'molto dolce espressivo' gives the cornetists full licence to use as much vibrato as the conductor can stand! The full name used in French 19th-century scores is ***cornet à pistons*** (often abbreviated to 'piston' or 'pist.').

The **euphonium** is the tenor instrument in a brass band, though its extensive range (approximately F_1-c^2) allows it to perform wide-ranging solos. The nomenclature of this agile instrument is bedevilled with confusion. In the USA baritone horn and euphonium are synonymous. In Germany *baryton* and *euphonium* refer to the same instrument (and they should know because the instrument was invented there in the third decade of the nineteenth century).

In his *Planets* Suite Holst calls it a tenor tuba, but performers who play the solo in C37 are likely to call their instruments euphoniums.

For other instruments used in brass bands see 6.7.2 and 6.7.3.

6.7.5 Ancient brass instruments

The ***cornetto*** (Italian) or **cornett** (English) should not be confused with the cornet (6.7.4). Although usually classified with brass instruments it has a wooden body with a cupped mouthpiece similar to those on brass instruments. In the late renaissance and early baroque periods it was commonly combined with early trombones in the performance of ensemble and choral works, notably in St Mark's and San Rocco in Venice. Cornetts can be heard in the upper parts of each of the three instrumental choirs of Giovanni Gabrieli's *Canzona noni toni a 12* (A58).

Elements of music

The **sackbut** can hardly be distinguished from the modern trombone in appearance and playing technique, though it could not be played as loudly as the modern instrument. (The use of the term sackbut to distinguish the baroque from the modern instrument is historically unjustified, since trombone is a term quite as old as sackbut, but it is commonly adopted for clarity.) A pair of sackbuts can be heard in the lower parts of each of the three instrumental choirs in A58, and the soft-toned sound of a solo 'saggbut' (*sic* – period English spelling) can be heard throughout A60.

The **ophicleide** is a large keyed bugle invented in Paris in 1817 as a vibrant alternative to the tuba. It features in French orchestral music of the nineteenth century, such as the 'Dies irae' in the 'Witches' Sabbath' from Berlioz's *Symphonie fantastique* (B63).

6.8 Percussion

The percussion section of the symphony orchestra can range from a couple of kettle drums to a vast battery of tuned and untuned instruments. There are various scientific methods of categorising these instruments (see, for example, **Membranophone** and **Idiophone** in the alphabetic entries), but what follows is more empirical, with percussion in common western use generally being listed before more exotic instruments.

6.8.1 Drums of definite pitch

Throughout the world there are many drums capable of producing definite pitches, but **timpani** or **kettle drums** are the only instruments of this type which are frequently used in the orchestra. They are made in different sizes, the precise pitch of each being determined by the tension of the membrane that covers the 'kettle'. The tension of the membrane is altered by adjusting a set of screws positioned round the circumference of the instrument or by moving a pedal. In baroque and classical music timpani are usually employed (often with trumpets) to enhance the effect of important cadences. To this end two timpani were tuned to the tonic and the dominant notes of the prevailing key (B36, bars 288–294). They could also be used at points of high drama, but only where chords contained either the tonic or the dominant (B36, bars 255–263).

Timpani are capable of a very wide dynamic range. In C27 two timpani are struck simultaneously with two sticks producing a sound that can be heard clearly against a wind band (including six trumpets) playing fortissimo.

Timpani can be equally effective at a low dynamic level. In bars 26–29 of B59 pianissimo strokes on a kettledrum are doubled by equally quiet pizzicato crotchets played on double basses.

Chromatic or **pedal timpani** are fitted with foot pedals that can alter the tension of the membrane without altering the position of the screws. This makes it possible to change the pitch of the drums instantly when there is a change of key or when the composer requires notes other than those first specified in the score. The foot pedal also allows microtonal slides such as the unaccompanied glissando heard in bars 68–69 of C82.

6.8.2 Drums of indefinite pitch

Untuned drums are of imprecise pitch, the size of the instrument determining its approximate pitch-level (large instruments sound deep, smaller ones sound high). The largest drum commonly found in orchestras is the

bass drum. It is usually played with a soft-headed stick to produce profoundly deep single notes (C42) or a roll like distant thunder (C52, bar 8).

The **tenor drum** has a higher pitch-level than the bass drum and is constructed like a side drum, but with a deeper cylinder and no snares. Varèse uses it in conjunction with two sizes of bass drum at the start of *Ionisation* (C52).

The **side drum** or **snare drum** has a higher pitch-level than the tenor drum. It has two heads. The uppermost is struck with wooden sticks, while the lower has a number of strings stretched across it (snares) which produce the dry rattling noise peculiar to this type of drum. When the snares are released the timbre of the instrument changes. Side drums with and without snares can be heard in C44 and a long side-drum solo can be heard in C74.

A contrasting sound can be produced by striking the snare drum on the rim instead of the head. The difference between this sound and the normal snare drum sound can be heard in bars 4–5 of C38 ('Nat.' above the first beat of bar 5 is an abbreviation of the Italian direction 'naturale', meaning a return to normal performance technique). Another special side-drum effect is the **rim shot**, in which the rim and the head of the side drum are struck simultaneously. Alternatively a stick can be laid on the drum so that the head rests on the membrane and the shank on the rim. This stick is then struck with the other stick. Simultaneous rim shots on a side drum and a tenor drum can be heard in the last bar of C43 and bar 31 of C53.

The **tambourine** is a small hand-held single-headed drum with tiny pairs of thin metal discs mounted in the wooden rim. When the instrument is shaken or struck with the knuckles these produce the characteristic jingling noise heard in C42 and the last two bars of C52. Some tambourines are without a membrane, but because some common tambourine performing techniques are not possible on this instrument they are rarely found in orchestras.

Bongos are small drums of Cuban origin which usually come in pairs (high and low). They can be played with the hands or with beaters. In C45 they are played with timpani sticks with felt heads. The same music can be heard in context in bars 9–12 of C52.

The most exotic drum heard in *Ionisation* is the ***tambour à corde*** (string drum) or **lion's roar** (the latter name giving a pretty fair impression of the instrument's timbre). This is a type of friction drum with a string attached to the centre of the membrane. The performer grips the string with rosined fingers and, pulling it tightly, lets the string slip through the fingers. It can be heard in the last bar of C46 and bar 12 of C52.

6.8.3 Cymbals, gongs and bells

Cymbals are large thin circular metal plates that can be clashed or rubbed together. A single cymbal can be suspended on a stand and struck with a variety of sticks or wire brushes. Suspended cymbals can also be struck with two sticks to produce a roll. All of these effects can be heard in C47 and, combined with other percussion, in C54. Both of these examples are quite soft, but a roll on a suspended cymbal can be tremendously powerful (C97, bars 7–8 and 21–22).

Antique cymbals are required in the last three bars of Debussy's *Prélude à L'Après-midi d'un faune* (C19). These small, very high-pitched cymbals

Elements of music

are modern reconstructions, possibly modelled on those depicted in the remains of Pompeii (though they were known in ancient Egypt and are mentioned in the Old Testament). Unlike other orchestral cymbals they can be made to sound definite pitches (in this case e^3 and b^3). Modern performers usually play these notes on *crotales*, small tuned cymbals mounted on a board).

Gongs are brass dishes like cymbals, but they are much heavier, more rigid, and almost always suspended vertically in a frame when used in an orchestra. They come in a variety of sizes, some of which are tuned to definite pitches (those with a raised boss). A pair of gongs tuned to F and B♭ can be heard at the start of bars 5 and 19 in C97.

The most common gong used in symphony orchestras is the **tam-tam**. Unlike bossed gongs it is of indefinite pitch, but a generalised difference of pitch-level is evident between the two tam-tams heard with a gong in C48 and C54.

Tubular bells or **chimes** are metal cylinders tuned to precise pitches and suspended in pitch-order in a rack. They are struck with mallets. Berlioz asks for real church bells in his *Symphonie fantastique* but it is known that he had to make do with a piano in a performance he himself conducted. Despite the use of period instruments, B63 does not have recourse to this last resort. An amazing tintinnabulation of tubular bells and hand bells can be heard in bars 36–38, 42–44 and 48–50 of C97.

Cowbells of a variety of pitches, precise or indeterminate, are hung around the necks of cattle in high alpine pastures. The bells contain loose clappers that strike the bells in a random fashion as the beasts move about. Some composers of programme music have taken advantage of the associations that such bells can summon. This is the case in the finale of Mahler's sixth symphony in which real cowbells are rung randomly. They can be heard soon after the start of C28.

Sleigh bells are mounted on a thick wooden stick, a leather strap or a metal frame that is held with one hand while the other makes a fist and bangs the other hand (C49 and bars 18–20 of C52).

6.8.4 Metal percussion instruments

The **triangle** is usually struck with a metal beater. At even the lowest dynamic level its very high pitch enables it to be heard distinctly above other instruments. Single notes and rolls are both possible and are demonstrated on C47 and C54.

The **anvil** can be a real blacksmith's anvil, but this is very heavy, so a small heavy metal block or cylinder struck with a mallet of hard wood or metal is sometimes substituted. Two of them, one higher-pitched than the other, may be heard in C48 and C54.

There are no substitutes for **brake drums**: only real motor-car brake drums struck with a metal mallet are ever used. Their pitch-level is largely determined by size. After the very loud crash of several percussion instruments at the start of bar 9 of C97 a set of three differently pitched brake drums can be heard playing a syncopated rhythm with muted brass until bar 14.

6.8.5 Wooden percussion instruments

True Spanish **castanets** consist of a pair of scallop-shell-shaped pieces of hardwood loosely held together with strings. They are attached to the thumb or finger of one hand (two pairs if both hands are used) and clapped together, often while the performer dances. Orchestral castanets may be mounted on a handle or frame. They can be heard with a bass drum in C50 and in a percussion ensemble in bars 18–20 of C52.

Cuban **claves** consist of two cylinders of hardwood, one held loosely in a cupped hand, the other striking the first. They can be heard with a güiro and wood blocks in C51, and in a larger percussion ensemble in bars 2–4 of C53.

The Latin-American **güiro** is a hollow gourd with a striated surface that is scraped with a stick. It can be heard with claves and wood blocks in C51, and in a larger percussion ensemble in C53.

Maracas are hollowed gourds of Latin-American origin. The gourds are mounted on sticks and filled with seeds which rattle when the maracas are shaken (one in each hand). They can be heard with a whip in C46 and in a percussion ensemble in bars 9–12 of C52.

Wood blocks consist of a set of hollowed wooden rectangles, cylinders or spheres of different pitch-levels that are struck, usually with wooden sticks. Three of them can be heard unaccompanied in the last bar of C51, and in a percussion ensemble in the last bar of C53.

The **whip** consists of two flat pieces of wood. The longer piece is grasped and the shorter piece is attached to the longer by a hinge. The two pieces are then clapped violently together to produce a noise approximating to the cracking of a whip. Two strokes of the whip can be heard in C46, and these sounds are repeated in the context of a percussion ensemble in bars 10–12 of C52.

6.8.6 Sound effects

In addition to those percussion instruments listed above which call to mind particular associations (such as the anvil and the whip), there are many more, the names of which are self-explanatory (car horns, thunder and wind machines and so on). One concrete example will suffice. The **sirens** at the start of Varèse's *Ionisation* bring to mind the wailing of emergency vehicles or wartime bombing raids. They do produce sounds of definite pitch but these are always in a state of flux (like glissandi) getting louder in ascent and softer in descent. Nevertheless, the two sirens heard in C44 are distinguishable because one has a higher pitch-range than the other. They can be heard in a large percussion ensemble in bars 1–7 and 13–17 in C52.

6.8.7 Keyed orchestral percussion instruments

This section includes those instruments that have wooden or metal keys, or strings struck with hand-held beaters as well as those that have keyboards.

The **piano** (see the folded insert) is usually thought of as a solo instrument capable of sustained melodic lines and figurative accompaniments (C2). But it is a percussion instrument in so far as the strings are struck by hammers. This aspect of the instrument has been widely exploited in twentieth-century solo piano music (C66 and C67). In C8 the two pianos (only piano 1 is shown in the reduced score) are as much percussion instruments as is the xylophone (the first piano repeats exactly what the xylophone has played, but in octaves).

Elements of music

The **celesta** (or, as orchestral musicians tend to call it, the celeste) was invented in the late nineteenth century. It looks like a small upright piano but has a smaller range (see the folded insert). The keyboard operates hammers which strike metal bars, the vibrations of which are sustained by resonators. It has a four-octave range based on middle C. Its delicate timbre can easily be swamped by other instruments. In the finale of Mahler's sixth symphony (C28) it is first heard with harps (bars 2–4) then with violins (bars 7–13). Mahler achieves a proper balance between these instruments by marking the celesta part 'forte', the harp part 'piano' and the violin parts *ppp*. In bars 15–18 the celesta's tremolo can be heard clearly against *pianissimo* woodwind parts.

The **glockenspiel** consists of metal bars arranged like the notes of a piano keyboard. These are struck with small hand-held beaters. The player might be required to hold two of these in each hand, thus enabling the performance of four-part chords. Alternatively some glockenspiels are fitted with a keyboard that is played in the same way as a piano keyboard. The orchestral glockenspiel commonly has a written range of two and a half octaves based on g, but it sounds two octaves above written pitch (see the folded insert). Two-part glockenspiel chords doubled at the lower octave by flutes can be heard in C3 and single notes in B35, bar 2.

The **xylophone** is similar to the glockenspiel, but the bars are made of resonant hardwood struck with beaters most often made of wood or plastic. Modern instruments have cylindrical resonators beneath each bar to amplify the sound. It commonly has a range of about three to four octaves (see the folded insert). Played loudly the xylophone's wooden timbre can cut through the densest of textures (C8).

The **marimba** is a type of xylophone with thinner and more delicate keys. It is pitched an octave below its counterpart (see the folded insert) and produces a softer and mellower timbre. It is played with two or four soft rubber-covered or yarn-wound mallets. Because of its more limited dynamic range it is not used in the orchestra as often as the xylophone. It is more at home in smaller ensembles such as the sextet of instruments used by Maxwell Davies in C90. In modern scores such as this the outer limits of virtuosity are explored. Particularly notable are the complex polyrhythms in bars 1–4, the tremolo in bar 12 and the double glissando at the end of the extract.

The **vibraphone** is another instrument that looks similar to a xylophone, but the bars are made of aluminium alloy. As in a modern xylophone cylindrical metal resonators are suspended beneath each bar. The single most important difference between this instrument and the xylophone and marimba is the fact that each resonator has an electrically-driven fan which gives each note an artificial vibrato (though the instrument can be played without the fan if desired). The vibraphone can be played with a variety of beaters which each produce their own timbral characteristics. Hard beaters are prescribed by Boulez in the opening bars of *Le marteau sans maître* (C87) in which the top two octaves of the instrument's three-octave range are exploited (see the folded insert).

6.9 Keyboard instruments

This section describes instruments with one or more keyboards. Instruments with keyboards include those in which sound is generated by vibrating columns of air (the organ and regal), by the vibrations of plucked strings (the harpsichord and spinet), and by the vibrations of struck strings (the clavichord and pianoforte). Thus keyboard instruments do not all belong to a single scientific category (the organ is an aerophone, the harpsichord a chordophone). Nevertheless, everyone recognises the kinship of instruments that are played in more or less the same manner and performers often move readily from one to another.

We tend now to think of these as being united in their omission from the orchestra, but this has not been consistently the case. The harpsichord and the fortepiano (the immediate precursor of the piano) both frequently appeared in eighteenth-century orchestras, and are now to be heard in performances of baroque and classical music on period instruments. Several twentieth-century composers have included keyboard instruments in their symphonic scoring (such as the organ in MacMillan's *Quickening* bars 35–39, 42–45 and 48–50, C97). With only one exception all of the keyboard instruments described below can be used as solo or accompanimental instruments (because of its soft tone the clavichord is rarely used for accompaniments).

6.9.1 Organ

The organ has a longer history than is usually realised, with references to it dating back to Graeco-Roman civilisations before the birth of Christ. The first hard evidence of the exact nature of particular instruments does not appear until the middle ages when Benedictine monks wrote about instruments used in their churches. The timbres which can be produced by particular types of pipe on a large organ (see the folded insert) are so varied that it is beyond the scope of this dictionary to try to identify them all. Suffice to say that from quite early in the history of the instrument there were two distinct types of timbre. The first is produced in a similar manner to bagpipes. A reservoir of pressurised air (produced by bellows rather than the player's lungs) provides the source for wind which is directed past a reed, the resulting sound usually being amplified by a pipe attached to the cap that contains the reed. A four-octave scale of C major is played on reed pipes in A3(a). The sixteenth- and seventeenth-century **regal** is an organ that contains only one or two ranks of such **reed pipes** (A63). The second type of organ timbre is produced in a similar manner to the recorder. In this case wind is directed against a sharp edge at the base of the pipe which amplifies the sound (A57). Most **positive organs** contain only **flue pipes** of this kind. They are commonly used as accompanimental instruments in baroque continuo groups (A68 and B7). A five-octave scale of C major is played on flue pipes in A3(b).

In baroque solo-organ music flue and reed **stops** are often used to clarify complex contrapuntal textures. In A92 the uppermost part (the *dux* of a canon) is played on flue pipes, the lower part (the *comes*) on reed pipes. When these two parts are incorporated into the four-part counterpoint of Bach's chorale prelude (A94) the canon of A92 can still be heard clearly because the *dux* is still in the uppermost part and because the *comes* is the only one of the four parts to be played on a reed stop. The effect of combining many flue and reed pipes on a large organ can be heard in the extract from Couperin's *Messe pour les paroisses* (A81) and the closing bars of Bach's Toccata in F major (A86). The latter is played on the **full organ** (*organo pleno*). It sounds quite different from the offertory because, despite being played on the same very large organ, the organist has selected different registrations for the two pieces. In the first reed sound predominates, while in the second reeds colour what is basically a flue chorus. Both registrations make use of a number of **mutation stops** (ranks of pipes that sound compound 5ths or 3rds above written pitch, so adding brilliance to the timbres of the organ choruses).

The Four Symphonic Meditations that make up Messiaen's *L'Ascension* were, as the title implies, originally written for orchestra. His arrangement of them for organ reflects the late nineteenth- and early twentieth-century trend towards the development of organs that could imitate the timbres of contemporary symphony orchestras. Instead of the boldly contrasted colours of the baroque organ these romantic instruments were designed to allow subtle combinations of stops. In C55 for instance, the lowest parts (including the pedals) are played on the *récit* (swell organ), a department of the instrument enclosed in a box with louvres to control the volume of sound emitted by the pipes within it. This allows the organist to balance these accompanimental parts against the right-hand solo (played on the unenclosed ***positif*** coupled to the *récit*) so that the melody is just that little bit louder than the other parts (and subtly differs from them in timbre). While playing the music the organist is able to alter the balance by adjusting the louvres with a foot pedal (which explains why the solo-plus-accompaniment effect is most noticeable at the end of each of the two phrases, bars 6–7 and 10–12).

Later in the twentieth century such 'orchestral' organs went out of favour as neoclassical ideals filtered through to the organ loft and real orchestral music became more widely available on radio and disc. Instead existing baroque instruments were refurbished and new organs built on similar principles to the sort of instruments that Couperin and Bach played. It was only towards the end of the century that composers saw the potential of the great romantic dinosaurs that were once emblems of civic pride. The terrific effect of *organo pleno* on one of these monsters (that in the Royal Albert Hall, London) is evident in the three greatest climaxes of C97 (bars 35–39, 42–45 and 48–50) in which organ tone can be clearly heard through massive orchestral textures.

6.9.2 Harpsichord and clavichord

The **harpsichord** rivalled the organ in popularity from the fifteenth century to the eighteenth century, after which time it fell into disuse until it was revived in the twentieth century with the advent of historical authenticity. The timbre of the harpsichord is determined by the way the strings are plucked by quill or leather plectrums. Its timbre and volume can be altered by the use of draw stops or pedals that activate registers of strings sounding at pitch, or sounding an octave above or below written pitch. On instruments with two **manuals** it is possible to preset the stops so that one will be louder than the other. This is the case in Jacquet de la Guerre's rondeau (A84), in which the first loud four-bar phrase (played on the lower manual) is echoed by the softer second four-bar phrase (played on the upper manual). A direct comparison of A84 with B17 reveals that the tonal qualities of harpsichords differ from instrument to instrument to a greater extent than pianos of comparable sizes.

Harpsichords were among the most favoured **continuo** instruments in the seventeenth and early eighteenth centuries because their clear, incisive tonal characteristics allowed melodic lines to be clearly heard while providing precisely articulated rhythms that could hold even quite large ensembles together. This role of the harpsichord is evident in A74 and A80.

The **clavichord**, dating from the mid-sixteenth century, is the most intimate of keyboard instruments. The sound is produced by a brass blade mounted on the end of the key furthest from the performer hitting a pair of strings. Although the instrument is soft-toned compared with other keyboard instruments, the player has more control of the sound than is the case in any other keyboard instrument. This made it an ideal instrument for the domestic performance of emotionally charged music of the proto-romantic idiom known as the *empfindsamer Stil*. The most important exponent of this style was C. P. E. Bach, who, like his father Johann Sebastian, declared that the clavichord was his favourite instrument. B20 is an extract from one of his fantasias which is remarkable for its detailed dynamic markings and improvisatory style (the absence of barlines is deliberate and meant to encourage metrically free performances). The slurred dots above the second minim of the first stave indicate a ***Bebung***, a type of vibrato that is impossible on any other keyboard instrument. Like the harpsichord, the clavichord fell into desuetude once the pianoforte became firmly entrenched at the beginning of the nineteenth century.

6.9.3 Fortepiano and pianoforte

The **fortepiano** was simply an early form of piano dating back to Christofori's 'gravicembalo col piano e forte' (harpsichord with soft and loud) at the beginning of the eighteenth century. But it was not until the second half of the eighteenth century that English and Viennese manufacturers introduced refinements that made the instrument an acceptable alternative to the harpsichord. These **pianofortes** (or fortepianos – the terms were then interchangeable) had wooden frames that were incapable of taking the strain of the heavy strings of a modern iron-framed instrument, consequently both the timbre and general dynamic level were different from a modern piano. The sound of the fortepiano recorded on B25 is less resonant than the modern grand piano recorded on B51–B56, but it has greater clarity and a lighter touch than the modern instrument, qualities that make it ideal for the performance of the rococo ornamentation heard in the repeat of Haydn's minuet.

6.10 Electric and electronic instruments

There is a wealth of twentieth-century electric instruments, but many of those developed for use in the performance of art music are rarely heard. However in pop music such instruments dominated the scene in the second half of the century. Many composers saw the possibilities of combining these instruments with traditional acoustic instruments. In C94 the contribution of an electric bass guitar (bars 6 and 12) is out of all proportion to the number of notes it is required to play. It is impossible to write in general terms about the characteristic timbres of electro-acoustic music since every sound is uniquely generated or modified by electronic instruments. However it is possible to comment on the **synthesiser** when used as a means of electronically recreating the sound of acoustic instruments. The

Elements of music

modern instrument stores tens of thousands of samples of notes originally played on real instruments. These are digitally encoded ready to be activated by the performer. But, as with acoustic instruments, the quality of sound of a synthesiser is determined by the quality of its components, as a comparison of electronically generated harpsichord timbres (A87) with the timbres of an acoustic harpsichord (A84) reveals. Nevertheless, many composers of the late twentieth century made effective use of the synthesiser, either to create new sounds or to recycle old ones. The common practice of electronic modification of the sound of live performers produced some of the most startling effects of the late twentieth century (C91 is an extract from a lengthy composition for electronically modified voices).

6.11 Texture

In its most literal sense texture refers to the appearance and tactile qualities of fabric. Thus many fine strands of silk may be closely woven to produce a smooth-textured cloth, or fewer thick strands of wool may be loosely woven to produce a rough-textured cloth. By analogy the word can be used to refer to the superficial impression the sounds of a passage of music makes on our ears. Just as fairly vague adjectives such as smooth or rough may be used to characterise the texture of cloth, so other vague adjectives (such as thick or thin, high or low) may be used with equal validity to characterise the texture of music. But just as closer inspection of fabric can reveal the type and density of the fibres which form the textures of particular types of cloth, so closer attention to music can reveal that musical texture is the product of the number of parts heard simultaneously, the **timbres** of these parts, and the way they relate to each other and to silence. Thus the texture of A87 can be described as thin, but it can be more precisely described as a homorhythmic two-part texture with just one timbre (that of the synthesised harpsichord on which both parts are played).

6.11.1 Monophony

The simplest possible musical texture is a single melodic line. Perhaps the largest extant corpus of this sort of music is the medieval **monophony** known as **plainsong** recorded on A4 and A5. In these examples a group of monks sing a single melodic line in unison and with no accompaniment. In some monophonic compositions the figuration often outlines chords when their constituent notes are played successively, thus clearly implying harmonic progressions. This can be seen in A96 where the monophonic arpeggios that the violinist plays (A96(i)) outline the chords of Bach's original notation (A96(ii)). So although A96(i) is monophonic, it sounds richer in texture than the plainsong of A4 or A5. When a melody is doubled by several instruments a similar enrichment of the texture is apparent (B59, bars 3–4 and 7–8 in which many violins play the same monophonic phrases). Similarly when a melody is doubled at the octave there is an even greater enrichment of a monophonic texture (bars 1–2 and 5–6 in the same example).

6.11.2 Monody

The term monody is sometimes used with reference to monophonic music such as the plainsong on A4, but more frequently it is reserved for accompanied Italian solo vocal music of the first half of the seventeenth century. In this music the texture is enriched by the accompanying instruments – a bass part played by one or more melody instruments (a trombone in A63, a cello in A68) together with harmonic filling provided by any number of plucked string or keyboard instruments (a regal in A63, ceterone and harp in A66).

6.11.3 Heterophony

In A63 the eponymous hero of Monteverdi's opera *Orfeo* comes face to face with Caronte (more familiar by his English name Charon). Since he ferries the dead to Hades a trombone, the musical signifier of grave matters, is used to provide a simple bass line. In this music the sepulchral tones of Caronte's resonant bass voice are shadowed by the trombone. When a simple melody (in this case the bass part provided by the trombone) sounds simultaneously with an elaborated version of it (in this case Caronte's solo) the texture formed between the two is said to be heterophonic.

6.11.4 Homophony

The sinfonia shown in A64 is played by an ensemble of string instruments with organ chords. All of the instruments play the same rhythm in the first 11 beats. Such a texture is described as **homorhythmic** or **chordal**, the most absolute type of homophony. Similar chordal textures are evident in A19 and A37. In the sixteenth century the term *stile familiare* was coined to refer to such textures to distinguish them from the contrapuntal textures of the renaissance. The term was reintroduced in the nineteenth century by scholars researching the works of Palestrina and is now frequently used in its English form – familiar style. This term is generally reserved for renaissance music, but chordal textures can be found in most styles and periods (C86, written in the mid-twentieth century, is an extreme example of a homorhythmic texture).

The term homophony also refers to those textures in which a prominent melodic line is accompanied by a subservient accompaniment whether it is homorhythmic or not. In B48 the chordal accompaniment is clearly subservient to the violin melody, but the rhythms of the melody and accompaniment could not be more contrasting. In its original form (B41, bars 1–4) the same passage is still dominated by the melody, but there is some melodic movement in the lower string parts, particularly in the cello part. In fact if the outer parts of this passage are taken out of context (B42) they form two-part counterpoint in the first two bars (the cello becomes subservient in the last two bars in which it simply provides dominant and tonic notes for the violin). The texture of most extended compositions is similarly varied by contrasting homophonic and contrapuntal textures (B40). In the second section of Mozart's minuet (B41, bars 9–16) a type of homophonic texture that was typical of the classical period can be heard. The first violin melody is still dominant, but the accompaniment is more varied. The cello supplies a simple functional bass, the second violin fills in missing harmony notes but has some independent movement in bars 10 and 12, and the viola provides a broken-chord accompaniment. The term melody-dominated homophony is sometimes used to distinguish this type of homophony from chordal homophony (similar textures may be found in B57, B61, B67, B74, C2, C7 and C73).

Elements of music

6.11.5 Polyphony and counterpoint

Monophony literally means 'one sound' and polyphony means 'many sounds'. Late medieval and renaissance church musicians (and monks to this day) used the term polyphony in this literal sense to refer to any music in more than one part as distinct from monophonic plainsong. Thus, rather confusingly, the term originally included homophonic music. In modern usage polyphony is almost synonymous with counterpoint: the sounding together of two or more melodies. The only real distinction between the two terms in current usage is that the word polyphony tends to be associated with church music written before about 1600, while counterpoint is used of music (whether secular or sacred) from that date onwards.

At its simplest counterpoint can manifest itself in the combination of two melodies that are almost entirely homorhythmic. This is the case in A85 in which the treble part is more melodious than the bass (especially when the latter begins to leap about to sketch the harmonic outline of the final cadence). In the two-part texture of C58 melodic interest is evenly shared between the two violins. The music sounds more contrapuntal because the second violin literally shares much of the first violin's melody by imitating it at the start, and instead of the note-against-note counterpoint of A85 the two parts are rhythmically independent (generally speaking, when one part moves in shorter note-values the other sustains a long note).

More complex textures are often clarified by the combination of dissimilar melodies. In A27 the three-part counterpoint in the first four bars is really a combination of a contrapuntal duet in short time-values in the upper voices with a slow-moving bass part. When the texture expands to four-part counterpoint in the next four bars the tenor and bass form a contrapuntal duet in which melodic interest is shared between the two voices. This duet contrasts with the continuing contrapuntal exchanges between the two upper voices because one duet uses long time-values that stand out against the short time-values of the other duet. The complex four-part texture of A94 is similarly clarified by the long notes of the first canon (A92) and the dancing triplet rhythms of the second canon (A93).

6.11.6 Antiphony and polychoral textures

Antiphonal textures probably first emerged when two groups of monks facing each other across the choir of their abbey church decided to take alternate verses when singing lengthy psalms to plainsong tones. This practice continues in monastic communities and in the antiphonal singing of homophonic settings of the psalms in Anglican cathedrals and churches.

Antiphonal textures were a feature of the late renaissance and early baroque polychoral music that was so much a part of the pomp and circumstance of elaborate ceremonies in the basilica of St Mark in Venice. In this sort of music choirs could be ensembles of instruments or voices or a mixture of both. In A58 three instrumental choirs begin with antiphonal exchanges of the same short phrase (A). The second phrase (B) is treated similarly. When phrase B is played for the third time antiphony overlaps with imitative counterpoint. Instead of three distinct brass choirs Gabrieli takes the figure beginning with a rising 4th from the bass part of the second antiphonal phrase (labelled C) and uses it in a point of

imitation. This point overlaps with the next (D) which ushers in a passage in which all 12 contrapuntal voices are heard for the first time. These fluid transitions between antiphony, imitative counterpoint and homophony typify the polychoral techniques of the late renaissance and early baroque periods in Italy and later in Germany.

Although the tradition of sacred polychoral music initiated in the sixteenth century declined in the eighteenth century, antiphonal textures were often a feature of instrumental music for the next three hundred years. C86 is an extreme example from the late twentieth century. Britten divides his large orchestra of 26 wind instruments and a symphonic string section into ten contrasting choirs ranging from full orchestra (bar 2) to just four horns (bars 10 and 12). The antiphonal exchanges between them are arranged in such a way that no two consecutive bars contain the same instrumental timbres.

6.11.7 Range and spacing

The first 19 bars of Giovanni Gabrieli's canzona (A58) highlight another aspect of texture: range. The term refers to the melodic interval encompassed by a single voice part as well as the harmonic intervals between the outermost voices. Both contribute to the texture of music, but it is the latter aspect of range that is most obvious at first hearing. In the first chord the range is only an octave (between the first cornett and second sackbut); in the last it is three octaves (between the first cornett of the first choir and the second sackbut of the third choir). The contrast in the ranges of the chords heard in C86 is even greater than that in A58. In bar 10 the interval between the outer parts is only a 5th – in bars 6 and 14 it is over five octaves.

Spacing refers to the differing intervals between adjacent parts. The first five chords of A59 are in close position, that is to say that the three parts are as close together as they possibly can be in a triad. In bar 9 a triad of B♭ major (B♭, D and F) is arranged in open position. Instead of two 3rds between parts (bar 1) there is a 5th between the two lowest parts and a 6th between the two upper parts. In bars 30–34 a triad in close position at the beginning of each bar contrasts with triads containing intervals as great as an octave. Such contrasting spacing does much to enliven three-voice textures that would otherwise become monotonous.

The stunning effect of unusual spacing is apparent as early as the first chord of Debussy's 'La Cathédrale engloutie' (C22). This six-part chord uses only the notes of a bare 5th on G. The mysterious, profoundly calm effect Debussy required is achieved by outlining this chord at the extremities of the piano, so leaving a massive space of more than three and a half octaves between them. The closing bars of C34 are at the other extreme. In bar 14 four-part piano chords are squashed together within an interval of a 7th in the lowest range of the keyboard. The bass clarinet and cello parts extend this range upwards somewhat, but they do little to alleviate the suffocating gloom that is largely a product of range and spacing.

6.11.8 Pointillist textures

Among Schoenberg's many inventions was **Klangfarbenmelodie**, in which the constituent notes of a melody are played on different instruments or different instrumental combinations. In atonal music it is often difficult to hear a melody as an entity which can be apprehended in the same way as a melody by Mozart. So if tonality is absent and pitches cannot be instantly related to each other in a coherent series of sounds (whether articulated as melody or chords), then timbre can come to the fore in a succession of sounds which are characterised by a series of varied **tone-colours**. In C35 the tone-colour melody consists of the notes B–C–B–E♭–G–D–G♯ played successively by a muted trumpet and harp, harp and viola harmonics with celesta, flutter-tongued flute with harp, three notes on a glockenspiel and finally an extended trill on the celesta. Texturally the effect of these first three bars is of detached points of sound similar to the points of light in paintings by Seurat. By analogy the term used by art historians for Seurat's technique, pointillism, has been applied to such sparse musical textures as these. Instruments playing more sustained pitches (notably the clarinet) enter from the end of bar 3 onwards to build quite substantial chords in bars 4–6. However, the texture thins again in the last few bars of the movement: a flutter-tongued flute plays a five-note figure between very high violin and cello parts, dots of sound are heard from the glockenspiel, muted trumpet and harp, then cello and celesta. The harp plays a seven-note figure unaccompanied using harmonics, and the movement ends with tremulous semiquavers heard successively on flute, muted trumpet and celesta. It is evident that in music like this it is quite impossible to separate texture and timbre: the relative density of the former determines the form (thin–thick–thin) and allows an amazing range of instrumental timbres to be heard within the half-minute duration of this remarkable movement.

7:
The structure of music

Form in music is the self-contained structure of a musical entity, whether it be a simple melody, a lengthy symphonic movement or a complete opera. Just as architectural forms present themselves as visible structures in space, so musical forms present themselves as audible structures in time. Thus the symmetrical disposition of a Palladian house, in which a colonnaded central block is flanked by identical wings on either side, is reflected in the symmetrical disposition of a da capo aria, in which a central section in a contrasting key is flanked by almost identical sections that begin and end in the tonic key (B15). Both depend upon repetition, but architectural form can be perceived at a glance while musical form depends upon memory (the ABA structure of Bach's aria will not be apparent if one has not remembered at least the broad outlines of bars 1–80). Just as architectural form presents itself in structures ranging from a bus shelter to a cathedral, so musical form is manifest in both the simplest song and the most complex operatic ensemble.

7.1 Motif

In the first bar of B41 a rhythmic pattern (long–short–short–short–short) on a single pitch is repeated in bars 3, 5, 9 and 11 (all identified by the letter x). This motif in its different manifestations is sufficiently distinctive for it to be recognised as a basic element which contributes to the whole melody of the minuet. In the second bar another very short but distinctive rhythmic pattern (y) is heard again in bars 6 (y^2), 7 (y^3), 10 (y^4), 12 (y^2), 14 (y^2), and 15 (y^3). Despite the fact that these motifs have different pitch patterns, the shared rhythm is sufficient to establish a relationship between them. Even the group of four semiquavers and a crotchet in bar 4 can be recognised as a variant of y^2, as B47(d) shows. Four variants of y are played consecutively in B47 to show how they are organically linked to one another. In a single performance of the minuet these derivations are only recognised retrospectively, but in its operatic context the whole minuet is heard many times, so allowing the listener to recognise (consciously or unconsciously) the way these motifs give the whole melody a sense of unity. In fact x and y are motifs that account for all but eight out of the 65 notes of the whole melody. This is a relatively simple example of motivic manipulation, but even here some idea of the subtlety with which motifs may be combined can be gained from bar 13 of B41. Here the initial crotchet of x is replaced by the dotted rhythm of y, and the final crotchet of y is in turn replaced with the first quaver of x, the two motifs thus coalescing organically to form a new motif (x^1).

7.2 Phrase

Just as a verbal phrase expresses a single idea without the complete sense expressed by a sentence, so a musical phrase expresses a single comprehensible but incomplete musical idea. B48 shows the melody of bars 1–4 of the minuet from Mozart's *Don Giovanni* discussed in 7.1. At the end of

Elements of music

bar 4 a crotchet rest in the violin part suggests a caesura similar to that which occurs when a comma appears in a sentence (at which point a breath might be taken if the text were spoken aloud or sung). This break emphasises the sense of closure which is implicit at this point in the melody alone and which is underlined by the perfect cadence played by the pianist. A single musical idea has been presented in bars 1–4 which is analogous to a verbal phrase, but, like a verbal phrase, the musical phrase is not of itself completely self-contained.

7.3 Period

In the same way that two or more phrases of English can form a sentence, so two or more **phrases** of music can express a complete utterance known as a period. B49 comprises two phrases separated from each other by silence (a caesura indicated by the crotchet rests). There is a sense of closure at the end of phrase 1, but the single musical idea of this phrase (the **antecedent**) is not completely self-contained. Only when the second four-bar phrase (the **consequent**) has been heard is there a sense that the musical idea presented in the antecedent has been answered (though the complete musical discourse comes to an end only when two more balanced phrases – bars 9–12 and 13–16 in B41 – bring the music back to a perfect cadence in the tonic).

Musical periods are not always formed from such balanced phrases. In the *corrente* by Frescobaldi shown in A67 phrases are defined by **cadences**. The key of D minor (absolutely clear despite some modality) is established in the first couple of bars by the use of chords I and V, but the first cadence (bars 5–6) is in F major. Since this is an imperfect cadence there is little sense of closure, but the cadence at the end of the next phrase (bars 9–10) suggests finality much more strongly than does the cadence at the end of the first period of B41 (because Mozart's perfect cadence is in the dominant, whereas Frescobaldi's perfect cadence is in the tonic key of D minor). Unlike Mozart's balanced phrases Frescobaldi's ten-bar period divides unevenly into a phrase of six bars and one beat and another of three bars and two beats. Even in the classical period Haydn often wrote periods which divide unevenly, as the 4+2+4 and 3+2+2+3 phrasing of the A and B sections of the minuet in B25 shows.

7.4 Binary forms

As its name suggests, binary form refers to movements which divide into two sections, A and B. But since both are repeated the structure can be more accurately represented as AABB (though these repeats are not observed in any of the binary dances discussed below). The two sections are not often differentiated by contrasting melodic material. Instead structure emerges thanks to the power of cadences and, in a majority of cases, modulations to related keys.

7.4.1 Non-modulating binary-form minuet

In B25 the two sections (identified as A and B in the score) could hardly be less differentiated melodically since the second section is a retrograde of the first. Every note (including the chords) of the second section can be replicated by playing the first section backwards, thus forming a musical **palindrome**. Nor could they be less differentiated tonally since the music never leaves the tonic key. What does distinguish A from B is the fact that the first section ends with an imperfect cadence (chords I–V, suggesting partial closure) while the second ends with a perfect cadence (chords V–I, affirming finality).

7.4.2 Binary-form minuet modulating to the dominant

It has already been observed (7.1–7.3) that Mozart's manipulation of a couple of motifs imparts a sense of unity to two phrases which together form a complete period. This **period** (B41, bars 1–8) is the first section (A) of a binary-form minuet which ends with a perfect cadence in the dominant key of D major. The second section (B) is dominated by the same two motifs used in the first section, and, like the first section, this one also ends with a perfect cadence, but this time it is in the tonic key of G major. In the same way that the imperfect cadence at the end of the first section of B25 imparts a sense of partial closure, so the same effect is achieved in B41 with a perfect cadence in the dominant key. Both composers achieve a sense of complete closure with a perfect cadence in the tonic at the end of the whole dance.

7.4.3 Binary-form corrente with identical cadences at the ends of both sections

The earliest binary-form movements often had a perfect cadence in the tonic at the end of both sections, and, like their classical counterparts, there was little melodic differentiation between them. In Frescobaldi's *corrente* (A67) a two-part structure is clarified by the use of passing or transitory modulations that ameliorate the effect of the identical cadences. In section A the music passes through the relative major (with an imperfect cadence in F major at the end of the first phrase) before returning to the tonic in bars 8–10. The second section (B) begins in A minor, a key which clearly distinguishes it from the first section. In the next phrase the music moves through C major before returning to the tonic in the last three bars. The *corrente* ends with two bars of music that replicates the last two bars of section A except that the melody is transposed up an octave.

7.4.4 Rounded binary-form allemande modulating to the dominant minor

Rameau's allemande (B17) is an example of a binary structure which, in its first section, modulates from the tonic key of A minor to the dominant key of E minor via a circle of 5ths. Much more significant though are the repetitions of passages from the first section towards the end of the second section. This was foreshadowed in the two-bar repeat in Frescobaldi's *corrente* discussed in the previous section, but here the recapitulations are on an altogether larger scale. The first section ends with two perfect cadences in the dominant minor (bars 15–16 and 17–18) and continuous triplet figuration that has not been heard before. The second section begins in this key at the end of bar 18, then, as expected, it moves through related keys back to the tonic key of A minor (bar 29). At this point Rameau repeats bars 3–4 in the same key, but, instead of moving through the circle of 5ths that occupied so much of the first section, he remains in the tonic key of A minor. It is in this key that he repeats six and a half bars from the end of the first section, thus rounding off the second section with the same music that rounded off the first section. The relationship of this repeated passage with

Elements of music

its original statement is made very clear by the perfect cadences and the triplet figuration that are common to both passages. Appropriately this more complex structure is called rounded binary form.

7.4.5 Monothematic binary-form bourrée modulating to the relative major

The two minor-mode dances discussed in 7.4.3 and 7.4.4 differ in the tonal schemes of their first sections. Section A of Frescobaldi's *corrente* (A67) remains in the tonic key of D minor (apart from a brief glimpse of F major) and ends with a perfect cadence in that key. Section A of Rameau's allemande (B17) modulates through several keys before reaching a perfect cadence in the dominant minor. By the end of the baroque era and throughout the classical period **modulation** to the relative major became the norm in the first sections of minor-mode dances. This is well illustrated by the bourrée from Bach's Lute Suite in E minor (A89). Here the first section consists of two balanced four-bar phrases, the first ending with a perfect cadence in the tonic (bar 4), the second modulating to a perfect cadence in G major (bars 7–8). As was often the case the second section is twice as long as the first. It consists of four four-bar phrases, the first and second ending with perfect cadences in related keys (bars 11–12 and 15–16), the third ending with an imperfect cadence in the tonic (bars 19–20) answered by the final perfect cadence in E minor. It is these strategically placed cadences and the phrases they define that give shape to a dance in which the tiny three-note motif at the start (short–short–long) is manipulated almost ceaselessly throughout this monothematic movement.

7.5 Ternary forms

These three-part structures (ABA) consist of a first section (A) which is self-contained in the sense that it begins and ends in the same key, a middle section (B) in a contrasting key or keys, and a repeat of the first section (A). Sections A and B may be differentiated by contrasting keys, by contrasting thematic material, or both.

7.5.1 Baroque da capo aria

The da capo aria is so called because, instead of a written-out repeat of the first section, the direction 'da capo al fine', or 'DC al fine' or just 'DC' at the end of the middle section indicates that the first section should be repeated (the movement ending when the word 'fine' at the end of the first section is encountered for the second time). Apart from a couple of brief references to related major keys the first section of the aria shown in B15 (bars 1–80) remains in D major throughout. The second section (bars 81–120) is distinguished from the first, not only by the absence of the obbligato trumpet at the start, but by the concentration on minor keys (24 bars) and the dominant (12 bars).

7.5.2 Classical minuet and trio

In the baroque suite a pair of minuets were often presented one after the other. When this was done it was a convention that the first minuet should be repeated after the second. The tradition continued in classical symphonies, though the second minuet was usually called a trio (because the texture was often reduced, sometimes to just three parts). This minuet–trio–minuet structure is more complex than the da capo aria since both the minuet and the trio were in binary form. This repeat of the minuet results in an overall structure that can be represented as AABB (minuet) – CCDD (trio) – AB (internal repeats in the minuet are usually omitted when it is played for the second time). Despite the apparent complexity the overall structure is the same as that of the da capo aria since both the minuet and the trio are similarly self-contained. This is the case in B25 except for the fact that the repeats of sections A and B in both the minuet and the trio have been omitted. As was customary, the repeat of the minuet after the trio is embellished with improvised ornamentation (which has been transcribed as symbols or in staff notation in the printed music).

7.5.3 Romantic ternary structures

In the nineteenth century there was a ready market for picturesque pieces which showed off young ladies' accomplishments and sensibilities (both of which qualities were apparently highly esteemed by romantically inclined young men of those times). What better way to demonstrate the range of the performer's affections than the contrast of mood between the first and second sections of a **ternary form** movement? A complete characteristic piece by Grieg is shown in C2. Introspection is suggested by the mournful aeolian melody of the Poco allegro (bars 1–16), while the Presto (bars 17–37) expresses a more flighty sensibility enhanced by piquant chromaticism and cross-rhythms. So in this case the central episode contrasts in key, thematic material and mood, the last being perhaps the most important element in a piece that is obviously written for amateur performance in a domestic environment.

7.6 Rondo forms

Rondos are structures in which a refrain (A) heard at the start is repeated more than once after contrasting material (B, C, D and so on), for instance ABABA or ABACA.

7.6.1 Medieval rondeau

The vocal rondeau of the middle ages was both a verse form and a musical structure, with repetitions in both text and music. Machaut was the author of both the text and the music of A23 and he would have regarded the poetic structure (with its rhyme scheme) as at least as important as his monophonic music. It will be seen that there are only two musical phrases, the first ending on the leading note (F♯ in bars 4, 11, 15, 19 and 26), the second on the tonic (G♯ in bars 7, 22 and 29) arranged to form the pattern ABAAABAB (which corresponds with Machaut's rhyme scheme). There are five different poetic lines arranged to form the pattern abcadeab (see the text printed at the foot of A23). Both of these are rondeaux in the sense defined above (Section 7.6). When music and text are combined they form a more complex structure that can be represented as ABaAabAB in which capital letters represent textual and musical refrains and lower-case letters represent repetitions of musical phrases with new words. This is the structure represented by letters in boxes at the start of the eight staves.

7.6.2 Baroque rondeau

In the seventeenth and eighteenth centuries an instrumental version of the rondeau was cultivated in France, especially by a famous school of

Elements of music

harpsichord composers including Elisabeth-Claude Jacquet de la Guerre. Her rondeau shown in A84 has a structure in which a **refrain** (or ***grand couplet***) alternates with **episodes** (or ***couplets***). It is typical of thousands of similar pieces written in *le grand siècle*. The refrain (A) always begins and ends in the tonic (and this particular refrain remains in G minor throughout), while the *couplets* (B and C) introduce new material in contrasting keys (B♭ major in the first *couplet*, F major and D minor in the second). The last four bars of the refrain is repeated at its last appearance. This ***petite reprise*** (bars 41–45) was common, not only in rondeaux, but also in French binary-form dances of the period. The form of the whole piece can therefore be represented as ABACA^{1}a, in which A is the eight-bar refrain in G minor, B and C are *couplets* in contrasting keys, A^1 is an ornamented version of the refrain and a is the *petite reprise*.

7.6.3 Baroque ritornello forms

The first section of the da capo aria shown in B15 is framed by substantial and thematically related instrumental passages, the first (bars 1–14) ending with an imperfect cadence, the second (bars 67–80) ending with a perfect cadence. These are ritornelli which frame the vocal solos (A and B) in this fashion:

| Ritornello 1 | A | Ritornello 2 | B | Ritornello 1 | A | Ritornello 2 |

This was a common pattern in baroque da capo arias, but Bach fuses his ritornelli with the vocal solos in a more intimate fashion than many of his contemporaries by introducing elements from the ritornelli within vocal solo B (y^3 and z in the ritornello of bars 96^2–104). Even more subtle is his introduction of elements from the first ritornello as counter-melodies against the vocal solo in passages like bars 50–57. Ritornello form was common in the flanking movements of late baroque concertos.

7.7 Sonata forms

Sometimes known as sonata-allegro or first-movement form, sonata form is a theoretical concept developed by Adolph Marx in the nineteenth century to explain the way in which many classical movements function. All three terms are confusing. Sonata-allegro is inadequate because there are many sonata-form types in slow tempi. First-movement form is just as misleading because the first movements of classical works might well be in a completely different form (for instance, Beethoven's Piano Sonata in A♭ Op. 26 begins with a set of variations), and movements other than the first are often in sonata form. Sonata form itself can lead to misconceptions: firstly, because the term applies not just to movements in sonatas, but to movements in symphonies, concertos and chamber-music genres; secondly, because the singular form of the term suggests that there is just one structural plan to which all sonata-form movements adhere.

The truth of the matter is that composers from Haydn onwards (particularly composers working in Vienna in the second half of the eighteenth century and the early years of the nineteenth century) developed principles of composition which manifested themselves in a wide variety of structures. The underlying principles that govern these sonata-form types are:

a) the dramatic opposition of contrasted tonal centres and very often of thematic materials, in an open-ended first section (the **exposition**)
b) the exploration of a range of keys in a central section which eventually returns to the tonic (the **development**)
c) the restatement of material from the first section in a way that reconciles the tonal conflicts of the first and second sections (the **recapitulation**).

7.7.1 Sonata-form movement with contrasting thematic material

The first movement of Mozart's Divertimento KA 229 (K439b) (B40) shows these principles at work. In the **exposition** (bars 1–51) a passage in the tonic key of F major (the **first subject** in bars 1–18^1) contrasts with a passage in the dominant key of C major (the **second subject** in bars 26–48^1). Between these two subjects is a **transition** (bars 18–25), the chief function of which is to modulate between the tonic key of the first subject and the dominant key of the second subject. At the end of the exposition a **codetta** (bars 48–51) asserts the dominant key of C major by repeated perfect cadences.

In the **development** (bars 52–71) the tonality becomes obscure. Several keys are implied, but they are never confirmed by definitive cadences, and the return to the tonic is left until the last possible moment. In fact just two chords effect the return to F major (VII^6 and I in bars 71–72). Nearly a half of the music in the development implies the key of D minor, and this casts a shadow over the whole section and contrasts strongly with the major keys of the flanking sections.

In the **recapitulation** (bars 72–123) nearly all of the music heard in the exposition is restated, but with a significant change. The transition (bars 89–94) is modified so that it ends on chord V of F major (instead of chord V of C major). There is to be no contrasting key in the recapitulation. Instead Mozart restates the second subject (bars 95–110^1) in the tonic key of F major, and the coda (an expanded version of the codetta at the end of the exposition) underlines the tonic with repeated perfect cadences in the tonic.

In addition to tonal contrasts this movement contains a number of thematic contrasts. Even within the first subject the lively, diatonic six-bar phrase heard at the opening contrasts with the more lyrical, chromatic four-bar phrase which follows (bars 7–10, repeated with a new cadence in bars 11–14). This in turn contrasts with the repeated anacrustic two-bar phrase (xD) that ends the first subject group (bars 14 to the first beat of bar 18). The theme of the second subject (bars 26–33, repeated with a new cadence in the next eight bars) is lyrical like the second phrase of the first subject, but it contrasts with it because the melody is entirely diatonic (though the accompanying chords are chromatic).

Balancing the tonal and thematic contrasts there are elements that make for unity. These are the kindred **motifs** which permeate most of the movement. The most significant of them is the on-beat motif of four repeated notes heard right at the beginning (x). Mozart immediately repeats the motif twice in rhythmic diminution (xD) and in bars 14–15 and 16–17 he uses xD to unify the whole of the first subject. In the same way motif x appears at the beginning of the second subject theme (bars 26–27, repeated at a higher pitch in bars 28–29), thus creating a thematic link between the first and second subjects. A subsidiary motif of two detached, on-beat, cadential chords (y in bar 6) recurs at the end of the exposition (bar 51) where it forms the end of a larger motif (z in bars 50–51). In the development tonal turbulence is enhanced by imitative development of motif z, and the section ends with four statements of motif y. The recapitulation restates almost all of the music of the exposition, so it follows that it is equally permeated with the three motifs that unify the whole movement. This balance between thematic variety and motivic unity is one of the many fine balances which distinguish classical music from that of other periods.

7.7.2 Monothematic sonata-form exposition

That tonality is the chief determinant of structure in sonata-form movements written before 1900 is apparent in the extract from the first movement of Haydn's String Quartet Op. 42 (B27). The first subject (bars 1–8) is in the key of D minor. Its theme contains the four **motifs** identified by the letters a, b, c and d. The transition (bars 9–12) modulates, as expected, to the relative major, but it consists entirely of two motifs from the first subject (a and b). The second subject group (bars 13–32) is in the new key of F major. Two themes are heard, both of them constructed from motifs first heard in the first subject. The first theme (bars 13–21) is entirely based on motif c with the exception of the tiny cadence-phrase (x and y in bars 18–19). The second theme of the second subject group (bars 22–32) similarly derives from the first subject. Apart from the three-note chromatic motif at the start (z in bars 22–23), this entire theme consists of manipulations of motif a (n and p being fragments of it) and a rhythmically altered version of the five-note descending figure c (part of which appeared at the end of IIa). Similarly, the codetta is constructed from rhythmically diminished and inverted versions of motif d (first heard in bar 7) and another version of motif c (the descent now encompassing the interval of a 5th). Thus almost the whole of the exposition is unified by four motifs heard within the first eight-bar phrase. In fact, were it not for the tonal structure B27 could be a development section. This was the sort of structure that Beethoven seized upon and expanded to form large-scale, thematically integrated symphonic movements.

7.7.3 Sonata-rondo forms

If it is difficult to generalise about the structure of sonata-form movements it is even more difficult to generalise about movements (most often finales) which classical composers entitled **rondo**. This might mean a simple French-style rondeau similar in structure to the ABACA form of A84. But in late eighteenth-century Viennese music the term is more likely to mean a fusion of the principles of French rondeau form and Austrian sonata form. Fusion might be as simple as repetition of a short, self-contained first-subject-cum-rondo-theme in the tonic between the exposition and the development, together with another repetition at the end of a movement that is otherwise in simple sonata form. If A is the first-subject-cum-rondo theme, B is the second subject (episodes 1 and 3) and C is the development (episode 2), this would give a symmetrical structure which can be represented as ABACABA (a type of **arch form**). In reality composers' creativity can rarely be so conveniently categorised.

7: The structure of music

This is evident from the beginning in the finale of Haydn's trumpet concerto (B36). It begins with an orchestral exposition in which two themes that later turn out to belong to the first and second subject are both heard in the tonic key of E♭ major. The first (A) is a repeated twelve-bar theme ending on V that is first played by upper strings and is then repeated by the full orchestra. The second (B, bars 26–43) is a contrasting 18-bar theme that ends with a definitive perfect cadence that marks the end of the orchestral **exposition**.

The rondo proper begins with a solo exposition that starts with the entry of the trumpet in bar 44. It begins with a restatement of most of theme A (which can now be viewed as the first subject or rondo theme) before the last few bars are modified to lead into the transition (bars 67–78). In this passage the music modulates via C minor to the dominant key of B♭ major ready for a lengthy second subject group or first episode (B, bars 79–123). In the last three bars of this section the trumpeter adds an A♭ to the tonic triad of B♭ major, thus turning it into chord V^7 of the tonic key of E♭ major. It is at this point that Haydn's rondo structure deviates from sonata form, for the dominant 7th heralds a return of the first-subject-cum-rondo-theme (A) in the tonic, starting at bar 124. (In a sonata-form structure the second subject, perhaps with a codetta appended, would not normally return to the tonic but would lead to a repeat of the whole exposition or proceed directly to the development.) After sixteen bars the theme is cut short and the music suddenly lurches into A♭ major and the **development** or second episode (C) is upon us (bars 141–179).

This central section is mostly concerned with motif x (first heard in bars 2–4). It is treated imitatively in bars 142–148. In bars 153^2–157^2 it acquires two more quavers (a) and a counter-subject (b) as an extended harmonic sequence begins. In bars 157^2–161 the subject (a) and counter-subject (b) are contrapuntally inverted. Then scalic figures (also derived from the first subject) are interrupted by dramatic fanfares on V of C minor. These twice interrupt variants of x (bars 167–171), but x wins the day and is bent to fit the dominant 7th of the home key (bars 178–179), a chord that heralds the **recapitulation**.

There are many delightful variations to the thematic material of the exposition in this section, but in broad outlines it follows the expected course by restating the first-subject-cum-rondo-theme (A, bars 180–198) and the second-subject-cum-first-episode (B, bars 199–236). Another version of A begins in bar 237 together with further development of motif x, but despite some chromatic posturing the music remains in the tonic key (affirmed by tonic–dominant kettle drums and perfect cadences) from this point to the end of the movement.

The overall form of this particular rondo structure is summarised below. It is unlikely that there exists another movement that replicates its form exactly.

Elements of music

The sonata-rondo structure of the first movement of Haydn's trumpet concerto			
Bars	**Keys**	**As sonata form**	**As rondo form**
1–43	E♭ major	orchestral exposition	–
1–25	E♭ major	first subject	A (rondo theme)
26–43	E♭ major	second subject	B (first episode)
44–140	E♭ and B♭ major	solo exposition	–
44–66	E♭ major	first subject	A (rondo theme)
67–78	E♭→B♭ major	transition	–
79–123	B♭ major	second subject group	B (second episode)
124–140	E♭ major	–	A (rondo theme)
141–179	A♭→V^7 of E♭	development	C (third episode)
180–278	E♭ major	recapitulation	–
180–190	E♭ major	first subject	A (rondo theme)
191–198	E♭ major	transition	–
199–236	E♭ major	second subject	B (fourth episode)
237–278	E♭ major	–	A^1 (rondo theme)
279–294	E♭ major	coda	A^2 (coda)

7.8 Variation forms

Variation of previously heard material is common in nearly all instrumental forms. But a set of variations as a form in its own right needs a self-sufficient theme which is then subjected to variation. The **theme** can be a melody (whether it be in the treble, bass or an inner part), a harmonic progression, or a combination of these. If the music is to be perceived as a set of variations the composer needs to fulfil two conditions. Firstly, at least one element of the theme needs to be retained in each variation. Secondly, at least one element of the theme needs to be changed in each variation.

7.8.1 Variations upon a ground

The **theme** of this type of variation form is the first cycle of an **ostinato bass**. In Purcell's *Song upon a Ground* this is a four-bar melody which is repeated unchanged throughout all 113 bars of the song. The first three complete cycles of the ground are shown in A75. It will be immediately obvious that the element which is most subject to change is the vocal melody (which limits the extent to which improvised or written-out chords can be varied). Comparison of the setting of the words 'O solitude' in bars 3–4 and 7–8 shows that although the bass is the same at these two points (F♯–E–F♯–F♯) both the rhythm and pitches of the vocal melody have changed (the dotted rhythm has been augmented and the leap is now a tritone instead of a 7th). Great craftsmanship is required of the composer in order to offset the mechanical repetitions of the ground. Purcell achieves both unity and variety in his three settings of the initial words (they all begin with a descending leap, but the precise intervals are different). Similarly, the dotted rhythms of the two melismas on the first syllable of 'sweetest' are subtly different. Equally important is the way Purcell's vocal melody relates to the ground. Instead of entering with the first note of the ostinato the voice enters in the middle of the first cycle, and the second vocal phrase overlaps the end of the first cycle and the beginning of the second. Voice and theorbo begin together in the third cycle, but variety has been achieved because the position of 'O solitude' has been changed in relation to the bass.

7.8.2 Retained-melody variations

In this type of variation the melody stays the same but elements such as texture and harmony are varied. It will not normally be continuous variation as in the ground bass. Instead a self-sufficient theme will be played at the beginning, and each variation will be a separate entity. This is the case in Haydn's set of variations on *Gott erhalte Franz der Kaiser*, the 'Emperor's Hymn'. The first eight bars of the theme and of variations 1, 2 and 4 are shown in B32–B35. The theme is the first violin melody shown in the first of these examples. It is accompanied by a simple, diatonic harmonisation. In the first variation (B33) the **theme** is transferred unchanged to the second violin while the first violin plays a florid counter-melody. In the second variation (B34) the theme (again unchanged) is transferred to the cello while the violins play counter-melodies (the viola providing the real bass at the cadences). In these two variations it is chiefly the texture that changes. The original theme is homophonic, the first variation is in two-part counterpoint and the second variation is in three-part counterpoint with a subservient viola part. In the fourth variation (B35) the theme returns to the first violin and the texture is once more largely homophonic, but the harmony is richer and more chromatic.

7.8.3 Retained-harmony variations

In these variations the harmonic progressions and phrase structure of the theme are retained, but the original melody is wholly or almost wholly abandoned. Bach's *Goldberg Variations* are based on a 32-bar binary-form theme of which just the first eight bars are shown in B1. Immediately beneath these bars is a harmonic reduction of the progression that, at least in outline form, underlies all of the variations (the reduction is not included among the accompanying recordings). Below the harmonic reduction the first four bars of Bach's thirtieth variation are shown (B2). It will be seen that, so far as the harmonic progression is concerned, three beats of B1 are equivalent to two beats of B2. Apart from the use of a C♯ in B1 (as against a C♮ in B2) and a slight displacement of chord V in bar 7 of B1 the harmonies are identical but the melodies (Bach's own in B1, folk tunes in B2) could hardly be more different.

7.8.4 Chaconne and passacaglia

Both of these forms function in the same way as the *Goldberg Variations*, but instead of self-contained movements the theme and variations are continuous, making one long movement. Scholars have attempted to differentiate between the chaconne and the passacaglia. They have had little success because composers have themselves been inconsistent in their use of these terms. They are both based upon a short **harmonic progression** that is repeated exactly or with some modifications in each variation.

Bach's Chaconne in D minor (A95–A98) contains sixty-four statements of the harmonic progression heard in the first four bars. It is this harmonic progression which is the theme of the chaconne. In the music examples the start of each new variation is identified by a number in a box. Underneath the theme the harmonic progression is shown in its simplest form and the chords are identified by Roman numerals. The extra stave continues beneath the first three variations and it will be seen that Bach slightly varies the theme itself. Roman numerals are appended only to those chords that have been changed. For instance chord IV in the theme becomes II_5^6 in Variation 1 and $V^{4-\sharp3}$ in Variation 2. Some of Bach's harmonic changes can be quite dramatic. For instance in A96 a chromatic diminished-7th chord replaces the two diatonic chords heard in bars 1, 5, 9 and 13. The most obvious harmonic changes comes in A97, where the key changes to the tonic major. What remains absolutely unchanged is the four-bar phrasing and the perfect cadence (sometimes inverted) that marks the end of each variation.

But these harmonic changes are a less obvious means of achieving variety than changes of texture and melody or figuration. The theme and first variation are characterised by three- and four-part chords and sarabande rhythms (dotted-crotchet-and-quaver figures that throw an accent onto the second beat of the bar). Three- and four-part textures are maintained in Variations 2 and 3, but the sarabande rhythms are abandoned in favour of a different type of dotted rhythm. These dotted-quaver–semiquaver rhythms are maintained as the texture thins to two parts in Variations 4 and 5. In Variation 6 Bach derives a lyrical melody from his harmonic progression (the bass of which is picked out on the G string). B95 ends with the first of a series of figural variations. Variation 23 (B96) is one of a series of frenetic arpeggio variations that suddenly stop for the lyrical *maggiore* (B97 shows the first two of 19 variations in the tonic major). B98 shows the lead up to the final climax of this monumental set of variations.

7.8.5 Canonic variations

This type of variation might take a form similar to that of the retained-harmony variation discussed in 7.8.3. Instead of integrating folk melodies with the harmonic progression of the theme (B1 and B2) the composer might fuse an independent **canon** with it (this is indeed the case in nine of Bach's *Goldberg Variations*). A second possibility is the use of a pre-existing melody as a theme for canonic elaboration. A third alternative is that a melodic theme is treated as a cantus firmus against which independent parts form a canon. The last two techniques of canonic variation were particularly favoured by composers of chorale preludes. A94 is a variation on the well-known carol *In dulci jubilo* (the melody of which is shown in A91). In this organ chorale Bach combines the last two variation types discussed above. A92 shows how Bach treats the chorale melody canonically while A93 shows the independent canon that Bach adds to the chorale canon. Together they form a canon 2 in 4 (see 4.4.4).

7.8.6 Divisions and doubles

The art of improvising ever more elaborate ornamentation on a given melody was widely cultivated by English violists in the seventeenth and eighteenth centuries. Not many of these were written down, but the same principle is at work in French ***doubles***. Handel's gavotte from his Suite in G major illustrates the principles of both types (the gavotte is a French dance, but Handel wrote this suite in England where he must have come across the treatises on division-playing by Christopher Simpson and John Playford).

The extracts shown in B18 clearly illustrate the origin of the word division in a musical context entirely in crotchets (there are a couple of quavers and a dotted rhythm in the second half of the complete eight-bar phrase played on B18). The crotchets are then divided into two (quavers in Variation 1), three (triplets in Variation 3) and four (semiquavers in Variation 5). In each of these groups of shorter notes the original pitches can be distinctly heard (pecked lines show how they form a part of the increasingly complex figuration).

7.8.7 Developmental variations

In this type of variation, one of the most popular in the nineteenth century, a **motif** is taken from the theme and consistently developed throughout a single variation. The theme of Brahms's Variations and Fugue Op. 24 is an instrumental aria by Handel (B76). The melody contains six written-out turns (marked with brackets). In Variation 16 Brahms takes the turn motif (also marked with brackets in B77) and adds a prefix and suffix (including near-sequences of the turn in the last beats of bars 2, 3, 5, 6 and 7) to make a longer motif. This he treats imitatively throughout most of B77. In Brahms's variation Handel's melody as an entity has disappeared. What is left is the 4+4 phrase structure and a development of just one of the motifs from the melody.

7.9 Vocal and instrumental forms of the middle ages and renaissance

Many of the forms so far discussed can be expressed through the medium of the human voice. The most obvious example is the ternary form of the da capo aria (B15). But there are some structures that are particularly associated with vocal music. It is these with which this section is concerned.

7.9.1 Bar form

A three-part structure which can be represented as AAB is as common in songs of all ages as is ternary form (ABA) in instrumental music. But it was particularly cultivated by German minnesingers in medieval times, and by their successors, the mastersingers (who coined the term *Bar* for this type of song). These monophonic songs could be sung with or without accompaniment or played instrumentally. A13 is a typical example of a melody in bar form from the thirteenth century. The first section, called the **Aufgesang**, consists of two identical eight-bar phrases called **Stollen** (the slight differences between them as recorded and transcribed is the result of improvised variations). The melody of the **Abgesang** differs from the *Stollen,* though there is usually some repetition of passages from the *Aufgesang* (these are identified as x and y in A13). The melody is dorian, and it will be seen that there are four cadences dividing the *Abgesang* into four four-bar phrases. Ending a phrase on the final of the mode (in this case D) produces a feeling of finality or closure (like a modern perfect cadence) while phrases ending on any other degree of the mode sound inconclusive (like a modern imperfect cadence). These open and closed endings differentiate the otherwise identical pair of four-bar phrases in each *Stollen*. The *Abgesang* also divides into four four-bar phrases, but a cadence on the final is avoided until the last bar.

In creating a corpus of chorale melodies, Luther drew on two main

Elements of music

sources, plainsong and secular German lieder. Both were rhythmically altered and supplied with new spiritual texts in German. It is not surprising therefore that many of the chorale melodies which Bach harmonised are in bar form. Luther's famous reformation hymn *Ein' feste Burg ist unser Gott* (B6) replicates the structure of *Der Kuninc Rodolp* almost down to the last detail. *Stollen* 1 consists of two phrases, the first (A) ending on the dominant (bar 3), the second ending on the tonic (bar 6). The second *Stollen* is identical to the first save for the new text and the regular metre (the first *Stollen* is taken from a sixteenth-century source, the second from Bach's harmonisation in Cantata No. 80). The *Abgesang* begins with four new phrases, but, like the ***Minnelied***, a phrase from the *Aufgesang* (B) is repeated to bring the chorale to a close with the same cadences as those at the end of the two *Stollen*.

7.9.2 Medieval formes fixes

The most important of the fixed forms of medieval France were the rondeau, the ballade and the virelai. The first of these has already been discussed in 7.6.1.

The monophonic **ballade** of twelfth-century aristocratic poet-musicians called troubadours (southern France) and trouvères (northern France) was almost identical in structure to the bar form of German minnesingers (7.9.1). A12 shows the AAB structure of a ballade by the most famous trouvère of them all, Richard the Lionheart. As in A13 sections A and B are linked by the use of common material (x). The melody is in the aeolian mode and, like the *Minnelied*, each section contains two phrases, the first of each pair ending on the subtonic (bars 4, 12 and 20), the second ending on the tonic (bars 8, 16 and 23).

The **virelai** was the least common of the *formes fixes*. Its musical structure can be represented as ABBAA, the first and last sections having the same words. The form was brought to a peak of perfection by the most important composer of the fourteenth century, Guillaume de Machaut. He wrote many polyphonic virelais, but also continued the tradition of the earlier monophonic type, of which A22 is a perfect specimen. The melody is in the dorian mode transposed to G (with some chromatic alterations suggestive of melodic-minor scales). Cadences on the fifth degree of the mode (bars 4, 13, 18, 22 and 30) and on the final (bars 8, 26 and 34) reflect the poetic structure. In fourteenth-century Italy the polyphonic **ballata** of composers such as Landini had the same AbbaA structure (capital letters indicating a musical and textual refrain).

7.9.3 Canonic structures

The **round** is a type of infinite canon in which each voice returns to the beginning every time it reaches the end of its part, the process only ending when the singers decide they have had enough. The most remarkable example of a round is a medieval English **rota** about the delights of summertime (sung by four male voices on A15). The canonic voices enter at two-bar intervals starting in bar 7. As soon as each singer reaches the end of the melody ('Ne swik thu naver nu') he returns to the start – a process which can be repeated endlessly. The whole round is accompanied by a two-voice ostinato and a bourdon that starts six bars before the first canonic voice enters.

7: The structure of music

7.9.4 Isorhythmic structures

The vocal forms of the middle ages that have been discussed in previous sections have all been quite short. In the '**Ars Nova**' composers sought means of unifying longer polyphonic compositions, such as motets and Mass movements. Plainsong had, from the very beginnings of polyphonic composition, been a point of departure, a framework around which contrapuntal lines could be woven. This was the case in the **organa** of the school of Notre Dame in which the plainsong (the *cantus prius factus* or **cantus firmus**) was stated in long notes in the tenor while one or two upper voices provided parallel or free contrapuntal parts. The trouble with this method of construction was that the plainsong was so distorted that it became unrecognisable and thus ceased to be a unifying factor. Machaut and his contemporaries therefore decided to impose a regular repeating rhythmic pattern called a ***talea*** on the tenor's cantus firmus. This **isorhythmic** organisation works on the same principle of unity by repetition as the baroque ground bass, but is not as audible because the *talea* is usually longer than one cycle of a ground and there is no simultaneous repetition of a pitch-pattern. (In some isorhythmic compositions a repeating pitch-pattern called a *color* was employed, but it was even less audible than the *talea*, and the two were often out of phase with each other.) A20 shows the plainsong upon which Machaut composed his setting of the Benedictus from his famous *Messe de Notre Dame* (believed to be the first complete setting of the Ordinary of the Mass by a single composer). In this case the *talea* in the isorhythmic tenor part (shown on an extra stave beneath A20) is a rhythmic pattern of eleven notes, the durations of which (in crotchet beats) are 31233111123. Each *talea* is separated from the next by a whole-bar rest (the start of each one is indicated by a Roman numeral in both B20 and B21).

7.9.5 Estampie and ductia

These related genres (which may be among the earliest surviving examples of purely instrumental composition) have in common a formal structure in which a number of paired phrases (called *puncta*) are differentiated by **open** and **closed endings** (just like first-time and second-time endings in late nineteenth- and twentieth-century popular music). Whether monophonic (A18) or polyphonic (A16) the principal melody in open endings (in Italian 'aperto') ends on a pitch other than the tonic or final, while closed endings (in Italian 'chiuso') end on the final. A16 shows the first two *puncta* of an English *ductia* while A18 shows a complete ***istampita*** (Italian) comprising four *puncta* (identified by the letters A, B, C and D).

7.10 Cyclic forms

A cyclic composition is one in which separate sections or movements are unified by common musical materials. The most obvious manifestations of cyclic form are the renaissance Mass and many of the instrumental genres of the nineteenth century.

7.10.1 Cyclic Mass

In the fifteenth century complete settings of the Ordinary of the Mass by one composer became the norm, and these composers sought means of unifying all five sections of the Ordinary (Kyrie, Gloria, Credo, Sanctus/

Elements of music

Benedictus and Agnus Dei). To achieve this they used the same or slightly varied **motifs** at the start of each movement. Obrecht's subtle manipulation of these head motifs can be heard distinctly in A28 and A29. The first and second (a and b in A28) are rhythmically transformed at the start of the Agnus Dei. A third motif (c) grows out of the end of motif b in the Kyrie and overlaps with its inversion (cI). In the Agnus Dei this motif is detached from motif b and appears three times transposed to other pitches (bars 4, 5 and 9). The only change made to the last motif (d in A28) is a lengthening of its last note in the Agnus Dei (bars 2–4). Settings that are unified in this way proliferated in the fifteenth century. They are known as cyclic Masses.

In the sixteenth century two special types of cyclic Mass reached a peak of perfection. The first, the **paraphrase Mass**, was based on a plainsong melody on which the composer elaborated in predominantly imitative textures. This type is illustrated by Palestrina's *Missa Iste confessor* (A52) based on the plainsong hymn shown in A49. The second, the **parody Mass**, was based on a motet or a chanson, utilising all of its polyphonic voices. This type is illustrated by Victoria's *Missa O quam gloriosum* (A45 and A46) based on his own motet *O quam gloriosum* (A44).

7.10.2 Cyclic forms in the romantic era

There are isolated examples of cyclic music in seventeenth- and eighteenth-century compositions, but the greatest flowering of cyclic instrumental composition emerged in the nineteenth century when Berlioz introduced the same *idée fixe* in all five movements of his *Symphonie fantastique* and Liszt used his technique of **thematic transformation** on a theme which appears in all three movements of his *Faust Symphony*. One of the most famous examples of cyclic form is Tchaikovsky's fifth symphony, in which a doom-laden 'fate motif' appears at climactic moments in all four movements. But it was late nineteenth-century French and Belgian composers who began to use cyclic processes with as much subtlety as Obrecht's head motifs. Right at the start of the first movement of his string quartet Debussy announces a dramatic theme (C18(a)) which permeates all four movements in transformed versions. C18(b) shows how the character of the theme is altered by a change from simple-quadruple metre to compound time accompanied by a change to a faster tempo, while C18(c) shows how augmentation and slight intervallic alteration cast a pensive shadow over a theme that unifies the whole quartet.

8:
Style, genre and historical context

The classification of musical styles and genres is fraught with difficulty because a single term could be used to mean one thing in one historical period and something quite different in another. Thus the term concerto could mean an ensemble of voices or instruments (or both) in the seventeenth century, Bach could use it as the title of what would now be called a cantata, Brahms could use it of a work for violin and cello soloists and orchestra, while in the twentieth century Bartók could use it for a work for orchestra with concertante roles for soloists from all instrumental families. In this chapter an attempt has been made to avoid such potential confusion by considering styles and genres within unfolding historical perspectives.

8.1 Style

Style is the individual character of a work of art or a collection of related art-works. It is this individual character which chiefly distinguishes one work from another, or the works of one school of artists from those of another. It has little to do with content or subject matter, and everything to do with the manner of expression. Plates 1 and 2 show that sails figure prominently in Francesco Guardi's *View of S. Giorgio Maggiore in Venice* and Monet's painting of a yacht race. In the depiction of sails the subject matter of the plates is the same, but the style of the two paintings is totally different. Another important subject in Guardi's painting is the great church of St George just across the Grand Canal from St Mark's Cathedral. Monet painted several pictures of a very different but equally grand church, Rouen Cathedral (Plate 3). Again the subject matter of Plates 1 and 3 is similar, but the styles are radically different. It is Guardi's own style that unites the images of the sails and the church in a single coherent and deeply satisfying composition. In Plates 2 and 3 it is Monet's unique and developing style which proclaims a kinship between these paintings of quite different subjects. A comparison of Plate 1 with Plates 2 and 4 again reveals that the style of the eighteenth-century Italian painting is, not unsurprisingly, quite unlike that of the two late nineteenth-century French paintings despite the similarity of subject matter. But there are stylistic features common to Monet's and Seurat's paintings of water and sails, and it is these common elements which have encouraged art historians to define an overarching late nineteenth-century style which encompasses the works of Monet, Seurat and other impressionist painters.

This categorisation of artists as members of distinct stylistic groups does not deny the existence of subgroups within larger art-historical periods. Thus Seurat's painting (Plate 4) is nearer in style to that of Signac (Plate 5) than it is to either of the paintings by Monet (Plates 2 and 3). All three of these French painters were impressionists, but the affinity between the two neo-impressionists (Seurat and Signac) is greater than that between them and most other impressionist painters. Nor do such categories deny that the styles of individual artists belonging to the same

Elements of music

Plate 1: Francesco Guardi, *View of San Giorgio Maggiore in Venice*

Reproduced by permission of the Trustees of the Wallace Collection, London

Plate 2: Claude Monet, *Yacht races at Argenteuil*

Musée du Louvre, Paris. Photo RMN

8: Style, genre and historical context

Musée du Louvre, Paris. Photo RMN

Plate 3: Claude Monet, *Rouen Cathedral in full sunlight*

school can be divergent (Seurat's neo-impressionism as represented in Plate 4 is more monumental than his disciple's vivid neo-impressionist style represented in Plate 5). Nor do they even deny that the style of an artist can radically change during his creative career (the stylistic differences between Plates 2 and 3 are almost as great as the stylistic differences between Monteverdi's works in the *stile antico* and his last works in the *stile moderno*).

Elements of music

Plate 4: Georges Seurat, *Bathers at Asnières*

Plate 5: Paul Signac, *Sailing boats in the harbour of St Tropez, 1893*

8: Style, genre and historical context

Because music is non-representational it is harder to distinguish between content and style. Only when a composer sets words to music, or when a title suggests a programme, is it possible to show with any degree of certainty how the style of the music relates to a concrete subject. Mendelssohn's *Venetian Gondola Song* Op. 19 No. 6 (B61) is a character piece from his collection of *Songs without Words*. We can be certain that the melody is in the general style of the **barcaroles** that the composer heard when he wrote the music in Venice in 1830. So the subject is almost as concrete as the gondolas seen in Plate 1, and it would not be at all out of place to allow images of Venice to float through the mind when listening to the music. The style of this particular gondolier's vocal effusion can be described by reference to the elements of music discussed in previous chapters. It has a moderate tempo with lilting rhythms in compound metre ($_8^6$ time). It is in G minor modified by aeolian flat 7ths (for example, the F♮s in bars 3 and 10), and the melody is further characterised by intervals of an augmented 2nd (for example, the leap from B♭ to C♯ in bars 14 and 16). The rhythmic features are common to the styles of all barcaroles, but elements of pitch are peculiar to the style of this particular barcarole. As a purely instrumental composition the style of the barcarole was characterised by a repetitive accompaniment suggesting the gentle rocking of a boat. Above this the melody was often doubled in 3rds or 6ths (for example, bars 7–8 and bar 9 respectively). It would then be possible to go on to consider the element of harmony and show how Mendelssohn's barcarole conforms to early romantic style (in this extract the dissonant appoggiatura above a diminished-7th chord in bar 14 is typical of the period). Thus, just as Seurat's painterly style is in part unique to himself, in part common to the work of other neo-impressionist artists, and in part contributes to the overarching style of impressionism, so Mendelssohn's musical style is stamped with his own unique creative imprint, yet it conforms to the melodic style of a Venetian song, the style of a barcarole, and the overarching style of romanticism.

In his old age Liszt wrote a number of piano pieces which give warning that the neat style-periods suggested by some historians are no more than generalisations about the common practice displayed in a majority of compositions within a particular span of years. In every period a very significant minority of works may be found which contradict many of the historian's generalisations. A striking example is the extract taken from the start of a character piece by Liszt entitled *La Lugubre Gondola* (*The Mournful Gondola*) (B74). Like Mendelssohn's *Venetian Gondola Song* discussed above it is in the style of a barcarole, and it too is an andante in a minor key. But there the resemblances end. Instead of Mendelssohn's uninterrupted rocking rhythm the accompaniment in Liszt's barcarole is disturbed by the halting effect of syncopations in the left-hand part every other bar. Instead of Mendelssohn's diatonic 'vocal' melody, Liszt's melodic line is unvocal and very chromatic. Instead of Mendelssohn's functional harmony that clearly defines the keys of G minor and D minor, Liszt's seemingly endless augmented triad barely defines the key of F minor. In fact this bleak piece is nearer in style to Debussyan impressionism than it is to Mendelssohn's picturesque romanticism. This is confirmed by the misty texture (produced by the extensive use of the sustaining pedal) and etiolated tone-colour (produced by the use of the

Elements of music

soft pedal throughout). By these means Liszt allows us to see the funeral gondola looming out of the mists with almost the same clarity that we can see Guardi's completely different vision of the city (Plate 1).

Another evocation of Italy, Tchaikovsky's *Capriccio italien* was written just two years before *La Lugubre Gondola*. The extract on C3 shows how widely styles can differ between composers normally bracketed together as romantic. The only common ground between the two is the compound metre and the fact that they are both based on ostinatos. But whereas Liszt's two-bar ostinato is in essence an arpeggiated augmented triad (shown below the first bar in close position) which only hints at the key of F minor, Tchaikovsky's one-bar ostinato is a deliberately crude oom-pah-pah on the tonic and dominant of A major (a key which could not possibly be more clearly defined than it is in this music). The melodic styles of the two are equally contrasting: Liszt's unvocal and extremely chromatic, Tchaikovsky's supremely vocal and diatonic (apart from the chromatic passing notes in 3rds that are so redolent of nineteenth-century Italian folk music).

Even within the works of one composer there can be considerable differences in style. Just as Monet's impressionist style changed in the two decades between *Yacht races at Argenteuil* (Plate 2) and *Rouen Cathedral in full sunlight* (Plate 3), so Debussy's impressionist style in 'Voiles' (C21) differs from the style he adopted for 'La Cathédrale engloutie' (C22–C26). In fact it is just as easy to draw stylistic parallels between Monet's and Debussy's sails, and between the painter's and the composer's cathedrals, as it is to draw parallels between each man's early and late works.

Because umbrella terms such as romanticism and impressionism tend to simplify and even obscure such widely different styles, two important caveats should be borne in mind when reading the following historical survey of styles. Firstly, any dates suggested for style-periods will be open to debate. They are nevertheless useful in approximately indicating common ground between composers in their historical contexts (the overlap of dates between style-periods is deliberate and avoids the artificially clinical impression given by the suggestion that the end of one period coincides with the beginning of the next). Secondly, only those compositions that most clearly illustrate commonly accepted generalisations about historical styles have been used as illustrations. This does not mean that there are no exceptions to the rule. On the contrary, there is in almost every style-period a significant minority of compositions that are atypical.

8.2 Genre

Like style, the term genre is by no means peculiar to music. There is also some overlap in the meaning of the two terms. If style refers to the general characteristics of a composer's musical language, then genre refers to the type, kind or species of particular compositions. The latter may be defined by the function of the composition. For example the **aria** is a genre associated with a larger creative concept (such as an opera or cantata). The aria functions as a more purely musical means of expression than recitative, the primary function of which is to convey narrative or dialogue as succinctly as possible. It can also function as a vehicle for the display of the soloist's vocal virtuosity. In this sense the term has little to do with form. But there can be some overlap between form and style in a particular and very common type of aria known as the **da capo aria** (B15). The use of this term

8: Style, genre and historical context

tells us what sort of musical structure to expect (ternary or ABA form), because the direction 'da capo' at the end of the printed music means that the performers must go back to the beginning and repeat the first (A) section. Another genre that is determined by its intended function is the dance. The primary purpose of the saltarello was to provide strongly defined rhythms for the conventional leaps and skips of a fast dance. As with the da capo aria there could be an overlap with form. In the case of the fourteenth-century saltarello, for instance, the music could take the form of an *estampie* (A18).

Genre can also be defined by the resources required for the performance of a particular type of composition. A string quartet, for example, requires two violinists, a viola player and a cellist. The use of this term may lead us to expect the use of certain musical structures (such as sonata form), and, because the genre reached a peak of perfection in the late eighteenth century, it might lead us to expect classical style. Both of these expectations (sonata form and classical style) are fulfilled in a work such as Haydn's String Quartet Op. 42 (B27), but both are defeated by a composition such as Debussy's string quartet (C12–C18).

A genre can manifest itself over hundreds of years. In this dictionary there are examples of the solo song ranging from Richard the Lionheart's *Ja nus hons pris* of the twelfth century (A12) to Hauer's *Hölderlin Lieder* of the twentieth century (C40). Other genres are confined to relatively short historical periods. The trio sonata (A74), for example, developed and died out within the baroque era. It should also be remembered that the same word can have different meanings when applied to genres of different periods. For example, the medieval rondeau was a vocal genre (A23), but the baroque rondeau was an instrumental genre (A84). What links them is not function or resources but similarity of form (though the structure of the medieval rondeau was determined as much by poetic form as by musical structure, whereas the form of the baroque rondeau was entirely determined by musical considerations).

8.3 Historical style-periods

Traditionally musical periods have followed the periods proposed by historians, notably art historians. The chief advantage of tracing the development of musical styles in this way is that music can thereby be more easily related to its social context and to developments in the other arts. The chief disadvantage is that radical changes of musical style rarely coincide neatly with the dates suggested by historians for changes in society at large. Nor does the rise and fall of musical genres neatly coincide with the rise and fall of the genres of the pictorial and plastic arts. There is, in any case, still much controversy about the dating of these periods. The categorisation of periods in the following historical survey is therefore based on a pragmatic approach which takes account of traditional style periods (such as the baroque era), but recognises that musical style-periods overlap one another and that some styles are peculiar to music.

8.4 Medieval monophony (c.500–c.1430)

Sacred plainsong and secular courtly song of the middle ages were often closely linked by their melodic modality. The modal system, particularly the system of **church modes**, was an attempt on the part of medieval theorists to classify the existing corpus of plainsong. Like modern major and minor keys the eight church modes can be defined by the relationships between a collection of seven different pitches. These seven pitches (with one of them repeated an octave higher) can be arranged in a scale containing five tones and two semitones between adjacent notes. It is the distribution of the five tones and two semitones which determines the particular modality of each scale, not the absolute pitch of the starting note (so, like modern major and minor scales, modal scales can start on any of the twelve pitch classes used in western music). The note to which all the other degrees of a modal scale gravitate (and on which plainsong melodies end) is the **final** (or *finalis*), the modal equivalent of the tonic.

A majority of **plainsong** melodies completely conform to one or other of the modes (eg A4, A8, A40 and A49). The exceptions are those melodies in which a modal B♮ is flattened by a semitone (often in order to avoid a tritonal effect with F♮). This type of chromatic alteration can be heard in A20 in which the fourth degree of Mode V is lowered by a semitone. The effect is to change the lydian mode (F to F on the white notes of a keyboard instrument) into what we now hear as music in the key of F major. In secular monophony chromatic alterations could affect several degrees of a modal scale, as Machaut's virelai *Comment qu'a moy lonteine* shows (A22). In addition there are many secular melodies which do not conform to any of the eight church modes. These are melodies which sixteenth-century theorists classified as aeolian (A to A on the white notes of a keyboard) or ionian (C to C), but which sound to modern ears like melodies in minor or major keys.

8.4.1 Gregorian chant (c.500–c.1250)

Little is known about the way music developed in the first few hundred years of the middle ages because there was no precise method of representing melodies on paper until neumatic notation began to appear in the ninth century. **Neumes** are symbols that fix the relative pitches of notes, but give little indication of rhythm (A4). This notational system was used to record the vast corpus of monophonic melodies known as *cantus planus* (**plainsong** or **plainchant**) that was sung in the **Mass** and **Divine Office** centuries before it was possible to transcribe it on paper. There were several different traditions of plainsong, the most famous being Gregorian chant (which soon became the officially approved liturgical music of the Roman Catholic Church).

Modern performances of plainsong are usually based on the researches of nineteenth- and twentieth-century monks of the Benedictine community at Solesmes in northern France. In this tradition rhythm is treated flexibly so that there is no sense of a regular pulse or metre. Melodic contours are predominantly conjunct and avoid the interval of a tritone and intervals greater than a perfect 5th.

More than 3,000 Gregorian chants have been classified according to their specific modality. Four of them (Modes I, III, V and VII) can be represented as scales very much like modern major and minor scales. But unlike modern scales the church modes were further defined by the approximate **range** (*ambitus*) of the melody. Those with a range spanning about an octave from the lower to the upper final of the mode were known as **authentic modes** (see 2.4.1). Those which had the same **final** as the corresponding authentic mode, but with a range approximately a 5th

8: Style, genre and historical context

higher or a 4th lower, were known as **plagal modes** (Modes II, IV, VI and VIII) (see 2.4.2). The modality of most of the plainsong melodies in this dictionary is identified by the modal scale with which it is associated.

A second important stylistic classification is based on the way in which plainsong melodies relate to their texts. The simplest style is **syllabic plainsong** in which there is just one note per syllable (A6). In **neumatic plainsong** most syllables bear two or more notes (A4). **Melismatic plainsong** is an elaborate style in which syllables of important words carry many notes (A5).

There are plainsong settings of all types of Latin liturgical texts, of which only a representative sample are included in the dictionary (polyphonic settings of other texts may be found by consulting the entries on the Mass and the Divine Office).

The core of the liturgies of monastic offices was (and still is) the chanting of **psalms**. A6 is a setting of a verse from Psalm 104. It is in a simple syllabic style and is sung to a psalm tone (a melodic formula adapted to each verse of the psalm) which in essence is a melodic decoration of a reciting note (the repeated C♯s). The narrow range, spanning only a 5th, is typical of this type of plainsong.

The final acclamation 'Benedicamus Domino – Deo gratias' (A8) is sung at the end of the services of the Divine Office. There are several plainsong melodies for this text, all of them sung responsorially: one or two soloists sing the first sentence ('Let us bless the Lord') to which the rest of the monastic choir respond with the second sentence ('Thanks be to God'). This particular example of responsorial plainsong is in a florid melismatic style. It begins and ends on D (the final of the dorian mode), but its *ambitus* (range) covers an octave on A, so it is in the plagal form of the dorian mode (Mode II, or the hypodorian mode).

Plainsong **hymns**, with texts associated with particular days of the liturgical calendar, were often sung at Lauds and Vespers (two of the services of the Divine Office, the first sung early in the morning, the second at sunset). These hymns consisted of a number of stanzas sung strophically (each stanza sung to the same plainsong melody). A49 shows the complete melody of a hymn sung on the feast day of a confessor (a saint who, by word and deed, witnessed to Christ, but who was not martyred for his faith). It is in a simple neumatic style. The melody begins and ends on G (the final of the mixolydian mode), but its ambitus covers an octave on C, so it is in the plagal form of the mixolydian mode (Mode VIII, or the hypomixolydian mode). A40 shows the beginning of a famous hymn in the dorian mode addressed to the Blessed Virgin Mary.

The **Ordinary of the Mass** consists of five texts that are sung at most celebrations of the sacrament. The first of these – 'Kyrie eleison, Christe eleison, Kyrie eleison' (Lord have mercy, Christ have mercy, Lord have mercy) – is the only Greek text to have been retained in the liturgies of the Roman Catholic Church. A42 shows the simple neumatic style of the **Kyrie** from Mass XI. It is usually sung responsorially, the word 'Kyrie' being allotted to one or two soloists who are answered by the whole choir or congregation singing 'eleison'. It is sung four semitones lower than its original pitch to facilitate comparison with Victoria's Kyrie (A45). In the Graduale (an officially approved book of chants for the Mass) it is classified as a Mode I melody (dorian: D to D on the white notes of a

Elements of music

keyboard instrument), but the sixth degree of the modal scale is flattened a semitone (B♭ at its original pitch) every time it appears. This effectively turns it into a melody in the aeolian mode (as A42 shows).

The fourth text of the ordinary – 'Sanctus, sanctus, sanctus Dominus Deus Sabaoth' (Holy, holy, holy Lord God of hosts) – is sung just before the consecration of the bread and wine. The last part of this text (the **Benedictus** which is detached from the **Sanctus** proper in some Anglican rites) is shown in A20 set in a fairly florid neumatic style. Again the use of a B♭ effectively changes a chant officially classified as lydian (Mode V) into a melody in the ionian mode (which in this case is the same as F major).

Perhaps the most famous plainsong melody is that associated with the *Dies irae*. This very late addition to the officially approved liturgical texts of the Roman Catholic Church is a **sequence** with a text attributed to Thomas of Celano who died in the middle of the thirteenth century. It is a terrifying vision of the Last Judgement sung in the **Requiem Mass** (the Missa pro defunctis or Mass for the Dead). In B62 the first few phrases of the dorian-mode melody are shown transposed down a tone so it is easier to compare the plainsong with Berlioz's use of it in his *Symphonie fantastique*. It should be noted that just as modern major and minor scales can start on any of the twelve chromatic pitches of western music so modes can be transposed from the nominal pitches indicated by ancient C and F clefs. All that is needed is the retention of the same order of tones and semitones of the modal scale as that in the original notation.

8.4.2 Medieval secular monophony (c.1150–c.1430)

The first flowering of secular music that can be transcribed into modern notation with any degree of accuracy is that of eleventh- and twelfth-century aristocratic poet-musicians known as troubadours in southern France and trouvères in northern France. The most common subject was courtly love. A12 is a **chanson** with words and music by Richard the Lionheart. In it the English king bewails his imprisonment and expresses his hope for a ransom that will ensure his release. As with plainsong, and in common with other songs of the period, there is some doubt about the rhythms and metre of King Richard's song, but what little evidence there is points to rhythms in triple metre. Also in common with plainsong is the narrow range (a minor 7th) and the modality of the melody. The frequent use of the leap of a 3rd (to the exclusion of all other leaps) imparts a more obviously tuneful style than is evident in most plainsong. The AAB melodic structure is that of the **ballade**, one of the medieval *formes fixes*. Medieval songs in this dictionary have been recorded entirely unaccompanied (A22 and A23), accompanied by an instrument (A12), or played as an instrumental dance (A13), reflecting the lack of conclusive information about original performance practices.

The **virelai**, another of the medieval *formes fixes*, was a poetic and musical genre which reached a peak of perfection in the chansons of Guillaume de Machaut (c.1300–77). In A22 the conventional musical form of the virelai (ABBAA) is clarified, not only by the contrasting melodies of sections A and B, but also by what is, in effect, contrasting tonality. Section A is in the dorian mode on C, but to modern ears the first phrase sounds as though it modulates from C minor to E♭ major (bars 2–4). Dorian modality returns with the A♮ in bar 5, and the section ends firmly on the final of the mode (bar 8). This 'modern' style is emphasised by periodic phrasing: a four-bar phrase with an open (*ouvert*) ending on G is answered by a four-bar phrase with a closed (*clos*) ending on C. Chromatic alterations in the repeated second section (B) dispel any suggestion of the dorian mode and so highlight the musical structure of the whole chanson.

The third and most complex of the medieval *formes fixes* is the **rondeau** which has a musical structure based on two phrases, the first with an open ending, the second with a closed ending. The musical phrases alternate in the pattern ABAAABAB. The eight-line verse form of A23 has a more complex structure: abcadeab (see the text printed beneath the music), although the rhyme scheme follows the same pattern as the musical form. When this is added to the musical structure the form has the pattern ABaAabAB, in which capital letters represent refrains containing repetitions of both words and music. Like much other secular music of the middle ages, Machaut's rondeau sounds more modern than contemporary sacred music such as Machaut's own Mass (A22). In this case the seven pitches that are heard throughout the chanson could be arranged to form an ascending melodic-minor scale (G–A–B♭–C–D–E–F♯–G). The impression of G-minor tonality is confirmed by the eight cadences on the supertonic halfway through each line and the cadences on the leading note (F♯) and tonic (G) at the ends of lines.

The German equivalent of the French trouvères were the minnesingers, aristocratic poet-composers who flourished from about 1150 through to the beginning of the fourteenth century. Like the French ballade, the German **Minnelied** (love song) typically has an AAB form with each open-ended phrase being repeated with a closed ending. In Germany this structure was called **bar form**, a structure that lasted well into the sixteenth century, as B6 shows. There was little or no distinction in the early middle ages between secular vocal and secular instrumental music, so it is not unusual to hear performances of a *Minnelied* on authentic instruments such as the citole and vielle heard in A13.

8.5 Medieval polyphony (c.900–c.1430)

Nowadays the term polyphony is most often used as a synonym for counterpoint or as an antonym for homophony. In the middle ages the term simply referred to music with two or more parts sounding simultaneously (whether or not the texture of the music was contrapuntal).

8.5.1 Medieval sacred polyphony (c.900–c.1430)

Medieval sacred polyphony grew out of plainsong and most of it was based on these officially approved melodies. They could be presented in their original form with one or more parts moving in the same rhythm, or the constituent notes could be lengthened and sounded against one or more faster moving and newly invented counter-melodies.

The earliest known polyphony is the **parallel organum** that was set down in an early type of notation and described in an anonymous treatise dating from about 900 AD entitled *Musica enchiriadis*. In its simplest form organum consisted of a **plainsong melody** with another voice singing the same melody in parallel 5ths below it. In A7(a) the plainsong melody of A6 appears as the ***vox principalis*** (the principal voice) and the added part is identified as the ***vox organalis*** (the added voice). It was possible to duplicate both parts at the octave in a style known as **composite organum**.

Elements of music

In A7(b) the original plainsong melody of the second phrase of the plainsong appears in the second part down (*vox principalis*) and this is doubled an octave below in the lowest part. Similarly the *vox organalis* (the second part up) is doubled an octave above in the uppermost part. In actual practice these two styles would not have been sung in such close proximity (but it was common for parts of a text to be sung in plainsong alternating with polyphonic settings of the remainder of the text). The original notation gives no indication of rhythm or metre, so on track A7 the organum is sung in the same non-metrical, freely flowing style as the plainsong on A6.

A much more elaborate style of polyphony known as florid or **melismatic organum** (A9) developed in the first half of the twelfth century in the Abbey of St Martial de Limoges in south-west France. As with parallel organum the music is based on plainsong, but it is heard as a *cantus prius factus* in long notes in the lower of the two parts (known as the **tenor** – the part that 'holds' the plainsong – in the middle ages). Above it the organal voice floats freely except at those points where it coincides with the articulation of one of the notes of the plainsong tenor. At these points the interval formed between the two parts is always consonant (unison, perfect 4th, perfect 5th or perfect octave). Like parallel organum the notation does not indicate the rhythms of either of the two parts. On track A9 the music is sung in the same non-metrical, freely flowing style as the plainsong on A8.

In the second half of the twelfth century the School of Notre Dame in Paris introduced the most important development in sacred music since the inception of polyphony – music which was **notated** in such a way that it is possible for modern scholars to determine its rhythm and metre. A10 shows a passage of liturgical polyphony based on the melismatic setting of the word 'Domino' shown in A8. Each note of the original plainsong becomes a dotted minim or a dotted crotchet plus a rest in the tenor part. To this is added a freely composed second voice-part called the ***duplum***. These two contrapuntal voices are unified by their common metre, but contrasted by their different rhythms. (Rhythms in compound or simple triple time were prominent stylistic features of medieval sacred music because the ratios of shorter to longer notes in these metres – 3:1 – were seen as musical representations of the Holy Trinity.) The two parts are further unified by consonant intervals of unison, 4th, 5th, or octave, heard at the beginning of almost every bar. This new, strictly measured metrical polyphony, characterised by a lively relationship between the plainsong and the added part or parts, was a feature of the **clausula**, a rhythmically notated polyphonic section based on a melismatic passage of plainsong heard within longer passages of monophonic chant or organum. The clausula heard on track A10 is preceded by the first phrase of the original plainsong ('Benedicamus') sung by cantors, and it is followed by the original plainsong response ('Deo gratias') sung by the whole choir. There are over 900 Parisian clausulae and it was from these that the independent medieval motet later emerged.

All of the medieval sacred music so far discussed has been monophonic plainsong or polyphony based on plainsong. The **conductus** was the only type of early medieval sacred music that was not always associated with Gregorian chant. It began life in the twelfth century as a monophonic song with a Latin text that was sung during ceremonial processions. A conductus might, for example, have been sung at that point in the Mass when the celebrant was 'conducted' by a deacon bearing the gospels to a lectern from which the gospel of the day was read. The polyphonic conductus was, with very few exceptions, based on a freely composed tenor, thus making it the first completely original type of polyphony. The note-against-note **discant style** of A11 is simpler than that of contemporary organa. There are only minor rhythmic differences between the parts and most of the text is set syllabically or with very short melismas. The exception is the *cauda*, the untexted or melismatic tail which was such a feature of many conducti (bars 33–38).

In the thirteenth century the **motet**, the descendant of the clausula, was cultivated at the expense of settings of the Ordinary of the Mass, but the fourteenth century saw a revival of interest in Mass settings. Indeed it is in this century that the first complete settings of the Ordinary of the Mass were written. Among the earliest of these is the anonymous *Messe de Tournai* It dates from the early fourteenth century and was probably compiled from several different sources since differences in style between the movements suggest that they were written in different periods. The Agnus Dei (A19) is among the most conservative in style. Like earlier medieval polyphony it extends over a very narrow range (a 5th in the *triplum*, a 4th in the motetus and tenor and only a 10th from the lowest tenor note to the highest note of the triplum). The tenor part is written in the third **rhythmic mode** (the repeating three-note rhythmic pattern shown beneath each system) which was a common feature of the Notre Dame school (A10). It is easy to hear the modal rhythm in the first five bars since all three parts conform to this mode. The largely homophonic texture harks back to the note-against-note style of the conductus (A11), a type of polyphony which had largely died out by the mid thirteenth century. Finally, its lydian modality is startlingly clear, there being only one chromatic inflection (the B♭ that features in the earliest sources of plainsong and which is here used to avoid the tritone that would otherwise occur between the outer parts).

The **Ars Nova** gained its name from a musical treatise of that name written in about 1322 by the priest, poet, theoretician and composer, Philippe de Vitry. The main thrust of the book is a comparison of the notational systems of the **Ars Antiqua** of the previous century with the more precise and flexible systems introduced at the start of the fourteenth century. An exploration of ancient forms of notation is outside the scope of this dictionary, but the effect notational changes had on musical style is well within our purview. The abandonment of the repetitive triple-time patterns of the old rhythmic modes in favour of a more modern notational system meant that compositions in simple duple and quadruple time became increasingly common (A17). Another effect that notational reforms had on the style of fourteenth-century music is evident in the greater range of note-values that became available to the composer (compare A10 and A11 with A21 and A23).

The greatest musical monument of the Ars Nova is *La Messe de Notre Dame*, written in about 1360 by Guillaume de Machaut (1300–77). It is probably the first complete setting of the Ordinary of the Mass by one composer and it epitomises the main achievements of the Ars Nova. It is in four parts as opposed to the two- or three-part textures that were most common in the Ars Antiqua. The longer texts of the Proper (the Gloria and

Elements of music

Credo) are set in conductus style similar to that found in the earlier *Messe de Tournai* (A19). However, passages in duple time with duple divisions of the beat are more common in these movements than the triple metre with triple divisions of the beat that dominated the style of the Ars Antiqua. The shorter movements of the Ordinary are based on plainsong melodies that are organised by a technique known as **isorhythm** (compare the tenor parts of A19 and A20). Instead of the two-bar rhythmic pattern of the Agnus Dei, the tenor cantus firmus of Machaut's Benedictus is organised into repeating seven-bar rhythms with a bar's rest between each statement of the *talea* (one complete isorhythmic pattern). There are slight differences between the pitches of the plainsong and Machaut's tenor (A20). No doubt some of these are deliberate decorations introduced by the composer. Others could reflect differences between a local version of the chant with which Machaut was familiar and the version printed in the modern *Liber usualis*. There are other more immediately obvious stylistic features in this music. Above the slowly moving melodies of the lowest two parts, the uppermost voices sing contrasting highly ornamented melodies characterised by syncopations and **hockets**. The latter was a medieval technique in which a single melodic line was broken up by two musicians singing alternate and overlapping notes (A21, bars 5–6, 13–14, 21–22 and 29–30). Whole compositions were written using this compositional technique. Of these, Machaut's *Hoquetus David* is the most famous example.

8.5.2 Medieval secular polyphony

Compared with the large corpus of sacred polyphonic music there are few extant examples of secular polyphony from the early middle ages. However, what has survived suggests that this lost repertoire was in no way inferior to church music. We have already seen that secular monophonic music was often more tonal than contemporary sacred music. This is the case in the remarkable Reading Rota which dates from the middle of the thirteenth century (A15). The sixteenth-century theorist Glareanus would probably have described it as music in the so-called ionian mode, but to our ears it is securely in the key of D major. The 'rota' of the title is a lengthy type of four-voice infinite canon known as a **round**, which is supported by two bass voices singing a four-bar ostinato (called a *pes* in the original manuscript). The harmonic progression that results from the combination of the canonic voice parts with the two-voice ostinato defines the key of D major with almost as much force as the individual melodies. A predilection for the major mode is a distinguishing feature of thirteenth-century English music, but what is most remarkable is a preference for intervals of the 3rd and 6th at a time when theorists were declaring them to be impure. When all voices have entered, the round produces the sort of triadic harmony shown beneath bars 15–18 in which there is an interval of a 3rd or a 6th (or both) on both beats of every bar.

The dancing, compound-time rhythms and major-mode tonality of the Reading Rota are equally pronounced in the anonymous English ***ductia*** recorded on A16, but since it is in two rather than in six parts triads cannot be formed. Nevertheless, there are on-beat 3rds in bars 5–7, 13 and 15. The *ductia* was similar to the *estampie* (A18) in that the first of each pair of phrases (called a ***punctus***) had an open ending (phrases A1 and B1) and the second a more conclusive closed ending (phrases (A2 and B2).

8: Style, genre and historical context

This pairing of phrases is not obvious on A16 until one listens to the lower of the two parts, when it will become apparent that the second rebec plays exactly the same melody in both phrases of the first *punctus*. The same is true of the second *punctus* except that phrase B1 ends the dominant (G♮) while phrase B2 ends on the tonic (C♮).

The early fifteenth century was a transitional period between the middle ages and the renaissance and it saw a great flowering of English music. In particular the homophonic style of the **faburden**, with its complete triads and consecutive first-inversion chords, had a profound influence on continental composers. It was during this period that the English polyphonic **carol** flourished. Many of the texts related to the Nativity and the Virgin Mary, but none of them were liturgical and most, like the anonymous *Agincourt Song* (A24), were secular. This carol is a song of thanksgiving for Henry V's victory over the French in 1415. Both style and form are typical of the genre. Its energetic triple-metre rhythms and complex syncopation (bars 34–35) enliven memorable melodies in the hypodorian mode (often chromatically altered to form a variety of idiomatic cadences). The form of all polyphonic English carols of the fifteenth century was determined by the alternation of one or two **burdens** (refrains which retained the same words each time they were repeated) alternating with strophic settings of a number of verses. The *Agincourt Song* has two burdens. The first begins monophonically (bars 1–4), then breaks into faburden-style polyphony with characteristic consecutive first-inversion chords (bars 4–8). The second is in three-voice counterpoint throughout, while the texture is reduced to two-voice counterpoint in the verses.

8.6 Renaissance music (c.1430–c.1600)

The literal meaning of the word renaissance is 'rebirth'. It refers to the new interest in classical civilisation that was greatly accelerated by the westward migration of secular scholars who fled Constantinople when it fell to the Turks in 1453. The new humanist learning began the long process of secularisation that was to have profound effects on the state, philosophy and the arts. In music this was reflected in the ascendancy of secular genres such as instrumental dances and madrigals. Eventually this was balanced by a corresponding decline of sacred genres such as the motet and settings of the Ordinary of the Mass. But the process was gradual. In fact many of the stylistic features of medieval secular music were evident in sacred music through to the beginning of the sixteenth century. The end of the same century saw the composition of what was probably the greatest corpus of liturgical music the world had seen since the emergence of Gregorian plainsong in the dark ages, and in some countries (notably England) these sacred styles were practised well into the seventeenth century. It was not until the rise of opera and the concerto that secular society could boast of musical achievements of comparable grandeur. Historians recognise that music hardly ever fits comfortably into the periods that were originally named after eras of comparative stability in the other arts. It is particularly difficult to think of the years from 1430 to 1600 as a musical rebirth since what little was known about Greek music had no effect whatsoever on the music of this period. Nevertheless, the name and approximate dates of the renaissance have stuck and they do, at the very least, help in an understanding of the way music relates to the

Elements of music

achievements of society at large during the fifteenth and sixteenth centuries.

Sacred and secular styles diverged more in this period than in the middle ages, the former most often being characterised by smoothly flowing melodic lines in predominantly contrapuntal textures, the latter being generally homophonic, often with strongly characterised dance rhythms. Of course there was cross-fertilisation between the two, but the styles are sufficiently distinct for it to be possible to generalise meaningfully about the differences between them.

8.6.1 Catholic music in the renaissance (c.1430–c.1600)

Guillaume Dufay (c.1400–74), born a century later than Guillaume de Machaut, shares more than his Christian name with his predecessor, for among his early music there are complex four-voice motets using isorhythmic techniques similar to those that are such a feature in Machaut's Mass (A21). For these he was justifiably famous in his own day, but in his old age he wrote a series of four-voice **tenor Masses** which are cornerstones of renaissance music. In the extract from his famous *Missa L'Homme armé* (A27) the *cantus prius factus* (A26) in the tenor part can be recognised more easily than can the plainsong in Machaut's isorhythmic tenor because the rhythms as well as the pitches of the original melody are retained. As in Machaut's Mass the bass part crosses the alto at certain points, but the melodic line is much smoother (compare the largely conjunct movement of the bass in the first seven bars of A27 with the angular bass part in the first seven bars of A21). The only exceptions are when the bass leaps to help form a cadence (bar 7), where it imitates the tenor (bars 16–17) and where it exploits the characteristic falling 5th of the melody to form the syncopated figures in bars 20 and 23. As in Machaut's Mass the soprano and alto parts have faster rhythms than the lower parts, but, whereas Machaut's upper parts start and stop irregularly and are interrupted by hockets, the rhythms of Dufay's upper voices are smoothly flowing. Indeed Dufay's soprano describes the arch-like shapes that were to become such a characteristic feature of Palestrinian style in the next century. This is particularly obvious in the first five bars, where the soprano begins on the final of Mode I (F♯ in this performance), rises to the dominant (C♯ in bar 2) then falls back beyond the final to the lower dominant (bar 4) before returning to the final in bar 5. In its other phrases the soprano is similarly contained within the plagal form of the mode as it revolves smoothly around the final. Dufay's early works form a link with late medieval music, but in these late masterpieces he had already achieved the classical sense of repose that was to become such a feature of late renaissance music.

There are 29 extant masses by Jacob Obrecht (c.1450–1505), all of them based on pre-existing music including plainsong, secular song and motets and chansons by other composers. Although most have a tenor cantus firmus (like the extract from Dufay's Mass discussed above) other voices also often contain borrowed material, sometimes from more than one source. If the same portion of the *cantus prius factus* is used in every one of the usual five movements of the Ordinary the whole Mass will thereby achieve a certain degree of cohesion. But in his *Missa O beate pater Donatiane* (A28 and A29) Obrecht achieves a more complete sense of unity

8: Style, genre and historical context

by using the same motifs at the beginning of each section of the mass. A setting of the Ordinary in which separate sections are thus unified is known as a **cyclic Mass**, while the repeated or subtly varied motifs heard at the beginning of each section are known as **head motifs**. The two extracts show a set of these motifs used in both the first and the last sections of the Ordinary. Motif a in the first Kyrie is heard in diminution in the second Agnus Dei. Motifs b and c are indivisible in the Kyrie but are heard separately in the Agnus Dei. Motif d is the only one to be heard virtually unchanged. It is probable that these motifs derive from an as yet unidentified *cantus prius factus*. Like Dufay, Obrecht's largely conjunct melodies are supremely vocal. When there is a leap the melody almost always returns to a pitch within the leap, and rising phrases (for instance, A28, tenor, bars 1–3) are balanced by falling phrases (for instance, the tenor in bars 4–6 of the same example). Obrecht's dissonance treatment is equally suave. The only discords heard on the crotchet beat are suspensions that foreshadow the style of the high renaissance. These are particularly evident just before cadences (for instance, the 7–6 suspensions in the penultimate bars of both examples) and in the suspensions formed between the falling phrases of bars 6–8 of A29.

A century later the cantus firmus techniques of Dufay and Obrecht had largely been replaced by more flexible ways of handling pre-existent musical materials. The **paraphrase Mass** was based on plainsong or a secular melody. The *Missa Iste confessor* by Giovanni Pierluigi da Palestrina (c.1525–94) is based on a plainsong hymn of the same name (A49). Instead of laying this out in long notes in the tenor, Palestrina takes a phrase (or part of a phrase) of the hymn and fashions a metrical version of it, the opening of which can be used as a motif for a passage of imitative counterpoint. A51 and A52 show how a complete phrase of the hymn is transformed into a complete phrase in the second Kyrie of Palestrina's Mass (A52, soprano, bars 9–14). In the opening bars of the Kyrie rhythmically altered versions of the first few notes of this phrase are heard at the beginning of each imitative entry (seven notes in the tenor, five in the other three voices). After each imitative entry the voices continue with smoothly flowing contrapuntal strands which may be quite independent of the plainsong (like the tenor in the first five bars), or might be decorated versions of the remainder of the plainsong phrase (as in A51). The overlapping of the cadence of one polyphonic strand with the entry of another voice produces a seamless flow of imitative counterpoint that is typical of much late sixteenth-century sacred music.

In the middle ages the **motet** had been based upon a tenor cantus firmus derived from a plainsong melody. By the end of the sixteenth century it had become a completely independent genre, every note of it written by the composer. The motet *O magnum mysterium* by Tomás Luis de Victoria (1548–1611) in A44 (staves 1, 3, 5 and 7) is more varied in style than is the Kyrie by Palestrina (A52). It begins with an imitative setting of the first two phrases of the text ('O magnum mysterium et admirabile sacramentum') that is similar to Palestrina's consistently contrapuntal texture. But after the cadence in bar 16 there is a contrasting homophonic passage, the cadence of which (bar 19) overlaps pairs of voices singing the beginning of the new phrase ('ut animalia'). Homophony returns for the next part of the phrase ('viderunt Dominum natum') and the extract ends with a return to the style

Elements of music

of pervasive imitation with which it began ('jacentem in praesepio').

The music printed with diamond note-heads in this score (A45 and A46) is Victoria's setting of Kyrie I (bars 1–14) and Kyrie II (bars 30–39) from his **parody Mass** *O magnum mysterium*. It will be seen that the Mass movements have been derived from the imitative passages at the beginning and end of the motet. This parody technique ranges from an almost exact quotation of the original music with new words (bars 30–36) to a subtle reworking of the melodies and contrapuntal textures of the original (bars 1–14). Parody and paraphrase techniques differ in that the former involves the reworking of entire contrapuntal passages while the latter makes use of a single pre-existent melody that is reworked in all contrapuntal parts of the new composition.

8.6.2 Protestant music in the renaissance (c.1525–c.1625)

Martin Luther (1483–1546), the prime mover of the reformation, was himself a musician, though it is not known whether all of the music attributed to him was in fact his own work. To develop a corpus of sacred songs for his newly founded church he skilfully adapted well-known plainsong chants and secular songs to newly composed spiritual texts in German. In addition he or his followers composed completely new melodies which soon became famous throughout northern Germany and beyond. Perhaps the best known of these is *Ein' feste Burg ist unser Gott* (B6), a **chorale**, supposedly written by Luther in 1529 and certainly printed in 1533, which epitomises the rock-like faith of the reformed church. Anxious to write melodies that ordinary laymen could sing, Luther ensured the popularity of this chorale by adopting a simple secular style and by the use of one major key throughout. Like the *Minnelied* (A13) the music is in **bar form** (XXY) of a type that was common in the sixteenth century. A repeated ***Stollen*** (XX) of two phrases (ABAB) is followed by an extended ***Abgesang*** (Y) of five phrases, the last of them repeating the melody of the second phrase of the *Stollen* (CDEFB). The text is a metrical version of part of Psalm 46 ('God is our hope and strength'). It is printed below together with an English version of it by Miles Coverdale (bishop and translator, during the reign of Henry VIII, of the first printed English Bible). The annotations in the table show how the musical form (represented by letters in brackets) relates to the rhyme scheme (represented by letters without brackets) of the German verse.

The musical and literary structure of a chorale melody in bar form

Stollen 1 (A):	Ein' feste Burg ist unser Gott,	A *Our God is a defence and towre*
(B):	ein gute Wehr und Waffen;	B *A good armour and good weapon,*
Stollen 2 (A):	er hilft uns frei aus aller Not,	C *He hath ben ever our helpe and sucoure*
(B):	die uns jetzt hat betroffen.	B *In all the troubles that we have been in.*
Abgesang (C):	Der alte böse Feind,	C *Therefore wyl we never drede*
(D):	mit Ernst er's jetzt meint,	C *For any wondrous dede*
(E):	gross Macht und viel List	D *By water or by londe*
(F):	sein grausam Rüstung ist,	D *In hilles or the sea-sonde.*
(B):	auf Erd' ist nicht seins gleichen.	E *Our God hath them all in his hond.*

8: Style, genre and historical context

On track B6 the first *Stollen* is sung in the original version which is notable for the rhythmic freedom that was a feature of much renaissance music. The rest of the melody is sung in the familiar version that Bach harmonised nearly two centuries later.

Although Thomas Tallis (1505–85) never forswore his Catholic faith, he was prepared to write music for the liturgies of the English Protestant church in the reign of Elizabeth I. Among these compositions there are settings of **metrical psalms** which, in intention and form if not in style, are similar to Lutheran chorales. A37 is a setting of a metrical version of Psalm 2, verses 1 and 2 from Archbishop Parker's *The Whole Psalter Translated into English Metre*. In form it closely resembles the bar form of *Ein' feste Burg* (a repeated *Stollen* – ABA^1B^1 – and an *Abgesang* of four phrases – CDEF). Like Luther's melody Tallis's psalm tune is rhythmically flexible with the metre changing from triple to duple time in the first nine bars, and changing from simple to compound time in the remaining bars. However, there are significant stylistic differences. Instead of a major key, the melody is in the phrygian mode. Where Luther wrote only the melody, Tallis's melody is part of a complete homophonic setting. Where Luther's melody is straightforward (in its original version the *Stollen* and its repeat are exactly the same), Tallis's melody is subtle (notice the slight but significant changes made to phrases A and B when they are repeated). But these differences are as nothing compared to the gulf that separates this Protestant music from contemporary Catholic music. The new churches had found their own musical voices.

For a hundred years from the mid-sixteenth century the **consort song** was cultivated in England. It was usually written for one or two treble voices accompanied by a consort of viols (or, more rarely, a broken consort) that together formed what was usually a five-part contrapuntal texture. Whether with secular or sacred words these songs were designed for domestic performance and successfully withstood the fashion for Italianate madrigals. A60 shows the opening of an anonymous consort song in which bars 1–7 are based on a short imitative point heard in each instrumental part and in the solo soprano part. After this the texture varies between the free counterpoint of bars 10–11 and the homophony of bar 16. A consort song such as this could easily be performed in an Anglican church service (perhaps with organ accompaniment instead of an instrumental consort). In this context the consort song is sometimes called a **consort anthem**.

The **verse anthem** was an expanded version of the consort anthem that included choral passages as well as vocal solos (called verse parts). It was designed to be sung at the end of the Anglican offices of Matins and Evensong. *See, see, the word is incarnate* (A61) by Orlando Gibbons (1583–1625) dates from the early seventeenth century, yet its style is essentially that of the late renaissance. The extract is based on six motifs which are used imitatively, each point of imitation overlapped with the next to produce a seamless contrapuntal texture like that in the first sixteen bars of Victoria's motet *O magnum mysterium* (A44). It differs from the Catholic motet in that the contrapuntal web is maintained by a consort of viols rather than *a cappella* voices. Three solo voices (verse alto, tenor and bass) are part of this texture. Contrast is provided at the end of the extract by the homophony of the full choir (just as the homophonic

Elements of music

passages in the middle of Victoria's motet contrast with the imitative counterpoint heard at the beginning and the end). Complete verse anthems are both unified and varied by alternations of sections for solo and choral voices.

8.6.3 Secular music of the renaissance

The ***frottola***, a simple **part song** that was popular in Italy in the late fifteenth and early sixteenth centuries, was the precursor of the madrigal. Because they make use of a limited harmonic vocabulary with obvious cadences and dancing rhythms, frottolas sound remarkably modern compared with contemporary church music. A30 is typical of the genre. It occurs in a printed collection published by Andrea Antico (c.1480–c.1539) in 1517, but it is not certain that he himself wrote either the words or the music. It is dominated by three major chords (C, F and G) which, to modern ears, define the tonality of C major (in which key they are primary triads). The chord of A minor (VI in C major) is heard only twice (on the last beat of bars 3 and 5), the chord of D major (bar 7) only once. All of the chords are in root position with the exception of the two first inversions identified by the figure 6. The only dissonances are the decorative passing notes (pn), accented passing notes (apn), escape notes (en) and cadential suspensions (figured '4–3'). Three of the four cadences correspond with tonal practice: imperfect (IV–V) in bar 2 and perfect (V–I) in bars 4 and 11 (though, in common with contemporary church music, the final chord lacks a 3rd). The only cadence that indicates the early date of this frottola is the one in bar 7 (twenty-first-century ears expect a chord of G major after the 4–3 suspension on the chord of D major). The repetitive dance rhythm (an anacrusis of three crotchet beats followed by an on-beat figure of two crotchets at the start of every phrase) was one of a number of common rhythmic patterns that characterised the genre. Finally, in common with a majority of frottolas, *Non resta in questa valle* is predominantly homophonic, with a largely conjunct melody in the treble and a strongly functional bass leaping perfect 4ths and 5ths.

The term **chanson** can refer to French songs or songs in French styles from the courtly **ballade** of the twelfth century (A12) through to ***mélodies*** of the nineteenth and twentieth centuries. In the renaissance it referred to polyphonic settings of French poetry that was not in one of the *formes fixes*. Among others Clément Janequin (c.1485–1558) was celebrated for his programmatic chansons, of which *La Bataille de Marignan* is one of the most famous. In A31 the sounds of battle coming from every side are suggested by martial motifs exchanged antiphonally between pairs of upper and lower voices. Generally speaking the style of the *chanson* was simpler, more homophonic and more tonal than contemporary sacred styles. Dance-like rhythms, often including repeated notes, contrast strongly with the sinuous contrapuntal melodic lines of contemporary sacred music (such as those shown in A28–A29). All of these stylistic features are evident even in such a short extract from *La Bataille*.

Several renaissance instrumental genres grew directly from the vocal music of the time. This was particularly true of the *chanson* and related dance forms. A32 is a **pavan** printed by Moderne in a collection of dances dating from the first half of the sixteenth century. A comparison of A31 and A32 will show that this dance is really nothing more than a fairly free instrumental arrangement of Janequin's famous chanson. The pavan was a courtly dance of the sixteenth and early seventeenth centuries in duple time (notated here in *alla breve* or $\frac{2}{2}$ time) which was often followed by a triple-time dance such as the **galliard** (A35). The instrumentation of renaissance music was largely determined by the setting in which it was performed. Soft-toned strings and flutes of various types were used for indoor performances, while the penetrating reedy sound of instruments such as shawms (used in this recording) were reserved for open-air performances.

The galliard (A35) is a sixteenth-century courtly dance in lively triple time that is characterised by dotted rhythms (like those in the drum part in every even-numbered bar) and a homophonic texture. It was often coupled with the pavan (A34).

The sixteenth-century French **basse dance** was performed with slow gliding steps. Most were in triple time, but some were in moderate duple time (the underlying beat in A36 is a minim).

Apart from dances there were several sixteenth-century instrumental genres which were intended for the delectation of the performer alone or a few connoisseurs. The anonymous *Guardame las vacas* (A34) is a set of *diferencias* (**variations**) for *vihuela de mano* (a plucked string instrument of the viol family). Variation forms were widely cultivated in renaissance Spain. This set is based on the **romanesca**, a nine-note bass melody that was used as a foundation for variations throughout sixteenth-century Europe. Its emphasis on the tonic and dominant of a major key followed by a move to the relative minor largely determines the harmonic progression. The romanesca bass is repeated for each variation with ever more inventive figuration above it. A34 shows just two variations. In the second the pitches of the romanesca are retained but they are decorated with passing notes.

The Italian **madrigal** was a genre which, in the early sixteenth century, was similar in style to the French *chanson*. In the hands of one of the first and greatest madrigalists, Jacques Arcadelt (c.1505–68), it could be equally homophonic and tonal, but modal inflections and occasional passages of imitative counterpoint were introduced, not only in the interests of contrast, but also as a means of discreet **word-painting**. In his justly famous *Il bianco e dolce cigno* (A33) the modal F-major chord in bars 6–7 is a musical illustration of 'io piangendo' (I weep), while the imitation in bars 23–25 reflects the 'thousand deaths' of the punning words in this passage.

After the publication of *Musica Transalpina* in 1588 the madrigal enjoyed a brief but brilliant flowering in England. One of the most familiar varieties of this genre, the **ballett**, is characterised by its fa-la-la refrains. A59 is a three-voice ballett by Thomas Morley (c.1557–1602). The style is dance-like (with an obvious hemiola in bars 25–27), homophonic and tonal (but with a few characteristic modal inflexions, such as the triad on the flattened seventh degree in bar 23).

In the late sixteenth century the Italian **ricercar** was the instrumental equivalent of the polyphonic motet and the progenitor of the baroque fugue. Among the most important exponents of this genre was Andrea Gabrieli (c.1510–86). A56 and A57 show that the influence of plainsong was still in evidence in late sixteenth-century Venice. The 'searching out'

Elements of music

implied by the name of the genre is evident in Gabrieli's imitative treatment of the first phrase of the plainsong hymn (A in bars 1–6 and 10–17).

At the end of the sixteenth century the Italian **canzona** was an instrumental genre which stood on the cusp of renaissance and baroque styles. It originated as a transcription of the French chanson (as in A31 and A32), but it soon became an independent genre, only its name ('canzona' means a song) revealing its parentage. On the one hand it could take the form of a modest multi-sectional keyboard piece. On the other it could be a large-scale ensemble piece that was the instrumental equivalent of contemporary sacred **polychoral compositions**. In this manifestation it was intended to be performed as processional music in great churches. This is the case with Giovanni Gabrieli's *Canzona noni toni a 12* (A58). Giovanni (c.1554–1612) was the the nephew of Andrea (A57) and, like him, organist at St Mark's in Venice. It is probable that the three instrumental choirs required for the performance of A58 would have been distributed around the four balconies that surround the central space of the basilica. The style varies from the homophonic antiphonal exchanges at the start to the overlapped points of imitation involving all twelve parts in bars 8–19.

8.7 Baroque era (c.1600–1750)

There is good reason for dating the baroque era from the year 1600, for it was then that the theorist Giovanni Artusi wrote an essay entitled *L'Artusi, overo delle imperfettioni della moderna musica* (*Artusi, or the Imperfections of Modern Music*). In it he brought to a head an argument that had been raging for some years about the relative merits of sixteenth-century polyphony and the new style embodied in the secular music of composers such as Claudio Monteverdi (1567–1643). This, and other polemical essays of the period, gave rise to the terms ***stile moderno*** (the new secular style) and ***stile antico*** (the old sacred style), and their rough equivalents, the ***prima prattica*** and ***seconda prattica*** (the first and second practices). As with all generalisations about musical style-periods there was, however, no clean break with the past. From the very start of the baroque era composers, including Monteverdi, continued to write music in the old sacred style alongside music in the new secular style. Nor did the term baroque come into common usage until the late eighteenth century (when it was used pejoratively of those manifestations of the art which, in the age of the Enlightenment, were considered to be grandiose, ornate and even bizarre).

8.7.1 Baroque opera and song

The impetus for change came from a desire to forge a new dramatic style of vocal music that would allow the words to be heard clearly and that could represent the meaning of the text better than the old polyphonic style. The result was **monody**, a style of early seventeenth-century Italian accompanied solo song that was radically different from the music of the *prima prattica* (the profundity of the gulf that separates them may be judged by comparing A52 with A62–A63). Monodic music divides into two chief classes. The first was known as the ***stile rappresentativo*** (representative style) in early seventeenth-century Italy. This is another term dating from 1600 (it first appeared in print on the title page of Caccini's opera *Euridice* which was published in that same year). It was embodied in

8: Style, genre and historical context

recitative (A62 and A63) a type of heightened speech in which a soloist declaims Italian verse or prose at the speed of spoken dialogue in rhythms corresponding to the natural rhythms of spoken language. The short phrases of the melodic line reflect the changing emotions of the singers as they interact in the drama. They are accompanied by unobtrusive **continuo** instruments playing the written bass part together with improvised chordal filling provided by plucked strings or keyboard instruments (or both).

The second type of monody was the **aria**, a self-contained song that could appear in the context of an opera, cantata or oratorio, or as a completely independent piece. The printed music was often very simple (A65), but seventeenth-century performance practice allowed virtuoso singers to embellish the melody with ornate decorations such as those shown in A66 (written out by Monteverdi himself). The aria only appeared when a pause in the unfolding drama allowed the singer to reflect on his predicament in a style of monody in which text and music were on a more equal footing.

In France and England the **air** was a genre which, like the Italian aria, could be an independent song (A75) or a part of an opera. The style was usually simpler than the contemporary Italian aria, though the dotted rhythms and angular melodic line of the air could be just as affecting as its Italian counterpart. Although the use of a **basso ostinato** was common in songs throughout Europe, Henry Purcell (1659–95) was justly famous for his masterful handling of the English version of it, the **ground bass**. In A75 this is the repeated four-bar bass melody of the theorbo part above which the soprano melody unfolds.

In early seventeenth-century opera the term **sinfonia** referred to a prelude or overture to an act, or an instrumental interlude within an act (A64). The genre was not associated with any specific form at this stage (though later operatic sinfonias were to become important in the development of baroque instrumental music). As with contemporary recitative the style was usually homophonic.

In the second half of the seventeenth century the **French overture** was a more extended instrumental composition which typically fell into two contrasted sections. The style of the first was largely homophonic with ceremonial dotted rhythms in a slow tempo, while the second was a fast, often fugal movement. Some French overtures ended with a brief return to the slow music of the first section. As A80 shows, this was a genre that was equally at home in Restoration England. This little French overture by Purcell exemplifies the stately dotted and double-dotted rhythms that were characteristic of the slow section, and it also illustrates the imitative texture of the following fast section.

8.7.2 Sacred music in the baroque era

The year 1600 is again significant in the early history of baroque music, for it was in this year that what was probably the first **oratorio** was performed in Rome. The genre was named after a reforming Catholic order known as the Congregation of the Oratory. The intention was to create a sacred equivalent of contemporary opera that could, usually through the medium of a vernacular libretto set to affective music, more directly impinge on the emotions than the formal Latin liturgy. Italian oratorios of the early seventeenth century are rarely performed nowadays, but the ***Christmas Story*** by Heinrich Schütz (1585–1672) was in a direct line of succession from these early examples of the genre. Like most oratorios the original title, *Historia der freuden- und gnadenreichen Geburth Gottes und Marien Sohnes, Jesu Christi* (*Story of the Joyful and Gracious Birth of Jesus Christ, Son of God and Mary*) gives little idea of what is to follow, but in its dramatic presentation of the Christmas story through recitatives, solos, ensembles and choruses it is more entitled to be classed as an oratorio than Bach's so-called *Christmas Oratorio* (which is really a collection of six cantatas).

Schütz was directly influenced by Monteverdi in his composition of recitatives (A68), particularly those in *Orfeo* (A62–A63). He used ***recitativo secco*** (dry recitative) to carry the biblical narration (in this case verse 15 from the second chapter of the Gospel according to St Luke). As in Monteverdi's recitatives, the Evangelist's melody follows the natural rhythms of the vernacular text, and it is supported by an unobtrusive continuo accompaniment (in this case a chamber organ).

From 1609 to 1612 Schütz studied under Giovanni Gabrieli in Venice. From him he learned the polychoral style illustrated by A58 and the new ***stile concertato***, a style which was to become a cornerstone of baroque music both in Italy, and, through Schütz's efforts, in Germany. It was based on the concept of the contrast and combination of differing ensembles of instruments and voices unified by a **basso continuo** (a continuous bass part played by any melodic bass instrument above which plucked string instruments or an organ supplied harmonic filling). Schütz's concertato style is illustrated by Intermedium III from his *Christmas Story* (A69), one of eight ensembles that punctuate the Evangelist's narration of the biblical account of the Nativity. The ***intermedium*** is like a dramatic tableau in which passages of direct speech are allotted to a soloist or vocal ensemble accompanied by one of a variety of instrumental groups, each appropriate to the scene described in the Gospel from which the text has been taken. Here a pair of recorders suggest shepherds' pipes. Their imitative counterpoint is extended by an obbligato bassoon part. After eight bars the ensemble is contrasted with a vocal trio whose imitative counterpoint suggests the image of the shepherds running after each other towards Bethlehem. Having contrasted the instrumental ensemble with the vocal ensemble Schütz combines them in the last three bars of the extract. The three-part instrumental counterpoint is both unified and contrasted with the three-part vocal counterpoint by the composer's inversion of the original motif (bar 1) in the section beginning at bar 9. This fusion of Italianate concertato style with rigorous Teutonic contrapuntal devices was to be a hallmark of German style throughout the remainder of the baroque era and beyond.

Schütz's settings of Gospel texts about the trial and crucifixion of Christ are quite unlike his oratorios. The Evangelist's narrative and the words of the principal characters are declaimed in unaccompanied mock-plainsong, while the *turbae* (the words of the crowds) are sung *a cappella* by a four-voice chorus: there are no Italian elements such as arias or recitatives with continuo accompaniments. More closely related to the oratorio, and more typical of German music in the late baroque are the Passions by Johann Sebastian Bach (1685–1750). The commonly used term **Passion** is taken

8: Style, genre and historical context

from the Latin titles of such works, for example *Passio secundum Joannem* (*The Passion According to John*). Many of the recitatives in Bach's *St John Passion* are as simple as that shown in A68, but B4 shows how dramatic they can be. In the simple secco recitative at the opening the narrator or Evangelist (St John) leaps to the highest note of his range as he relates how the crowd cry out for Barabbas. The crowd's vivid *turba* dramatically interrupts the Evangelist's narration. When he resumes he enters on the same high note as he reveals that Barabbas was a murderer. Finally the lashing rhythms of the extended melisma (bars 8–10) bring the brutal scourging of Jesus to life in a way that words alone cannot achieve. In order to highlight particularly important words, especially direct speech, the continuo group were sometimes joined by other instruments in a style of recitative known as **recitativo accompagnato** or **recitativo stromentato** (accompanied recitative and instrumental recitative respectively). In B16 the Evangelist's reported speech is accompanied by a continuo group consisting of just three instruments, but the direct speech of the angel is sung against a halo of upper strings.

The **cantata**, another early seventeenth-century Italian invention, reached a peak of perfection in early eighteenth-century Germany. In its sacred form it was, in effect, a small-scale oratorio consisting of any combination of recitatives, arias, vocal ensembles and choruses. In the Lutheran cantata **chorales** were added, either as relatively simple four-voice harmonisations of chorale melodies that were often rhythmically simplified versions of pre-existent melodies, or as cantus firmi in instrumental concerto-style movements. B6 shows the evolution of the first type. Luther's original chorale melody of 1529 is represented by its first two phrases (bars 1–6), while bars 6–10 show the same two phrases in their simplified eighteenth-century form. Phrases C, D, E and F are shown with cadences from Bach's harmonisations of the chorale melody, while the last phrase is shown completely harmonised as it appears at the end of Cantata No. 80.

The second type of chorus is exemplified by the extract in B8. This, the fifth movement of Cantata No. 80, is a perfect example of Bach's fusion of Italian and German styles. It takes the form of an orchestral **concerto** movement against which the choir sings the third verse of the chorale as a cantus firmus. The degree of integration of the two styles is evident in the first two bars of the opening **ritornello** in which Bach fashions his first instrumental motif from the first phrase of the chorale melody (as shown by the extra stave beneath the first two bars). The instruments pursue their own purely musical logic throughout the movement. Against this orchestral counterpoint the chorale melody, broken up into its constituent phrases, is superimposed in stark octaves (bars 13–17). The scoring is typically baroque in its contrast and combination of two homogenous choirs of instruments (double-reed woodwind and upper strings), all underpinned by the ubiquitous continuo group.

The **chorale prelude** or **organ chorale** was cultivated in northern Europe from the beginning of the seventeenth century. It developed from the combination of English variation techniques with chorale melodies. The chorale fantasias of the Dutch Calvinist composer Jan Pieterszoon Sweelinck (1562–1621) consist of several variations on a chorale melody that appears in long notes surrounded by independent contrapuntal parts.

Elements of music

In his youth Bach wrote three sets of chorale variations, but by this time the chorale prelude had achieved independence as a short organ composition based on a chorale melody that was intended to be performed immediately before a congregational rendition of the same melody. Several different types of chorale prelude were developed including the cantus firmus chorale in which the complete chorale melody is combined with independent contrapuntal parts. In his Chorale Prelude BWV 608 (A94) Bach's cantus firmus is the familiar carol *In dulci jubilo* (A91). The whole of this melody, with some very slight ornamentation, appears as a canon between manuals and pedals (A92). Meanwhile two independent melodic lines form another canon (A93). The complete chorale prelude is recorded on A94.

The third movement of Bach's Cantata No. 80 is a secco recitative running directly into an **arioso** (B7, bars 7–16), the latter a vocal style that emerged in the early seventeenth century. It is halfway between the declamatory style of recitative and the song-like style of the aria. This particular arioso features most of the common elements of the style. It grows seamlessly out of a recitative, but is more lyrical. Clear quadruple metre is established after the speech rhythms of the recitative. The text is repeated in a melodic sequence. Expressive melismas focus attention on melody as well as text. The continuo bass line is itself melodic, and the harmonies change more frequently and move with a greater sense of purely musical purpose than they do in many recitatives. By the end of the baroque era the balance between words and music had tipped even further in favour of the latter. This is evident in the evolution of arioso, which, beginning as a musical intensification of recitative, eventually became an independent movement distinguished from the aria only by its relative brevity and lack of repeats (B5).

The **da capo aria** is a solo vocal genre that gained its name from the instruction 'da capo al fine' (or just 'DC al fine') printed at the end of the second section. This directed the performers to repeat the first section, thus giving the aria an overall ternary form (ABA). Many of these arias were further unified by the repetition of phrases from an introductory instrumental passage known as a ritornello. In the aria by Johann Sebastian Bach (1685–1750) shown in B15 these 'little returns' frame the first section to form a structure which can be represented as rArBrAr (where r represents recurring phrases of the ritornello, and A and B the main vocal sections). The style of the aria is typical of the baroque era in that motifs heard in the opening ritornello are manipulated to form contrapuntal strands throughout the movement. Contrast between the two main sections is achieved by the use of contrasting but related keys (D major in bars 1–80 and minor keys in bars 81–108). This movement is an example of an **obbligato aria**, a baroque genre in which the most important melodic ideas are shared between one or more instruments and the singer. In this case the extremely taxing trumpet part is both contrasted and combined with the vocal melodies.

In the Roman Catholic Church settings of the Ordinary of the Mass continued to be written in the baroque era, some of them on a vast scale, but the perfect marriage of text and music achieved by composers such as Palestrina (A52) was never again equalled. Instead a relatively new type of music began to develop as soon as the organ had been accepted as a suitable instrument for use in church. This was the **organ Mass**, a genre that reached a peak of perfection in France during the reign of Louis XIV. The structure was based on the same principle as that used for centuries in antiphonal psalmody. In the organ Mass, plainsong is retained for certain phrases of the liturgical texts, but others are replaced by an organ solo called a **verset** (during which the celebrant would say the omitted words privately). Since direct or varied textual repetition is a feature of the Ordinary of the Mass, this makes more sense than is immediately apparent. For instance, the ninefold **Kyrie** was, after standardisation of the organ Mass in 1600, divided between plainchant and organ as shown below.

The ninefold Kyrie in an organ mass

Kyrie eleison – organ	Kyrie eleison – chant	Kyrie eleison – organ
Christe eleison – chant	Christe eleison – organ	Christe eleison – chant
Kyrie eleison – organ	Kyrie eleison – chant	Kyrie eleison – organ

---

In the same year it was decreed that two of the texts of the Proper of the Mass (the **Offertory** and **Communion**) could be replaced by an independent organ piece. Again this made perfectly good sense, since the focus of prayerful attention is on action, not words, at these points (during the Offertory the bread and wine are brought in procession to the altar, during the Communion the faithful receive the consecrated elements). A81 is an extract from the 'Offertoire sur les grands jeux' ('Offertory on Full Organ') from one of the greatest of French baroque organ Masses, François Couperin's *Messe pour les paroisses*. Although written specifically for parish churches Couperin adds that the music is intended for solemn feasts. This is reflected in the style of this slow, dissonant and extremely chromatic music. There is evidence that the ***sonata da chiesa*** (8.7.3) was similarly used as a replacement for plainsong graduals and communions.

8.7.3 Baroque suite

The **suite**, a collection of instrumental pieces in contrasting styles, grew from the paired **dances** of the renaissance (see 8.6.3). As more dances were added, so a basic core of dance types evolved, of which the **allemande**, **courante** (or its Italian relation, the **corrente**), **sarabande** and **gigue** (usually in that order) occurred most frequently. Additional dances were often added between the sarabande and gigue. If these are regarded as 'optional' numbers a popular order of dances represented by the acronym ACSOG emerges (Allemande–Courante–Sarabande–optional movements–Gigue). Finally these movements were sometimes prefaced by a prelude not in dance style. It could be in the style of a toccata (like A86 – though this prelude precedes a fugue, not a set of dances), or it could be in the style of a French overture (like A80 – though, again, this overture precedes an opera, not a dance suite). Confusingly some composers entitled an entire suite *Ouverture* when the first movement was a French overture. For example, the original title of Bach's four Orchestral Suites is *Vier Ouverturen*. This way of ordering a suite (Prelude–Allemande–

Elements of music

Courante–Sarabande–optional movements–Gigue) was favoured by Bach in his English Suites. But this scheme was not adopted by all composers (differing arrangements are noted below in the descriptions of each particular dance style). There was usually no effort to achieve unity across the movements of a suite other than the fact that the dances were usually all in the same key (though one or two dances might be in the parallel major or minor). In some cases (notably Bach's suites) it is probable that all of the dances were meant to be played in a single performance. In other cases (notably François Couperin's *ordres*) the great number of movements suggests that the performer was at liberty to treat the suite as a sort of anthology from which he could choose to play as few or as many items as were appropriate to particular circumstances. The most favoured form for each dance was a binary structure, but there were exceptions such as the French rondeau (A84). With few exceptions each movement of a baroque suite is based upon one or more motifs heard within the first bar or two. These are manipulated consistently throughout the movement, giving each dance a strong sense of unity.

The **allemande** is more of a style than a dance. It is usually in $\frac{4}{4}$ time, moderately slow in tempo, and with phrases characterised by an anacrusis of one or more semiquavers. The style is serious and the texture contrapuntal, usually with some imitative treatment of the most pervasive motifs. Rarely are these textures rigorous in term of the number of contrapuntal parts. Rather are they broken up in the quasi-polyphony known as **style brisé** (very much in evidence in B17 in which the texture varies between one and four real parts). This allemande by Jean-Philippe Rameau (1683–1764) is in rounded binary form with the first section (A) moving through a circle of 5ths to the dominant key of E minor. The second section (B in bar 18) returns to A minor in bar 29 and the movement ends with repeats of passages from the A section (this time all in the home key of A minor). As with most French baroque harpsichord music in slow tempi the melodic line is encrusted with a variety of **ornaments** (some of which are written out on the extra staves beneath bars 1–4). Equally French in style is the harpsichordist's consistent use of **notes inégales** (again written out on the extra stave below bar 1). Only in a few isolated passages (such as bars 22–23) are the semiquavers played evenly as *notes égales*.

The **corrente** was an Italian dance in lively triple time with characteristic scalic figures and a predominantly homophonic texture. The *corrente* shown in A67 is by the Roman composer Girolamo Frescobaldi (1583–1643) and comes from a collection of harpsichord pieces entitled *Toccate d'intavolatura di cimbalo et* [sic] *organo, partite di diverse arie, e correnti, balletti, ciaconne, passacagli* and so on. Clearly this is more like a menu than a suite. From it the performer is at liberty to select whatever he wants in any number of possible permutations. The result would be a **partita** (the Italian equivalent of a suite, though Frescobaldi's 'partite di diverse arie' are, confusingly, sets of variations). The simple, largely three-part texture is dominated by a melodic line that sometimes betrays its relatively early date by its modality. It divides into the usual two sections of binary form, but the first section (bars 1–10) finishes in the tonic key, and only at two points are there brief references to other keys (bars 5–6 and 15–16).

The French **sarabande** was a stately slow dance in triple time with a

8: Style, genre and historical context

notable accent on the second beat of the bar (frequently emphasised by a dotted rhythm). In its mature baroque form it fell into regular four- or eight-bar phrases. All of these features are evident in the first section of a binary-form sarabande shown in A88.

Composers could choose from scores of dance styles for the 'optional' movements of the suite. These tended to be shorter, simpler, and more elegantly French in style than the serious allemande and sarabande. The textures were either homophonic or in two parts, with the upper voice more melodic than the lower. The phrasing was usually periodic – four- or eight-bar antecedents answered by four- or eight-bar consequents. In all of these ways these **Galanterien** (as Bach called them) were harbingers of the galant style of the middle and late eighteenth century.

The **bourrée** was a fast French dance in duple metre with periodic phrases beginning on the fourth crotchet of the bar and dactylic rhythms (quaver–quaver–crotchet) throughout. The bourrée by Johann Sebastian Bach (1685–1750) shown in A89 begins with two balanced four-bar phrases, the first ending with a perfect cadence in the tonic, the second modulating to the relative major. In the longer B section (bars 8–24) similar cadences define the four four-bar phrases which pass through related minor keys before returning to the tonic.

The **gavotte** was a moderate to fast French dance also in duple metre but with anacrustic phrases beginning at the half-bar. Its binary-form theme was often followed by a set of variations like those shown in B18. In this example only the first three bars of the theme and Variations 1 and 3 are shown, but track B18 contains more complete versions (like that shown for Variation 5).

Dances from other countries were sometimes included among the 'optional' movements. The **siciliana** by George Frideric Handel (1685–1759) shown in B19 is typical of this pastoral Italian dance in compound time. It often appeared in sonatas and concertos as well as the suite (in which it sometimes replaced the sarabande as the main slow movement).

The last movement of the suite was usually a **gigue**, a lively dance in compound metre. The most common time signatures were $\frac{3}{8}$, $\frac{6}{8}$ and $\frac{12}{8}$, and, although some gigues are notated in $\frac{3}{4}$ time, they are played at a speed at which a dotted minim is heard as the beat. Thus the aural effect is exactly the same as that of a gigue notated in compound time. The gigue often proclaims its rustic origins by a drone bass (suggesting bagpipes). Two drones, one on a G, the other on a D can be heard in bars 25–40 of A90 (which shows just the first part of Bach's binary-form dance). Gigues for keyboard were often fugal in style. The last movement of Bach's Partita, BWV 829 shows how a gigue in binary form can be combined with a double fugue. B10 shows the fugal exposition in the first eight bars, B11 shows a second fugal exposition in the second half of the binary structure, and B12 shows how Bach combines of the two subjects towards the end of the movement.

Not all suites or partitas ended with a gigue. Bach's monumental **Chaconne** (A95–A98) is the last movement of his second partita for unaccompanied violin. The theme (bars 0–4) has all of the hallmarks of sarabande style. It is in slow triple time with obvious second-beat accents and dotted rhythms. But there the similarity between the two types of dance ends, for instead of following the binary-form structure of more

Elements of music

common suite movements the chaconne consists of a set of continuous variations on a harmonic progression heard at the start. In this particular chaconne the theme is four bars long and there are a total of 64 variations (identified by numbers in boxes in A95–A98). Since this is such a lengthy set of variations Bach modifies his harmonic progression to some extent in each varation. In the first 16 bars Roman numerals beneath the harmonic reduction on the extra stave show where Bach changes his initial harmonic progression (where there are no numerals there are no changes). But the chief means of variation is stylistic change. In Variations 2–5 sarabande style gives way to a different sort of dotted rhythm reminiscent of the French overture (A80, bars 1–12). This in turn gives way to the smoothly flowing cantilena of Variation 6 and the semiquaver figuration of the next variation. Variation 23 (A96) is a virtuoso display of arpeggio figuration which contrasts strongly with the major mode and the return to sarabande rhythms in Variation 33 (A97). Finally virtuosic figuration builds through Variations 57–61 culminating in the demisemiquaver scales to the end of A98 (just after this point the theme returns in its original form). The whole partita consists of an allemande, a courante, the sarabande shown in A88, a gigue, and finally the Chaconne itself. By the time Bach wrote this music the constituent dances of the suite had become stylistic representations of dance music rather than music for dancing. That being so it should come as no surprise that style (sarabande) and form (binary) were no longer necessarily yoked together.

8.7.4 Baroque sonata

The **trio sonata** was a multi-movement chamber composition unique to the baroque era. It was written for two melody instruments (most often violins or flutes) and a continuo group (usually comprising a cello or bassoon and harpsichord, organ or plucked string instruments such as the theorbo). The genre earned its generic title 'sonata a tre' from the fact that it is notated on three staves, one each for the melody instruments and a figured bass part for the continuo instruments. The texture of this sort of music is sometimes described as polarised because of the large gap between the two high melody instruments and the much lower range of the instrument playing the bass part.

There were two types of trio sonata. The *sonata da chiesa* was intended for use in church, possibly as a substitute for a plainsong Offertory or Communion. By the end of the seventeenth century it was most commonly in four movements (slow–fast–slow–fast), though there were many exceptions to prove the rule. The style was usually serious and the texture often contrapuntal. When a particular continuo instrument is specified it is usually the organ. The *sonata da camera* was intended for domestic performance. It is distinguished from the *sonata da chiesa* by having several dance movements (whether so designated or not). As such this type of trio sonata is a close relative of the baroque suite. This generalisation is illustrated by the twelve *Sonate da camera a tre* Op. 2 of Arcangelo Corelli (1653–1713), which contain eight preludes, eleven allemandes, four *correnti*, four sarabandes and seven gigues, thus covering all of the most common dances of the contemporary suite. Matters became less clear-cut in his Op. 3 sonatas. They are entitled *Sonate da chiesa*, but the styles and forms of some movements make them indistinguishable

8: Style, genre and historical context

from the dances of his *Sonate da camera* Op. 4. This is true of the last movement of the second sonata of his Op. 3 (A74). Despite specifying an organ for the continuo group, this movement is in every other respect typical of the gigues which are so often the final movements of baroque dance suites and church sonatas. Like the gigue at the end of Bach's Partita BWV 829 (B10–B12) it is in binary form, in compound time, and the texture is fugal. It has one other feature of many contemporary gigues – the beginning of the second section (bars 20–24) is based on an inversion of the subject heard in the first two bars. Thus do composers confound the generalisations of unwary musical historians.

8.7.5 Concerto grosso

The principles of contrast and combination of disparate ensembles in early seventeenth-century concertato style are evident later on in the baroque era in the concerto grosso (or, as Handel anglicised the term, the grand concerto). Although born in Germany, he was for many years a naturalised English citizen. George Frideric Handel (1685–1759) continued to write in the Italian style he had learned as a young man for the rest of his life. In particular he followed in the footsteps of Corelli, whose own concerti grossi were built upon the contrasting textures of a solo trio-sonata combination of two violins and continuo (see 8.7.4), and a fuller string band including viola and double bass. The thematic material of these two groups (known as the **concertino** and **ripieno**) was the same, the groups being differentiated only by dynamics (soft and loud) and texture (three as opposed to four parts). There is no set number of movements in a Handelian concerto grosso, nor are there set styles (some of them consist entirely of abstract music while others include dance movements). The concerto from which B19 is taken has five movements and includes an allemande as well as this siciliana. Indeed, if it were not for the contrasting textures of the concertino and ripieno, it would be difficult to distinguish this concerto from an orchestral suite.

8.7.6 Baroque prelude, fugue and toccata

The **fugue** as an independent movement was often prefaced by a **prelude**. A87 shows part of the Prelude in C minor from Book 1 of *The Well-Tempered Clavier* by Johann Sebastian Bach (1685–1750), while B14 shows the whole of the Fugue in C minor from Book 2 of the same collection of preludes and fugues. The preludes are usually improvisatory in style: in A87 Bach consistently manipulates the motif heard in the first two beats in a way which many baroque performers could play extempore. The fugue, on the other hand, was the most consistently contrapuntal genre of the period. It was based on a memorable theme known as a subject (for instance, B9 is easy to remember because of its wedge shape). Most, if not all of the fugue, consisted of contrapuntal manipulations of the subject and other motifs heard in the fugal exposition. It must not be thought that B14 represents a blueprint for all fugues. In fact the only generalisation about the structure of a fugue is that it will begin with some form of fugal exposition such as that described above. What happens thereafter is entirely at the discretion of the composer. Even the fugal exposition itself can be altered by introducing two subjects simultaneously (B13), and there can be two fugal subjects, each with its own fugal exposition

Elements of music

(B10–B12). Both of these types are known as **double fugues** (triple fugues and even quadruple fugues are not unknown, but they are very rare indeed).

The fugal exposition shown in B13 is the start of a very short fugue known as a *fughetta* (in this case a self-contained section heard in the context of a substantial harpsichord piece which Bach called a toccata). The whole work consists of an improvisatory prelude, the *fughetta*, another improvisatory section marked 'Adagio', and a final complete fugue for three voices. The **toccata** was a genre designed to show off both the virtuosity of the performer and the scope of the instrument. In Bach's hands the toccata, without its fugal sections, became an independent movement of equal or greater stature than the prelude. This is the case in the great toccata which dwarfs the ensuing double fugue in the Toccata and Fugue in F, BWV 540 (A86).

8.7.7 Baroque variations

In a sense most baroque instrumental music is based upon variation principles since it is unusual to find contrasting themes within a movement. Instead the music most often consists of continuous manipulation of a limited number of motifs heard in the first few bars. The basic principle underlying sets of variations is the retention of one element of the theme (to ensure unity) while other elements are modified or replaced with new material. In the case of the ground or basso ostinato a memorable, short bass melody is repeated throughout all or most of the piece while the melody (and sometimes the harmony) constantly changes. The extract from an air by Henry Purcell (1659–95) shown in A75 is based on a four-bar ground.

B18 is taken from a gavotte with *doubles* (variations) by George Frideric Handel (1685–1759). It illustrates the principles of figural variation or **divisions**. In this type of variation technique the bare bones of the original melody (in this case an ascending and descending scale of G major) are retained, but are overlaid with ever-increasing layers of ornamentation which progressively divide each note of the original theme into shorter and shorter note-values.

Although the **chaconne** and **passacaglia** began life as distinct genres, by the eighteenth century the chaconne had lost its identity as a dance, the passacaglia was no longer a type of formulaic ritornello, and the styles of both had converged to a point where it becomes impossible to tell them apart. Both depend on the retention of the harmonic progression of the theme while all other elements (rhythm, melody, texture and so on) can be changed. In his Chaconne in D minor (A95–A98) Johann Sebastian Bach (1685–1750) retains the same basic four-bar harmonic progression throughout all 256 bars. For fuller discussion of this chaconne see the last paragraph of 8.7.3.

This example of continuous variation contrasts with Bach's last great essay in the genre, the *Goldberg Variations* (B1 and B2). Here the theme is a complete binary-form aria, and each of the thirty variations is a strongly characterised independent movement following the same or a very similar harmonic and structural scheme as the aria. The last variation is a **quodlibet** in which Bach combines these constant elements with a contrapuntal treatment of a number of popular folk tunes.

8: Style, genre and historical context

8.8 Eighteenth-century pre-classical styles

During the eighteenth century there were two remarkable flowerings of musical art. In the first half of the century Bach and Handel summed up the achievements of baroque music. In the second half Haydn and Mozart brought Viennese classical music to a peak of perfection. Yet there were common stylistic elements in some of the works of all four composers and their lesser contemporaries. These styles, which often shelter under the epithet 'pre-classical', are the subject of this section.

8.8.1 French rococo style (c.1700–c.1760)

This is one of a number of styles that form bridges between monumental baroque art and the classicism of late eighteenth-century Viennese music. The term, as usual, derives from the visual arts where it denotes the decorative styles of painters such as Antoine Watteau, whose elegantly dressed aristocrats disport themselves in arcadian surroundings where it never rains and never a real peasant is seen. The parallels between the visual arts and music have probably never been so close as they were in France in the period encompassed by the lives of François Couperin le Grand (1668–1733) and Jean-Philippe Rameau (1683–1764). Among the thousands of pieces that have survived by composers of this period there are some that are as profound and monumental as the works of contemporary German masters. For instance Couperin's majestic Passacaille in B minor from his eighth *Ordre* (1717) does not suffer from a comparison with Bach's Chaconne in D minor (A95–A98). Nor is Rameau's Allemande from his second book of harpsichord pieces (B17) any less serious than an allemande by Bach. But the rondeau by Elisabeth Jacquet de la Guerre (1666–1729) in A84 is, in both form and style, more typical of rococo elegance. It is characterised by thin textures, extensive ornamentation of the melody and a clear tonal scheme that helps clarify the ABACAA structure of the whole rondeau. The same observations apply with equal force to the Forlane by Couperin shown in C36.

8.8.2 Galant style (c.1730–c.1782)

The ***style galant*** is seen by some historians to encompass French rococo music. There is some justification for this since the archetypical rococo artist, Antoine Watteau, entitled one of his paintings *Fêtes galantes*. But the first manifestations of the *galanter Stil* are to be found in the *galanteries* of the early eighteenth-century suite. ***Galanterien*** (the German word for ***galanteries***) include those 'optional' movements of the suite which are characterised by simple triadic, scalic and sequential melodies, thin two-part or homophonic textures, and simple tonic–dominant harmony. The dance which most perfectly encapsulates this style is the **minuet**, which Rousseau described as being 'elegant and nobly simple'. This was the only dance of the baroque suite to survive as a movement in new eighteenth-century genres such as the symphony and sonata. The minuet from the Sonata No. 26 by Joseph Haydn (1732–1809) shown in B25 reveals the fact that galant style survived well into the second half of the eighteenth century. The melody begins by outlining the notes of the dominant triad (x). This is followed by a scalic ascent (y) that is immediately repeated in sequence (z). Similar melodic devices can be found in the remainder of Haydn's simple diatonic melody. The thin two-part texture is sometimes

Elements of music

padded out with completely subservient inner parts to form three- or four-note chords. Of the thirteen chords heard in the first section (bars 1–10) all but two are tonic or dominant chords and none of them includes any chromatic notes. The fact that the second section (bars 11–20) is a retrograde version of the first section is no indication of serious intent. Rather is it an example of that elegantly sophisticated galant art which conceals art, and any connoisseur of the Age of Enlightenment who recognised what was going on would have congratulated Haydn on his wit rather than his scholarship.

8.8.3   Cult of sentiment (c.1740–c.1788)

It is almost impossible to translate into English the meaning of the German noun *Empfindsamkeit*. Sensitivity, sensibility and even sentimentality get near the mark if one thinks of how these related words were used by authors of the English Enlightenment. The very titles of Laurence Sterne's *A Sentimental Journey* and Jane Austen's *Sense and Sensibility* give a clue to the meaning of *Empfindsamkeit*. Sterne's assertion that sensibility is a 'source inexhausted of all that's precious in our joys, or costly in our sorrows' gets very close to the passion of the *empfindsamer Stil*, while Dr Johnson's observation that 'the happiest conversation [is that] where there is no competition, no vanity, but a calm quiet interchange of sentiments' reflects the more decorous aspect of the cult of sentiment. Carl Philipp Emanuel Bach (1714–88) could write music in the fashionable galant idiom, but he is chiefly remembered for those keyboard pieces which seem like harbingers of romanticism. In his unbarred **fantasias** (B20) he positively encourages the performer to indulge in passionate sentiment on the one hand (letter A) and delicate sensibility on the other (letter B). In purely musical terms Bach achieves these effects by the use of pathetic suspensions over ambiguous diminished-7th chords (the minim tied to a quaver above the first chord of the extract is a suspension that does not achieve resolution until the minim D♯). Also notable are the use of a sort of vibrato called a *Bebung* (indicated by the dots over the second minim of the extract), the sudden dynamic changes, the equally sudden changes of tonality (G minor at letter B and F minor after the key signature) and the varied textures (ranging from five-part chords after the key signature to the thinnest possible texture at the end of the extract). Beethoven himself admitted his indebtedness to C. P. E. Bach, a debt which is only too clear when one compares Bach's clavichord fantasias with the romantic quasi-recitative passages in Beethoven's middle- and late-period piano sonatas.

8.8.4   Storm and stress (c.1765–c.1775)

For once it seems that, in the second half of the eighteenth century, music was ahead of the other arts, for it was in the late 1760s and early 1770s that Haydn and several of his contemporaries wrote a series of instrumental works in minor keys, the tempestuous style of which prefigured the ***Sturm und Drang*** movement of authors such as Goethe and Schiller. There are historians who would limit the use of the expression to little-known German melodramas of the 1770s, but they are too late – the term has stuck to these earlier instrumental works and been validated by eminent scholars such H. C. Robbins Landon. Comparing the

8: Style, genre and historical context

literary and musical manifestations of the *Sturm und Drang* movement he writes, 'It will be seen that the same demonic strain runs through Austrian music, beginning with Haydn and his school c.1766, finding a superb flowering in the 'dark' side of Mozart and reaching a culmination in Beethoven'. 'Demonic' is the right adjective for the last movement of the *Trauersinfonie* ('Mourning Symphony') by Joseph Haydn (1732–1809) shown in B21. Passionate intensity is palpable within the first few bars. At the fastest possible tempo, breathless, staccato, two-bar phrases are delivered loudly in bare octaves, then repeated quietly in spectral two-part counterpoint (bars 12–18), then again loudly and in minatory tones by the full orchestra (bars 18–28). The complex canonic counterpoint of bars 28–42 winds the tension up still further until all of the violins in unison resume the staccato style of the opening (bars 42–49), but this time with wildly leaping intervals as large as a 10th and even a 12th. This is followed by measured tremolandi (a symbol of warlike affection since Monteverdi's time) and *forzando* accents in bars 50–55. Despite the limited instrumentation (two oboes, two horns and strings) there is no other symphonic music that exceeds this finale in demonic intensity before 1808 (when Beethoven's fifth symphony was first performed).

8.9 Viennese classical styles (c.1770–c.1820)

Some historians reckon that classical styles emerged in the mid-eighteenth century, others that Viennese classicism began only in 1780. The year in which Beethoven was born, 1770, seems as good a year as any for the inception of classical styles since it includes Haydn's Op. 17 quartets, but excludes his earlier divertimenti. It includes all of Mozart's extant concertos and string quartets, but excludes his earliest galant-style instrumental works. Similarly, some historians maintain that the classical period extended to the death of Beethoven (1827) or Schubert (1828), but long before they died both composers had moved far away from classical ideals and the first indisputably romantic operas had been written in Germany. 1820 was the year in which Weber's *Der Freischütz* (B59 and B60) was first performed and it is a date that admits the inclusion of all of Beethoven's symphonies other than the ninth (a lodestar for the romantics) within the classical canon. This also allows the inclusion of all of Schubert's chamber music up to the tempestuous *Quartettsatz* of 1820, but it excludes the romantic quartet known as *Death and the Maiden*. Of course these suggestions beg the question, for the criteria by which works should be included in the classical canon have not been set out. To attempt this would require not a paragraph but a book. Suffice to say that classical composers gathered up the threads of the elegant galant style (8.8.2), the sensitivity of the *empfindsamer Stil* (8.8.3) and the turbulence of the *Sturm und Drang* movement (8.8.4) and wove them together to create musical styles which, in their balance of formal perfection and emotional content, have probably never since been excelled. Certainly romantic composers were always aware of the supreme achievements of Haydn, Mozart, Beethoven and Schubert, and they measured their own essays in classical genres against the yardsticks these four composers had laid down.

8.9.1 Classical chamber music

There is a wealth of chamber music genres written by classical composers, ranging from duo sonatas to octets, but by far the most important type was the **string quartet**. These were usually in four movements, often comprising an allegro, a slow movement, a minuet and trio and a fast finale. B27 shows the first section of the first movement of the Quartet Op. 42 by Joseph Haydn (1732–1809). This movement, like the first movements of most classical quartets, is in **sonata form**. The extract shows the exposition. Within these few bars many of the stylistic traits of mature classical style are evident. The first subject (bars 1–8) reminds us that just over a decade before the composition of this music Haydn had been writing his minor-key *Sturm und Drang* symphonies. It is in D minor and is heavily marked with dramatic *forzandi* (like the end of B21). But the first subject is a classically balanced eight-bar melody which dominates the homophonic accompaniment and ends with a typical galant/classical cadence formula (I_4^6–V–I in bars 7–8). In the transition (bars 9–12) the strings converse with each other in a sort of dialogue which Haydn called his 'new and special manner'. By 1785 the simple melody-dominated homophony of the galant style had given way to much subtler textures, such as that heard in the first part of the second subject (bars 13–21). In this passage the violins' imitative counterpoint is supported by a subservient cello playing the tonic and dominant of F major and a viola that provides harmonic filling. The 'new and special manner' is also evident in the imitative treatment of the motif from the first bar (bars 23–26). After another I_4^6–V^7–I cadence (bars 32–33) the serious mood of the first and second subjects is replaced by frivolous exchanges in the codetta (which ends with a feminine cadence – another classical harmonic cliché). Two elements unify this extract. Firstly, the two stable keys of the first subject (D minor) and second subject (F major) are clearly defined by simple tonic–dominant harmonic progressions. Secondly, all of the thematic materials are derived from the first eight bars of the movement (such **monothematic sonata-form** structures are hallmarks of Haydn's mature style).

The second movement of a classical string quartet often consisted of a **theme and variations**. Perhaps the most famous are those based on the melody which has come to be known as the 'Emperor's Hymn'. B32 shows the theme in the first violin with a simple homophonic accompaniment. In the first variation (B33) the second violin sings the same melody against the first violin's ornate counter-melody. In the second variation (B34) the cello has the melody. This is doubled (mostly in 3rds) on the second violin and combined with a new, syncopated violin counter-melody, while the viola provides a real bass for the two cadences. In the fourth variation (B35) the 'Emperor's Hymn' theme returns to the first violin while the lower parts provide a new homophonic accompaniment.

In other slow movements Haydn's chromatic harmony and rich textures prefigure romantic practice (B30 and B31). C. P. E. Bach's harmony was often just as chromatic (see 8.8.3 and B20), but there is an important distinction between the harmony of the *empfindsamer Stil* and Haydn's mature harmonic style. Whereas C. P. E. Bach's chromatic chords could lead anywhere (and presumably did when he was improvising in this style), Haydn's chromatic chords are a very important part of the structure of the music. In B30 Haydn uses just twenty chords to modulate from E major and to firmly establish the new key of B major. It is easy to move temporarily to the dominant (producing an effect like an imperfect cadence), but to give the new key equal standing with the old one it is necessary to destroy the listener's memory of the first key. This Haydn does by means of a massively scored German-6th chord in bar 8. This is the hinge on which the modulation turns, and it is with chromatic harmony of this sort that Haydn balances emotional content with carefully controlled classical tonal structures.

The third movement of an eighteenth-century string quartet was usually a **minuet and trio**. This grew out of the paired minuets of the baroque suite, in which the first minuet was repeated after the second minuet had been played. Similarly, although both the minuet and the trio of a classical string quartet were in binary form, the repetition of the minuet after the trio gave the movement an overall ternary structure: Minuet–Trio–Minuet. The rhythmic and metrical simplicity of some classical minuets made them suitable for dancing. This is true of the minuet by Wolfgang Amadeus Mozart (1756–91) shown in B41. But in other string quartets the minuet became a sophisticated stylisation of the original dance. This is evident in the minuet from Mozart's String Quartet in G, K387 (B38). Here the abrupt alternation of loud and soft notes comes close to destroying the stately triple metre of the dance, while the imitative treatment of the motif identified by the letter c is clearly intended for the delectation of connoiseurs, not dancers.

The last movement of a classical string quartet, like the finale of other classical genres, was most often another sonata-form movement or a **rondo** in a lighter style than the first movement.

8.9.2 Classical concerto

The classical concerto usually had three movements (fast–slow–fast). The first movement was typically in sonata form, often with two expositions, the first for orchestra alone, the second for soloist accompanied by the orchestra. The second movement could be in any one of a variety of forms – abbreviated sonata form, ternary form or a set of variations. The last movement was often in **sonata-rondo form**. B36 is a skeleton score of the whole finale from a trumpet concerto by Joseph Haydn (1732–1809). It begins with an orchestral exposition (bars 1–43) in which both first subject (A) and second subject (B) are heard in the tonic key of E♭ major. The solo exposition (bars 44–104) begins with the first subject (now played by the soloist) and this is followed by a much longer second subject group (B) which is now in the dominant key of B♭ major. Up to bar 119 the solo exposition follows the same course as the exposition of the first movement of Haydn's String Quartet Op. 42 (B27) discussed in the first paragraph of 8.9.1. In bars 121–122, however, the music modulates back to the tonic key of E♭ major and the first subject (A) returns. This leads to a development section (C) in which Haydn explores minor keys for the first time. As expected the recapitulation (bars 180–278) consists of the first subject (A) and second subject group (B) in the tonic key. A variant of the first subject (A1) returns at bar 237, and another (A2) appears in the coda (bars 279–294). There are two significant differences between the structure of this movement and the structure of most sonata-form movements. Firstly, the exposition proper is prefaced by an orchestral exposition. Secondly, the first subject (always in the tonic key) reappears between the exposition and development and at the end. In fact the first subject behaves exactly

Elements of music

like a refrain in a baroque rondo (A84). Thus the overall form of Haydn's finale can be represented by reference to the letters in the score as: ABACABA, a classically balanced synthesis of sonata form and rondo form.

The mature classical style of this finale can seamlessly accommodate the cheerful melody-dominated homophony of the first subject, the dialogue of bars 85–92, the double counterpoint of bars 157–161, the mock-serious chromatic tremolo of bars 265–269 and the boisterous tonic–dominant figurations of the closing bars.

8.9.3 Classical cassation, divertimento, notturno and serenade

Up to about 1770 composers used the title **divertimento** for a wide range of instrumental genres. Only after this time did they begin to differentiate between serious affairs such as the string quartet, and lighter works such as the divertimento. A comparison of the extract from the Op. 42 quartet by Joseph Haydn (1732–1809) shown in B27 with the first movement of the Divertimento KA229 (K439b) by Wolfgang Amadeus Mozart (1756–91) shown in B40 reveals how different they are (despite the fact that they were both written in 1785). The first is in a minor key; the second in F major. The first subject of the first contains a number of motifs which are manipulated and developed throughout the rest of the extract; the second contains long lyrical melodies. The first contains a good deal of imitative counterpoint; the second does not.

There is, however, hardly any difference between the style and form of this divertimento and works which Mozart called **cassations**, ***notturni*** and **serenades**. All of them are multi-movement works, perhaps containing one or two minuets and a march as well as a sonata-allegro, a slow movement and a rondo. They are all intended to be light-hearted instrumental entertainments, and are written in idioms that are nearer to the galant style than to the mature classical styles of the post-1770 concerto, quartet, sonata and symphony (though even in these works Mozart's dark side sometimes briefly emerges). His works of these types were scored for widely differing ensembles, ranging from full orchestra (the so-called 'Haffner' Serenade) to a trio of basset-horns (B40).

The first movement of B40 is a concise sonata-form structure of great clarity, and the first six bars immediately establish its light-hearted galant style. Only a few subtleties betray it as a work of Mozart's maturity: the sinuous chromatic bass in the first subject, and a similarly chromatic inner part in bar 28; the free contrapuntal inversion of the second subject (compare bars 26–33 with bars 34–41); the syncopated chromatic chords in the codetta (which delay the final tonic pedal of the exposition); the ambiguous chords at the end of the development (which, at the last moment, pull the recapitulation out of the hat like a conjuror's rabbit); and the extension of the chromatic chords (bars 110–117) – all of these are elements of Mozart's mature artistry.

8.9.4 Classical symphony

After 1770 most symphonies consisted of a fast sonata-form movement (similar in structure to B40), a slow movement (which might take the form of a theme and variations such as B32–B35), a minuet and trio (probably more elaborate in structure than B25) and a fast finale (which might be a light-hearted rondo like B36). The scope of the creativity of Joseph Haydn

(1732–1809) is evident when one compares the passionate *Sturm und Drang* style of his sparsely scored *Trauersinfonie* (B21) with the mature classical style of his *Oxford* Symphony (scored for flute, two each of oboes, bassoons, horns, trumpets and drums and the usual string band). The sonata-form structure begins with a periodically phrased first subject (B28). In the development the same theme becomes the subject of a learned fugato (appropriately, since the symphony was performed in Oxford when Haydn received an honorary doctorate there). The integration of counterpoint in both of these movements is a stylistic feature that separates the symphonies of the giants of the classical period from the elegant superficiality of the galant symphonies of composers such as J. C. Bach.

8.9.5 Classical sonata

There is a direct line of succession from the keyboard sonatas of Carl Philipp Emanuel Bach (1714–88), through the 62 keyboard sonatas by Joseph Haydn (1732–1809), to the early piano sonatas of Ludwig van Beethoven (1770–1827). From C. P. E. Bach's multi-faceted sonatas Haydn inherited both the *empfindsamer Stil* and the galant style. However Haydn's Op. 13, a set of six sonatas dedicated to his patron Prince Nicolaus Esterházy, are more diverse in style and form than his later, more famous sonatas. Only one of them contains all three movements commonly found in Bach's sonatas (Allegro–Adagio–Presto), four of them have only two movements, and the middle movement of the last sonata of the set is a minuet (B25). Although this movement can be played on a harpsichord, clavichord or fortepiano, this is not idiomatic keyboard writing. The explanation is that this movement is a transcription (done by Haydn himself) of the minuet in his Symphony No. 47 in G (written a year before the sonata was composed). The styles of the flanking movements of Sonata No. 26 are much more idiomatic, but the fact that Haydn could transfer a movement from a symphony to a keyboard sonata shows that, at this stage in his musical development, he did not see the need to develop this genre with as much enthusiasm as he lavished on his quartets and symphonies (it is significant that he called 16 of his sonatas 'divertimenti').

Twenty years later Beethoven wrote the first of his cycle of 32 piano sonatas. These are more varied in style and form than the sonatas of any other composer, having from two to five movements and including unusual movements such as a funeral march and a complete and very long fugue. B51–B54 are extracts from the exposition of the sonata-allegro with which Beethoven's Sonata in F Op. 10 No. 2 begins. Broken-chord figuration in B51 supports syncopated melodic fragments, while a syncopated melody dominates a chordal accompaniment in B52. At the start of the second subject (B53) another syncopated melody is accompanied by continuous semiquavers in the bass, and in the last extract (B54) detached chords alternate between the left and right hands (the printed music shows only the uppermost notes of these chords). So within the first 53 bars of the movement at least four different textures have been heard, all of them in idiomatic piano styles.

Beethoven is famous for the rumbustious **scherzos** (jokes) that he wrote as a replacement for the courtly minuet and trio. B55 (the first 24 bars of the scherzo from his *Pastoral* Sonata Op. 28) gives some idea of the style of these movements. It is very fast (Allegro vivace) and begins with

Elements of music

mysterious octaves answered by the simplest possible three-note triadic figures accompanied by equally simple staccato chords (I–IIb–V^7–I). The whole passage is then repeated in the dominant (bars 9–16). This elfin music is then interrupted by one of Beethoven's crude jokes – the quiet octaves unexpectedly become loud 3rds (each one marked *f* by the composer), answered by a return to the innocent little cadence formula. The phrase structure is as naïve as the harmonic progressions: three eight-bar phrases all divide in exactly the same way into two shorter phrases. Are these the country bumpkins of this *Pastoral S*onata?

The piano sonatas of Franz Schubert (1797–1828), like Beethoven's, span the end of the classical period and the beginning of the romantic era. Their connection with romanticism is evident when one compares the song-like lyricism of B56 and B75. They are both profoundly meditative in mood, with slowly changing harmonies featuring dominant dissonances that enrich the deep-hued texture (note especially the dominant major 13ths in the final cadences of both passages).

8.9.6 Classical opera

Opera buffa was born in the early eighteenth century when comic intermezzi between the acts of opera seria became independent of their host. The plots of the early eighteenth-century opera buffa concerned ordinary folk rather than figures from classical antiquity, and the music reflected this. Melodies were triadic or scalic and were short enough to be remembered after the opera was over. The texture was homophonic, often with Alberti figuration, and completely dominated by the melody. The harmony was simple, often staying on the tonic for several bars before briefly changing to chord V (possibly IV or I$^6_4$ as well) before the cadence that marked the end of each phrase of the melody. Wolfgang Amadeus Mozart (1756–91) contributed to both of these genres, notably *Idomeneo* (opera seria) and *Le nozze di Figaro* (opera buffa). Another operatic genre to which he contributed two masterpieces was the **Singspiel**, a sort of elaborate pantomime with spoken German dialogue, solo songs, ensembles and choruses in any of the current musical styles. Osmin's aria from *Die Entführung aus dem Serail* (*The Abduction from the Harem*) shown in B37 is typical of songs in buffo style which Mozart wrote for this opera. Songs in the style of an aria from an opera seria are found in his other great *Singspiel Die Zauberflöte* (*The Magic Flute*), notably the Queen of the Night's aria in Act 2 (B50). Here every vocal, orchestral and harmonic device is exploited to characterise the vindictive rage of the Queen. The vocal solo is often chromatic (bars 7–10), exploits extreme vocal ranges (bars 30–31) and includes virtuoso **coloratura** passages (bars 69–72). The wind band punctuates the vocal line with dramatic minor triads and discords (bars 2–6) while the string band contributes sudden dynamic changes (bars 1–11). The harmony includes an array of dissonant and chromatic chords, notably the Neapolitan 6th in bars 80–81 and the diminished 7ths in bars 93–94.

8.10 Nineteenth-century romantic music (c.1820–c.1900)

From about the third decade of the nineteenth century the tendency to allow music to express intense emotion at the expense of formal beauty is apparent in a high proportion of the works of a new generation of composers. This led to the transformation of old genres such as opera and

8: Style, genre and historical context

the symphony, and the establishment of new genres that were often inspired by romantic literature. In return music itself was apotheosised by contemporary writers, who viewed it as the highest manifestation of the human spirit because of its ability to stir the 'finer feelings' (and, one might add, the baser instincts) without recourse to concrete images. Romanticism, the seeds of which were planted in the terror which followed the French Revolution, was a movement of extremes, and this is apparent even in the purely musical genres of the nineteenth century. On the one hand there is the musical gigantism of operatic composers such as Richard Wagner (1813–83) and symphonists such as Anton Bruckner (1824–96). On the other hand there are the poetic fragments of song-writers such as Robert Schumann (1810–56) and pianist-composers such as Fryderyk Chopin (1810–49).

8.10.1 Romantic opera

Der Freischütz by Carl Maria von Weber (1786–1826) was completed in 1820. Although it is technically a **Singspiel** like Mozart's *Die Zauberflöte* (see 8.9.5), it can be viewed as the first romantic German opera that still retains a place in the modern repertoire. The overture (B59) is constructed out of music that appears in the opera itself. In fact the passage beginning at bar 25 (a *locus classicus* of romantic harmony and orchestration) appears at several points in the opera like a **leitmotif**. The most impressive return of this passage is in the **melodrama** at the end of Act 2 when the wicked Caspar summons the devil (in the shape of Samiel) in the Wolf's Glen (B60). The melodrama (spoken dialogue between, or superimposed on, short evocative passages of orchestral music) was not new (Beethoven used it in *Fidelio*), but what is new is the way music is used purely as a means to an end. B60 begins with the midnight bell which is followed by a **tritone** (A♮–E♭): the famous *diabolus in musica* that helps Caspar wake the devil, Samiel. In bar 5 a C♮ and G♭ is added to the tritone so that it becomes a chord of the diminished 7th (beloved of romantic composers because of its tonal ambiguity). The dark-hued scoring is just as revolutionary. In bar 5 two oboes at the bottom of their range are doubled by violins playing on their lowest strings. Similarly, clarinets in their chalumeau register are doubled by violas playing on their two lowest strings. The fourth note of the diminished-7th chord is supplied by the dull thud of pizzicato cellos and double basses with menacing soft strokes on a kettle drum. In the final bars string tremolos add urgency as the music builds to a fortissimo chord of C minor that coincides with the entrance not only of the devil but of three trombones (traditionally associated with the solemn rites of death).

In his early operas Richard Wagner (1813–83) began where Weber left off, but by the time he completed *Tristan und Isolde* in 1859 he had developed the genre into what he variously called the 'total artwork' and the 'artwork of the future'. In both cases his immodest claims are justified. He did his own research in medieval literature to arrive at the plot of the opera (a new historical awareness was one of the many strands of romanticism). He wrote his own libretto, and persuaded King Ludwig of Bavaria to part with large sums of money, which eventually enabled him to build his own theatre consecrated to 'holy German art' (meaning his own). But most importantly he developed a style based upon the deployment of

Elements of music

several distinctive **leitmotifs** in contrapuntal textures of great complexity. His technique of 'unending melody' integrated these motifs into long and extremely **chromatic** melodic strands which often verged on atonality (B68(i) shows how Wagner uses all twelve chromatic notes within the first seven bars of the prelude). Three leitmotifs can be identified in the first 18 bars. They are shown separately in B68(i) and B68(ii). The first is a rising minor 6th followed by a chromatic descent heard on cellos. The second begins with the last note of the first leitmotif. It consists of a rising four-note chromatic figure heard on an oboe then repeated on a clarinet. The third is the figure shown in B68(ii). It first appears on cellos in bars 17–18 (where it is identified by the letter z). From this leitmotif two smaller units can be abstracted (a and b) and it is through manipulations of these that Wagner constructs the long 'unending' chromatic melody of bars 17–24.

Wagner was a demigod in the pantheon of the New German School, a group of musicians who supported the progressive tendencies of composers such as Berlioz and Wagner. The foremost composer of this group was Franz Liszt (1811–86), and it has to be admitted that Wagner derived much benefit from studying Liszt's music (as B70 and B71 show). Of course this does nothing to detract from Wagner's pre-eminence among romantic composers (Machaut, Palestrina and Handel all borrowed freely from other sources in some of their greatest works). There are two important differences between these passages. Firstly, Wagner changes Liszt's D♮ (in the first chord) to a D♯. This not only creates a more biting dissonance, it changes a romantic commonplace (a chord of the diminished 7th) into the *Tristan* chord, a chord that generates tension not only throughout the prelude but throughout the whole opera. Secondly, Liszt immediately resolves the second chord to the tonic chord of the whole song while Wagner leaves his dominant 7th unresolved (B68, bar 3). In fact he leaves two more dominant 7ths unresolved (B68, bars 7 and 11), and a fourth dominant 7th (bar 16) only partially resolved (to the submediant rather than the tonic). B72 (which uses exactly the same four pitches as the melody in bars 2–3 of the prelude) shows how pervasive Wagner's influence was in early twentieth-century music.

8.10.2 Romantic song

One of the most important new genres of the romantic era was the **lied**, a setting of a German poem for voice and piano (or, in some late examples, for voice and orchestra). The earliest and most prolific composer of genius to write lieder was Franz Schubert (1797–1828). His songs range from short **strophic settings** with melodies that sound like folk songs to lengthy through-composed settings of dramatic poems in which new music reflects the contrasting moods of each successive verse. The piano part is typically as important as the vocal melody. This is the case in 'Wohin?' (B57), the second setting from a song cycle entitled *Die schöne Müllerin* (*The Fair Maid of the Mill*). In twenty songs the cycle tells how a young man sets out from home to follow a brook from its source to the sea. The cheerfully bubbling brook is represented by a sextuplet figure that runs through the whole song, while the young man's jaunty strides are represented by a continuous 'walking bass' in quavers. But this accompaniment is not just crude pictorialism, for Schubert is able to mould the sextuplets and bass so they reflect the changing moods of the young man. At the

8: Style, genre and historical context

beginning the harmony is simple: just chords I and V^7 over a drone bass (the latter suggesting rustic delights). The vocal melody is equally simple: just repeated notes and triadic figures outlining the piano chords. Bars 1–10 are in G major with not a single chromaticism to spoil the mood of joyful innocence. In bars 11–14 a slight chromatic shadow falls over the music as the singer wonders what prompted him to begin the journey, but diatonic G-major tonality returns when the poet speaks of the young man's determination to continue (bars 15–22). In bars 35–41 the youth begins to wonder if he has taken the right path. This question can be taken at face value, but Schubert's use of minor keys and chromaticism tell us more: the youth's indecision runs deeper than doubts about which path to take – he is beginning to decide the future course of his life (as the rest of the song cycle confirms).

Harmony and tonality are used to more devastating effect in 'Der Doppelgänger', one of the last songs Schubert wrote. Beginning in A minor the piano part in B58 rises chromatically to reach the distant key of C♯ minor (representing both horror at seeing the image which presages the poet's death and the remembered torture of unrequited love). The return to A minor is achieved through the German 6th in bar 9, which, at its resolution in the next bar, accompanies the highest note of the agonised vocal part. In this terrifying song tonality and chromatic harmony are used solely as a means of expression, not as a means of clarifying a musical structure. In this way 'Der Doppelgänger' is an extreme manifestation of musical romanticism.

8.10.3 Romantic character piece

This romantic genre (most often taking the form of a short piano solo) was written for the burgeoning middle classes of the nineteenth century, for whom the possession of a piano was as much of a status symbol as the possession of a Mercedes Benz is today. The title *Songs without Words* immediately defines the aims of the composer, Felix Mendelssohn (1809–47). Each 'song' is to be a **programmatic** representation of a single mood (and possibly the circumstances which gave rise to it), or an expression of changing emotions. The *Venetian Gondola Song* (B61) from this collection is typical of the romantic character piece. The title (Mendelssohn's own) invites us to imagine Venice, so when the gently swaying accompaniment begins we know that Mendelssohn is evoking the atmosphere of a calm day on a Venetian canal through the medium of a barcarole. But the minor key and modal melodic inflections evoke that sort of melancholic response which is engendered by cold leaden days in La Serenissima. This is just one possible interpretation, for the character piece deliberately leaves much to the imagination in a way that is impossible in a 'Song *with* Words' (because of the concrete images of the poem). This poetic ambiguity is one of the most prominent features of romantic instrumental miniatures.

Romantic tonal ambiguity is carried to extremes in another character piece that evokes a water-borne funeral cortège in Venice. In the extract from *La Lugubre Gondola* (*The Mournful Gondola*) by Franz Liszt (1811–86) shown in B74 an extremely chromatic melody is accompanied by broken chords outlining an atonal augmented triad. By this means the composer creates a sense of total desolation. It was often the case that the romantic

Elements of music

desire to evoke particular emotions led to stylistic changes. In pieces like this, written at the end of his life, Liszt could have claimed to be more a musician of the future than Wagner.

In compositions such as the prelude by Fryderyk Chopin (1810–49) shown in B66 there is no title to help us imagine a scene, but the major key, the fleet-footed figuration and the luminous harmony leave us in no doubt about the mood Chopin so persuasively expresses. (Mendelssohn said that, far from being ambiguous, music was so precise a language of the emotions that it could not possibly be translated into mere words.) There has been much discussion about the E♭ that intrudes into the tonic chord of F major at the end of this prelude. But this is a fairly common feature of music from an generation that admired fragmentary romantic ruins. The E♭ turns the last chord into the dominant 7th of a foreign key (B♭ major). In the silence after the music has ended we are left to imagine our own ending, or perhaps just to admire the deliberately inconclusive ending.

The romantics loved the night for its mystery and its boundless imagined or real amorous possibilities. It is not surprising then that a species of the character piece known as the **nocturne** should have been so popular. Chopin's Nocturne in F♯ minor (B67) is typical of this lyrical genre. Over an arpeggiated accompaniment a cantabile melody slowly unwinds very much like a slow aria in a romantic Italian opera. The chromatic route from F♯ minor to its relative major (A major) is characteristic of Chopin's regard for both romantic expressiveness and classical poise (the progression in bars 7–8 is almost the same as Wagner's, but it links the related keys of F♯ minor and A major).

In one sense of the term an **intermezzo** is a movement sandwiched between acts of an opera or between two more substantial instrumental movements. This is the case in those romantic symphonies in which the classical minuet or scherzo is replaced by a movement in a lighter, more lyrical style. These movements are really orchestral versions of the character piece (C1, brief though it is, gives some idea of the style of a movement that comes between a lengthy and profoundly beautiful adagio and a terrifically festive yet cerebral finale). But the intermezzo is more commonly encountered as an independent instrumental work, most often a characteristic piano solo. The extracts from two intermezzi by Johannes Brahms (1833–97) shown in B78 and B79 typify the composer's late style. Although the first intermezzo begins in a tonal haze (the inversions of the supertonic and tonic chord in the first two bars do not establish the tonic key of B♭ minor with any degree of clarity). But the circle of 5ths in the remainder of the extract harks back to baroque harmonic usage and directs the listener towards the dominant-7th chord of B♭ minor with which the extract ends. The chief feature of the second intermezzo is a blurring of the triple metre in bars 9–15 and 30–37 achieved by cross-phrasing and non-periodic chord changes. Such metrical ambiguity is common in the nineteenth century (especially in Schumann's songs and piano music) and it is especially characteristic of the late works of Brahms.

The nineteenth-century character piece could be more programmatic and light-hearted than the nocturne or intermezzo. Indeed the parodistic wit of the *Carnival of the Animals* by Camille Saint-Saëns (1835–1921) looks forward to the ironic humour of music such as Satie's *Trois morceaux en forme de poire* (1903) rather than backwards to the romantic generation of the early nineteenth century. 'L'Éléphant' (C7) begins as an ungainly minuet in E♭ major which, by the end of the extract, has modulated to the 'wrong' key of G minor (given the melodic style and the balanced eight-bar phrases the music ought to have modulated to the dominant or relative minor). Saint-Saëns innovative use of the xylophone as a member of a romantic symphony orchestra (in his *Danse macabre* of 1874) merited a special note in the score in which the composer explained what the instrument was ('de bois et paille') and informed those intending to conduct the work that the instrument could be obtained from the publishers. In C8 he uses it with ironic intent to suggest, not the real skeletons of the *Danse macabre,* but the fossilised remains of skeletons (perhaps a reference to the more academic of his colleagues in the French Academy?).

8.10.4 Nationalism and characteristic dances

In the ballet *The Nutcracker* by Pyotr Ilyich Tchaikovsky (1840–93) there are six short movements entitled 'Danses caractéristiques'. In using this term Tchaikovsky was not introducing a new genre, but following in the footsteps of Robert Schumann (1810–56) whose set of piano pieces entitled *Davidsbündlertänze* (*Dances of the League of David*, composed in 1837) are subtitled '**Charakterstücke**' (*'Character Pieces'*). Clearly Schumann and Tchaikovsky saw stylised **dances** for piano or orchestra as a subgenre of the ubiquitous character piece (see 8.10.3).

The **polonaise**, a song and dance genre which incorporates features of a number of ancient Polish folk dances, dates back to the sixteenth century, but only in the early eighteenth century did composers of art music begin to imitate some of its stylistic features in movements entitled 'Polonaise'. A notable stylisation of the polonaise can be found in Bach's Orchestral Suite in B minor. The polonaises of Fryderyk Chopin (1810–49) are more directly based on the original folk dance as the extract from his Polonaise in E♭ Op. 22 shows (B64(a)). The dance is in moderate triple time with phrases beginning on the first beat of the bar. Specific types of rhythm are associated with the dance, one of the most common being the rhythm shown on an extra stave beneath bar 1 and heard in the left-hand accompaniment in bars 1, 3, 4 and 5. As with most **folk music** the melodic line includes extensive repetition of motifs or whole phrases. The phrase in bars 1–2, for instance, is repeated in bars 5–6 transposed down a semitone. Unlike the original folk dance, however, Chopin's melody is encrusted with idiomatic piano **arabesques**. It is the combination of the rhythmic complexity and chromaticism of these elaborate melodic lines with the simple polonaise rhythms and diatonic harmony of the accompaniment that characterises Chopin's unmistakable stylistic fusion of folk idioms with pianistic versions of contemporary operatic coloratura.

Chopin, who lived most of his life in self-imposed exile, is in touch with his roots to an even greater extent in his **mazurkas**. He was born in Mazovia near Warsaw, a province that lends its name to the original Polish name for the genre (*mazur* or *mazurek*). There were many styles of mazurka, but they all share in common triple metre with accents on the second or third beat of the bar, and a range of distinctive and oft-repeated

Elements of music

rhythmic patterns and melodic motifs. The melodies are often modal, the lydian mode being most closely associated with the original dance and song genres. The most commonly used instruments were violins and flutes (playing the melody) and bagpipes (with one or two drones) providing a sparse accompaniment. In his Mazurka in C♯ minor Op. 30 No. 4 (B65) all of these elements are present. Accents on the third beat of the bar are caused by the harmonic rhythm: changing chord on the third beat of the bar and remaining on it throughout the ensuing bar shifts the metrical accent forward a beat (as in bars 6 and 8 where dominant harmony in the first two beats changes to tonic harmony on the third beat). Where there is no change of chord Chopin uses other means to create a third-beat accent (in bar 15 an octave leap from the grace notes suggests a violinistic portamento and Chopin has marked the third beat with a dynamic accent). The rhythmic pattern marked x in bar 6 is typical of the *mazur* and, as a melodic motif, it is heard in its original or transposed form no fewer than fourteen times, and variants of it are heard ten times in this short extract. The melody is in the aeolian mode throughout bars 5–32 and 37–43, while a tonic–dominant drone imitates a bagpipe accompaniment in bars 5–8 and 13–16. Although united by common motifs the harmonic style of bars 5–16 contrasts strongly with the Neapolitan 6ths in bars 21–27, the chromatically sliding non-functional 'dominant 7ths' in bars 33–36, and the unusual plagal cadence at the end (in which chord II^7 serves as a substitute for chord IV).

If the minuet is the dance that most clearly evokes the eighteenth century, the **waltz** is for many the epitome of the nineteenth-century ballroom. It began life as the rustic ***Deutscher Tanz*** (B44), a fast romp in triple time dating from the late eighteenth century that was closely related to a slower version known as the ***Ländler***. Both varieties were admitted to polite society in the late eighteenth century, but both were superseded by the waltz. The waltz is particularly associated with Vienna, but it soon spread throughout Europe and America. C2 is taken from a collection of character pieces which the Norwegian composer Edvard Grieg (1843–1907) called *Lyric Pieces*. Like many such compositions it is in simple ternary form (Poco allegro–Presto–Poco allegro). But what is more interesting is the way Grieg mates the characteristic features of the Viennese waltz with third-beat syncopations (bars 9 and 11), cross-phrased quavers (bars 21–24 and 29–31) and his own brand of modality in the flanking sections. In this character dance the waltz has become a naturalised Norwegian.

In its original guise the ***furiant*** was a fast, boisterous Bohemian folk dance in alternating triple and duple metres. It was taken up by Czech nationalist composers and introduced into art music as an independent piano piece, as a dance in an opera, or as a replacement for the scherzo in multi-movement instrumental works. The third movement of the Piano Quintet Op. 81 by Antonín Dvořák (1841–1904) is a *furiant* which, like most examples in art music, remains in triple time throughout but retains the weak-beat accents that characterise the dance. This is evident in C9 in which the pervasive four-note motif x is rhythmically altered so it can fit the exhilarating hemiolas in bars 26–29 (effectively six bars of $\frac{2}{4}$ time conflicting with the established triple metre). Equally notable is the idiomatic leaping counter-melody heard in the viola at the start of the

8: Style, genre and historical context

extract. These folk-derived features are combined with Dvořák's special mixture of chromaticism and modality. Both are evident in bars 26–29 where melodic chromaticism (D♯s and B♯s) combines with the modal sound of chords I, III and VI in root position. The use of chords VI and I (instead of IV and I) to form the final 'plagal' cadence is equally modal. Together all of these elements define a unique late romantic nationalist style that is instantly recognisable as coming from the pen of Dvořák.

Although Tchaikovsky was not counted among the self-proclaimed Russian nationalist composers known as the 'Mighty Handful' (Balakirev, Borodin, Cui, Mussorgsky and Rimsky-Korsakov), Stravinsky, surveying a century of musical nationalism from a vantage point in the twentieth century, declared that Tchaikovsky was 'the most Russian of us all'. Even the tiny **trepak** from his ballet *The Nutcracker* (C5) confirms Stravinsky's assertion. This Cossack dance in very fast duple time has many of the hallmarks of Russian folk music. It is based throughout on repetitions (exact and varied) of a three-note motif (x) and of a complete eight-bar melody (y). The prominent strong-beat accents (f or ff) and weak-beat accents (sf) coincide with the athletic kicking of the squatting dancers. Although this character dance is in ternary form (like Greig's waltz), there is no rhythmic relaxation in the central section (B), which, instead of presenting a contrasting idea, further develops motif x. The reprise ends with a tonic pedal over which repetitions of motif x become faster and faster until the abrupt final cadence.

8.10.5 Romantic ballet music

Ballet as theatrical entertainment grew out of the groupings of courtly dances performed by courtiers themselves in sixteenth- and seventeenth-century France and Italy. In this form it reached a peak of perfection and sophistication in the *ballet de cour* of the second half of the seventeenth century when the fifteen-year-old Louis XIV appeared as Apollo in the *Ballet de la nuit* (1653). With his foundation of the Académie Royale de Danse in 1661 and the Académie Royale de Musique et de Danse in 1672 Louis ensured the future of ballet in France. It was during this *grand siècle* that ballet dancing (performed by professionals) was introduced into stage plays. But it was not until a century later that the first great ballet as a completely independent art form appeared (Gluck's *Don Juan*, a *ballet d'action* first performed in Vienna in 1761). France retained its pre-eminence in ballet in the nineteenth century with productions of works such as *Giselle* (Adam, 1841) and *Sylvia* (Delibes, 1876).

When the French dancer and choreographer Marius Petipa became ballet-master at the Maryinsky Theatre in St Petersburg in 1847 he began to build a repertoire that rivalled that of Paris. In particular he devised the structure of the *pas de deux* and brought the staging of the *corps de ballet* to an unrivalled level of perfection. Among his greatest successes were his major collaborations with Pyotr Ilyich Tchaikovsky (1840–93): *The Sleeping Beauty* (1890) and *The Nutcracker* (1892). Tchaikovsky, like many romantic composers, sought escape from the overheated emotionalism of his own times in the classical perfection of the past (witness his magnificent *Rococo Variations*). He was therefore delighted with the setting of *The Sleeping Beauty* in the time of the boy-dancer Louis XIV since it gave him ample opportunity to write music in styles reminiscent of the *grand*

Elements of music

siècle (the ballet features a 'Tempo di Menuetto', a 'Tempo de Gavotte' and a 'Sarabande'). One of the chief stylistic influences that is evident to a greater or lesser extent in most of his music is that of nineteenth-century French composers such as Adolphe Adam (he was taken to see *Giselle* as a schoolboy and he read the score when he was writing *The Sleeping Beauty*) and Léo Delibes (he wrote to his benefactress Madame von Meck that his own *Swan Lake* was 'not fit to hold a candle to *Sylvia*').

These two strands – the purity of style of French classical music and the elegance of nineteenth-century French operatic music – come together in C6. It is music for a transformation scene in which the Lilac Fairy leads Prince Charming through an enchanted wood to the palace where the Sleeping Beauty lies dormant. The sixteen-bar violin melody divides into two balanced eight-bar phrases. The first (an antecedent) ends with an imperfect cadence in the tonic key of G major, and the second (a consequent that begins with the same three bars as the antecedent) ends with a perfect cadence in the dominant key of D major. This has the same classical poise as the refrain of Couperin's Forlane (C32, bars 1–9) – an eight-bar phrase dividing into two balanced four-bar phrases that begin in the same way but diverge in the last three beats. The orchestral texture of C6 has the clarity and elegant charm of Adam and Delibes. It consists of just four elements: a melody in octaves on violins, pizzicato strings marking the two beats of $^6_8$ time, woodwind alternating with horns to provide a harmonic filling, and harp arpeggios that mark the end of each of the four-bar phrases into which both antecedent and consequent divide. The other two elements that go towards the style of the Panorama (C6) are pure Tchaikovsky. Firstly, the gently dissonant chords add an astringency that avoids potential sentimentality. Secondly, the polymetric conflict between the $^6_8$ metre of the accompanying instruments and the triple-time melody allows the latter to float freely above the accompaniment (in C6 the antecedent is printed as Tchaikovsky wrote it while the consequent is notated in $^3_4$ time to clarify this conflict). The scope of Tchaikovsky's genius as a composer of ballet music is evident when this wonderfully subtle music is compared with the manic frenzy of the 'Russian dance' from his last ballet *The Nutcracker* (see 8.10.4 and C5).

8.10.6 Romantic programme music

Programme music – music that seeks to paint a picture or tell a story – was not a new phenomenon in the nineteenth century. It can be traced back at least as far as the sixteenth century, when the programme chanson and its instrumental progeny realistically imitated extra-musical phenomena such as the din of battle (A31 and A32). But the most revolutionary romantic composers went far beyond such onomatopoeia, raising programmatic music to an ideological principle opposed to what they saw as the dry-as-dust absolute music of the eighteenth century (and the music of those who continued to use classical genres and forms in the nineteenth century). **Character pieces** (see 8.10.3), such as the evocations of Venice by Mendelssohn (B61) and Liszt (B74), are small-scale manifestations of the urge to link music with real or imaginary texts. On a much larger scale, two new orchestral genres emerged as a result of this desire to pin music to concrete images.

The first was the **programme symphony**, a multi-movement genre that

8: Style, genre and historical context

was inspired by, among other works, Beethoven's *Pastoral* Symphony. First in the field was Hector Berlioz (1803–29), whose *Symphonie fantastique* was accompanied by a lengthy programme note which was to be distributed to audiences whenever the work was performed. No one could explain his reasons for going to such lengths better than this most articulate of composers himself. He wrote: 'The composer's intention has been to represent different scenes from the life of an artist, as far as their own musicality allows. Given that the plan of the instrumental drama is unsupported by words, it needs to be revealed in advance. The following programme should be considered the equivalent of the spoken text of an opera, serving to introduce the fragments of music, the character and expressive qualities of which it determines.'

In essence the programme tells how an artist's obsessive but unrequited love for a woman leads him to kill the object of his desire. He is executed, but meets the beloved in the witches' orgy of the last movement. In order to conjure up the dark doings of the witches' sabbath Berlioz draws on a plainsong melody from the Mass for the Dead (B62) which, in the early nineteenth century, was obviously well known, not only to believers, but also to agnostics like Berlioz himself. Even without the composer's programme note ('funeral bell and ludicrous parody of the **Dies irae**') the intention of B63 is crystal clear.

The next important composer to figure in the development of romantic programme music was Franz Liszt (1811–86), the inventor of the **symphonic poem** (a single-movement work for orchestra based upon a programme that was most often printed and read by the audience before the music was played). Although his *Mephisto Waltz* No. 1 (B73) is sometimes not classified as a symphonic poem it deserves to be. It is based on an episode from Lenau's *Faust* and its original title was *The Dance in the Village Inn*. Faust and Mephisto (an abbreviation of Mephistopheles – the Devil) join the locals. While Faust engages the landlord's daughter in conversation Mephisto grabs a violin from the village band. He tunes all four strings (bars 19–26), then intoxicates the dancers with his wild virtuosity – just as Paganini (on the violin) and Liszt (on the piano) had intoxicated their audiences in the first half of the nineteenth century. Romantic texts often inspired composers to go far beyond generally accepted musical norms. The terrific dissonances at the start of the *Mephisto Waltz* were welcomed by the audience because they knew from their programmes what these dissonances were about. The biting sounds would have added to the enjoyable *frisson* of horror they must have felt as the music led them on to an unfettered orgy presided over by the devil himself.

The title '**Capriccio**' never implied that the music that followed could be regarded as an example of a clearly defined genre. The word is Italian for a whim or a fancy (the English adjective 'capricious' derives from this Italian noun). The only common element between pieces bearing the title is succinctly described by the seventeenth-century French lexicographer, Antoine Furetière: 'Capriccios are pieces of music, poetry or painting wherein the force of imagination has more success than observation of the rules of art'. This definition is as true of Frescobaldi's fugal capriccios as it is of the *Capriccio italien* by Pyotr Ilyich Tchaikovsky (1840–93). The composer left no printed programme for this pot-pourri of popular Italian songs, but its evocation of Mediterranean warmth, colour and gaiety places it firmly among similar works that do have a programme. In C3 the oom-pah-pah, tonic–dominant accompaniment, the cornet duet and the vulgar chromatic passing notes at the end of bar 5 suggest the music of a village band that Tchaikovsky might have heard when he visited Italy in 1880.

In essence the term **tone poem** refers to the same sort of one-movement orchestral work as Liszt's 'symphonic poem'. The late nineteenth-century tone poems of Richard Strauss (1864–1949) represent the final full flowering of the genre. Not only are the programmes brilliantly realised in sound, but also the coherence of his musical structures is ensured by **thematic transformation**, and by more traditional formal devices. Although *Till Eulenspiegel's Merry Pranks* does not bear the label 'tone poem' it is as obviously programmatic as any of the five works which Strauss assigned to this genre. The composer did, however, add 'in Rondeauform' to the title, and the use of rondo form certainly helps overcome the problems which the episodic structure of his programme presented. C10 is taken from the last of these episodes. Till is hung as retribution for his 'merry pranks' (the mode of execution being verified by a literal 'drop' of a minor 7th on brass and bassoons at the start of the extract). Then he is throttled by the rope (represented by the high-pitched screech of a D clarinet in its highest register). Finally he expires (represented by the slow descent of the clarinet). But of course this is only a story for children, so the work ends, as it began, with a soothing transformation of Till's theme (C11). In this way the thematic transformation at the start of the epilogue ('and so it was that ...') serves as a programmatic reminder of the *Gemächlich* (comfortable or leisurely) introduction ('Once upon a time ...') and provides purely musical coherence between the last episode and the epilogue.

Like Strauss, Claude Debussy (1862–1918) does not acknowledge that his ground-breaking *Prélude à L'Après-midi d'un faune* is a tone poem (it was originally intended as the first part of a Prelude, Interlude and Paraphrase to be played in association with a reading of Mallarmé's poem of the same name). Yet this piece, the first fruit of musical **impressionism**, certainly accords with the *aims* of Debussy's radical German contemporaries, even if it is expressed in a *style* far removed from that of Strauss. It was inspired by Mallarmé's obscure *symboliste* eclogue about a faun – a mythological creature with a human face and trunk, but with goat's horns, legs and tail – who, in the shimmering heat of the afternoon drowsily recalls his passionate encounter with a pair of nymphs. He remembers how the lips that caress his panpipes once caressed these beautiful creatures. At length he succumbs to the languorous vision, and, dreaming, falls asleep. The poet intended his eclogue to be read aloud because its effect is as much dependent on sound as it is on sense. The passage which corresponds with the end of Debussy's tone poem (C19) reads as follows:

...*mais l'âme*
de paroles vacante et ce corps alourdi
tard succombent au fier silence de midi
... but the soul
empty of words and this heavy body
at last succumb to the proud silence of noon.

Mallarmé expected that Debussy's music would 'present no dissonance with my text, [but would] go much further into its nostalgia and light it with subtlety, malaise and richness'. The clue to musical impressionism lies in the poet's use of the word light. Just as contemporary artists sought to give an impression of their perception of the play of light, so Debussy's score relies on the colouristic effect of chords and instrumental **timbres**. In the first bar of C19 unrelated triads float timelessly (at the very slow tempo set by the composer it is almost impossible to detect a regular time-defining beat). The veiled sonority comes from the use of muted horns with muted violins playing on their lowest strings. In the next bar tonality remains unclear until the flute rises from the dotted minim C♯ to the dotted minim E (the root of chord I) and the violins rise from their lydian A♯ to B♮ (the fifth of chord I). In the last three bars the orchestral sonorities are even more delicate than they were in the first bar. Nostalgic antique cymbals sound four octaves and more above the double basses, harp harmonics in mid-register climb up a C♯-minor triad in crotchets and horns and violins fall silent. Then, in the last bar, only pizzicato cellos and double basses (*ppp*) are heard against the dying sounds of low flutes and antique cymbals. Although written only one year after Wagner died, and three years before Brahms's death, this music stands at the beginning not only of musical impressionism but of a path that leads directly to the music of Messiaen and, through byways, to many of the divergent styles of twentieth-century music.

8.10.7 Romantic symphony

Despite the tendency to pictorialism of much nineteenth-century orchestral music there were many composers who attempted to continue the classical tradition of the symphony as a four-movement abstract composition. Among those who succeeded most brilliantly in this mission were Mendelssohn in the first half of the century and Johannes Brahms (1833–97) in the second half. In his four symphonies Brahms expanded classical structures (such as sonata form) and maintained the Beethovenian tradition of motivic development. Nevertheless, he was able to combine these elements with romantic harmony and rich orchestral textures in a style that is instantly recognisable as his alone. This synthesis is evident even in the short extract from his second symphony shown in C1. Classicism is apparent in the way he builds melodies by manipulating short motifs such as the three-note crotchet figure (x) and the four-note quaver figure (y). It is evident, too, in the two-part counterpoint of bars 10–14 and the firmly rooted tonality of the whole passage. Romanticism is evident even in the tempo mark. This is the third movement of the symphony and instead of a Beethovenian scherzo Brahms has written a graceful allegretto in the style of an intermezzo (as he did in his first and third symphonies). Classical composers sometimes opposed passages in the major with passages in the tonic minor, but the way Brahms slides in and out of these parallel keys in bars 1–15 is a romantic effect that has nothing to do with the structure of the music. At the end of this passage the lyricism of the string melody (bars 7–10) and its scoring (doubled at the octave above and below) contrasts with the motivic melody of the first six bars. But most romantic of all is the way a secondary dominant major 9th (bars 17^3–19^1) interrupts the gently rocking woodwind melody that seems to be winding down to a final tonic chord.

Elements of music

The scoring in these bars is equally romantic: a widely spaced woodwind chord overlapped with a very soft, closely spaced string chord. But when the cadence eventually arrives it could hardly be more classical (I_4^6–V^7–I).

Although Pyotr Ilyich Tchaikovsky (1840–93) maintained the four-movement structure of the symphony as a whole and wrote sonata-form movements, the balance is tipped in favour of romantic expressiveness at the expense of classical balance in his six symphonies. This is evident in C4 in which a horn and an oboe sing a love duet over a throbbing string accompaniment, both of them indulging themselves with sighing appoggiaturas (horn, bar 2, beat 1; oboe, bar 5, beat 1; horn, bar 6, beat 1). When the first bar of the oboe melody is detached and played by a clarinet and bassoon (bars 7–9) no attempt is made to develop this motif: the clarinets simply answer the lovers' sighs with their own appoggiaturas. Although no publicly available programme was printed, Tchaikovsky's letters to Madame von Meck and his markings in sketches for the symphony ('consolation', 'O how I love you! O my friend!' and so on) confirm what is already manifest in the music itself. Tchaikovsky is sometimes regarded as a purveyor of delectable ballet music whose symphonic works are spoiled by self-indulgent displays of emotion. In fact his dramatic symphonic music has for a century been among the most often performed of all nineteenth-century music, and his influence on twentieth-century composers as diverse as Sibelius, Stravinsky, Shostakovich and Britten has been at least as important as the influence of more obviously revolutionary composers such as Liszt and Wagner.

8.10.8 Romantic renewal of early genres

Abstract genres such as the symphony, sonata and quartet continued to flourish in the early nineteenth century, and, once the fruits of scholarly enquiries into early music bore fruit, some composers began to find inspiration in baroque and even renaissance music. Johannes Brahms (1833–97) was just such a composer. From his earliest years he took an interest in ancient music and later worked with some of the greatest scholars of the day in producing complete editions of the works of earlier composers. Perhaps the greatest of these tasks was the edition of Couperin's *Pièces de clavecin* that he made for Chrysander, the general editor of *Denkmäler der Tonkunst* (*Monuments of Musical Art*). For Chrysander's complete edition of Handel's works Brahms realised the continuo parts of several of the vocal compositions. In his library he had the first edition of Handel's Suite in B♭ (which was published in 1733 and contained three pieces written before 1720). The last movement of this suite is an air (B76) with five simple variations (or *doubles*) similar to those shown in B18. In his own set of 25 variations on this theme Brahms sticks rigidly to the periodic phrasing of Handel's little binary-form theme, but invests it with a wealth of detail, such as the canonic display of Variation 16 (B77) which grows naturally from motifs in Handel's theme. Despite the contrapuntal two-part texture this is not simply pastiche; rather it is a witty commentary on Handel that uses the whole range of the nineteenth-century piano in the service of an idiomatic keyboard style.

Chamber music genres continued to flourish throughout the nineteenth century, but the string quartet did not dominate the repertoire quite so

8: Style, genre and historical context

much as it had in the classical era. Instead there was a considerable interest in ensembles in which the piano played a central role, such as the Piano Quintet Op. 81 by Antonín Dvořák (1841–1904), an extract from which is shown in C9. The Czech master's Quartet No. 14 Op. 105 (completed in December 1895) can be regarded as the last great romantic example of the genre. Like the piano quintet it contains a *furiant*, and its rich variety of textures includes some quasi-orchestral passages which threaten to overwhelm the even temper of the music. But adherence to sonata form in the outer movements ensures a balance between form and content that was soon to be destroyed or just ignored by early twentieth-century composers.

Dvořák's joyfully romantic last quartet contrasts strongly with the String Quartet Op. 10 by Claude Debussy (1862–1912). Although it was written seven years before the end of the century, it is one of the seminal works of the late nineteenth century that in spirit belong to twentieth-century music. There are four movements, but their relationship one to another and their internal structures are quite different from Dvořák's flexible sonata-form movements. Nor does Debussy's use of cyclic form correspond to that of Tchaikovsky. Debussy was much more systematic in his use of thematic transformation than the Russian master (who used a motto theme as a quasi-programmatic prompt in each of the four movements of his fifth symphony). In Debussy's quartet the character of the opening theme of the first movement (C18(a)) is radically altered in the second and fourth movements (C18(b) and (c)). Rather than being alien intruders in movements of quite different moods from a motto theme, Debussy's transformations themselves help to define the characteristics of the three movements in which they occur. C12–C17 show how, in the second movement, Debussy builds up a complex polyrhythmic texture from varied fragments of the theme in much the same way as an artist builds a mosaic from tiny fragments of brightly coloured ceramic. It is by techniques such as this that Debussy integrates his movements into a single coherent design. In doing this he was rejecting Teutonic doctrines of thematic development and recapitulation and, as with the *Prélude à L'Après-midi d'un faune* (C19), laying the foundations for twentieth-century music.

8.11 Divergent trends in twentieth-century music

Never before had there been so many radically different styles of music coexisting alongside each other as there were in the twentieth century. The tonal language of romantic and earlier music survived and, in some quarters, flourished until the end of the century. Musical impressionism sought and found new ways of organising tonality. The introspection of expressionist painters was reflected in the early works of those composers who thought that nothing new could be expressed in tonal styles. Composers of art music woke up to the fact that jazz had become a vital force that could not be ignored. Others reached back to pre-romantic music in the hope that they would find styles that could purge tonal music of romantic excess and be adapted to their own needs. A more scientific exploration of folk music revealed rhythmic and melodic possibilities far removed from the picturesque modality of late nineteenth-century nationalist composers. Similarly, deeper acquaintance with the exotic music of other cultures profoundly altered the course of western music

Elements of music

and opened yet wider horizons to young composers of both art and pop music. New technology enabled composers to record bird song in order to notate it with great accuracy, and the use of more advanced technology in pop and art music became so widespread that electronically generated sound was, and still is, an often unremitting accompaniment to everyday life. This Tower of Babel of musical styles reached a high point of complexity in the work of avant-garde composers of the 1960s and 1970s. Yet even as Pierre Boulez (b.1925) and Karlheinz Stockhausen (b.1928) were engaged in their cerebral investigations into the nature of sound, other composers began to respond to the postmodern groundswell that was emerging in all the arts. At the start of a new millennium it is still too early to see clearly defined stylistic trends in late twentieth-century music – perhaps the fragmentation and coalescence of styles is just so complex that the attempt will forever prove futile. For the moment the many 'isms' with which twentieth-century historians have attempted to categorise the proliferating styles and genres of the last 100 years will have to suffice.

8.11.1 Late romanticism and neoromanticism

The spirit of Brahms lived on in academic circles at least until the world war one. Exciting though it is, the Magnificat from the Service in C major by Charles Villiers Stanford (1852–1924) uses a harmonic idiom with which the young Brahms would have been familiar (compare, for instance, the dominant 13ths in B75 with those in C30).

The vast **symphonies** of Gustav Mahler (1860–1911) show that the genre was sufficiently flexible to be 'like the world – [embracing] everything' (Mahler in conversation with Sibelius). In several of his symphonies the composer makes his programmatic intentions clear by introducing sung texts. The sixth symphony (1906) is entirely orchestral, but the listener can be in no doubt about the meaning of the solemn chorale (C27), the hammer-blows delivered by the timpani and the fearful trumpet chords changing from major to minor. The passage shown in C28 comes just after a terrifying, dissonant development of the main motifs (including an inversion of the demisemiquaver figure in bars 4–5). The cowbells heard 'in the distance' and the icy timbre of a celesta with muted and divided violin tremolo immediately suggest an Alpine scene. At the end of the extract large tubular bells sound like church bells in the distance, suggesting that the listener is high above a valley where a church lies. But this is not a picture-postcard evocation. Although a pedal D♮ (heard on double basses then cellos in the first 12 bars of C28) anchors the music in D minor, the chords above it are unsettling. Some are diatonic but dissonant (harps bars 2–4), some are modal (the F-major triad on the last beats of bars 7–9) and some are chromatic triads which are totally unrelated to the key of D minor (the D♭ and G♭ major triads in bars 12–14). The length of this movement (at just under half an hour it is longer than many complete classical symphonies) and the huge instrumental resources it demands are both characteristics of late romantic orchestral music. Yet apart from climactic points Mahler uses these resources with great restraint. C29 is typical of the delicate chamber-like scoring of many similar passages in his symphonies. The extract is taken from a movement entitled 'Nachtmusik' (Night Music). The title and the performance direction (Andante amoroso) make Mahler's programmatic use of a mandolin quite clear. The serenading mandolin is one of three instrumental parts, and the style in bars 5–6, with its dominant–tonic bassoon, is a **pastiche** of similar passages in classical serenades and divertimenti (see B40). In the next bar pastiche gives way to sardonic humour when the bassoon plays a B♮ instead of a B♭. This mood of affectionate mockery is maintained in 'wrong-note' chords in the remainder of the extract.

The symphony was kept alive in Soviet Russia, partly as a result of the communists' insistence that composers should help shape the new Utopia by adopting the conservative styles of 'socialist realism'. Realism meant the depiction of the workers' struggle against capitalism, and their inevitable triumph over it. Every street corner was adorned with pictures of Lenin (and later Stalin) and unnaturally virile young Russians of both sexes urging the workers to contribute towards industrial and agrarian productivity. Similarly musicians were required to contribute by depicting the struggle in sometimes dissonant but always tonal music, and by showing the triumph of communism through the eventual resolution of dissonance in a major-key apotheosis. Though often unwilling, Dmitri Shostakovich (1906–75) spent much of his creative energies writing a series of mammoth quasi-Mahlerian symphonies which, at least superficially, toed the ideological line (his sprawling twelfth symphony is dedicated to the memory of Lenin). Realism and romantic pictorialism are exemplified by his seventh symphony. It depicts the Russian army's heroic defence of Leningrad. In the lead up to the climax of the first movement the approaching German forces are represented by a brutally repetitive and deliberately vulgar march. C74 shows the militaristic side drum ostinato and the sinister beginning of the march theme (which is repeated no fewer than twelve times in the symphony) with the sequential phrase (x) that Bartók parodied in his *Concerto for Orchestra* (C75, bars 2–10).

The **suite** was given a new lease of life by Gustav Holst (1874–1934) in his musical portraits of the astrological characteristics of the seven planets that were known to exist at the start of the twentieth century (excluding the Earth). But, unlike the baroque genre, *The Planets* is a suite only in the sense that it is a collection of contrasting movements linked by a common idea. It is romantic in so far as there is, to a greater or lesser extent, a **programmatic** element in every one of the movements. Its romanticism is also evident in its reliance on tonal harmony (liberally coloured by modality) both to define structure and to enhance the emotional effect of other musical elements such as rhythm and melody. Like Mahler's symphonies (C27–C29) the suite is scored for a very large romantic orchestra (with a hidden choir of female voices in the last movement). Every element contributes to the portrait of Mars as 'The Bringer of War' (C36 and C37). The insistent rhythmic ostinato in $\frac{5}{4}$ time played with the dry rattle of wood on strings (*col legno*); the persistent falling chromatic semitones of the melody (each marked with a bracket in C36); the dissonances heard between these chromatic notes and the ever-present tonic pedal; the menacing bare octaves and hollow parallel 5ths on penetrating double-reed instruments (contrabassoon, bassoons, bass oboe, cor anglais and oboe) – all of these make an immediate and unforgettable impression. In their historical context the parallel harmonies in bars 10–14 are in themselves not new (they hark back to the parallel organum of A7), nor is the use of quintuple metre exceptional

Elements of music

(Tchaikovsky wrote a whole movement of his sixth symphony in $\frac{5}{4}$ time). What is new is the fusion of these elements in a late romantic style that is quite unlike that of any of Holst's contemporaries.

Benjamin Britten (1913–76) was an eclectic composer whose early music shows an intimacy with the work of the most progressive composers of continental Europe, including members of the Second Viennese School. However his mature music, though often extremely dissonant and chromatic, is nearly always tonal. Indeed **tonality** is used as one of the expressive elements in what might be called his neoromantic style. His *Serenade for Tenor, Horn and Strings* (1943) is an orchestral song cycle consisting of settings of six contrasting poems about evening, night and sleep. The songs are framed by a prologue and an identical epilogue for unaccompanied horn (C84). The improvisatory nature of the music ('sempre ad libitum'), the use of natural harmonics throughout, the clearly established key of F major (coloured by 'out of tune' harmonics), and the movement's brevity (a romantic fragment) are in a direct line of succession from nineteenth-century romantic composers. The originality of the concept and the extreme economy of means are hallmarks of Britten's style.

Both of these qualities are equally evident in the extract from his **opera** *Billy Budd* shown in C86. The music is played as the captain of the *Indomitable* (an early nineteenth-century warship) leaves a court martial to tell the eponymous hero that he has been found guilty and is to be hanged from the yardarm. The captain knows that Billy Budd is morally innocent but is unable to prevent the hanging, and it is he who must convey the news to the victim. The audience is never allowed to witness their meeting: the terrifying music of the orchestral interlude is allowed to speak directly to our imagination. Britten achieves this devastating effect by the simplest of means. Limiting himself to major and minor triads he relies on the dissonant effect of false relations between unrelated chords (for instance, C♮ and C♯ in the first two chords) and on extreme dynamic and timbral contrasts. The originality of the concept lies in the fact that every one of these unrelated chords contains an F♮, an A♮, or a C♮ (as shown on the extra stave above the orchestral reduction). This 'horizontal' use of the tonic triad of F major ensures tonal cohesion in what might otherwise be a series of sound effects.

The tonal centre of the 'Elegy' from Britten's *Serenade* (C85) is E major/ minor. The change of mode from major to minor in the first bar links this music directly to Mahler's use of the same expressive device in his sixth symphony (C27, bars 5–6). But where Mahler uses six trumpets, Britten achieves an equally remarkable effect with a few solo cellos and a tenor voice. The semitonal shift (G♯/G♮) is central to the structure of the whole 'Elegy', since the ubiquitous semitones (x) of the horn melody (and the double bass part in bars 23–24) are derived from the semitones with which the vocal recitative begins and ends. The concept no doubt derives from the possibility of changing the pitch of a note on a horn by a semitone by pushing a fist up the bell of the instrument instead of using valves. The effect can be heard with great clarity in the last two bars, in which four cellos sustain a bare 5th on E♮ while the horn alternates between G♯ and G♮ (thus changing the tonic chord from major to minor and back again). The sinister timbre of the stopped notes (marked with a cross), the change in mode of the tonic chord and the obsessive semitones reflect Blake's nightmare text and simultaneously ensure musical cohesion. Whether or not Britten remembered the minatory semitones of Holst's portrait of the warlike Mars (C36), the two composers use them to similar ends.

8.11.2 Impressionism

Claude Debussy (1862–1918) is best known for those of his works which have come to be thought of as impressionist in style (even though Debussy himself disliked the term, particularly as applied to his own music). To achieve musical effects akin to the colouristic effects of impressionist painters Debussy drew upon a formidable variety of techniques in his two books of preludes. Each of these pieces is a musical impression of subjects that are vaguely defined by titles printed at the end of the music (printed there, one suspects, as if to suggest that the performer ought not to pay too much attention to the concrete images which mere words are bound to evoke). In 'Voiles' (C21) an impression of sails reflected in calm water is achieved by the use of just six pitch classes which can be arranged to form a **whole-tone scale** (shown above the first four bars). Like the chromatic scale (in which every successive interval is a semitone) this scale lacks the goal of a tonic note, so were it not for the oft-repeated B♭ pedal the prelude would be atonal. Similarly, the deliberately complex rhythms cut across the barlines so that the metrical pulse is barely audible. The music floats in what is an almost total tonal and rhythmic vacuum. In 'La Cathédrale engloutie' the tonality is sometimes clear (C major in C24 and C26), but is often obscured by streams of parallel, unrelated dissonances (C25). Tonality and texture both serve Debussy's programme: the bells of the sunken cathedral of Ys (represented by the long-held, widely spaced chord in C22) are heard 'in a quietly echoing mist' of tonally ambiguous parallel harmony derived from a pentatonic scale on G. Then 'little by little the mist clears' to reveal the splendour of the clearly defined key of B major (C23). In music of this complexity one becomes acutely aware how much musical terminology changes its meaning as composers constantly renew the art. The prelude, which began life in the seventeenth century as an improvisatory genre intended to establish the key of an ensuing and more substantial composition, has become a programmatic impression of an ancient legend in the hands of Debussy.

Debussy's influence on Olivier Messiaen (1908–92) was profound. In fact the whole-tone scale which dominates both melody and harmony in Debussy's 'Voiles' (C21) became the first of Messiaen's seven **modes of limited transposition**. In his 'Prière du Christ montant vers son Père' (C55) Messiaen uses his seventh mode, a collection of ten pitch classes shown as a scale below the last system. Although he rarely made such systematic use of his first mode of limited transposition (the whole-tone scale), the colouristic harmonies derived from the seventh mode in the 'Prière du Christ' float as timelessly and as impressionistically as do Debussy's whole-tone harmonies in 'Voiles'. Messiaen's early style often betrays Debussyan influence in his reliance on the peculiarly impressionistic effect of streams of dissonant chords moving in parallel motion (compare the descending stream of 7ths in bars 2–3 of C25 with the ascending stream of discords at the start of C55). When Messiaen does arrive on a chord that is notated as a dominant 7th (bars 2–4 and 7–8) it is, like the other

Elements of music

discords, devoid of tonal significance. Only with the arrival of the last chord (an unsullied triad of C major) does a tonal centre emerge. But this is simply because, at the extremely slow tempo indicated at the start, it seems to last an eternity (which, of course, is precisely the effect Messiaen intended it to have). It is probably not an accident that both of the pieces are about churches – the first giving an impression of a cathedral rising from the waves, the second giving an impression of Christ, the head of the Church, rising towards his heavenly father.

8.11.3 Expressionism

Where impressionist painters, poets and composers looked outwards to the objective reality of the natural world, expressionist artists looked inwards to the often disturbing subjective reality of their own subconscious minds. In both cases painters were the first to find means of representing these realities, but poets and musicians soon found analogous means of representation in their own media. In expressionist music there is a particularly close connection between paintings and music, since the prime mover of the artistic movement, Wassily Kandinsky, was a close associate of the prime mover of the musical movement, Arnold Schoenberg (1874–1951). Both gave vivid expression to feelings of longing, loneliness, alienation and morbidity bordering on madness. In the process Kandinsky's paintings became non-representational and Schoenberg's compositions became atonal. *Pierrot Lunaire*, one of the monuments of expressionist music, is a setting by Schoenberg of 21 poems about a pathetic clown who tells of his tribulations in a type of speech-song (**Sprechgesang** or **Sprechstimme**) that is halfway between Monteverdian recitative (A61 and A62) and Sitwellian metrical speech (C38). In 'Nacht' ('Night' – C34) Pierrot imagines he sees great black creatures that blot out the light of the sun and vapours rising from the depths that destroy memory. This nightmare world is expressed through a contorted vocal melody and accompanimental parts that explore the extremities of the instruments' ranges (as shown on the extra staves at the end of Schoenberg's music). At no point is tonality suggested. Schoenberg preferred to use the term **pantonality** for the atonal style of his own music and that of his disciples Berg and Webern. At a literal level this makes good sense because their music uses all twelve chromatic notes without giving pre-eminence to any one of them, but the term **atonality** has stuck and is now almost universally used to describe their music.

When atonal music like this is associated with a poem the verse-form can offer the composer a prop on which to hang his music. When the prop of a text as well as the prop of tonality were removed composers found it difficult to give perceptible shape to their music. That being so, atonal instrumental compositions were for some years limited to tiny, concentrated utterances such as the *Five Pieces for Orchestra* by Anton Webern (1883–1945). Speaking of miniatures such as these Schoenberg tellingly said that 'a whole novel is expressed in a single sigh'. The whole of the first of the *Five Pieces* is shown in C35. It is completely atonal, and the few chords that are heard lack any sense of tension or resolution because any aurally perceptible feelings of consonance and dissonance have been lost along with tonality. What is left is a variety of **textures** and disjointed melodic lines articulated in a wide array of contrasting **timbres**. It is this

8: Style, genre and historical context

melody of **colours** (*Klangfarbenmelodie*) and the varying density of the textures that are chiefly responsible for the music's expressiveness. Beginning with a single harp note doubled by a muted trumpet the music rises to a textural climax in bars 7–8 then falls through harp harmonics and stuttering flute and trumpet notes to a single lonely semiquaver on the celesta, then, almost before the piece has begun, silence. By analogy with the painterly technique of Seurat, textures such as the isolated points of sound heard at the beginning and end of this piece have been described as **pointillist**, but there are many who doubt the validity and usefulness of the term in this context, given its very different effects.

8.11.4 Serialism

In order to compose longer instrumental pieces than those of Webern's *Five Pieces for Orchestra* (C35) it became clear that a new structural principle would have to be found if tonality were to be abandoned. The answer came in the shape of **dodecaphony**, which was more of a technique than a style. The principle was very simple. A row consisting of all 12 chromatic pitch classes could replace the tonic key as the backbone of the composition. This could be articulated horizontally (as in bars 0–8 of C40), or vertically as a series of chords (bars 9–12 of the same example). In its strictest form none of the pitch classes could be repeated until all 12 had been sounded (to avoid the possibility of one note assuming undue prominence in a way similar to the privileged status of the tonic in tonal music). Variety could be achieved without a loss of cohesion by inverting the row or playing it backwards (or both), and each of these rows could be transposed by up to eleven semitones. The flexibility and durability of this new technique becomes apparent when one compares the extract from the second song of the *Hölderlin-Lieder* Op. 21 by Josef Matthias Hauer (1883–1959) shown in C40 with the extract from the second movement of the *Canticum sacrum* by Igor Stravinsky (1882–1971) shown in C88. The first, with its chords of the diminished 7th and its quotation from Wagner (compare B71 with B72), now seems like an intensification of late romantic styles, but the diamond-bright textures of the second still sound remarkably modern nearly half a century after they were composed.

8.11.5 Neoclassicism

One of the reactions to the super-heated emotionalism of late romantic and expressionist music was an urge to seek renewal through the genres, forms and, to a limited extent, the styles and techniques of pre-nineteenth-century music. Neoclassicism refers to a much wider range of historical styles than that conveyed by the term 'classical' as commonly used by musical historians, but a narrower range than that implied by the sign 'classical music' in a record store. In *Le Tombeau de Couperin* by Maurice Ravel (1875–1937) the classical period to which the music refers is the French *grand siècle* that was dominated by *Le Roi soleil*, Louis XIV (at whose court François Couperin Le Grand was the chief musical ornament). This homage to Couperin takes the form of a six-movement **suite** for solo piano that begins with a prelude and fugue, and ends with a toccata. Between these typical baroque genres are three dances that were common in seventeenth- and eighteenth-century France. The *forlane* was a courtly dance in moderately fast compound time. These rhythmic characteristics

Elements of music

are evident in C32, but Couperin (who wrote only one dance of this type) would have been surprised by the modality of Ravel's melody. In this respect Ravel's music refers back to French music of the renaissance (another French golden age), while the piquantly dissonant harmony is entirely characteristic of Ravel's own style. The fusion of these elements – baroque dance rhythms, **modal** melodies and twentieth-century harmonies – is typical of many neoclassical compositions.

Music that does not have such obvious connections with the past is sometimes regarded as being neoclassical, at least in some respects. The earliest masterpiece by Béla Bartók (1881–1945) is a symphonic poem, but in a majority of his instrumental works he spurned this typically romantic genre in favour of classical species such as the string quartet. Of his fourth quartet he wrote: 'The work is in five movements, their character corresponding with classical sonata form'. So, despite the almost aggressively modern style both genre and form are neoclassical. His sixth quartet has the normal four movements of a classical string quartet, but they are linked by the melody heard at the beginning of each movement. This melody dominates the last movement, and the final repeat of its opening can be heard in the viola part of bars 6–8 of C72.

The 'Giuoco delle coppie' ('Game of the couples') from Bartók's *Concerto for Orchestra* reminds us that neoclassicism can be fun. The game of the title consists in a series of **parodies** of the instrumental duets in parallel 3rds or 6ths that were such a feature of baroque, classical and romantic music, for example bars 219–231 of B36 (violins in 6ths and woodwind in 3rds) and bars 3–6 of C3 (cornets in 3rds). In C77 Bartók makes a travesty of classical propriety by ensuring that two bassoons in 6ths form grating false relations. For instance, in bar 1 the second bassoon plays an A♮ that is immediately followed by an A♭ played by the first bassoon. In C78 two oboes outline 'forbidden' intervals such as the tritone between an F♯ and a C♮ in the first two bars. Other delights include the wonky figuration in bars 4–5 and the augmented 2nd (C♮–D♯) in the first oboe part at the end of bar 5. In C79–C81 the humour is more sardonic as all three pairs of instruments play parallel 'forbidden' intervals (clarinets in 7ths, flutes in 5ths and trumpets in 2nds).

The *Concierto de Aranjuez* by Joaquín Rodrigo (1902–99) is cast in the three-movement form of the late baroque and classical concerto. The colourful but delicate textures of the first movement evoke the aristocratic atmosphere of eighteenth-century Aranjuez, a royal retreat south of Madrid. Rodrigo achieved his neoclassical effects by an astute use of late baroque mannerisms, such as the hemiolaic bars in C83. The music is clearly tonal, but characterised by the sort of dissonances that are to be found in some of Domenico Scarlatti's eighteenth-century harpsichord sonatas (Scarlatti spent the last twenty eight years of his life at the Spanish royal court where his music acquired a decidedly Iberian flavour). While the strummed chords of bars 1–17 remind one of more earthy traditions of guitar playing (*rasgueado*), the ensuing dancing triadic and scalic figures played by plucking individual notes with the fingertips (*punteado*) reflect the courtly life of Aranjuez in much the same way as Ravel's Forlane reflects the civilisation of eighteenth-century Versailles.

8: Style, genre and historical context

8.11.6 Nationalism

In the nineteenth century the influence of **folk music** on art music was often apparant only in a vague colouring of pan-European tonal styles (as in the 'Norwegian' modality of C2). In the twentieth century composers began to take a more scientific interest in the music of their own countries. In eastern Europe Kodály and Bartók transcribed thousands of folk tunes, and their work in this field brought a new authenticity to the styles of those pieces that were meant to reflect national characteristics. At its simplest these could be harmonisations of original folk melodies, as is the case in the *Romanian Dances* by Béla Bartók (1881–1945), a collection of seven piano pieces dating from 1915 which the composer orchestrated in 1917. C56 is based on a pentachord in which the 'eastern' interval of an augmented 2nd is particularly prominent (the extract is taken from a transcription for violin and piano made by Zoltán Székely in 1926). In his *44 Duos* for two violins he cast his ethno-musicological net wider by including Arabic as well as eastern European folk music among his arrangements. C57 shows a folk melody in the hypolydian mode, while C58 shows Bartók's arrangement of the same melody for two violins. Less closely pinned to authentic folk sources are Bartók's *Six Dances in Bulgarian Rhythm*, in which the asymmetrical metres of folk dances are reproduced (quavers grouped 3+3+2), but the music is otherwise original (C66 and C67).

In 1926 Bartók's fellow ethnomusicologist Zoltán Kodály (1882–1967) made a major contribution to twentieth-century Hungarian music with his folk opera *Háry János*. It is in the tradition of the *Singspiel* in that it consists of individual solos, duets and ensembles with spoken dialogue. It includes a Viennese carillon melody, a minuet and Austrian marches, but at its centre are original Hungarian folk songs which Kodály, a great pedagogue, wished to bring to the attention of a broader public. He succeeded brilliantly, for the orchestral suite he made from the opera is now in the regular repertoire of major orchestras throughout the world. One of the movements combines **modal** melodies with an extended solo for the Hungarian national instrument, the **cimbalom** (C41).

Nationalism could also be expressed by programmatic elements within a work painted on a much larger canvas. This is true of the seventh symphony by Dmitri Shostakovich (1906–75) which the composer said was meant to express 'the majestic ideas of the patriotic war'. He went on to say that 'neither savage raids ... nor the grim atmosphere of the beleaguered city [of Leningrad, now St Petersburg] could hinder the flow of ideas'. In the first movement a menacing side drum accompanies a vulgar march tune which is meant to represent the approaching German army (C74). This **parody** of a German march is made all the more bitter by its jerky, detached articulation and the simultaneous use of bowed, *col legno* and pizzicato violins. Of his parody of this march in the 'Intermezzo interrotto' from his *Concerto for Orchestra* Bartók wrote: 'The artist declares his love for his native land in a serenade which is suddenly interrupted in a crude and violent manner; he is seized by rough, booted men who even break his instrument'. The extract from this movement (C75) begins with another Bulgarian rhythm in $\frac{8}{8}$ time (with quavers grouped 3+2+3). The 'interruption' takes the form of a parody of a parody: the scalic figure x (in both C74 and C75) becomes increasingly encrusted with triplet figures as the sequence continues and accelerates until cut

Elements of music

short by derisory laughter from the rest of the orchestra. The final irony is that neither composer could have been unaware of the connection between this melody and the melody by Franz Lehár (1870–1948) shown in C73 (from *The Merry Widow*, perhaps the most successful operetta of the early twentieth century).

8.11.7 Synthesis of east and west

Béla Bartók (1881–1945) said that his life's work was to achieve 'a synthesis of eastern [European] **folk music** and western **art music**'. This synthesis is apparent in his *Six Dances in Bulgarian Rhythm* (C66 and C77). However, like many twentieth-century composers, he was also inspired by the music of other, non-European cultures. In 'From the Island of Bali' (C64) he makes use of a pentatonic scale characterised by semitones enclosing a perfect 4th that corresponds almost exactly with one of the pentatonic scales of Indonesia to which a **gamelan** is tuned. After a monophonic melody derived from this scale (bars 1–4) the Bartókian synthesis begins when the first four notes of this scale (motif x on the first stave of C64) are used as the opening of the peculiarly western device of a canon at the 6th (the second stave). Motif x is then inverted (in an almost Bachian manner) to form a canon by inversion with the original form of motif x (bars 6–8). Additionally both of these canonic passages are based upon a collection of eight pitch sets that can be represented as an octatonic scale of alternating tones and semitones (famously used by Stravinsky in *Les Noces* of 1922). The extract ends with complex cross-phrasing (see 1.10.2) that is more typical of Brahms (B79) than of Balinese music.

In the last 11 bars of the extract from Bartók's *Concerto for Orchestra* (C82) the composer makes use of an anhemitonic **pentatonic scale**. This five-note scale contains no semitones and is prevalent in folk music throughout the world. In western folk music and in nineteenth- and twentieth-century art music this type of pentatonic scale is often treated in a way which gives one of the five notes more prominence than any of the others. The most-favoured note becomes, in effect, the tonic of a major or minor scale. In bars 69–79 of C82 there can be no doubt about which of the five pitches is the tonic since B-major triads are played for three bars before the pentatonic melody and the harp and both sets of violins end on the tonic (B♮).

A similar though more subtle effect can be heard in the first two bars of Debussy's 'La Cathédrale engloutie' (C22). Here G♮ is given pre-eminence over the other four notes because it is sustained in the bass, so the music feels as though it is in G major. In the last three bars of C65 the E♭ achieves a similar status (it is heard on its own on every beat, and the piece ends on E♭). The pentatonic scale based on this note differs from both of the more familiar types in the intervals formed between each successive pair of notes. This less-tonal-sounding scale is common in eastern Russia and central Asia. It is shown on the first of the three staves beneath the extract (the other two show how the same pitches could be arranged to form an incomplete major scale and an incomplete aeolian-mode scale). Bartók's synthesis is between music based on this exotic scale and the decidedly twentieth-century western quartal harmony and melodies that are dominated by intervals of a perfect 4th (vertical and horizontal brackets show harmonic and melodic 4ths respectively).

8: Style, genre and historical context

In Bartók's 'Five-tone Scale' (C63) the more familiar 'major' pentatonic scale can be heard in the four-bar phrase cadencing on G (C60), and the 'minor/modal' version of the same pitches can be heard in the second four-bar phrase cadencing on E (C61). In bars 9–16 Bartók displays his 'synthesis between east and west' by combining the melody of bars 1–8 (pentatonic on E) with a different scale (pentatonic on D as shown in C62). Such **bimodality** is extremely rare in folk music, but there are plenty of examples of the style in twentieth-century western music. Similarly, Bartók combines two pentachords in his **bitonal** 'Melody against Double Notes' (C59), one from the scale of F♯ major (F♯, G♯, A♯, B♮ and C♯), the other from the scale of D minor (D, E, F, G and A).

Superficially, it would seem that Edgard Varèse (1883–1965) was a radical whose aim was not so much a synthesis of east and west but a total rejection of the post-renaissance western musical tradition. Until the closing bars of *Ionisation* (C42–C54) he rejects any possibility of western developmental processes by renouncing pitch altogether (the sirens excepted – but with these instruments pitch is in a constant state of flux). The work is scored for thirty-seven percussion instruments that produce a primitive, visceral sound-world of repetitive rhythmic cells that mirror the ceaseless clamour of the twentieth-century megalopolis. Among these instruments there are many that remind us that modern urban society is multicultural: bongo drums of Afro-Cuban origin, Cuban clappers, Latin American maracas and güiro, the string drum that is still known as *bukai* in eastern Europe (because it sounds like a bellowing bull), Chinese blocks, Chinese and Turkish cymbals, Oriental gongs, Spanish castanets, as well as the decidedly western sirens that evoke images of air raids, fires and road accidents. At the end of the work pitched instruments appear (piano, chimes and glockenspiel) as the scrapings, thuddings and clankings die away. So in the end this enormously influential composition can be seen, not as a rejection of western society, but as a celebration of multicultural society.

8.11.8 Populism and pastiche

From the beginning of the twentieth century there was a constant stream of composers of art music who were intrigued by the idioms of popular music. The recreative pastiche of a **cakewalk** by Claude Debussy (1862–1918) shown in C20 is among the earliest examples. It exhibits most of the stylistic features of this nineteenth-century strutting dance, which, by the turn of the century, had become a subspecies of ragtime. It is a duple-metre march with a pervasive syncopated rhythm heard right at the beginning (x). It begins with a four-bar introduction, a one-bar rest and four bars of 'till ready' harmony featuring a typical oom-pah **ragtime** bass. The melody (bars 10–25) is 16 bars long and divides into an eight-bar antecedent (bars 10–17) and an eight-bar consequent that modulates to the dominant key of B♭ major (bars 18–25). Both of these eight-bar phrases themselves divide into four-bar phrases with the first and third being identical (thus forming the pattern ABAC). Such regular phrasing is typical of ragtime melodies. The simple diatonic style is relieved by **added-note chords** (bar 6) and **blue notes** (see bars 15–23 and the blues scale shown on an extra stave), both of them features of the many-faceted styles of **jazz**.

William Walton (1902–83) described *Façade* as a 'melodrama', then,

Elements of music

perhaps because it smacked too much of the opera house (see 8.10.1), he changed the subtitle to 'entertainment'. The fact that it is impossible to assign the work to a traditional genre is, of itself, symptomatic of the extreme divergency of trends in twentieth-century music (it is equally impossible to assign Schoenberg's *Pierrot Lunaire* – C34 – to any single traditional genre). These two works were among the first to combine elements of music, poetry and drama in new ways that owe nothing to opera. As such they are prototypes for a specifically twentieth-century genre which has come to be known as **music theatre**. *Façade* is a setting of 21 nonsense poems which the author, Edith Sitwell (1887–1964), described as 'studies in rhythm, sound and association of ideas'. At the first performance the instrumentalists and reciter were hidden behind a curtain on which a face had been painted. The mouth was shaped like a megaphone through which Sitwell declaimed her verses in a sing-song manner to the accompaniment of seven instrumentalists playing Walton's parodies of ancient and modern popular song and dance styles. The 'Popular Song' (C38), with its jazz quavers, substitution chords (C39(b)) and humorous use of off-beat percussion, is a satirical evocation of contemporary music-hall songs.

8.11.9 Modernism

'Modern music' often means music composed within the life span of whoever uses the phrase (Varèse's percussive *Ionisation* (C42–C54) would certainly have sounded modern to someone hearing it for the first time in the 1930s). But 'modernism' has acquired a special meaning in the history of twentieth-century music. In its broadest sense it refers to styles based on the **serial techniques** of Schoenberg as opposed to twentieth-century tonal styles. But composers who began work after the second world war rightly regarded some early serial styles as being an intensification of romanticism rather than a clean break with the past. This was the generation of composers who embraced Webern's more rigorous serial style and developed compositional methods that allowed every element of the music – rhythm, metre, dynamics, timbre and so on – to be controlled according to the same sort of principles as governed pitch series.

Le marteau sans maître, a masterpiece of modernism by Pierre Boulez (b.1925), shows that serial music can make its impression on a sympathetic ear without any necessity for getting to grips with the composer's creative techniques. The clue to the music, as with Schoenberg's *Pierrot Lunaire* (C34), lies in the surreal texts which are the launching pads for the purely instrumental movements. These are 'commentaries' on the vocal movements, though Boulez deliberately confuses the issue by placing some of the commentaries *before* the songs to which they are related – the reverse of Debussy's practice of revealing the titles of his preludes at the end of each piece (see 8.11.2). What strikes the ear at a first hearing of the opening bars of *Le marteau* (C87) is the sheer speed with which angular motifs and varied tone-colours race by (at twice the speed of the music in the vocal movement upon which this instrumental movement is a commentary). The impression is of chaotic fragmentation (Boulez described it as 'controlled delirium') rather than predetermined order. The exotic ensemble of instruments cannot fail to impress (Boulez hoped the vibraphone would suggest a Balinese gamelan and the guitar a Japanese koto).

8: Style, genre and historical context

Igor Stravinsky (1882–1971), who had adopted most twentieth-century styles and impressed upon them his own unmistakable fingerprints, turned, near the end of his long life, towards the modernist camp. But his serial technique was less rigorous than that of Boulez. Analysis of 'Surge, aquilo' from his *Canticum sacrum* of 1955 (C88) shows a polyphonic web of serial melodies that are modified by oscillations between pairs of notes in the row that lend the music an almost baroque exuberance. This can clearly be heard in bar 3, where the tenor alternates between notes 7 and 8 of the prime order while the cor anglais alternates between notes 2 and 3 of the retrograde inversion.

The musical culture of post-war England was for some time largely unaffected by continental European **avant-garde music**. For many musicians and their audiences Benjamin Britten was the last word in modernity. But in the 1950s, by a staggering coincidence, five young men came together at the Royal Manchester College of Music and the Faculty of Music of the University of Manchester. All were extraordinarily gifted, and all were rebels against the stultifying conservatism of the English musical establishment. The eldest, Alexander Goehr (b.1932), went on to study with Messiaen, became a respected exponent of serialism, and carried the banner of modernism to Cambridge when he became professor of music there in 1976. Harrison Birtwistle (b.1934) has become famous as the composer of modernist operas, notably *Gawain* (Covent Garden 1990), and he too became a professor of music (at King's College London). Elgar Howarth (b.1935) achieved distinction, first as a virtuoso trumpeter, then as a conductor and composer. John Ogdon (1937–89) contributed terrific pianism that was recognised throughout the world when he won the Moscow Tchaikovsky Competition in 1962 (he too was a composer, but illness and premature death prevented him from achieving lasting fame).

One of the most remarkable members of the Manchester School is Peter Maxwell Davies (b.1934). On a bedrock of post-Webernian serialism (he knew the music of Boulez while still a student), his style can accommodate crude pastiche as well as arcane references to medieval and renaissance music. Indeed several of his compositions make overt use of specific pre-classical melodies or polyphonic compositions that form the structural foundations of his own 'recompositions'. This is the case in *Ave maris stella* (1975), a sextet for flute/alto flute, clarinet, viola, cello, piano and marimba (shades of *Le marteau sans maître*). Most of this atonal composition is derived from the plainsong (A40) by permutations of a 'magic square' of pitches, but the process, like total serialism, is aurally imperceptible. What is quite perceptible is the terrific virtuosity of the performers, the Fires of London. This ensemble, dedicated to contemporary music, had originally been formed as the Pierrot Players – a reference to the instrumental and vocal resources required for performances of Schoenberg's *Pierrot Lunaire* (C43), a work which was an icon of modernism throughout most of the twentieth century. *Ave maris stella* is one of the earliest compositions in which the marimba is given such a prominent role, so much so that the work has been aptly described as a chamber concerto. Its dominance is particularly evident in C90, a cadenza-like passage in which the marimba is accompanied by a sustained string chord and a ghostly **cluster chord** on the piano. The latter effect is achieved by silently depressing two and a half octaves of white notes with the arm (thus releasing the mutes that normally prevent the strings from vibrating) then playing the detached bass chords shown in the score without using the sustaining pedals. This causes the notes of the cluster chord to sound, not because the strings have been struck in the usual way, but because the overtones of the bass chords have induced **sympathetic vibrations** in the strings set free by the pianist's right arm.

Tone clusters are common in twentieth-century music (perhaps beginning with those written by the American composer Henry Cowell as early as 1912), and one of the pieces in Bartók's *Mikrokosmos* Book 4, No. 102, is devoted to the exploration of piano harmonics. What is novel here is the combination of the two procedures. Such exploration of advanced instrumental techniques is characteristic of post-war modernism. Notable, too, is the bare texture and huge pitch range (the two notes of the second chord of bar 9 are separated from each other by an interval spanning more than five and a half octaves). The simultaneous black- and white-note glissandi with which the extract ends are characteristic of much music for tuned percussion instruments. *Ave maris stella* is a true chamber work in the sense that it is designed to be performed without a conductor (despite its rhythmic complexity). Coordination is achieved by assigning a principal role to one or other of the instrumentalists whom the others must follow. In C90 pecked lines and arrows pointing at particular notes in the soloistic marimba part show the exact points at which the clarinet and flute are to enter, and the points at which the detached piano chords are to be articulated.

8.11.10 Minimalism

The complexity of post-war modernist compositions alienated all but a small minority of listeners and widened the gulf between jazz and pop on the one hand and twentieth-century 'classical music' on the other. Among the most influential composers who reacted against the dominance of the avant-garde were minimalist composers such as Terry Riley. His seminal composition *In C* (1964) consists of 53 tiny melodic fragments that can be played in any order by any number of instrumentalists for as long as they like (so long as they maintain the same pulse throughout). This **aleatoric** or indeterminate element gives rise to a variety of ostinato patterns which, together with the static harmony, has a mildly hallucinatory effect directly opposed to the intellectual rigour of contemporary modernist compositions. Indeed its effect is nearer to the ethos of oriental music, even though there is no deliberate attempt to imitate the sound-worlds of Indian, Indonesian or Sino-Japanese cultures. Steve Reich (b.1936) played in the first performance of *In C*, and, like Riley, he made a particular study of non-western music. In *Writings about Music* (1974) Reich confirms that, although minimalist composers were inspired by world music, they did not find it necessary to attempt to imitate the music of any specific culture: 'One can study the rhythmic structure of non-western music, and let that study lead one where it will while continuing to use the instruments, scales, and any other sound one has grown up with'.

Reich's *Clapping Music* is, on one level, as minimal as can be since one of the fundamental elements of music, defined pitch, is entirely absent. In its place there is a rhythmic complexity that has its roots in the drumming techniques he heard in Ghana. In C89 the two performers begin clapping synchronously, but thirteen seconds into the track the second performer suddenly omits the first quaver of the basic rhythm and tags it on to the end of bar 2, thus effectively moving the whole rhythm forward a quaver. At 24 seconds into the track the same process is repeated by the second performer. Meanwhile the first performer continues with the original rhythm in its original temporal position. Since there are twelve quavers per bar, it follows that after twelve of these shifts the performers will once again achieve synchronicity. For ears and minds accustomed to the development of musical ideas in classical music a willingness to listen in a completely different way is required if minimalist music of this sort is to be appreciated. Like the patterns of the myriad tiny crystals embedded in granite Reich's complex rhythmic patterns are simply there, signifying nothing beyond themselves.

8.11.11 Postmodernism

Postmodernism first declared itself in architecture when, in the final decades of the twentieth century, a reaction set in against the hi-tech functionalism of modernist buildings of plate-glass and cement. The reaction often manifested itself in a return to some of the characteristic features of much earlier styles, such as pilasters and round arches. Like practitioners of all of the other arts, musicians soon followed the example set by architects, but it would be wrong to imagine that there was a direct correspondence between architectural and musical changes in the late twentieth century. Essentially musicians realised that a majority of the population (even those who regularly listened to 'classical' music) found it impossible to relate to atonal modernist compositions (8.11.9), but were impressed by music which maintained tonal terms of reference (such as jazz, pop and most types of non-western music). Minimalism (8.11.10) sought to return to the primal elements of music, and it was from minimalism, pop music and all manner of world music, as well as tonal western styles, that the protean idioms of postmodern music began to develop.

This is apparent in one of the earliest and most remarkable compositions of the new tonal era of late twentieth-century 'serious' music, *Cry*, by Giles Swayne (b.1946). This monumental composition for 28 unaccompanied and electronically amplified solo voices lasts as long as a symphony by Mahler. In seven movements it tells the story of creation and comments on man's place in the universe. Each movement is based on a key note a whole tone above the preceding movement so that together they traverse a complete whole-tone scale returning to the original pitch in the last movement. Apart from three crucial words – 'adama' (Adam), 'eva' (Eve) and 'anima' (spirit) – the text of *Cry* is non-verbal. Vowels are used to sustain notes (as shown in C91) while consonants engage the lips, teeth, tongue and palate in an innovative manner to produce a huge range of unpitched percussive sounds (some of which can be heard in the background in the first ten bars of the extract). These purely acoustic effects are emphasised by artificial reverberation and phasing effects (induced by the sophisticated use of such electronic devices as digital delay, an echo simulator and a flanger).

C91 clearly shows a return to tonality. Beginning on a unison D♯ three soloists climb chromatically to form a **cluster chord** on this sustained note

Elements of music

(bar 2). In the next four bars the D♮ is abandoned as the chromatic ascent continues, but at the end of bar 7 it returns as a sustained note around which another cluster chord is formed (bar 8). In bars 9–11 the final chromatic ascent excludes the D♮, but after a brief silence in bar 11 this note is reaffirmed as the tonic by a blazing triad of D major, first in four parts, then in twelve real parts.

A comparison of this music with Boulez's *Le marteau sans maître* (C87) reveals just how deep was the gulf between modernism and post-modernism. Swayne made his position clear in the notes he wrote for the insert that accompanies the recording: 'The origins of *Cry* are very complicated, and hard for me to write about. My discovery, in 1977, of the importance of African music was certainly one element. Another was my dissatisfaction with the stale and negative gestures of so-called serious music. An awful lot seemed to be wrong with or missing from the musical culture within which, so far, I had moved; the realisation that I admired the work of David Bowie much more than that of Boulez or Stockhausen set me thinking and worrying ... When the BBC offered me a commission in 1977, I was already casting around for ways in which to translate into my own work the lessons I was learning from African music, from listening to rock music, and from generally opening my ears to the world around me.'

John Tavener (b.1944) began his musical pilgrimage when, at the age of 12, he heard Stravinsky's *Canticum sacrum*, a work that he said woke him up and inspired him to become a composer. He became particularly attached to the second movement, a setting of words from the Song of Songs – 'Awake, O north wind; and come, thou south wind' (C88). In his maturity, he described the *Canticum sacrum* as 'the pinnacle of twentieth-century music, which brings together Webern, organum and Gregorian and Byzantine chant'. In his identification of these four elements he was not only accurately describing Stravinsky's masterpiece, he was also referring to his own postmodern pilgrimage from serialism to simplicity. In 1987 (the same year that he composed his famous *Protecting Veil*) he wrote a short unaccompanied choral work for the choir of Christ Church Cathedral Oxford (where his namesake and putative ancestor John Taverner had been choirmaster in the sixteenth century). This *Hymn to the Holy Spirit* (C92) illustrates his use of two of the elements he identified in the *Canticum sacrum*.

The first is his imaginative adaptation of chant. Both Gregorian **plainsong** and Byzantine **chant** are derived from a set of four **authentic modes** (dorian, phrygian, lydian and mixolydian, the white notes of a keyboard from D to D, E to E, F to F and G to G respectively) and four variants of them known as **plagal modes** (see 2.4.1 and 2.4.2). In both traditions the most primitive melodies are the psalm tones based on these modes. The extant tones of the two traditions are different, but they have in common the use of a limited number of modal pitches, short phrases cadencing on the final, a largely conjunct style and a lack of a regular pulse. All of these features are evident in the ancient psalm tone shown in A6, and they are also evident in the tenor part of the first five bars of C92. In the former there are five pitches: in the latter there are just four. In the former both phrases cadence on C: in the latter all five phrases cadence on E. Both are entirely conjunct apart from two leaps of a 3rd. In neither of them is there any suggestion of regular metre. All that has been said about the tenor part applies equally to the second bass part which exactly

8: Style, genre and historical context

mirrors the tenor melody. Consequently a different set of pitches emerges, only one of which corresponds to a note in the tenor's pitch set (D♮). This bimodal style is characteristic of much of Tavener's later music.

The second element mentioned by Tavener is **organum**. In its most primitive form the author of *Musica enchiriadis* (c.900 AD) observes that any plainsong melody may be sung in parallel octaves, just as the tenor and first bass do in the first five bars of C92. A second type of parallel organum consisted of the original plainsong (the *vox principalis* in A7(a)) doubled at the 5th below by the *vox organalis* – exactly the technique Tavener employs in the soprano and alto parts of bars 6–10. In a third type of parallel organum the *vox principalis* or *vox organalis* (or both) were doubled at the octave (A7(b)) in the same way as Tavener does when the soprano part is doubled at the lower octave in bars 6–10. Thus it is that Tavener's particular brand of postmodern simplicity can be seen to have its roots in styles dating back more than a millennium.

After the collapse of Soviet communism in the early 1990s, musicians from Russia and its formerly subjugated peripheral states stumbled into the garish light of western capitalism. They came bearing gifts, notably music by composers that westerners knew only by repute, or not at all. Many of them had lived all their lives under the cultural dictatorship that Stalin imposed when he came to power. Consequently they were hardly aware of the forbidden fruits of western modernists, and the struggle between **modernism** and the more approachable emergent styles of **minimalism** and **postmodernism**. One such composer is Giya Kancheli (b.1935), a Georgian who has lived in Berlin since 1992. In his earliest works the influence of Bartók and Transcaucasian folk music is evident. With the cultural thaw that followed the death of Stalin he was able to get to know contemporary western music better, and was particularly influenced by cool jazz and the music of American composers such as Copland and Crumb.

Since the 1970s Kancheli's music has included enigmatic and unacknowledged quotations from baroque and classical music. This is particularly evident in *Abii ne viderem* ('I turned away so that I might not see'), a twenty-five-minute composition for solo viola, string orchestra, piano (often played directly on the strings rather than via the keyboard) and bass guitar. This haunted music, interrupted by cataclysmic outbursts, makes it clear that the title refers to images of unbearable brutality (perhaps not unlike the images of savagery in the Balkans from which many turned away in horror at the end of the twentieth century). At the start of C94 the first six degrees of the scale of A minor (x) are sustained to form a ghostly **cluster chord** answered by another segment of the scale played on plucked piano strings (x^1). The initial scale is then inverted (y). Finally an imperfect cadence in A minor (bars 5–7) is distorted by the tonic (A♮ in the strings) forming a protracted dissonance against the leading note (G♯ on solo viola). These first seven bars contain a hidden message, for it turns out that the melody (x and y) together with harmony notes in the cadence form a distorted and transposed quotation from the start of Bach's Two-part Invention in D minor (C93). Panic sets in at the end of bar 9 with the sudden disorienting shift to the unrelated key of C minor. This accompanies another distortion of the first bar of Bach's invention (x^2) culminating in two more cluster chords (the second encompassing all seven degrees of the natural minor scale). The extract ends with a conventional baroque melodic figure (bars 10–12) which derives from the last three bars of Bach's invention. But the harmony, texture and scoring (especially the terrific resonance of the tonic note played by the bass guitar in the last chord) turn Bach's eighteenth-century rationality into a late twentieth-century nightmare.

Terezín has a tragic history. It lies about 60 kilometres to the north of Prague and was built by Emperor Joseph II as a fortress to defend the Austrian Empire from the forces of the aggressive Prussian armies of Frederick II. In 1940 the fortress became a Gestapo prison. In 1941 the SS evicted the population of the town and turned it into a ghetto with 160,000 Jews from 35 different countries. At first it was largely self-governing and normal cultural activities thrived. Between 1943 and 1944 twenty performances of Verdi's Requiem were given there. But in 1944 the town and fortress were turned into a transit camp for Auschwitz and other extermination camps. On 8 May 1945 the remaining prisoners were freed by Soviet tank detachments, but they were too late to save the 33,000 Jews who died in Terezín and the 87,000 who were taken from the town to be exterminated elsewhere.

The *Terezín Ghetto Requiem* by the Czech composer Sylvie Bodorová (b.1954) was commissioned by the Warwick Arts Foundation, inspired by the performances of Verdi's Requiem in the ghetto and dedicated to the victims of the Holocaust. In all of its three movements Jewish and Catholic texts are juxtaposed. In the extract from the end of the second movement (C96) the text of the sequence 'Dies irae, dies illa' (shown in B62) is set to angular melodic phrases in the unrelated keys of A minor, C minor and B♭ minor. But tonality is no match for the atonal, quasi-orchestral textures of the string quartet whose accompaniment is based on a series of interlocking **tritones** (shown on an extra stave beneath bars 1–7). In the context of this particular Requiem the words of the medieval Latin sequence become horrendously relevant, especially the phrase 'solvet saeclum in favilla' (the earth dissolves in ashes), for the crematorium at Terezín was just as efficient as that at Auschwitz. After only seven bars the baritone falls silent as the strings continue their *Totentanz* around a tritone that forms an internal double pedal. Shifting tritones (bars 23–26) precipitate the climax ('Full of wrath') in bar 27. Suddenly tritones give way to a G minor chord (bar 29) as the baritone re-enters with the Hebrew word 'Gael' (Redeemer) sung to a rising minor 3rd. When the same word is sung for a second time the interval is augmented to a major 3rd (bar 31), then a perfect 4th at the start of a phrase setting the words 'Gael Yisrael!' ('Redeemer of Israel!') in which, quite unexpectedly, the string quartet, now purged of tritones, forms a completely tonal perfect cadence in C major. Sylvie Bodorová's own words seem particularly relevant to the release that this remarkable cadence brings: 'When my composition was almost finished I too, like the prisoners in 1943 and 1944, heard Verdi's Requiem at Terezín. I was dwarfed by the walls surrounding the ghetto ... But when the music started I looked up and felt an extraordinary sense of liberation, and as the music came to an end the small group of survivors gathered in front of the stage were suddenly and magically illuminated by the setting sun'.

James MacMillan (b.1959) is a composer whose music is informed by Catholicism as well as by his catholicism. In the former sense much of his

8: Style, genre and historical context

music reflects his deeply held beliefs, but he rejects the notion that his religious position makes his music exclusive. In an interview he said that 'there is definitely a connection between the extra-musical stimulus and the musical outcome, but there has to be some element of (to use a theological analogy) transubstantiation of the extra-musical into the musical, so that the idea communicates itself fully as music'. In the second sense he is catholic in his attitude towards the work of composers whom he admits influenced him. These range from Palestrina (A52) and Bach (A88–B16) to Messiaen (C55), Boulez (C87) and Stravinsky (C88), as well as twentieth-century eastern-European composers. He clarified his position on modernism and postmodernism when he said: 'Postmodernity means many things and has a lot of negative attributes ... but some positive ones too. Postmodernity as a negative thing implies a robbing, a pillaging of musical history with no real moral intent or respect for tradition. But I think that when you talk about postmodernity in music in a positive way you take on board an openness to a wider spectrum of human experiences ...'

That wider spectrum is evident in MacMillan's *Quickening*, a major BBC commission that received its world premiere at a Promenade Concert in the Royal Albert Hall in September 1999. The title derives from English versions of the psalms, from St Paul's Epistles and from the metaphysical verse of Henry Vaughan (1622–95). In these contexts it means 'to animate, to inspire, to hasten or to become viable (as a child in the womb)'. It was this multi-layered word that inspired MacMillan's poet, Michael Symmons Roberts, to compose the text about the literal birth of a child and the birth, or rebirth, of the soul. C97 is an extract from the end of the last movement in which water, the traditional Christian symbol of life and the element in which the unborn swim, is symbolised in musical terms by temple bowls (bars 53–68). The resources for which MacMillan writes represent the many meanings of the word that gave birth to the whole piece. The intimacy of the unaccompanied solo vocal quartet (bars 2–5 and 15–19) allows the references to John the Baptist and Mary the Mother of God to be heard clearly, while the clangorous and partially **aleatoric** orchestral interludes (bars 5–14 and 19–25) joyfully celebrate the pregnancy of Elisabeth (whose 'babe leaped in the womb' when Mary visited her in the city of Judah). The full chorus emphasise the universality of their joy in a tonal climax that moves from a modal F minor (bar 27) to a sudden unrelated chord of E minor (bar 35), the latter expressing both the force and the strangeness of the coming of the life-giving Holy Spirit at Pentecost. This sparks off the first instrumental ritornello (bars 36–39) and an aleatoric choral rendition of the Lord's Prayer in Aramaic for women's voices (bars 39–41) answered by ecstatic tenors and basses. These two elements alternate in bars 42–50, with the ritornello growing in power each time. Suddenly the joyous ritornello is cut short and boys' voices, hundreds of feet away, are heard intoning the Lord's Prayer to the accompaniment of a solo violin (playing the theme of the ritornello), a whispering harp, mysterious rolls on steel drums and the just-perceptible hum of temple bowls that fade at the last into stunned silence.